INTERNATIONAL ENVIRONMENTAL LAW

International Environmental Law is a new textbook written for students, practitioners, and anyone interested in the subject. The overall aim of the book is to provide a fresh understanding of international environmental law as a whole, seen in the light of climate change, biodiversity loss and the other serious environmental challenges facing the world. The book has also been kept deliberately manageable in size by careful selection of topics and by adopting a cross-cutting synthesis of regulatory interaction in the field. This enables the reader to place international environmental law in the broader context of public international law in general, revealing at the same time that international environmental law is experimental ground for developing new legal approaches towards global governance. To this end, the authors have combined theory and practice.

Apart from discussing concepts, rule-making and compliance, the book looks at options for improved co-ordination, harmonisation and even integration of existing multilateral environmental agreements, analysing how conflicts between various environmental regimes can be avoided or, at least, adequately managed. The authors argue that an appropriate management of international environmental relations must address the North–South divide, which continues to be a major obstacle to global environmental co-operation. Furthermore, the authors emphasise the growing human rights dimension of international environmental law.

This book is an ideal 'door opener' for the further study of international environmental law. Focusing on 'international environmental governance' in a comprehensive way, it serves to explain that each institution, each actor, and each instrument is part of a multidimensional process in international environmental law and relations.

International Environmental Law

Ulrich Beyerlin and Thilo Marauhn

Verlag CH Beck

Published in the United Kingdom by Hart Publishing Ltd
16C Worcester Place, Oxford, OX1 2JW
Telephone: +44 (0)1865 517530
Fax: +44 (0)1865 510710
E-mail: mail@hartpub.co.uk
Website: http://www.hartpub.co.uk

Published in North America (US and Canada) by
Hart Publishing
c/o International Specialized Book Services
920 NE 58th Avenue, Suite 300
Portland, OR 97213-3786
USA
Tel: +1 503 287 3093 or toll-free: (1) 800 944 6190
Fax: +1 503 280 8832
E-mail: orders@isbs.com
Website: http://www.isbs.com

British Library Cataloguing in Publication Data
Data Available

ISBN: 978-1-84113-924-1 (Hart Publishing)
ISBN: 978-3-406-62874-0 (Verlag CH Beck)

Typeset by Forewords Ltd, Oxford
Printed and bound in Great Britain by
TJ International Ltd, Padstow, Cornwall

Preface

This book is being published in the run-up to the UN Conference on Sustainable Development (UNCSD) to be held at Rio de Janeiro in June 2012. The preparatory process has already begun. 'Rio+20' invites the international community's environmental and developmental players to critically review their efforts to sustainably preserve the Earth's ecosystem. Even if all actors involved have managed to ward off some serious environmental threats in the past, are they able and willing to identify ways and means to overcome the current global environmental crisis?

Mankind has recently experienced devastating natural catastrophes—the tsunamis in the Indian Ocean (December 2004) and off the Japanese coast (March 2011), the Hurricane Katrina (August 2005) and the Pakistan floods (August 2010). Man has learned how limited human capacities and capabilities are. The effects of natural catastrophes have often been exacerbated by human-induced incidents, such as the explosion of the offshore oil platform *Deepwater Horizon* in the Mexican Gulf (April 2010) and the destruction of the Fukushima nuclear power plant (March 2011), which proved not to be strong enough to withstand a tsunami. Apart from such 'headline' disasters, a myriad of simultaneously occurring multifaceted processes of environmental degradation are presenting unprecedented ecological challenges for the international community and global civil society.

It is not just the responsibility of politicians but also of scholars, including those skilled in international law, to actively engage in the global discourse on finding new ways and means to address these threats and to enhance global environmental governance in order to preserve the Earth from its worst environmental threats. Indeed, the potential contribution of international environmental law to cope with this growing global environmental crisis is more than just an added value, it is a matter of urgency.

There is already a number of well-known textbooks on international environmental law of high academic standard available, headed by P Sands, *Principles of International Environmental Law*, 2nd edn (2003), A Kiss and D Shelton, *International Environmental Law*, 3rd edn (2004), and P Birnie, A Boyle and C Redgwell, *International Law and the Environment*, 3rd edn (2009). As these and other books certainly provide comprehensive information and analysis of current international environmental law, our new textbook *International Environmental Law* is far from being unrivalled. However, primarily written for students and practitioners interested in the subject, this book tries to make the reader familiar with the system of international environmental law as a whole. We have tried hard to keep up with the inherent dynamics and with all new developments that have driven practice and theory in this field of international law. Apart from discussing key concepts, rule-making and compliance by a careful selection of topics and by adopting a cross-cutting synthesis of regulatory interaction, the book looks at options for improved co-ordination, harmonisation and even integration of existing multilateral environmental agreements, and also analyses how conflicts between various environmental regimes can be avoided or, at least, adequately managed. Notwithstanding this comprehensive and multifaceted conceptual approach, the book has been kept deliberately manageable in size. It presents the law as of late 2010, with data on pertinent treaty ratifications referred to as of 31 October 2010.

It is with gratitude we note that many people contributed to the completion of this book in different ways. To begin with, we want to express our thanks to Professors Armin von Bogdandy and Rüdiger Wolfrum, both Directors of the Heidelberg Max Planck Institute for Comparative Public Law and International Law, for their twofold support of our book project. They not only allowed us to make use of the rich facilities of the Heidelberg Max Planck Institute, but also enabled us to enjoy the support of Jenny Grote Stoutenburg and Vanessa Holzer as research fellows; given their excellent skills in law and language, they both critically assessed, commented and improved parts of our manuscript, even after having left Heidelberg for the United States and the United Kingdom, respectively. Likewise, we also thank Justus Liebig University, Gießen, for employing Ayse Martina Böhringer and Stefan Weiß as research assistants. They contributed to the successful completion of our efforts by assessing, commenting on and improving the text; they also significantly engaged in proof-reading and revising the final version of the whole text. In addition, we are grateful to Nora Phoebe Erler's contribution, who—notwithstanding a scholarship provided for doctoral studies by the Land Hessen—managed the book's index, table of treaties and list of abbreviations. Furthermore, we appreciate the academic and organisational support of a number of student assistants at Justus Liebig University, Gießen, namely Cora Baumann, Johannes Krombach, Mariana C Ruiz Lopez, Frederic Schneider, Veronika Semenova, Lydia Seng, Maribel Soto Sobrino, Michael Suter and Judith Thorn. Irrespective of all the support, all mistakes remain ours.

No book will ever be published without the active support and a lot of patience on the part of the publisher. Apart from expressing our gratitude to Richard Hart who was convinced of our project from the very outset, we want to thank Rachel Turner, Tom Adams and Mel Hamill and all the others who supported this publication.

We are grateful to our wives, Isolde and Katja, who tolerated our passion; we dedicate this book to our children, Friederike and Jörg, and Simon and Tabea. We hope that they themselves, their children and all the generations to come will have a chance to enjoy the richness of our precious global environment. This largely depends on our own responsibility and on our ability to establish sustainable modes of environmental governance. Let us recall the words of then 12-year-old Severn Cullis-Suzuki, speaking for the Environmental Children's Organization at the 1992 Rio Summit: 'Do not forget why you're attending these conferences, who you're doing this for—we are your own children. You are deciding what kind of world we will grow up in'.

Ulrich Beyerlin and Thilo Marauhn
Heidelberg and Gießen, June 2011

Contents

List of Abbreviations

AAU	Assigned Amount Unit
ABS	Access and Benefit-Sharing
ACCOBAMS	Agreement on the Conservation of Cetaceans of the Black Sea, Mediterranean Sea and Contiguous Atlantic Area (1996)
AIA	Advance Informed Agreement
AJIL	*American Journal of International Law*
AMU	Arab Maghreb Union
AOSIS	Alliance of Small Island States
ASCOBANS	Agreement on the Conservation of Small Cetaceans of the Baltic, North East Atlantic, Irish and North Seas (1992)
ASEAN	Association of Southeast Asian Nations
AWG-KP	Ad Hoc Working Group on Further Commitments for Annex I Parties under the Kyoto Protocol
AWG-LCA	Ad Hoc Working Group on Long-term Cooperative Action under the (UNFCCC) Convention
BAP	Bali Action Plan
BAPA	Buenos Aires Plan of Action
BGBl	Bundesgesetzblatt
CBD	Convention on Biological Diversity (1992)
CCAMLR	Commission for the Conservation of Antarctic Marine Living Resources
CCSBT	International Commission for the Conservation of Southern Bluefin Tuna
CCW	UN Convention on Certain Conventional Weapons (1980)
CDM	Clean Development Mechanism
CER	Certified Emission Reduction
CERES	Coalition for Environmentally Responsible Economies
CESCR	Committee on Economic, Social and Cultural Rights
CFC	Chlorofluorocarbon
CGIAR	Consultative Group of the International Agricultural Research
CILSS	Permanent Inter-State Committee for Drought Control in the Sahel
CITES	Convention on International Trade in Endangered Species of Wild Fauna and Flora (1973)
CMP	Conference of the Parties serving as the Meeting of the Parties to the Kyoto Protocol
CMS	Convention on the Conservation of Migratory Species of Wild Animals (1979)
COP	Conference of the Parties
COP/MOP	Conference of the Parties serving as the Meeting of the Parties
CPF	Collaborative Partnership on Forests
CSD	Commission on Sustainable Development
CTE	Committee on Trade and Environment
CTS	Canada Treaty Series

CWC	Chemical Weapons Convention (1993)
DSB	Dispute Settlement Body
DSU	Dispute Settlement Understanding
EC	European Commission
ECE	United Nations Economic Commission for Europe
ECHR	European Convention on Human Rights
EComHR	European Commission of Human Rights
ECOSOC	Economic and Social Council
ECSC	European Coal and Steal Community
ECtHR	European Court of Human Rights
EEC	European Economic Community
EEZ	Exclusive Economic Zone
EIA	Environmental Impact Assessment
EJIL	*European Journal of International Law*
EMAS	EU Eco-Management and Audit Scheme
EMEP	Cooperative Programme for Monitoring and Evaluation of the Long-range Transmission of Air Pollutants in Europe
EMS	Environmental Management System
EMuT	International Environmental Law – Multilateral Treaties
ENMOD Convention	Convention on the Prohibition of Military or Any Other Hostile Use of Environmental Modification Techniques (1976)
ERU	Emissions Reduction Unit
ET	Emissions Trading
EU	European Union
EURATOM	European Atomic Energy Community
FAO	Food and Agriculture Organisation of the United Nations
FSC	Forest Stewardship Council
GATS	General Agreement on Trade in Services
GATT	General Agreement on Tariffs and Trade
GEF	Global Environment Facility
GESAMP	Joint Group of Experts on the Scientific Aspects of Marine Environmental Protection
GFCM	General Fisheries Commission for the Mediterranean
GHG	Greenhouse gas
GMEF	Global Ministerial Environment Forum
GPA	Global Programme of Action
GRI	Global Reporting Initiative
HBFC	Hydrobromochlorofluorocarbon
HCFC	Hydrochlorofluorocarbon
HELCOM	Helsinki Commission
HNS Convention	International Convention on Liability and Compensation for Damage in Connection with the Carriage of Hazardous and Noxious Substances (1996)
HNS Fund	International Hazardous and Noxious Substances Fund
IAEA	International Atomic Energy Agency
IBRD	International Bank for Reconstruction and Development
IBSFC	International Baltic Sea Fisheries Commission
ICC	International Co-ordinating Council

ICCAT	International Commission for the Conservation of Atlantic Tuna
ICCPR	International Covenant on Civil and Political Rights
ICESCR	International Covenant on Economic, Social and Cultural Rights
ICJ	International Court of Justice
ICLQ	*International and Comparative Law Quarterly*
ICPR	International Commission for the Protection of the Rhine against Pollution
ICRC	International Committee of the Red Cross
ICRW	International Convention for the Regulation of Whaling (1946)
IDA	International Development Association
IDI	Institut de Droit International
IDP	Internally displaced person
IELR	International Environmental Law Reports
IFF	Intergovernmental Forum on Forests
IFS	Integrated Financing Strategies
IGAD	Intergovernmental Authority on Development
IITA	International Institute of Tropical Agriculture
IJC	US-Canadian International Joint Commission
ILA	International Law Association
ILC	International Law Commission
ILM	International Legal Materials
ILO	International Labour Organization
ILR	International Law Reports
IMO	International Maritime Organization
INFCIRC	IAEA Information Circular
IOTC	Indian Ocean Tuna Commission
IPCC	Intergovernmental Panel on Climate Change
IPE	International Protection of the Environment: Treaties and Related Documents
IPF	Intergovernmental Panel on Forests
ISO	International Organization for Standardization
ITFF	Interagency Task Force on Forests
ITLOS	International Tribunal for the Law of the Sea
ITPGRFA	International Treaty on Plant Genetic Resources for Food and Agriculture (2001)
ITTA	International Tropical Timber Agreement (1994 and 2006)
ITTO	International Tropical Timber Organization
IUCN	International Union for Conservation of Nature
IUPGR	International Undertaking on Plant Genetic Resources (1983)
IUU	Illegal, Unreported and Unregulated (Fishing)
IWC	International Whaling Commission
JLG	Joint Liaison Group
JWP	Joint Work Plan
LBS	Land-Based Sources
LDCs	Least developed countries
LMO	Living Modified Organism
LNTS	League of Nations Treaty Series
LRTAP Convention	Geneva Convention on Long-Range Transboundary Air Pollution (1979)

LULUCF	Land Use, Land-Use Change and Forestry
MAB	UNESCO Man and the Biosphere Programme (1977)
MARPOL 73/78	London Convention for the Prevention of Pollution from Ships (1973, as modified by Protocol of 1978)
MATs	Mutually Agreed Terms
MDGs	Millennium Development Goals
MEA	Multilateral Environmental Agreement
MEPC	Marine Environment Protection Committee
MERCOSUR	Mercado Común del Sur
MOP	Meeting of the Parties
MOU	Memorandum of Understanding
MSC	Marine Stewardship Council
NAAEC	North American Agreement on Environmental Cooperation (1994)
NACEC	North American Commission for Environmental Cooperation
NAFO	Northwest Atlantic Fisheries Organization
NAFTA	North American Free Trade Agreement (1992)
NAMMCO	North Atlantic Marine Mammal Commission
NBI	Nile Basin Initiative
NEAFC	North East Atlantic Fisheries Commission
NGO	Non-Governmental Organisation
NIEO	New International Economic Order
NPAFC	North Pacific Anadromous Fish Commission
NYIL	*Netherlands Yearbook of International Law*
ODS	Ozone-depleting substances
OECD	Organisation for Economic Cooperation and Development
OJ	Official Journal of the European Union
OPCW	Organisation for the Prohibition of Chemical Weapons
OPRC Convention	London International Convention on Oil Pollution Preparedness, Response and Co-operation (1990)
OPRC-HNS Protocol	London Protocol on Preparedness, Response and Co-operation to Pollution Incidents by Hazardous and Noxious Substances (2000)
OSPAR Convention	Convention for the Protection of the Marine Environment of the North-East Atlantic (1992)
PCA	Permanent Court of Arbitration
PCIJ	Permanent Court of International Justice
PIC	Prior Informed Consent
POP	Persistent organic pollutant
PPP	Public-Private Partnership
RAP	Regional Action Programme
RCAP	Canadian Royal Commission on Aboriginal Peoples
RECIEL	*Review of European Community & International Environmental Law*
REDD-plus	Reducing emissions from deforestation and forest degradation
RIAA	Reports of International Arbitral Awards
RMP	Revised Management Procedure
SADC	Southern African Development Community
SBSTA	Subsidiary Body for Scientific and Technological Advice
SDR	Special Drawing Rights

SEAFO	South-East Atlantic Fisheries Organization
SMTA	Standard Material Transfer Agreement
SPFFA	South Pacific Forum Fisheries Agency
SPS Agreement	Agreement on the Application of Sanitary and Phytosanitary Measures (1994)
STCP	Sustainable Tree Crops Program
TBT Agreement	Agreement on Technical Barriers to Trade (1994)
TFEU	Treaty on the Functioning of the European Union (2007)
TOMA	Tropospheric Ozone Management Area
TRIPS	Agreement on Trade-Related Aspects of Intellectual Property Rights (1994)
UKTS	United Kingdom Treaty Series
UN	United Nations
UNCCD	United Nations Convention to Combat Desertification (1994)
UNCED	United Nations Conference on Environment and Development
UNCESCR	UN Committee on Economic, Social and Cultural Rights
UNCLOS	United Nations Convention on the Law of the Sea (1982)
UNCSD	United Nations Conference on Sustainable Development
UNCTAD	United Nations Conference on Trade and Development
UNDP	United Nations Development Programme
UNDRIP	United Nations Declaration on the Rights of Indigenous Peoples
UNECE	United Nations Economic Commission for Europe
UNEP	United Nations Environment Programme
UNESCO	United Nations Educational, Scientific and Cultural Organization
UNFCCC	United Nations Framework Convention on Climate Change (1992)
UNFF	United Nations Forum on Forests
UNGA	United Nations General Assembly
UN GAOR	United Nations General Assembly Official Records
UNITAR	UN Institute for Training and Research
UNTS	United Nations Treaty Series
VCLT	Vienna Convention on the Law of Treaties (1969)
VOC	Volatile Organic Compound
WBCSD	World Business Council for Sustainable Development
WHO	World Health Organization
WMO	World Meteorological Organization
WRI	World Resources Institute
WSSD	World Summit on Sustainable Development
WTO	World Trade Organization
WWF	World Wide Fund for Nature
YIEL	*Yearbook of International Environmental Law*
ZaöRV	*Zeitschrift für ausländisches öffentliches Recht und Völkerrecht* (*Heidelberg Journal of International Law*)

Table of Treaties

Part I

Historical Development

1

From the Beginnings of International Environmental Law to the Stockholm Conference (1972)

1.1 Early Stages and the Interwar Period

Instruments of international law that focus on the protection of the environment only emerged in greater number after the end of the Second World War. Symptomatic of the deficient environmental consciousness of the founding fathers of the United Nations is the fact that the UN Charter of 1945 made neither environmental protection nor the conservation of the natural resources the explicit task of the United Nations. The great mass of international environmental protection norms that deserve this name was only generated in the last 35 years. In comparison with other fields of international law, such as the law of armed conflict, the law of diplomatic relations or the law of the sea, international environmental law is thus a rather young branch of law.

However, the first treaties relevant to environmental protection can be found much earlier. Thus, a number of—mostly bilateral—agreements concerning fisheries,[1] problems of the equitable utilisation of watercourses by riparian states[2] or the protection of wild birds[3] date from the late nineteenth century. The international agreements in the first two areas pursued mainly a utilitarian objective, ie the balancing of competing interests of neighbouring states; their benefit, if any, for the environment was hardly more than a side effect. In contrast, the above-mentioned bilateral agreements on the protection of wild

[1] *Eg* the Fisheries Convention between France and Great Britain of 11 November 1867; the Agreement between Great Britain and the United States of America for a *Modus Vivendi* in Relation to the Fur Seal Fisheries in the Bering Sea of 15 June 1891.

[2] *Eg* the Convention between Great Britain and the United States of America Relating to Boundary Waters and Boundary Questions between the USA and Canada of 11 January 1909.

[3] *Eg* the Convention for the Protection of Birds Useful to Agriculture of 19 March 1902; the Convention for the Protection of Migratory Birds in the United States and Canada of 16 August 1916.

birds, like some later multilateral agreements on nature conservation—*eg* the Convention destinée à assurer la conservation des diverses espèces animales vivant à l'état sauvage en Afrique qui sont utiles à l'homme ou inoffensives of 19 May 1900, the Convention Relative to the Preservation of Fauna and Flora in the Natural State of 8 November 1933, which primarily relates to Africa, and the Convention on Nature Protection and Wild Life Preservation in the Western Hemisphere of 12 October 1940—come closer to pursuing genuine ecological aims. However, it should be noted that the efforts of this time to protect the flora and fauna only resulted in very sporadic and selective contractual agreements with limited regulatory effect. On the other hand, the International Convention for the Regulation of Whaling of 24 September 1931 contained rudimentary regulation on the preservation of the whale population obviously for the sole purpose of enhanced utilisation of this natural resource.

Nevertheless in the early stages of international environmental law, namely on 11 March 1941, the famous international arbitral award in the *Trail Smelter* case[4] was rendered, which subsequently proved to be a milestone for the further development of transboundary environmental protection. This dispute between the USA and Canada dealt with the settlement of damages incurred by the agriculture and forestry in the US state of Washington by the discharge of sulphur dioxide emissions from a lead and zinc smelting plant in British Columbia, Canada. The arbitral tribunal ascertained that

> under the principles of international law . . . no state has the right to use or permit the use of its territory in such a manner as to cause injury by fumes in or to the territory of another or the properties or persons therein, when the case is of serious consequences and the injury is established by clear and convincing evidence.[5]

The arbitral award held Canada liable not only for the damages already incurred, but also for possible further lead and zinc smelter activities with adverse transboundary effects for the environment in the neighbouring state. The judges further declared that Canada would have to ensure that detrimental activity in its territory ceased if persistent and grave environmental damage was to be expected. However, this statement cannot be understood as obliging every state to avoid causing transboundary environmental damage of a certain gravity to its neighbouring states from the outset. Nevertheless, the arbitral award rendered in the Trail Smelter case has turned out to be an important precedent for the development of the principle of limited territorial sovereignty and integrity,[6] the eminent legal principle that determines transboundary environmental protection.

1.2 From 1945 to 1972

After the Second World War, the United Nations, in spite of the silence of the UN Charter on ecological matters, soon addressed questions of international environmental protection,

[4] (1949) 3 RIAA 1903 *et seq*.
[5] *Ibid*, at 1965.
[6] See in detail Chapter 6.

in particular those concerning the conservation of natural resources which might come into conflict with resource utilisation. Special mention should be made in this respect of the UN Conference on the Conservation and Utilization of Resources of 1949, convened by the Economic and Social Council (ECOSOC), where the interrelation of the utilisation and the conservation of resources was exhaustively discussed for the first time. It is exactly this tension between the competing regulatory aims of resource utilisation and conservation that is symptomatic of the subsequent international agreements dealing with the law of the sea and the law of freshwater resources.

This holds true for the Convention on Fishing and Conservation of Living Resources of the High Seas of 29 April 1958, concluded during the first UN Conference on the Law of the Sea in Geneva, as well as for the numerous regional fisheries conventions concluded between 1949 and 1969.[7] In the 1950s, states made initial sporadic attempts to regulate by treaty certain aspects of the protection of the marine environment. Here, Articles 24 and 25 of the Convention on the High Seas of 29 April 1958 should in particular be referred to: these require the states parties to commit to taking measures to prevent pollution of the seas by the discharge of oil or radioactive waste. The International Convention for the Prevention of Pollution of the Sea by Oil had already been adopted (12 May 1954). Still further agreements on the abatement of these specific sources of pollution were adopted in the late 1960s. A comprehensive regulation of marine environmental protection, however, was only achieved with the Convention on the Law of the Sea of 10 December 1982, which had been concluded during the third UN Conference on the Law of the Sea, but did not enter into force until 1994.

The efforts by riparian states of international rivers and lakes in the 1950s and 1960s to apportion equitably between them the usage rights for these watercourses and to agree on protection measures were more successful in producing contractual solutions. The focus of the activities had been on North America before the Second World War, but now shifted to Europe and other continents. Although the states still mainly cared about the regulation of fisheries and navigation and other economic uses, they increasingly attended to the problems of freshwater protection in numerous international multilateral agreements, concerning for example the protection against pollution of the Moselle, the Rhine, Lake Geneva or Lake Constance. On the basis of these agreements, joint commissions for the protection of these watercourses were established. The commissions, however, act in a purely advisory capacity.[8]

The arbitral award in the *Trail Smelter* case of 1941, which resulted in the principle of limited territorial sovereignty and integrity, received early confirmation from a decision of the International Court of Justice in the *Corfu Channel* case of 9 April 1949.[9] In the *Corfu Channel* case, the judges assumed the obligation of every state 'not to allow knowingly its territory to be used for acts contrary to the rights of other States',[10] although in

[7] See generally K Bangert, 'Fisheries Agreements' in R Wolfrum (ed), *Max Planck Encyclopedia of Public International Law* (Heidelberg/Oxford 2008) paras 19 *et seq*, available at www.mpepil.com.

[8] See for details Chapter 11.1.

[9] *UK and Northern Ireland v Albania* (1949) ICJ Reports 4 *et seq*.

[10] *Ibid*, at 22.

a completely different context. In the *Lac Lanoux* case[11] an international arbitral tribunal had to deal with a conflict of sovereignty, namely the problematic relationship between the upper and lower riparian states of a transboundary watercourse. In its decision of 16 November 1957 settling the dispute between Spain and France, the arbitral tribunal arrived at the important conclusion that the upper riparian state can only make use of its right to water utilisation insofar as no serious harm to the lower riparian state is caused by the alteration of the natural watercourse. Thus, conflicting interests of sovereignty and integrity were once again—as in the *Trail Smelter* case—balanced.

The international protection of flora and fauna by treaty was further expanded. Of particular note are the African Convention on the Conservation of Nature and Natural Resources of 15 September 1968 and the Convention on Wetlands of International Importance Especially as Waterfowl Habitat (Ramsar Convention) of 2 February 1971. The latter agreement for the first time protected primarily the habitats of certain species, *ie* specific ecosystems.

However, the enumeration of all these international agreements cannot conceal the fact that in the early stages, *ie* in the period before 1972, international environmental law seen as a whole was still far from being fully developed. Important subareas of environmental protection were not yet subject to regulation by treaty. For instance, states did not perceive air pollution as a global environmental problem since they obviously were not aware that the release of pollutants into the atmosphere entails far-reaching, severe environmental risks. Nor was the handling of hazardous waste a topic at that time. In fact, transboundary movements of hazardous waste have only become a serious international problem in the last 30 years.

Another characteristic of international relations prior to 1972 is that environmental treaty-making was clearly dominated by the industrialised states. Most of the relevant treaties concluded during this period show clear traces of the close interrelation between natural conservationism and colonialism; almost none of these treaties refer to the economic and social needs of underdeveloped countries and their societies. Only since the late 1960s did the international community of states become increasingly aware of the close interdependence between environmental and developmental interests and needs. This change in states' attitude came along with the growing activism of the developing countries in the international arena. As the number of developing countries which are members of the United Nations grew from 27 originally in 1945 to almost 150 at present, the so-called 'Third World' states slowly gained considerable bargaining power, at least in the plenary organs of the United Nations and their specialised agencies. Thus, starting with the 1972 Stockholm Conference, the developing countries, formed up in the 'Group of 77' since 1964,[12] could increasingly become a serious opponent to the industrialised world.[13]

[11] (1963) 12 RIAA 281 *et seq*.

[12] Today, the Group of 77 comprises 130 developing countries; the members include fast-developing countries such as China, India and Brazil.

[13] See below Chapter 2.2.

2

From Stockholm to the Rio Conference (1992)

2.1 The Stockholm Conference

The UN General Assembly, with its Resolution 2398 (XXIII) of 3 December 1968, established the basis for the convocation of the Stockholm Conference on the Human Environment. With this initiative, the General Assembly reacted to two trends, namely on the one hand the rapidly increasing risk potential of environmental pollution and its globalisation, of which the world public was becoming increasingly aware, and on the other hand the fact that the time was ripe for effective international environmental protection as the ability of science to identify the causes and effects of complex environmental pollution had constantly improved, and more effective techniques and technologies for environmental protection had been developed.

According to the UN General Assembly, the UN Conference on the Human Environment was destined to provide states with a high-ranking, central forum for treating environmental problems as a whole and for discussing options for coping with them in a coordinated, effective manner. Convening this conference was a reaction to the finding that the disparate and often uncoordinated activities to protect the environment undertaken by UN specialised agencies and other international organisations in the previous decade had not succeeded in this respect.

The results of this first universal conference[1] on questions of international environmental protection, held 5–15 June 1972 in Stockholm, are mainly reflected in two legally non-binding documents: (i) the final declaration of the Conference, the so-called Stockholm Declaration, with its remarkable catalogue of rather clear-cut principles;[2] and (ii) an Action Plan consisting of 109 recommendations.[3]

The Stockholm Declaration, in spite of not being legally binding, proved to be par-

[1] The former Eastern Bloc states did not belong to the 114 participating states. However, representatives of numerous international institutions and NGO observers took part in the conference.

[2] See its text in the Report of the UN Conference on the Human Environment, Stockholm, UN Doc A/CONF48/14/Rev1, 3 *et seq*; (1972) 11 ILM 1416.

[3] *Ibid*, 6 *et seq*.

ticularly conducive to the further development of international law. Principle 1 needs to be highlighted here, as it clearly and firmly determined the leitmotif and the programme for the future intergovernmental protection of the environment by stating:

> Man has the fundamental right to freedom, equality and adequate conditions of life, in an environment of a quality that permits a life of dignity and well-being, and he bears a solemn responsibility to protect and improve the environment for present and future generations.

Special attention needs to be given to Principle 21, which emphasises, on the basis of the *Trail Smelter* arbitration, the responsibility of states

> to ensure that activities within their jurisdiction or control do not cause damage to the environment of other States or of areas beyond the limits of national jurisdiction.

However, this obligation of states is considerably qualified by the concurrent allusion to their 'sovereign right to exploit their own resources pursuant to their own environmental policies' in Principle 21. Furthermore it is most remarkable that already at the Stockholm Conference the close interdependency between environment and development was recognised, which is mainly reflected in Principles 8 and 11 of the Stockholm Declaration. The latter principle reads:

> The environmental policies of all States should enhance and not adversely affect the present or future development potential of developing countries, nor should they hamper the attainment of better living conditions for all.

Twenty years later, the pursuit of an integrated environment and development policy on the international and national level, referred to as 'sustainable development', was to become the central concern of the second major UN environment conference in Rio de Janeiro.

The first visible outcome of the Stockholm Conference was the United Nations Environment Programme (UNEP), established in December 1972, which was the first institution within the UN system to have environmental protection as its main task. It was thus destined to assume a leading and coordinating function within the United Nations in this area. Since UNEP was only established on the basis of a UN General Assembly resolution,[4] it does not possess international legal personality of its own, unlike, for example, the UN specialised agencies. Nevertheless, UNEP has taken part in the subsequent process of generating international environmental norms with considerable success.[5]

2.2 Impacts of the North–South Divide on International Environmental Law

As already indicated, Principle 11 of the Stockholm Declaration pursued a new conceptual approach by stating that environmental protection should be an integral part of any

[4] UNGA Res 2997 (XXVII) (15 December 1972).

[5] For more details see Chapter 17.2.2.

developmental measure, and vice versa. However, at the Stockholm Conference many developing countries clearly resisted this paradigmatic shift in environmental and developmental thinking. In their view, pollution of the environment was primarily the result of industrialisation and therefore only of concern for the developed states. It was this scepticism of the South about the environmental dedication of the North that induced Indira Gandhi, the Indian Prime Minister, to make the following statement in Stockholm:

> The rich countries may look upon development as the cause of environmental destruction, but to us it is one of the primary means of improving the environment of living, of providing food, water, sanitation and shelter. . . . We cannot forget the grim poverty of large numbers of people. . . . How can we speak to those who live in villages and in slums about keeping the oceans, rivers and the air clean when their own lives are contaminated at the source? Environment cannot be improved in conditions of poverty. Nor can poverty be eradicated without the use of science and technology.[6]

Consequently, in the post-Stockholm era the economic and social concerns of the underdeveloped societies in the South clearly became predominant in interstate relations.

In 1974 the developing states, organised in the Group of 77, succeeded in their efforts to make the UN General Assembly adopt the Declaration on the Establishment of a New International Economic Order,[7] as well as the Charter of Economic Rights and Duties of States.[8] These instruments, both legally non-binding in nature, were inspired by the idea of overcoming injustices in the then existing international legal system. Accordingly, they called upon the industrialised states to take action towards reaching the following seven objectives: opening of their markets for the products of developing countries; acknowledging the developing countries' full and permanent sovereignty over natural resources; increasing the official development aid of industrialised states to 0.7 per cent of their GNP; increasing the developing countries' share in the worldwide process of manufacturing industrial products; facilitating their access to modern technology and enhancing their infrastructure; solving the debt crisis of developing countries; and increasing their participation in relevant decision-making processes of international financial institutions.

At first sight, the adoption of the 1974 Declaration on the Establishment of a New International Economic Order may be seen as an increase in prestige of the Third World states. However, their optimism, as expressed in the 1974 Cocoyoc Declaration, 'that ways of life and social systems can be evolved that are more just, less arrogant in their material demands, and more respectful of the whole planetary environment',[9] was to dissipate all too quickly in the 1980s—a decade that was marked by the superpowers' cold war attitudes and a dramatic increase in the debt burden of poor countries. Symptomatic of the deep political and ideological gap between the North and South is RP Anand's sar-

[6] Cited according to RP Anand, 'Development and Environment: The Case of the Developing Countries' (1980) 20 *Indian Journal of International Law* 1, 10.

[7] UNGA Res 3201 (S-XV) (1 May 1974).

[8] UNGA Res 3281 (XXIX) (12 December 1974).

[9] The Declaration was adopted at the UNEP/UNCTAD Symposium on Resource Use, Environment, and Development Strategies held in Cocoyoc, Mexico, in October 1974; see its text in: The International Law of Development: Basic Documents, 1753, 1776.

castic comment on the finding that due to their backwardness in the past the developing countries inflicted less harm on the environment than the rich countries:

> For the survival of mankind the poor developing countries should remain in a state of underdevelopment because if the evils of industrialization were to reach them, life on the planet would be in jeopardy.[10]

After all, in the aftermath of the Stockholm Conference the protagonists of both the North and South were far from heeding in practice what they had conjointly committed to in Principle 11 of the Stockholm Declaration.

2.3 International Treaty Practice since 1972

Notwithstanding these discrepancies between the North and the South, the Stockholm Conference gave new momentum to the development of international environmental law. In particular the net of bilateral and multilateral environmental agreements (MEAs) grew considerably tighter in the years that followed. Some environmental problems that had hitherto been neglected or not even addressed were now made the subject of international agreements. Some particularly important MEAs are:

- the Washington Convention on International Trade in Endangered Species of Wild Fauna and Flora (CITES) of 3 March 1973;
- the International Convention for the Prevention of Pollution from Ships of 2 November 1973, as modified by the Protocol of 1978 relating thereto (MARPOL 73/78);
- the Geneva Convention on Long-Range Transboundary Air Pollution of 13 November 1979, with eight subsequent protocols;[11]
- the Convention on the Conservation of Antarctic Marine Living Resources of 20 May 1980;
- the environmental protection norms in Part XII of the United Nations Convention on the Law of the Sea of 10 December 1982 (but which only entered into force on 16 November 1994);
- the Vienna Convention for the Protection of the Ozone Layer of 22 March 1985 with its Montreal Protocol on Substances that Deplete the Ozone Layer of 16 September 1987;
- the two IAEA Conventions on Early Notification of a Nuclear Accident and on Assistance in the Case of a Nuclear Accident or Radiological Emergency of 26 September 1986;
- the Basel Convention on the Control of Transboundary Movements of Hazardous Wastes and Their Disposal of 22 March 1989;
- the International Convention on Oil Pollution Preparedness, Response and Co-operation of 30 November 1990;

[10] Anand, above n 6, 8.
[11] For details on the protocols see Chapter 13.2.1.

- the UNECE Convention on Environmental Impact Assessment in a Transboundary Context of 25 February 1991;
- the UNECE Convention on the Protection and Use of Transboundary Watercourses and International Lakes of 17 March 1992; and
- the UNECE Convention on the Transboundary Effects of Industrial Accidents of 17 March 1992.

This small selection of MEAs concluded between the two eminent UN environment conferences of Stockholm and Rio de Janeiro demonstrates that the treaty practice now covered a much broader spectrum of environmental problems than before. It is striking that although many agreements still aim at transboundary environmental protection in the stricter sense, some, in particular the Vienna Convention for the Protection of the Ozone Layer, now also try to solve global environmental problems. However, the approach adopted by most agreements on resource conservation of that time is still utilitarian rather than ecological.

More than a hundred universal and regional MEAs were concluded between 1972 and 1992. However, these agreements were still far from constituting an effective international legal order of environmental protection. The net of agreements had certainly grown tighter, partly in reaction to the increasing number of environmental catastrophes with global consequences—*Amoco Cadiz*, *Exxon Valdez*, Seveso, Bhopal, Chernobyl, Sandoz. Nevertheless, international environmental treaty law in the early 1990s still had some large gaps, and the quality of the MEAs often left a great deal to be desired— in particular, the operative norms of many agreements were rather poor in legal substance. The fact that the contracting states far too often did not comply in practice with the obligations they had committed to further worsened the situation.

2.4 Other Activities

The intensity and seriousness of the efforts to extend and improve the system of international environmental norms are not only reflected in legally binding MEAs, but also in legally non-binding instruments that have considerably influenced the further development of international environmental law.

Among these are in particular the Draft Principles of Conduct in the Field of the Environment for the Guidance of States in the Conservation and Harmonious Utilization of Natural Resources Shared by Two or More States, adopted by the UNEP Governing Council in 1978.[12] Starting from the concept of 'shared natural resources', these Draft Principles posit procedural obligations of conduct for the riparian states of surface waters which are determined by the principles of good faith and good neighbourliness. Thus, Draft Principle 4 urges states to make environmental impact assessments before engaging in any activity which may create a significant risk for the environment of another state.

[12] (1978) 17 ILM 1091.

This prepared the ground for the later conclusion of the respective Espoo Convention of 1991 within the framework of the UNECE.

With the 1982 Montevideo Programme for the Development and Periodic Review of Environmental Law,[13] the UNEP Governing Council defined the environmental objectives of its future activity. In this (legally non-binding) programme, the further development of international environmental law especially in three problem areas—marine pollution from land-based sources, protection of the stratospheric ozone layer, and the control of the handling and transboundary movement of hazardous waste— was declared exceedingly urgent. The latter two matters were made the subject of legally binding agreements years later.

The World Charter for Nature, adopted in 1982 by the UN General Assembly in the form of a resolution,[14] stands out against most instruments of that time in that it clearly focuses on the protection of nature for its own sake. Based on this ecocentric approach, it posits a 'standard of ethical conduct' which has greatly inspired subsequent international treaty practice.

Finally, the work done by the World Commission on Environment and Development (the so-called 'Brundtland Commission'), established by the UN General Assembly in 1983, warrants attention. With its famous report 'Our Common Future' of 1987,[15] this commission provided decisive impulses for the programmatic direction of the Rio Conference of 1992.

Important initiatives for the further development of international environmental protection were also taken outside of the system of the United Nations during the period in question. Here, the Recommendations of the OECD Council of the 1970s on specific problems of transfrontier environmental protection need to be highlighted.[16] These OECD Recommendations presented innovative ways and means to intensify international co-operation with regard to solving transfrontier pollution problems. They have strongly influenced subsequent state practice. Thus, Recommendations C (76)55 and C (77)28 paved the way for foreign neighbours to have recourse to and standing in domestic administrative and judicial procedures.[17] Other important OECD Recommendations of the 1980s concerned questions of the transboundary movement of waste.[18]

[13] UNEP/GC.10/5/Add2, Annex (1981), at 5; UNEP GC Dec 10/21 (31 May 1982).

[14] UNGA Res 37/7 (28 October 1982); (1983) 22 ILM 455.

[15] World Commission on Environment and Development, *Our Common Future* (Oxford 1987).

[16] Special mention should be made of Recommendation C (74)224 (14 November 1974) on 'Principles Concerning Transfrontier Pollution'; Recommendation C (76)55 (11 May 1976) on the 'Equal Right of Access in Relation to Transfrontier Pollution'; Recommendation C (77)28 (17 May 1977) on the 'Implementation of a Regime of Equal Right of Access and Non-Discrimination in Relation to Transfrontier Pollution'; and Recommendation C (78)77 (21 September 1978) on 'Strengthening International Co-operation on Environmental Protection in Frontier Regions'.

[17] *Our Common Future*, above n 15, 413 *et seq*.

[18] See for details Chapter 15.1.

3

From Rio to the Johannesburg Conference (2002)

3.1 The Rio Conference

The United Nations Conference on Environment and Development (UNCED) took place in Rio de Janeiro, 3–14 June 1992. Remarkably, more than 30000 participants from 176 states took part.

The decision to convene UNCED had been adopted by the UN General Assembly in its Resolution 44/228 of 22 December 1989.[1] According to the Resolution, the objective of the conference was to

> elaborate strategies and measures to halt and reverse the effects of environmental degradation in the context of increased national and international efforts to promote sustainable and environmentally sound development in all countries.[2]

The Resolution prescribed a comprehensive catalogue of measures in the field of environment and development for the conference. In doing so, the General Assembly drew on its two Resolutions 42/186 and 42/187 of 11 December 1987 on the 'Environmental Perspective to the Year 2000 and Beyond' and on the Brundtland Commission report 'Our Common Future'.

The actual preparatory process for the planned conference was entrusted by the General Assembly to the UNCED Preparatory Committee, which had been established especially for this purpose. Independently from the Committee, two Intergovernmental Negotiating Committees had during the same time elaborated drafts for two international agreements on climate change and on biological diversity, which were open for signature by states at the Rio Conference.

[1] With this, the General Assembly followed a proposition by the Brundtland Commission; see its report *Our Common Future* (Oxford 1987) 343.

[2] Resolution available at www.un.org/documents/ga/res/44/ares44-228.htm.

UNCED itself was characterised, like the whole preparatory process, by the tenacious struggle of the state representatives to overcome the conflict of interests between the different groups of states. The North–South divide was present all too clearly in Rio. The industrial states showed little willingness to meet the demands of the developing countries for more distributive justice and for a change in their own ecologically harmful production and consumption patterns. The developing countries, on the other hand, opposed the request by the industrialised states to ensure the democratisation of their societies and to take better care of their natural resources. The depth of the clashes between the North and the South in weighing their opposing interests at the Rio Conference is best reflected by the statement of the former Prime Minister of Malaysia, Mahathir Mohamad:

> The poor are not asking for charity. When the rich chopped down their own forests, built their poison-belching factories and scoured the world for cheap resources, the poor said nothing. Indeed they paid for the development of the rich. Now the rich claim a right to regulate the development of the poor countries. And yet any suggestion that the rich compensate the poor adequately is regarded as outrageous. As colonies we were exploited. Now as independent nations we are to be equally exploited.[3]

Thus, the demeanour of states during the Rio Conference fully confirmed environmentalists in their fears that states would only relinquish their traditional conception of sovereignty through a very tedious and protracted process.

A novelty in the practice of outstanding international state conferences was the degree to which non-governmental organisations (NGOs) were actively involved in the conference proceedings. More than 700 NGOs were accredited to UNCED as observers via a simplified admission procedure. Moreover, more than 800 NGOs from all over the world met in the 'Global Forum '92', an event held in parallel to the official conference, in order to elaborate 'alternative treaties'—in contrast to the positions held by the states at the Rio Conference.

3.2 Rio Outcomes

Positive outcomes of the Rio Conference are the Rio Declaration, the Statement of Forest Principles, and Agenda 21, as well as the two conventions on climate change and biological diversity. However, as mentioned above, the two latter instruments had been negotiated earlier. They are ascribed to Rio because there they were signed by an exceptionally large number of states. All instruments mentioned are characterised substantially by the concept of 'sustainable development', which likewise had been developed before UNCED, but which since Rio has become a widely accepted benchmark in international environment and development relations. Therefore, the concept deserves mention in the context of Rio.[4]

[3] Cited according to K Mickelson, 'Rhetoric and Rage: Third World Voices in International Legal Discourse' (1998) 16 *Wisconsin International Law Journal* 353–419, 390 *et seq*.

[4] As to the normativity and the (legal) status of 'sustainable development' see below Chapter 10.

3.2.1 The Concept of 'Sustainable Development'

The notion of 'sustainable development' points to the close relationship between environment and development. While 'development' explicitly appears as one of the components of the term 'sustainable development', environmental protection as the second component finds expression in the rather cryptic attribute 'sustainable'. However, that 'sustainability' relates to environmental protection follows from the genesis of the concept of 'sustainable development'[5] as well as from the fact that this concept constitutes the dominant leitmotif of numerous subsequent MEAs.

The origins of the concept of 'sustainable development' are hard to trace. The close linkage between development politics and environmental protection was emphasised for the first time in the UN Declaration proclaiming the Second United Nations Development Decade of 1970.[6] Principles 9, 10 and 11 of the Stockholm Declaration of 1972 then urged all states to ensure that their environmental policies enhance and do not adversely affect the present or future development potential of developing countries, and that they do not hamper the attainment of better living conditions for all. That environment and development have to be equal components of an indivisible policy objective was made especially clear in the International Development Strategy for the Third Development Decade, adopted by the UN General Assembly in 1980,[7] which states *inter alia*:

> It is essential to avoid environmental degradation and give future generations the benefit of a sound environment. There is need to ensure an economic development process which is environmentally sustainable over the long run and which protects the ecological balance.

With this, the General Assembly explicitly called attention for the first time to a fundamental element of 'sustainable development', namely the necessary persistence of the required policy.

The 1980s were characterised by manifold international efforts to implement this still very abstract strategic concept of the UN General Assembly. Noteworthy in this respect are the 1980 World Conservation Strategy,[8] jointly developed by the IUCN, UNEP and the WWF, and the 1982 UN World Charter for Nature.[9] They both are much more definite as to what kind of actions states should take with the aim of achieving 'sustainable development'. The characterisation of the concept of 'sustainable development' in the Brundtland Commission report of 1987 as 'development that meets the needs of the present without compromising the ability of future generations to meet their own needs'[10] gained general recognition. Understood in this sense, the concept infiltrated the Rio documents in various forms. Thus, according to Principle 3 of the Rio Declaration, '[t]he right to development must be fulfilled so as to equitably meet developmental and environmental needs

[5] See for details U Beyerlin, 'The Concept of Sustainable Development' in R Wolfrum (ed), *Enforcing Environmental Standards: Economic Mechanisms as Viable Means?* (Berlin 1996) 95, 96 *et seq*.

[6] UNGA Res 2626 (XXV) (24 October 1970).

[7] UNGA Res 35/56 (5 December 1980); (1981) 20 ILM 480.

[8] IUCN *et al*, *World Conservation Strategy: Living Resource Conservation for Sustainable Development* (Gland 1980).

[9] UNGA Res 37/7 (28 October 1982); (1983) 22 ILM 455.

[10] *Our Common Future*, above n 1, 43.

of present and future generations'. Legal scholarship has developed in this context the formula of 'intergenerational equity and responsibility', which constitutes a core element of the concept of 'sustainable development'.

Hence, essential attributes of 'sustainable development' are the close linkage between the policy goals of environment and development, the consideration of environmental protection as an integral part of development politics, and the intergenerational dimension of this concept. 'Sustainable development' thus needs to be conceived as a holistic policy goal with development and environmental protection as its equal-ranking components.[11]

3.2.2 Legally Non-Binding Instruments

The Rio Declaration on Environment and Development,[12] the Non-legally Binding Authoritative Statement of Principles for a Global Consensus on the Management, Conservation and Sustainable Development of all Types of Forests,[13] and Agenda 21[14] are generally qualified as being 'soft law' instruments, *ie* agreements without immediate international binding force.[15]

The Rio Declaration of 1992—like the Stockholm Declaration of 1972 had done before—addresses states with a catalogue of 27 recommendations (named 'Principles'). These recommendations are all guided, as already indicated, by the idea of 'sustainable development'. Principle 1 proclaims human beings to be 'at the centre of concerns for sustainable development' and emphasises their entitlement 'to a healthy and productive life in harmony with nature'. Principle 3 contains a commitment to intergenerational equity as a guideline for efforts to do justice to the developmental and environmental needs of present and future generations. Consequently, Principle 4 demands that 'environmental protection' be 'an integral part of the development process'. Although most of these recommendations are programmatic, there are some that—due to their more precise wording and concrete content—either confirm already existing rules of customary international law or allude to emerging customary rules. Among the Principles confirming international customary law are the responsibility not to cause transboundary harm to the environment of other states or of areas beyond the limits of national jurisdiction (Principle 2), and the duty to provide mutual information and warnings (Principles 18 and 19). Belonging to the second category are the two requirements of public participation in environmental decision-making (Principle 10) and the undertaking of environmental impact assessments for proposed activities that are likely to have a significant adverse effect on the environment (Principle 17), and arguably also the precautionary approach (Principle 15) and the 'polluter pays' principle (Principle 16).[16]

The Statement of Forest Principles, which explicitly declares itself to be 'authoritative'

[11] See for details Chapter 10.

[12] See its text in Report of the UN Conference on Environment and Development, Rio de Janeiro, UN Doc A/CONF151/26/Rev1 (vol I), 3 *et seq*; (1992) 31 ILM 874.

[13] *Cf ibid*, 480 *et seq;* (1992) 31 ILM 881.

[14] Available at www.un.org/esa/sustdev/documents/agenda21/english/agenda21toc.htm.

[15] See for details Chapter 20.

[16] See for details Chapters 6–8.

yet 'non-legally binding', contains for the first time 15 globally applicable principles relating to forest management, conservation and sustainable development. However, these 'principles' are very vaguely worded and thus offer little substantive content. In a normative respect, the Statement therefore contributes little to the better protection of forests. For instance, Principles 1(a) and 2(b) affirm the sovereign right of states to exploit their own resources to the benefit of their citizens and for the development of the country, a right which is only restricted by the vague obligation to consider environmental concerns. As its genesis shows, the Statement of Forest Principles is a mere stopgap. This holds true for its content as well as for its form. Originally, the industrialised states had pushed for the conclusion of a legally binding agreement, but in the end they had to be satisfied with a 'soft law' instrument, mainly because of strong resistance from the timber-producing countries of the Third World. It was also unfortunate that no obligation of states to negotiate a legally binding instrument on forest protection resulted from the Forest Statement.[17]

Agenda 21 is—like the 1972 Stockholm Action Plan—a dynamic political action programme for the implementation of the Rio Declaration. It addresses all actors operating in international environment and development relations in 40 chapters containing more or less concrete recommendations for action. In Chapter 1.6, Agenda 21 refers to itself as 'a dynamic programme'. It further states that the programme

> will be carried out by the various actors according to the different situations, capacities and priorities of countries and regions in full respect of all the principles contained in the Rio Declaration on Environment and Development. It could evolve over time in the light of changing needs and circumstances. This process marks the beginning of a new global partnership for sustainable development.

Permeated by the integrative approach of 'sustainable development', according to which no environmental protection measure shall be taken which does not at the same time promote socioeconomic development, Agenda 21 attempts to balance the inherent tension between environmental protection and development and to convert it into operable strategic concepts. Its very complex catalogue of duties, which is divided into several programme areas, has still not been completely implemented to date. It includes *inter alia* the protection of the atmosphere, the planning and management of land resources, combating deforestation and desertification, the conservation of biological diversity, the protection of oceans and coastal areas as well as the rational use of their living resources, the protection of freshwater resources, and the environmentally sound management of wastes. Chapter 38 of Agenda 21 develops ideas on the institutionalisation of an effective co-operation between the UN bodies dealing with environmental and developmental matters and the still to be established UN Commission on Sustainable Development (CSD).[18] Chapter 39 calls on all relevant actors to further develop the 'international law on sustainable development'[19] and establishes guidelines to this end.

[17] On these efforts see Chapter 14.4.
[18] See on this institution Chapter 38, para 3.2.4.
[19] This term has not yet succeeded in replacing the notion of 'international environmental law'.

3.2.3 Multilateral Environmental Agreements (MEAs)

The Conventions on Climate Change (UNFCCC) and on Biological Diversity (CBD) were not, as already mentioned, actual outcomes of the Rio Summit. They had been elaborated before by special intergovernmental negotiating committees and adopted in May 1992 in New York and Nairobi, respectively. However, Rio was the place where both Conventions were signed by more than 150 states and by the European Community. CBD entered into force on 29 December 1993, UNFCCC on 21 March 1994. The objectives, regulative strategies and contents of both Conventions will be described and assessed in detail in later chapters.[20]

3.2.4 Institutional Innovations

UNEP was established in 1972 as a follow-up to the Stockholm Conference. For 20 years this was the only institution within the UN framework that was specifically entrusted with the duty of addressing global environmental problems. Although UNEP performed its broad range of tasks quite satisfactorily in practice, there soon developed ample discussion on possible ways and means of strengthening UNEP, but also on innovative forms of international environmental institution-building.

In the run-up to UNCED there had already been numerous calls for the establishment of a 'Green Security Council' or a new UN specialised agency for environmental protection.[21] Measured by these ideas, the institutional innovations agreed on at Rio were rather modest. At any rate, the ECOSOC decided—following a recommendation by the UN General Assembly[22] which in turn was based on Chapter 38 of Agenda 21—in its Resolution 1993/207 of 12 February 1993 to establish the intergovernmental CSD. According to Chapter 38.11 of Agenda 21, this functional commission of the ECOSOC was supposed to

> ensure the effective follow-up of the Conference, as well as to enhance international cooperation and rationalize the intergovernmental decision-making capacity for the integration of environment and development issues and to examine the progress in the implementation of Agenda 21 at the national, regional and international levels.[23]

Today, the CSD has developed into a high-level forum for information and discussion of environmental, developmental, social and economic issues among the different environmental actors, including NGOs. Moreover, the CSD endeavours to open up new problem areas, primarily those referred to in Agenda 21, for law-making, particularly by way of identifying 'negotiable' questions to be made the subject of subsequent treaty negotiations by UNEP.[24]

[20] See Chapters 13.4.1. and 14.3.1.

[21] See for details Chapter 17.

[22] UNGA Res 47/191 (22 December 1992).

[23] See n 14 above.

[24] See for a more detailed discussion U Beyerlin and T Marauhn, *Law-Making and Law-Enforcement in International Environmental Law after the 1992 Rio Conference* (Berlin 1997), 58–59, 152–153.

3.2.5 Rio Evaluated

As presaged by the difficult preparatory process, the Rio Conference was not sufficiently successful to warrant the assertion that it prepared the ground for a new global environmental legal order. It was not, however, surprising that the long-standing North–South conflict could not be overcome in a single conference. The severe conflict of interests between these two groups of states was inevitably reflected in the outcomes of the Rio Conference. But even if, from a present-day perspective, the states gathered at the Rio Conference did not move on to pastures new, the conference was not a failure. Rio was the first time that an intensive and serious dialogue between industrialised states and developing countries had unfolded. And although it was a controversial dialogue, it clearly indicated the willingness of both the North and the South to cooperate. In view of the immense global environmental problems, which had been seen like never before to affect the common interests of the universal state community, no state in Rio could afford, for reasons of prestige, to abstain from international environmental co-operation. Rio might therefore have marked the beginning of a learning process for states, culminating in the insight that elementary ecological concerns of the state community must have supremacy over national interests in order to achieve effective international environmental co-operation. However, the perseverance of the states' sovereign thinking in the aftermath of the Rio Conference clearly revealed that this learning process would be protracted and gradual at best.

While the beginnings of broader public participation in environmental negotiations can arguably be traced back to Stockholm, UNCED can certainly be seen as a decisive stage in a process that PH Sand has called 'participatory revolution'.[25] In fact, the manifold activities at the Rio Conference of a very large number of NGOs, some of which showed considerable expertise, gained vast respect. This was rendered possible by an informal agreement on rules that gave NGOs access to UNCED's intergovernmental negotiations.

3.3 Post-Rio Process

Those environmentalists who believed that the community of states, driven by the spirit of the Rio Conference, would considerably enhance, and then perfect, the international environmental legal order were badly disappointed.

The post Rio-process up to 2002 can be credited to some of the newly created MEAs. The UN Convention to Combat Desertification (UNCCD) of 17 June 1994 deserves particular interest.[26] Based on a respective recommendation contained in Agenda 21,[27] this

[25] PH Sand, 'Environmental Summitry and International Law' (2002) 13 *Yearbook of International Environmental Law* 21, 25–26. See also *id*, 'The Evolution of International Environmental Law' in D Bodansky *et al* (eds), *The Oxford Handbook of International Environmental Law* (Oxford 2007), 29, 41.

[26] The United Nations Convention to Combat Desertification in Those Countries Experiencing Drought and/or Desertification particularly in Africa came into force in December 1996. For more details see below Chapter 14.5.

[27] Agenda 21, Chapter 12.40.

convention was the first legally binding instrument established in the post-Rio process. In its operative part the UNCCD imposes general obligations on the affected developing country parties to elaborate action programmes for the purpose of combating desertification at the national, sub-regional and regional levels, as well as duties on the developed country parties to take supportive measures in favour of the developing country parties. These treaty rules at the universal level are complemented by rules contained in five separate Regional Implementation Annexes for Africa, Latin America and the Caribbean, Asia, the Northern Mediterranean, and Central and Eastern Europe, designed to specify and facilitate the respective regional processes of treaty implementation. This technique of intertwining two different levels of norm-setting is a novelty in modern international treaty practice. Another important post-Rio instrument is the Straddling Fish Stocks Agreement of 4 August 1995.[28] This instrument can also be traced back to a stipulation contained in Agenda 21.[29] It addresses questions of sustainable use and conservation of fish populations that habitually cross the boundaries between the high seas and the exclusive economic zones controlled by the coastal states concerned. Also worth mentioning are the Protocol of 7 November 1996 to the London Convention on the Prevention of Marine Pollution by Dumping of Wastes of 1972,[30] as well as the Rotterdam Convention on the Prior Informed Consent Procedure for Certain Hazardous Chemicals and Pesticides in International Trade of 10 September 1998[31] and the Stockholm Convention on Persistent Organic Pollutants (POPs Convention) of 22 May 2001.[32] Finally, with the Aarhus Convention on Access to Information, Public Participation in Decision-Making and Access to Justice in Environmental Matters of 25 June 1998, an innovative instrument has been established within the framework of the UNECE that creates far-reaching intra-state procedural environmental obligations.[33]

Apart from these MEAs newly created in the ten years between UNCED and the Johannesburg Summit, a number of already existing MEAs have been further developed, notably international framework conventions, including the 1979 Geneva Convention on Long-Range Transboundary Air Pollution, the 1992 UNFCCC and the 1992 CBD. Because of their indefinite wording, the original framework agreements had little practical effect: they had to wait for the establishment of more concrete implementation protocols to achieve their aims.

The 1979 Geneva Convention, which had already been complemented by four protocols adopted prior to Rio, was further refined four more times by protocols elaborated in the years between Rio and Johannesburg. With the Oslo Sulphur Protocol (1994), the Aarhus Protocol on Heavy Metals (1998), the Aarhus Protocol on Persistant Organic Pollutants (1998), and the Gothenburg Protocol to Abate Acidification, Eutrophication

[28] Agreement for the Implementation of the Provisions of the United Nations Convention on the Law of the Sea of 10 December 1982 Relating to the Conservation and Management of Straddling Fish Stocks and Highly Migratory Fish Stocks. For more details see below Chapter 12.4.2.

[29] Agenda 21, Chapter 17.49(a).

[30] 1996 Protocol to the 1972 Convention on the Prevention of Marine Pollution by Dumping of Wastes and Other Matters. For more details see below Chapter 12.3.4.

[31] See for a more detailed discussion below Chapter 15.3.1.

[32] For a more detailed account of the POP Convention see Chapter 15.3.2.

[33] For more details see Chapter 16.

and Ground-Level Ozone (1999), this convention was again specified in certain respects. Meanwhile, the total of eight protocols has turned the Geneva Convention into a workable instrument. The Climate Change Convention, in its vague Article 2, calls upon its states parties 'to achieve . . . stabilization of greenhouse gas concentrations in the atmosphere at a level that would prevent dangerous anthropogenic interference with the climate system', without giving any further guidance as to the methods and means to be used in doing so. Only five years later, with the Kyoto Protocol of 11 December 1997, concrete emission reduction targets and a timetable for a first commitment period from 2008 to 2012 were set. This is at least a modest first step in the ongoing struggle against global climate change which seriously threatens the earth's ecosystem as a whole. The Cartagena Protocol on Biosafety of 29 January 2000 also fulfils the function of implementing and further specifying a framework convention, namely the CBD; however, compared to the Kyoto Protocol, its scope is rather limited, as it binds its parties only with respect to the field of safe handling of biotechnology and distribution of benefits (Article 19 CBD). The elaboration and adoption of legally binding protocols for the purpose of implementing rather vaguely formulated framework conventions is a crucial task that is mostly entrusted to the Conferences of the Parties (COPs) to be established under these conventions.[34]

As envisaged by Agenda 21,[35] in June 1997, five years after Rio, the UN General Assembly convened a special session in New York to review the progress achieved in the field of environmental protection and development in the post-Rio process ('Rio + 5'). The state representatives' evaluation of the post-Rio process made at this meeting was disillusioning. It showed that in the aftermath of UNCED the global environmental situation had worsened rather than improved, and that the endeavours to bridge the North–South divide had not made any noteworthy progress. The Final Document of 'Rio + 5' only confirms the obligations states had assumed at the Rio Summit; it lacks any innovative feature. As it became clear that the Special Session's outcomes would be rather poor, the heads of government of Brazil, Germany, Singapore and South Africa felt compelled to promulgate a common 'Global Initiative for Sustainable Development' which called for including environmental protection as an express goal in the UN Charter, reforming UNEP, finalising a protocol relating to the UNFCCC with clear-cut reduction obligations, and elaborating a global convention on forest protection. The fact that this initiative was made by only four states reveals the deep disagreement among states on these matters.

An important step on the road to the Johannesburg Summit was the '2000 Millennium Declaration', *ie* Resolution 55/2 of the UN General Assembly adopted on 8 September 2000. In Part IV of the Declaration, entitled 'Protecting our Common Environment', the UN Member States reaffirmed their 'support for the principles of sustainable development, including those set out in Agenda 21'. Moreover, they resolved 'to adopt in all our environmental actions a new ethic of conservation and stewardship'; in this respect, they resolved, 'as a first step', *inter alia*, to ensure the rapid entry into force of the 1997 Kyoto

[34] For a more detailed discussion on the functions and legal status of COPs see below Chapters 17.2.3 and 18.4.3.

[35] See Agenda 21, Chapter 38.9.

Protocol, to intensify their collective efforts for the conservation and sustainable use of all types of forests, to press for the full implementation of the CBD and the UNCCD, and, last but not least, 'to stop the unsustainable exploitation of water resources by developing water management strategies . . . which promote both equitable access and adequate supplies'. Apart from Part IV, the 2000 Millennium Declaration solemnly confirms the UN Member States' commitment to: common values and principles; peace, security and disarmament; development and poverty eradication; human rights, democracy and good governance; protecting the vulnerable; meeting the special needs of Africa; and strengthening the United Nations.

From this Declaration eight Millennium Development Goals (MDGs) to be achieved by 2015 were drawn which 'form a blueprint agreed to by all the world's countries and all the world's leading development institutions'.[36] These eight MDGs are directed at: eradicating extreme poverty and hunger; achieving universal primary education; promoting gender equality and empowering women; reducing child mortality; improving maternal health; combating HIV/AIDS, malaria and other diseases; ensuring environmental sustainability; and developing a global partnership for development.

As a closer look at the preparatory process and the final agenda of the 2002 Johannesburg Summit will reveal,[37] the 2000 Millennium Declaration and the eight MDGs derived from it considerably predetermined the bargaining process of the Johannesburg Summit, as well as its outcomes.

With the Doha Ministerial Declaration of the World Trade Organization (WTO) of November 2001 and the Monterrey Consensus, negotiated by the International Conference on Financing for Development in spring 2002, two other events gave direction to the forthcoming Johannesburg Summit's discussion on two facets of the broader issue of 'sustainable development in a globalizing world'.[38] While the Doha Ministerial Declaration stressed the 'mutually supportive' relationship of trade and environmental protection and the 'integrity of WTO instruments' in the face of MEAs, the Monterrey Consensus centred on raising development assistance and mitigating the effects of globalisation on developing countries.[39]

[36] See for this characterisation of the Millennium Development Goals www.un.org/millenniumgoals/.

[37] See below Chapter 4.1.

[38] Formula used as headline preceding paras 47 *et seq* of the later Plan of Implementation of the Johannesburg Summit.

[39] *Cf* U Beyerlin and M Reichard, 'The Johannesburg Summit: Outcome and Overall Assessment' (2003) 63 *ZaöRV* 213, 214.

4

Johannesburg and Beyond

4.1 The Johannesburg Summit

Ten years after Rio, the World Summit on Sustainable Development (WSSD) took place in Johannesburg, 26 August–4 September 2002. Its preparatory process from April 2001 (New York session) to early June 2002 (Bali session) had already indicated that the WSSD would differ considerably from its antecedent in Rio, both with respect to its programme and its target. The WSSD in Johannesburg gathered more than 21000 participants, among them some 9000 delegates from 191 governments, as well as a large number of NGOs. It comprised seven thematic partnership meetings, four high-level round tables and a multi-stakeholder event, the closing plenary. Thus, the WSSD exceeded UNCED's level of participation; however, it lagged far behind the latter with regard to its results.

4.2 Johannesburg Outcomes

From the outset, the states participating in the WSSD were not expected to agree upon any meaningful new legally binding environmental commitments. Instead, they concentrated on enhancing the implementation of those already in existence. In fact, notwithstanding some remaining lacunae in international environmental law-making, such as the lack of an international instrument for halting the ongoing process of worldwide degradation of forests and related biodiversity, the current weakness of global environmental protection results first and foremost from shortcomings in the post-Rio process of law implementation.

The states participating in the Johannesburg Summit pursued two different strategies for redressing this implementation gap. In the end, two types of outcomes were reached. While the so-called 'type 1 outcome' of the WSSD consists of two 'soft law' instruments, namely the 'Johannesburg Declaration on Sustainable Development'[1] and the 'Johannes-

[1] See its text in Report of the World Summit on Sustainable Development, Johannesburg, UN Doc A/CONF199/20, 1 *et seq*.

burg Plan of Implementation',[2] the Summit's 'type 2 outcome' is composed of so-called 'public–private partnerships'.

4.2.1 'Type 1 Outcome': The Political Declaration and the Plan of Implementation

The seven-page 'Johannesburg Declaration' contains a number of political commitments of the participating states relating to global sustainable development. As they are generally rather poorly worded, they can hardly influence the multilevel process of future actions aimed at sustainable development. Among these commitments, only the states' resolve

> through decisions on targets, timetables and partnerships, to speedily increase access to such basic requirements as clean water, sanitation, adequate shelter, energy, health care, food security and the protection of biodiversity[3]

is worthy of being expressly mentioned here. With its one-sided developmental orientation, this pledge mirrors the character of the Declaration as a whole.

The other 'type 1 outcome' of the Johannesburg Summit is the 72-page 'Plan of Implementation'. Instead of defining new fields where treaty-making is needed, the Plan develops a broad range of strategies for implementing existing instruments on sustainable development. It covers a very broad spectrum of issues that encompasses poverty eradication; changing unsustainable patterns of consumption and production; protecting and managing the natural resource base; sustainable development in a globalising world; health and sustainable development; sustainable development of small island developing states; sustainable development for Africa; other regional initiatives; means of implementation; and the institutional framework for sustainable development.

The majority of the Plan's 170 provisions are so vaguely worded that they can hardly be expected to produce any clear effect in practice. Only few of them are promising because they call upon states to take meaningful action directed at reaching well-defined targets within fixed periods of time, thereby quite often referring to the 2001 MDGs mentioned above. Among the latter type of clauses are the following:

- The call to take actions to halve, by the year 2015, the proportion of the world's people whose income is less than US$1 per day, who suffer from hunger and who do not have access to safe drinking water and basic sanitation.[4]
- The request for taking measures to enhance health education by 2010, to reduce, by 2015, mortality rates for infants and children under five by two-thirds, and maternal mortality rates by three-quarters of the rate prevailing in 2000; and to reduce HIV prevalence among young men and women by 25 per cent in the most affected countries by 2005, and globally by 2010.[5]
- The understanding of states that, by 2020, chemicals need to be produced and used

[2] See its text *ibid*, 6 *et seq*.

[3] Johannesburg Declaration, n 1, para 18.

[4] See para 7(a) of the Plan which reiterates the respective MDG.

[5] Paras 54(e)(f) and 55 of the Plan.

in ways that minimise any significant adverse effects on human health and the environment.[6]

- The demand for applying, by 2010, the ecosystem approach, as featured by the Conference of the Parties to the CBD in its decision V/6, with regard to oceans, seas, islands and costal areas; and the order, with regard to achieving sustainable fisheries, to restore depleted fish stocks to levels that can produce the maximum sustainable yield on an urgent basis and where possible by 2015.[7]

Unfortunately, all other commitments contained in the Plan lack clarity in determining the kind and scope of measures to be taken. This was probably the price to be paid for agreeing upon an all-encompassing political programme of action for sustainable development.

4.2.2 'Type 2 Outcome': Partnership Initiatives

'Public–private partnerships' (PPPs), some 220 of which had been officially announced at the Johannesburg Summit, form the 'type 2 outcome' of the WSSD. These partnerships allow different stakeholders, *ie* governments, local authorities, non-governmental actors, international institutions and the private sector, to join forces in order to achieve some designated common objectives relating to sustainable development. The states participating in the Johannesburg Summit adopted a 'Consolidated List of Partnerships for Sustainable Development', which as of 3 February 2003 encompassed a total of 255 PPPs.[8] In 2004, a Partnerships Database, administered by the Commission on Sustainable Development (CSD) as the institution designated to promote and facilitate partnerships, was established.[9] The CSD Partnerships Database as of January 2008 listed 334 partnerships.

PPPs cannot even be classified as 'soft law' because they clearly lack any normative force. Partnerships for promoting sustainable development to be entered into by state and non-state actors on a voluntary basis are complementary action-oriented tools which in the future may prove to be capable of filling the implementation gap in international environmental treaty practice. However, they do not alleviate the need for respective interstate commitments that are legally binding. Thus, they can never be used as surrogates to the latter. To date, a first step at best has been made towards 'the vision of a new and innovative type of environmental governance' that JM Witte had observed at Johannesburg.[10] The Bali 'Guiding Principles for Partnerships for Sustainable Development' of June 2002[11] may help in the future to put this new type of partnership between

[6] Para 23 of the Plan.

[7] Paras 30(d) and 31(a) of the Plan.

[8] See www.un.org/jsummit/html/sustainable_dev/consolidated_*list*_091202.pdf. For a more thorough discussion of the phenomenon of 'public–private partnerships' in today's international environmental and developmental relations see below in Chapter 21.4.3.

[9] See http://webapps01.un.org/dsd/partnerships/public/browse.do.

[10] JM Witte and C Streck, 'Introduction' in JM Witte *et al* (eds), *Progress or Peril? Partnerships and Networks in Global Environmental Governance. The Post-Johannesburg Agenda* (Berlin/Washington, DC 2003), 1, 2.

[11] Text in UN Doc A/CONF199/4, Report of the Commission on Sustainable Development acting as

state governments and the civil society in international environmental and developmental relations on a firm footing. So far its echo in practice is rather weak.

4.2.3 Johannesburg Evaluated

The formula 'Rio – 10'[12] implies that, at least from a genuine ecological perspective, the Johannesburg Summit was, compared to the Stockholm and Rio Conferences, a step backwards. Johannesburg may stand for a critical shift from 'sustainability' to 'development'.[13] In any case, it is fair to say that quite a number of commitments contained in the WSSD's Plan of Implementation, in particular those referring to sustainable development in a globalising world and trade,[14] pursue a policy approach that gives economics clear preponderance over the environment. Thus, the WSSD has been rightly blamed for its failure to bring new life to the environmental agenda.[15]

This shift from environmental protection to development at the Johannesburg Summit is clearly reflected in the Political Declaration and the Plan of Implementation, both of which stated that 'the integration of the three components of sustainable development—economic development, social development and environmental protection—as interdependent and mutually reinforcing pillars' should be reaffirmed and promoted.[16] 'Sustainable development' was then widely understood as a concept consisting of two equivalent components, *ie* development and environmental protection. If one splits up 'sustainable development', as the WSSD documents do, into three 'interdependent and mutually reinforcing' coequal pillars, this allows the assumption that the weight given to the protection of the environment is lowered.[17] Thus, this new mode of balancing out the constitutive elements of sustainable development appears to be prototypic for the WSSD's proceedings and outcomes.

The Johannesburg Summit, especially in its Plan of Implementation, was certainly right to advance the Third World's developmental concerns much more definitely than its predecessors in Stockholm and Rio did. However, it can be blamed for having done so by giving the developmental needs of the South undue preference over the environmental interests that are usually ascribed to the North. This is why, in the final result, the Johannesburg Summit has not brought about any substantial progress in bridging

the preparatory committee for the World Summit on Sustainable Development (Fourth Session), Annex III Appendix, at 34–35.

[12] See K Conca, 'Environmental Governance after Johannesburg: From Stalled Legislation to Environmental Human Rights?' (2005) 1 *Journal of International Law and International Relations* 121, 122.

[13] In this sense U Beyerlin and M Reichard, 'The Johannesburg Summit: Outcome and Overall Assessment' (2003) 63 *ZaöRV* 213, 236, referring to K Bosselmann's statement: 'while Rio aimed for sustainability to guide economic and social progress, Johannesburg aimed for economic and social progress to guide sustainability' (K Bosselmann, 'Rio + 10: Any Closer to Sustainable Development?' (2002) 6 *New Zealand Journal of Environmental Law* 297, 314. See also L Rajamani, 'From Stockholm to Johannesburg: The Anatomy of Dissonance in the International Environmental Dialogue' (2003) 12 *RECIEL* 23.

[14] Paras 47–55, respectively paras 90–99 of the Plan.

[15] See P Galizzi, 'From Stockholm to New York, via Rio and Johannesburg: Has the Environment Lost its Way on the Global Agenda?' (2006) 29 *Fordham International Law Journal* 952, 1005.

[16] Plan of Implementation, para 2; very similar Political Declaration, para 5.

[17] See for a more thorough discussion V Barral, 'Johannesburg 2002: Quoi de neuf pour le développement durable?' (2003) 107 *Revue Générale de Droit International Public* 415, 426 *et seq*.

the North–South divide.[18] Measured against the objective the United Nations pursued, namely to organise the Johannesburg Summit in order to reinvigorate the process of implementing Agenda 21 and the Rio Declaration, Pring is certainly right to state that in Johannesburg the 'UN's vision was taken hostage by both the South and the North'.[19]

4.3 From Johannesburg to Copenhagen (2009)

The trend to treat environmental issues as part of the development agenda which hallmarked the Johannesburg Summit and its outcomes has continued to determine the environmental interstate relations in the post-Johannesburg era. For instance, the '2005 World Summit Outcome',[20] referring to the UN Millennium Declaration, affirmed

> that development is a central goal in itself and that sustainable development in its economic, social and environmental aspects constitutes a key element of the overarching framework of United Nations activities,

and acknowledged

> that good governance and the rule of law at the national and international levels are essential for sustained economic growth, sustainable development and the eradication of poverty and hunger.[21]

In April 2007 the UN Security Council held a debate on 'Energy, Security and Climate' and stressed:

> Climate change must be treated in line with other major global threats in order to prevent very serious consequences from occurring. Climate change may undermine the carrying capacity of many developing countries, exacerbate tensions over scarce water resources and fertile land, lead to an increasing number of environmental refugees, drive conflict over strategic trade routes and newly accessible resources, and lead to territorial loss. It is therefore crucial to acknowledge the security implications of climate change.[22]

In June 2009 the UN General Assembly adopted a resolution which invites

> the relevant organs of the United Nations, as appropriate and within their respective mandates, to intensify their efforts in considering and addressing climate change, including its possible security implications.[23]

So far, the post-Johannesburg era has not evidenced any meaningful progress as regards

[18] *Cf* U Beyerlin, 'Bridging the North–South Divide in International Environmental Law' (2006) 66 *ZaöRV* 259, 263.

[19] G Pring, 'The 2002 Johannesburg World Summit on Sustainable Development: International Environmental Law Collides with Reality, Turning Jo'Burg into "Joke'Burg"' (2002) 30 *Denver Journal of International Law and Policy* 410, 413.

[20] See High-Level Plenary Meeting of the 60th Session of the UN General Assembly in mid-September 2005. See for its outcome UNGA Res 60/1 (24 October 2005).

[21] *Ibid*, paras 10 and 11.

[22] See the statement of the representative of Denmark Staur in: UN Security Council Verbatim Record (17 April 2007) UN Doc S/PV/5663 (Resumption 1), 15.

[23] UNGA Res 63/281 (11 June 2009).

further development of the 'hard law' components of international environmental law. Since the Johannesburg Summit was more aimed at enhancing the implementation of existing MEAs rather than creating new ones, this does not come as a surprise. Among the few legally binding instruments established over the past eight years are: the Framework Convention for the Protection of the Marine Environment of the Caspian Sea of 4 November 2003; the Revised African Convention on the Conservation of Nature and Natural Resources of 11 July 2003 (Maputo Convention); the Amendment of 28 November 2003 to Articles 25 and 26 of the 1992 UNECE Convention on the Protection and Use of Transboundary Watercourses and International Lakes; the Protocol on Strategic Environmental Assessment of 21 May 2003 to the respective 1991 UNECE Espoo Convention; the Protocol on Pollutant Release and Transfer Registers of 21 May 2003 to the respective 1998 UNECE Aarhus Convention; the International Convention for the Control and Management of Ships' Ballast Water and Sediments of 13 February 2004; the Protocol on Civil Liability and Compensation Caused by the Transboundary Effects of Industrial Accidents on Transboundary Waters of 23 May 2003 to the respective 1992 UNECE Helsinki Convention; the International Tropical Timber Agreement (ITTA) of 27 January 2006; the South Indian Ocean Fisheries Agreement of 7 July 2006; and the Madrid Protocol on Integrated Coastal Zone Management in the Mediterranean of 21 January 2008 to the Convention for the Protection of the Marine Environment and the Coastal Region of the Mediterranean (Barcelona Convention). Most of these international agreements have not entered into force as yet.

Likewise, in other areas of international environmental law states have not yet succeeded in ultimately meeting the problems concerned. This holds especially true for two most crucial environmental issues, namely access and benefit sharing in the field of biodiversity and combating climate change in the post-2012 era.

In order to reach one of the complementing objectives laid down in Article 1 CBD, COP 6 to the CBD adopted the Bonn Guidelines on Access to Genetic Resources and Fair and Equitable Sharing of the Benefits Arising out of their Utilization in 2002 which had been developed by the Ad Hoc Open-ended Working Group on Access and Benefit Sharing.[24] By 2010 this body has elaborated the contours of an international regime on access and benefit sharing (Nagoya Protocol) with the aim of ensuring that the developing countries hosting the biological resources being accessed, as well as their indigenous and local communities, will substantially participate in all relevant decision-making processes regarding the utilisation of genetic resources and have a fair and equitable share in the benefits arising from foreign use of these resources.[25]

With regard to climate change,[26] the Kyoto Protocol has left many questions, such as the specification of the Protocol's flexibility mechanisms, the establishment of a non-compliance procedure, and the details of funding and technology transfer for developing country parties to the Protocol, to be solved by subsequent decision-making of the COP to the UNFCCC and the Kyoto Protocol, respectively. The so-called Marrakesh Accords,

[24] Decision VI/24 in UNEP/CBD/COP/6/20 (7–19 April 2002); the Bonn Guidelines were adopted during COP 6 in the Hague, 7–19 April 2002.

[25] For a more detailed discussion see below Chapter 14.3.2.

[26] See Chapter 13.4 for more details.

which contain detailed rules for the implementation of the Kyoto Protocol, were formally adopted at COP 11/MOP 1[27] shortly after the Protocol's entry into force on 16 February 2005. As it was clear from the outset that the measures provided for under the first commitment period from 2008 to 2012 would not suffice to redress climate change with all its fatal ecological effects, interstate negotiations on drafting a greenhouse gas emissions reduction scheme for the following commitment period commenced in 2005. These negotiations centred on the determination of the group of states bound to reduce their greenhouse gas emissions in the commitment periods subsequent to 2012. In this respect, the question whether the rapidly developing countries, such as China, India and Brazil, should be included into the prospective mandatory emissions reduction scheme gained pivotal importance. While COP 12/MOP 2, held in Nairobi in 2006, did not yield any tangible results, COP 13/MOP 3, held in Bali in late 2007, agreed on the 'Bali Roadmap' setting the agenda for negotiation on an agreement on post-2012 commitments to be reached in December 2009 at COP 15/MOP 5 in Copenhagen. Unfortunately, this conference did not meet the hopes placed on it. It ended with the drafting of the so-called Copenhagen Accord, a political minimum consensus on the long-term strategy for combating climate change, which, however, was only taken note of by the convening states rather than formally adopted.[28] Thus, one of the most serious environmental threats to the earth's ecosystem and to the whole of humankind has yet to be averted, or at least mitigated.

Further Reading (Chapters 1–4)

V Barral, 'Johannesburg 2002: Quoi de neuf pour le développement durable?' (2003) 107 *Revue Générale de Droit International Public* 415–432.

U Beyerlin and J Grote Stoutenburg, 'Environment, International Protection', in R Wolfrum (ed), *Max Planck Encyclopedia of Public International Law* (Heidelberg/Oxford 2011) paras 3–19, available at www.mpepil.com.

U Beyerlin and M Reichard, 'The Johannesburg Summit: Outcome and Overall Assessment' (2003) 63 *Heidelberg Journal of International Law (ZaöRV)* 213–237.

E Brown Weiss, 'International Environmental Law: Contemporary Issues and the Emergence of a New World Order' (1993) 81 *Georgetown Law Journal* 675–710.

C Bruch and J Pendergrass, 'Type III Partnerships, International Law, and the Commons' (2003) 15 *Georgetown International Environmental Law Review* 855–886.

J Brunnée, 'The Stockholm Declaration and the Structure and Processes of International Environmental Law' in A Chircop *et al* (eds), *The Future of Ocean Regime-Building* (Leiden/Boston 2009) 41–62.

K Conca, 'Environmental Governance after Johannesburg: From Stalled Legislation to Environmental Human Rights?' (2005) 1 *Journal of International Law and International Relations* 121–138.

[27] This term indicates that the Conference of the Parties (COP) to the UNFCCC serves as the Meeting of the Parties (MOP) to the Kyoto Protocol.

[28] See Decision 2/CP.15 (18–19 December 2009) in UN Doc FCCC/CP/2009/11/Add.1 (30 March 2010).

D Freestone, 'The Road from Rio: International Environmental Law after the Earth Summit' (1994) 6 *Journal of Environmental Law* 193–218.

P Galizzi, 'From Stockholm to New York, via Rio and Johannesburg: Has the Environment Lost its Way on the Global Agenda?' (2006) 29 *Fordham International Law Journal* 952–1008.

K Mickelson, 'South, North, International Environmental Law, and International Environmental Lawyers' (2000) 11 *Yearbook of International Environmental Law* 52–81.

A Najam, 'Developing Countries and Global Environmental Governance: From Contestation to Participation to Engagement' (2005) 5 *International Environmental Agreements: Politics, Law and Economics* 303–321.

J Ntambirweki, 'The Developing Countries in the Evolution of an International Environmental Law' (1991) 14 *Hastings International and Comparative Law Review* 905–928.

G Pring, 'The 2002 Johannesburg World Summit on Sustainable Development: International Environmental Law Collides with Reality, Turning Jo'Burg into "Joke'Burg"' (2002) 30 *Denver Journal of International Law and Policy* 410–420.

L Rajamani, 'From Stockholm to Johannesburg: The Anatomy of Dissonance in the International Environmental Dialogue' (2003) 12 *RECIEL* 23–32.

PH Sand, 'Environmental Summitry and International Law' (2002) 13 *Yearbook of International Environmental Law* 21–41.

——, 'The Evolution of International Environmental Law' in D Bodansky *et al* (eds), *The Oxford Handbook of International Environmental Law* (Oxford 2007) 29–43.

SJ Scherr and RJ Gregg, 'Johannesburg and Beyond: The 2002 World Summit on Sustainable Development and the Rise of Partnerships' (2006) 18 *Georgetown International Environmental Law Review* 425–463.

JM Witte *et al* (eds), *Progress or Peril? Partnerships and Networks in Global Environmental Governance. The Post-Johannesburg Agenda* (Berlin/Washington, DC 2003).

Part II

Key Concepts in International Environmental Law

5

'Key Concepts': Meaning, Underlying Ideas and Classification

5.1 'Key Concepts' of International Environmental Law: Meaning and Role

The 1992 Rio Declaration[1] features a catalogue of 27 multifaceted concepts which it expressly denominates 'Principles'. According to its preamble, these 'Rio Principles' are designed to determine the road which all states and other actors in international environmental and developmental relations should take in order to achieve 'the goal of establishing a new and equitable global partnership through the creation of new levels of [environmental] co-operation among States, key sectors of societies and people' (3rd recital). It continues to state that the Rio Conference establishes the Rio Principles in its endeavour to work towards 'international agreements which respect the interests of all and protect the integrity of the global environmental and developmental system' (4th recital).

The Rio Declaration, in its operative part, starts with the statement that '[h]uman beings are at the centre of concerns for sustainable development. They are entitled to a healthy and productive life in harmony with nature' (Principle 1). It then points to the 'responsibility [of states] to ensure that activities within their jurisdiction or control do not cause damage to the environment of other States or of areas beyond the limits of national jurisdiction' ('no harm' – Principle 2). A brief hint follows that '[t]he right to development must be fulfilled so as to equitably meet developmental and environmental needs of present and future generations' ('intergenerational equity' – Principle 3). Of the remaining 24 Rio Principles, of particular note are 'sustainable development' (Principles 1, 4, 5, 6, 8 and 12), 'common but differentiated responsibilities' (Principle 7), 'precautionary action' (Principle 15), and 'polluter pays' (Principle 16).

[1] *Cf* Chapter 3.2.

It is clear from the outset that the Rio Declaration belongs to the sphere of international 'soft law'[2] and does not therefore impose on its addressees[3] any legally binding obligations. The Rio Principles do not altogether have the same status. While some of them may prove to be recognised as customary international norms, others are located in a 'twilight' zone at the bottom of the international environmental law system. Their normative quality and status is far from clear.

Some Rio Principles, particularly 'no harm', 'polluter pays', 'precautionary action', 'common but differentiated responsibilities', 'sustainable development' and 'intergenerational equity', can be said to considerably determine the objectives and structure of international environmental law. Denoted here as 'key concepts', they will be discussed in more detail in the following chapters. The focus of their examination will be on the question of whether or not they have normative quality in the sense that they produce direct or indirect steering effects on the addressees' behaviour. Only those concepts which possess normative quality have the potential to gain the status of customary international norms. Our analysis of the said Rio Principles will be based on Dworkin's theory of policies, principles and rules.[4] It will reveal that these 'principles' are far from being co-equal as to their nature and effects. Some of them will prove to be 'legal principles' or 'legal rules'; others will be allocated to the sphere of mere 'policies' (see Section 5.3).

International environmental law can be imagined as a system of heterogeneous concepts grouped into three layers: a thin layer consisting of highly abstract ideals, a thicker one with less abstract concepts, and a huge one with concrete norms. In this three-layer normative system[5] few fundamental ideas, such as 'international solidarity' and 'international justice', have to be placed in the first layer.[6] Due to their abstractness and vagueness, these ideas are *per se* not able to immediately steer the behaviour of states. However, they are important as ethical sources from which less abstract concepts can flow. As ethical roots of the key concepts in question, they possibly contribute to a better understanding of the latter. This is why they deserve closer attention (see Section 5.2).

The above-named key concepts derive from the ideas of solidarity and justice. The majority of them belong to the second layer of the international environmental law

[2] *Cf* Chapter 20.

[3] Many 'Rio Principles' address states only, others address states and private actors, and few of them seem to remain without identifiable addressees.

[4] See R Dworkin, *Taking Rights Seriously* (London 1977).

[5] The designation of international environmental law as a three-layer system should be distinguished from the characterisation of international law as a hierarchical pyramid system with *jus cogens* at its top and soft law at its bottom.

[6] As far as 'solidarity' is concerned, this understanding is not in line with the opinions taken by other authors. See in particular RStJ Macdonald, 'The Principle of Solidarity in Public International Law' in C Dominicé *et al* (eds), *Etudes de Droit International en l'Honneur de Pierre Lalive* (Basel 1993) 275–308; *id*, 'Solidarity in the Practice and Discourse of Public International Law' (1996) 8 *Pace International Law Review* 259–303, but also K Wellens, 'Solidarity as a Constitutional Principle: Its Expanding Role and Inherent Limitations' in RStJ Macdonald and DM Johnston (eds), *Towards World Constitutionalism: Issues in the Legal Ordering of the World Community* (Leiden 2005) 775–807. Other works on international solidarity include R Wolfrum, 'Solidarity amongst States: An Emerging Structural Principle of International Law' in PM Dupuy *et al* (eds), *Völkerrecht als Wertordnung* (Kehl 2006) 1087–1101; WD Verwey, 'The Principle of Solidarity as a Legal Cornerstone of a New International Economic Order' in C Philotheou and PC Spiliakos (eds), *North-South Dialogue: A New International Economic Order* (Thessaloniki 1982) 483–518; C Wellmann, 'Solidarity, the Individual and Human Rights' (2000) 22 *Human Rights Quarterly* 639–57; R Wolfrum and C Kojima (eds), *Solidarity: A Structural Principle of International Law* (Heidelberg *et al* 2010).

system. Functioning like a 'transmission belt' between abstract ideas and concrete norms of international law, they help transform the two non-enforceable extralegal ideas of international solidarity and justice into enforceable legal principles or rules which make up the great mass of norms in the international environmental law system.[7]

Many states still adhere to traditional sovereignty thinking. They often hesitate to swiftly become parties to MEAs with unambiguous legally binding obligations. Instead, as a cautious first step, they typically enter into agreements containing rather abstract and vague commitments to one or another second-layer concept.

5.2 Ethical Sources of International Environmental Law Key Concepts

5.2.1 Solidarity

In the view of Macdonald, 'solidarity' is 'both a fundamental and fundamentally sound principle of international law'.[8] Attempting to clarify what solidarity means, he considers the UN General Assembly's debates on the adoption of the New International Economic Order in 1974 to be evidence for 'a will to establish a new cooperative system of economic relations informed by the principle of solidarity'.[9] However, he rightly rejects the understanding of solidarity as a concept that imposes a one-sided obligation on the developed states actively to assist the less developed countries. Solidarity is indeed not tantamount to charity in the sense that rich states must support the poorer ones, *eg* by granting development aid. It should rather be conceived as 'an understanding among formal equals that they will refrain from actions that would significantly interfere with the realization and maintenance of common goods or interests'.[10] However, solidarity does not only command non-interference, but also requires the pertinent actors to become active in pursuing a common interest.

Solidarity is an intensified form of interstate co-operation that reaches beyond 'normal' partnership, *ie* a relationship driven by mutual respect and a soundly balanced give-and-take. Solidarity additionally requires any state to become affiliated to a particular community that acts in concert to achieve certain common benefits that prevail over its own interests. As Macdonald put it:

> As a member of a community that benefits from the protection of the community, a state acting in a manner that preserves the good of the community also preserves its own individual good.[11]

Solidarity can be expected to arise rather easily among states that become aware of 'a

[7] See U Beyerlin and J Grote Stoutenburg, 'Environment, International Protection' in R Wolfrum (ed), *Max Planck Encyclopedia of Public International Law* (Heidelberg/Oxford 2011), available at www.mpepil.com.

[8] Macdonald (1993), above n 6, 275 *et seq*; *id* (1996), above n 6, 259 *et seq*.

[9] Macdonald (1993), above n 6, 291.

[10] *Id* (1996), above n 6, 290. In the same sense P Cullet, *Differential Treatment in International Environmental Law* (Aldershot 2003) 18, 42.

[11] Macdonald (1996), above n 6, 301.

specific convergence of interests'.[12] Thus, states that have become or are likely to become victims of a global environmental harm appear to be predestined to be motivated by a sense of solidarity and to form a solidarity-driven community for the purpose of self-preservation, *eg* the Alliance of Small Island States. The same might apply to states which have jointly caused a particular environmental problem. They should feel commonly responsible for taking joint remedial action. However, solidarity which remains within a specific group of states is not very helpful. It should rather impel states belonging to antagonistic state groups to make every effort towards bridging the gap between them. Consequently, the idea of solidarity has become, or will become, a significant moral incitement for states to overcome the North–South dichotomy that still exists in international environmental law.[13]

5.2.2 Justice

Akin to 'solidarity', 'justice' claims authority both in the national and international arena. As already indicated above, it is an abstract moral imperative from which more concrete concepts may be derived. Despite its vague contents and contours, justice is a fundamental ideal to which states all over the world adhere—or at least pretend to adhere.

As to its meaning and effects, 'justice' comes very close to 'fairness' and 'equity'. Franck comprehends 'distributive justice' as an aspect of 'fairness', pleads for an equation of fairness with equality, and brings 'equity' together with 'justice'.[14] Brown Weiss speaks partly of 'justice among generations', partly of 'fairness to future generations', and eventually of 'intergenerational equity'.[15] Anand, who deals specifically with 'international environmental justice', also uses 'fairness' and 'equity' as synonymous notions of 'justice'.[16] In her analysis of the inequities at the international level, she distinguishes between 'procedural justice implying fairness of decision-making processes, and distributive justice, focusing on norms for equitable resource distribution in terms of costs and benefits'.[17]

Procedural justice in interstate relations, especially in the form of equitable participation of states in international decision-making irrespective of their development status, seems to be best achieved by providing for formal equality of states. Accordingly, Article 2(1) of the UN Charter proclaims the principle of sovereign equality of all UN Member States. Correspondingly, the voting procedure of the UN General Assembly is governed by the requirement 'one state–one vote' (Article 18(1) of the UN Charter). However, formal equality ensures international justice only in situations where the members of a community are perfectly equal in all respects. This is not always the case in today's

[12] Cullet, above n 10, 173.

[13] On the whole paragraph *cf* U Beyerlin, 'Bridging the North–South Divide in International Environmental Law' (2006) 66 *ZaöRV* 259, 268 *et seq*.

[14] See TM Franck, *Fairness in International Law and Institutions* (Oxford 1995) 8, 19 and 47.

[15] See E Brown Weiss, *In Fairness to Future Generations: International Law, Common Patrimony and Intergenerational Equity* (Tokyo 1989) 17 *et seq*.

[16] See R Anand, *International Environmental Justice. A North-South Dimension* (Aldershot 2004) 16.

[17] *Ibid*, 15.

interstate relations, especially in their North–South dimension. Therefore, formal equality needs to be complemented by substantive equality. Substantive equality implies the need to treat unequal states unequally in view of providing distributive justice in interstate environmental and developmental affairs. It is aimed at ensuring that the 'outcomes' of relevant interstate decision-making processes meet the requirements of justice or fairness. The more these processes will be determined by procedural justice, the better are the chances of coming close to distributive justice. We shall see that procedural and distributive justice are rich sources for generating more concrete concepts, which in turn will be able to influence significantly the further development of international environmental law, especially in its North–South dimension.[18]

5.3 Classification of International Environmental Law Norms

Dworkin's legal theory separates 'policies' from 'legal principles' and 'legal rules'.[19] It deals with the distinction between principles and rules very extensively, but neglects the borderline between policies and principles, which is, especially in international environmental law, also crucial. While policies stipulate mere political ideals instead of deploying any appreciable direct or indirect steering effect on states' behaviour, principles and rules both have normative quality, *ie* they do generate such a steering effect. What distinguishes principles and rules from each other is that rules are norms immediately aimed at making the addressees take action, refrain from action or achieve a fixed result, while principles are norms that are first and foremost designed to give guidance to their addressees for future conduct in rule-making processes, and to shape the interpretation and application of rules already in existence. Rules, especially those contained in international treaties, may be subdivided into rules which impose on states parties broadly formulated obligations to work towards a rather abstractly defined objective (action-oriented rules) and rules that contain strictly worded obligations to achieve a clearly defined result within a fixed time limit (result-oriented rules). While the former rules create obligations of conduct, the latter entail obligations of result. What both types of rules have in common is that they 'set out legal consequences that follow automatically when the conditions provided are met',[20] irrespective of the determinateness or indeterminateness of the action or result prescribed by them. By contrast, principles do not prescribe or proscribe a particular state behaviour. They rather aim at influencing the states' decision-making, which otherwise remains open to choice, as well as their interpretation of rules.[21]

Despite their different effects, both international rules and principles possess a normative quality that makes them eligible for claiming the legally binding effects of either a

[18] *Cf* Beyerlin, above n 13, 270 *et seq*.

[19] See Dworkin, above n 4, 22.

[20] *Ibid*, 25.

[21] See U Beyerlin, 'Different Types of Norms in International Environmental Law: Policies, Principles, and Rules' in D Bodansky *et al* (eds), *The Oxford Handbook of International Environmental Law* (Oxford 2007) 425, 437.

rule or a principle. If the questionable norm, be it a rule or a principle, has been incorporated into the operative part of an international treaty, it shares the treaty's legal status. Otherwise it can become legally binding only if it meets the requirements of a norm of customary international law. While it is quite easy to judge whether rules entailing 'action-oriented' or 'result-oriented' obligations have grown into customary international norms, principles raise more difficulties in this respect. Proving that a state was directed by a certain principle when it took a decision on a particular action may be difficult in practice because clear evidence for such psychological moments of states' decision-making is hardly available. This is why to date few principles, if any, have passed the threshold for having gained the status of a customary international norm.

In Chapters 6–10, the key concepts of international environmental law as identified above will be allocated, one after the other, to Dworkin's tripartite typology of norms. According to its individual function and effects, each concept will be assessed in the following terms: (i) Does it have normative quality? (ii) Does it have the status of an international legally binding norm? If both questions are answered in the affirmative, the concept in question constitutes either a rule or a principle, both being legal in nature. If only the first question is answered positively, the concept belongs to the realm of morally steering 'soft law'. If neither of the two questions is answered positively, the concept belongs to the sphere of non-normative policies.

Further Reading

A Aarnio, 'Taking Rules Seriously' in W Maihofer and G Sprenger (eds), *Law and the States in Modern Times, Proceedings of the Fourteenth IVR World Congress in Edinburgh, August 1989* (Stuttgart 1990) 180–192.

U Beyerlin, 'Different Types of Norms in International Environmental Law. Policies, Principles, and Rules' in D Bodansky *et al* (eds), *The Oxford Handbook of International Environmental Law* (Oxford 2007) 425–448.

R Dworkin, *Taking Rights Seriously* (London 1977).

J Ebbesson and P Okowa (eds), *Environmental Law and Justice in Context* (Cambridge 2009).

V Lowe, 'Sustainable Development and Unsustainable Arguments' in A Boyle and D Freestone (eds), *International Law and Sustainable Development: Past Achievements and Future Challenges* (Oxford 1999) 19–37.

N MacCormick, *Legal Reasoning and Legal Theory* (Oxford 1978, reprinted in 1995).

N de Sadeleer, *Environmental Principles: From Political Slogans to Legal Rules* (Oxford 2002).

P Sands, 'International Law in the Field of Sustainable Development: Emerging Legal Principles' in W Lang (ed), *Sustainable Development and International Law* (London 1995) 53–66.

J Verschuuren, *Principles of Environmental Law: The Ideal of Sustainable Development and the Role of Principles of International, European, and National Environmental Law* (Baden-Baden 2003).

P Weil, 'Towards Relative Normativity in International Law' (1983) 77 *AJIL* 413–442.

R Wolfrum and C Kojima (eds), Solidarity: A Structural Principle of International Law (Heidelberg *et al* 2010).

6

'No Harm'

6.1 Historical Development

Under the so-called Harmon Doctrine, developed in the late nineteenth century, every state, due to its absolute territorial sovereignty, was held to be free to engage in, or permit, environment-related activities within its territorial boundaries regardless of whether these activities were likely to have adverse transboundary environmental impacts. This doctrine finally became obsolete in 1941 when the arbitral tribunal in the famous *Trail Smelter* case settled an environmental utilisation conflict between the United States and Canada[1] by stating that

> [u]nder the principles of international law . . . no state has the right to use or permit the use of territory in such a manner as to cause injury by fumes in or to the territory of another of the properties or persons therein, when the case is of serious consequences and the injury is established by clear and convincing evidence.[2]

Three decades later, the prohibition on causing transboundary environmental harm, the so-called 'no harm' concept, was included in the 1972 Stockholm Declaration as Principle 21, which stipulates:

> States have . . . the responsibility to ensure that activities within their jurisdiction or control do not cause damage to the environment of other states or of areas beyond the limits of national jurisdiction.

This formulation makes very clear that 'no harm' does not only protect the environmental integrity of other states, but also the environment in common areas, such as Antarctica, the high seas, the deep seabed and outer space.[3]

The 1992 Rio Declaration, in Principle 2, reaffirmed this responsibility of states not to cause transboundary harm, as defined in Stockholm Principle 21, as a correlate to states' sovereign right to exploit their own natural resources. Moreover, 'no harm', in its various forms, has been widely reflected in declarations adopted by the United Nations

[1] For details see above Chapter 1.1.

[2] (1941) 3 RIAA 1907.

[3] See *eg* PW Birnie, AE Boyle and C Redgwell, *International Law and the Environment* (3rd edn Oxford 2009) 145.

and international environmental agreements,[4] in Article 3 of the 2001 ILC 'Draft Articles on Prevention of Transboundary Harm from Hazardous Activities',[5] as well as in the jurisprudence of the International Court of Justice. In its 1996 Advisory Opinion on the *Legality of the Threat or Use of Nuclear Weapons* the Court endorsed this concept by emphasising:

> The existence of the general obligation of States to ensure that activities within their jurisdiction and control respect the environment of other States or of areas beyond national control is now part of the corpus of international law relating to the environment.[6]

In its 1997 judgment in the case concerning the *Gabčíkovo-Nagymaros Project (Hungary v Slovakia)* the ICJ recalled 'the great significance that it attaches to respect for the environment, not only for States but also for the whole of mankind'.[7]

The dogmatic roots of 'no harm' are disputed. In the 1941 *Trail Smelter* award this concept was grounded on principles of US constitutional law and a number of US Supreme Court decisions.[8] Subsequent international legal writings have traced it back to the Roman law principle *sic utere tuo ut alienum non laedas* or to the principle of 'good neighbourliness'.[9] Alternatively, 'no harm' may result from a concept of international law which forbids sovereignty being exercised in an abusive manner as a substratum of the doctrine of abuse of rights.[10] 'No harm' is perhaps best characterised as a compromise between the territorial sovereignty of the state of origin of the environmental harm, on the one side, and the territorial integrity of the state likely to be affected by this harm, on the other. Ultimately, it is a compromise clearly favouring territorial integrity over territorial sovereignty.

6.2 Function and Normative Quality

'No harm' entails prohibitive and preventive steering effects on states. In its prohibitive function, it forbids any state from causing significant transboundary environmental harm. In its preventive function, 'no harm' obliges every state of origin 'to take adequate measures to control and regulate in advance sources of potential significant transboundary

[4] See *eg* Art 194(4) UNCLOS; Art 3 CBD; Preamble of the LRTAP Convention; Preamble of the UNFCCC.

[5] Draft Art 3 stipulates that '[t]he State of origin shall take all appropriate measures to prevent significant transboundary harm'. See for the ILC Draft Articles on the Prevention of Transboundary Harm from Hazardous Activities ILC, 'Report of the International Law Commission on the work of its 53rd Session' (23 April–1 June and 2 July–10 August 2001) UN Doc A/56/10 and ILC, 'Report of the International Law Commission on the work of its 56th Session' (3 May–4 June and 5 July–6 August 2004) UN Doc A/59/10.

[6] (1996) ICJ Reports 226, 241 *et seq*, para 29.

[7] (1997) ICJ Reports 7, 41, para 53.

[8] For references see A Kiss and D Shelton, *International Environmental Law* (3rd edn New York 2004) 184. Nevertheless, the *Trail Smelter* award formed the historical starting point for the emergence of 'no harm' as a concept of customary international law. For a more thorough discussion see below at Section 6.3.

[9] *Cf* Kiss and Shelton, *ibid*, 179 *et seq*; G Handl, 'Transboundary Impacts' in D Bodansky *et al* (eds), *The Oxford Handbook of International Environmental Law* (Oxford 2007) 531, 533.

[10] See in particular A Kiss, 'Abuse of Rights' in R Bernhardt (ed), *Encyclopedia of Public International Law* vol I (Amsterdam *et al* 1992) 4.

harm'.[11] It is exactly this obligation to prevent that makes 'no harm' so meaningful in practice, especially in cases where neighbouring states are involved in environmental utilisation conflicts.

The obligation to prevent transboundary environmental harm or to minimise the risk thereof is primarily a substantive one. However, in order to achieve the objective of harm prevention, the state of origin is generally required to enter into close procedural co-operation with one or more potentially affected states for the purpose of solving the environmental utilisation conflict in a way that best respects their integrity interests. Thus, the substantive obligation to prevent is complemented by certain procedural duties. In both dimensions, 'no harm' possesses normative quality and, consequently, the capacity to gain the status of a customary international norm.[12]

'No harm' immediately commits every state to take all measures needed to achieve its aim of respecting the environment beyond the state's boundaries. The state concerned has discretion only as to the manner in which it reaches this end. If assigned to Dworkin's theory of norms, 'no harm' is, albeit with some uncertainties such as whether it proscribes only significant or also less serious transboundary environmental harm (see Section 6.3.1), a rule rather than a principle.

6.3 Substantive Obligations

6.3.1 Preventing Significant Transboundary Harm

In the *Trail Smelter* case the arbitral tribunal emphasised, as indicated above, that the prohibition on causing transboundary environmental harm should only apply to cases 'of serious consequence'. Astonishingly, Principle 21 of the Stockholm Declaration and Principle 2 of the Rio Declaration, as well as the two statements of the ICJ cited above, appear to ignore this restriction of the 'no harm' duty of states. Today, however, it is widely accepted in relevant doctrine and interstate practice that the state of origin is enjoined only from causing transboundary environmental harm that reaches a certain threshold level of significance or seriousness. Thus, the injury expected to result, or already resulting, from an activity undertaken within the jurisdiction of the state of origin must be more than *de minimis*. Consequently, a state that has become a victim of only an insignificant environmental damage cannot be entitled to claim reparation.[13]

The task of defining 'significant harm' and deciding whether the transboundary environmental harm that was caused in the particular case surmounts the said threshold level can raise considerable difficulties, if not trigger a downright dispute between the state of origin and the victim state. Interestingly, under the 1991 Espoo Convention on Environmental Impact Assessment in a Transboundary Context, states parties that disagree

[11] Handl, above n 9, 539.
[12] *Cf* Chapter 5.3.
[13] *Cf* Birnie, Boyle and Redgwell, above n 3, 186 *et seq*; VP Nanda and G Pring, *International Environmental Law & Policy for the 21st Century* (Ardsley 2003) 22.

whether the given transboundary harm is 'significant' may submit their controversy to an enquiry commission which, according to Article 3 (7) of the Convention, is able to adopt a respective 'final conclusion' that, although legally non-binding in character, may help the parties concerned to settle their dispute.[14]

6.3.2 No Balancing of Interests

Another possibility for curtailing the scope and effectiveness of 'no harm' may lie in weighing the interest of one state in not becoming victim of a significant environmental harm against the interest of another state making use of its territorial sovereignty as widely as possible. Such a balancing of interests of the concerned states might be appropriate in cases where the management of international watercourses is at stake. However, Handl is right to argue that 'in relation to transboundary environmental interference generally, it would be inappropriate to condition the threshold of significant harm to considerations of equitable sharing'.[15] This conforms with the statement of the ILC's special rapporteur for the 2001 'Draft Articles on Prevention of Transboundary Harm' that the draft article on equitable balancing of interests was not intended to dilute the obligation of prevention enshrined in draft Article 3.[16]

6.3.3 Disregard of 'Due Diligence'

Unlike the doctrine of 'abuse of rights', 'no harm' does not require that the state of origin causes the transboundary damage with the intent to injure. The obligation to prevent or minimise the transboundary environmental harm originating from an activity within its jurisdiction is rather one to be fulfilled with 'due diligence'. Accordingly, the state of origin has to comply with the objective standard of care of due diligence. It has to take all measures to control and restrain likely harmful activities that it can reasonably be expected to take.

However, what is 'reasonable' in this respect? Answering this question certainly depends on the particular circumstances, which vary from case to case. This is why the criterion of 'reasonableness' entails a considerable degree of uncertainty in determining the operative effects of 'no harm' in practice. It requires the state of origin to do the 'best it can'.[17] Relevant technical standards, such as 'best available technology' and 'best environmental practice', may serve as benchmarks for making pertinent judgments.[18]

Moreover, the state of origin must have been able to recognise that its act or omission would result in a serious infringement of the integrity of the environment beyond its

[14] *Cf* below Chapter 16.3.

[15] Handl, above n 9, 537.

[16] PS Rao, *Third Report on International Liability for Injurious Consequences Arising Out of Acts Not Prohibited by International Law*, UN Doc A/CN4/510 (9 June 2000), 11, para 21.

[17] This may also be the underlying philosophy of Art 3 of the 2001 ILC Draft Articles on the Prevention of Transboundary Harm, as cited above (n 5). *Cf* R Verheyen, *Climate Change Damage and International Law* (Leiden/Boston 2005) 159.

[18] See Handl, above n 9, 538.

jurisdiction. Thus, the injury incurred must have been foreseeable for the state of origin; the respective reference point is today's best scientific knowledge.[19]

6.3.4 Standard and Burden of Proof

'No harm' is, as indicated above, a concept that generally tends to favour territorial integrity over territorial sovereignty. Consequently, a state affected or likely to be affected by a significant transboundary environmental harm deserves to the best possible protection. If a state that has already become victim of such harm brings an action against the state of origin before an international court, it must show 'clear and convincing evidence' for having been significantly affected by this harm.[20] However, what is the standard of proof or who bears the burden of proof in cases where a state is not yet victim of, but is severely at risk of becoming affected by such harm?

There are good reasons for arguing that the more serious the consequences of the impending harm, the lower should be the standard of proof regarding the probability of the occurrence of the respective harm. Accordingly, in cases where the feared consequences of the risk of environmental harm are most serious, the very demanding 'clear and convincing' proof standard should be gradually alleviated in favour of the victim state. In case of an ultra-hazardous activity that shows a low probability of causing transboundary environmental harm, but a high probability that the harm once occurred entails catastrophic consequences for the environment,[21] the state of origin should bear the burden of proof for having diligently fulfilled its obligation of prevention. The state of origin should thus be required to show that it has taken all adequate and reasonable measures to control and regulate in advance all intrinsically hazardous activities planned within its jurisdiction, such as the operation of a nuclear plant close to its national border.[22]

Lowering the standard of proof for the benefit of the victim state or shifting the burden of proof to the detriment of the state of origin in such a way is closely interrelated to the idea of the so-called 'precautionary approach' which, as laid down in Principle 15 of the Rio Declaration, stipulates:

> Where there are threats of serious or irreversible damage, lack of full scientific certainty shall not be used [by states] as a reason for postponing cost-effective measures to prevent environmental degradation.

However, the standard and burden of proof in the context of 'no harm' is admittedly as much a matter of debate as the meaning and implications of the 'precautionary approach'.[23]

[19] See Birnie, Boyle and Redgwell, above n 3, 152 *et seq*; Verheyen, above n 17, 178 *et seq*.

[20] This is the standard of proof established in the *Trail Smelter* arbitration; *cf* above n 2.

[21] Correspondingly, 'risk' is defined in Art 2(a) of the ILC Draft Articles on Prevention of Transboundary Harm to encompass both 'a low probability of causing disastrous harm' and 'a high probability of causing significant harm'; see above n 5.

[22] See Birnie, Boyle and Redgwell, above n 3, 152 *et seq*; Handl, above n 9, 539 *et seq*; Nanda and Pring, above n 13, 21.

[23] See for a more thorough discussion Birnie, Boyle and Redgwell, above n 3, 152 *et seq*. *Cf* for a general treatment of the 'precautionary action' approach Chapter 7.

6.3.5 Status

As indicated above in section 6.2, 'no harm' is a substantive norm that entails immediate prohibitive and preventive steering effects. It therefore has the normative quality of a rule rather than a principle. First laid down in general form by Principle 21 of the Stockholm Declaration in 1972, it has been so widely accepted in international treaty practice, numerous declarations of international organisations, the codification work of the ILC, and in the jurisprudence of the ICJ that it can be considered to be a customary substantive rule at the universal level.

6.4 Procedural Obligations

6.4.1 Contents and Scope

Current practice of environmental utilisation conflicts between neighbouring states reveals that the substantive obligation of the state of origin to prevent significant transboundary environmental harm implies by its very nature certain procedural duties. Among the procedural obligations designed to safeguard states' right to be protected against significant transboundary injurious impacts[24] are particularly the following:

(1) to consult each other with the aim of preventing transboundary harm;
(2) to exchange in a timely fashion information regarding projects likely to cause transboundary harm;
(3) to notify of environmental emergency situations and give early warnings in case of imminent harm;
(4) to assess nationally the projects' potential transboundary environmental impacts; and
(5) to grant non-residents equal access to environmental information, equal participation in relevant decision-making processes, and equal access to justice in environmental matters.

A closer look at relevant international treaty practice reveals that the procedural obligations under (1) and (2) have been repeatedly included in bilateral and multilateral environmental agreements at all levels,[25] while those referred to under (3) and (4) have even been made the subject of specific MEAs.[26] The obligations mentioned under (5) trace back to a number of soft law instruments established by the Council of the Organi-

[24] Handl, above n 9, 541.

[25] The obligations to consult and inform each other are almost typical for international environmental agreements, particularly bilateral ones concluded between neighbouring states; see only Arts 4 and 5 of the 1979 Geneva LRTAP Convention. *Cf* also Chapter 13.2.1.

[26] Most important in this respect are the two Conventions on Early Notification of Nuclear Accidents, and on Assistance in the Case of a Nuclear Accident or Radiological Emergency respectively, both concluded in 1986 under the auspices of the IAEA, as well as the already mentioned 1991 Espoo Convention. *Cf* particularly Chapter 16.1.

sation for Economic Co-operation and Development in the 1970s,[27] on the basis of which the UNECE Aarhus Convention was concluded in 1998.[28] Whether all these procedural obligations, apart from their validity as treaty norms, have meanwhile become part of customary international law is a question to be dealt with in the following.

6.4.2 Status

It might be argued that the above-named procedural obligations flowing from 'no harm', *eg* to exchange information, to consult and to undertake transboundary impact assessments, are auxiliary sub-concepts of the substantive rule of 'no harm' which automatically share the latter's status. However, what militates against this solution is the finding that there is no closed circle of procedural sub-concepts of 'no harm' with clear-cut contours. Rather, it can be better argued that these procedural emanations of 'no harm' have been emancipated from the 'mother concept' to such a degree that it is necessary to provide evidence for each of them that it has gained customary status on its own. It can, however, be generally concluded that out of the five procedural sub-concepts named above, only the duties aimed at the exchange of information, early warnings and consultation appear to have already become part of universal customary law.[29]

6.5 Breach of the 'No Harm' Rule

In case of non-compliance with the 'no harm' rule, the state of origin runs the risk of being made internationally responsible for its adverse consequences. Any breach of an obligation flowing from the 'no harm' rule constitutes an internationally wrongful act which entails the state of origin's international responsibility. The state has to bear the legal consequences set out in the ILC's Draft Articles 28–41 on the 'Responsibility of States for Internationally Wrongful Acts', as adopted in 2001, which, in large part, reflect the state of relevant customary international law.[30] They include in particular the obligation of the state of origin to cease its wrongful act and to make full reparation for the injury caused by it (Draft Articles 30 and 31). Consequently, a state that has become

[27] See 'Recommendation on Principles Concerning Transfrontier Pollution', C(74)224 (14 November 1974); 'Recommendation on Equal Right of Access in Relation to Transfrontier Pollution', C(76)55 (Final) (11 May 1976); 'Recommendation on Implementation of a Regime of Equal Right of Access and Non-Discrimination in Relation to Transfrontier Pollution', C(77)28 (Final) (17 May 1977); 'Recommendation on Strengthening International Co-operation on Environmental Protection in Transfrontier Regions', C(78)77 (Final) (21 September 1978). *Cf* Chapter 16.2.

[28] For a more detailed discussion *cf* Chapter 16.2.

[29] *Cf* Chapter 16.1.

[30] ILC, 'Report of the International Law Commission on the work of its 53rd Session', above n 5; A/CN4/L602/Rev1 (26 July 2001). On state responsibility *cf* Chapter 24.2.

a victim of a significant environmental damage is entitled to claim reparation from the state of origin.

Further Reading

RM Bratspies and RA Miller (eds), *Transboundary Harm in International Law—Lessons from the Trail Smelter Arbitration* (Cambridge 2006).

N Craik, 'Trail Smelter Redux: Transboundary Pollution and Extraterritorial Jurisdiction' (2004) 14 *Journal of Environmental Law and Practice (Special Issue)* 139–163.

F Francioni and T Scovazzi (eds), *International Responsibility for Environmental Harm* (London 1991).

G Handl, 'Transboundary Impacts' in D Bodansky *et al* (eds), *The Oxford Handbook of International Environmental Law* (Oxford 2007) 531–549.

X Hanqin, *Transboundary Damage in International Law* (Cambridge 2003).

N Horbach, *Liability Versus Responsibility under International Law—Defending Strict State Responsibility for Transboundary Damage* (Leiden 1996).

R Lefeber, *Transboundary Environmental Interference and the Origin of State Liability* (The Hague 1996).

PN Okowa, *State Responsibility for Transboundary Air Pollution in International Law* (Oxford 2000).

DP Piscitello and GE Andrés, 'The Conflict Between Argentina and Uruguay Concerning the Installation and Commissioning of Pulp Mills Before the International Court of Justice and MERCOSUR' (2007) 67 *Heidelberg Journal of International Law (ZaöRV)* 159–183.

R Verheyen, Climate Change Damage and International Law (Leiden/Boston 2005).

7

Precautionary Action

The precept of 'precaution' in international environmental law is usually addressed in international legal writings in terms of the 'precautionary principle' or the 'precautionary approach'. Since, however, 'precaution' has the potential of an action-oriented rule rather than a mere principle,[1] for our purposes the terminology 'precautionary action' (PA) is preferred. We will first look at the historical development of PA and its use in international environmental practice before attempting to clarify the meaning and (legal) effects of PA. In this respect, there are three questions that must be addressed: Does PA merely preclude states from arguing that scientific uncertainty commands inaction? Does it operate as a 'license to act'? Or does it even establish a duty to act?

7.1 Historical Development

The concept of PA provides the basis for early action to address serious environmental threats in cases where there is ongoing scientific uncertainty with regard to these threats. Although its exact meaning and effects are the subject of continuing controversy, PA is certainly one of the most prominent concepts in current international environmental law.[2] Bodansky even observed that '[i]f international environmental law were to develop Ten Commandments, the precautionary principle would be near the top of the list'.[3]

Originating from the sphere of domestic law, the evolution of PA started with the Swedish Environment Protection Act of 1969 which introduced the concept of 'environmentally hazardous activities' for which the burden of proof was reversed with the consequence that the mere risk of an environmental hazard was a sufficient basis for the Swedish regulatory authorities to take protective measures or to even ban the activity in question. In the 1970s, the other Nordic states, West Germany and Switzerland followed the Swedish example of establishing a rather strict approach to PA. Thus, PA became an

[1] See Section 7.5.

[2] *Cf* JB Wiener, 'Precaution' in D Bodansky *et al* (eds), *The Oxford Handbook of International Environmental Law* (Oxford 2007) 597, 599.

[3] D Bodansky, 'Deconstructing the Precautionary Principle' in DD Caron and HN Scheiber (eds), *Bringing New Law to Ocean Waters* (Leiden/Boston 2004) 381, 381.

environmental 'core principle' in the legal systems of several European states.[4] France included PA in its legislation through the so-called 'Loi Barnier' only in 1995.[5] In 1999, PA became part of the revised Canadian Environmental Protection Act.[6] US environmental law contains elements of PA in many settings, but it appears at best in a highly diluted and compromised fashion.[7]

Given the prior inclusion of PA in the domestic legal systems of many Western European states, it was relatively easy for the European Union (EU) to base its environmental policy on PA. First introduced by the 1992 Maastricht Treaty, current Article 191(2) of the Treaty on the Functioning of the European Union (TFEU) (formerly Article 174(2) EC Treaty) stipulates that

> Union policy on the environment . . . shall be based on the precautionary principle and on the principles that preventive action should be taken, that environmental damage should as a priority be rectified at source and that the polluter should pay.[8]

Thus, PA has been recognised as a core principle of EU law since 1992.[9] In February 2000, the EC Commission issued its 'Communication on the Precautionary Principle'[10] which outlined the Commission's approach to the use of the principle of PA and established guidelines for its application. In this respect, the Commission stated:

> Recourse to the precautionary principle presupposes that potentially dangerous effects deriving from a phenomenon, product or process have been identified, and that scientific evaluation does not allow the risk to be determined with sufficient certainty. . . . Decision-makers need to be aware of the degree of uncertainty. . . . Decision-makers faced with an unacceptable risk, scientific uncertainty and public concerns have a duty to find answers.[11]

At the international level, PA began to appear in a number of 'soft law' instruments in the 1980s, including the UN World Charter for Nature of 1982[12] and the ministerial declarations issued at the 1984, 1987 and 1990 North Sea Conferences, respectively.[13]

[4] For a comprehensive survey of the inclusion of PA in the domestic law of European states and EC Law see PH Sand, 'The Precautionary Principle: A European Perspective' (2000) 6 *Human and Ecological Risk Assessment* 445, 448 *et seq* with ample references.

[5] Loi Relative au Renforcement de la Protection de l'Environnement of 2 February 1995, Art 1(1)(3).

[6] Canadian Environmental Protection Act of 1999, in force since 31 March 2000.

[7] For a critical account see JS Applegate, 'The Precautionary Preference: An American Perspective on the Precautionary Principle' (2000) 6 *Human and Ecological Risk Assessment* 413 *et seq*.

[8] Originally, when the 1986 Single European Act introduced Art 130(r) into the then existing EEC Treaty, there was only mention of a principle 'that preventive action should be taken' (*cf* Art 25 of the Single European Act).

[9] *Cf* again Sand, above n 4, 449.

[10] Commission (EC), 'Communication from the Commission on the Precautionary Principle' COM(2000) 1 final, 2 February 2000.

[11] Summary of the Communication, *ibid*, paras 4 and 5.

[12] UNGA Res 37/7 (28 October 1982); (1983) 22 ILM 455.

[13] The 2nd North Sea Conference (1987) stated that '[i]n order to protect the North Sea from possibly damaging effects of most dangerous substances, a precautionary approach is necessary which may require action to control inputs of such substances even before a causal link has been established by absolutely clear scientific evidence' (Ministerial Declaration of the Second International Conference on the Protection of the North Sea, London, 25 November 1987). The 3rd North Sea Conference (1990) declared that the participating states 'will continue to apply the precautionary principle, that is to take action to avoid potentially damaging impacts of substances that are persistent, toxic and liable to bioaccumulate even where there is no scientific evidence to prove a causal link between emissions and effects' (Ministerial Declaration of the Third International Conference on the Protection of the North Sea, The Hague, 8 March 1990).

In 1992, PA was enshrined as Principle 15 of the Rio Declaration,[14] which reads as follows:

> In order to protect the environment, the precautionary approach shall be widely applied by States according to their capabilities. Where there are threats of serious or irreversible damage, lack of full scientific certainty shall not be used as a reason for postponing cost-effective measures to prevent environmental degradation.

This definition of PA is almost[15] a *verbatim* quote of sentence 3 of the Bergen UNECE Ministerial Declaration on Sustainable Development of 16 May 1990.[16] During the Rio negotiations, PA initially encountered resistance from developing states which considered it a typical 'Northern' demand. However, they subsequently agreed to PA in return for acceptance of other 'Southern' concerns by developed states in the Rio bargaining process.[17]

In the post-Rio era, PA has been increasingly referred to in numerous MEAs and in the case law of international courts. Relevant practice will now be discussed in more detail. This may help eventually to identify the conception, meaning and effects of PA.

7.2 References to Precautionary Action in International Environmental Practice

7.2.1 Multilateral Environmental Agreements

More than 50 currently existing MEAs explicitly refer to PA or have adopted its rationale in one way or another. Among the first ones were the 1985 Vienna Ozone Convention[18] and the accompanying 1987 Montreal Protocol.[19]

The 1992 UNECE Water Convention expressly commits itself to

> [t]he precautionary principle, by virtue of which action to avoid the potential transboundary impact of the release of hazardous substances shall not be postponed on the ground that scientific research has not fully proved a causal link between those substances, on the one hand, and the potential transboundary impact, on the other hand.[20]

[14] Report of the UN Conference on Environment and Development, Rio de Janeiro, UN Doc A/CONF151/26/Rev1 (vol I), 3 *et seq*; see Chapter 3.2.2 for details.

[15] Principle 15 contains the rather ominous rider that states must not postpone 'cost-effective' preventive measures.

[16] Para I.7 of the Bergen Declaration (text in (1990) 1 *Yearbook of International Environmental Law* 431) reads as follows: 'In order to achieve sustainable development, policies must be based on the precautionary principle. Environmental measures must anticipate, prevent and attack the cause of environmental degradation. Where there are threats of serious or irreversible damage, lack of full scientific certainty should not be used as a reason for postponing measures to prevent environmental degradation.'

[17] See in particular Sand, above n 4, 447, with references.

[18] See Preamble, indent 5.

[19] See Preamble, indent 8.

[20] Art 2(5)(a) of the Convention.

The 1992 Biodiversity Convention notes in its preamble that 'where there is a threat of significant reduction or loss of biological diversity, lack of full scientific certainty should not be used as a reason for postponing measures to avoid or minimize such a threat'.[21]

The related 2000 Cartagena Biosafety Protocol explicitly points to PA in its Article 1 without, however, explaining its meaning. Elsewhere the Protocol states, without expressly referring to PA, that

> [l]ack of scientific certainty due to insufficient relevant scientific information and knowledge regarding the extent of the potential adverse effects of a living modified organism on the conservation and sustainable use of biological diversity in the Party of import, taking also into account risks to human health, shall not prevent that Party from taking a decision, as appropriate, with regard to the import of that living modified organism intended for direct use as food or feed, or for processing, in order to avoid or minimize such potential adverse effects.[22]

The 1992 Climate Change Convention refers to PA as one of its guiding principles by stating that

> [t]he Parties should take precautionary measures to anticipate, prevent or minimize the causes of climate change and mitigate its adverse effects. Where there are threats of serious or irreversible damage, lack of full scientific certainty should not be used as a reason for postponing such measures, taking into account that policies and measures to deal with climate change should be cost-effective so as to ensure global benefits at the lowest possible cost.[23]

The 1996 London Protocol to the 1972 Convention on the Prevention of Marine Pollution by Dumping of Wastes and Other Matter is also based on PA. It stipulates that

> [i]n implementing the Protocol, Contracting Parties shall apply a precautionary approach to environmental protection from dumping of wastes . . . whereby appropriate preventative measures are taken when there is reason to believe that wastes . . . introduced into the marine environment are likely to cause harm even when there is no conclusive evidence to prove a causal relation between inputs and their effects.[24]

These references to PA in modern MEAs show that states tend to accept that a lack of scientific certainty concerning an identified environmental risk must not be a reason to postpone action. Furthermore, the above-cited clauses of the 1996 London Dumping Protocol and the 2000 Cartagena Biosafety Protocol could even be read as implying an understanding of PA as a concept that entitles states to take all necessary measures to ward off or minimise serious or irreversible environmental risks. Understood as a 'license to act', PA is a concept that gives states considerable leeway in determining the kind and quality of their action as well as the level at which it will be taken. However, so far there is no clear evidence in treaty practice suggesting that PA might impose a duty on states to take definable action.

[21] Preamble, indent 9.
[22] Arts 10(6) and 11(8) of the Protocol. The wording of both provisions is almost identical.
[23] Art 3(3) UNFCCC.
[24] Art 3(1) of the Protocol.

7.2.2 Decisions of International Courts

In the 1995 *Nuclear Tests* case brought before the International Court of Justice (ICJ),[25] two dissenting judges considered PA to be an emerging feature of international environmental law.[26]

In the 1997 case concerning the *Gabčíkovo-Nagymaros Project* before the ICJ,[27] Hungary and Slovakia invoked, *inter alia*, the precautionary principle. However, the ICJ did not feel the need to deal with PA in detail. This is all the more plausible as in 1989, when Hungary suspended work on the Gabčíkovo-Nagymaros Project, the precautionary principle was, if not nonexistent, at least too greatly blurred in content.[28] Judge Weeramantry, in his separate opinion, addressed 'sustainable development' and 'environmental impact assessments' (EIAs) but avoided dealing with PA in more detail. He just stated that 'EIA, being a specific application of the larger general principle of caution, embodies the obligation of continuing watchfulness and anticipation'.[29]

More telling is the following statement of the International Tribunal for the Law of the Sea (ITLOS) in the 1999 *Southern Bluefin Tuna* case:

> [Although there is] scientific uncertainty regarding measures to be taken to conserve the stock of southern bluefin tuna and . . . although the tribunal cannot conclusively assess the scientific evidence presented by the parties, it finds that measures should be taken as a matter of urgency to preserve the rights of the parties and to avert further deterioration.[30]

Judge Treves, in his concurring opinion to the Order, considered 'a precautionary approach' to be 'inherent in the very notions of provisional measures'; however, he signalled understanding for 'the reluctance of the Tribunal in taking a position as to whether the precautionary approach is a binding principle of customary international law'.[31]

Traces of PA can also be found in the *MOX Plant* case which was first dealt with by the ITLOS in 2001 and then transferred to the Permanent Court of Arbitration in 2003.[32] Although the Court was blocked from addressing the merits of the case, the submissions of the two parties showed that both considered the precautionary principle to be

[25] *Request for an Examination of the Situation in Accordance with Paragraph 63 of the Court's Judgment of 20 December 1974 in the Nuclear Tests (New Zealand v France)* case (1995) ICJ Reports 288. The ICJ dismissed the request of New Zealand in its order of 22 September 1995. Three judges dissented and relied in their dissenting opinions on developments in international environmental law.

[26] See the dissenting opinions of judge Weeramantry (*cf ibid*, 342 *et seq*) and judge ad hoc Palmer (*cf ibid*, 412).

[27] *Hungary v Slovakia* (1997) ICJ Reports 7 (Judgment of the ICJ of 25 September 1997).

[28] JM Van Dyke, 'The Evolution and International Acceptance of the Precautionary Principle' in Caron and Scheiber (eds), above n 3, 357; P Sands, *Principles of International Environmental Law* (2nd edn Cambridge 2003) 274 *et seq*.

[29] Separate Opinion of Judge Weeramantry, above n 26, 113.

[30] *Australia v Japan; New Zealand v Japan* (Provisional Measures, Order of 27 August 1999) ITLOS cases Nos 3 and 4, paras 79 *et seq*. See also *ibid*, para 77.

[31] Separate Opinion of Judge Treves, para 9.

[32] *Ireland v United Kingdom* (Provisional Measures, Order of 3 December 2001) ITLOS case No 10; Permanent Court of Arbitration, (Suspension of Proceedings on Jurisdiction and Merits, and Request for Further Provisional Measures) Order No 3 of 24 June 2003.

a possible key for solving the dispute, without elucidating its contents and scope more closely.[33]

After all, international courts have shown reluctance to apply PA as a legal yardstick for solving interstate disputes, because of the still ambiguous contents and normativity of this concept. This is why today's relevant international judicial decision-making is rather inconclusive as to determining the exact meaning of PA.

7.3 Conception and Meaning

PA appears to be premised on the idea that policy-makers at all levels should feel compelled to administer and conserve the earth's ecosystem as an indispensable basis for the wellbeing of humankind, both now and in the future. They should realise that sound environmental policy-making must not be limited to warding off identified environmental dangers but must additionally comprise timely action that inhibits the emergence of such dangers in the first place. Due to its strongly future-oriented approach, the concept of PA can be considered as promoting the idea of intergenerational solidarity.[34]

It may contribute to a better understanding of the concept of PA in international environmental law initially to contrast it with similar concepts in states' domestic environmental law and in relevant EU law.

Taking Germany's environmental law as an example, this distinguishes two regulatory situations which, at least in theory, are clearly opposed to each other: firstly, the situation of warding off an environmental danger where it is clear that a particular environmental harm resulting from an identified source will occur unless inhibited by timely state intervention; secondly, the situation of an environmental risk where it is necessary to take precautionary action in order to inhibit this risk from becoming an immediate danger. However, relevant German legislation[35] does not differentiate between preventive and precautionary action. In contrast, Article 191(2) TFEU, leaving aside the regulatory situation of 'averting environmental dangers', discerns the 'precautionary principle' and that of 'preventive action' without explaining the differences that might exist between both concepts.

As demonstrated, there is no conclusive evidence for identifying the role of PA in current international environmental law. What seems to be clear is that PA responds to the limitations of science in assessing global ecological risks which typically raise serious difficulties as to understanding the chain of causation and predicting the outcomes. This is in line with de Sadeleer's observation that

> [a]lthough unpredictable risks are rising, authorities tend to wait in the face of uncertainty and to react only to crisis events. . . . In this respect, precaution aims to bridge the gap between

[33] For a more thorough discussion on all these decisions see JM Van Dyke, above n 28, 370 *et seq*.

[34] *Cf* Chapter 5.2.1.

[35] See *eg* § 5(1) nos 1 and 2 of the German Federal Immission Control Act. The legal situation in other Western European states is similar.

scientists working on the frontiers of scientific knowledge and decision-makers willing to act to prevent environmental degradation.[36]

Notwithstanding the lacking clarity regarding the meaning of PA, there is common understanding in today's doctrine and state practice that PA applies to situations where scientific uncertainties make it difficult for the authorities concerned to decide whether and, if so, how they should encounter environmental risks. However, there is ongoing discord regarding the reference point of such scientific uncertainty in a given case. As shown above,[37] the practice of MEAs in this respect is rather inconclusive. While the 1992 Biodiversity Convention and the 1992 Climate Change Convention leave this question unanswered, the 1992 Water Convention and the 1996 Dumping Protocol make plain that the required scientific uncertainty refers to the 'causal relation between inputs and their effects'.[38] By contrast, according to Articles 10(6) and 11(8) of the Biosafety Protocol, the reference point of 'insufficient relevant scientific information and knowledge' seems to be the extent of potential harm.

Thus, two difficult questions regarding the conditions of PA's applicability remain to be answered. Firstly, does the required scientific uncertainty refer to the cause of the potential harm, its extent and/or the probability of its occurrence? Secondly, how are 'precautionary action' and 'preventive action' related to one another and what kind of legal effects do both concepts entail?

If PA were a broad concept functionally designed to ward off serious environmental threats by anticipatory action, it would be hardly distinguishable from what is called the 'principle of preventive action' or the 'preventive principle'.[39] What makes PA gain specific importance aside from the 'preventive principle' is its applicability in situations where the authorities concerned realise that a serious or irreversible environmental harm might occur, but they are also aware of the insufficient scientific basis, whether empirical or theoretical, for demonstrating the causal link between one or more identified human activities and the prospective harm.[40] Contrary to the concept of PA just defined, the 'preventive principle'[41] seems to apply to situations where the authorities concerned have reason enough to fear that one or more identified activities might cause a serious or irreversible environmental harm; it only remains uncertain whether their fear will materialise.

By contrast, Trouwborst considers '[t]he precautionary principle . . . alternatively as effectively comprising the preventive principle, as presupposing its application, or as

[36] N de Sadeleer, 'The Precautionary Principle as a Device for Greater Environmental Protection: Lessons from EC Courts' (2009) 18 *RECIEL* 3, 4.

[37] See Section 7.2.1.

[38] Art 3(1) Dumping Protocol; *cf* also Art 2(5)(a) Water Convention.

[39] See Sands, above n 28, 246 *et seq*; A Trouwborst, *Evolution and Status of the Precautionary Principle in International Law* (The Hague 2002) 37 *et seq; id*, *Precautionary Rights and Duties of States* (Leiden/Boston 2006) 94.

[40] See Trouwborst (2006), *ibid*, 87; L Boisson de Chazournes, 'Precaution in International Law: Reflections on its Composite Nature' in TM Ndiaye and R Wolfrum (eds), *Law of the Sea, Environmental Law and Settlement of Disputes,* Liber Amicorum *Judge Thomas A Mensah* (Leiden 2007) 21, 24. She states: 'The element of uncertainty is a *sine qua non* condition to the application and even to the legitimacy of the precautionary principle' (*ibid*).

[41] This 'principle' is related to the 'no harm' rule (*cf* Chapter 6), but broader in scope. *Cf* Sands, above n 28, 246.

constituting its most developed form'.[42] However, for the sake of clarity 'precautionary action' and 'preventive action' should be distinguished from one another as separate, coexisting concepts which due to their differing conditions of applicability may claim different normative qualities and statuses in international environmental law.

7.4 Effects

There is ongoing controversy on the question of what kind of legal effects PA may have in situations where there is a serious or irreversible environmental risk, but scientific uncertainty regarding its cause(s).

As indicated above, Principle 15 of the Rio Declaration, stating that scientific uncertainty must not be used as a reason to postpone action, reflects a widely accepted minimum understanding of PA in doctrine.[43] However, simply saying that uncertainty is no excuse for inaction, PA does not bar governments from remaining inactive for other reasons, *eg* because taking precautionary action is unnecessary in the given situation or because it would bring about excessive costs. If it had nothing but this effect, PA would be a rather blunt instrument.

This is why PA has also been interpreted as a concept signifying that 'uncertainty justifies action'.[44] Understood in this way, PA operates as 'a license to act'. For instance in the trade context, it can be considered to justify the taking of environmental measures 'that might otherwise be questionable as disguised barriers to trade'.[45] However, it does not indicate at which level PA should be taken and of what kind that action should be.[46] It gives at best rough guidance to a state facing serious or irreversible environmental risk.

Thus, there is reason enough to reflect on a third version of PA according to which this concept implies a duty of states to take action for responding to a given environmental risk.[47] In this respect, the most rigid form of action would be to abjure entirely the action most likely suspected to cause the questionable harm. However, taking such a draconian response would hardly be a realistic option in practice. Hence, there is discussion on several other substantive and procedural duties that may flow from PA. Among them are granting equal access to information on the environment, employing EIAs, as well as setting obligatory quantified emission limitation and reduction targets, or requirements to use the best available technology or clean production methods. However, there are doubts whether this strongest version—PA as a 'command to act'—has been sufficiently echoed in current international environmental practice.

[42] By contrast, Trouwborst (2006), above n 39, 117 *et seq*, 159 takes the position that uncertainty does not only refer to the cause of an environmental risk, but also to its extent and/or probability.

[43] See *eg* Bodansky, above n 3, 383 *et seq*; Wiener, above n 2, 604 *et seq*.

[44] See again Bodansky, *ibid*, 385; Wiener, *ibid*, 605. *Cf* Trouwborst (2006), above n 39, 159 *et seq*, 286 *et seq*.

[45] *Cf* Bodansky, *ibid*, 385.

[46] For a thorough discussion on the requirements any precautionary action must meet in order to fulfil its function, such as effectiveness and proportionality, see in particular Trouwborst (2006), above n 39, 147 *et seq*.

[47] See generally for interpreting PA as a concept from which a 'duty to act' flows *ibid*, 159 *et seq*, 287 and Bodansky, above n 3, 386.

A very specific procedural duty flowing from PA is that of 'shifting the burden of proof' to the proponent of the potentially risky undertaking who will benefit from it and 'setting a standard of proof' that must be demonstrated.[48] A positive effect of this particular version of PA might be that in case the initiator of an activity has failed to demonstrate that it is of no or tolerable risk, this activity should be forbidden. On the other hand, there is danger that imposing such a standard of proof 'could invite overregulation'.[49]

7.5 Normative Quality and Status

As shown above, there is a growing number of MEAs which explicitly refer to PA. However, they are still far from reflecting a uniform understanding of its meaning and effects. At least, they agree in two important respects: (i) scientific uncertainty is a *conditio sine qua non* for applying PA; (ii) it is no argument that alone justifies inaction. Practice of MEAs seems also to reveal a growing readiness of states to accept PA as grounds for justifying the taking of remedial action in cases of serious or irreversible threats to the environment. On the other hand, it may be a theoretically sound and politically desirable option to understand PA as a concept that imposes a duty on states to take remedial action of a particular kind and extent. However, as yet this option of construing PA has not been sufficiently reflected in MEAs.

After all, PA is a concept which, despite its abstractness and indeterminateness in content, deploys the steering effects of an action-oriented rule rather than being a mere principle that gives guidance to states for future rule-making as well as interpreting or applying rules already in existence.

What remains to be determined is the question whether the PA rule has become part of customary international law.[50] Since it has been included in more and more MEAs, there are good reasons for arguing that it is applied in today's general state practice accompanied by the *opinio iuris* of the states. However, the reluctance of international courts to rely on PA suggests that there are still certain doubts as to whether PA has already grown to a universally accepted rule of customary international law. On the other hand, it is clear

[48] Wiener, above n 2, 606. For an extensive discussion on this particular procedural effect of PA see also Trouwborst (2006), above n 39, 193 *et seq*; Sands, above n 28, 272 *et seq*; PW Birnie, AE Boyle and C Redgwell, *International Law and the Environment* (3rd edn Oxford 2009) 155 *et seq*. The International Court of Justice, in its judgment of 20 April 2010 in the case concerning *Pulp Mills on the River Uruguay (Argentina v Uruguay)*, in paras 160–164 rejected the Argentine contention 'that the 1975 Statute [a treaty signed by Argentina and Uruguay on 26 February 1975] adopts an approach in terms of precaution whereby "the burden of proof will be placed on Uruguay for it to establish that the … mill will not cause significant damage to the environment"' (*ibid*, para 160) by arguing 'that while a precautionary approach may be relevant in the interpretation and application of the provisions of the Statute, it does not follow that it operates as a reversal of the burden of proof' (*ibid*, para 164). The judgment is available at www.icj-cij.org/docket/index.php?p1=3&p2=3&k=88&case=135&code=au&p3=4.

[49] See Wiener, above n 2, 606.

[50] See for this question A Trouwborst, 'The Precautionary Principle and the Ecosystem Approach in International Law: Differences, Similarities and Linkages' (2009) 18 *RECIEL* 26; Boisson de Chazournes, above n 40, 25 *et seq*; Van Dyke, above n 28, 375 *et seq*; Sands, above n 28, 279; Birnie, Boyle and Redgwell, above n 48, 159 *et seq*.

that PA, notwithstanding the remaining uncertainties as to its legal effects, is an emerging rule of customary international environmental law that can claim eminent importance.

Further Reading

JS Applegate, 'The Precautionary Preference: An American Perspective on the Precautionary Principle' (2000) 6 *Human and Ecological Risk Assessment* 413–443.

A Arcuri, 'Reconstructing Precaution, Deconstructing Misconceptions' (2007) 21 *Ethics and International Affairs* 359–379.

D Bodansky, 'Deconstructing the Precautionary Principle' in DD Caron and HN Scheiber (eds), *Bringing New Law to Ocean Waters* (Leiden/Boston 2004) 381–391.

L Boisson de Chazournes, 'Precaution in International Law: Reflections On Its Composite Nature' in TM Ndiaye and R Wolfrum (eds), *Law of the Sea, Environmental Law and Settlement of Disputes,* Liber Amicorum *Judge Thomas A. Mensah* (Leiden/Boston 2007) 21–34.

J Cameron, 'The Precautionary Principle in International Law' in T O'Riordan *et al* (eds), *Reinterpreting the Precautionary Principle* (London 2001) 113–142.

J Cazala, *Le principe de précaution en droit international* (Paris 2006).

N de Sadeleer (ed), *Implementing the Precautionary Principle. Approaches from the Nordic Countries, EU and USA* (London 2007).

——, 'The Precautionary Principle as a Device for Greater Environmental Protection: Lessons from EC Courts' (2009) 18 *RECIEL* 3–10.

D Freestone and E Hey (eds), *The Precautionary Principle and International Law* (The Hague 1996).

D Maurmann, *Rechtsgrundsätze im Völkerrecht am Beispiel des Vorsorgeprinzips* (Baden-Baden 2008).

PH Sand, 'The Precautionary Principle: A European Perspective' (2000) 6 *Human and Ecological Risk Assessment* 445–458.

CR Sunstein, 'Irreversible and Catastrophic' (2006) 91 *Cornell Law Review* 841–897.

A Trouwborst, *Evolution and Status of the Precautionary Principle in International Law* (The Hague 2002).

——, *Precautionary Rights and Duties of States* (Leiden/Boston 2006).

——, 'The Precautionary Principle and the Ecosystem Approach in International Law: Differences, Similarities and Linkages' (2009) 18 *RECIEL* 26–37.

JM Van Dyke, 'The Evolution and International Acceptance of the Precautionary Principle' in DD Caron and HN Scheiber (eds), *Bringing New Law to Ocean Waters* (Leiden/Boston 2004) 357–379.

JB Wiener, 'Precaution' in D Bodansky *et al* (eds), *The Oxford Handbook of International Environmental Law* (Oxford 2007) 597–612.

8

Polluter Pays

8.1 Origin

Polluter pays (PP), as articulated in Principle 16 of the 1992 Rio Declaration, provides that

> [n]ational authorities should endeavour to promote the internalisation of environmental costs and the use of economic instruments, taking into account the approach that the polluter should, in principle, bear the costs of pollution.

Prior to the 1992 UN Conference on Environment and Development (UNCED), the PP concept could be found in a number of legally non-binding international instruments that have been established within the framework of the Organisation for Economic Co-operation and Development (OECD), such as the 1972 OECD Council Recommendation on Guiding Principles Concerning the International Economic Aspects of Environmental Policies,[1] the 1974 OECD Council Recommendation on the Implementation of the Polluter-Pays Principle,[2] and the 1989 OECD Council Recommendation on the Application of the Polluter-Pays Principle to Accidental Pollution.[3] PP was also included in several EU documents, such as EC Council Recommendation 75/436/EURATOM, ECSC, EEC of 3 March 1975 regarding Cost Allocation and Action by Public Authorities on Environmental Matters,[4] the EC Environment Action Programmes, as well as Article 130(r)(2) of the 1986 Single European Act and the 1992 Maastricht Treaty, respectively.

At the global level, there are a number of MEAs which expressly refer to PP, such as the 1990 International Convention on Oil Pollution Preparedness, Response and Cooperation[5] and the 1992 UNECE Convention on the Transboundary Effects of Industrial Accidents,[6] both pointing to PP as 'a general principle of international environmental law'. The 1992 Convention for the Protection of the Marine Environment of the North-

[1] Recommendation C(72) 128 (1972).

[2] Recommendation C(74) 223 (1974).

[3] Recommendation C(89) 88 (1989).

[4] According to the Annex (para 2) to this Recommendation, 'the European Communities at Community levels and the Member States in their national legislation on environmental protection must apply the "polluter pays" principle, under which natural or legal persons governed by public or private law who are responsible for pollution must pay the costs of such measures as are necessary to eliminate that pollution or to reduce it'.

[5] Preamble, indent 7.

[6] Preamble, indent 9.

East Atlantic provides in its Article 2(2)(b) the application of PP as a principle 'by virtue of which the costs of pollution prevention, control and reduction measures are to be borne by the polluter'. The 2001 Stockholm Convention on Persistent Organic Pollutants, in its preamble, reaffirms Principle 16 of the Rio Declaration by quoting it and providing its text with the rider 'with due regard to the public interest and without distorting international trade and investment'. However, all these MEAs have contributed little to the clarification of the meaning and effects of PP.

8.2 Applicability and Meaning

At first sight, the PP concept seems simply to state the obvious. It directly calls upon the national authorities of states to ensure that in every case where the environment has been, or runs the risk of being, polluted, the accountable natural or legal person bears the costs resulting from the pollution or from the measures taken for the purpose of preventing pollution. However, on closer examination, PP shows considerable uncertainties and ambiguities as to its applicability and meaning.

PP has originally been designed to apply within the state's domestic sphere because it is best applied in a geographic region that is subject to uniform environmental law, such as within a state. However, the more EU law became harmonised, the more PP gained importance in the EU context too. Thus, with respect to the territorial range of its applicability, PP clearly differs from the concept of 'common but differentiated responsibilities' (CBDR). It is limited to the internal sphere of a single state or an international organisation, while CBDR, as expressed in Principle 7 of the Rio Declaration, is designed to govern global environmental interstate relations, particularly in the North–South context.

Moreover, both concepts, PP and CBDR, considerably differ from each other regarding their function. While PP indicates the most efficient way of allocating the costs of pollution prevention and control measures, CBDR induces both the industrialised states and developing countries to cooperate appropriately in combating global environmental degradation and/or mitigating its detrimental effects.[7]

As defined by the OECD in a series of recommendations, PP provides 'that the polluter should bear the expense of carrying out . . . measures decided by public authorities to ensure that the environment is in an acceptable state' and that 'the cost of these measures should be reflected in the costs of goods and services which cause pollution in production and/or consumption'.[8] This explanation reflects the acknowledgement that allocating the costs of preventive or remedial environmental measures to the polluter in the given case implies a significant negative economic incentive for the latter to abstain from any future behaviour to the detriment of the environment. Thus, PP is a concept which can deploy considerable steering effects on private actors, although its meaning remains open to interpretation in various respects.

[7] *Cf* Chapter 9.

[8] OECD Council Recommendation C(72)128 (1972) of 26 May 1972, Annex A(4); see its text in (1975) 14 ILM 236.

The nature and extent of the costs included and the circumstances in which the concept exceptionally does not apply are subject of particular debate.[9] Both the choice of methods used for making polluters pay—taxation, charges, liability laws—and the degree of implementation have as yet shown little consistency in state practice.[10] Moreover, PP is totally silent as to how to determine the link of the chain of polluters on which the costs should best be imposed. Both questions are particularly crucial in case of 'pollution chains'. For instance, it may be asked whether the producer of a harmful merchandise or the consumer should bear the costs. And who is in charge of the costs for clearing oil pollution or mitigating its effects? Is it the operator of the oil tanker or the cargo owner? It is first and foremost this indeterminacy of contents and scope that prevents PP from giving meaningful guidance for solving liability issues. Ensuring full implementation of a PP approach requires consideration of the question of civil liability and compensation, especially if accidental damage to the environment is to be included. The extent to which civil liability makes the polluter pay for environmental damage depends on a variety of factors which cannot be controlled by the concept of PP itself.

8.3 Normative Quality and Status

PP, as expressed in Principle 16 of the Rio Declaration, has normative quality as a rule rather than as a principle. It is neither designed to be taken into account in relevant decision-making as a mere consideration inclining in one or another direction, nor intended to be used merely for interpretative guidance.[11] It rather directly calls upon states to ensure that in every case where the environment has been, or is going to be, polluted, the accountable person bears the costs resulting from clearing or preventing pollution. It fulfils the typical functions of a legally binding rule rather than those of a principle. Thus, notwithstanding its indeterminateness in content and scope, PP meets all prerequisites that are needed for gaining the status of a norm of customary international law.

Regarding the question of whether PP has already become part of customary international law, the 'softened' wording in Principle 16 ('should endeavour to promote') indicates that to date it has not yet received support or attention by states to such a degree that it might have already gained the status of a rule of universal customary law. As yet, it is at best recognised as a legal rule within the framework of the EU and OECD.[12]

Further Reading

F Böhm and H Trabold, 'Das Verursacherprinzip in der globalen Umweltpolitik: Argumente für eine Weltumweltorganisation' (2004) 2 *Zeitschrift für Umweltpolitik und Umweltrecht* 201–229.

HC Bugge, 'The Polluter Pays Principle: Dilemmas of Justice in National and International Con-

[9] P Sands, *Principles of International Environmental Law* (2nd edn Cambridge 2003) 280.

[10] PW Birnie, AE Boyle and C Redgwell, *International Law and the Environment* (3rd edn Oxford 2009) 323.

[11] In this sense R Dworkin, *Taking Rights Seriously* (London 1977) 26. *Cf* Chapter 5.3.

[12] In this sense also Sands, above n 9, 280.

texts' in J Ebbesson and P Okawa (eds) *Environmental Law and Justice in Context* (Cambridge 2009) 411–428.

U Kettlewell 'The Answer to Global Pollution? A Critical Examination of the Problems and Potential of the Polluter-Pays Principle' (1992) 3 *Colorado Journal of International Environmental Law and Policy* 429–478.

HJ Kim, 'Subsidy, Polluter Pays Principle and Financial Assistance Among Countries' (2000) 34 *Journal of World Trade* 115–141.

ET Larson, 'Why Environmental Liability Regimes in the United States, the European Community, and Japan Have Grown Synonymous with the Polluter Pays Principle' (2005) 38 *Vanderbilt Journal of Transnational Law* 541–575.

JR Nash, 'Too Much Market? Conflict between Tradable Pollution Allowances and the "Polluter Pays" Principle' (2000) 24 *Harvard Environmental Law Review* 465–535.

9

Common but Differentiated Responsibilities

9.1 Historical Development of CBDR

Prior to 1972[1] the industrialised states clearly dominated international environmental treaty-making or even kept international environmental treaty-making to themselves. Accordingly, early international environmental agreements usually provided identical treatment to all contracting states by means of employing 'absolute' norms that treat all parties uniformly.[2] Since the 1972 Stockholm Conference, however, things have changed considerably. To encourage universal participation of states in global environmental treaty-making, modern MEAs typically provide for a differential treatment of developing country parties, thereby abrogating the traditional sovereign equality which guarantees that all states parties have formally equal rights and obligations.

The struggle of the newly independent developing countries in the late 1960s and 1970s for a 'new international economic order' (NIEO) was aimed at eliminating the enduring inequalities between states which were, at least in part, a product of colonial imperialism. The NIEO movement strived to remedy the inequality of the then existing legal order governing economic interaction. It was based on and inspired by the ideas of Prebisch, the most influential Third World economist and first Secretary General of the United Nations Conference on Trade and Development (UNCTAD) in the 1960s,[3] as well as demands of French academic lawyers in the mid-1960s to establish an international law of development ('droit international du développement'), conceived as a new approach to the whole body of international law and directed to shaping anew the North–South relations particularly by means of concepts such as co-operation, solidarity and mutual aid.[4]

[1] *Cf* Chapter 1.

[2] DB Magraw, 'Legal Treatment of Developing Countries: Differential. Contextual, and Absolute Norms' (1990) 1 *Colorado Journal of International Environmental Law and Policy* 69, 73 *et seq*, separates 'absolute' norms from 'differential' and 'contextual' norms.

[3] See C Fortin, 'United Nations Conference on Trade and Development (UNCTAD)' in R Wolfrum (ed), *Max Planck Encyclopedia of Public International Law* (Heidelberg/Oxford 2006) 3 *et seq*, available at www.mpepil.com; *cf* also A Mahiou, 'Development, International Law of' in Wolfrum, *ibid*, 1 *et seq*.

[4] See L Rajamani, *Differential Treatment in International Law* (Oxford 2006) 13 *et seq*; P Cullet, 'Differential

With the NIEO, the developing countries tried to bring about effective equality among states by creating new rules that would allow them to benefit better from the international economic system. Accordingly, their efforts focused on the 'denunciation of injustice in economic relations among developed and developing countries'.[5] The NIEO movement was marked by calls from developing countries for gaining effective control over their natural resources and economic development, as well as strengthening the position of states as economic actors against foreign private investors. Since the developing countries felt that technology transfer might help them to realise economic self-determination, getting easier access to modern technologies was most prominent among the NIEO demands. The developing countries managed to draw attention to their demands in the UN General Assembly, but they encountered strong resistance from the industrialised states. The failure to bring about significant changes in the field of commodities at UNCTAD IV in 1976, the outbreak of the debt crisis in 1982, the collapse of the socialist regimes and a shift away from state-controlled economies to *laissez-faire* in the late 1980s marked the beginning of the eventual decline of the NIEO movement. Since the early 1990s, differential treatment for developing countries was on the wane in broad fields of international economic law, particularly in international trade agreements. At the same time, differential treatment increasingly gained importance as a means for organising North–South co-operation in international environmental law.[6]

The internationalisation and, in part, globalisation of environmental concerns, together with the ongoing integration of developing countries in the world economy and the growing entanglement of economic technological and environmental affairs, led to 'a profound change in international environmental policy-making and to the search for new ways to ensure the participation of all countries in relevant agreements', and, in this context, to a 'revival' of differential treatment 'under a different guise'.[7]

With 'common but differentiated responsibilities' (CBDR), a specific form of differential treatment found its way into the 1992 Rio Declaration as Principle 7 which should play a pivotal role in further developing international environmental law. Principle 7 reads as follows:

> States shall cooperate in a spirit of global partnership to conserve, protect and restore the health and integrity of the Earth's ecosystem. In view of the different contributions to global environmental degradation, States have common but differentiated responsibilities. The developed countries acknowledge the responsibility that they bear in the international pursuit of sustainable development in view of the pressures their societies place on the global environment and of the technologies and financial resources they command.

The following considerations will start with identifying the underlying ideas and the

Treatment in International Law: Towards a New Paradigm of Inter-State Relations' (1999) 10 *European Journal of International Law* 549, 565.

[5] *Ibid*, 566.

[6] *Cf* Cullet, above n 4, 564 *et seq*; *id*, *Differential Treatment in International Environmental Law* (Aldershot 2003) 62 *et seq*; L Rajamani, above n 4, 17 *et seq*; Y Matsui, 'Some Aspects of the Principle of "Common But Differentiated Responsibilities"' (2002) 2 *International Environmental Agreements: Politics, Law and Economics* 151, 152.

[7] Cullet, above n 4, 569.

theoretical concept of CBDR, as expressed in Principle 7 of the 1992 Rio Declaration. This will be followed by a discussion of the relevance of CBDR to international environmental treaty practice, as well as its normative quality and status. Finally, perspectives of CBDR in the North–South context will be scrutinised.

9.2 Underlying Ideas and Conceptual Approach of CBDR

CBDR appears to reflect a wisdom originating from the times of Plato according to which '"equality among unequals" may be inequitable and . . . differential treatment may be essential for "real equality"'.[8] It goes without saying that in a world characterised by disparities in resources and capabilities, sovereign equality of states alone does not guarantee just interstate relations. As long as the world *de facto* consists of unequal states, formal equality must be complemented by substantive equality as a constitutive element of international justice. In order to ensure that the outcomes of interstate decision-making processes are just and fair, unequal states must be treated unequally. Differential treatment even proves to be the only means to achieve substantive equality.[9] In so far as it is 'premised on commonalities of interest in the face of divergent material conditions', differential treatment, as specified in the concept of CBDR, can also be seen as 'a reflection of solidarity in the international field'.[10]

Today, all states, both the industrialised and developing ones, are responsible for meeting the immense global environmental challenges they commonly face by taking joint large-scale remedial action. However, the factual preconditions under which both state groups are acting differ considerably. Firstly, the historical contribution of industrialised states to the processes of global environmental degradation, such as ozone depletion, climate change and loss of biodiversity, has been by far greater than that of developing countries. Secondly, both state groups have long shown significant differences regarding their respective levels of economic development. The more developed a state is, the more it is capable to engage in cost-intensive environmental action.

CBDR, as articulated in Principle 7 of the Rio Declaration, responds to this divergent situation of both state groups by pursuing a twofold conceptual approach. It starts with emphasising the states' common responsibility for the preservation of the global environment and the need for co-operation. It then goes on to declare this responsibility to be both 'common' and 'differentiated'. In the latter respect, Principle 7 takes notice of the 'different contributions' of states to global environmental degradation, but avoids directly allocating the costs of pollution to those states which historically inflicted most harm on the environment. It points to 'the need to take account of differing circumstances, particularly in relation to each state's *contribution* to the creation of a particular environmental

[8] O Schachter, *Sharing the World's Resources* (New York 1977) 7.

[9] See Cullet, above n 4, 553 *et seq*; *id*, above n 6, 21 *et seq*. *Cf* Chapter 5.2.2.

[10] Rajamani, above n 4, 7. *Cf* also Cullet, above n 4, 558 *et seq*; *id*, above n 6, 18. PW Birnie, AE Boyle and C Redgwell, *International Law and the Environment* (3rd edn Oxford 2009) 134 *et seq* take the position that Principle 7 of the Rio Declaration entails 'obligations of solidarity assistance to developing states'.

problem and its *ability* to prevent, reduce and control the threat'.[11] As a result, the industrialised states must carry most of the burden which effective remedial and preventive environmental action necessarily brings about. This includes their responsibility to support developing countries by financial and technological means, especially for purposes of compliance assistance. Accordingly, CBDR calls on the industrialised states to pursue a strategy of differential treatment for the benefit of developing countries.

Principle 8 of the Rio Declaration states that

> [t]o achieve sustainable development and a higher quality of life for all people, States should reduce and eliminate unsustainable patterns of production and consumption and promote appropriate demographic policies.

This principle can be understood as a specific variant of CBDR. It formally addresses all states. However, *de facto* the call for changing unsustainable patterns of production and consumption is solely directed to the industrialised states, while, conversely, propagating appropriate demographic policies is aimed at the developing countries only.[12]

At the 1992 UN Conference on Environment and Development (UNCED) in Rio de Janeiro, the industrialised states tried hard to avoid the inclusion of any terminology in the Rio outcome documents that might be interpreted as an explicit admission of having caused the most serious threats to the global environment. Ultimately, the industrialised states succeeded in convincing the developing countries to incorporate 'polluter pays' and CBDR into the Rio Declaration as two separate principles.

Principle 16 of the Rio Declaration, which stipulates 'polluter pays', reads as follows:

> National authorities should endeavour to promote the internalization of environmental costs and the use of economic instruments, taking into account the approach that the polluter should, in principle, bear the cost of pollution, with due regard to the public interests and without distorting international trade and investment.[13]

This formulation shows that 'polluter pays' diametrically differs from CBDR as to its field of application. While 'polluter pays' concerns the internal relationship between the states' national authorities and the polluters which mostly originate from the civil society, CBDR comes into play in interstate relations, namely in the antagonistic relationship between industrialised states and developing countries. Thus, both concepts are not antithetical in character.

9.3 Interpretation of CBDR

The interpretation of Principle 7 raises considerable difficulties which centre on the question whether CBDR propagates the '*ability* to pay or a *responsibility* to pay'[14]. Mickelson

[11] P Sands, *Principles of International Environmental Law* (2nd edn Cambridge 2003) 286.

[12] In this sense also Matsui, above n 6, quoting the Report of the UN Secretary-General to the Commission on Sustainable Development, 'Rio Declaration on Environment and Development: Application and Implementation' (1997) UN Doc E/CN17/1997/8, at para 51.

[13] For a more detailed discussion on 'polluter-pays' *cf* Chapter 8.

[14] K Mickelson, 'South, North, International Environmental Law, and International Environmental Lawyers' (2000) 11 *Yearbook of International Environmental Law* 52, 70.

stresses that 'depending on the perspective brought to bear on it, it can reflect totally different ways of thinking about the respective roles of South and North in addressing environmental degradation'.[15] She puts the problem in a nutshell when she states:

> On the one hand, it [Principle 7 of the Rio Declaration] can simply reflect a pragmatic acceptance of, and response to, the fact of differing levels of financial and technological resources available to countries in different economic circumstances. On the other hand, it can be said to reflect an acknowledgement of the historic, moral, and legal responsibility of the North to shoulder the burdens of environmental protection, just as it has enjoyed the benefits of economic and industrial development largely unconstrained by environmental concerns.[16]

Notwithstanding these uncertainties, Principle 7 of the Rio Declaration appears to be a compromise, or at least an 'agreement to disagree', between both state groups. This becomes evident if one compares the existing Principle 7 with the original text proposal of the 'Group of 77' (G-77) which, *inter alia*, emphasised that

> [t]he major cause of the continuing deterioration of the global environment is the unsustainable pattern of production and consumption, particularly in the developed countries. . . . In view of their main historical and current responsibility for global environmental degradation and their capability to address this common concern, developed countries shall provide adequate, new and additional financial resources and environmentally sound technologies on preferential and concessional terms to developing countries to enable them to achieve sustainable development.[17]

What results from the comparison of this text with the final version of Principle 7 is that contrary to the original aspiration of the G-77, the ultimately adopted Principle 7 does not make any reference to legal responsibility in the context of the historical contributions of the industrialised states to global environmental degradation. It rather emphasises the idea of future responsibility in achieving global sustainable development, and is generally far less accusatory in its terms.[18]

Nonetheless, the United States felt compelled at the Rio Conference to issue an interpretative statement to Principle 7 according to which this principle

> highlights the special leadership role of the developed countries, based on our industrial development, our experience with environmental protection policies and actions, and our wealth, technical expertise and capabilities.[19]

The United States went on to assert that it does

> not accept an interpretation of Principle 7 that would imply a recognition or acceptance by the United States of any international obligation . . . or any diminution in the responsibilities of developing countries.[20]

[15] See *ibid.*

[16] *Cf ibid.*

[17] Proposal submitted on behalf of the G-77, UN Doc A/CONF151/PC/WGIII/L20/Rev1 (19 March 1992).

[18] See in particular D French, 'Developing States and International Environmental Law: The Importance of Differentiated Responsibilities' (2000) 49 *ICLQ* 35, 36 *et seq*; Mickelson, above n 14, 70 *et seq*; Rajamani, above n 4, 138 *et seq*.

[19] Cited by J Kovar, 'A Short Guide to the Rio Declaration' (1993) 4 *Colorado Journal of International Environmental Law* 119, 129 *et seq*.

[20] *Ibid.*

This statement clearly reflects the then existing reluctance of the whole group of industrialised states to accept a direct responsibility to pay for its past behaviour.

A closer look at the practice of MEAs will reveal whether and, if so to what extent, this understanding of CBDR has governed and still governs interstate co-operation in global environmental matters.[21]

9.4 CBDR in International Environmental Treaty Practice

In addition to the Rio Declaration several other legally non-binding international documents make explicit reference to the specific situation, needs and concerns of developing countries. Among them are Agenda 21 of 1992, another Rio outcome document, and the Plan of Implementation of the 2002 World Summit in Johannesburg. While Agenda 21, in its Chapter 38.3(c), stipulates what CBDR requires, without expressly referring to it,[22] the Johannesburg Plan repeatedly points to CBDR, but avoids giving any specification of this concept.[23] In this respect, modern MEAs are much more telling.

9.4.1 Reference to CBDR in Single MEAs

In order to win over as many developing countries as possible to global environmental co-operation, since the late 1980s the industrialised states increasingly entered into MEAs that impose on them stricter obligations than those incumbent on developing country parties. Thus, most of the MEAs existing today pursue a conceptual approach that conforms to CBDR.

There are essentially two ways an MEA can differentiate in favour of the developing country parties. It can either impose on its developing country parties lesser substantive environmental obligations or totally exempt them from such obligations. Alternatively, it can impose identical substantive environmental obligations on its parties, but grant a longer compliance period only to its developing country parties, considering that their economic underdevelopment prevents them from meeting their obligations in due time.

Theoretically, the parties to an MEA pursuing a CBDR approach can opt for two different categories of norms.[24] They can either rely on 'differential' norms which *per se* provide explicitly different, presumably more favourable, treatment to developing countries, or they can use 'contextual' norms, *ie* norms which on the face of it provide identical treatment to all states parties, but require or allow 'considerations of factors that

[21] *Cf* at Section 9.4.1.

[22] Chapter 39.3(c) of Agenda 21 recommends '[t]o promote and support the effective participation of all countries concerned, in particular developing countries, in the negotiation, implementation, review and governance of international agreements or instruments, including appropriate provision of technical and financial assistance . . ., as well as the use of differential obligations where appropriate'.

[23] *Cf eg* paras 2, 4 and 81 of the Plan of Implementation.

[24] The third category of 'absolute' norms (see above at Section 9.1) does not fit to the strategy of CBDR.

might vary from country to country'.[25] While the use of 'contextual' norms in an MEA allows the parties concerned to conceive the most flexible solutions possible with a range of beneficiaries, the use of this type of norms in an MEA pursuing a strategy of CBDR that typically only benefits developing countries appears to be suboptimal. This is why the MEAs that follow primarily rely on norms that are 'differential' in nature.

The 1987 Montreal Protocol on Ozone Depleting Substances was perhaps the first important MEA[26] to pursue a clear strategy of CBDR. Opting for temporal rather than substantive differentiation, it imposes in its Article 2A–H on all parties identical substantive environmental obligations, but allows in its Article 5 developing countries with an annual consumption of substances controlled in the Protocol of less than 0.3 kilograms per capita to postpone for ten years compliance with their obligations to reduce or freeze the consumption and production of these 'controlled substances'. This 'differential norm', which unilaterally benefits the developing country parties, is accompanied by the obligation of the industrialised state parties under Article 10 of the Montreal Protocol to create a financial mechanism, including a Multilateral Fund, that provides financial and technical co-operation, including the transfer of chlorofluorocarbon-free technology to developing countries. In this way, the Montreal Protocol creates strong incentives for developing countries to join its regime.[27]

Both the 1992 Climate Change Convention (UNFCCC) and the thereto related 1997 Kyoto Protocol explicitly refer to CBDR.[28] The Kyoto Protocol is perhaps the most striking example of an instrument that makes use of CBDR in the form of construing an asymmetric environmental obligation scheme which consists exclusively of 'differential norms'. According to the abstract parameters established by Article 4 UNFCCC, the Kyoto Protocol applies CBDR in its most rigid form. It imposes solely on the developed country parties strict substantive environmental obligations aimed at the reduction of their greenhouse gas emissions within fixed time limits, while the developing country parties only must meet some minor procedural obligations such as reporting. More precisely, under Article 3(1) of the Kyoto Protocol, certain Annex I parties to the Climate Change Convention which are listed in Annex B of the Protocol, namely industrialised states and states in transition to market economies, agreed to reduce their overall emissions of greenhouse gases by at least 5 per cent below 1990 levels in the commitment period of

[25] See for the distinction between 'absolute', 'differential' and 'contextual' norms Magraw, above n 2, 73 *et seq*. *Cf* also B Kellersmann, *Die gemeinsame, aber differenzierte Verantwortlichkeit von Industriestaaten und Entwicklungsländern für den Schutz der globalen Umwelt* (Heidelberg 2000) 60 *et seq*; M Weisslitz, 'Rethinking the Equitable Principle of Common but Differentiated Responsibility: Differential Versus Absolute Norms of Compliance and Contribution in the Global Climate Change Context' (2002) 13 *Colorado Journal of International Environmental Law and Policy* 473, 485 *et seq*.

[26] An earlier one is the 1982 Law of the Sea Convention which already in its preamble takes into account the 'special interests and needs of developing countries' and which contains in its operative part numerous contextual norms (*eg* Article 194 UNCLOS) and few differential norms (*eg* Article 202 UNCLOS) that provide for substantive equality among unequal states. See for a more detailed analysis again Magraw, above n 2, 94 *et seq*.

[27] See *eg* Kellersmann, above n 25, 91 *et seq*, 105 et seq; Weisslitz, above n 25, 480 *et seq*. *Cf* Chapters 13.3.2 and 23.2.

[28] See Art 3(1) UNFCCC and Article 10 Kyoto Protocol.

2002–2012.[29] Moreover, the industrialised states are committed to transferring financial resources and technology to the developing countries in order to enable them to fulfil their procedural duties. Thus, CBDR, as applied in the Kyoto Protocol, results in asymmetric substantive environmental obligations of states and in a mechanism of compliance assistance.[30] Both components of this concept one-sidedly benefit the developing countries and lead to what may be called 'benign' or 'positive' discrimination in favour of the Third World.[31]

Taking into account that 'the conservation of biological diversity is a common concern of humankind',[32] the 1992 Biodiversity Convention stipulates the common responsibility of both industrialised states and developing countries for the conservation of biological diversity. Correspondingly, the parties' respective obligations under the Convention are formally symmetric, but have *de facto* different effects. The task of conserving biological resources is mainly incumbent on the hosting states, which are quite often developing countries. They are obliged to promote and facilitate the access of industrialised states and their companies to the genetic resources existing within their territories. In return to the benefits drawn from the economic use of these resources, the industrialised states must provide financial, scientific and technological assistance to the hosting developing countries. Apparently inspired by the concept of CBRD, the Convention thus creates a sophisticated system of mutual economic incentives that benefits both state groups.[33]

Regarding its regulatory design, the 1994 Convention to Combat Desertification stands out from the other MEAs just described. Firstly, the Convention, pursuing an innovative bottom-up approach, devolves the totality of environmental obligations, namely to combat desertification and mitigate the effects of drought, upon the developing countries themselves affected by these ecological conditions (Article 5). Secondly, the industrialised states are legally bound under the Convention to provide substantial financial resources and other forms of support to assist affected developing country parties and to promote the mobilisation of new and additional funding (Articles 6 and 20). However, compared to other MEAs, the Convention less clearly determines the extent to which affected developing countries can practically count on financial and technological support by the industrialised states. In this respect, the imprint of CBDR in the Convention appears to be rather weak.[34]

[29] See *eg* Rajamani, above n 4, 191 *et seq*; Weisslitz, above n 25, 483 *et seq*; AM Halvorssen, 'Common, but Differentiated Commitments in the Future Climate Change Regime Amending the Kyoto Protocol to Include Annex C and the Annex C Mitigation Fund' (2007) 18 *Colorado Journal of International Environmental Law and Policy* 247, 256 *et seq*. *Cf* also Chapter 13.4.2.

[30] The Kyoto Protocol pursues what M Bothe, 'The United Nations Framework Convention on Climate Change: an Unprecedented Multilevel Regulatory Challenge' (2003) 63 *ZaöRV* 239, 252, has called the 'North first' approach. According to him this approach 'is a special form of intergenerational equity: The generation living in the industrialised countries of today assumes a responsibility for the emissions produced by the generations of yesterday' (*ibid*).

[31] AM Halvorssen, *Equality among Unequals in International Environmental Law. Differential Treatment for Developing Countries* (Boulder 1999) 28, classifies the concept of 'differential treatment' of developing countries 'as a kind of "international affirmative action" notion'.

[32] Third recital of the preamble of the Biodiversity Convention.

[33] See for a more detailed discussion Kellersmann, above n 25, 208 *et seq*, 338 *et seq*. *Cf* also Chapter 14.3.1.

[34] In this sense also Kellersmann, *ibid*, 256 *et seq*, 340. *Cf* Chapter 14.5.

9.4.2 Conditionality of Environmental Protection and Compliance Assistance?

MEAs pursuing a strategy of CBDR typically combine their schemes of differential substantive environmental obligations with the respective schemes of compliance assistance. It might be argued that rendering compliance assistance on the part of the industrialised state parties is a *quid pro quo* for the readiness of the developing country parties to comply with their environmental treaty obligations. Indeed, Article 5(5) of the Montreal Protocol states that 'implementation by . . . [developing country] Parties will depend upon the effective implementation of the financial co-operation as provided by Article 10A'. Thereby it seems to bring both obligation schemes into a relationship of legal conditionality. The same might apply to the Biodiversity Convention, which in its Article 20(4) states that '[t]he extent to which developing country Parties will effectively implement their commitments under this Convention will depend on the effective implementation of the developed country Parties of their commitments under this Convention related to financial resources and transfer of technology', as well as to the Climate Change Convention with its identical wording in Article 4(7).[35] However, this reading of the treaty clauses in question is detrimental to the aim of environmental protection, because it allows the developing countries to withhold the fulfilment of their environmental obligations under the Convention as long as the industrialised states abstain from providing compliance assistance.

This is why, alternatively, the above-mentioned clauses may be either understood as plain statements of facts or as provisions designed to give the developing countries the opportunity if necessary to defend their own non-compliance with environmental treaty obligations as long as the industrialised states have failed to provide adequate compliance assistance.[36] Even so, there are good reasons for arguing that

> it becomes irrelevant whether developed states have a legal duty to provide assistance: if they want developing states to participate actively in securing the goals of each agreement they must honour the expectation that the necessary resources will be provided.[37]

9.5 Normative Quality and Status

Based on the findings of section 9.4, CBDR can be seen as a concept with a strong driving force which is not 'immediately aimed at making the addressees take action, to refrain form action, or achieve a fixed result', but designed 'to give guidance to all states for future conduct in rule-making processes as well as to shape the interpretation and

[35] Art 11 of the Kyoto Protocol explicitly refers to Art 4(7) UNFCCC.

[36] U Beyerlin and T Marauhn, *Law-Making and Law-Enforcement in International Environmental Law after the 1992 Rio Conference* (Berlin 1997) 129, 155.

[37] Birnie, Boyle and Redgwell, above n 10, 135. In this context, they emphasise that 'it is in this sense that solidarity is a key element' of CBDR (*ibid*).

application of rules already in existence'.[38] Accordingly, in Dworkin's typology of norms, CBDR is a principle rather than a rule. Due to its steering effects it possesses a normative quality which makes it eligible for gaining the status of a principle of customary international law. However, since the attitudes of states to CBDR are as yet rather ambivalent, this principle still waits to be accepted in general state practice. It is not consolidated enough in terms of content to have the authority to uniformly determine and control the conclusion, interpretation and implementation of MEAs.[39]

9.6 CBDR and Future North–South Co-operation

From its very beginning, CBDR was designed as a conceptual approach for bridging the North–South divide, which hampers global environmental and developmental co-operation between antagonistic state groups almost as seriously as it did in the 1970s and 1980s. Although it is at best an emerging principle of customary international law, CBDR politically legitimises the conclusion of MEAs which combine highly asymmetric environmental obligations with mechanisms of compliance assistance. The Kyoto Protocol is prototypical for this innovative approach and puts it to the test in practice. The total exemption of the entire group of developing countries from any obligations to reduce greenhouse gas emissions, combined with the Protocol's financing mechanism at the expense of the industrialised states, leads to what can be called 'benign discrimination' in favour of the South. This solution might have been just and fair at the time when the Kyoto Protocol was made. However, it is doubtful whether it will also prove to be wise environmental policy in the long run.

As any splitting of treaty obligations entails the risk of diminishing the effectiveness of the treaty regime concerned, compensatory benign discrimination of the South under the Kyoto Protocol should only be granted on a temporary basis.[40] Accordingly, there is much in favour of arguing that in the commitment periods subsequent to 2012, the circle of states bound to reduce their greenhouse gas emissions should be considerably broadened. While the least developed countries and the developing countries which are particularly vulnerable to the effects of climate change may be left outside the scheme of emissions reduction obligations also in the future, this can hardly be valid for rapidly industrialising developing countries such as China, India and Brazil. The greater the number of developing states to be included in the mandatory emissions reduction scheme, the more the industrialised states will have to provide for technological and financial transfers that help the developing countries meet the costs arising from the fulfilment of their reduction obligations under the Kyoto Protocol.

[38] U Beyerlin, 'Different Types of Norms in International Environmental Law. Policies, Principles, and Rules' in D Bodansky *et al* (eds), *The Oxford Handbook of International Environmental Law* (Oxford 2007) 425, 437. *Cf* Chapter 5.3.

[39] *Cf* Kellersmann, above n 24, 321 *et seq*; Matsui, above n 12, 166 *et seq*; Birnie, Boyle and Redgwell, n 10, 135 *et seq*.

[40] Also in this sense Matsui, above n 12, 158.

Casting doubt on whether it really conforms to the idea of international justice any longer to exempt developing countries altogether from being bound to reduce their greenhouse gas emissions does not mean discarding the principle of CBDR. Quite the contrary, it only takes account of the quintessence of CBDR, *ie* the insight that the responsibility of states from the North and the South for the global environment is both common and differentiated.[41]

Further Reading

R Anand, *International Environmental Justice. A North-South Dimension* (Aldershot 2004).

P Cullet, 'Differential Treatment in International Law: Towards a New Paradigm of Inter-State Relations' (1999) 10 *European Journal of International Law* 549–582.

——, *Differential Treatment in International Environmental Law* (Aldershot 2003).

D French, 'Developing States and International Environmental Law: The Importance of Differentiated Responsibilities' (2000) 49 *ICLQ* 35–60.

C Glass, *Die gemeinsame, aber unterschiedliche Verantwortlichkeit als Bestandteil eines umweltvölkerrechtlichen Prinzipiengefüges. Konkretisierungsvorschläge für künftige Übereinkommen zum Schutz globaler Umweltgüter* (Berlin 2007).

AM Halvorssen, *Equality among Unequals in International Environmental Law. Differential Treatment for Developing Countries* (Boulder 1999).

——, 'Common, but Differentiated Commitments in the Future Climate Change Regime Amending the Kyoto Protocol to Include Annex C and the Annex C Mitigation Fund' (2007) 18 *Colorado Journal of International Environmental Law and Policy* 247–265.

B Kellersmann, *Die gemeinsame, aber differenzierte Verantwortlichkeit von Industriestaaten und Entwicklungsländern für den Schutz der globalen Umwelt* (Heidelberg 2000).

DB Magraw, 'Legal Treatment of Developing Countries: Differential, Contextual, and Absolute Norms' (1990) 1 *Colorado Journal of International Environmental Law and Policy* 69–99.

Y Matsui, 'Some Aspects of the Principle of "Common But Differentiated Responsibilities"' (2002) 2 *International Environmental Agreements: Politics, Law and Economics* 151–171.

K Mickelson, 'South, North, International Environmental Law, and International Environmental Lawyers' (2000) 11 *Yearbook of International Environmental Law* 52–81.

L Rajamani, *Differential Treatment in International Law* (Oxford 2006).

C Stone, 'Common but Differentiated Responsibilities in International Law' (2004) 98 *AJIL* 276–301.

M Weisslitz, 'Rethinking the Equitable Principle of Common but Differentiated Responsibility: Differential Versus Absolute Norms of Compliance and Contribution in the Global Climate Change Context' (2002) 13 *Colorado Journal of International Environmental Law and Policy* 473–509.

[41] *Cf* U Beyerlin, 'Bridging the North–South Divide in International Environmental Law' (2006) 66 *ZaöRV* 259, 277 *et seq*.

10

Sustainable Development

10.1 Historical Development

The roots of the concept of sustainable development go back to the early 1970s when the UN General Assembly proclaimed the Second UN Development Decade[1] and the Founex Report 'Development and Environment' of 1971[2] pointed to the linkage of long-term development goals and environmental protection. In 1972, the UN Stockholm Declaration on the Human Environment,[3] particularly in its Principles 9, 10 and 11, first emphasised that environmental protection and economic development must be understood as compatible and mutually reinforcing goals. Particularly telling in this respect is Principle 11 which states that

> the environmental policies of all States should enhance and not adversely affect the present and future development potential of developing countries, nor should they hamper the attainment of better living conditions for all, and appropriate steps should be taken by States and international organizations with a view to reaching agreement on meeting the possible national and international economic consequences resulting from the application of environmental measures.

A first clear but legally non-binding commitment by states to sustainable development can be found in UN General Assembly Resolution 35/56 on the International Development Strategy for the Third UN Development Decade of 5 December 1980 which stressed in paragraph 41 that

> [a]ccelerated development in the developing countries could enhance their capacity to improve their environment. The environment implications of poverty and under-development and the interrelationships between development, environment, population and resources must be taken into account in the process of development. It is essential to avoid environmental degradation and give future generations the benefit of a sound environment. There is need to ensure an economic development process which is environmentally sustainable over the long run and which protects the ecological balance.

[1] UNGA Res 2626 (XXV) (24 October 1970).

[2] Founex Report on Development and Environment, elaborated by a Panel of Experts convened in June 1971 to set the agenda of the then upcoming Stockholm Conference. Text in: International Conciliation no 586.

[3] (1972) 11 ILM 1416.

The World Conservation Strategy, developed by the IUCN, UNEP and the WWF in 1980, as well as the UN World Charter for Nature of 1982 transformed the still very abstract concept of sustainable development into more specific programmes of action.

In its famous report 'Our Common Future' of 1987, the World Commission on Environment and Development, the so-called 'Brundtland Commission', understood sustainable development as 'development that meets the needs of the present without compromising the ability of future generations to meet their own needs'.[4] In December 1987 the UN General Assembly endorsed the Brundtland Report.[5] Ever since, the conceptualisation of sustainable development has proven particularly challenging for the international environmental law community.

Taken together, all these documents already contain the key elements of the concept of sustainable development as it was later employed in the run-up to the 1992 United Nations Conference on Environment and Development (UNCED) in Rio de Janeiro, during the negotiations at Rio, as well as in the Rio outcome documents, namely the Rio Declaration and Agenda 21. The latter set in motion an almost universal process ultimately aimed at establishing 'a new global partnership for sustainable development'.[6] Agenda 21 did not try to transmute sustainable development into a set of specific behaviour patterns, but developed a broad catalogue of recommendations without any further specification of the concept of sustainable development. Agenda 21 promoted sustainable development also in institutional respects by proposing the establishment of the Commission on Sustainable Development (CSD). Pursuant to ECOSOC Resolution 1993/207, this Commission was indeed set up in early 1993. Designated 'to ensure the effective follow-up of the [Rio] Conference, as well as to enhance and rationalize the intergovernmental decision-making capacity for the integration of environment and development issues',[7] the CSD has developed into a platform for high-level policy information and discussion regarding environmental protection and development.[8]

At least since UNCED, the concept of sustainable development has left significant traces in a broad number of international instruments, both of a legal and non-legal nature. The notion of 'sustainable development' and a variety of sub-notions that are derived from it, such as 'sustainable use', 'sustainable utilisation', 'maximum sustainable yield' or 'sustainable management', have been included in almost all important post-Rio instruments.

For instance, the 1992 Climate Change Convention (UNFCCC) and the Kyoto Protocol both refer to sustainable development as an integral objective of combating climate change (Article 2 UNFCCC and Article 2(1) Kyoto Protocol); moreover, Article 3 UNFCCC makes clear that '[t]he parties have a right to, and should, promote sustainable development'. The Convention to Combat Desertification (UNCCD) is particularly telling

[4] World Commission on Environment and Development, *Our Common Future* (Oxford 1987) 43.

[5] UNGA Res 42/187 (11 December 1987).

[6] Preamble of Agenda 21 para 1.6. For the text of Agenda 21, see *Report of the United Nations Conference on Environment and Development, Rio de Janeiro, 3–14 June 1992, Vol I: Resolutions Adopted by the Conference*, Resolution 1, Annex II, UN Doc A/Conf15/26/Rev1 (New York 1993). The text is also available at www.un.org/esa/sustdev/documents/agenda21/english/agenda21toc.htm.

[7] Chapter 38.11 of Agenda 21, for the text see *ibid.*

[8] *Cf* Chapter 17.2.2.

as regards the close interdependence between development and ecology. It emphasises that sustainable economic growth, social development and poverty eradication are priorities of developing countries experiencing drought and/or desertification, particularly in Africa, and are essential to 'meeting sustainability objectives' (recital 8 of the preamble of the UNCCD). Consequently, UNCCD calls upon its parties to take effective action at all levels for combating desertification and mitigating the effects of drought, thereby contributing to the achievement of sustainable development in affected areas (Articles 2(1) and 4(2)(b)). As regards the 1992 Convention on Biological Diversity (CBD), the goal of sustainable use of the components of biological diversity (instead of sustainable development) is complementary to that of conservation of biological diversity. They both constitute the CBD's main objectives (Article 1 CBD). Accordingly, sustainable use of the components of biological diversity, and hence biological resources, is a central concern of the CBD (*cf* Articles 5, 8 and 10 CBD). All in all, numerous MEAs at different levels expressly refer to sustainable development or sustainable use. However, they typically abstain from defining these terms.[9]

In September 2000, the UN General Assembly adopted the Millennium Declaration[10] which stipulates eight millennium development goals (MDGs) to be achieved by 2015. MDG 7 focuses on environmental sustainability. In this Declaration, the General Assembly reaffirmed its support for the principles of sustainable development as agreed upon at UNCED.[11]

In April 2002, the non-governmental organisation International Law Association (ILA) published its New Delhi Declaration on the Principles of International Law Relating to Sustainable Development.[12] This Declaration points to the duty of states to ensure sustainable use of natural resources, as well as a conglomeration of 'principles' that encompasses 'equity and the eradication of poverty'; 'common but differentiated responsibilities'; a 'precautionary approach to human health, natural resources and ecosystems'; 'public participation and access to information and justice'; 'good governance'; and 'integration and interrelationship, in particular in relation to human rights and social, economic and environmental objectives'.[13] However, it does not address the question of what sustain-

[9] An exception in this respect is the Antigua Convention for Cooperation in the Protection and Sustainable Development of the Marine and Coastal Environment in the Northeast Pacific of 18 February 2002 (not yet in force). According to its Art 3(a), sustainable development means 'the process of progressive change in the quality of life of human beings, which places it as the centre and primordial subject of development, by means of economic growth with social equity and the transformations of methods of production and consumption patterns, and which is sustained in the ecological balance and vital support of the region. This process implies respect for regional, national and local ethnic and cultural diversity, and the full participation of people in peaceful coexistence and in harmony with nature, without prejudice to and ensuring the quality of life of future generations.' This definition at best expresses what sustainable development means in the common understanding of the parties to the convention concerned. However, it is far from representing a definition that is uniformly accepted by the parties to MEAs in general.

[10] UNGA Res 55/2 (8 September 2000). *Cf* Chapter 3.3.

[11] UNGA Res 55/2, *ibid*, para 22.

[12] UN Doc A/CONF199/8 (9 August 2002). The New Delhi Declaration has been commented by N Schrijver, 'The New Delhi Declaration of Principles of International Law Relating to Sustainable Development' in MC Cordonier and CG Weeramantry (eds), *Sustainable Justice. Reconciling Economic, Social and Environmental Law* (Leiden/Boston 2005) 549.

[13] New Delhi Declaration, *ibid*, paras 2–7.

able development in itself legally means. The ILA presented its New Delhi Declaration to the World Summit on Sustainable Development (WSSD) which took place in 2002 in Johannesburg.

As suggested by its name, the World Summit focused on sustainable development. In its Plan of Implementation it developed a wide range of strategies for implementing existing instruments on sustainable development. The Plan emphasises that sustainable development consists of 'three components . . .—economic development, social development and environmental protection—as interdependent and mutually reinforcing pillars'.[14] It must be noted that the WSSD paid particular attention to the social needs of humankind, such as health and education, which in essence lack any significant environmental dimension. This observation is not, however, tantamount to criticising the WSSD for being primarily concerned with the social development aspect of sustainable development. The Plan covers a very broad spectrum of sustainability-related issues, including sustainable development in a globalising world; health and sustainable development; sustainable development of small island states; sustainable development in Africa; and the institutional framework for sustainable development.[15]

In October 2005, the UN General Assembly adopted the '2005 World Summit Outcome'[16] which, *inter alia*, reaffirmed sustainable development as a key element of UN activities.[17]

All these documents confirm that since UNCED at the latest, sustainable development has become the worldwide dominating leitmotif for shaping international environmental and developmental relations. They also illustrate the immense proliferation of this concept in international relations which resulted in confusion rather than clarity as regards its contours, meaning and effect.

10.2 Meaning and Function

Notwithstanding doubts as to whether sustainable development can claim normative quality in the sense of entailing meaningful guidance for relevant state behaviour, it has developed at the international, regional and national levels to a crucial political precept that governs virtually every sphere of activity aimed at balancing and integrating economic, social and environmental policies.

The composite term 'sustainable development' describes an abstract political value that deserves respect in today's international relations. It provides for a close interdependence between the policy goals of development and environmental protection. An indispensable prerequisite for any developmental policy or action which merits the label 'sustainable' is that it meets the essentials of environmental protection. Thus, the notion

[14] Para 2 of the Plan; UN Doc A/CONF199/20, Annex, 8.

[15] *Cf* Chapter 4.2.1.

[16] *Cf* Chapter 4.3.

[17] High-Level Plenary Meeting of the 60th Session of the UN General Assembly, UNGA Res 60/1 (24 October 2005) para 10.

of 'sustainability' is tantamount to that of 'environmental soundness'. As indicated by the term 'development', sustainable development points at a process of interaction to be set in motion, without saying by whom and in which form. As to the impact of the environment on development and vice versa, the 1992 Rio Declaration, particularly in its Principle 4, clearly stresses the interdependence between both:

> In order to achieve sustainable development, environmental protection shall constitute an integral part of the development process and cannot be considered in isolation from it.

While there is continuing uncertainty among states regarding the exact meaning and scope of sustainable development, it is widely accepted that the concept entails two temporal dimensions which Principle 3 of the Rio Declaration addresses by stating that '[t]he right to development must be fulfilled so as to equitably meet developmental and environmental needs of present and future generations'. Thus, sustainable development necessarily implies the inter- and intragenerational responsibility of states. It is concerned with relationships both among members of the present generation, and between the present and future generations.[18]

In both dimensions, the primary concern of sustainable development is 'sustained human development ("weak sustainability")'.[19] This reading is in line with Principle 1 of the 1992 Rio Declaration, which states:

> Human beings are at the centre of concerns for sustainable development. They are entitled to a healthy and productive life in harmony with nature.

Accordingly, from an ethical perspective, sustainable development is by its very essence an anthropocentric concept. This does not mean, however, that any attempt to interpret sustainable development also in ecocentric terms must be categorically rejected. On the contrary, Bosselmann is right to consider sustainable development to be 'a new, extended form of justice' that 'expands our traditional concept of justice in terms of space and time' by including 'the entire global community and future generations', comprising both 'the human and nonhuman world'.[20] Therefore, states should feel prompted to leave the earth's ecosystem to future generations in as sound a condition as possible. They should take all efforts to conserve the 'diversity of the natural and cultural resource base' and maintain 'the quality of the planet',[21] including the nonhuman nature. Thus, the intergenerational component of sustainable development gives reason enough to interpret this concept as if it were conceived in ecocentric terms.

[18] G Mayeda, 'Where Should Johannesburg Take Us? Ethical and Legal Approaches to Sustainable Development in the Context of International Environmental Law' (2004) 15 *Colorado Journal of International Environmental Law and Policy* 29, 59 *et seq*, considers the concept of 'common but differentiated responsibility' and the 'precautionary principle' to offer appropriate conceptual approaches for curing the uncertainties resulting from 'the absence of information about the interests of future generations and their conception of the good' (*ibid*, 61).

[19] K Bosselmann 'The Concept of Sustainable Development' in K Bosselmann and D Grinlinton (eds), *Environmental Law for a Sustainable Society* (Auckland 2002) 81, 84.

[20] *Ibid*, 96.

[21] E Brown Weiss, *In Fairness to Future Generations: International Law, Common Patrimony and Intergenerational Equity* (New York 1989) 38.

Since intergenerational equity ideally cannot be isolated from intragenerational equity,[22] the concept of sustainable development in its entirety calls for an interpretation that is anthropocentric in essence, but gives also leeway to ecocentric deliberations. On the one hand, sustainable development comprehends 'humanity as the centre of existence', thereby allocating to nature 'an instrumental value for humans'.[23] On the other hand, it respects the view 'that nature with all its life forms has intrinsic value independently from any instrumental values for humans'.[24]

Unfortunately, neither the Rio Declaration of 1992 nor the subsequent Political Declaration adopted at the Johannesburg WSSD in 2002 definitely answer the question of how exactly development and environmental protection should be balanced. At least, the statement in Article 3 of the Rio Declaration that '[t]he right to development must be fulfilled so as to equitably meet developmental and environmental needs of present and future generations' suggests that striking an equitable balance between the competing interests of development and environmental protection presupposes their equivalence in substance. There is no evidence for assuming that development prevails over environmental protection, or vice versa. Developing countries which face economic deficiencies and social disruption are tempted to give preference to developmental needs over environmental ones, while industrialised states are inclined to take the opposite view. However, the concept of sustainable development ultimately does not lend support to either of the positions. Consequently, in any individual case an equitable compromise between both the developmental and environmental needs must be sought, even though, since the WSSD at the latest, sustainable development is widely understood as a concept with three pillars. However, it should be clear that this tripartition must not minimise the concept's protective effect on the environment.

By contrast, Bosselmann takes the position that ecology should have general priority over development. In his view

> [i]t is crucial . . . to realize the ecological core of the concept [of sustainable development]. Not realizing it means that social, economic and environmental interests have nowhere to go. There is only ecological sustainable development or no sustainable development at all. To perceive environmental, economic and social as equally important components of sustainable development is arguably the greatest misconception of sustainable development and the greatest obstacle to achieving social and economic justice.[25]

Admittedly, intergenerational equity, understood as an integral part of sustainable development, requires the present human generation to abstain strictly from systematically degrading the earth's ecosystem to such an extent that future generations will be deprived of the basic ecological prerequisites for meeting their own needs. However, giving ecology general preponderance over development, thereby paying respect to the future-oriented

[22] K Bosselmann, 'A Legal Framework for Sustainable Development' in Bosselmann and Grinlinton (eds), above n 19, 150, balances intergenerational justice and intragenerational justice in a way 'that the former is a prerequisite for the latter, but that intragenerational justice itself shapes the commitments coming from intergenerational equity'.

[23] A Gillespie, *International Environmental Law, Policy and Ethics* (Oxford 1997) 2, 4.

[24] Bosselmann, above n 22, 151.

[25] K Bosselmann, *The Principle of Sustainability: Transforming Law and Governance* (Aldershot 2008) 23.

dimension of sustainable development as embodied by the concept of intergenerational equity,[26] hardly reflects the current state of thinking in international environmental and developmental relations and doctrine. It merely points to an ambitious long-term goal.

All in all, sustainable development is a concept characterised by (i) the close linkage between the policy goals of economic and social development and environmental protection; (ii) the qualification of environmental protection as an integral part of any developmental measure, and vice versa; and (iii) the long-term perspective of both policy goals, namely states' intergenerational responsibility that widens the conceptual and temporal dimension of sustainable development.

10.3 Normative Quality and Status

The question of whether sustainable development has normative quality and thus in structural terms the capacity to grow into a legally binding norm, be it a principle or a rule, depends on whether it can be considered to be a concept with steering effects on its addressees. If it lacks such effects, it can merely be classified as a policy goal to be pursued by all actors in international environmental and developmental relations.

The practice of MEAs is hardly instructive in this respect. As indicated above (at section 10.1), most MEAs even lack a clear definition of sustainable development, let alone indicate whether sustainable development has normative quality thus meeting the precondition for one day growing into a customary international norm.

The case law of international judicial and arbitral tribunals also gives little insight into the normative quality and status of sustainable development. Only once, in its judgment in the 1997 case concerning the *Gabčíkovo-Nagymaros Project (Hungary v Slovakia)*, has the International Court of Justice (ICJ) dealt with sustainable development. The Court expressly invoked the concept of sustainable development as an apt expression of the 'need to reconcile economic development with protection of the environment'.[27] In its view, as a consequence of this concept, the parties 'together should look afresh at the effects on the environment of the operation of the Gabčíkovo power plant'.[28] However, the question whether this concept is of legal or non-legal quality has been left undecided by the ICJ's majority judgment. Judge Weeramantry, in his separate opinion, considered sustainable development to be 'a principle with normative value' rather than 'a mere concept'.[29] In his view, this principle 'is a part of modern international law by reason not only of its inescapable logical necessity, but also by reason of its wide and general acceptance by the global community'.[30] Whether the majority judgment in the *Gabčíkovo-Nagymaros*

[26] Bosselmann observes that 'if sustainable development would be used merely for integrating and balancing conflicting interests, nothing would be achieved. Without a benchmark, we are left at a guess *how* environmental, social and economic interests should be balanced. The Brundtland definition offered some direction by demanding not to compromise "the ability of future generations to meet their own needs"' (*ibid*, 25).

[27] *Gabčíkovo-Nagymaros* case *(Hungary v Slovakia)* (1997) ICJ Reports 78, para 140.

[28] *Ibid*.

[29] *Ibid*, 92.

[30] *Ibid*, 95.

case shares this understanding of sustainable development, as Sands suggests,[31] appears to be uncertain at least.[32]

In the arbitration regarding the Iron Rhine Railway between the kingdoms of Belgium and the Netherlands, the Arbitral Tribunal stated in its Award of 24 May 2005, referring to the ICJ judgment in the *Gabčíkovo-Nagymaros* case:

> Environmental law and the law on development stand not as alternatives but as mutually reinforcing, integral concepts, which require that where development may cause significant harm to the environment there is the duty to prevent, or at least mitigate such harm. . . . This duty, in the opinion of the Tribunal, has now become a principle of general international law.[33]

This last sentence undoubtedly refers to 'no harm' rather than sustainable development.[34] Thus, it is clear that the latter's status has been left undecided by the Arbitral Tribunal in its 2005 award.

The spectrum of doctrinal views on the normative content and status of sustainable development in relevant international legal writings is broad and multifaceted. While some scholars take the straightforward position that sustainable development is a principle of customary international law,[35] others place it within the realm of 'soft law'[36] or explicitly allocate it to the sphere of political ideals which do not possess normative value.[37] Most scholars shy away from a clear answer to this question,[38] or consciously leave this issue undecided.[39] For instance, Magraw and Hawke argue

> that sustainable development is more than just a policy goal and that neither the category of non-normative policy statement nor the category of customary international law accurately characterizes sustainable development.[40]

[31] P Sands, *Principles of International Environmental Law* (2nd edn Cambridge 2003) 254.

[32] The case concerning *Pulp Mills on the River Uruguay (Argentina v Uruguay)*, Order of the ICJ of 13 July 2006 regarding provisional measures (text in (2006) 45 ILM 1025) also induced the ICJ to address sustainable development. However, its rather poor hints to sustainable development (paras 67 and 80 of the Order) hardly expedite the debate on the normative quality and status of sustainable development.

[33] *Iron Rhine Arbitration (Belgium v The Netherlands)*, Award of 24 May 2005, Permanent Court of Arbitration. The text of the Award is available in Permanent Court of Arbitration Award Series, (Cambridge 2007).

[34] Contrary to the Arbitral Tribunal's view, 'no harm' must be understood as a universal international rule for reasons explained above in Chapter 6.3.5.

[35] See *eg* A Epiney and M Scheyli, *Strukturprinzipien des Umweltvölkerrechts* (Baden-Baden 1998) 171, and H Hohmann, *Precautionary Legal Duties and Principles of Modern International Environmental Law* (London 1994) 166. In the view of P Sands (above n 31, 254) '[t]here can be little doubt that the concept of "sustainable development" has entered the corpus of international customary law'. Bosselmann (above n 25, 57) speaks of 'the normative character that the principle of sustainability has for the meaning of sustainable development. It follows that sustainability possesses the quality of a legal principle. We have defined it as the duty to protect and restore the integrity of the Earth's ecological systems.'

[36] See *eg* TA Mensah, 'Soft Law: A Fresh Look at an Old Mechanism' (2008) 38 *Environmental Law and Policy* 50, 52.

[37] See *eg* U Beyerlin, 'Sustainable Development' in R Wolfrum (ed), *Max Planck Encyclopedia of Public International Law* (Heidelberg/Oxford 2009), paras 15 *et seq*, available at www.mpepil.com.

[38] See *eg* E Louka, *International Environmental Law. Fairness, Effectiveness and World Order* (Cambridge 2006) 53.

[39] See VP Nanda and G Pring, *International Environmental Law & Policy for the 21st Century* (Ardsley 2003) 22 *et seq*.

[40] DB Magraw and LD Hawke, 'Sustainable Development' in D Bodansky *et al* (eds), *The Oxford Handbook of International Environmental Law* (Oxford 2007) 613, 624.

Birnie, Boyle and Redgwell cautiously state that

> [w]hether or not sustainable development is a legal obligation, and as we have seen this seems unlikely, it does represent a policy which can influence the outcome of cases, the interpretation of treaties, and the practice of states and international organizations, and may lead to significant changes and developments in the existing law.[41]

Lowe argues that sustainable development is a 'meta-principle', exercising 'a kind of interstitial normativity',[42] and concludes by stating that '[i]f employed by judges, a norm of such type gains normative force'.[43] Cordonier Segger seems to support Lowe's sophisticated thesis by stating that sustainable development

> is a purpose of treaty law rather than a principle in itself, though States may agree on certain principles in order to achieve their sustainable development purpose. If this were the case, the objective might, of course, still have a certain interstitial normativity when other principles come into conflict.[44]

None of these views has been able to identify and explain clearly enough what sustainable development specifically contributes to the normative system of international environmental law. Thus, the question of whether sustainable development has normative quality as a prerequisite for gaining the status of a customary international norm remains unsolved. If anything, relevant doctrine shows a certain tendency towards considering sustainable development to be a concept somewhere in between a legally binding international principle and a mere political ideal.

After all, there are ongoing controversies in determining the meaning and nature of the concept of sustainable development. Notwithstanding the acknowledgement that it is susceptible to varied explanations, the current state of debate gives reason to the following tentative assessment of sustainable development: Be it part of an international treaty or not, it is not an action-oriented rule but rather a principle that guides states in their decision-making. However, as indicated above,[45] the borderline between legal principles and political ideals is often blurred. The 'normative language' of sustainable development is so ambiguous that it cannot deploy any appreciable steering effect on states' environmental behaviour. For these reasons, there is much in favour of the assumption that sustainable development remains below the threshold of normative quality that is an indispensable prerequisite for ascribing the quality of a (legal) principle to it. Thus, it stipulates a political aim to be reached, or, alternatively, constitutes a political ideal to be pursued, rather than a legal principle that entails indirect steering effects on the conduct of its addressees.

In spite of their lacking normativity, political ideals can be catalysts in the process

[41] PW Birnie, AE Boyle and C Redgwell, *International Law and the Environment* (3rd edn Oxford 2009) 127.

[42] V Lowe, 'Sustainable Development and Unsustainable Arguments' in AE Boyle and DAC Freestone (eds), *International Law and Sustainable Development: Past Achievements and Future Challenges* (Oxford 1999) 19, 31.

[43] *Ibid*, 33. Also in this sense Birnie, Boyle and Redgwell, above n 41, 127.

[44] MC Cordonier Segger, 'Sustainable Development in International Law' in HC Brugge and C Voigt (eds), *Sustainable Development in International and National Law. What Did the Brundtland Report Do to Legal Thinking and Legal Development, and Where Can We Go from Here?* (Groningen 2008) 85, 118.

[45] *Cf* Chapter 5.3.

of further developing international law. Thus, there is much in favour of deducing some self-contained norms (*eg* intergenerational equity, sustainable use, equitable use and intragenerational equity) from the 'principle of sustainable development' irrespective of the latter's current nature.[46]

10.4 Sustainable Use—A Special Emanation of Sustainable Development

Sustainable development proves to be a source from which subordinate norms may be derived, one of which is 'sustainable use' in so far as it relates to natural resources. This precept calls upon states owning valuable natural resources on their territories, as well as third states seeking access to these resources for exploitation, to use these resources in a sustainable manner, thereby ensuring their continuance. Both groups of states should act as co-equal members of a community committed to the preservation of biological diversity as a goal of common welfare. Thus, sustainable use of natural resources does not only reflect the idea of distributive justice, but also that of international solidarity.[47] It helps preserve the earth's ecosystem for the sake of present and future generations.

'Sustainable use' is a special emanation of sustainable development. As such it may have become a self-contained norm in international law. However, it only gains normative quality if linked with a defined object of use. For example, the CBD puts sustainable use together with components of biological diversity, such as flora and fauna, and other natural resources. As defined in Article 2[48] and specified by Article 10(b) CBD, the contracting parties are called upon to take measures directed to ensure the sustainable use of natural resources. Notwithstanding its remaining indeterminateness, sustainable use is a legal rule in this context. Interstate practice reveals that it has been integrated in a very large number of international environmental agreements at all levels, *eg* in Article 1 of the 2000 Biosafety Protocol, the preamble of the 1968 African Nature Convention (Algiers Convention) and Article II of the 2003 Revised African Nature Convention (Maputo Convention), and Article 1(1) of the 1985 ASEAN Nature Agreement. Moreover, particularly for marine living resources, with the requirement of 'sustained' or 'optimal' exploitation, a standard approach has emerged which is very closely related to that of 'sustainable use'.[49] Thus, there is even much in favour of arguing that the duty to make 'sustainable use' of natural resources has gained the status of a universal customary rule.

[46] In this sense Sands, above n 31, 253.

[47] *Cf* Chapter 5.2.

[48] According to Art 2 CBD, 'sustainable use' means 'the use of components of biological diversity in a way and at a rate that does not lead to the long-term decline of biological diversity, thereby maintaining its potential to meet the needs and aspirations of present and future generations'.

[49] See for a more detailed discussion Sands, above n 31, 257 *et seq*.

10.5 Sustainable Development—An Approach for Bridging the North–South Divide

The 1992 Rio Declaration, in its Principles 5 and 6, assigns to the concept of sustainable development an important role in the process of bridging the continuing North–South divide in international environmental and developmental relations between industrialised states and developing countries. Indeed, sustainable development is a concept that directs states to preserve and protect the earth's ecosystem without compromising the interests and needs of the developing world's poor peoples. It provides for a very close interdependence between the competing policy goals of development and environmental protection. Thus, it pursues an integrative approach according to which economic and social development is an integral part of environmental protection, and vice versa.

Understood as a concept pursuing a combined anthropocentric and ecocentric approach, sustainable development cannot be suspected of being 'a force of ideological imperialism' featuring 'the idea of nature as separate from man'.[50] It rather gives meaningful direction to the process of bridging the North–South divide by reminding all actors in international environmental and developmental relations, coming both from the industrialised and developing world, to administer and conserve the earth's ecosystem as an indispensable natural resource basis for the good of present and future humans. It hinders actions that give intragenerational needs undue predominance over intergenerational ones, as well as actions that are designed to meet human needs at the expense of nonhuman natural goods.

In both its intra- and intergenerational dimension, sustainable development reflects the idea of distributive justice. It transposes this idea into a concept that gives important impetus to all actors involved in the endeavour to converge the conflicting interests and needs of the North and the South, although it is not able to deploy immediate steering effects on states' behaviour. It is not a principle of customary international law, but an important catalyst in the process of the further development of international law.[51]

Further Reading

TB Adams, 'Is There a Legal Future for Sustainable Development in Global Warming? Justice, Economics, and Protecting the Environment' (2003–2004) 16 *Georgetown International Environmental Law Review* 77–126.

U Beyerlin, 'Sustainable Development' in R Wolfrum (ed), *Max Planck Encyclopedia of Public International Law* (Heidelberg/Oxford 2009), available at www.mpepil.com.

——, 'The Concept of Sustainable Development' in R Wolfrum (ed), *Enforcing Environmental Standards: Economic Mechanisms as Viable Means?* (Berlin 1996) 95–121.

K Bosselmann, 'A Legal Framework for Sustainable Development' in K Bosselmann and D Grinlinton (eds), *Environmental Law for a Sustainable Society* (Auckland 2002) 145–161.

[50] A Geisinger, 'Sustainable Development and the Domination of Nature: Spreading the Seed of the Western Ideology of Nature' (1999) 27 *Boston College Environmental Affairs Law Review* 45.

[51] *Cf* Beyerlin, above n 37, paras 21 *et seq*.

K Bosselmann, 'The Concept of Sustainable Development' in K Bosselmann and D Grinlinton (eds), *Environmental Law for a Sustainable Society* (Auckland 2002) 81–96.

——, *The Principle of Sustainability. Transforming Law and Governance* (Auckland 2008).

E Brown Weiss, *In Fairness to Future Generations: International Law, Common Patrimony and Intergenerational Equity* (New York 1989).

AE Boyle (ed), *International Law and Sustainable Development. Past Achievements and Future Challenges* (Oxford 1999).

MC Cordonier Segger, 'Sustainable Development in International Law' in HC Brugge and C Voigt (eds), *Sustainable Development in International and National Law. What Did the Brundtland Report Do to Legal Thinking and Legal Development, and Where Can We Go from Here?* (Groningen 2008) 85–189.

MC Cordonier Segger and A Khalfan, *Sustainable Development Law. Principles, Practices, & Prospects* (Oxford 2004).

MC Cordonier and CG Weeramantry (eds), *Sustainable Justice. Reconciling Economic, Social and Environmental Law* (Leiden/Boston 2005).

D French, *International Law and Policy of Sustainable Development* (Manchester 2005).

KF Gärditz, 'Nachhaltigkeit und Völkerrecht' in W Kahl (ed), *Nachhaltigkeit als Verbundbegriff* (Tübingen 2008) 137–179.

A Gillespie, *The Illusion of Progress. Unsustainable Development in International Law and Policy* (London 2001).

E Hey, 'Sustainable Development, Normative Development and the Legitimacy of Decision-Making' (2003) 34 *NYIL* 3–54.

V Lowe, 'Sustainable Development and Unsustainable Arguments' in A Boyle and D Freestone (eds), *International Law and Sustainable Development: Past Achievements and Future Challenges* (Oxford 1999) 19–37.

DB Magraw and LD Hawke, 'Sustainable Development' in D Bodansky *et al* (eds), *The Oxford Handbook of International Environmental Law* (Oxford 2007) 613–638.

G Mayeda, 'Where Should Johannesburg Take Us? Ethical and Legal Approaches to Sustainable Development in the Context of International Environmental Law' (2004) 15 *Colorado Journal of International Environmental Law and Policy* 29–69.

PJ Sands, 'International Courts and the Application of the Concept of "Sustainable Development"' in J Hatchard and A Perry-Kessaris (eds), *Law and Development Facing Complexity in the 21st Century. Essays in Honour of Peter Slinn* (London 2003) 147–157.

N Schrijver, *The Evolution of Sustainable Development in International Law. Inception, Meaning and Status* (Leiden 2009).

P Schwarz, 'Sustainable Development in International Law' (2005) 5 *Non-State Actors and International Law* 127–152.

D Tladi, 'Strong Sustainability, Weak Sustainability, Inter-generational Equity and International Law: Using the Earth Charter to Redirect the Environmental Ethics Debate' (2003) 28 *South African Yearbook of International Law* 200–210.

J Verschuuren, *Principles of Environmental Law: The Ideal of Sustainable Development and the Role of Principles of International, European, and National Environmental Law* (Baden-Baden 2003).

TW Wälde, 'Natural Resources and Sustainable Development: From "Good Intentions" to "Good Consequences"' in N Schrijver and F Weiss (eds), *International law and Sustainable Development. Principles and Practice* (Leiden/Boston 2004) 119–150.

Part III

Key Issues in Current International Environmental Law

11

Freshwater Resources

11.1 Survey

Secure and safe water supply is essential for human, animal and plant life or health. Water scarcity combined with poor demand-and-supply management inevitably results in serious shortages of water supply and sanitation. Today, about 884 million people still have no access to safe drinking water and 2.6 billion lack access to adequate sanitation services.[1] Some 2 million deaths are caused by water-related diseases every year. By 2025, at least 3–5 billion people are expected to face water scarcity. Water losses in irrigated agriculture amount to 25–40 per cent of the water used. These figures alone demonstrate that freshwater scarcity is one of the greatest challenges the world is facing today.[2]

The relationship between the use of international freshwaters and their protection from the impact of that use has become one of the most pressing issues in international policy-making. To name some of the causes of the current crisis, firstly, environmental degradation and overexploitation reduce the available amount of freshwater; secondly, increasing agricultural and industrial demand, and pressure from population growth contribute to water scarcity; thirdly, the infrastructure for water delivery is deficient in many states.[3] Conflicting interests on the use of freshwater resources are not new. However, today, water scarcity has reached an unprecedented level, and some even fear that wars will be fought over water.

The management of freshwater resources, in particular in a transboundary context, continues to be a truly complex issue involving multiple challenges, including those resulting from climate change and desertification. One-third of the more than 250 river basins of the world is shared by more than two countries and some even involve five or more states.[4] Treaties and institutions established by those states—most commonly river basin

[1] WHO and UNICEF Joint Monitoring Programme for Water Supply and Sanitation, *Progress on Sanitation and Drinking-Water: 2010 Update* (New York/Geneva 2010) 6 *et seq*.

[2] See U Beyerlin, 'Sustainable Use of Natural Resources—A Key to Combating Poverty' (2003) 63 *ZaöRV* 417, 428; *id*, 'Nachhaltige Nutzung natürlicher Ressourcen und Menschenrechtsschutz' in K Dicke *et al* (eds), *Weltinnenrecht. Liber amicorum Jost Delbrück* (Berlin 2005) 47.

[3] HM Gregersen, PF Ffolliott and KN Brooks, *Integrated Watershed Management: Connecting People to their Land and Water* (Wallingford/Cambridge 2007), 6; K Bourquain, *Freshwater Access from a Human Rights Perspective: A Challenge to International Water and Human Rights Law* (Leiden *et al* 2008) 3–5.

[4] MA Giordano and AT Wolf, 'Sharing Waters: Post-Rio International Water Management' (2003) 27 *Natural Resources Forum* 163, 164.

commissions—contribute to reducing the potential for conflicts. Attention has recently moved from surface water to groundwater since in many areas this is an important source of drinking water. The 1997 UN Convention on the Law of the Non-Navigational Uses of International Watercourses (UN Watercourses Convention) addresses groundwater only in so far as it is related to surface waters; the remainder is unregulated. In light of the fact that groundwater constitutes 97 per cent of all freshwater reserves of the earth, and that these resources are threatened by pollution, in particular salinisation, it is urgent that groundwater aquifers be covered by more comprehensive international regulation. Just a few regional agreements partly address groundwater, namely Article III of Annex II to the Treaty of Peace between the State of Israel and the Hashemite Kingdom of Jordan (1994 Israel–Jordan Peace Treaty) and the 1973 Mexico–US Agreement on the Permanent and Definitive Solution to the Salinity of the Colorado River Basin.[5] Only the 1977 Arrangement on the Protection, Utilization, and Recharge of the Franco-Swiss Genevese Aquifer is specifically dedicated to the allocation and protection of groundwater.[6] In 2008, the International Law Commission (ILC) adopted its Draft Articles on the Law of Transboundary Aquifers.[7]

Most of the agreements discussed below share a number of common elements, including the rules applicable to the allocation of water resources, the (lack of) rules on water quality and water efficiency, and the trend towards integrated water resources management or integrated river basin management.

In light of the particular dynamics of the upper–lower riparian relationship and the role which hegemonic co-riparians may play, the allocation of transboundary water resources among states was one of the first problems addressed by international agreements. While in principle, the upper riparian enjoys physical control of a river basin, this does not necessarily mean effective control. States have, until today, presented various arguments with regard to their rights as co-riparians;[8] these include doctrines such as absolute territorial sovereignty (typically inferred by upstream states), absolute territorial integrity (a claim made by downstream states), limited territorial sovereignty (including the obligation not to cause significant harm) and equitable use (sometimes also referred to as 'community of interests').

Today, states will hardly ever successfully claim absolute positions as to the use of transboundary freshwater resources. The concept of equitable utilisation of water resources and the obligation not to cause significant harm, now included in the 1997 UN Watercourses Convention, are, however, only loosely related to each other. Regional agreements concretise the concept of equitable utilisation. As has been argued,

[5] *Cf* IJ Silverbrand, 'The History and Potential Future of the Israeli-Palestinian Water Conflict' (2008) 44 *Stanford Journal of International Law* 221; A Hardberger, 'What Lies Beneath: Determining the Necessity of International Groundwater Policy Along the United States–Mexico Border and a Roadmap to an Agreement' (2004) 35 *Texas Tech Law Review* 1211, 1238 and 1254 *et seq.*

[6] For a background analysis see G Loibl, 'Groundwater Resources—A Need for International Legal Regulation?' (2000) 5 *Austrian Review of International and European Law* 81.

[7] For an analysis see K Mechlem, 'Moving Ahead in Protecting Freshwater Resources: The International Law Commission's Draft Articles on Transboundary Aquifers' (2009) 22 *Leiden Journal of International Law* 801.

[8] E Louka, *International Environmental Law. Fairness, Effectiveness, and World Order* (Cambridge 2006) 173.

> [r]egional water agreements are appraised as fair not because they are above the rules of the game . . . but because they have followed the rules of the game to extract the optimal outcomes for coriparians, based on these rules. Water agreements are based on a notion of fairness that is guided by the foresight that the circumstances of states may change.[9]

Procedural equity and institutional arrangements thus form part and parcel of modern treaty-based approaches to the management of transboundary water resources.

Institution-building normally facilitates the fulfilment of procedural co-operational duties among the parties to an agreement. These include, in particular, mutual information on the planned water use, and in cases of controversial plans, mutual consultation with the intention of agreeing upon a solution which meets the utilisation interests of one state as well as the environmental interests of the other. To this end, community institutions have increasingly been established, assuming the task of 'common management'. Early examples of such institutional co-operation include the International (US–Canadian) Joint Commission of 1909[10] and the International Commission for the Protection of the Rhine against Pollution, operational since 1950.[11] However, commissions have not normally been equipped with legislative powers in relation to the protection of water resources.

Many agreements dealing with freshwater resources have long concentrated on water allocation, not including detailed environmental provisions. More recently, agreements, in particular those concluded between developed states, have focused on environmental problems, among others, the 1972 US–Canada Great Lakes Water Quality Agreement (revised in 1978), the 1994 Convention on Co-operation for the Protection and Sustainable Use of the River Danube (Danube Convention), and the 1999 Convention on the Protection of the Rhine. As far as developing countries are concerned, only the 1995 Protocol on Shared Watercourse Systems in the Southern African Development Community (SADC) Region, the 1995 Agreement on the Cooperation for the Sustainable Development of the Mekong River Basin, and the 2002 Tripartite Interim Agreement between the Republic of Mozambique and the Republic of South Africa and the Kingdom of Swaziland for Co-operation on the Protection and Sustainable Utilisation of the Water Resources of the Incomati and Maputo Watercourses address water quality and environmental concerns. The insight that efficient water allocation necessitates appropriate development of public utilities and often costly water production (including extraction, purification and distribution) has not yet found its way into bilateral or multilateral agreements on freshwater resources. Recognition of water as a scarce, public and economic resource has given rise to discussions about the human rights dimension of freshwater access.[12] This may contribute to the development of agreements on water quality and water efficiency.

Integrated water resources management in general, and integrated river basin manage-

[9] *Ibid*, 179.

[10] *Cf* SJ Toope and J Brunnée, 'Freshwater Regimes: The Mandate of the International Joint Commission' (1998) 15 *Arizona Journal of International and Comparative Law* 273.

[11] See, among others, A Nollkaemper, 'The River Rhine. From Equal Apportionment to Ecosystem Protection' (1996) 5 *RECIEL* 152, 154.

[12] See, among others, S Tully, 'The Contribution of Human Rights to Freshwater Resource Management' (2003) 14 *Yearbook of International Environmental Law* 101.

ment in particular, is a recent approach to improve freshwater management by conceiving the river basin as a hydrological unit in need of consistent and coherent management. This necessitates taking into account the physical, ecological and chemical characteristics of the water resources; the interests of all the different users; the environmental aspects of water use; decision-making processes including all stakeholders; and interdepartmental and interagency co-ordination in the management of resources.[13] Based upon national experiences to this end, the concept of an integrated water resources programme has been primarily introduced and pursued by UN agencies and international programmes for development co-operation. Emerging from the 'catchment management approach' referred to in Chapter 18 of Agenda 21,[14] the WSSD Implementation Plan includes an explicit reference to integrated water resources management and water efficiency plans.[15]

Historically, the use of transboundary water resources has become one of the most intensely regulated topics of international environmental law. Case law has contributed to these developments, particularly the judgement of the Permanent Court of International Justice (PCIJ) in the case concerning jurisdiction of the International Commission of the River Oder (the *River Oder* case) of 1929,[16] the international arbitral award in the French–Spanish dispute over Lac Lanoux in 1957,[17] the 1997 ruling of the International Court of Justice (ICJ) in the case concerning the *Gabčíkovo-Nagymaros Project*,[18] and finally, in 2010, the judgement of the ICJ in the case concerning *Pulp Mills on the River Uruguay*.[19]

As far as law-making is concerned, the adoption of the Helsinki Rules on the Uses of the Waters of International Rivers by the International Law Association (ILA) in 1966[20] led to the adoption of the ILC Draft Rules on the Non-Navigational Uses of International Watercourses in 1994[21] and the already mentioned UN Watercourses Convention in 1997. In 2004, the ILA adopted the Berlin Rules on Water Resources,[22] superseding the Helsinki

[13] See Principle 1 of the Dublin Statement on Water and Sustainable Development (31 January 1992), available at www.un-documents.net/h2o-dub.htm.

[14] Agenda 21 Chapters 18.1–18.6, 18.12, 18.23, 18.24, 18.26, 18.27, 18.35, 18.37–18.40, 18.76 and 18.85, among others.

[15] WSSD, Plan of Implementation, www.un.org/jsummit/html/documents/summit_docs/2309_planfinal.htm, para 25.

[16] Case relating to the *Territorial Jurisdiction of the International Commission of the River Oder (United Kingdom v Poland)* PCIJ Report Series A No 23; case relating to the *Territorial Jurisdiction of the International Commission of the River Oder (United Kingdom v Poland)* PCIJ Report Series C No 17/2.

[17] *Lac Lanoux* case *(Spain v France)* (1957) 12 RIAA 281 *et seq*.

[18] *Hungary v Slovakia* (1997) ICJ Reports 7.

[19] *Argentina v Uruguay*, Judgement of 20 April 2010, available at www.icj-cij.org/docket/index.php?p1=3&p2=3&k=88&case=135&code=au&p3=4.

[20] The Helsinki Rules on the Uses of the Waters of International Rivers Adopted by the International Law Association at the fifty-second conference, held at Helsinki in August 1966. Report of the Committee on the Uses of the Waters of International Rivers (London 1967), available at www.unece.org/env/water/meetings/legal_board/2010/annexes_groundwater_paper/Annex_II_Helsinki_Rules_ILA.pdf.

[21] Draft Articles on the Law of the Non-Navigational Uses of International Watercourses and Commentaries Thereto and Resolution on Transboundary Confined Groundwater (1994); for the report and commentaries see Yearbook of the International Law Commission, 1994, vol II (Part Two).

[22] The text of the Berlin Rules on Water Resources is available at http://internationalwaterlaw.org/documents/intldocs/ILA_Berlin_Rules-2004.pdf.

Rules, and, in 2008, the ILC adopted its Draft Articles on the Law of Transboundary Aquifers.[23]

From an ecological perspective, it is important that transboundary agreements are not limited to surface water alone. The 'drainage basin' must be placed under a uniform treaty regime, covering 'a geographical area extending over two or more states determined by the watershed limits of the system of waters, including surface and underground waters, flowing into a common terminus'.[24] Even though this 'drainage basin' approach is the basis of numerous international freshwater agreements, it still meets with resistance, in particular from upstream riparians because of the inclusion of too many land areas bordering a watercourse. The ILC thus did not follow the 'drainage basin' approach in its 1994 Draft Articles but relied on the concept of an 'international watercourse'. This is defined as 'a system of surface waters and groundwaters constituting by virtue of their physical relationship a unitary whole and normally flowing into a common terminus' (Article 2 of the 1994 Draft Rules and Article 2 of the UN Watercourses Convention). It is obvious that this narrows down the geographical scope of pertinent agreements. The 2008 Draft Articles on the Law of Transboundary Aquifers do not include the notion of river basin but instead apply to transboundary aquifers and to transboundary aquifer systems consisting of a series of two or more hydraulically connected aquifers. According to the Draft Articles, aquifer means 'a permeable water-bearing geological formation underlain by a less permeable layer and the water contained in the saturated zone of the formation'. An aquifer system is defined as 'a series of two or more aquifers that are hydraulically connected'.[25] The 2004 ILA Berlin Rules, however, refer to the concept of an 'international drainage basin' which is defined as 'a drainage basin extending over two or more States' (Article 2), though unfortunately no further specification is given.

Although there still seems to be reluctance over adopting the concept of 'drainage basin', the idea of 'shared resources' appears to have developed into a standard pattern. The 1978 UNEP Draft Principles of Conduct[26] called for the 'harmonious utilization of natural resources shared by two or more states'. Even if the UN Watercourses Convention does not define international watercourses as 'shared resources', it follows from Article 5 of the Convention that riparian states are not only entitled to use international watercourses 'in an equitable and reasonable manner', but are also obligated to take part in the use, development and protection of the waters in the same manner, and to co-operate appropriately. The ILC's mandate, eventually leading to the 2008 Draft Articles, has been running under the heading of 'shared natural resources'. In addition, the 2004 ILA Berlin Rules refer to 'internationally shared waters'.

While there is agreement in principle that the customary international law obligation to prevent transboundary environmental harm extends to international water law, there is uncertainty as to the relationship between 'no harm' and the concept of 'equitable utiliza-

[23] For the report and commentaries see ILC, 'Report of the International Law Commission on the work of its 60th Session' (5 May–6 June and 7 July–8 August 2008) UN Doc A/63/10.

[24] Art 2 of the Helsinki Rules.

[25] Art 2(c) of the 2008 ILC Draft.

[26] UNEP, 'Environmental Law Guidelines and Principles on Shared Natural Resources', available at www.unep.org/law/PDF/UNEPEnvironmental-Law-Guidelines-and-Principles.pdf.

tion'. Unfortunately, Article 7 UN Watercourses Convention weakens the obligation to prevent transboundary environmental harm to an obligation 'to prevent the causing of significant harm to other watercourse States', thus only addressing significant harm. The second paragraph further dilutes this obligation:

> Where significant harm nevertheless is caused to another watercourse State, the State whose use causes such harm shall, in the absence of agreement to such use, take all appropriate measures . . . in consultation with the affected State, to eliminate or mitigate such harm and, where appropriate, to discuss the question of compensation.

In the following, after a brief discussion of pertinent case law, the general instruments governing water law will be discussed, including the UN Watercourses Convention, the 1992 UNECE Convention on the Protection and Use of Transboundary Watercourses and International Lakes (UNECE Water Convention), and the 2008 ILC Draft. Subsequently, specific basin instruments will be addressed, covering watercourses from all continents and providing an overview of regulatory approaches. Finally, the interrelationship between general and specific instruments as well as the role of institution-building will be assessed.

11.2 Case Law

One of the first important cases on international rivers was the PCIJ's ruling concerning the *River Oder* case.[27] The Versailles Treaty placed the Oder River under the administration of an international commission. Disagreement arose between Poland and the other six governments concerned with regard to the territorial scope of the international regime of the river. In its judgment of 10 September 1929, the PCIJ held that the Commission enjoyed jurisdiction also with regard to two tributaries situated in Polish territory. The Court referred to 'principles governing international fluvial law in general' and found that while access to the sea had been an essential consideration to develop the principle of freedom of navigation on international rivers, it was not decisive alone. Rather, the Court went beyond the 'idea of a right of passage in favour of upstream States' and introduced the notion of 'a community of interest of riparian States'.[28]

Another significant case is the *Meuse (Diversion of Water)* case between the Netherlands and Belgium, decided by the PCIJ on 28 June 1937.[29] The Meuse is an international river rising in northeastern France and flowing through Belgium and the Netherlands to the North Sea. The conflict arose out of the construction of new canals diverting water from the Meuse. In contrast to the *River Oder* case, the PCIJ did not take into account 'the general rules of international law' but based its judgement on an interpretation of the Meuse Treaty only. In addition, the Court strongly applied the principle of reciprocity in international law, arguing that, in the absence of a treaty provision to the contrary, both

[27] *River Oder* case, above n 16.

[28] *Ibid*, 27.

[29] *The Diversion of Water from the Meuse (Netherlands v Belgium)* (1937) PCIJ Report Series A/B No 70.

states should be treated equally. It is also noteworthy that the Court concluded that each of the two states was free in its own territory to enlarge canals as long as the water division, the volume of water and the flow of water were not thereby affected.

A third case referred to in this section is the *Lac Lanoux* arbitral award, delivered on 16 November 1957.[30] Lac Lanoux is one of the largest Pyrenean lakes situated in French territory. The dispute arose over a French proposal to carry out works in order to utilise the waters of the lake; Spain objected, fearing that these works would adversely affect Spanish rights and interests, and arguing that such works could not be undertaken without the previous agreement of both parties. The Tribunal, finding that its competence also included the examination of general international law, held that the French scheme did not constitute an infringement of the rights of Spain recognised by bilateral treaty law; however, it reaffirmed the rule not to cause substantial damage to the environment of other states. The Tribunal even specified that the doctrine must be understood as meaning that any damage to the environment of another state must be serious. With regard to principles for the use of shared water resources, the Tribunal found that international law does not require prior agreement but stated that riparian states have an obligation to notify and consult with others who may be potentially affected prior to engaging in activities which may harm a shared river resource.[31]

The dispute between Hungary and Czechoslovakia, now Slovakia, over the massive common project Gabčíkovo-Nagymaros on the Danube, which was eventually settled by the judgement of the ICJ on 25 September 1997,[32] must also be briefly addressed. The case arose out of a bilateral treaty, agreed upon in 1977,[33] which related to the construction and operation of two series of locks on the Danube River on both Czechoslovak and Hungarian territory. The project was aimed at producing hydroelectricity, improving navigation on the Danube and protecting the areas along the banks against flooding. It included the creation of a reservoir, the construction of a dam, a bypass canal, a barrage and two hydroelectric power plants. Work had begun when the Hungarian government, responding to internal pressures, on 13 May 1989 decided to suspend construction at Nagymaros pending completion of a number of scientific studies. Czechoslovakia responded by seeking an interim solution which involved, among others, a unilateral diversion of the Danube on its territory. In 1992, Hungary terminated the Treaty and Czechoslovakia began to dam the river. The case finally ended up with the ICJ. In its ruling, the Court considered a broad variety of legal issues and included some reflections on international environmental law. In particular, the Court endorsed the concept of sustainable development with a view to 'reconcil[ing] economic development with protection of the environment' and requiring the parties to a treaty and to a dispute to 'look afresh' at the effects of an agreed project on the environment. While refraining from clarifying the legal nature of sustainable development, the ICJ relied upon it as a basis

[30] *Lac Lanoux* case, above n 17.

[31] For further details see A Epiney, 'Lac Lanoux Arbitration' in R Wolfrum (ed), *Max Planck Encyclopedia of Public International Law* (Heidelberg/Oxford 2006), available at www.mpepil.com.

[32] *Gabčíkovo-Nagymaros Project*, above n 18.

[33] The Treaty concerning the Construction and Operation of the Gabčíkovo-Nagymaros System of Locks was signed on 16 September 1977 and entered into force on 30 June 1978.

for specifying the future conduct of Hungary and Slovakia with respect to the Danube.[34] The ICJ avoided any determination of the status and legal implications of other relevant concepts of international environmental law, including the precautionary principle, the concept of environmental impact assessment or the duty of consultation.[35]

Most recently, the ICJ decided a case between Argentina and Uruguay concerning pulp mills on the River Uruguay.[36] The case arose out of Argentina's claim that Uruguay had violated the Statute of the River Uruguay[37] by authorising, constructing and commissioning two pulp mills on the river, which would have serious adverse effects on the quality of the waters of the river and on its environment. Most important is the Court's finding that the parties to the dispute must, for the purposes of protecting and preserving the aquatic environment with respect to activities which may be liable to cause transboundary harm, carry out an environmental impact assessment.[38] The Court asserted

> a requirement under general international law to undertake an environmental impact assessment where there is a risk that the proposed industrial activity may have a significant adverse impact in a transboundary context, in particular, on a shared resource.[39]

It is noteworthy that this finding is based on 'general international law' and not on treaty law.[40]

11.3 General Instruments

11.3.1 The UN Convention on the Law of the Non-Navigational Uses of International Watercourses

The UN Watercourses Convention is the outcome of extensive ILC codification efforts. Built upon an ILC Draft of 1994,[41] the Watercourses Convention was adopted by UNGA Resolution 51/229 of 21 May 1997 by 103 votes with 3 against and 27 abstentions. It was open for signature until 20 May 2000 and will enter into force after 35 ratifications; however, at the time of writing only 19 states had submitted their instruments of ratification.[42]

The Convention[43] establishes a regulatory framework for the management of non-

[34] *Cf* JG Lammers, 'The Gabčíkovo-Nagymaros Case Seen in Particular from the Perspective of the Law of International Watercourses and the Protection of the Environment' (1998) 11 *Leiden Journal of International Law* 287.

[35] See A A-Khavari and D Rothwell, 'The ICJ and the Danube Dam Case: A Missed Opportunity for International Environmental Law?' (1998) 22 *Melbourne University Law Review* 507.

[36] *Pulp Mills on the River Uruguay*, above n 19.

[37] The 1975 Statute of the River Uruguay entered into force on 18 September 1976.

[38] See also below Chapter 16.3.

[39] *Pulp Mills on the River Uruguay*, above n 19, para 204.

[40] *Ibid*, paras 215, 216.

[41] *Cf* n 21 above.

[42] For the latest status *cf* http://treaties.un.org/Pages/ViewDetails.aspx?src=UNTSONLINE&tabid=2&mtdsg_no=XXVII-12&chapter=27&lang=en#Participants.

[43] For a comprehensive analysis of the Convention see SC McCaffrey, *The Law of International Watercourses* (2nd edn Oxford *et al* 2007).

navigational uses of international watercourses (as defined in Article 2). It does not affect the rights or obligations of a watercourse state arising from agreements in force (Article 3). It invites states to harmonise such agreements with the basic principles of the Convention.

The Convention includes a number of 'general principles', such as equitable and reasonable utilisation and participation (Article 5), the obligation not to cause significant harm (Article 7), the obligation of riparian states to co-operate on the basis of sovereign equality, territorial integrity, mutual benefit and good faith (Article 8), the regular exchange of data and information (Article 9), and general equality of all relevant uses of an international watercourse (Article 10).[44]

Most importantly, the Convention includes detailed procedural obligations for co-operation among riparian states with a view to the envisaged usage of a common watercourse (Articles 11–19). The basic obligation is laid down in Article 11 which stipulates that '[w]atercourse states shall exchange information and consult each other and, if necessary, negotiate on the possible effects of planned measures on the condition of international watercourses'. Subsequent provisions on notification and consultation ensure that a state which is potentially affected by measures planned by another riparian state receives substantive and timely information about the environmentally harmful consequences of such measures and may subsequently (within a period of six months) submit a written statement to the notifying riparian state (Articles 12–15). If the submission includes an objection to the realisation of the project, both states have to enter into consultations and, if necessary, negotiations with the aim of finding an 'equitable resolution' to the controversy (Article 17(1)); each state must 'pay reasonable regard' to the interests of the other. As a rule the notifying state may not proceed with the project without the approval of the affected state (Article 14), unless, as laid down in Article 19, the project 'is of the utmost urgency in order to protect public health, public safety or other equally important interests'.

Articles 20–28 impose detailed obligations upon riparian states towards the protection and conservation of international watercourses and their ecosystems, individually and 'where appropriate' jointly. These include measures to prevent, reduce and control water pollution which includes 'any detrimental alteration in the composition or quality of the waters . . . which results directly or indirectly from human conduct' (Article 21(1) and (2)). Upon the request of any riparian state, consultations have to be held in order to find 'mutually agreeable measures and methods' to protect waters (Article 21(3)). Article 23 requires riparian states to take all necessary measures for the protection and preservation of the marine environment, taking into account 'generally accepted international rules and standards'. The Convention remains fairly general with regard to the management of an international watercourse, only establishing an obligation of riparian states to enter into appropriate consultations upon a request of another riparian to that end; the establishment of a 'joint management mechanism' is only referred to as an option (Article 24). Article 25 says little about co-operation among riparian states, and Article 26 (2) only calls for

[44] *Cf* M Fitzmaurice, 'General Principles Governing the Cooperation between States in Relation to Non-Navigational Uses of International Watercourses' (2003) 14 *Yearbook of International Environmental Law* 3.

consultations if one of the riparian states has reasonable grounds to fear that certain installations will have a substantial negative impact.

If natural developments or human impact change the character of the watercourse and lead to significant transboundary environmental harm, Article 27 merely requires riparian states to co-operate. In the event of a sudden natural emergency with potentially significant transboundary environmental harm, the state concerned is under an obligation to warn other riparian states and to take measures to reduce damage; if need be concerned states should get involved in emergency planning.

11.3.2 The UNECE Convention on the Protection and Use of Transboundary Watercourses and International Lakes

Negotiated under the auspices of the UNECE and signed on 17 March 1992, the UNECE Water Convention has been ratified by 36 states and the European Union. It entered into force on 6 October 1996.

Even though the UNECE Water Convention also builds upon the work of the ILC and largely mirrors existing customary international law, it differs from the UN Watercourses Convention in a number of respects. Some of its provisions go beyond existing customary law and further develop international water law.[45] They are much more inspired by practical considerations and, to this end, more specific and detailed.

According to Article 2, the parties take all appropriate measures to prevent, reduce and control pollution of waters causing or likely to cause transboundary impact. To this end they agree that the pollution of waters with a potentially significant transboundary environmental harm must be avoided, reduced and controlled, and that the respective measures should 'where possible' be taken at the source. Parties also agree that there must be environmentally sound management of transboundary water resources with the aim of preserving these resources and protecting the environment. None of these measures must result in a transfer of pollution to other parts of the environment. According to Article 2(5) of the Convention, parties have to consider both the 'precautionary principle' and the 'polluter pays principle' as well as to the concept of intergenerational equity.[46] None of the parties is prevented from taking stricter measures, individually or jointly.

According to Article 3, the parties must adopt legal, administrative, economic, financial and technical measures to prevent, control and reduce the transboundary pollution of waters. These measures have to be co-ordinated in order to address particular types of pollution such as the disposal of sewage. To this end, each party will set emissions limits for particular discharges into surface waters on the basis of the 'best available technology'. These limits shall be industry-specific. It is envisaged that parties partially or totally ban the use or production of pertinent substances. In addition, parties set water-

[45] See M Papaconstantinou, 'The ECE Convention on the Protection and the Use of Transboundary Watercourses and International Lakes and the UN Convention on International Watercourses' (1999) 52 *Revue Hellénique de Droit International* 263.

[46] Art 1(5)(c) refers to intergenerational equity as follows: 'Water resources shall be managed so that the needs of the present generation are met without compromising the ability of future generations to meet their own needs.'

quality levels and issue criteria to determine these levels. The Convention provides for the monitoring of transboundary waters (Article 4) and calls for co-operation in researching and developing technology 'for the prevention, control and reduction of transboundary impact' (Article 5).

Article 9 of the Convention envisages the development of new bilateral and multilateral agreements among riparian states. These agreements shall provide for the establishment of joint bodies for the management of transboundary waters. Article 11 specifies the obligation of riparian states to establish and implement joint programmes to monitor and assess the state of international waters, as well as the effectiveness of the measures taken.

The Convention prescribes obligations to provide comprehensive and timely mutual information (Articles 6 and 13). Riparian states are generally required to consult each other in a spirit of good neighbourliness (Article 10). They have to inform each other of every critical situation which might cause significant transboundary environmental harm, and they must establish co-ordinated or joint systems of information, warning and alarm (Article 14). Riparian states are under an obligation of mutual assistance (Article 15) and they have to inform the public about the state of transboundary waters, protective measures taken and their effectiveness (Article 16).

In order to improve water quality, the parties to the Convention adopted a Protocol on Water and Health in 2000.[47] According to Article 4 of this Protocol, the parties shall

> take all appropriate measures to prevent, control and reduce water-related disease within a framework of integrated water-management systems aimed at sustainable use of water resources, ambient water quality which does not endanger human health, and protection of water ecosystems.[48]

To this end, the parties shall

> take all appropriate measures for the purpose of ensuring adequate supplies of wholesome drinking water which is free from any micro-organisms, parasites and substances which . . . constitute a potential danger to human health; adequate sanitation . . .; effective protection of water resources used as sources of drinking water . . .; sufficient safeguards for human health against water-related disease.

In particular, the Protocol requires parties to set targets in areas covering the entire water cycle as well as dates by which they will achieve such targets (Article 6). Furthermore, the Protocol provides for the establishment and maintenance of comprehensive national and local surveillance as well as early warning systems to prevent and respond to water-related disease, along with contingency and outbreak response plans (Article 8). Article 10 of the Protocol includes a set of procedural rights similar to the Aarhus Convention.[49]

[47] For its text see UN Doc EUR/ICP/EHCO 020205/8Fin. The Protocol entered into force on 4 August 2005. Currently, there are 24 parties to the Protocol. For a commentary on the Protocol see B Bosnjakovic, 'Regulation of International Watercourses under the UN/ECE Regional Agreements' (2000) 25 *Water International* 544, 547 *et seq*.

[48] For the human rights dimension of freshwater access see Chapter 26.2.1.

[49] See below Chapter 16.4.2.

11.3.3 The 2008 Draft Articles on the Law of Transboundary Aquifers

The protection and management of groundwater resources—a subject long neglected[50]—has gained prominence through the adoption of draft articles for an international framework convention on transboundary aquifers by the ILC.[51] Based upon its work on the law of international watercourses (1971–94), the ILC, after inclusion of the topic 'Shared Natural Resources of States' in its long-term programme of work in 2002, and on the basis of five reports presented by its Special Rapporteur,[52] adopted the 2008 Draft Articles. It is not yet clear whether these articles will lead to a legally binding convention or a non-binding set of guidelines.

According to Article 2(b) the draft articles apply to transboundary aquifers and to transboundary aquifer systems. The Draft covers the utilisation of transboundary aquifers; other activities that have or are likely to have an impact upon those aquifers; and measures for the protection, preservation and management of transboundary aquifers (Article 1). Based upon existing customary international law on water resources, the Draft includes the principle of equitable and reasonable utilisation (Article 4), the obligation not to cause significant harm (Article 6) and the obligation to co-operate (Article 7). According to the Draft, equitable and reasonable utilisation means utilisation of an aquifer in a manner that is consistent with the equitable and reasonable accrual of benefits from the aquifer; the aim of maximising the long-term benefits to be derived from the use of aquifer waters; the establishment of individual or joint comprehensive utilisation plans, taking into account present and future needs and alternative water sources; and not utilising a recharging aquifer at a level that would prevent the continuance of its effective functioning. The obligation not to cause significant harm (Article 6) includes a duty 'to take all appropriate measures' to prevent such harm to aquifers, thus establishing an obligation of due diligence. In addition to a broadly phrased obligation to co-operate, the Draft includes an obligation to exchange data and information (Article 8). Articles 10–12 deal with issues of protection and preservation, and Articles 13–15 include obligations of monitoring and management as well as a notification requirement with regard to planned activities. The Draft refers to precautionary action in Article 12, stipulating that '[a]quifer States shall take a precautionary approach in view of uncertainty about the nature and extent of a transboundary aquifer or aquifer system and of its vulnerability to pollution'. The ILC's decision to prioritise development of the international law on transboundary groundwater resources is to be welcomed.

[50] *Cf* K Mechlem, 'International Groundwater Law' (2003) 14 *Yearbook of International Environmental Law* 47.

[51] ILC 'Text of the Draft Articles on the Law of Transboundary Aquifers adopted by the Commission on First Reading' in ILC, 'Report of the International Law Commission on the work of its 58th Session' (1 May–9 June and 3 July–11 August 2006) UN Doc A/61/10, 192; for a comprehensive analysis see Mechlem, above n 7.

[52] Reference may be made to the final report of the ILC Special Rapporteur C Yamada, *Fifth Report on Shared Natural Resources: Transboundary Aquifers*, UN Doc A/CN4/591 (21 February 2008).

11.4 Specific Instruments

11.4.1 Africa

The Nile River is the longest river in Africa (6700 km). Its basin includes ten states: Egypt, Sudan, Ethiopia, Eritrea, Burundi, Uganda, Kenya, Tanzania, Rwanda and the Democratic Republic of the Congo. Primary water uses include irrigation, industry, domestic supply, hydroelectricity and navigation.

Utilisation of the River Nile is still governed by treaty law originating from colonial times[53] even though a new agreement was opened for signature in May 2010. The most important agreement in force is the 1959 Agreement for the Full Utilization of the Nile Waters concluded between Egypt and Sudan.[54] The Agreement includes provisions on the distribution of the annual water flow (Article 1) and the construction of hydroelectric power stations (Article 2). Article 4 provides for the establishment of a Permanent Joint Technical Commission. In practice, the Commission, which does not enjoy legislative or judicial competence, has been tasked with studies on the regulation of Nile water, plans for the utilisation of water, hydrological measurements and the elaboration of recommendations. In addition, Egypt and Sudan agreed to take a common position in negotiations with third states.

The 1959 Agreement did not fully replace an earlier exchange of notes on the utilisation of Nile water for irrigation purposes, signed by Egypt and the United Kingdom in 1929.[55] Confirming Egypt's natural and historic rights to Nile water, the exchange of notes supported Egypt's position *vis-à-vis* upstream riparians, making the establishment of irrigation plants and power stations along the Nile and its tributaries, the lakes of Sudan or in countries under British administration dependent on Egypt's consent.

After decolonisation most upstream riparians have questioned the binding nature of the agreements of 1929 and 1959. It was only in 1999 that a major step towards better management of the River Nile among all riparian states was taken with the creation of the Nile Basin Initiative (NBI).[56] The NBI, which lacks a treaty basis, has been granted legal status in Uganda according to its national law. It serves as a political and developmental institution and may provide a starting point for the reconsideration of co-operative Nile Basin governance. The NBI consists of three main bodies: the Nile Council of Ministers of Water Affairs, providing policy guidance and taking decisions; the NBI Technical Advisory Committee, made up of senior civil servants and providing technical advice and

[53] See AM Fahmi, 'The Legal Regime of the River Nile' (1986) 37 *Österreichische Zeitschrift für öffentliches Recht und Völkerrecht* 51 and CM Carroll, 'Past and Future Legal Framework of the Nile River Basin' (1999) 12 *Georgetown International Environmental Law Review* 269.

[54] Agreement (with Annexes) between the United Arab Republic and the Republic of Sudan for the full Utilization of the Nile Waters, signed at Cairo on 8 November 1959; entered into force on 22 November 1959.

[55] Exchange of Notes between His Majesty's Government in the United Kingdom and the Egyptian Government in Regard to the Use of the Waters of the River Nile for Irrigation Purposes.

[56] J Brunnée and SJ Toope, 'The Changing Nile Basin Regime: Does Law Matter?' (2002) 43 *Harvard International Law Journal* 105, 137.

assistance to the Council of Ministers; and the NBI Secretariat, which provides administrative support to the Council of Ministers and the Technical Advisory Committee.

Meanwhile, within the NBI framework, a Cooperative Framework Agreement has been negotiated.[57] Under this Agreement, the NBI will be transformed into an intergovernmental organisation. While the signing of the agreement had first been envisaged for 2007, signature was deferred several times at the request of Egypt. The agreement includes provisions on the equitable and reasonable use of the Nile waters (Article 4), on the prevention of harm to the waters of the Nile (Article 5), on the protection and conservation of the basin and its ecosystem (Article 6) and procedural obligations, including prior informed consent before using the waters (Article 8). Most contentious is Article 14 which, recognising 'the vital importance of water security' to each of the basin states, decrees that these states 'work together to ensure that all states achieve and sustain water security' and that they do not 'significantly affect the water security of any other Nile Basin State'.

Notwithstanding the objections of Egypt and Sudan to this latter clause, which they fear will negatively affect their current status, the agreement has been signed by most of the other riparian states in May 2010.

The Congo River, with a total length of approximately 4700 km, is the second largest river in Africa. There is, however, no all-encompassing treaty regime for the management of the Congo River. Basin countries include the Democratic Republic of the Congo, the Republic of the Congo, Cameroon, the Central African Republic, Rwanda, Burundi, Tanzania, Zambia and Angola. While the focus of treaties concluded during the colonial era was upon navigation and trade rights, current international law governing the Congo River basin deals with water allocation, development and conservation issues.[58] As far as water allocation is concerned, two Congo River basin states (Tanzania and Zambia) are bound by the 2000 SADC Revised Protocol on Shared Watercourse Systems.[59] The Protocol, which entered into force in 2003, supports integrated management of shared basins. It includes provisions for equitable utilisation and the obligation not to cause significant harm. In 1999, Cameroon, the Central African Republic, the Democratic Republic of the Congo and the Republic of the Congo signed the Accord Instituting a Uniform River Regime, creating the International Commission for the Congo-Oubangui-Sangha Basin,[60] which affects the Congo River since the Oubangui is one of its major tributaries. The Commission is charged with advising and managing sustainable development and integrated water resources management of the rivers' waters.

[57] Agreement on the Nile River Basin Cooperative Framework. For an in-depth analysis concerning the negotiation process see Y Arsano, 'Negotiations for a Nile Cooperative Framework Agreement: Process and a Way Forward' (2011) Institute for Security Studies—Working Paper (manuscript on file with the authors) and DZ Mekonnen, 'The Nile Basin Cooperative Framework Agreement Negotiations and the Adoption of a "Water Security" Paradigm: Flight into Obscurity or a Logical Cul-de-sac?' (2010) 21 *EJIL* 421.

[58] G (Rock) Pring and CC Witkus, 'Congo River' in R Wolfrum (ed), *Max Planck Encyclopedia of Public International Law* (Heidelberg/Oxford 2007), available at www.mpepil.com.

[59] Revised Protocol on Shared Watercourses in the Southern African Development Community (SADC).

[60] The Accord was signed on 6 November 1999 and entered into force in 2003. Its French text is available at www.cicos.info/siteweb/fileadmin/documents/Accords/Accord_Instituant_un_Regime_Fluvial_Uniforme_et_creant_la_CICOS.pdf.

The Niger River extends over a distance of 4200 km. The riparian states include Guinea, Mali, Niger, Benin and Nigeria, and, with a view to tributaries, Burkina Faso, Cameroon, Chad and Côte d'Ivoire. The Niger is currently governed by the 1980 Convention Creating the Niger Basin Authority.[61] However, earlier agreements must be taken into account, in particular, the 1963 Act on Navigation and Economic Co-operation[62] and the (supplementary) 1964 Agreement on the Niger River Commission,[63] with the latter being revised in 1973.[64]

On the basis of the 1980 Agreement, the Niger Basin Authority replaced the earlier Niger River Commission. According to Article 1(3) of the Agreement, the Commission 'assumes all the obligations of the River Niger Commission'. The Authority enjoys legal personality (Article 16) and acts through a number of organs (Articles 5–9). Today, the objectives of the Authority include the integrated development of the resources of the Niger River, 'particularly in the fields of energy, water resources, agriculture, animal husbandry, fishing and fisheries, forestry and forestry exploitation, transport, communications and industry' (Article 3). To this end, the Authority seeks to harmonise development policies of its members 'through the implementation of integrated development projects and programmes'. Among others, Article 4 includes 'environmental control and preservation' as part of the Authority's activities. According to Article 4(4), Member States keep the Authority's Secretariat 'informed of all projects and works they might intend to carry out in the Basin' and 'pledge not to undertake any work . . . under their territorial jurisdiction which pollute the waters or modify the biological features of the fauna and the flora'.

While the Niger Basin Authority forms the institutional background for the management of the river basin,[65] obligations of riparian states can still be taken from the 1963 Agreement. Defining utilisation in a broad sense (Article 2), the agreement includes an obligation among participating states to co-operate with regard to the study and the execution of any project 'likely to have an appreciable effect' on certain features of the regime, including 'the sanitary conditions of their waters, and the biological characteristics of their fauna and flora' (Article 4). The 1964 Agreement requires the riparian states to inform the Commission 'at the earliest stage' about all studies and works which they want to perform (Article 12). In addition, they undertake, within their jurisdiction, to abstain from carrying out 'any works likely to pollute the waters, or any modification likely to affect biological characteristics of its fauna and flora, without adequate notice to, and prior consultation with, the Commission' (Article 12).[66]

[61] The Convention (with a Protocol relating to the Development Fund of the Niger Basin) was adopted on 21 November 1980 and is in force since 3 December 1982.

[62] The Act (of Niamey) regarding Navigation and Economic Co-operation between the States of the Niger Basin was adopted on 26 October 1963 and entered into force on 1 February 1966.

[63] The Agreement concerning the Niger River Commission and the Navigation and Transport on the River Niger which was adopted on 25 November 1964 is in force since 12 April 1966.

[64] The Agreement Revising the Agreement concerning the Niger River Commission and the Navigation and Transport on the River Niger of 25 November 1964, adopted on 15 June 1973, entered into force on 15 December 1973.

[65] I Andersen, O Dione, M Jarosewich-Holder, and JC Olivry, *The Niger River Basin: A Vision for Sustainable Management* (Washington, DC 2005).

[66] For a broader analysis of the Niger basin regime *cf* SMA Salman, 'Niger River' in R Wolfrum (ed), *Max Planck Encyclopedia of Public International Law* (Heidelberg/Oxford 2007), available at www.mpepil.com.

The Zambezi River is the largest river in southern Africa. Starting in Zambia, it flows over 2500 km before emptying into the Indian Ocean. As an intensely shared resource, the river is governed by the Agreement on the Action Plan for the Environmentally Sound Management of the Common Zambezi River System between Botswana, Mozambique, Tanzania, Zambia and Zimbabwe of 28 May 1987.[67] This treaty can be considered to be one of the most ambitious efforts to protect river basins in Africa.[68] Apart from addressing utilisation as such, the agreement sets up a comprehensive action plan for the environmentally sound management of the Zambezi River. The Plan is implemented through specific projects (Article 1(4)) some of which are already included in the Action Plan annexed to the Agreement. Parties are under an obligation to take all appropriate measures to meet the policies and objectives agreed upon. To this end, 'focal points' are established by all parties (Article 3) to harmonise nationally all measures related to the Action Plan. An intergovernmental commission is charged with monitoring the Agreement (Article 2 and Annex II), though without being equipped with regulatory powers.

Lake Victoria, with a surface area of 68800 square kilometres, is Africa's largest lake. Basin states include Kenya, Tanzania and Uganda. The lake has been covered by several treaties. These include the Agreement on the Preparation of a Tripartite Environmental Management Programme for Lake Victoria of 1994 and the Protocol for the Sustainable Development of Lake Victoria Basin of 2003. Most interesting from an environmental perspective is the Convention for the Establishment of the Lake Victoria Fisheries Organization of 30 June 1994[69] which aims at co-operation among the parties, harmonisation of national measures for the sustainable utilisation of the living resources of the Lake Victoria, and the development and adoption of conservation and management measures (Article II). To this end, the Organization, among others, promotes 'the proper management and optimum utilization of the fisheries and other resources of the Lake'.

11.4.2 America

In 1909, Canada and the United States concluded the Treaty Relating to Boundary Waters.[70] This Treaty is still the basic document governing Canadian–US water issues, focusing on the Great Lakes. Affirming each party's exclusive jurisdiction and control over the use and diversion of all waters on its own side (Article II), Article IV of the Treaty includes the agreement among the parties that boundary waters and waters flowing across the boundary 'shall not be polluted on either side to the injury of health or property on the other'. In light of its limited effectiveness, the Treaty was supplemented by the 1972 and 1978 Great Lakes Water Quality Agreements and an amendment to the latter of 1987.[71] According to Article II of the 1978 Agreement, its purpose is 'to restore and

[67] For its text see www.fao.org/docrep/w7414b/w7414b0j.htm.

[68] For further details *cf* G (Rock) Pring and K Allison, 'Zambezi River' in R Wolfrum (ed), *Max Planck Encyclopedia of Public International Law* (Heidelberg/Oxford 2008), available at www.mpepil.com.

[69] Available at www.fao.org/docrep/w7414b/w7414b0l.htm.

[70] The Treaty between the United States and Great Britain relating to Boundary Waters between the United States and Canada was signed on 11 January 1909 and entered into force on 5 May 1910.

[71] The 1972 Agreement on Great Lakes Water Quality (with Annexes and Attachments) entered into force

maintain the chemical, physical, and biological integrity of the waters of the Great Lakes Basin Ecosystem'.[72] The waters, among others, should be free from substances adversely affecting aquatic life, free from debris, oil and other immiscible substances in amounts that are deleterious, as well as free from heat and nutrients with a negative impact on aquatic life (Article III). Special objectives are included in Article IV which together with Annex I lists maximum permissible values for certain substances. According to Article V, water quality standards and other regulatory requirements must be consistent with these objectives, and Article VI ensures that the parties develop and implement programmes and other measures to fulfil the purpose of the Agreement. Details are included in Annexes II–IV.

Most importantly, the 1909 Treaty Relating to Boundary Waters had already established the International Joint Commission (IJC).[73] The Commission, composed of an equal number of representatives from the USA and from Canada (Article VII) is competent in cases involving the use or obstruction or diversion of the waters (Article VIII). Decision-making takes place by majority vote. The IJC is empowered to examine and report on all matters arising between the parties involving the rights, obligations or interests of either in relation to the other or to the inhabitants of the other along the border (Article IX). It may adopt binding decisions in cases of dispute (Article X).

The tasks of the IJC were adapted to the Great Lakes Water Quality Agreements (Article VII of the 1978 Agreement), including the collection, analysis and dissemination of various types of data. Semi-annual reporting is formalised; it precedes the adoption of appropriate measures (Article X). Under Article VIII of the 1978 Agreement, the IJC is supported by a Great Lakes Water Quality Board and a Great Lakes Science Advisory Board.

The Treaty Relating to Boundary Waters also affected the management of the Columbia River, which is 2044 km in length and runs from Canada to the United States. Discussions related to the use of the river for hydroelectric purposes were finally submitted to the IJC in 1959. In 1961, the IJC's report led to the conclusion of the Treaty Relating to the Co-operative Development of the Water Resources of the Columbia River Basin. The Treaty, which entered into force in 1964, committed Canada to provide reservoir storage behind three large dams and to operate them for increased power generation and flood control downstream in the US (Article II). In return, the United States agreed to give Canada half of the increased power. Even though the Treaty does not explicitly address issues of fish, irrigation and environmental protection, its implementation through detailed annual operating plans has resulted in increased awareness of fishing and environmental concerns.[74]

on 15 April 1972; the 1978 Agreement on Great Lakes Water Quality (with Annexes) entered into force on 22 November 1978; the Protocol amending the 1978 Agreement between the Government of Canada and the Government of the United States of America on Great Lakes Water Quality, as amended on 16 October 1983, entered into force on 18 November 1987.

[72] For a discussion of the Agreements and their implementation see BC Karkkainen, 'Managing Transboundary Aquatic Ecosystems' (2006) 19 *Pacific McGeorge Global Business & Development Law Journal* 209.

[73] *Cf* Toope and Brunnée, above n 10.

[74] G (Rock) Pring and K Whitehead, 'Columbia River' in R Wolfrum (ed), *Max Planck Encyclopedia of Public International Law* (Heidelberg/Oxford 2007), available at www.mpepil.com.

The Amazon is similar in length to the River Nile (around 6700 km), and is the largest single source of freshwater in the world. In July 1978, after a number of agreements concerning commerce, navigation, exploration and territorial issues, most of the riparian states on the Amazon (Bolivia, Brazil, Columbia, Ecuador, Guyana, Peru, Surinam and Venezuela, with the exception only of French Guiana) concluded the Treaty for Amazonian Cooperation[75] with a view to 'promote the harmonious development of the Amazon region [and] to permit an equitable distribution of the benefits' (Preamble). According to Article I of the Treaty, which entered into force in 1980, the parties co-operate in order to preserve the environment and to conserve and rationally utilise the natural resources of their respective Amazonian territories. To this end, they agree to exchange information and prepare operational agreements and understandings. While Article IV reaffirms the right of each party exclusively to utilise natural resources within their respective territories, Article V stipulates that the parties to the Agreement 'shall make efforts aimed at achieving rational utilization' of water resources. Under Article VII the parties agree upon information exchange with regard to 'the exploitation of the flora and fauna of the Amazon region' in order to maintain 'the ecological balance within the region'. In particular, the parties agree to submit annual reports on the conservation measures adopted, or to be adopted. The Treaty recognises the need to maintain a balance between economic growth and environmental conservation and calls for equitable distribution of the benefits of development.

The Paraná River in South America runs through Brazil, Paraguay and Argentina for some 2570 km. Together with the Paraguay, Uruguay and La Plata Rivers, the Paraná makes up the La Plata Basin, the continent's second largest watershed. In 1968 the Inter-Governmental Coordinating Committee of the River Plate Basin Nations was established by a ministerial decision of the five basin states (the three riparian states, plus Bolivia and Uruguay). This was formalised by the 1969 Treaty of the River Plate Basin.[76] The Treaty establishes an institutional framework for 'harmonious and balanced development' of the resources of the La Plata Basin (Preamble). It includes rules for the reasonable utilisation of water resources and conservation obligations (Article I). Final decision-making rests with the foreign ministers; however, the Committee is charged with implementing the programmes adopted (Article III). In 1971, the ministers adopted the Act of Asunción on the Use of International Rivers.[77] This added substance to the Treaty, by requiring prior bilateral agreements before making use of the waters, by preventing 'appreciable damage' from the use of waters, by exchanging hydrological-meteorological information, and by ensuring conservation of living resources.[78] In 1979, Argentina, Brazil and

[75] For an analysis see GD Landau, 'The Treaty for Amazonian Cooperation: A Bold New Instrument for Development' (1980) 10 *Georgia Journal of International and Comparative Law* 463.

[76] *Cf* G (Rock) Pring and H Shelton, 'Paraná River' in R Wolfrum (ed), *Max Planck Encyclopedia of Public International Law* (Heidelberg/Oxford 2008), available at www.mpepil.com.

[77] Act of Asunción on the Use of International Rivers (3 June 1971), signed by the Ministers for Foreign Affairs of the States of the River Plate Basin at their Fourth Meeting (1–3 June 1971); *cf* to the whole Yearbook of the International Law Commission, 1974, vol II (Part II) 322–324.

[78] For a case study see JR Walsh, 'Major Infrastructure Projects, Biodiversity and the Precautionary Principle: The Case of the Yacyretá Dam and Iberá Marshes' (2004) 13 *RECIEL* 61.

Paraguay entered into an Agreement on Paraná River Projects,[79] focusing on the use of the river for hydroelectric purposes. However, the Agreement also includes obligations to preserve the environment and to avoid contamination of the river.

11.4.3 Asia

The Indus River, with a length of 2900 km, flows through the Indian subcontinent. China, India and Pakistan are riparian states; the river basin also includes parts of Afghanistan. Conflicts related to the Indus River have typically concerned the quantity of water available, not the quality of the river's waters or its environment. The Indus Waters Treaty of 1960,[80] concluded between India and Pakistan, has successfully prevented serious water disputes between the parties with regard to the Indus, and even during times of armed hostilities, the provisions of the Indus Waters Treaty have been observed by the parties. Part of its success may be attributed to the fact that the Treaty singles out water from other contentious issues and does not even aim at integrated water management of the river basin as a whole. Basically, the river basin is divided between the parties and the Treaty ensures control by each state of its own water resources. The Treaty has been perceived as 'a demonstration that realistic arrangements, although not optimal may be more durable than integrated management'.[81]

The River Ganges, with a total length of about 2500 km, runs from the Himalayas to the Bay of Bengal, with Nepal, India and Bangladesh as riparian states. The sharing and utilisation of the river have been matters of controversy, with a major dispute between India and Bangladesh going back to the partition of India in 1947. The main issue surrounded the construction of the Farakka dam, with Bangladesh accepting temporary diversion of the river for a short period in 1975 for testing purposes, but not thereafter. Since India continued with the diversion, Bangladesh sought international support to have its rights recognised against the upper riparian state. Only in 1996 was the Treaty between the Government of the Republic of India and the Government of the People's Republic of Bangladesh on Sharing of the Ganga/Ganges Waters at Farakka (Ganges Treaty) concluded.[82] Articles I–III of the Treaty lay down a formula for sharing the waters of the River Ganges at Farakka. According to Article III of the Treaty, the water released to Bangladesh from Farakka will not be further reduced before the Bangladeshi border, unless for 'reasonable use' and to a limited amount. The Treaty does not include provisions on the conservation of water nor on the protection of the ecosystem or the aquatic life.

In 1996, India and Nepal also entered into an agreement, the Treaty concerning the

[79] The Agreement between Argentina, Brazil and Paraguay Concerning the Hydroelectric Facilities of Corpus and Itaipú (with Annexes) was signed on 19 October 1979.

[80] Text available at http://siteresources.worldbank.org/INTSOUTHASIA/Resources/223497-1105737253588/IndusWatersTreaty1960.pdf; SP Subedi, 'Indus River' in R Wolfrum (ed), *Max Planck Encyclopedia of Public International Law* (Heidelberg/Oxford 2008), available at www.mpepil.com.

[81] Louka, above n 8, 213.

[82] SP Subedi, 'Ganges River' in R Wolfrum (ed), *Max Planck Encyclopedia of Public International Law* (Heidelberg/Oxford 2008), available at www.mpepil.com.

Integrated Development of the Mahakali River between India and Nepal (Mahakali River Treaty).[83] The Mahakali River, with a length of approximately 550 km, forms part of the border between India and Nepal. Replacing an agreement of 1992, the Treaty concerns the integrated development of the Mahakali River, awarding Nepal a right to water from the Sarada dam, and authorising the earlier Tanakpur dam built by India; Nepal receives water and electricity in turn. Article 3 of the Treaty provides for the implementation of a joint multipurpose project on the river, and Article 4 includes an obligation of India to supply Nepal with water for irrigation purposes. It is noteworthy that the Treaty, in its Article 5, stipulates that '[w]ater requirements of Nepal shall be given prime consideration in the utilization of the waters of the Mahakali River'. According to Article 7 of the Treaty, 'each party undertakes not to use or obstruct or divert the waters of the Mahakali River adversely affecting its natural flow and level except by an agreement between the parties provided'. The use of the waters by local communities living alongside the River is, however, exempted from this. The Treaty establishes the Mahakali River Commission (Article 9), which may propose recommendations for the conservation and usage of the river, evaluate projects and contribute to dispute settlement among the parties. Unfortunately, it seems that the implementation of the Treaty has suffered from a number of problems and the arrangements have largely remained defunct.

The longest river in Southeast Asia, at about 4350 km, is the Mekong. Riparian states are China, Myanmar, Laos, Thailand, Vietnam and Cambodia. Due to the contrast in physical conditions before and after the Mekong's descent from the Yunnan highlands, the river is divided into the upper and the lower Mekong. With regard to the lower Mekong, Cambodia, Laos, Thailand and Vietnam, in 1995, concluded the Agreement on the Cooperation for the Sustainable Development of the Mekong River Basin[84] with an associated Protocol establishing the Mekong River Commission. China and Myanmar, in 1996, became so-called dialogue partners to the Commission. Article 9 of the Agreement recognises the freedom of navigation throughout the mainstream of the Mekong without regard to the territorial boundaries, for transport and communication. Co-operation, according to Article 1 of the Agreement, is not limited to navigation and commerce but covers

> all fields of sustainable development, utilizations, management and conservation of the water and related resources of the Mekong River Basin including, but not limited to irrigation, hydropower, navigation, flood control, fisheries, timber floating, recreation and tourism, in a manner to optimize the multiple-use and mutual benefits of all riparians and to minimize the harmful effects that might result from natural occurrences and man-made activities.

Article 3 of the Agreement provides that the parties involved are committed 'to co-operate to protect the environment, natural resources, aquatic life and conditions, and ecological balance of the Mekong River Basin from pollution or other harmful effects resulting from any development plans and uses of water and related resources in the Basin'. According

[83] For a comparative analysis see SMA Salman, 'Hydro-politics in South Asia. A Comparative Analysis of the Mahakali and the Ganges Treaties' (1999) 39 *Natural Resources Journal* 295.

[84] See generally E Morgera, 'Mekong River' in R Wolfrum (ed), *Max Planck Encyclopedia of Public International Law* (Heidelberg/Oxford 2007), available at www.mpepil.com.

to Article 7 of the Agreement, parties undertake to make every effort to avoid, minimise and mitigate harmful effects on the environment, and to cease immediately an alleged cause of harm, upon notification by another party, until such cause is determined in accordance with international law on state responsibility. Utilisation of the waters must be in a reasonable and equitable manner in the respective territories (Article 5). Article 11 establishes the Mekong Basin Commission, consisting of a Council, a Joint Committee and a Secretariat. Decision-making in the Council is by unanimity (Article 20). The same applies to the Joint Committee which is charged primarily with information exchange (Articles 21 and 24). Overall, the Mekong Basin Commission can be considered as a positive example. The Commission has not only successfully managed a shared natural resource but it has also attained some important environmental objectives, such as water conservation and broader ecosystem protection.[85]

11.4.4 Europe

The Danube, with a length of 2860 km, is the second longest river in Europe, ranging from Germany to the Black Sea with ten states (Germany, Austria, Slovakia, Hungary, Croatia, Serbia, Romania, Bulgaria, Moldova and Ukraine) as riparians. Originally, pertinent treaty law focused on navigation.[86] In 1994, however, the Convention on Co-operation for the Protection and Sustainable Use of the Danube River (Danube Convention) was adopted, with now 13 out of 20 basin states being parties to the Convention, plus the European Union.[87]

Article 2 of the Danube Convention lays down the objectives and principles of the Convention, including the goals of a sustainable and equitable water management, encompassing the conservation, improvement and the rational use of surface waters and ground water in the catchment area as far as possible. Among others, the Convention, according to its Article 3, covers the discharge of waste waters, nutrients and hazardous substances; planned activities and measures in the field of water construction works; other planned activities and measures for the purpose of water use, such as water power utilisation, water transfer and withdrawal; the operation of the existing hydrotechnical constructions such as reservoirs and water power plants; and the handling of substances hazardous to water and the precautionary prevention of accidents. As to forms of co-operation, Article 4 envisages consultations and joint activities in the framework of the International Commission for the Protection of the Danube River (ICPDR) and a fairly broad exchange of information. Parties are invited to develop, adopt and implement rel-

[85] AS Rix, 'The Mekong River Basin: A Resource at the Cross-Roads of Sustainable Development' (2003) 21 *Temple Environmental Law & Technology Journal* 103. For a different, more critical view see N Van Duyen, 'The Inadequacy of Environmental Protection Mechanisms in the Mekong River Basin Agreement' (2001) 6 *Asia Pacific Journal of Environmental Law* 349.

[86] See, *eg*, Convention concerning the Regime of Navigation on the Danube (signed 18 August 1948, entered into force 11 May 1949).

[87] Text available at www.icpdr.org; for an overview, however, in the context of a particular environmental problem, see C Hudson, 'The Role of International Environmental Law in the Protection of the Danube River Basin' (2001) 12 *Colorado Journal of International Environmental Law and Policy* 367, 386–389.

evant legal, administrative and technical measures (Article 5) and to adopt specific water resources protection measures (Article 6). According to Article 7, the parties, taking into account the recommendations of the Commission, set emissions limits as well as water quality goals and criteria. They establish periodic inventories about sources of pollution as well as about prevention and abatement measures (Article 8). Article 9 calls for harmonised monitoring and assessment methods in order to ensure comparability of data. Obligations to consult among the parties are included in Article 11. While Article 12 requires parties to exchange data among themselves, Article 14 ensures that information is made available to the public, more specifically, 'to any natural or legal person, with payment of reasonable charges, in response to any reasonable request, without that person having to prove an interest'. Article 17 provides for mutual assistance of parties 'in particular where a critical situation of riverine conditions should arise'.

Article 18 of the Convention establishes the already-mentioned ICPDR . The Commission is tasked with implementing the objectives and provisions of the Convention. Its structure and procedures are detailed in Annex IV to the Convention which is the Statute of the Commission. Decision-making within the Commission is by consensus, unless this cannot be attained; then decisions must be taken by a four-fifths majority vote of the delegations present and voting. Decisions will be binding upon all members, unless they notify, within ten months, the Executive Secretary in writing that they are unable to accept the decision. Recommendations and decisions with financial implications can only be adopted by consensus. Dispute settlement takes place with the help of the Commission, otherwise, but not later than 12 months after notification of the Commission by reference to the International Court of Justice or arbitration (Article 24).

So far, the 1994 Convention and the Commission have contributed to better environmental protection of the Danube river basin. To a large extent, the 1994 Convention includes similar obligations as the UNECE Water Convention. However, its focus on environmental aspects is stronger than that of the UNECE Water Convention.[88] The river's water quality has been continuously improving and the Commission has adopted numerous recommendations to ensure that the best techniques available are applied by the main industrial polluters of the river basin.

In order to protect the Elbe River, which runs, over a distance of 1165 km, from the Czech Republic through Germany to the North Sea, from pollution the Convention on the International Commission for the Protection of the Elbe was agreed upon between Germany, Czechoslovakia and the European Economic Community in October 1990, entering into force in October 1992.[89] The aim of the Commission is to prevent the pollution of the Elbe and its drainage area (Article 1), and to enable use to be made of the river, to achieve as natural an ecosystem as possible with a healthy diversity of species; and to reduce substantially the pollution of the North Sea from the Elbe area. The Commission is charged with the management of a comprehensive and detailed set of tasks. In addition, it is responsible for all other matters assigned to it by contracting parties on

[88] See A Schwabach, 'From Schweizerhalle to Baia Mare: The Continuing Failure of International Law to Protect Europe's Rivers' (2000) 19 *Virginia Environmental Law Journal* 431, 447.

[89] *Cf* [1991] OJ L/321/25; see D Rauschning, 'Elbe River' in R Wolfrum (ed), *Max Planck Encyclopedia of Public International Law* (Heidelberg/Oxford 2008), available at www.mpepil.com.

the basis of an agreement. The Commission consists of delegations of the parties (Article 5). It meets once a year (Article 7). Decision-making is by consensus, with abstentions having no effect as long as all delegations are present (Article 8). The Commission is assisted by a secretariat (Article 10).

The Rhine, with a length of 1320 km, flows through four riparian states (France, Germany, Switzerland and the Netherlands) and its basin affects eight countries. In 1999, the Convention on the Protection of the Rhine was signed; it entered into force on 1 January 2003.[90] Replacing the 1963 Convention on the Creation of an International Commission for the Protection of the Rhine against Pollution (ICPR) and the 1976 Convention on the Protection of the Rhine against Chemical Pollution, the 1999 Convention is now the principal basis for international co-operation for the protection of the Rhine within the ICPR.[91]

The 1999 Convention is broad in scope. According to its Article 2 it is applicable to the Rhine, its catchment area, as well as groundwater and aquatic and terrestrial ecosystems interacting with the Rhine. The objectives laid down in Article 3 of the Convention include the sustainable development of the Rhine ecosystem, the production of drinking water from the Rhine, the improvement of sediment quality, flood protection and prevention, and help towards restoring the North Sea. Article 4 of the Convention includes an impressive list of 'principles' which the parties agree to apply in order to meet the objectives stipulated by Article 3: precautionary action; preventive action; rectification, as a priority at source; polluter pays; not increasing damage; compensation in the event of major technical measures; sustainable development; the application and development of the state of the art and best environmental practice; and not transferring environmental pollution from one environment to another. The parties agree to take a broad variety of measures, including co-operation and information sharing, international measuring programmes, analyses at various levels, national measures in conformity with the objectives of the Convention, and many others (Article 5). Article 6 of the Convention refers to the already existing Commission for the Protection of the Rhine which enjoys legal personality, with details of its tasks laid down in Article 8. The Commission consists of delegations of the parties (Article 7). Its decisions are taken unanimously (Article 10(1)) and '[a]bstention of only one delegation shall not constitute an impediment to unanimity' (Article 10(4)). Parties must report on the implementation of the decisions of the Commission (Article 11).

Whereas the Convention on the Protection of the Rhine against Chemical Pollution has been replaced by the 1999 Convention, the 1976 Convention on the Protection of the Rhine against Pollution by Chlorides (Chlorides Convention), which entered into force in 1985, and its Additional Protocol remain in force.[92] The Chlorides Convention,

[90] Text reprinted in [2000] EC OJ L/289/31.

[91] For an overview of the environmental protection of the River Rhine *cf* A Nollkaemper, 'The Evolution of the Regime for the River Rhine' in SP Subedi (ed), *International Watercourses Law for the 21st Century: The Case of the River Ganges Basin* (Aldershot/Burlington, VT 2005), 151–166.

[92] Convention for the Protection of the Rhine from Pollution by Chlorides modified by Exchanges of letters, text available at www.ecolex.org/server2.php/libcat/docs/TRE/Multilateral/En/TRE000488.txt. Parties to the agreement are France, the Netherlands, Germany, Luxembourg and Switzerland.

which had been negotiated in order to address the dumping of chlorides in the river by French mining companies in Alsace, was signed in 1976 but only entered into force in 1985 after France had managed to overcome internal opposition related to underground storage of chlorides in Alsace. The Convention aims at co-operation in fighting against the pollution of the Rhine by chloride ions (Article 1). Article 2 sets an obligation to reduce the discharge of chloride ions by at least 60 kg/s thereof (annual average). This was to be achieved gradually and in French territory, originally by 1 January 1980. On 11 December 1986, after protests in Alsace, the governments of all parties within the ICPR agreed that France could temporarily store the salt residues on the ground. In a second phase beginning in January 1989 France should have kept another 40 kg/s out of the Rhine. The Additional Protocol of 25 September 1991 set another limit in order to reduce the burden of chloride ions at the German–Dutch border to 200 mg/l. The modalities to this end were finally agreed upon at a plenary meeting of the ICPR in July 1999.

According to Article 3 of the Chlorides Convention, the parties will take the necessary measures to prevent an increase in the amounts of chloride ions discharged into the Rhine basin in their own territory. Increases of chloride ions are only permissible in exceptional situations to the extent that parties will offset such concentration in their respective territories. As laid down in Article 4, the French government may halt the process 'when there is evidence of serious danger to the environment and particularly to the water table'. Article 7 includes a detailed cost-sharing arrangement. Parties are obligated, according to Article 11 of the Convention, to report to the Commission, without delay, should they note a sudden and sizeable increase in chloride ion concentrations in the waters of the Rhine or have knowledge of an accident that may seriously endanger the quality of those waters. Measurement systems have to be installed and operated according to Article 12. Finally, the Convention includes dispute settlement provisions (Article 13).

In practice, the contribution of the ICPR to the improvement of the ecological situation of the Rhine is multifaceted. In 1982, members agreed upon an international warning and alarm plan for the Rhine which has been updated and continues to be operative. In response to a massive fire at a chemical production facility in Switzerland in November 1986, the 'Sandoz accident', a Rhine Action Plan against Chemical Pollution was agreed upon.[93] In addition, measures to protect the North Sea, and in particular the Wadden Sea, were agreed upon.

There are many other European examples of environmental protection of transboundary watercourses, including rivers and lakes, which cannot be discussed here in detail. To mention some of them, the Convention Concerning the Canalization of the Moselle of 1956[94] includes a number of provisions to protect the Moselle against pollution; in 1960 the Treaty on the Protection of Lake Constance against Pollution was concluded by Baden-Württemberg, Bavaria, Austria and Switzerland;[95] the Convention

[93] *Cf* www.iksr.org/fileadmin/user_upload/Dokumente_en/apr_iksr_engl.pdf. The successor of the Rhine Action Plan which ended in the year 2000 is the 'Rhine 2020—Program on the Sustainable Development of the Rhine'. For more information concerning this new programme see www.iksr.org/fileadmin/user_upload/Dokumente_en/rhein2020_e.pdf.

[94] UN Doc TRANS/SC3/R158/Add3, 2.

[95] This Treaty with the German title 'Übereinkommen über den Schutz des Bodensees gegen Verunreinigung' was signed on 27 October 1960 and entered into force on 10 November 1961.

Concerning Protection of the Waters of Lake Geneva Against Pollution was signed at Paris in 1962;[96] and in 1996 Germany, Poland, the Czech Republic and the European Community concluded the Convention on the International Commission for the Protection of the Oder which entered into force in 1999.[97]

11.4.5 Middle East

Water-related conflicts have long been of concern in the Middle East. In particular, the Jordan River Basin has been a major source of conflict.[98] While the river itself is a small international watercourse, it is the most important freshwater source for Israel, Lebanon, Syria, Jordan and the Palestinian territories. All these entities comprise the Basin.

The most important legal instrument to date is the 1994 Israel Jordan Peace Treaty.[99] It includes a detailed annex on allocation and development of basin waters. General principles are laid down in Article 6 of the Treaty. They include a commitment not to harm each other's water resources; to provide mutual assistance during water shortages; to prevent pollution; to develop existing and new water resources together; to share information and undertake joint research and development; and otherwise to co-operate in water-related matters. Annex II to the Treaty spells out the details, in particular, of water allocation. A Joint Water Committee is established for the purpose of implementing the Annex (Article 7 and Annex II). Unfortunately, matters of finance, water quality and drought seem to lack sufficient clarity and have given rise to problems in the implementation of the Peace Treaty, even though it seems likely that most issues will eventually be settled on the basis of bilateral arrangements.[100] Agreements between Jordan and Syria concluded in 1953 and 1987 did not produce the hoped-for results.[101] Rather, their disproportionate allocation and disagreement about the building of dams prevented the further development of co-operation between these two riparian states in respect of the River Jordan.

The Euphrates and Tigris have historically been of overall importance in the Middle East. The pertinent basin includes Turkey, Syria, Iraq, Iran, Saudi Arabia and Jordan, but only Turkey, Syria and Iraq are riparian states. Currently, there are no multilateral agreements for the management of shared resources in the Tigris–Euphrates basin.[102] While in 1946 Iraq and Turkey, in a protocol to their Treaty of Friendship and Good

[96] This Convention came into force on 1 November 1963.

[97] For the Treaty text and the Commission see www.mkoo.pl/index.php.

[98] *Cf* A Wolf and J Ross, 'The Impact of Scarce Water Resources on the Arab-Israeli Conflict' (1992) 32 *Natural Resources Journal* 919; H Elver, 'Palestinian/Israeli Water Conflict and Implementation of International Water Law Principles' (2005) 28 *Hastings International and Comparative Law Review* 421.

[99] Treaty of Peace between the State of Israel and the Hashemite Kingdom of Jordan; *cf* also Silverbrand, above n 5, 233 *et seq.*

[100] G (Rock) Pring and DE Frick, 'Jordan River' in R Wolfrum (ed), *Max Planck Encyclopedia of Public International Law* (Heidelberg/Oxford 2008), available at www.mpepil.com.

[101] Agreement between the Republic of Syria and the Hashemite Kingdom of Jordan concerning the Utilization of the Yarmuk Waters (signed on 4 June 1953, entered into force on 8 July 1953); in 1987, Jordan and Syria renewed their bilateral 1953 treaty on developing the Yarmuk.

[102] See G (Rock) Pring and BS Banaei, 'Tigris and Euphrates Rivers' in R Wolfrum (ed), *Max Planck Encyclopedia of Public International Law* (Heidelberg/Oxford 2008), available at www.mpepil.com.

Neighborly Relations,[103] called for discussion of water development plans in the interests of both parties, their positions have significantly changed since the 1960s. There is increasing potential for conflict in light of dams being built and water demand likely to outstrip water supply in the near future. None of the many attempts to achieve greater co-operation in the 1980s proved to be successful. It has been argued that this is due to a number of factors, including lack of communication, lack of agreement over data, conflicting national priorities, inefficient water management, uncoordinated planning and development, and unwillingness to engage in multilateral negotiations.

11.5 Conclusions

International watercourse law has been one of the most important areas for the development of rules on shared natural resources. For many years, the primary concern of states was about navigation and quantitative aspects of sharing water. Since the adoption of the 1997 UN Watercourses Convention, however, this multilateral effort has served as a model for further agreements taking a broader approach than before, in particular with regard to preserving the environment of international watercourses.

As far as river (basin) management is concerned, and in respect of environmental regulation, Europe with its many recent treaties and river commissions may serve as a model for future-oriented regime-building in other parts of the world. This does not necessarily mean that integrated water management is the only way ahead since there are also examples of successful selective regulation, such as the Indus Waters Treaty. States should, however, be aware of the fact that competition for resources will not necessarily aggravate existing conflicts but may also be an incentive to establish a meaningful regime for the benefit of populations concerned.

Institution-building has been strong in the field of watercourse regulation. Typically, commissions are established with a clear but narrow mandate, excluding legislative powers. Tailor-made institutions seem to pave the way for closer integration, possibly at a supranational level[104]–even if only for practical purposes.

Further Reading

E Benvenisti, 'Asian Traditions and Contemporary International Law on the Management of Natural Resources' (2008) 7 *Chinese Journal of International Law* 273–283.

G Eckstein, 'Water Scarcity, Conflict, and Security in a Climate Change World: Challenges and Opportunities for International Law and Policy' (2009) 27 *Wisconsin International Law Journal* 409–461.

MS Helal, 'Sharing Blue Gold: The 1997 UN Convention on the Law of the Non-Navigational

[103] Protocol on Flow Regulation of the Tigris and Euphrates Rivers and of Their Tributaries; *cf* A Kibaroğlu, *Building a Regime for the Waters of the Euphrates–Tigris River Basin* (London *et al* 2002) 222 *et seq.*

[104] See E Benvenisti, *Sharing Transboundary Resources: International Law and Optimal Resource Use* (Cambridge *et al* 2002) 131 *et seq.*

Uses of International Watercourses Ten Years on' (2007) 18 *Colorado Journal of International Environmental Law and Policy* 337–378.

U Lall, T Heikkila, C Brown and T Siegfried, 'Water in the 21st Century: Defining the Elements of Global Crises and Potential Solutions' (2008) 61 *Journal of International Affairs* 1–17.

J Lautze and M Giordano, 'Transboundary Water Law in Africa: Development, Nature, and Geography' (2005) 45 *Natural Resources Journal* 1053–1087.

SC McCaffrey, 'The International Law Commission Adopts Draft Articles on Transboundary Aquifers' (2009) 103 *AJIL* 272–293.

——, 'International Watercourses' in R Wolfrum (ed), *Max Planck Encyclopedia of Public International Law* (Heidelberg/Oxford 2009), available at www.mpepil.com.

O McIntyre, 'International Water Resources Law: Relative Priority Accorded to Environmental Protection' (2008) 38 *Environmental Policy and Law* 131–140.

AL Parrish, 'Trail Smelter Déjà-Vu: Extraterritoriality, International Environmental Law, and the Search for Solutions to Canadian-US Transboundary Water Pollution Disputes' (2005) 85 *Boston University Law Review* 363–429.

SMA Salman, 'Legal Regime for Use and Protection of International Watercourses in the Southern African Region: Evolution and Context' (2001) 41 *Natural Resources Journal* 981–1022.

A Schulz, 'Creating a Legal Framework for Good Transboundary Water Governance in the Zambezi and Incomati River Basins' (2007) 19 *Georgetown International Environmental Law Review* 117–183.

EJ Thorson, 'Sharing Himalayan Glacial Meltwater: The Role of Territorial Sovereignty' (2009) 19 *Duke Journal of Comparative and International Law* 487–514.

MJ Vick, 'International Water Law and Sovereignty: A Discussion of the ILC Draft Articles on the Law of Transboundary Aquifers' (2008) 21 *Pacific McGeorge Global Business & Development Law Journal* 191–221.

12

Oceans and Marine Resources

12.1 Survey

Until the end of the Middle Ages, states did not take a particular interest in extending their control over the seas; they left the oceans to the merchants. Things changed fundamentally with the start of European expansionism in the late fifteenth century. In 1609, Hugo Grotius, in his famous treatise *Mare liberum*, argued that the sea may not be subjected to national sovereignty because it was a common good of all mankind. This was the actual birth of the freedom of the seas, which later became a generally recognised principle of international law. This principle was upheld in the nineteenth century by Britain, the then paramount sea power, although the 'British Age' witnessed important codification projects which, however, mainly concerned the law of maritime warfare. It was only in the twentieth century, and especially after World War II, that the law of the sea underwent a process of 'terraneisation',[1] which was driven by the increasing importance of fisheries and the desire to exploit the newly discovered natural resources beneath the sea-bed. Accordingly, coastal states started to claim exclusive rights over as much of the maritime areas as possible, including their continental shelves.[2]

In 1958, the Second United Nations Conference on the Law of the Sea, held at Geneva, did not stop the creeping extension of coastal states' rights to the detriment of the global commons and the freedom of the seas. However, with the insertion of Articles 24 and 25 into the 1958 High Seas Convention which require states to prevent oil pollution from ships, pipelines and sea-bed operations, and pollution from radioactive substances, an initial, though cautious, attempt was made to provide for a rudimentary protection of the marine environment of the high seas.[3] Another important outcome of the 1958 Law of the Sea Conference was the Convention on Fisheries Conservation and Management,

[1] See W Graf Vitzthum, 'The Terraneisation of the Ocean' (1977) 15 *Law and State* 124.

[2] See the more thorough observations made by W Graf Vitzthum, 'From the Rhodian Sea to UNCLOS III' in P Ehlers *et al* (eds), *Marine Issues: From a Scientific, Political and Legal Perspective* (The Hague *et al* 2002) 1.

[3] With the clauses 'taking account' of 'existing treaty provisions', both provisions were designed to cover states' obligations flowing from the 1954 London Convention for Prevention of Pollution of the Sea by Oil.

which has been described as the first multilateral treaty designed to codify and develop international fisheries law.[4]

In 1967 the disastrous *Torrey Canyon* tanker accident greatly alarmed the public at large. States reacted by adopting the 1969 Brussels Convention Relating to Intervention on the High Seas in Cases of Oil Pollution Damage, which was rapidly followed by the two companion agreements, namely the 1969 Brussels Convention on Civil Liability for Oil Pollution Damage and the 1971 Brussels Oil Pollution Fund Convention.

Benefiting from the new impetus which the 1972 Stockholm Conference had given to the development of international environmental law,[5] a significant global instrument for the prevention of marine pollution was soon adopted—the 1972 London Dumping Convention. Only one year later, this treaty was followed by another important one, namely the International Maritime Organization (IMO, formerly IMCO) Convention for the Prevention of Pollution by Ships (MARPOL). 1973 also marks the beginning of the elaboration of the Law of the Sea Convention (UNCLOS) by the Third United Nations Conference on the Law of the Sea. After nine years of negotiations, UNCLOS was signed at Montego Bay, Jamaica, on 10 December 1982. Twelve years were still to pass before UNCLOS entered into force on 16 November 1994. The stumbling block for the entry into force of UNCLOS, Part XI relating to deep sea-bed mining, which met with persistent resistance from several industrialised states, was removed in late July 1994 by the UN General Assembly. With Resolution 48/263,[6] the General Assembly adopted the Agreement relating to the Implementation of Part XI of UNCLOS. In accordance with Annex VIII to UNCLOS, the first international court dealing exclusively with matters concerning the law of the seas, the International Tribunal for the Law of the Sea (ITLOS), was established in 1997.

In the aftermath of the Stockholm Conference, the United Nations Environment Programme (UNEP) developed its Regional Seas Programme. Starting with the 1976 Barcelona Convention for the Protection of the Mediterranean Sea against Pollution, which was adopted under the auspices of UNEP, a network of regional MEAs emerged that covers both the protection of the oceans' marine environment and their living resources.

With the adoption of the legally non-binding Agenda 21, the 1992 Rio Conference gave fresh impetus to fostering the protection and sustainable development of the marine and coastal environment and its resources. Noteworthy is Chapter 17 of Agenda 21, which pursues a holistic approach by recognising the need for combating cross-media pollution, subjecting marine and coastal areas to a common regime of action, and pointing to the urgent need for further developing and intensifying interstate co-operation at all levels.[7]

Today, the most important actors other than states in the field of managing and conserving fisheries resources are: (i) international organisations, such as the IMO which addresses all environmental concerns of shipping, and the Food and Agriculture Organization (FAO) which is engaged in the field of fisheries and aquaculture; (ii) the European

[4] See PW Birnie, AE Boyle and C Redgwell, *International Law and the Environment* (3rd edn Oxford 2009) 709.

[5] *Cf* Chapter 2.1.

[6] UNGA Res 48/263 (17 August 1994).

[7] For a more detailed discussion of Agenda 21's impact on the further development of relevant international law see U Beyerlin, 'New Developments in the Protection of the Marine Environment: Potential Effects of the Rio Process' (1995) 55 *ZaöRV* 544, 565 *et seq*.

Union, which due to its exclusive competence for fisheries is entitled to enter into international fisheries agreements with third states or other international organisations;[8] and (iii) treaty-based regional fisheries organisations.[9]

In addition to these actors, reference may be made to various international arbitral tribunals and courts.[10] Their diversified case law has significantly influenced the law concerning the protection of the oceans and the conservation of marine resources. Arbitration has often been successfully used as a means to settle environmental disputes. Best known is the *Bering Sea Fur Seals* arbitration award of 1893,[11] which settled a dispute between the US and the UK concerning the right of states to adopt regulations for the conservation of fur seals in areas beyond national jurisdiction. Another important arbitral decision in the field of marine environmental protection was adopted by an arbitral tribunal established under Annex VII of UNCLOS in the *Southern Bluefin Tuna* dispute.[12] The MOX Plant, a British nuclear reprocessing facility on the shores of the Irish Sea (at Sellafield), has given rise to proceedings in the Permanent Court of Arbitration (PCA) under Annex VII of UNCLOS and under the 1992 OSPAR Convention.[13] As these examples demonstrate, international courts and tribunals have the 'capacity to adopt a more independent stance, oriented towards public interest considerations'.[14] This also applies to the International Court of Justice (ICJ), and the ITLOS. While the ICJ, in the 1972 *Fisheries Jurisdiction* cases, has only been indirectly concerned with the issue of marine resource conservation,[15] the ITLOS handled cases relating to the prompt release of foreign vessels arrested by coastal states on suspicion of illegal, unregulated and unreported fishing.[16] Three of these cases have raised significant issues relating to the conservation and management of marine living resources.[17] Finally, in the *Swordfish Stocks* case, the ITLOS was concerned with an issue similar to that dealt with in the 1893 *Pacific Fur Seal* arbitration.[18]

[8] See for a thorough discussion on the EU's involvement in international fisheries N Wolff, *Fisheries and the Environment* (Baden-Baden 2002).

[9] They deserve closer attention; see below at Section 12.4.2.

[10] For a critical account of the role of international adjudicative bodies in international environmental law in general see T Stephens, *International Courts and Environmental Protection* (Cambridge 2009). *Cf* also below Chapter 25.3.

[11] *Moore's International Arbitration Awards*, vol 1 (1893) 755. For a more detailed discussion see P Sands, *Principles of International Environmental Law* (2nd edn Cambridge 2003) 561 *et seq*.

[12] See *Southern Bluefin Tuna* cases: *(New Zealand v Japan; Australia v Japan)* (Provisional Measures, Order of 27 August 1999) ITLOS Cases Nos 3 and 4, (1999) 38 ILM 1624; (*Australia and New Zealand v Japan)* (Award on Jurisdiction and Admissibility) (2000) 39 ILM 1359. For a detailed discussion see Stephens, above n 10, 220 *et seq*.

[13] See *MOX Plant* cases: *Ireland v United Kingdom* (Provisional Measures, Order) ITLOS Case No 10, (2002) 41 ILM 405; *Ireland v United Kingdom* (Suspension of Proceedings on Jurisdiction and Merits, and Request for Further Provisional Measures, Order No 3) (2003) 42 ILM 1187; *OSPAR* arbitration (*Ireland v United Kingdom*) (Final Award) (2003) 42 ILM 1118. See for more details Stephens, above n 10, 232 *et seq*. As regards the OSPAR Convention see below at Section 12.3.2.

[14] Stephens, above n 10, 36.

[15] See these judgments of the ICJ in *Fisheries Jurisdiction* cases *(United Kingdom v Iceland; Germany v Iceland)* (1974) ICJ Reports 3 and 175.

[16] In late 2009, combating IUU fishing has been made the subject of a FAO agreement; see below at Section 12.4.2.

[17] *Camouco* case (*Panama v France*) (2000) 125 ILR 151, (2000) 39 ILM 666; *Monte Confurco* case (*Seychelles v France*) (2000) 125 ILR 203; *Volga* case (*Russian Federation v Australia*) (2003) 42 ILM 159. For detailed information and critical comment see Stephens, above n 10, 214 *et seq*.

[18] *Conservation and Sustainable Exploitation of Swordfish Stocks in the South-Eastern Pacific Ocean* (*Chile

12.2 The Legal Framework: UNCLOS

Tommy TB Koh of Singapore, the then president of the Third United Nations Conference on the Law of the Sea, praised UNCLOS at the final session of the Conference on 10 December 1982 as 'a comprehensive constitution for the oceans which will stand the test of time'.[19] Although having been signed by 119 states on the very first day on which it was opened for signature, UNCLOS only entered into force on 16 November 1994. Today there are 161 ratifications; however, the US has still to sign.

Even prior to its entry into force, UNCLOS already had an impact on the further development of the law of the sea at both the global and regional level. Meanwhile, Tommy Koh's understanding of UNCLOS as a 'constitution for the oceans' seems adequately to reflect the role of the Convention, at least as far as the protection of the oceans' marine environment and resources is concerned.

The 1958 Geneva Conventions on the Law of the Sea contained only a few rudimentary rules regarding marine environmental protection. By contrast, UNCLOS, particularly in its Part XII, establishes a comprehensive legal framework for the management and protection of the oceans and their living resources. The total of its rules reflects 'a fundamental shift from power to duty'[20] in the sense that it imposes numerous obligations on states which supersede the formerly valid principle that pollution is implicit in the freedom of the seas. UNCLOS provides for a balance of power between coastal states and flag states. While the latter are primarily interested in the best possible use of the traditional freedom of navigation and fishing, the former are primarily concerned with protecting the waters and marine resources under their control. Furthermore, UNCLOS places more weight on preventing and reducing environmental harm by way of regulation and co-operation than on responsibility or liability for environmental damage.[21] However, UNCLOS's preventive approach does not meet the specific requirements of the concept of precautionary action which was unknown at the time it was drafted.[22]

In large parts, UNCLOS is a mere codification of the then existing rules of relevant customary and conventional international law. For instance, Article 193 UNCLOS refers to already accepted international customary rules when it seeks a compromise between two traditionally antagonistic interests of states by providing that '[s]tates have the sovereign right to exploit their natural resources pursuant to their environmental policies and in accordance with their duty to protect and preserve the marine environment'.

Furthermore, Articles 208, 210 and 211 essentially incorporate pre-existing treaty law, *eg* the standards laid down in the 1972 London Dumping Convention and the 1973/1978

v European Community) (Proceedings Suspended) (2001) 40 ILM 475. See again Stephens, above n 10, 228 *et seq*, and Sands, above n 11, 218 *et seq* and 582 *et seq*.

[19] See www.un.org/Depts/los/convention_overview_convention.

[20] AE Boyle, 'Marine Pollution under the Law of the Sea Convention' (1985) 79 *AJIL* 347, 350.

[21] See *eg* Birnie, Boyle and Redgwell, above n 4, 383. Also in this sense already Beyerlin, above n 7, 547 and 553.

[22] See Beyerlin, *ibid*, 554.

MARPOL Convention Annexes, when they require all states parties to prevent marine pollution from sea-bed activities, by dumping and from vessels.

Obviously, UNCLOS also includes a number of provisions which appear to reflect 'law in progress' rather than 'established law'. Among them are, for instance, Article 198 (obligation to notify imminent or actual damage), Article 199 (obligation to develop contingency plans against pollution), Article 204 (obligation to monitor the risks or effects of pollution) and Article 206 (obligation to assess the potential effects of activities).[23]

It should also be mentioned that UNCLOS shows some normative lacunae. One of them relates to straddling and migratory fish stocks which raise specific difficulties as to their utilisation and conservation. As states were not prepared to solve these problems in 1982, they did not touch upon this issue in UNCLOS. This lacuna has meanwhile been filled by the 1995 Fish Stocks Agreement.[24]

UNCLOS largely abstains from issuing substantive environmental rules. One of the few exceptions is Article 119(1)(a) UNCLOS which provides that

> [i]n determining the allowable catch and establishing other conservation measures for the living resources in the high seas, States shall . . . take measures which are designed . . . to maintain or restore populations of harvested species at levels which can produce the maximum sustainable yield.

UNCLOS compensates for its own lack of substantive standards in a twofold way. Firstly, it provides a system of norms which determine who is competent to generate pertinent substantive rules and who is responsible for enforcing these rules. Secondly, Article 197 UNCLOS imposes on all states parties the fundamental duty to

> co-operate on a global and, as appropriate, on a regional basis, directly or through competent international organisations, in formulating and elaborating international rules, standards and recommended practices and procedures consistent with this Convention, for the protection and preservation of the marine environment, taking into account characteristic regional features.

Several other UNCLOS rules covering all kinds of pollution sources, namely Articles 207(1) and (4), 208(3) and (5), 209(1) and (2), 210(4), 211(2), (5) and (6), and 212(1) and (3), explicitly refer to these 'internationally agreed rules, standards and recommended practices and procedures' mentioned in Article 197. Typical of them is Article 211(2) which provides that

> [s]tates shall adopt laws and regulations for the prevention, reduction and control of pollution of the marine environment from vessels flying their flag or of their registry. Such laws and regulations shall at least have the same effect as that of generally accepted international rules and standards established through the competent international organization or general diplomatic conference.

The above-mentioned UNCLOS rules provide a general framework to be filled by substantive norms in other international legal instruments. Some of these norms, *eg* the standards laid down in the Annexes of the 1973/1978 MARPOL Convention, were already

[23] See Birnie, Boyle and Redgwell, above n 4, 388.
[24] See below at Section 12.4.2.

in existence at the time when UNCLOS was signed. Others remained to be developed by international organisations such as the IMO in their future norm-setting processes.

Part XII of UNCLOS starts with a set of 'umbrella norms' (Articles 192–206)[25] establishing some fundamental obligations to protect and preserve the marine environment which must be met by all states parties. These general norms apply in the various fields of marine environmental protection. They are complemented by more specialised rules in UNCLOS's subsequent sections which address different types of marine environment pollution, such as dumping (Articles 210 and 216),[26] from ships (Articles 211 and 217–221),[27] through the atmosphere (Articles 212 and 222),[28] from land-based sources (Articles 207 and 213), and from sea-bed activities (Articles 208, 209, 214 and 215). All of these rules will be discussed below in more detail.

UNCLOS also contains framework rules on marine living resources that must be implemented by more concrete treaty norms at the universal and regional level. In particular, Parts V and VII of UNCLOS deal with states' rights and duties concerning the conservation and management of marine living resources, including marine mammals, in the exclusive economic zones (Articles 56, 61, 62 and 65) and the high seas (Articles 116–120). Just a few UNCLOS provisions address the issue of protecting and managing non-living marine resources.[29]

In a nutshell, UNCLOS's regulatory system of marine environmental protection is a 'package deal' which provides a general framework of states' rights and obligations. This framework must be filled by way of establishing, particularly at the regional level, internationally agreed norms which impose on states clear-cut environmental obligations, including substantive ones. Due to its strong emphasis on preventing marine environmental harm rather than compensating for environmental losses, UNCLOS exerted, and still exerts, a considerable steering effect on all further law-making processes concerning the protection of the oceans' marine environment and living resources. Therefore, it deserves Tommy Koh's label of a 'constitution for the oceans'.

[25] These UNCLOS norms appear under the headings 'General Provisions' (s 1), 'Global and Regional Co-operation' (s 2), 'Technical Assistance' (s 3), and 'Monitoring and Environmental Assessment' (s 4).

[26] UNCLOS contains two provisions which regulate marine pollution from dumping of wastes in rather abstract terms. Firstly, under Art 210(1) and (4) the states parties to UNCLOS are required to adopt laws and regulations to prevent, reduce and control pollution of the marine environment by dumping, and endeavour to establish relevant global and regional rules, standards and recommended practices and procedures. Secondly, Art 216 UNCLOS provides that the enforcement jurisdiction regarding these laws and regulations is shared by the flag state, the coastal state and the port state.

[27] Art 211 UNCLOS deals exclusively with deliberate or accidental pollution from ships. Under this provision states are required to establish international rules and standards to prevent, reduce and control such kind of marine pollution. Arts 217–221 regulate questions of enforcement by flag states, coastal states and port states. Art 217 requires flag states to take measures necessary for the implementation and effective enforcement of international rules and standards, and Art 218 gives port states express power to investigate and prosecute discharge violations wherever they have taken place.

[28] According to Art 212(1) UNCLOS, '[s]tates shall adopt laws and regulations to prevent, reduce and control pollution of the marine environment, from or through the atmosphere, applicable to the air space under their sovereignty and to vessels flying their flag or vessels or aircraft of their registry '.

[29] Art 208 concerns seabed activities in areas subject to the jurisdiction of coastal states. Under Art 145 the International Seabed Authority can adopt rules etc for the seabed and ocean floor and subsoil.

12.3 Protection of the Marine Environment

12.3.1 State of the Marine Environment

Up until the 1980s, the main sources of marine pollution were oil, persistent organic compounds, chemical substances, nuclear wastes, as well as urban and industrial effluents. Whereas sea-based marine pollution has been successfully addressed since 1954, land-based marine pollution has remained a matter of serious concern. This can be illustrated by comparing studies prepared in the 1970s and 1980s by GESAMP[30] with more recent analyses of the state of the marine environment.[31] According to the findings made in UNEP's Global Programme of Action for the Protection of the Marine Environment from Land-Based Sources (UNEP/GPA)[32] the state of the marine environment is as follows:

Progress has been achieved in protecting the marine environment against persistent organic pollutants, radioactive substances and oil. In several regional seas, particularly in the Baltic Sea and in the northeast Atlantic, there has been a considerable reduction in the pollution loads and levels of persistent organic pollutants, *ie* long-lived industrial chemicals, pesticides or by-products of combustion. A certain reduction of disposal levels is also reported for radioactive substances; today most degradation of the marine environment results from natural radioactive sources. Considerable progress has been achieved regarding pollution of the sea by oil. Total oil inputs decreased to 37 per cent of 1985 levels; spills from tanker accidents went down by 75 per cent, from tanker operations by 95 per cent, and from municipal and industrial discharges by close to 90 per cent. Mixed progress is reported for combating marine pollution by heavy metals and the movement of sediments and soils. While lead, cadmium and mercury inputs in the North Sea, the northeast Atlantic and the Mediterranean Sea dropped, in other regional seas, *eg* the Caspian Sea, concerns remain; and rising amounts of electronic waste are reported in the seas of East Asia. The story of the movement of sediments and soils is ambivalent: while some coastlines are shrinking because the soils are being trapped by upstream barrages, other coasts have been cut off from river sediment flows by dam building. Changes for the worse are reported regarding marine pollution by sewage, nutrients and litter, as well as with respect to population growth and destruction of habitats: a rising tide of wastewater threatens the oceans. While the loads of untreated wastewater amount to 50 per cent for the Mediterranean Sea and 60 per cent from total wastewater for the Caspian Sea, the respective figures for Latin America, the Caribbean, East Asia, the South East Pacific

[30] See IMO/FAO/UNESCO/WMO/WHO/IAEA/UN/UNEP Joint Group of Experts (GESAMP), *The State of the Marine Environment: GESAMP Reports and Studies no 39* (Nairobi 1990). GESAMP is a Group of Experts on Scientific Aspects of Marine Environmental Protection which was established in 1969 as an advisory body within the United Nations system.

[31] In the 1990s, 77% of total marine pollution newly originated from land-based sources and airborne depositions, 12% from shipping and 10% from dumping. See *ibid*; *id*, *Estimates of Oil Entering the Marine Environment From Sea-Based Activities: Reports and Studies no 75* (London 2007). *Cf* also *id*, *The State of the Marine Environment: UNEP Regional Seas Reports and Studies no 115* (Nairobi 1990) 88.

[32] See for the information that follows UNEP, Press Releases (The Hague, 4 October 2006). The data and facts are taken from UNEP/GPA, *The State of the Marine Environment: Trends and Processes* (The Hague 2006).

and West and Central Africa reach 80–90 per cent. Coastal 'dead zones', areas of bottom waters too oxygen depleted to support most ocean life, have developed. The problem of marine litter is reported to have steadily grown worse. Much of the litter is not biodegradable. 70 per cent of marine litter ends up on the sea-bed, 15 per cent on beaches and another 15 per cent is floating. Finally, many states, especially the developing ones, are facing a serious deterioration of their coastal environments. Phenomena such as losses of coral reefs, wetlands, loss of coastal habitats and mangroves are often aggravated by large population growth.

The ocean floors are vulnerable ecosystems in various respects. Firstly, at least in part they suffer from the remnants of war.[33] Both chemical and conventional munitions have been extensively dumped at sea since World War I. This is especially true for the Baltic Sea area.[34] Secondly, to date there are more than 400 identified oceanic 'dead zones' worldwide.[35] They are caused by the runoff of fertilisers and the consumption of fossil fuels, both of which feed massive algae blooms in the coastal oceans. More algae means more oxygen-burning, and thereby less oxygen in the water. This results in a massive flight by those fish, crustaceans and other ocean-dwellers able to relocate as well as the mass death of immobile creatures.[36] Thirdly, the newly emerging technological possibility of carbon capture and storage on the seafloor is praised as a promising option of tackling climate change, because such sites may absorb carbon dioxide (CO_2) as carbon sinks. However, there are fears that these kinds of CO_2 inputs might severely imperil the ocean floors which are valuable habitats for living and non-living marine resources. There are even voices arguing that carbon storage is nothing but a new form of dumping, falling under the scope of the 1996 London Protocol.[37] An amendment of 2006 to the 1996 Protocol allows for the storage of captured CO_2 in sub-sea-bed geological formations.[38]

12.3.2 All Types of Pollution

Apart from UNCLOS, there is no instrument at the global level which pursues a holistic regulatory approach in such a way that it addresses all of the sources of marine pollution. Such instruments can only be found at the regional level.

The 1992 Paris Convention for the Protection of the Marine Environment of the North-

[33] This will be addressed in Chapter 27.

[34] Due to the relatively shallow depths of the munitions dumping sites, *eg* east of Bornholm, south of Gotland, and in the Little Belt region, the Baltic Sea appears to provide a 'worse-case' scenario. For a more detailed information see T Stock, 'Sea-Dumped Chemical Weapons under the CWC—More Questions than Answers?', 52nd Pugwash CBW Workshop, *10 Years of the OPCW: Taking Stock and Looking Forward*, Noordwijk, The Netherlands, 17–18 March 2007; and Council of Europe, 'Chemical Munitions Buried in the Baltic Sea', Parliamentary Assembly Doc 11601 (28 April 2008).

[35] The world's largest 'dead zone' is the Baltic Sea whose bottom waters lack oxygen all the year round.

[36] See the Report 'Oceanic Dead Zones Continue to Spread', available at www.scientificamerican.com/article.cfm?id=oceanic-dead-zones-spread.

[37] See *eg* J Friedrich, 'Carbon Capture and Storage: A New Challenge for International Environmental Law' (2007) 67 *ZaöRV* 211. *Cf* also Chapter 13.4.

[38] U Beyerlin and J Grote Stoutenburg, 'Environment, International Protection' in R Wolfrum (ed), *Max Planck Encyclopedia of Public International Law* (Heidelberg/Oxford 2011), para 54, available at www.mpepil.com.

East Atlantic (OSPAR Convention) is designed to implement the relevant framework rules of UNCLOS for the area of the northeast Atlantic, the North Sea and adjacent Arctic waters.[39] Upon its entry into force on 25 March 1998, it replaced the 1972 Oslo Dumping Convention and the 1974 Paris Convention for the Prevention of Marine Pollution from Land-Based Sources.

The OSPAR Convention consists of 34 articles and five annexes, which form an integral part of the Convention. It 'addresses all sources of pollution of the marine environment . . ., takes into account the precautionary principle and strengthens regional cooperation' (Preamble, last indent). It imposes general obligations on states parties regarding pollution from land-based sources (Article 3), by dumping (Article 4), from offshore sources (Article 5) and from other sources (Article 7). Four annexes relating to pollution from land-based sources (I), pollution by dumping or incineration (II), pollution from offshore sources (III) and assessment of the quality of the marine environment (IV) are destined to substantiate these rather scantly worded obligations.

Articles 3–5 and 7 are preceded by Article 2(2)(a) and (b), according to which the contracting parties 'shall apply' what the drafters of the OSPAR Convention call the 'precautionary principle' and the 'polluter pays principle'. The former 'principle'[40] is understood as preventing the parties from interfering with the marine environment even in cases where there is no conclusive evidence of a causal relationship between the activities and the harmful effects. For the purpose of implementing the 'precautionary principle', the parties must adopt programmes and measures of preventive environmental protection which have to meet standards such as the 'best available techniques' and 'best environmental practice' (Article 2(3)).[41] As 'sustainable development', another key concept of international environmental law, is referred to only in the OSPAR Convention's preamble, there are doubts at least as to whether it entails immediate legal effects.[42]

The Convention also shows some significant procedural and institutional characteristics which were, at the time of signature, rather innovative in nature. Most important is Article 10, on the basis of which the OSPAR Commission was established. As successor to the two commissions that had been established under the 1972 Oslo Convention and the 1974 Paris Convention, it administers and further develops the OSPAR Convention. The Commission, *inter alia*, supervises the implementation of the Convention, considers and, where appropriate, adopts amendments of the Convention, related annexes and appendices, as well as amendments to the latter (Articles 15–19). Remarkably, the OSPAR Commission, made up of representatives of each of the contracting parties, is authorised under Article 13 to adopt decisions and recommendations by unanimous vote and, when this is not attainable, by a three-quarters majority vote of the parties (Article 13(1)). Moreover, the OSPAR Commission, on the basis of reports submitted to it by the contracting parties, assesses their compliance with the Convention and, when appropriate,

[39] Art 1(a) gives an exact definition of the 'maritime area' that is covered by the Convention.

[40] For a more thorough discussion on 'precautionary action' see Chapter 7.

[41] The criteria for the definition of both terms are specified in Appendix 1 to the OSPAR Convention.

[42] In its third indent, the preamble speaks of the need 'to achieve sustainable management of the maritime area, that is, the management of human activities in such a manner that the marine ecosystem will continue to sustain the legitimate uses of the sea and will continue to meet the needs of present and future generations'.

decides upon and calls for steps to bring about full compliance (Articles 22 and 23).[43] Thus, it belongs to the treaty bodies which may contribute to a flexible and dynamic evolution of MEA regimes.[44]

The OSPAR Commission has widely used its implementing and 'law-making' powers: at its 1998 Ministerial Meeting it adopted Annex V to the Convention which pursues a combined strategy of protecting and conserving the ecosystems and biodiversity of maritime areas, thereby bringing together the respective obligations of the parties under the OSPAR Convention and the Biodiversity Convention.[45] At the same meeting the OSPAR Commission adopted strategies to direct its future work in the areas of hazardous substances, radioactive substances and eutrophication.[46] Since 1998, the OSPAR Commission has adopted a large number of decisions and recommendations that are complemented by (legally non-binding) 'other agreements'.[47] Noteworthy are in particular OSPAR Decision 2007/1 to Prohibit the Storage of Carbon Dioxide Streams in the Water Column or on the Sea-bed, and OSPAR Decision 2007/2 on the Storage of Carbon Dioxide Streams in Geological Formations.[48] The latter issue led to amendments to Annexes II and III of the OSPAR Convention.[49]

In 1992 the Convention for the Protection of the Marine Environment of the Baltic Sea Area (Helsinki Convention) was adopted. Applying to the 'Baltic Sea Area' as defined in Article 1, it comprises 38 provisions and seven annexes forming an integral part of the Convention; six of them are amended annexes to the former Helsinki Convention, only one of them is new (Annex VII). Upon the entry into force of the new Helsinki Convention on 17 January 2000, its predecessor, the 1974 Helsinki Convention, ceased to apply.

In many respects the 1992 Helsinki Convention is similar to the OSPAR Convention. Analogous to the latter it addresses marine pollution caused by substances[50] from all sources, including the land-based ones (Articles 5 and 6), refers to 'precaution' and 'polluter-pays', both classified as 'principles' (Article 3(2) and (4)). It calls upon the contracting parties to 'promote the use of Best Environmental Practice and Best Available Technology' in order to prevent and eliminate pollution of the Baltic Sea Area (Article 3(3)).[51] Conforming to their 'firm determination to assure the ecological restoration of the

[43] See for a more thorough discussion Chapter 22.2.

[44] *Cf* Chapter 17.2.3.

[45] Annex V is entitled 'The Protection and Conservation of the Ecosystems and Biological Diversity of the Maritime Area'; the text is available at www.ospar.org/eng/html/convention/ospar_conv10.htm. It is in force for 15 states and the European Union (Art 15(5) OSPAR Convention). Annex V has been accompanied by Appendix 3, entitled 'Criteria for Identifying Human Activities for the Purpose of Annex V'; the text can be found at www.ospar.org/eng/html/convention/ospar_conv9.

[46] See the following documents of the Ministerial Meeting of the OSPAR Commission held in July 1998: 'OSPAR Strategy with regard to Hazardous Substances' Ref no 1998-16, Annex 34, Ref § B-6.3; 'OSPAR Strategy with regard to Radioactive Substances' Ref no 1998-17, Annex 35, Ref § B-6.5; 'OSPAR Strategy to Combat Eutrophication' Ref no 1998-18, Annex 36, Ref § B-6.6.

[47] See OSPAR Commission, 'List of Decisions, Recommendations and Other Agreements Applicable within the Framework of the OSPAR Convention (last updated 01/12/08)' available at www.ospar.org/html_documents/ospar/html/ospar_decs_recs_other_agreements.pdf.

[48] Meeting of the OSPAR Commission (25–29 June 2007), Annex 5 (Ref §2.9b) and Annex 6 (Ref §2.10c).

[49] See amended Art 3(2)(f) in Annex II and amended Art 3(3) in Annex III.

[50] Annex I to the Helsinki Convention offers criteria for identifying and evaluating 'harmful substances'.

[51] Criteria for the use of both strategies are laid down in Annex II to the Helsinki Convention.

Baltic Sea, ensuring the self-regeneration of the marine environment and preservation of its ecological balance' (Preamble, fourth indent), the contracting parties

> shall individually and jointly take all appropriate measures with respect to the Baltic Sea Area and its coastal ecosystems influenced by the Baltic Sea to conserve natural habitats and biological diversity and to protect ecological processes. Such measures shall also be taken in order to ensure the sustainable use of natural resources within the Baltic Sea Area.

In some respects, however, the Helsinki Convention differs from the OSPAR Convention. Contrary to the latter, it covers not only the maritime area, but also the respective coastal ecosystems. This is in line with Agenda 21 which demands an 'integrated management and sustainable development of coastal and marine areas'.[52]

Moreover, unlike the OSPAR Convention, the Helsinki Convention clearly commits itself to a holistic policy of protecting the marine environment and conserving the natural conditions of marine living resources, as may be taken from Article 4(1) which determines that the Convention applies 'to the marine environment of the Baltic Sea Area which comprises the water-body and the sea-bed including their living resources and other form of marine life'.[53]

As regards its institutional setting, the Helsinki Convention builds on the Baltic Marine Environment Protection Commission that had been established under the predecessor Convention of 1974. Accordingly, Article 19(2) of the 1992 Helsinki Convention merely states that this former body 'shall be the Commission'.

Compared to the OSPAR Commission, the Helsinki Commission (HELCOM) is less innovative as to its rights and duties under Article 20 of the Helsinki Convention. Unlike the OSPAR Commission, it is limited to adopting legally non-binding recommendations and is not empowered to engage in compliance control.

Perhaps the most important outcome of HELCOM's activities is the Baltic Sea Action Plan (BSAP), adopted on 15 November 2007 in Krakow, Poland.[54] It contains an ambitious program of co-ordinated action 'to achieve a Baltic Sea in good environmental status by 2021'. It seeks to establish a Baltic Sea unaffected by eutrophication, undisturbed by hazardous substances, with environmentally friendly maritime activities, and with a favourable conservation status. In 2003, HELCOM and the OSPAR Commission started to co-operate at ministerial level.[55]

As part of UNEP's Regional Seas Programme, the 1978 Kuwait Regional Convention for Cooperation on the Protection of the Marine Environment from Pollution was adopted on 24 April 1978. In force since 1 July 1979, it has been accompanied by an 'Action Plan for the Protection of the Marine Environment and the Coastal Areas of Bahrain, Iran, Iraq, Kuwait, Oman, Qatar, Saudi Arabia and the United Arab Emirates', and followed by four implementing protocols.

[52] Agenda 21, Chapter 17.1 *et seq*.

[53] However, Art 27 provides that nothing in the Convention shall be construed as infringing upon, *inter alia*, fishing.

[54] Its text is available at www.helcom.fi/stc/files/BSAP/BSAP_Final.pdf.

[55] See *eg* Declaration of the Joint Ministerial Meeting of the Helsinki and OSPAR Commission, Bremen, 25–26 June 2003, Doc JMM 2003/3 (final version)-E.

The 2003 Tehran Framework Convention for the Protection of the Marine Environment of the Caspian Sea[56] pursues an integrated approach by protecting the marine environment and marine living resources. It addresses all kinds of pollution sources. As indicated by its denomination as 'framework convention', most of its provisions remain rather abstract and are therefore in need of further specification.

12.3.3 Pollution from Ships

Pollution from ships comprises any deliberate or accidental discharge from vessels that inflicts harm on the marine environment. Examples for deliberate discharges are the cleaning of tanks and discarding ballast. Accidental discharges of dangerous pollutants resulting from collision, stranding or explosion, especially oil pollution accidents, such as the *Torrey Canyon* (1967), *Amoco Cadiz* (1978), *Exxon Valdez* (1989) and *Prestige* (2002), quite often highly alarmed the world public.

The leading instrument regulating pollution from ships at the universal level is the 1973 London International Convention for the Prevention of Pollution by Ships (MARPOL Convention). It replaced the 1954 London Convention for the Prevention of Pollution of the Sea by Oil, which, despite several amendments, had not been particularly successful in practice.

First adopted in 1973, the MARPOL Convention required for its entry into force ratification by 15 states, with a combined merchant fleet of not less than 50 per cent of world shipping by gross tonnage. By 1976, it had only received three ratifications—notwithstanding the fact that states could become party to the Convention by only ratifying Annexes I (pollution by oil) and II (pollution by noxious liquid substances), while Annexes III–V (covering pollution by packaged harmful substances, sewage and garbage) were optional.

In February 1978, the IMO held a Conference on Tanker Safety and Pollution Prevention in order to amend the initial text of the 1973 MARPOL Convention. On 17 February 1978 the Conference adopted a protocol[57] the result of which is the (amended and consolidated) International Convention for the Prevention of Pollution from Ships, as Modified by the Protocol of 1978, commonly referred to as the 1973/78 MARPOL Convention, which entered into force on 2 October 1983. This had been achieved by allowing states to become parties to the Convention by only implementing Annex I thereto (Article I(1) of the Protocol), as it was decided that Annex II would not become binding 'for a period of three years from the date of entry into force of the present Protocol or for such longer period as may be decided by a two-thirds majority of the Parties to the present Protocol' (Article II(1) of the Protocol). In September 1997 the 1973/78 MARPOL Convention was complemented by the adoption of Annex VI covering air pollution from ships.[58]

Due to the fact that in 2007 the parties to the 1973/78 MARPOL Convention com-

[56] It is not part of UNEP's Regional Seas Programme.

[57] Its official name is Protocol of 1978 Relating to the International Convention for the Prevention of Pollution from Ships.

[58] It entered into force on 19 May 2005. The other five MARPOL Annexes are also in force.

prised more than 98 per cent of merchant tonnage, the MARPOL Annexes I and II can be considered to be 'generally accepted international rules and standards' as referred to in Article 211 UNCLOS. The same can be said for optional Annexes III–VI, whose tonnage participation rates in 2007 were 94, 75, 96 and 74 per cent, respectively.[59]

The states parties to the 1973/78 MARPOL Convention are allowed to agree upon designating certain sea areas as 'special areas' which, for technical reasons relating to their specific geographical and ecological condition and to their sea traffic, must be provided with a higher level of protection than other areas of the sea.[60]

The 1973/78 MARPOL Convention applies to ships flying the flag or operating under the authority of a state party, except warships, naval auxiliary or other ships used only in government non-commercial service (Article 3). Compared to the 1954 London Convention, the 1973/78 MARPOL Convention disposes of a much more effective enforcement scheme (Articles 4–6) which, apart from penalising any violation of the Convention's requirements, involves

> the cooperation of coastal states, port states, and flag states in a system of certification, inspection, and reporting whose purposes are to make the operation of defective vessels difficult or impossible and to facilitate the performance by flag states of their primary jurisdiction to prosecute and enforce applicable laws.[61]

A specific 'tacit amendment procedure'[62] allows the IMO Marine Environment Protection Committee (MEPC) to adopt an amendment to a MARPOL Annex provided that it has been accepted by two-thirds of the parties, constituting at least 50 per cent of the tonnage of the world's merchant fleet (Article 16(2)(f) of the 1973/78 MAROL Convention).[63] In recent years IMO's MEPC has made wide use of this procedure. Thus, for instance, in 2001 and 2003 the MEPC adopted amendments to Regulation 13G in Annex I of the 1973/78 MARPOL Convention to bring forward the phasing-out date for single-hull tankers and replacing them by double-hull tankers.[64]

There are a number of other universal MEAs which contain international standards on the safety of shipping, including those for the prevention of collisions at sea, the safety of life at sea, and the training of seafarers and fishing vessel personnel.[65]

[59] These figures are taken from Birnie, Boyle and Redgwell, above n 4, 404.

[60] The establishment of such 'special areas' requires the adoption of a respective amendment to the MARPOL Annex concerned. Thus, for instance, in 2006 the Southern South African Waters were designated as a Special Area under MARPOL Annex I by amendment which entered into force on 1 March 2008.

[61] *Cf* Birnie, Boyle and Redgwell, above n 4, 405.

[62] *Cf* below Chapter 18.4.

[63] *Cf* D Freestone and SMA Salman, 'Oceans and Freshwater Resources' in D Bodansky *et al* (eds), *The Oxford Handbook of International Environmental Law* (Oxford 2007) 337, 346.

[64] See Resolution MEPC 95(46) (27 April 2001); Resolution MEPC 111(50) (4 December 2003) and Resolution MEPC 114(50) (4 December 2003). See www.imo.org/Conventions/contents.asp?doc_id=678&topic_id=258#2001.

[65] Among them are the 2001 IMO Convention on the Control of Harmful Anti-Fouling Systems which entered into force on 17 September 2008, and the 2004 IMO Convention for the Control and Management of Ships' Ballast Water and Sediments which has not yet entered into force. For more information see Sands, above n 11, 444, with references.

12.3.4 Pollution by Dumping of Wastes

The 1972 London Convention on the Prevention of Marine Pollution by the Dumping of Wastes (1972 London Convention) established the first comprehensive regime against the dumping of wastes at the global level with detailed rules.

Central to the 1972 London Convention is Article IV which regulates waste dumping on the basis of three lists: Highly hazardous wastes that are included in the 'black list' (Annex I) are prohibited. However, there are a considerable number of exceptions to this ban. The dumping of wastes perceived as less dangerous which are contained in the 'grey list' (Annex II) requires a 'prior special permit'. The dumping of all other wastes requires a prior general permit. The grant of 'special' and 'general' permits must meet the requirements set forth in Annex III. In practice the 1972 version of the London Convention proved to be an instrument that regulated rather than prohibited the dumping of waste.

The three-year process of reviewing the Convention resulted in the 1996 Protocol to the London Dumping Convention (1996 London Protocol). Upon its entry into force on 24 March 2006, it replaced the 1972 London Convention for those of its parties which ratified the Protocol. As of 31 October 2010, 39 states were parties to the Protocol. Among them are all important industrialised states except Russia and the United States.

The purpose of the 1996 London Protocol is the same as that of the 1972 Convention. Contrary to the latter, the states parties to the Protocol are required to apply a 'precautionary approach'[66] to environmental protection against dumping of wastes in implementing this Protocol, and to take into account the polluter-pays principle[67] (Article 3(1) and (2)). The Protocol also adopts a listing system. However, unlike the 1972 London Convention, it pursues a reverse list approach: states parties are required to prohibit the dumping of 'any wastes or other matters with the exception of those listed in Annex 1' which need to be permitted in accordance with the requirements laid down in Annex 2 (Article 4(1)). The incineration of wastes at sea, as well as the export of wastes or other matter to other countries for dumping or incineration at sea is prohibited (Articles 5 and 6). A transitional period assists new contracting parties towards gradually achieving full compliance with the Protocol over a maximum period of five years (Article 26). In 2007 the Meeting of Contracting Parties met its obligation under Article 11 of the 1996 Protocol to establish mechanisms and procedures of compliance control.[68]

In 2005, upon the withdrawal of Russia's objection to Resolution LC.51(16), the ban on all radioactive waste dumping became binding on all parties to the Protocol. In 2006 the first Meeting of the Parties to the Protocol adopted amendments to the Protocol's Annex 1 to regulate the sequestration of 'CO^2 streams from carbon dioxide capture processes in sub-seabed geological formations for permanent isolation'.[69]

At the regional level, the Oslo Convention for the Prevention of Marine Pollution by

[66] *Cf* Chapter 7.

[67] *Cf* Chapter 8.

[68] See Report of the 29th Consultative Meeting, Doc IMO, LC 29/17 (2007) para 5 and Annex 7. *Cf* Chapter 22.2.

[69] MOP 1, Resolution LP 1(1) of 2 November 2006; Doc IMO, LC 28/15, Annex 6. Upon its entry into force on 10 February 2007 it is binding for each party to the Protocol unless it has notified the IMO of its objections.

Dumping from Ships and Aircraft was established in 1972. It has since been replaced by the 1992 OSPAR Convention.[70] There are also three UNEP Regional Seas Protocols, *ie* the Dumping Protocols of Barcelona (1976), Noumea (1986) and Paipa (1989) to the respective framework conventions; they require parties to prevent dumping from ships and aircraft.[71]

12.3.5 Pollution from Land-Based Sources and Atmospheric Pollution

Article 207 UNCLOS confines itself to require states to adopt laws and regulations to prevent, reduce and control marine environmental pollution from land-based sources, such as rivers, estuaries, pipelines and outfall structures, as well as to establish the respective 'global and regional rules, standards and recommended practices and procedures' (paragraphs 1 and 4). Article 213 UNCLOS requires states to enforce their laws and regulations with respect to this kind of pollution.

The 1974 Paris Convention for the Prevention of Marine Pollution from Land-Based Sources (Paris Convention) was the only universal international treaty ever to deal exclusively with this kind of pollution. It required states to adopt programmes and measures to eliminate pollution of the maritime area from land-based sources of substances listed in Part I of Annex A, and to limit strictly pollution by less harmful substances listed in Part II of Annex A. However, upon the entry into force of the 1992 OSPAR Convention in 1998, the 1974 Paris Convention ceased to apply between the parties to the latter.[72] In 1985, the legally non-binding UNEP Montreal Guidelines for the Protection of the Marine Environment against Pollution from Land-based Sources were adopted.[73] Building on these guidelines, and in response to Agenda 21,[74] the legally non-binding 1995 Global Programme of Action for the Protection of the Marine Environment from Land-based Activities (GPA) and the accompanying Declaration were adopted in Washington, DC on 1 November 1995 by 108 states and the EC.[75] At present, the GPA, apart from the UNCLOS rules mentioned above, is the sole (politically binding) instrument at the universal level that deals with the threats to the marine environment resulting from human activities on land. The GPA is designed to be a source of conceptual and practical guidance for national and/or regional authorities in devising and implementing sustained action to prevent, reduce, control and/or eliminate marine degradation from land-based activities.[76]

[70] See Section 12.3.2.

[71] *Cf* Sands, above n 11, 427.

[72] See Art 31(1) OSPAR Convention. Like the 1992 Helsinki Convention, the OSPAR Convention belongs to a group of MEAs aimed at combating pollution from a total of sources, including the land-based ones. See at Section 12.3.2.

[73] UNEP GC Dec 13/18 on 'Environmental Law' (24 May 1985). For its text see www.unep.org/law/PDF/UNEPEnv-LawGuide&PrincN07.pdf.

[74] Para 17.26.

[75] UN Doc UNEP(OCA)/LBA/IG2/7 (5 December 1995).

[76] See the Summary Report of the Second Intergovernmental Review Meeting of the GPA, 16–20 October 2006, Earth Negotiations Bulletin, vol 25 no 37 (23 October 2006) 2. As an outcome of this meeting the Beijing Declaration on Furthering the Implementation of the GPA was adopted (UN Doc UNEP/GPA/IGR2/CRP2).

At the regional level, four UNEP Regional Seas Protocols exclusively address pollution from land-based sources: the 1980 Athens Protocol; the 1983 Quito Protocol; the 1990 Kuwait Protocol; and the 1992 Black Sea Protocol. Following the same regulatory approach as the 1974 Paris Convention, these protocols require their respective parties to prohibit the discharge of 'black list' substances and limit less noxious 'grey list' substances.[77]

As already pointed out, a significant proportion of atmospheric pollution results from land-based activities, a smaller one from ships and aircraft. Accordingly, Article 212 UNCLOS requires all states to 'prevent, reduce and control pollution of the marine environment, from or through the atmosphere, applicable to the air space under their sovereignty and to vessels flying their flag or vessels or aircraft of their registry'. The 1992 OSPAR Convention, the 1992 Baltic Convention, as well as the above-mentioned protocols of Athens, Quito and Kuwait include rules against pollution through the atmosphere as a land-based source.[78]

Persistent organic pollutants (POPs) can be considered to be among the most dangerous threats to the marine environment because of the long-range spread of these substances. Therefore, two legally binding instruments that deal specifically with atmospheric pollution should also be mentioned here. Firstly, the 1998 Aarhus Protocol to the 1979 Geneva Convention on Long-Range Transboundary Air Pollution on Persistent Organic Pollutants, which recognises in its Preamble that measures to control emissions of POPs also contribute to the protection of the environment in areas outside UNECE's region, 'including the Arctic and international waters'. Secondly, the 2001 Stockholm Convention on Persistent Organic Pollutants can be expected to produce similar protective effects on the marine environment.[79]

12.3.6 Pollution from Sea-Bed Activities

Under Article 208(1) and (2) UNCLOS coastal states are obliged to prevent, reduce and control marine environmental pollution 'arising from or in connection with sea-bed activities subject to their jurisdiction and from artificial islands, installations and structures under their jurisdiction'. Their respective measures 'shall be no less effective than international rules, standards and recommended practices and procedures'.

The sea-bed and ocean floor beyond the limits of national jurisdiction, *ie* the 'Area' (Article 1(1) UNCLOS), and its resources, are the common heritage of mankind, the exploration and exploitation of which shall be carried out for the benefit of mankind. Acting on behalf of the latter, the International Sea-Bed Authority (the 'Authority') is empowered under Article 145 UNCLOS to adopt rules, regulations and procedures for

> (a) the prevention, reduction and control of pollution and other hazards to the marine environment, including the coastline, and of interference with the ecological balance of the marine environment, particular attention being paid to the need for protection from harmful

[77] *Cf* Sands, above n 11, 436, with references.
[78] *Cf ibid*, 437 *et seq*.
[79] For a more detailed discussion of these instruments see Chapters 13.2.1. and 15.3.2.

> effects of such activities as drilling, dredging, excavation, disposal of waste, construction and operation of maintenance of installations, pipelines and other devices related to such activities; [and]
> (b) the protection and conservation of the natural resources of the Area and the prevention of damage to the flora and fauna of the marine environment.

In addition, the Council of the Authority is required under Article 162(2)(x) UNCLOS to disapprove areas for exploitation 'where substantial evidence indicates the risk of serious harm to the marine environment'. Based on Articles 160(2)(f)(ii) and 162(2)(o)(ii) UNCLOS, the Authority adopted the 2000 Regulations on Prospecting and Exploration for Polymetallic Nodules in the Area which apply to all private and public entities under contract with the Authority. Part V of these Regulations deals with marine environmental protection.[80] Regulation 31(1)–(3) requires (1) the Authority to 'establish and keep under periodic review environmental rules, regulations and procedures to ensure effective protection of the marine environment from harmful effects which may arise from activities in the Area'; (2) the Authority and the sponsoring states to apply 'a precautionary approach, as reflected in Principle 15 of the Rio Declaration'; and (3) each contractor to 'take the necessary measures to prevent, reduce and control pollution and other hazards to the marine environment arising from its activities in the Area as far as reasonably possible using the best technology available to it'.[81] The Authority is currently working on additional regulations on prospecting and exploration for cobalt-rich crusts and polymetallic sulphides. These will all form part of what is called the 'Mining Code'.[82] Protecting the seafloor from pollution is increasingly important as newly discovered animal species live there amidst the mineral deposits. The coexistence of non-living and living resources should prompt states to develop a regime that combines sustainable use of both resources with preserving the ecosystem concerned.[83]

In addition to UNCLOS, two protocols established within the framework of UNEP's Regional Seas Programme deal with pollution arising from sea-bed activities, namely the 1989 Kuwait Exploration Protocol[84] and the 1994 Madrid Offshore Protocol.[85]

[80] At the time when the UNCLOS was negotiated (1973–1982) the so-called manganese nodules, *ie* polymetallic deposits known to occur on the deep ocean bed of the Pacific, were the main resources under consideration for being exploited. Today, it is rather unlikely that they will be economically mined in the foreseeable future. Polymetallic crusts, found in slightly shallower water, and polymetallic sulphides containing some precious metals are more recently discovered deep sea-bed non-living resources. For more information, see Freestone and Salman, above n 63, 341.

[81] *Cf* M Bothe, 'The Protection of the Marine Environment against the Impacts of Seabed Mining: An Assessment of the New Mining Code of the International Seabed Authority' in Ehlers *et al* (eds), above n 2, 221.

[82] The 'Mining Code' refers to the whole of the comprehensive set of rules, regulations and procedures issued by the International Seabed Authority to regulate prospecting, exploration and exploitation of marine minerals in the Area.

[83] See www.isa.org.jm/en/documents/mcode. *Cf* also United Nations Division for Ocean Affairs and the Law of the Sea, Office of Legal Affairs, and the International Seabed Authority, *Marine Mineral Resources: Scientific Advances and Economic Perspectives* (New York 2004).

[84] 1989 Protocol Concerning Marine Pollution Resulting from Exploration and Exploitation of the Continental Shelf. See its text in www.unep.org/regionalseas/Programmes.

[85] 1994 Protocol Concerning the Protection of the Mediterranean Sea against Pollution Resulting from Exploration and Exploitation of the Continental Shelf and the Seabed and its Subsoil; see its text *ibid*.

12.3.7 Intervention in Case of Marine Pollution Incidents

The 1982 UNCLOS requires states, once they are aware of imminent or actual pollution of the marine environment, to give immediate notification to others likely to be affected, and 'to cooperate, to the extent possible, in eliminating the effects of pollution and preventing or minimizing the damage', and to jointly develop contingency plans (Articles 198 and 199).

In response to the 1967 *Torrey Canyon* disaster, the 1969 Brussels Convention Relating to Intervention on the High Seas in Cases of Oil Pollution Damage (Intervention Convention) was established. In force since 6 May 1975, the Intervention Convention enables a coastal state to take all necessary measures on the high seas to prevent, mitigate or eliminate grave and imminent danger to its coastline from imminent or actual pollution by oil resulting from a maritime incident. Before taking action, a coastal state should notify the flag state of the ship, consult independent experts and notify any person whose interests may be reasonably expected to be affected. However, in cases of extreme urgency measures can be taken at once. The related 1973 London Protocol extended the Intervention Convention to cover harmful substances other than oil. The list of substances attached to the 1973 Protocol has been revised by amendment three times.[86]

In 1990 the London International Convention on Oil Pollution Preparedness, Response and Co-operation (OPRC Convention) was elaborated within the framework of the IMO. Having entered into force on 13 May 1995, the OPRC Convention requires parties to take, individually or jointly, all appropriate measures to prepare for and respond to an oil pollution incident (Article 1). The spectrum of measures to be taken encompasses oil pollution emergency plans on ships, offshore units, seaports and oil-handling facilities; oil pollution reporting procedures; and national and regional systems for preparedness and response (Articles 3, 4 and 6). In addition, the OPRC Convention establishes rules concerning the action to be taken by a party on receiving an oil pollution report and provides for international co-operation in pollution response (Articles 5 and 7). The related 2000 London Protocol on Preparedness, Response and Co-operation to Pollution Incidents by Hazardous and Noxious Substances (OPRC-HNS Protocol), in force since 21 November 2008, extends the scope of co-operation between the parties to include incidents involving hazardous and noxious substances which are defined by reference to lists of substances included in other IMO conventions and codes.

At the regional level, a first instrument to address marine environmental emergencies was the 1969 Bonn Agreement for Co-operation in Dealing with Pollution of the North Sea by Oil. It was superseded by the 1983 Bonn Agreement for Co-operation in Dealing with Pollution of the North Sea by Oil and Other Harmful Substances. In force since 1 September 1989, the 1983 Agreement goes beyond the 1969 Agreement by requiring states parties to develop guidelines for joint action in response to large maritime oil pollution emergencies, to provide information on pollution incidents of this kind, and to establish a standard form for the reporting of pollution.[87]

[86] *Cf* Resolution MEPC 49(31) (4 July 1991), Resolution MEPC 72(38) (10 July 1996) and Resolution MEPC 100(48) (11 October 2002). See www.imo.org/Conventions/mainframe.asp?topic_id=258&doc_id=680.

[87] All the information needed for counter-pollution operations is compiled in the Bonn Agreement Counter Pollution Manual. See www.bonnagreement.org/eng/html/counter-pollution_manual/welcome.

The 1990 Lisbon Cooperation Agreement for the Protection of the Coasts and Waters of the North-East Atlantic against Pollution between Spain, France, Morocco, Portugal and the European Community, in force since 20 October 1993, is aimed at establishing a mechanism to co-operate in the case of an incident of pollution at sea such as pollution caused by hydrocarbons or other harmful substances.[88] In addition, Spain and Morocco concluded the bilateral 1996 Co-operation Agreement on Combating Pollution and on Maritime Search and Rescue which is aimed at co-ordinating the means at their disposal for combating pollution and for rescue at sea.

Within the framework of UNEP's Regional Seas Programme there are eight environmental emergency protocols, namely those of Barcelona (1976), Kuwait (1978), Abidjan (1981), Lima (1981), Jeddah (1982), Cartagena (1983), Nairobi (1985) and Noumea (1986).[89]

12.4 Conservation and Management of Marine Living Resources

12.4.1 State of the Marine Living Resources[90]

Oceans cover 71 per cent of the earth's surface and contain more than 90 per cent of the earth's living biomass. More than 50 per cent of the world's population live within 60 kilometres of a coast; by 2020 this figure could have risen to as much as 75 per cent. The basic nutrition of 3.5 billion people depends on oceanic products. Several direct pressures cause overexploitation of fish stocks and the decline of marine mammals and turtles worldwide. Population growth and rising wealth have resulted in an almost 50 per cent increase in fish harvest from 95 million tonnes in 1987 to 141 million tonnes in 2005. Fish represent the fastest-growing food commodity traded internationally, causing increasingly serious ecological problems.

Global fishing fleets are estimated to have a capacity 250 per cent greater than needed to catch what the oceans can sustainably produce.[91] Global fishing practices affect the spawning and nursery grounds of many marine species. Destructive fishing gear and practices, such as bottom trawlers, dynamite and poison, also compromise the productivity of global fishing. Trawlers in particular produce 'by-catch', often consisting of large quantities of non-target species. Apart from these unsustainable fishing practices which widely neglect the essentials of conservation of marine habitats and spawning

[88] A dispute over the borders in Western Sahara preventing Spain and Morocco from ratifying the Agreement was cleared by an Additional Protocol signed on 20 May 2008. See for the whole Commission (EC), 'Proposal for a Council Decision concerning the conclusion, on behalf of the European Community, of the Additional Protocol to the Cooperation Agreement for the Protection of the Coasts and Waters of the North-East Atlantic against Pollution', COM(2009) 436 final, 27 August 2009.

[89] For details see Sands, above n 11, 453.

[90] The marine living resources include marine fish, cephalopods, crustaceans and marine mammals (*ibid*, 559).

[91] United Nations Environment Programme (UNEP), *Global Environment Outlook (GEO 4): Environment for Development* (Nairobi 2007) 122.

grounds, climate change driven phenomena such as sea-level rise and changes in water temperatures and wind patterns are progressively degrading marine habitats and creating great pressures on many marine species.[92] Based on estimates made by the Food and Agriculture Organization (FAO) in 2007, it appears that the global state of exploitation of the world marine fishery resources has remained relatively stable over the past 10–15 years: 2 per cent of the fish stock groups monitored by FAO were underexploited, 18 per cent moderately exploited and 52 per cent fully exploited. A quarter of the stocks were either overexploited (19 per cent), depleted (8 per cent) or recovering from depletion (1 per cent). Most of the stocks of the top ten species, which account for about 30 per cent of the world fish catches, were fully exploited or overexploited in 2007.[93]

As regards the issue of whaling, it should be noted that despite the moratorium on commercial whaling in force since 1986, the current status of whales is unsatisfactory. There is ongoing scientific uncertainty over the numbers of whales of different species and in different geographical stocks. This is why reliable whale population figures are only available for a few species/stocks which have been assessed in some detail.[94] Estimates of the International Whaling Commission (IWC) show that in 2004, several populations of great whales remained highly endangered and numbered 500 or less, including most bowhead whale stocks, grey whales in the western Pacific, all stocks of northern right whales, and various stocks of blue whales. It has been reported that some of the small Arctic bowhead populations have been deliberately caught in contravention of IWC regulations, trapped accidentally by fishing gear, or killed by ship strikes. In 2009 Norway, Denmark and Iceland were believed to have killed more whales than Japan for the first time in many years.[95]

12.4.2 Fish

In line with the basic understanding of the *Bering Sea Fur Seals* arbitration of 1893 that the freedom to fish the high seas and the need for restraint in exploitation must be properly balanced,[96] UNCLOS tries to balance the utilisation interests of fishing states and the state community's interest in conserving marine fauna. Rather than declaring the high seas and their living resources to be a 'common heritage of mankind',[97] UNCLOS entitles all states to allow their nationals to engage in fishing. Yet, at the same time, UNCLOS requires them also, individually or jointly, to take the measures necessary for the conservation of the high seas' living resources (Articles 116–120 UNCLOS).

However, the extent of the high seas regime has been limited by the growth of mari-

[92] See *eg* Birnie, Boyle and Redgwell, above n 4, 702.

[93] All figures are taken from FAO, *The State of World Fisheries and Aquaculture* (Rome 2009) particularly 30 *et seq*.

[94] See the IWC's estimates for the whale stocks by 1 September 2009 at www.iwcoffice.org/conservation/estimate.

[95] According to a report of Guardian News and Media Limited, said European states intended to hunt 1478 whales compared to Japan's 1280 in 2009; this would mean an increase of nearly 20% by these states in 2008. See www.guardian.co.uk/environment/2009/jun/19/whaling-europe-japan/print.

[96] See for a more detailed discussion on this arbitral award Birnie, Boyle and Redgwell, above n 4, 707.

[97] *Cf* Art 136 UNCLOS.

time areas controlled by coastal states, *ie* a process of terraneisation. In their territorial seas, which extend up to 12 nautical miles from the coastline, coastal states can exercise their sovereign rights freely except for their duty to protect and preserve the marine environment according to the general rules of Articles 192–194 UNCLOS. Within the newly established 200 nautical mile exclusive economic zones (EEZs),[98] the coastal states have sovereign rights for the purpose of exploiting, conserving and managing the natural (living or non-living) resources (Article 56(1)(a) UNCLOS). Moreover, they have to determine the allowable catch, to protect marine living resources against overexploitation, and to maintain or restore populations of harvested species at levels which can produce the 'maximum sustainable yield' (Article 61(1)–(3) UNCLOS). Due to their utilisation interests, coastal states are better prepared to protect 'their' resources. This was the assumption when the EEZ was introduced. However, practice sometimes seems to prove the opposite.[99]

UNCLOS addresses four categories of marine species which migrate in various ways, namely (1) highly migratory species listed in its Annex I, such as species of tuna, swordfish and shark (Article 64); (2) marine mammals, such as whales, dolphins and seals (Article 65); (3) anadromous species, such as salmon (Article 66), which mostly live in the ocean, and breed in fresh water; and (4) catadromous species, such as eels (Article 67), which live in fresh water, and breed in the ocean.

Under Article 64 UNCLOS, coastal and other states fishing in a region for highly migratory species 'shall co-operate directly or through appropriate international organizations with a view to ensuring conservation and promoting the objective of optimum utilization of such species throughout the region, both within and beyond the exclusive economic zone'.

As called for by Agenda 21, the UN General Assembly convened a special conference in 1993 to identify and assess existing problems related to the conservation and management of such fish stocks, and to give full effect to this rather ambiguous provision of UNCLOS.[100] As a result, in August 1995 the conference adopted the Agreement for the Implementation of the UNCLOS Provisions Relating to the Conservation and Management of Straddling Fish Stocks and Highly Migratory Fish Stocks (1995 Fish Stocks Agreement), which entered into force on 11 December 2001. As of 30 November 2010 it was binding on 78 parties.

The object and purpose of the 1995 Fish Stocks Agreement is to ensure the long-term conservation and sustainable use of straddling and highly migratory fish stocks. With the exceptions laid down in Articles 6 and 7 it applies to said fish stocks 'beyond areas under national jurisdiction' (Article 3(1)). Under Article 5, coastal states and states fishing on the high seas are required to, *inter alia*, adopt measures to ensure long-term sustainability of relevant fish stocks and promote the objective of their optimum utilisation; to base such measures on the 'best scientific evidence available' and to design them 'to maintain

[98] See Arts 55–75 UNCLOS.

[99] See D Hunter, J Salzman and D Zaelke, *International Environmental Law and Policy* (3rd edn New York 2007) 757 *et seq*.

[100] See UNGA Res 47/192 (22 December 1992). See also UN Doc A/CONF164/9, Report on the Organizational Session of the United Nations Conference on Straddling Fish Stocks and Highly Migratory Fish Stocks.

or restore stocks at levels capable of producing maximum sustainable yield'; to apply the precautionary approach as specified in Article 6; to minimise pollution of all kinds; to protect biodiversity in the marine environment; to prevent or eliminate overfishing and excess fishing capacity; and to provide effective monitoring, control and surveillance. Article 7 requires coastal states and states fishing on the high seas to co-operate with each other to achieve compatible measures with the aim of harmonising the respective conservation and management measures for the EEZs and the high seas. Article 8 stipulates the duty of coastal states and states fishing on the high seas to co-operate in order to 'ensure effective conservation and management of such stocks'. Articles 9–14 deal with 'subregional and regional fisheries management organisations and arrangements' and their functions in a very detailed form.

Although conceptualised as a tool for implementing UNCLOS's framework rules, the 1995 Fish Stocks Agreement itself contains hardly more than framework rules which need further implementation. This has largely been accomplished by agreements concluded within the framework of Regional Fisheries Management Organisations (RFMOs).

Apart from these developments, the legally non-binding Code of Conduct for Responsible Fisheries deserves closer consideration. Unanimously adopted by the FAO Conference on 31 October 1995, the Code, according to its preface, provides 'a necessary framework for national and international efforts to ensure sustainable exploitation of aquatic living resources in harmony with the environment'.[101] The Code itself is further implemented by other FAO 'soft law' instruments, such as the 1999 Declaration on the Implementation of the Code of Conduct for Responsible Fisheries,[102] and the 2008 International Guidelines for the Management of Deep-Sea Fisheries in the High Seas.[103]

Based on two earlier legally non-binding instruments[104] the FAO adopted on 25 November 2009 the Agreement on Port State Measures to Prevent, Deter and Eliminate Illegal, Unreported and Unregulated Fishing (Agreement on Combating IUU Fishing),[105] which will enter into force after ratification by 25 states. The ultimate objective of this agreement is 'to ensure the long-term conservation and sustainable use of living marine resources and marine ecosystems' (Article 2). It requires port states to conduct regular inspections of ships according to minimum standards set forth in Annex B (Articles 12 and 13) and to ensure that ports are adequately equipped and inspectors properly trained

[101] See the text of the Code of Conduct for Responsible Fisheries in www.fao.org/fishery/ccrf. Integral part of the Code of Conduct is the (legally binding!) 1993 FAO Agreement to Promote Compliance with International Conservation and Management Measures by Fishing Vessels on the High Seas which came into force on 24 April 2003, after acceptance by 25 parties.

[102] The so-called Rome Declaration was adopted by the FAO Ministerial Meeting on Fisheries held in Rome in March 1999. Its text is available at www.fao.org/DOCREP/005/X2220e/X2220e00.HTM. For a general overview see also DJ Doulman, 'Coping with the Extended Vulnerability of Marine Ecosystems: Implementing the 1995 FAO Code of Conduct for Responsible Fisheries' (2007) 46 *Social Science Information* 189.

[103] The Guidelines were adopted by the FAO Technical Consultation on 29 August 2008, as requested by UNGA Res 61/105 (8 December 2006). See the Guidelines' text in (2008) 47 ILM 994.

[104] See the 2001 FAO International Plan of Action to Prevent, Deter and Eliminate Illegal, Unreported and Unregulated Fishing (available at ftp://ftp.fao.org/docrep/fao/012/y1224e/y1224e00.pdf) and the 2005 FAO Model Scheme on Port State Measures to Combat Illegal, Unreported and Unregulated Fishing (available at ftp://ftp.fao.org/docrep/fao/010/a0985t/a0985t00.pdf).

[105] See its text in www.fao.org/legal/treaties/037t-e.

(Articles 16 and 17). When a vessel is denied access, port states must promptly notify the flag state and, as appropriate, relevant coastal states and regional fisheries organisations (Article 18). Moreover, port states must ensure that the national authorities of the country whose flag the vessel is flying investigate and take enforcement action if necessary (Article 20). In addition, the FAO Agreement provides for assistance to developing countries to adopt and implement port state measures in a very comprehensive way (Article 21). In a nutshell, the FAO Agreement is the first MEA under which port states become actively involved in combating illegal, unreported and unregulated fishing, alongside flag states which are primarily responsible for the conduct of their vessels on the high seas.

At the regional level there is an abundance of agreements on the management and conservation of marine living resources.

Firstly, there is the 2000 Convention on the Conservation and Management of Highly Migratory Fish Stocks in the Western and Central Pacific Ocean. It serves to implement the 1995 Fish Stocks Agreement in this region.

Secondly, appropriate agreements have been entered into within the framework of UNEP's Regional Seas Programme. Among them are the 1982 Geneva Protocol Concerning Mediterranean Specially Protected Areas (related to the 1976 Barcelona Convention); the 1990 Kingston Protocol Concerning Specially Protected Areas and Wildlife (related to the 1983 Cartagena Convention); the 1985 Nairobi Protocol Concerning Protected Areas and Wild Flora and Fauna in the Eastern African Region (related to the 1985 Nairobi Convention); the 1986 Noumea Convention for the Protection of the Natural Resources and Environment of the South Pacific Region; and as an independent partner programme the 1980 Convention on the Conservation of Antarctic Marine Living Resources.

Thirdly, the 1989 Convention for the Prohibition of Fishing with Long Driftnets in the South Pacific may serve as an example for singling out a particular segment of marine resource conservation.[106] Inspired by this regional convention, the UN General Assembly adopted Resolution 44/225 of 22 December 1989 which recommended the imposition of moratoria on all large-scale pelagic driftnet fishing activities by 30 June 1992.[107] However, as is well known, resolutions of the General Assembly are *per se* legally non-binding.[108]

Fourthly, there are numerous treaty-based regional fisheries organisations the majority of which was established at times prior to the adoption of the 1995 Fish Stocks Agreement. Among them are: the International Pacific Halibut Commission (1923); the FAO Asia-Pacific Fisheries Commission (1948); the General Fisheries Commission for the Mediterranean (GFCM) (1949); the Inter-American Tropical Tuna Commission (1949); the North Pacific Anadromous Fish Commission (NPAFC) (1952); the South Pacific Permanent Commission on the Exploitation of the Marine Resources (1952); the Inter-

[106] This regulatory strategy may be called 'piecemeal approach'; see U Beyerlin and T Marauhn, *Law-Making and Law-Enforcement in International Environmental Law after the 1992 Rio Conference* (Berlin 1997) 26 *et seq*.

[107] (1990) 29 ILM 1555. On 21 December 1990 the UN General Assembly passed Resolution 45/197 ((1991) 17 LSB 7) which reaffirms Resolution 44/225 and calls for its full implementation by all members of the international community. With the adoption of Resolution 46/215 on 20 December 1991 ((1992) 31 ILM 241) the full implementation of the moratorium was envisaged by 31 December 1992.

[108] Some authors argue that the moratorium called for by the UNGA driftnet Resolutions may have eventually become customary law. See GJ Hewison, 'The Legally Binding Nature of the Moratorium on Large-Scale High Seas Driftnet Fishing' (1994) 25 *Journal of Maritime Law and Commerce* 557.

national Commission for the Conservation of Atlantic Tuna (ICCAT) (1966); the South-East Atlantic Fisheries Organization (SEAFO) (1973); the International Baltic Sea Fisheries Commission (IBSFC) (1973); the Northwest Atlantic Fisheries Organization (NAFO) (1978); the South Pacific Forum Fisheries Agency (SPFFA) (1979); the Commission for the Conservation of Antarctic Marine Living Resources (CCAMLR) (1980); the North East Atlantic Fisheries Commission (NEAFC) (1980); the North Atlantic Salmon Conservation Organization (1982); the Pacific Tuna Organization (1989); the International Commission for the Conservation of Southern Bluefin Tuna (CCSBT) (1993); and the Indian Ocean Tuna Commission (IOTC) (1993).[109] As already indicated, all these commissions are based on regional fisheries agreements which show considerable variances in their priorities. While some of them appear to be more aimed at proper management than conservation of fish stocks, others give clear priority to the latter aspect. Notwithstanding these conceptual disparities, all of these commissions have much in common as to their structure and function. Typically they combine an information and research function with a regulatory function which enables them to adopt legally binding or non-binding conservation measures.[110] In the latter respect, each measure which a regional fisheries commission takes with regard to fish stocks covered by the 1995 Fish Stocks Agreement must meet the requirements laid down in Articles 8–12 of the Agreement. Particularly important is Article 10(a) and (c) of the Fish Stocks Agreement according to which states, '[i]n fulfilling their obligation to cooperate through subregional or regional fisheries management organizations or arrangements' must, *inter alia*, 'agree on and comply with conservation and management measures to ensure the long-term sustainability of . . . fish stocks', as well as 'adopt and apply any generally recommended international minimum standards for the responsible conduct of fishing operations'.[111]

12.4.3 Mammals

Article 65 UNCLOS does not itself prohibit the taking of marine mammals or whaling, but allows coastal states and international organisations to do so. By virtue of Article 120 UNCLOS, Article 65 UNCLOS also applies to the high seas. However, it requires states to co-operate with a view to conserving marine mammals and, in the case of cetaceans, to 'work through the appropriate international organization'.[112]

At the universal level there is just one MEA that specifically deals with the problems of whaling,[113] namely the 1946 International Convention for the Regulation of Whaling

[109] For more information and references see Sands, above n 11, 584 *et seq* and 597 *et seq*.

[110] Most regional fisheries agreements include provisions on an objection procedure which, if used, ensures that a state party which objects a Commission's decision does not become bound by it.

[111] For a more thorough discussion on the regional fisheries organisations see particularly Sands, above n 11, 584 *et seq*; Birnie, Boyle and Redgwell, above n 4, 739 *et seq*; Wolff, above n 8, 78 *et seq*; E Louka, *International Environmental Law. Fairness, Effectiveness, and World Order* (Cambridge 2006) 264 *et seq*.

[112] Much speaks in favour of assuming that the International Whaling Commission (IWC) is that body. However, this understanding is not compelling.

[113] The 1973 CITES Convention (by 1983, Appendix I lists a number of whales) and the 1979 Bonn Convention on Migratory Species include marine mammals amongst many other species in their protection regimes (Sands, above n 11, at 591).

(ICRW).[114] Designed 'to provide for the proper conservation of whale stocks and thus make possible the orderly development of the whaling industry',[115] it originally pursued a rather utilisation-oriented approach. The ICRW only provides the procedural framework for the establishment of the IWC, as well as its composition, tasks and rules of decision-making.

The regulation of all substantive questions concerning whaling is reserved to what is named 'Schedule', an annex to the ICRW, which forms an integral part thereof. The Schedule's regulations with respect to the conservation and utilisation of whale resources (*eg* the determination of protected and unprotected species, open and closed seasons, open and closed waters, including the designation of sanctuary areas, etc (Article V ICRW)) can be added or amended by a three-quarter majority vote of those members to the Commission voting (Article III(2)); however, objecting members may opt out of such an amendment (Article V(3)). The more non-whaling and anti-whaling states became members of the IWC over the years, the more the IWC was able to make ample use of this amendment option. Today, its Schedule differs from its original version so fundamentally that the ICRW and the IWC appear to be committed to the preservation rather than the management of whaling resources. In 1982 the IWC adopted an amendment to the Schedule for prohibiting commercial whaling from 1985/86.[116] Although reviewed at each meeting of the IWC, the moratorium has as yet not been lifted.

In 1992, in protest against the moratorium, Iceland withdrew from the ICRW and concluded, together with the Faroe Islands, Greenland and Norway, the Agreement on Cooperation in Research, Conservation and Management of Marine Mammals in the North Atlantic (NAMMCO Agreement) on 9 April 1992. On the basis of this Agreement, the North Atlantic Marine Mammal Commission (NAMMCO) was established. Although practically competing with the ICRW, the NAMMCO Agreement does not directly conflict with the former in terms of international law for the following reasons: (1) Norway, although party to the latter, is not bound by the moratorium since it lodged a formal protest against it at the time of its adoption; (2) Iceland, after rejoining the ICRW in 2002, has since 2003 relied on its asserted right to scientific whaling; and (3) the inhabitants of Greenland and the Faroe Islands benefit from the right to aboriginal subsistence whaling according to Rule 13 of the ICRW Schedule. Nevertheless, most commentators consider the NAMMCO to be a symbol of dissatisfaction with the ICRW.[117]

In 1979 and 1994, the IWC established two sanctuaries, namely the Indian Ocean Sanctuary and the Southern Ocean Sanctuary, as areas in which commercial whaling is prohibited.[118] Moreover, in 1994 the Revised Management Procedure (RMP) for deter-

[114] It is a successor to the 1937 International Agreement for the Regulation of Whaling.

[115] Preamble, last indent.

[116] The amended para 10(e) of the Schedule provides that 'catch limits for the killing for commercial purposes of whales from all stocks for the 1986 coastal and the 1985/86 pelagic seasons and thereafter shall be zero. This provision will be kept under review'. See the text of the Schedule as amended by the Commission at the 61st Annual Meeting in June 2009 at www.iwcoffice.org/_documents/commission/schedule.pdf.

[117] See A Proelß, 'Marine Mammals' in R Wolfrum (ed), *Max Planck Encyclopedia of Public International Law* (Heidelberg/Oxford 2009), paras 19, 20, available at www.mpepil.com.

[118] Both were preceded by an IWC sanctuary in the Antarctic in 1938. Two additional proposals for the establishment of sanctuaries in the South Atlantic and South Pacific failed to achieve the three-quarters majority of votes needed to amend the Schedule; see www.iwcoffice.org/conservation/sanctuaries.

mining allowable catches of some whale species was agreed by an IWC Resolution, but not formally adopted into the Schedule.[119]

Thus, due to its secondary rule-making activities over more than six decades, the IWC developed into what may be called an anti-whaling body, although its annual meetings are marked by notorious controversies between pro- and anti-whalers on issues such as lifting the moratorium on commercial whaling, whale killing methods, Japan's requests for 'scientific whaling', and aboriginal subsistence whaling.[120]

The ICRW is complemented by some regional agreements on the conservation of marine mammals. Among them are, apart from the previously mentioned 1992 NAMMCO Agreement, the 1992 Agreement on the Conservation of Small Cetaceans of the Baltic, North East Atlantic, Irish and North Seas (1992 ASCOBANS), adopted as an agreement under the 1979 Bonn Agreement on Migratory Species; the 1996 Agreement on the Conservation of Cetaceans of the Black Sea, Mediterranean Sea and Contiguous Atlantic Area (1996 ACCOBAMS); and the 1999 Agreement Concerning the Creation of a Marine Mammal Sanctuary in the Mediterranean between France, Italy and Monaco.

12.5 Conclusions

The appeal of the current legal system concerning the protection of the oceans and their resources lies in the broad range of normative strategies and sophisticated regulatory techniques. This system is multidimensional, but nonetheless substantially determined by the pertinent framework rules of UNCLOS. At the global level, the number of relevant instruments is still rather limited. However, among them are important ones such as the 1973/78 MARPOL Convention, the 1996 London Dumping Protocol and the 1995 Fish Stocks Agreement. At the regional level, there is a multitude of relevant international agreements, each of them constructed so as to meet the specific ecological and socio-economic needs of the regional sea concerned. At both levels, legally binding agreements are often complemented by 'soft law' instruments, sometimes designed to make legally binding rules operative in practice. To date, all these instruments constitute a dense network of norms steering the behaviour of all actors involved in marine environmental protection and fisheries. Unfortunately, in practice the achievements of all these forms of interstate co-operation have so far been rather modest.

UNCLOS strikes a balance between the competing national interests of coastal, navigating and fishing states, on the one hand, and the state community's fundamental interest in protecting the marine environment and conserving the oceans' living and non-living resources, on the other, by way of framing a package-deal of rules which seek to make

[119] See www.iwcoffice.org/conservation/rmp.htm. Work on a 'Revised Management Scheme' (RMS) started the same year. The RMS is a comprehensive inspection and observation scheme which includes the scientific aspects of the RMP but also deals with non-scientific issues such as enforcement of the agreed catch limits. See www.iwcoffice.org/conservation/rms.htm.

[120] For an account of the 60th IWC Annual Meeting in 2008 see J Depledge, 'Winds of Change' (2008) 38 *Environmental Policy and Law* 251.

compromises between these rival interests. It pursues a sectoral rather than integrative approach by controlling marine pollution source by source, and orienting its rules along the lines of strictly defined maritime zones. While coastal states are controlling the territorial seas and the EEZs, on the high seas individual fishing states compete strongly with each other, often with the result that the state community's interest in the conservation of marine resources lags behind. As the extension of the concept of 'common heritage of mankind' from the deep sea-bed area and its mineral resources to the high seas is hardly an option, in future all states involved, especially the coastal states, should be more strictly obliged to engage in marine resource conservation—as 'trustees' acting on behalf of the state community.

Another means to cure the existing shortcomings in the protection of the oceans and their resources could be to rely henceforth more on international agreements pursuing a regulatory approach which is more integrative than sectoral, and more precautionary than preventive. In both respects, new methods of protection and conservation should be devised, such as agreeing upon protecting 'marine ecosystems' or preserving the 'marine biodiversity' as a whole. Instead of strictly separating maritime zones from coastal areas, both should be considered as a whole. The establishment of more comprehensive regimes for the protection of the marine and coastal environment and its resources might help to mitigate the underdevelopment of poor people living in the Third World's coastal areas.[121] In 1995, the Conference of the Parties to the Convention on Biological Diversity (CBD) adopted the Jakarta Mandate on Marine and Coastal Biological Diversity[122] which is driven by the idea to extend the CBD's concept to protect all life on earth, understood as a variety of life forms including plants, animals and micro-organisms, the genes that they contain and the ecosystems that they form,[123] to the law of the sea. This conceptual approach has been recently echoed in three resolutions of the UN General Assembly focussing on 'conservation and sustainable use of marine biological diversity beyond areas of national jurisdiction'.[124] An UN Ad Hoc Open-ended Informal Working Group has been mandated to consider all threats to marine biodiversity and to identify their various causes. The issue remains to be solved.[125]

Both overfishing and degradation of the habitats of marine species continue to seriously impede the achievement of long-term sustainability of marine fish stocks. One of the reasons why this target has so far been missed, apart from the undue proliferation

[121] This is in line with Agenda 21 which propagates in its Chapter 17.2 an 'Integrated Management and Sustainable Development of Coastal and Marine Areas, Including Exclusive Economic Zones (Programme Area A)'. See www.un.org/esa/dsd/agenda21/res_agenda21_17.shtml.

[122] UNEP/CBD/COP/2/19, Decision II/10, 16; *cf* also MM Goote, 'Convention on Biological Diversity: The Jakarta Mandate on Marine and Coastal Biological Diversity' (1997) 12 *International Journal of Marine and Coastal Law* 377.

[123] See CA de Fontaubert, DR Downes and TS Agardy, *Biodiversity in the Seas: Implementing the Convention on Biological Diversity in Marine and Coastal Habitats*, IUCN Environmental Policy and Law Paper no 32 (1966), cited in Centre for Biodiversity, www.marinebiodiversity.ca/cmb/education/what-ismarine-biodiversity.

[124] See UNGA Res 61/222 (20 December 2006); UNGA Res 62/215 (22 December 2007); UNGA Res 63/111 (5 December 2008).

[125] For more details see K Hakapää, 'Protection of the Marine Environment in the Light of New Uses and Old Dangers' in T Giegerich and A Proelß (eds), *Bewahrung des ökologischen Gleichgewichts durch Völker- und Europarecht* (Berlin 2010) 237, 243 *et seq*.

of fisheries organisations operating worldwide, is the lack of co-ordination of the latter's activities. Moreover, an effective enforcement of international rules and standards for ensuring the sustainable use and conservation of the oceans' living resources is still lacking. This is why there is a need for renewed endeavours to strengthen flag state jurisdiction and make port state control more effective. As it is feared that effective flag jurisdiction will continue to be circumvented by 'outflagging', *ie* the choice of 'flags of convenience', port state control, as advocated by the 2009 FAO Agreement on Combating IUU Fishing, may become the most promising enforcement means in future.

Further Reading

K Bangert, 'Fisheries Agreements' in R Wolfrum (ed), *Max Planck Encyclopedia of Public International Law* (Heidelberg/Oxford 2009), available at http://www.mpepil.com.

J Basedow and U Magnus (eds), *Pollution of the Sea: Prevention and Compensation* (Berlin/Heidelberg 2007).

M Bowman, '"Normalizing" the International Convention for the Regulation of Whaling' (2008) 29 *Michigan Journal of International Law* 293–499.

V Bou, 'The Critical Environmental Situation of the Black Sea Region' in K Koufa (ed), *Protection of the Environment for the New Millennium* (Athens/Thessaloniki 2002) 521–542.

A Broggiato, 'Marine Biological Diversity Beyond Areas of National Jurisdiction' (2008) 33 *Environmental Policy and Law* 182–188.

WCG Burns and G Wandersforde-Smith, 'The International Whaling Commission and the Future of Cetaceans in a Changing World' (2002) 11 *RECIEL* 199–210.

J Ebbesson, 'A Critical Assessment of the 1992 Baltic Sea Convention' (2000) 43 *German Yearbook of International Law* 38–64.

P Ehlers *et al* (eds), *Marine Issues: From a Scientific, Political and Legal Perspective* (The Hague *et al* 2002).

L de la Fayette, 'The OSPAR Convention Comes into Force: Continuity and Progress' (1999) 14 *International Journal of Marine and Coastal Law* 247–297.

D Freestone, 'A Decade of the Law of the Sea Convention: Is It a Success?' (2007) 39 *George Washington International Law Review* 499–540.

D Freestone and SMA Salman, 'Oceans and Freshwater Resources' in D Bodansky *et al* (eds), *The Oxford Handbook of International Environmental Law* (Oxford 2007) 337–361.

J Friedrich, 'Carbon Capture and Storage: A New Challenge for International Environmental Law' (2007) 67 *Heidelberg Journal of International Law (ZaöRV)* 211–227.

K Hakapää, 'Protection of the Marine Environment in the Light of New Uses and Old Dangers' in T Giegerich and A Proelß (eds), *Bewahrung des ökologischen Gleichgewichts durch Völker- und Europarecht* (Berlin 2010) 237–253.

D Hassan, *Protecting the Marine Environment from Land-Based Sources of Pollution. Towards Effective International Cooperation* (Hampshire 2005).

T Henriksen, G Hønneland and A Sydnes, *Law and Politics in Ocean Governance. The UN Fish Stocks Agreement and Regional Fisheries Management Regimes* (Leiden/Boston 2006).

I Lutchmann, 'Beyond National Jurisdiction: The Emergence of Regional Fisheries Management Organizations (RFMOs)' in C de Fontaubert and I Lutchmann (eds), *Achieving Sustainable Fisheries. Implementing the New International Legal Regime* (Cambridge 2003).

F Orrego Vicuña, 'The International Law of High Seas Fisheries: From Freedom of Fishing to

Sustainable Use' in OE Stokke (ed), *Governing High Seas Fisheries. The Interplay of Global and Regional Regimes* (Oxford 2001) 23–52.

C Pinon Carlarne, 'Saving the Whales in the New Millennium: International Institutions, Recent Developments and the Future of International Whaling Policies' (2005–2006) 24 *Virginia Environmental Law Journal* 1–48.

A Proelß, 'Marine Mammals' in R Wolfrum (ed) *Max Planck Encyclopedia of Public International Law* (Heidelberg/Oxford 2009), available at www.mpepil.com.

RG Rayfuse, 'Natural Resource Management and Conservation: Fisheries and Marine Mammals' (2007) 18 *Yearbook of International Environmental Law* 317–346.

J Roberts, *Marine Environment Protection and Biodiversity Conservation. The Application and Future Development of the IMO's Particularly Sensitive Sea Area Concept* (Berlin/Heidelberg 2007).

T Stephens, *International Courts and Environmental Protection* (Cambridge 2009).

AKJ Tan, *Vessel-Source Marine Pollution. The Law and Politics of International Regulation* (Cambridge 2006).

Y Tanaka, 'Reflections on the Conservation and Sustainable Use of Genetic Resources in the Deep Seabed Beyond the Limits of National Jurisdiction' (2008) 39 *Ocean Development & International Law* 129–149.

——, 'Regulation of Land-Based Marine Pollution in International Law: A Comparative Analysis Between Global and Regional Legal Frameworks' (2006) 66 *Heidelberg Journal of International Law (ZaöRV)* 535–574.

D VanderZwaag and A Daniel, 'International Law and Ocean Dumping: Steering a Precautionary Course aboard the 1996 London Protocol, but still an Unfinished Voyage' in A Chircop (ed) *The Future of Ocean Regime-Building* (Leiden/Boston 2009) 515–550.

D Vidas (ed), *Protecting the Marine Environment. Law and Policy for Pollution Prevention* (Cambridge 2000).

R Warner, *Protecting the Oceans beyond National Jurisdiction: Strengthening the International Law* (Leiden 2009).

N Wolff, *Fisheries and the Environment* (Baden-Baden 2002).

R Wolfrum and N Matz, 'The Interplay of the United Nations Convention on the Law of the Sea and the Convention on Biological Diversity' (2000) *Max Planck Yearbook of United Nations Law* 445–480.

R Wolfrum, V Röben and FL Morrison, 'Preservation of the Marine Environment' in FL Morrison and R Wolfrum (eds), *International, Regional and National Environmental Law* (The Hague 2000).

United Nations Environment Programme, *The Revision of MAP Legal Framework: The Barcelona Convention and its Protocols* (Athens 2002).

13

Air, Ozone, Climate and Outer Space

13.1 Survey

Transboundary air pollution, depletion of the ozone layer and global climate change are phenomena which are closely interlinked as to their causes and detrimental effects on the environment. Resulting largely from human activities, all three anthropogenic atmospheric degradations seriously affect the ecosystem of the earth in its entirety, including human life and health. Compared to these phenomena, human activities in outer space have so far had only a marginal impact on the environment, although orbital space debris may, in the longer run, cause considerable environmental damage on earth; this is all the more so as space tourism is currently beginning to be promoted.

Notwithstanding their ecological interrelationship, air pollution, ozone layer depletion and global warming must be treated separately because they have developed at different times and, in light of their diverse environmental impacts, need to be solved in different ways.

Gaseous substances which contaminate the atmosphere have the capacity to be highly noxious and persistent. By their very nature, they spread over great distances, thereby easily transcending national borders. In the twentieth century the progressive industrialisation of the 'First World' societies almost inevitably gave rise to the phenomenon of long-range transboundary air pollution which harbours much potential for conflict between neighbouring states. It is therefore not by chance that the *Trail Smelter* arbitration of 1941, which significantly influenced early international environmental law, dealt with a severe air pollution dispute between Canada and the United States.[1]

With the conclusion of the Geneva Convention on Long-Range Transboundary Air Pollution (LRTAP Convention) in 1979 states reacted to the discovery made in the late 1960s that the immense acid damage to lakes and rivers in Scandinavian countries originated from pollution sources located in central Europe and the United Kingdom hundreds of kilometres away from the areas of acid deposition ('acid rain').[2] Conceived as a UNECE

[1] *Cf* above Chapter 1.1.

[2] Acid deposition is primarily the result of emissions of sulphur dioxide (SO_2) and nitrogen oxides (NO_x) that have substantial international spillover effects.

framework convention, the LRTAP Convention binds primarily European states, but also the United States and Canada as parties. In 1991 the latter states bilaterally agreed on the Air Quality Agreement, which primarily addresses the problem of 'acid rain' then hitting especially the eastern Canadian provinces.[3] Due to the existence of the LRTAP Convention the subsequent making of sub-regional or bilateral agreements on air pollution became superfluous. The Convention would have remained a blunt instrument if it had not been specified by subsequent implementing protocols which oblige states parties to reduce a variety of specific pollutant emissions. Substantiated in this way, the LRTAP Convention developed into an efficient international treaty regime, although geographically limited to Europe and North America. It remains the only regional multilateral instrument which comprehensively regulates and controls transboundary air pollution. The Association of Southeast Asian Nations (ASEAN) Agreement on Transboundary Haze Pollution of 10 June 2002 only deals with a subproblem of transboundary air pollution, *ie* large-scale smoke resulting from uncontrolled land and forest fires with deleterious effects on human health and the environment.[4]

When the LRTAP Convention was signed states were not yet aware that the atmosphere needs to be protected as a global environmental resource. Things changed fundamentally in the 1980s when scientists discovered that the stratospheric ozone layer was disappearing, in particular over the Antarctic, but also over the northern hemisphere. This finding was alarming because the ozone layer protects the earth from excessive ultraviolet radiation that endangers human health and damages natural ecosystems. Scientists discovered that the process of ozone depletion was caused by a number of noxious anthropogenic gases, such as chlorofluorocarbons (CFCs), halons, methane, nitrous oxides and carbon dioxide. As 'the impact of ozone-depleting substances is the same wherever or however they originate, and would affect all states',[5] it was clear that, unlike transboundary air pollution, ozone depletion was a global environmental threat. Accordingly, with the 1985 Vienna Convention on the Protection of the Ozone Layer (Ozone Convention) the international community responded promptly to this challenge. Remarkably, only two years later states succeeded in adopting the Montreal Protocol on Substances that Deplete the Ozone Layer, which was intended to implement and specify the rather vague and abstract framework rules of the Ozone Convention. With its amendments adopted in 1990, 1992 and 1997, this Protocol, *inter alia*, requires industrialised states to limit production and consumption of ozone-depleting substances by quantitatively specified amounts, shows interesting attempts at institution-building, and provides for an unprecedented non-compliance procedure. Due to these innovative features the Montreal Protocol has been seen as a 'key moment' in the endeavours of states to establish an effective system of global environmental protection. This is all the more so as the measures fostered by the Protocol appear to have slowed down the process of stratospheric ozone depletion.

A range of atmospheric gases absorb infra-red radiation, making the earth's atmos-

[3] See below at Section 13.2.2.

[4] The agreement was a response of Southeast Asian states to the haze disaster in Indonesia in the late 1990s that was caused by uncontrolled burning for clearing land. In force since 25 November 2003, it is binding on nine ASEAN Member States. *Cf* http://haze.asean.org/hazeagreement/status.

[5] P Birnie, A Boyle and C Redgwell, *International Law and the Environment* (3rd edn Oxford 2009) 349.

phere warmer than it otherwise would be. Principally, this natural phenomenon, known as the 'greenhouse effect', is beneficial because, without it, the earth would be deprived of life as we know it. As early as the nineteenth century scientists had anticipated that adding CO_2 to the atmosphere could change the earth's climate. Initially they expected that the CO_2 caused by the growing industrialisation would be absorbed by the oceans. However, as human activities entailed the release of 'greenhouse gases' (GHGs) into the atmosphere at an ever faster rate, human-induced global climate change became a key environmental challenge. It results from increasing concentrations of anthropogenic GHG emissions which primarily, if not exclusively, originate from the industrialised world. However, awareness with regard to this alarming phenomenon has developed in the international community only in the mid-1980s. The first international scientific conference on the greenhouse effect, held at Villach, Austria, in 1985, predicted that in the first half of the twenty-first century GHGs will cause a rise of global average temperature greater than ever before in history of mankind. In 1988, in the aftermath of the Toronto Conference on the Changing Atmosphere, the World Meteorological Organization (WMO) and the United Nations Environment Programme (UNEP) established the Intergovernmental Panel on Climate Change (IPCC), a scientific body for the assessment of the current state of climate change and its environmental and socioeconomic consequences. Two years later, the IPCC issued its first report which provided a scientific basis for initiating the UN negotiations on building a legally binding climate change regime.

It was clear from the outset that meeting the challenge of global climate change would be much more difficult than halting ozone depletion. While the latter problem could be technologically solved by replacing the most dangerous ozone-depleting substances by less detrimental ones, states soon realised that curbing global warming would require a considerable behavioural change of humankind, especially in the industrialised world. Nevertheless, in June 1992, after a short period of negotiation under the auspices of the United Nations, the UN Framework Convention on Climate Change (UNFCCC) was adopted and opened for signature by states at the Rio Conference. As indicated by its name, the UNFCCC contains a legally binding framework under which the industrialised states bear the main responsibility for taking action towards reaching the ultimate objective of stabilising GHGs at levels that avoid dangerous climate change. Entailing only weak immediate legal effects, the UNFCCC was ratified by as many states as necessary to enter into force as early as 1994. However, the UNFCCC would have remained toothless unless followed by a legally binding implementing protocol.

In late 1997, after tough negotiations, especially in the North–South context, states agreed on the Kyoto Protocol. Although containing commitments on the part of the industrialised states to reduce their GHG emissions by specified amounts within a fixed period of time, the Kyoto Protocol fulfils its implementing function at best imperfectly. It provides for a rather modest reduction in GHG emissions to be achieved during a first commitment period of 2008–2012, leaving the developing countries, including the rapidly industrialising ones, completely outside its emissions reduction scheme. Many questions, such as the specification of the flexibility mechanisms introduced by the Protocol, the establishment of a non-compliance procedure, and the details of funding and technology transfer for developing country parties to the Protocol, were left to be solved by subsequent decision-making of the Conferences of the Parties (COPs) to the UNFCCC and the Kyoto Protocol, respectively.

The period between the signature of the Kyoto Protocol and its entry into force in February 2005 was marked by highly controversial negotiations on these matters between four groups of states pursuing rather heterogeneous interests, *ie* the European Union, the so-called Umbrella Group, including the United States, Canada, Japan, Australia and Russia, the Group 77/China, and the Alliance of Small Island States (AOSIS). However, especially with the Marrakesh Accords adopted at COP 7 in November 2001 considerable progress was reached in defining important details concerning the flexibility mechanisms and the compliance-control procedure under the Protocol, thereby politically paving the way for its ratification by China, Canada and Russia.

Aware of the fact that the first commitment period under the Kyoto Protocol will expire in 2012, political discussion on the key elements of a successor agreement commenced shortly after the Protocol's entry into force. From the outset it centred on the determination of the group of states obliged to reduce their GHG emissions in the commitment periods subsequent to 2012. In this respect, the question of whether the rapidly industrialising developing countries, such as China, India and Brazil, should be included into the prospective mandatory emissions reduction scheme gained pivotal importance.

Shortly before COP 13 was held in Bali, Indonesia, in December 2007, the IPCC, based on its Fourth Assessment Report, summarised its view of climate change by stating that

> [w]arming of the climate system is unequivocal, as is now evident from observations of increases in global average air and ocean temperatures, widespread melting of snow and ice and rising global average sea level;

and

> [g]lobal GHG emissions due to human activities have grown since pre-industrial times, with an increase of 70% between 1970 and 2004. . . . Most of the observed increase in global average temperatures since the mid-20th century is *very likely* due to the observed increase in anthropogenic GHG concentrations. It is *likely* that there has been significant anthropogenic warming over the past 50 years averaged over each continent (except Antarctica).[6]

It should be added that warmer temperatures result in unprecedented permafrost degradation, with the consequence that almost all near-surface permafrost will disappear by the end of this century, thereby exposing large carbon stores to decomposition and consequent release of GHGs.[7]

These predictions are the more alarming as there are serious threats driven by climate change which may occur in different regions of the world, such as conflict over natural

[6] IPCC, 'Summary for Policymakers' in The Core Writing Team *et al* (eds), *Climate Change 2007: Synthesis Report* (Geneva 2008) 2 and 5.

[7] *Cf* the following publications for an in-depth analysis: IPCC, 'Chapter 4: Observations: Changes in Snow, Ice and Frozen Ground' in S Solomon *et al* (eds), *Climate Change 2007: The Physical Science Basis: Contribution of Working Group I to the Fourth Assessment Report of the IPCC* (Cambridge *et al* 2007) 371 *et seq*; IPCC, 'Chapter 1: Assessment of observed changes and responses in natural and managed systems' in M Parry *et al* (eds), *Climate Change 2007: Impacts, Adaptation and Vulnerability. Contribution of Working Group II to the Fourth Assessment Report of the IPCC* (Cambridge *et al* 2007) 88 *et seq*.

resources; loss of territory and border disputes; environmentally induced migration; destabilisation of weak or failing states; tension over energy supply; and increasing pressure on the international security architecture.[8]

With the adoption of the Bali Action Plan, the COP 13/MOP 3 charted the course for a new negotiating process designed to tackle climate change with the aim of completing this process at the 2009 Copenhagen Conference (COP 15). However, COP 15 did not meet the hopes placed on it. It ended with the so-called 'Copenhagen Accord', a political minimum consensus on future climate change action which eventually was merely taken note of rather than formally adopted by the Conference of the Parties.[9]

The Ozone Convention and the UNFCCC are aimed at protecting global environmental goods from serious degradation which threatens the very existence of present and future generations of humankind. This is why the achievement of the objectives of both MEAs fundamentally concerns the community of states as a whole. Accordingly, the preamble of the UNFCCC explicitly declares climate change to be a 'common concern of mankind'. However, this alone cannot mean a paradigm shift in the sense that states entering into such an MEA principally accept to subordinate their sovereign rights to fundamental state community interests. An MEA is rather 'common interest' oriented when it contains in its operative part clear elements of collective institution-building. In this respect, rules such as those contained in Articles 11(4) and 2(9) Montreal Protocol, which provide the possibility for states parties to entrust treaty bodies with the performance of certain tasks on their behalf, are particularly telling.

13.2 Transboundary Air Pollution

13.2.1 LRTAP Convention and Related Protocols

The LRTAP Convention of 13 November 1979 entered into force on 16 March 1983. At present, there are 51 parties.[10]

Under Article 2 states parties 'shall endeavour to limit and, as far as possible, gradually reduce and prevent air pollution including long-range transboundary air pollution'. Based on this broadly worded obligation, Articles 3–8 commit the parties to a broad spectrum of activities, ranging from exchange of information, consultation, research and monitoring to developing and reviewing policies, strategies and measures for combating and reducing air pollution. Article 5 requires that consultations shall be held between parties 'actually affected by or exposed to a significant risk of long-range transboundary air pollution' and parties 'within which and subject to whose jurisdiction a significant contribution to [such kind of pollution] originates, or could originate'. With regard to their obligations under

[8] 'Climate Change and International Security', paper from the High Representative and the European Commission to the European Council, Doc S113/08 (14 March 2008) 3 *et seq*.

[9] See the text of the Copenhagen Accord in UN Doc FCCC/CP/2009/11/Add1, Decision 2/CP15 (18–19 December 2009) 5 *et seq*.

[10] See the information available at www.unece.org/env/lrtap/status/lrtap_st.htm.

Articles 2–5, each party 'undertakes to develop the best policies and strategies', including air quality management and control measures, 'in particular by using the best available technology which is economically feasible and low- and non-waste technology' (Article 6). All these provisions are weak in substance.

The intrinsic value of the LRTAP Convention is that it subjects states parties to a procedural framework of co-operation. For this reason, an Executive Body, composed of representatives of the parties, has been established under Article 10 LRTAP Convention. Although only endowed with the task of reviewing the implementation of the Convention, the Executive Body has also served as a forum for the subsequent elaboration and adoption of implementing protocols to the LRTAP Convention. Today, eight protocols are in force. They will now be reported in some detail.

The Geneva Protocol on Long-term Financing of the Cooperative Programme for Monitoring and Evaluation of the Long-range Transmission of Air Pollutants in Europe (EMEP) of 28 September 1984[11] provides for financing the costs of EMEP, which collects data on all pollutants regulated under the LRTAP Convention and measures air quality in various areas in Europe. According to the Protocol, the financing of this innovative instrument for the review and assessment of air pollution in Europe consists of mandatory contributions, supplemented by voluntary contributions.

The Helsinki Protocol on the Reduction of Sulphur Emissions or their Transboundary Fluxes by at Least 30 Per Cent of 8 July 1985[12] was established in response to the widespread damage to natural resources, such as forest, soil and water, in parts of Europe and North America caused by acidification. The core obligation of the parties to the Protocol is to 'reduce their national annual sulphur emissions or their transboundary fluxes by at least 30 per cent as soon as possible and at the latest by 1993, using 1980 levels as the basis for calculation of reductions' (Article 2). Parties are required to report annually to the Executive Body of the LRTAP Convention on the levels of national sulphur emissions, as well as on the progress made towards achieving the set sulphur emissions reduction target (Articles 4–6). The envisaged further reductions of sulphur emissions (Article 3) were reached nine years later with the adoption of the second Sulphur Protocol (see below).

The Sofia Protocol Concerning the Control of Emissions of Nitrogen Oxides or their Transboundary Fluxes of 31 October 1988[13] addresses a problem more difficult to solve because a principal source of nitrogen oxide emissions is the politically sensitive issue of motor traffic. This is why the Sofia Protocol establishes an emissions reduction scheme for nitrogen oxides which is more comprehensive and flexible than that under the Helsinki Sulphur Protocol. Under Article 2(1) of the Sofia Protocol, parties 'shall, as soon as possible and as a first step, take effective measures to control and/or reduce their national annual emissions of nitrogen oxides or their transboundary fluxes' at the latest by 31 December 1994 to the 1987 emissions level. All parties must apply national emissions standards to new mobile sources and introduce pollution control measures for major

[11] The Protocol is in force since 28 January 1988. Currently, there are 43 parties to it.

[12] In force since 2 September 1987, the Protocol is binding on 25 parties.

[13] In force since 14 February 1991, the Protocol is binding on 34 parties.

existing stationary sources. These standards must be based on 'best available technologies which are economically feasible' (Article 2(2)). Within six months of the entry into force of the Sofia Protocol the parties must 'commence negotiations . . . on further steps to reduce national annual emissions of nitrogen oxides . . ., taking into account the best available scientific and technological developments, internationally accepted critical loads and other elements' (Article 2(3)(a)).

The Geneva Protocol Concerning the Control of Emissions of Volatile Organic Compounds (VOCs) or their Transboundary Fluxes of 18 November 1991,[14] in its Article 2(1) requires the parties to 'control and reduce their emissions of VOCs[15] in order to reduce their transboundary fluxes and the fluxes of the resulting secondary photochemical oxidant products'. According to Article 2(2)(a)–(c), states parties have three options for meeting their reduction obligation. The first option involves a reduction in national annual emissions of VOCs by at least 30 per cent by 1999, using any year between 1984 and 1990 as a basis. The second option is available only to states parties whose VOC emissions originate from zones called Tropospheric Ozone Management Areas (TOMAs) as designated in Annex I to the 1991 Geneva Protocol. Annual emissions in TOMAs must also be reduced by 30 per cent; additionally the total national annual emissions of VOCs by 1999 must not exceed the 1988 levels. The third option can only be used by states parties whose 1988 emissions do not exceed certain limits. Article 2(3) provides that no later than two years after the entry into force of the 1991 Geneva Protocol each party has to '[a]pply appropriate national or international emissions standards to new stationary sources based on the best available technologies which are economically feasible, taking into consideration annex II' (Article 2(3)(i)). Moreover, the parties are required, as a second step, to commence negotiations, within six months after the entry into force of the 1991 Geneva Protocol, 'on further steps to reduce national annual emissions of [VOCs] . . ., taking into account the best available scientific and technological developments, scientifically determined critical levels and internationally accepted target levels' (Article 2(6)). They must co-operate, *inter alia*, to develop control strategies, and measures and a timetable commencing not later than 1 January 2000 for achieving such emissions reductions (Article 2(7)). Parties are not relieved by the Protocol from their other obligations to reduce gaseous emissions that may contribute significantly to climate change, the formation of tropospheric background ozone or the depletion of stratospheric ozone, or that are toxic or carcinogenic (Article 3(1)); moreover, they have to establish a mechanism for monitoring compliance with the Protocol (Article 3(3)).

The Oslo Protocol on Further Reduction of Sulphur Emissions of 14 June 1994,[16] unlike the Helsinki Sulphur Protocol, explicitly pursues an innovative precautionary approach.[17] In Article 2(1) it requires states parties to

> control and reduce their sulphur emissions in order to protect human health and the environment

[14] In force since 29 September 1997, the Geneva Protocol is binding on 24 parties.

[15] 'VOCs' means 'all organic compounds of anthropogenic nature, other than methane, that are capable of producing photochemical oxidants by reactions with nitrogen oxides in the presence of sunlight' (Art 1(9) of the Protocol).

[16] The Protocol entered into force on 5 August 1998. It is binding on 29 parties.

[17] See the Preamble of the Protocol, 3rd indent.

> from adverse effects, in particular acidifying effects, and to ensure, as far as possible, without entailing excessive costs, that depositions of oxidized sulphur compounds in the long term do not exceed critical loads for sulphur given, in annex I, as critical sulphur depositions, in accordance with present scientific knowledge.

As a first step to the achievement of the critical loads objective, the parties must meet the targets and timetables for reductions of sulphur emissions specified in Annex II to the Protocol (Article 2(2)).[18] Furthermore, they must make use of the most effective measures for the reduction of sulphur emissions for new and existing sources, including, *inter alia*, measures to increase energy efficiency and the use of renewable energy, as well as the application of 'best available control technologies not entailing excessive cost, using the guidance in annex IV' (Article 2(4)). In addition, the parties may 'apply economic instruments to encourage the adoption of cost-effective approaches to the reduction of sulphur emissions, and agree upon the joint implementation of the Protocol with other parties' (Article 2(6) and (7)). The Oslo Protocol establishes, for the first time within the LRTAP Convention regime, an implementation committee that is mandated to review the compliance of parties and provide solutions in cases of non-compliance (Article 7).[19]

The Aarhus Protocol on Heavy Metals of 24 June 1998[20] is designed to control anthropogenic emissions of 'heavy metals'. As a first step, Article 3(1) and (2) of the Protocol requires states parties to reduce their total annual emissions of three particularly harmful metals, namely lead, cadmium and mercury (listed in Annex I) by industrial sources, combustion processes and waste incineration into the atmosphere, applying the best available techniques (identified in Annex III). Moreover, parties undertake to phase out leaded petrol and to take measures to reduce the heavy metal content of various products (Article 3(3) and Annex VI). Even weaker formulated is Article 3(4), according to which each party 'should consider applying' management measures for products containing mercury (Annex VII). Parties must develop and maintain emission inventories for the heavy metals listed in Annex I (Article 3(5)). Exemptions are provided for parties that cannot achieve the limit values established under the Protocol (Article 3(6) and (7)).

The Aarhus Protocol on Persistent Organic Pollutants (POPs), adopted by the Executive Body likewise on 24 June 1998,[21] is aimed at eliminating discharges, emissions and losses of POPs.[22] It focuses on a list of 16 substances singled out according to agreed risk criteria, comprising pesticides, industrial chemicals and contaminants. Each party must take effective measures to (i) eliminate the production and use of the substances listed in Annex I, such as aldrin, chlordane, DDT, dieldrin, endrin, heptachlor, hexachlorobenzene,

[18] Contrary to the 1984 Sulphur Protocol which imposed on all parties the duty to reduce relevant emissions by 30%, the 1994 Protocol specifies the levels of reduction per state.

[19] For a more detailed discussion on the institutional setting of modern compliance control see below Chapter 22.4.

[20] The Protocol entered into force on 29 December 2003 and is binding on 29 parties. It runs parallel to the global Stockholm POPs Convention of 22 May 2001 which entered into force on 17 May 2004. The latter will be dealt with in more detail below in Chapter 15.3.2.

[21] In force since 21 October 2003; at present it is binding on 29 parties.

[22] 'POPs' are 'organic substances that: (i) possess toxic characteristics; (ii) are persistent; (iii) bioaccumulate; (iv) are prone to long-range transboundary atmospheric transport and deposition; and (v) are likely to cause significant adverse human health or environmental effects near to and distant from their sources' (Art 1(7) of the Protocol).

mirex and PCB; (ii) restrict the substances listed in Annex II to the uses described, *eg* DDT for public health protection from diseases such as malaria or encephalitis; and (iii) reduce the total annual emissions of substances listed in Annex III, namely polycyclic aromatic hydrocarbons (PAHs), dioxins/furans and hexachlorobenzene, from the level of emissions in a reference year between 1985 and 1995 (Article 3(1) and (5)(b)). For emissions of dioxins and furans (PCDD/F), parties are required to apply limit values for major stationary sources specified in Annex IV, based on best available techniques to control emissions of POPs laid down in Annex V (Article 3(5)(b)). The Protocol also includes provisions for dealing with the wastes containing, or generated from, listed substances (Article 3(1) and (3)). Moreover, parties must develop strategies, policies and programmes to meet their obligations under the Protocol; promote the provision of information to the general public, including direct users of POPs; facilitate the exchange of information and technology; and encourage related research, development, monitoring and co-operation (Articles 5–8). Parties must report periodically to the Executive Body on measures taken to implement the Protocol (Article 9). Compliance of each party is supervised by the Implementation Committee established by a decision of the Executive Body in 1997 (Article 11).

The eighth and, for the time being, last Protocol to the LRTAP Convention is the Gothenburg Protocol to Abate Acidification, Eutrophication and Ground-Level Ozone of 30 November 1999.[23] Its objective is to control and reduce emissions of sulphur, nitrogen oxides, ammonia and VOCs caused by anthropogenic activities which are likely to cause adverse effects on human health and natural ecosystems, due to acidification, eutrophication or ground-level ozone, and to ensure, 'as far as possible', that 'in the long term in a stepwise approach' atmospheric depositions or concentrations by 2010 do not exceed certain specified critical levels (Article 2). Parties whose emissions have a particularly severe impact on the environment or health and whose emissions are relatively economical to reduce have to make the biggest cuts. Once the Protocol is fully implemented, in Europe sulphur emissions will be cut by 63 per cent, nitrogen oxides by 41 per cent, VOC emissions by 40 per cent, and ammonia emissions by 17 per cent, compared with the 1990 levels (Article 3 and Annex II). In addition, the Protocol sets tight limit values for specific emission sources (*eg* combustion plants, electricity production, dry cleaning and motor vehicles) and requires the best available technologies to be used to keep emissions down (Article 3(2)–(6)). For the first time within the LRTAP Convention framework, the 1999 Protocol specifically requires farmers to take the ammonia control measures specified in Annex IX (Article 3(8)). The remaining provisions, especially Articles 5–9, are similar to the respective provisions in the Protocol on POPs.

13.2.2 Canada–US Air Quality Agreement

For a long time the International Joint Commission, established on the basis of the 1909 Treaty Relating to Boundary Waters,[24] not only managed the shared water resources of

[23] The Protocol entered into force on 17 May 2005 and is binding on 25 parties.
[24] See Chapter 11.4.2.

the United States and Canada, but also dealt with problems of transboundary air pollution between both states, such as those leading to the *Trail Smelter* case. Eventually, on 13 March 1991, the governments of the United States and Canada entered into the Agreement on Air Quality aimed at controlling transboundary air pollution leading to 'acid rain'. In order to achieve this objective the parties committed themselves to establishing specific objectives for emissions limitations or reduction of air pollutants (Articles III and IV). The respective obligations regarding the reduction of emissions of sulphur dioxide and nitrogen oxides are set forth separately and differently for both sides in Annex 1.

In December 2000 the United States and Canada signed a Protocol which added to the 1991 Agreement a new Annex 3, entitled 'Specific Objectives Concerning Ground-level Ozone Precursors' (these precursors had been identified as a major component of smog). Since 2007 both states have engaged in negotiations on a 'Particulate Matter Annex' to the Air Quality Agreement to complement the 2000 Annex, and the original Annex 1 on acid rain.

The United States and Canada are reported to have made considerable progress in reducing emissions of acid rain precursors and smog-forming compounds since 1991. The United States has reduced sulphur dioxide emissions from covered sources by 52 per cent, and nitrogen oxide emissions by 55 per cent, both from 1990 levels. Canada has made similar progress in reducing emissions of these substances.[25]

13.3 Ozone Layer Depletion

13.3.1 Ozone Convention

Alarmed by scientific warnings of the ongoing destruction of the stratospheric ozone layer, resulting in dangerous levels of ultraviolet radiation reaching the earth, in May 1981 the UNEP Governing Council launched negotiations on a global agreement for protecting the ozone layer. By the mid-1980s CFCs[26] were widely suspected of being responsible for this global environmental threat, but scientists had not yet reached absolute certainty about the causes of ozone layer depletion. This is why during the international negotiations from 1982 to 1985 states disagreed about the question whether they should prohibit only the use of CFCs or also their production. In spite of this controversy, the Ozone Convention was signed on 22 March 1985 in Vienna and entered into force on 22 September 1988.

As a framework convention, the Ozone Convention is characterised by its abstractness and broad language. Typical is Article 2(1), which stipulates that '[t]he Parties shall take appropriate measures . . . to protect human health and the environment against adverse effects resulting or likely to result from human activities which modify or are likely to modify the ozone layer'.

[25] See the official statement of the Spokesman of the US Department of State of 19 November 2009, available at www.state.gov/r/pa/prs/ps/2009/nov/132173.htm.

[26] Since long these substances were widely used in air conditioners, refrigerators and hair sprays.

The Ozone Convention neither requires its parties to take concrete measures to reduce ozone-depleting substances, nor gives a precise definition of these substances. It only binds its parties, 'in accordance with the means at their disposal and their capabilities', to co-operate by using 'systematic observations, research and information exchange in order to better understand and assess the effects of human activities on the ozone layer'; to adopt appropriate legislative or administrative measures; to co-operate in formulating 'agreed measures, procedures and standards for the implementation of this Convention, with a view to the adoption of protocols and annexes'; and to 'co-operate with competent international bodies to implement effectively this Convention' (Article 2(2)). According to Article 3, the parties 'undertake, as appropriate, to initiate and co-operate in, directly or through competent international bodies, the conduct of research and scientific assessments', as specified in Annexes I and II. Article 4(2) requires the parties to 'co-operate, consistent with their national laws, regulations and practices and taking into account in particular the need of the developing countries, in promoting . . . the development and transfer of technology and knowledge'. This overly soft obligation 'proved inadequate to satisfy the concerns of developing states that CFC substitutes might not be available to them, or would be prohibitively expensive, and the issue was reopened in later negotiations'.[27] With the COP and a permanent secretariat, the Ozone Convention commands the typical institutional setting of a modern MEA (Articles 6 and 7).[28]

All in all, the Ozone Convention was hardly more than a first step towards an effective international ozone protection regime. Accordingly, states felt prompted to elaborate and adopt, through the COP, a more substantial implementing protocol, as envisaged in Article 6(4)(h).

13.3.2 Montreal Protocol

In late 1986, startled by the discovery of an almost complete destruction of the ozone layer above Antarctica, an Ad Hoc Working Group on the Ozone Convention started to develop a draft for such a protocol under the guidance of UNEP. As early as 16 September 1987, at a diplomatic conference in Montreal, states formally adopted the Montreal Protocol, which entered into force on 1 January 1989. With its ratification by Timor-Leste on 16 September 2009, the Montreal Protocol was the first MEA in history that has achieved universal participation by 196 parties; the same applies to the underlying Ozone Convention.

The strategy pursued by parties under the Montreal Protocol is best reflected in its preamble,[29] which declares them to be

> [d]etermined to protect the ozone layer by taking precautionary measures to control equitably total global emissions of substances that deplete it, with the ultimate objective of their elimination on the basis of developments in scientific knowledge, taking into account technical and economic considerations and bearing in mind the developmental needs of developing countries.

[27] Birnie, Boyle and Redgwell, above n 5, 350.
[28] *Cf* Chapter 17.2.3.
[29] Montreal Protocol, Preamble, 6th indent.

In its original text, the Montreal Protocol set firm targets for reducing and eliminating consumption and production of a range of ozone-depleting substances. Article 2 and Annex A of the Montreal Protocol provided for a complex scheme of 'control measures'. Annex A discerned two groups of 'controlled substances', adding for each of them its ozone-depleting potential, with five CFCs in Group I and three halons in Group II. Article 2 Montreal Protocol, in its original wording, established a limitation and reduction scheme for the consumption and production of all substances listed in Annex A. Under Article 4, within one year of the entry into force of the Protocol, each party was required to ban the import of controlled substances from any non-party state. Article 6 required parties to assess the Article 2 control measures on the basis of available scientific, environmental, technical and economic information.

Ab initio the Montreal Protocol has clearly differentiated between industrialised states ('non-Article 5 parties') and developing countries ('Article 5 parties'): the industrialised states parties have been required to take control measures for some CFCs and halons, while the developing country parties have been granted a grace period allowing them to increase the use of said ozone-depleting substances (ODS) before taking on respective commitments. Thus, the Montreal Protocol was a forerunner of 'common but differentiated responsibilities'.[30] Laid down in Principle 7 of the 1992 Rio Declaration, this concept has gained considerable importance in the post-Rio environmental and developmental relations between North and South.

Aware of the necessity to keep the scheme of ODS controls and reductions as dynamic and flexible as possible, the parties to the Montreal Protocol have provided for the establishment of 'Meetings of the Parties' (MOPs) with the mandate to consider and adopt adjustments and amendments to the Protocol (Article 11(4)(b) and (h)). While adjustments, as referred to in Article 2(9), become legally binding by consensus, and if this cannot be attained, by a two-thirds majority vote by the parties present and voting (simplified procedure), amendments to the Protocol, once adopted by the MOP, become legally binding only if they have been subsequently ratified by a sufficient number of parties.[31]

After the entry into force of the Montreal Protocol the MOPs made ample use of these powers. They have adjusted and/or amended the Protocol four times: in London (1990), Copenhagen (1992), Montreal (1997) and Beijing (1999).

At MOP 2 in London (1990) parties placed more substances under control of the Protocol in two new Annexes. Annex B adds three new groups of controlled substances (additional CFCs, carbon tetrachloride and methyl chloroform); Annex C contains a list of numerous transitional substances. In addition, the parties agreed on the establishment of the 'Multilateral Fund'. There are currently 195 parties to the London Amendment.[32]

MOP 4 in Copenhagen (1992) added controls on methyl bromide, hydrobromochlo-

[30] *Cf* Chapter 9 for details on the concept of common but differentiated responsibilities.

[31] *Cf* Chapters 17.2.3, 17.3.2 and 18.4.2.

[32] See the information available at the website of the UNEP, Ozone Secretariat, Evolution of the Montreal Protocol/Status of Ratification, at http://ozone.unep.org/Ratification_status.

rofluorocarbons (HBFCs) and hydrochlorofluorocarbons (HCFCs), which emerged in the 1990s as substitutes for the older and more ozone-damaging CFCs. Moreover, parties have enacted an innovative non-compliance procedure and established an Implementation Committee with the mandate to examine cases of non-compliance by parties and to recommend ways and means to secure full compliance.[33] To date, 192 parties have ratified the Copenhagen Amendment.[34]

MOP 9, held in Montreal (1997), has not extended controls to new substances, but has provided for controls on the trade in ODSs and licensing procedures: if a party is unable to phase out production of a substance for domestic consumption, it must ban the export of the substance to other states parties for purposes other than its destruction (Article 4A). Moreover, by 1 January 2000 each party had to establish and implement a system for licensing the import and export of new, used, recycled and reclaimed controlled substances in Annexes A, B, C and E (Article 4B). At the time of writing there are 181 parties to the Montreal Amendment.[35]

MOP 11, held in Beijing (1999), listed bromochloromethane as a new controlled substance and introduced additional controls on HCFCs (Annex C, Group I substances). Moreover, it instituted new reporting obligations for quarantine and pre-shipment uses of methyl bromide. To date, the Beijing Amendment is binding on 165 parties.[36]

Before MOP 19 was held in Montreal in autumn 2007, the ODS control schedule of the Montreal Protocol, as amended and adjusted over the years, was as follows: Non-Article 5 parties (*ie* industrialised states parties) were required to phase out production and consumption of halons by 1994; CFCs, CTC, HBFCs and methyl chloroform by 1996; bromochloromethane by 2002; and methyl bromide by 2005. Consumption of hydrochlorofluorocarbons (HCFCs) is to be phased out by non-Article 5 parties by 2030 and by Article 5 parties by 2040, with production to have been stabilised by 2004. Article 5 parties (*ie* developing states parties) were required to phase out production and consumption of bromochloromethane by 2002. They must still phase out production and consumption of CFCs, halons and CTC by 2010, and methyl chloroform and methyl bromide by 2015. Production of HCFCs in Article 5 countries must be stabilised by 2016. As for non-Article 5 parties, there are exemptions to these phase-outs to allow for certain uses for which no feasible alternatives exist or in particular circumstances.[37]

At MOP 19, the parties decided to adjust their commitments related to the phase-out of HCFCs as follows: Non-Article 5 (developed country) parties are required to reduce production and consumption of HCFCs by 75 per cent by 2010, by 90 per cent by 2015 with a final phase-out in 2020. Article 5 (developing country) parties must freeze production and consumption of HCFCs by 2013, and cut both production and consumption

[33] For a more detailed discussion see Chapter 22.3.

[34] *Cf* the website of the UNEP Ozone Secretariat, above n 32.

[35] See *ibid*.

[36] *Cf ibid*.

[37] See Summary of the Nineteenth Meeting of the Parties to the Montreal Protocol, 17–21 September 2007, Earth Negotiations Bulletin, vol 19 no 60 (24 September 2007) 3. *Cf* E Louka, *International Environmental Law. Fairness, Effectiveness and World Order* (Cambridge 2006) 347 *et seq*.

by 10 per cent by 2015, 35 per cent by 2020, and 67.5 per cent by 2025 with a final phase-out in 2030.[38]

MOP 19, in its 'Montreal Declaration', has celebrated

> the successful conclusion of a landmark agreement on the accelerated phase-out of hydrochlorofluorocarbons thereby making great strides in the global effort to protect the ozone layer and at the same time providing opportunities for further beneficial impacts on the environment including for climate change.[39]

As a result of the accelerated process of phasing-out HCFCs, the use of hydrofluorocarbons (HFCs) as replacement chemicals for the proscribed HCFCs has increased considerably. While HFCs do not show any adverse impact on the ozone layer, there is a fear among scientists that these synthetic gases may contribute considerably to global warming; at worst, HFCs could by the year 2050 be contributing the equivalent of 45 per cent of CO_2 emissions.[40]

This is why the debates at MOP 21, held in Port Ghalib, Egypt (November 2009), have centred on two proposals to add HFCs to the list of controlled substances under the Montreal Protocol.[41] Concerns that the Kyoto Protocol already covers HFCs can be rebutted by arguing that the Kyoto Protocol addresses emissions, whereas the ozone regime targets production and consumption. Thus, both protocols can be considered to complement each other in their effort to combat global warming rather than to be in conflict.[42]

Meanwhile, the stringent control and reduction regime operating under the repeatedly amended and adjusted Montreal Protocol has been beginning to take long-term effect. Today, 97 per cent of all ozone-depleting substances are controlled. It is estimated that 'without the Montreal Protocol, by the year 2050 ozone depletion would have risen to at least 50 per cent in the northern hemisphere's mid latitude and 70 per cent in the southern mid latitudes, about ten times worse than current levels'.[43] Global observations have verified that atmospheric levels of key ozone-depleting substances are going down. With the full implementation of the Montreal Protocol's provisions, the ozone layer can be hoped to return to pre-1980 levels by the years 2050–2075.[44]

[38] UN Doc UNEP/OzLPro19/7, 21 September 2007, Annex II: Adjustments agreed by the Nineteenth Meeting of the Parties relating to the controlled substances in group I of Annex C of the Montreal Protocol (hydrochlorofluorocarbons), 62 *et seq*.

[39] Annex IV, *ibid*, 64 *et seq*.

[40] UNEP Press Release, 'Upgrading Ozone Layer Treaty to Assist in Combating Climate Change Key Issue at International Meeting in Egypt: 21st Meeting of the Parties to the Montreal Protocol on Substances That Deplete the Ozone Layer' (2 November 2009), available at www.unep.org/Documents.Multilingual/Default.asp?DocumentID=602&ArticleID=6356&l=en&t=long.

[41] The proposals have been submitted by the Federal States of Micronesia and Mauritius, on the one hand, and Canada, Mexico and the United States, on the other. At the end of COP 21 the issue was left undecided. See for the whole UN Doc UNEP/OzLPro21/3 (27 August 2009), and UN Doc UNEP/OzLPro21/3/Add1 (17 September 2009).

[42] See J Depledge, 'The "Climate MOP"' (2009) 39 *Environmental Policy and Law* 274 *et seq*.

[43] See UNEP Press Release, 'Ozone Treaty Anniversary Gifts Big Birthday Present to Human Health and Combating of Climate Change' (16 September 2009), available at www.unep.org/Documents.Multilingual/Default.asp?DocumentID=596&ArticleID=6305&l=en&t=long.

[44] *Cf ibid*.

13.4 Global Climate Change

13.4.1 Climate Change Convention

Based on the UN General Assembly Resolution 45/212 (1990)[45] the Intergovernmental Negotiating Committee (INC) was established to elaborate a framework convention on climate change. As a result of a short negotiating process, the UNFCCC was adopted by the INC in May 2002. Only one month later it was signed at the Rio Conference by 155 states and the European Community. In force since 21 March 1994, with currently 194 parties the UNFCCC enjoys an almost universal membership.[46]

The UNFCCC pursues what has been called a 'double track approach': Its primary objective is 'to achieve . . . stabilization of greenhouse gas concentrations in the atmosphere at a level that would prevent dangerous anthropogenic interference with the climate system' (Article 2). This primary objective, usually referred to as 'mitigation', is complemented by the secondary objective of 'adaptation' to the change which is reflected in various provisions, such as Article 3(2) and Article 4(1)(e) UNFCCC.[47]

In their actions to achieve this objective, the parties to the UNFCCC shall be guided by a number of precepts that are classified in Article 3 as 'principles' from which some rather weakly formulated obligations flow: the parties, according to Article 3(1),

> should protect the climate system for the benefit of present and future generations of humankind, on the basis of equity and in accordance with their common but differentiated responsibilities. Accordingly, the developed country Parties should take the lead in combating climate change and the adverse effects thereof.

All parties 'should take precautionary measures to anticipate, prevent or minimize the causes of climate change and mitigate its adverse effects' (Article 3(2)). Moreover, all parties 'have a right to, and should, promote sustainable development' (Article 3(3)).

Article 4 sets up a system of clearly differentiated commitments of developed countries on the one hand, and developing countries on the other. The developed country parties and the country parties 'undergoing the process of transition to a market economy' listed in Annex I to the UNFCCC (Annex I parties) are required to adopt national policies to mitigate climate change by limiting GHG emissions and protecting and enhancing GHG sinks[48] and reservoirs,[49] 'with the aim of returning individually or jointly to their 1990 levels of anthropogenic emissions of carbon dioxide and other greenhouse gases not

[45] UNGA Res 45/212 (21 December 1990).

[46] See http://unfccc.int/essential_background/convention/status_of_ratification/items/2631.php.

[47] See M Bothe and E Rehbinder, 'Climate Change as a Problem of Law and Policy' in M Bothe and E Rehbinder (eds), *Climate Change Policy* (Utrecht 2005) 1, 4.

[48] 'Sink' means 'any process, activity or mechanism which removes a greenhouse gas, an aerosol or a precursor of a greenhouse gas from the atmosphere' (Art 1(8) UNFCCC). *Eg* forests absorbing carbon from the atmosphere are 'sinks' whilst forests with balanced carbon flows act as 'reservoirs'. As a result of deforestation, they can also become sources of GHGs; see F Yamin and J Depledge, *The International Climate Change Regime. A Guide to Rules, Institutions and Procedures* (Cambridge 2004) 76 *et seq*.

[49] 'Reservoir' means 'a component or components of the climate system where a greenhouse gas or a precursor of a greenhouse gas is stored' (Art 1(7) UNFCCC). *Eg* oceans and soils are reservoirs of carbon (*ibid*).

controlled by the Montreal Protocol'(Article 4(2)(a) and (b)). By contrast, the developing country parties only have to meet a couple of procedural obligations, such as establishing inventories of anthropogenic emissions by sources and removals by sinks; developing and implementing national and, where appropriate, regional programmes containing measures to mitigate climate change; and communicating information related to implementation (Article 4(1)(a), (b), (j)). As to the question of who bears the compliance costs of developing countries, the developed country parties listed in Annex II are required to provide 'new and additional financial resources to meet the agreed full costs incurred by developing country Parties in complying with their obligations' under the UNFCCC (Article 4(3)).

The institutional setting of the UNFCCC comprises a conference of the parties as supreme treaty body, a permanent secretariat, two subsidiary bodies (*ie* the Subsidiary Body for Scientific and Technological Advice, and the Subsidiary Body for Implementation), and a financial mechanism (Articles 7–11).

13.4.2 Kyoto Protocol

The first meeting of the Conference of the Parties to the UNFCCC (COP 1) took place at Berlin in spring 1995. Conforming to Article 4(2)(d), it reviewed the obligations incurred by the Annex II parties under Article 4(2)(a) and (b) and found them inadequate. Accordingly, COP 1 adopted a ministerial declaration known as the 'Berlin Mandate'[50] in which it agreed 'to take appropriate action for the period beyond 2000', including the strengthening of the commitments of the Annex I parties in Article 4(2)(a) and (b) UNFCCC, 'through the adoption of a protocol or another legal instrument'. Moreover, the 'Berlin Mandate' prescribed that the new negotiating process 'should begin without delay and be conducted as a matter of urgency, in an open-ended ad hoc group of Parties hereby established'.

Only two years later, in December 1997, COP 3, held at Kyoto, fulfilled the 'Berlin Mandate' and adopted the Protocol to the UN Framework Convention on Climate Change (Kyoto Protocol). The US Clinton administration signed the Kyoto Protocol on 12 November 1998, but the US Congress refused to ratify it, citing potential damage to US economic development. On 28 March 2001 the Bush administration even announced the withdrawal of the United States from the Kyoto Protocol, arguing that the Protocol was 'too costly' and describing it as 'an unrealistic and ever-tightening straitjacket'.[51] As prescribed in its Article 25 the Kyoto Protocol cannot enter into force unless it is ratified by at least 55 parties to the UNFCCC, incorporating Annex I parties accounting for at least 55 per cent of the total Annex I CO_2 emissions for 1990. As the United States—which, in 1990, alone produced 36.1 per cent of global CO_2 emissions[52]—could not be expected to ratify the Protocol in the medium term, the latter's fate hinged on its ratification by

[50] See Decision 1/CP1 (7 April 1995) in UN Doc FCCC/CP/1995/7/Add1 (6 June 1995) 4.

[51] *Cf* P Saundry (topic ed), 'Kyoto Protocol and the United States' in CJ Cleveland (ed), *The Encyclopedia of Earth* (Washington, DC 2006), available at www.eoearth.org/article/Kyoto_Protocol_and_the_United_States.

[52] Report of the Conference of the Parties on its Third Session, Held at Kyoto from 1 to 11 December 1997, UN Doc FCCC/CP/1997/7/Add1 (25 March 1998) 60.

Canada and the Russian Federation.[53] Eventually, in November 2004, Russia ratified the Kyoto Protocol, thus clearing the way for its entry into force on 16 February 2005.[54] Currently, there are 192 parties to the Kyoto Protocol, with the United States still refusing to participate.

Driven by the concept of 'common but differentiated responsibilities' as expressed in Principle 7 of the Rio Declaration,[55] the Kyoto Protocol imposes on its parties highly asymmetric obligations. The Annex I (developed country) parties to the UNFCCC are required under the Protocol to reduce their GHG emissions, while the developing country parties must only meet some procedural obligations, such as reporting. Thus, the latter states could defend their position of 'no emissions cut' reached in the UNFCCC. Not even the rapidly developing countries which show considerable increases of GHG emissions, such as China, India and Brazil, are required to make any emissions cuts.

Unlike the UNFCCC, the Kyoto Protocol sets out quantified emissions reduction targets and a timetable for their achievement. All Annex I parties listed in Annex B to the Protocol[56] are obliged to reduce their overall emissions of defined GHGs[57] by at least 5 per cent below 1990 levels in the commitment period from 2008 to 2012. The said Annex B lists differentiated targets for individual parties. For instance, the United States agreed to an emission cut of 7 per cent, Japan of 6 per cent, and the EC of 8 per cent. Canada and Japan each accepted a 6 per cent reduction, while New Zealand and the Russian Federation were permitted to stabilise their GHG emissions at 1990 levels. Australia and Iceland were even allowed to make emissions increases of respectively 8 and 10 per cent above 1990 levels. Considering that the Annex B parties are burdened with reducing their GHG emissions and, at the same time, transferring financial resources and technology to the developing country parties in order to help them fulfil their procedural duties, the asymmetry of the parties' obligations under the Kyoto Protocol is striking, resulting in what may be called 'benign' or 'positive' discrimination in favour of the Third World.[58]

Like the UNFCCC, the Kyoto Protocol favours the strategy of 'mitigating climate change through the reduction of GHG emissions' over the complementary strategy of 'adaptation to climate change'. As will be shown below, the latter option has been more clearly advanced in the subsequent period between the 1998 Buenos Aires Plan of Action and the 2001 Marrakesh Accords.[59]

The Annex I parties to the UNFCCC can meet their obligations under the Kyoto

[53] In 1990, Russia emitted 17.4% of global greenhouse gases while Canada accounted for 3.3% (*ibid*).

[54] Altogether the parties to the Kyoto Protocol are responsible for 63.7% of emissions, see http://unfccc.int/kyoto_protocol/status_of_ratification/items/2613.php.

[55] *Cf* Chapter 9.

[56] The Annex B parties include Australia, Canada, the European Community (EC), France, Germany, Italy, Japan, New Zealand, Poland, the Russian Federation, Spain, Sweden, the United Kingdom, and the United States.

[57] The list of GHGs in Annex A to the Protocol includes: carbon dioxide, methane, nitrous oxide, hydrofluorocarbons, perfluorocarbons and sulphur hexafluoride.

[58] *Cf* U Beyerlin, 'Bridging the North–South Divide in International Environmental Law' (2006) 66 *ZaöRV* 259, 278.

[59] See at Section 13.4.3. *Cf* L Nurse and R Moore, 'Adaptation to Global Climate Change: An Urgent Requirement for Small Islands Developing States' (2005) 14 *RECIEL* 100; EL Schipper, 'Conceptual History of Adaptation in the UNFCCC Process' (2006) 15 *RECIEL* 82.

Protocol either by cutting their GHG emissions or increasing their removals by sinks, or both. Under Article 3(3) and (4) Kyoto Protocol Annex I parties are permitted to take into account land use, land-use change and forestry (LULUCF) activities in meeting their emissions reduction commitments under Article 3(1) of the Protocol. Article 3(3) of the Protocol provides that

> [t]he net changes in greenhouse gas emissions by sources and removals by sinks resulting from direct human-induced land-use change and forestry activities, limited to afforestation, reforestation and deforestation since 1990, measured as verifiable changes in carbon stocks in each commitment period, shall be used to meet the commitments under this Article of each Party included in Annex I.

Each Annex I party must report on and account for emissions and removals in the first commitment period on lands on which these activities have occurred. Article 3(4) of the Protocol requires the COP 'serving as the meeting of the Parties to this Protocol' (MOP), as soon as possible, to

> decide upon modalities, rules and guidelines as to how, and which, additional human-induced activities related to changes in greenhouse gas emissions by sources and removals by sinks in the agricultural soils and the land-use change and forestry categories shall be added to, or subtracted from, the assigned amounts for Parties included in Annex I.

While any such decision mandatorily applies in the second and subsequent commitment periods, a party may choose to apply such a decision for the first commitment period provided that the 'additional human-induced activities' have taken place since 1990 (Article 3(4), sentences 3 and 4).

As the wording of Article 3(3) and (4) left many questions of definition and interpretation unsolved, both provisions were sources of considerable disagreement among the parties to the Protocol. The disputes ranged from definitional problems, raised by some key terms in Article 3(3) such as 'human-induced land-use change', 'forestry activities' or 'afforestation, reforestation and deforestation', to some inconsistencies with regard to the conditions for accounting LULUCF activities under Article 3(3) and (4). Thus, it was clear from the outset that it would be incumbent on subsequent COPs/MOPs to clarify and/or specify the meaning and effects of these provisions.[60]

Perhaps the most innovative feature of the Protocol's regulatory system is the high degree of flexibility in achieving climate change mitigation. The Protocol enables Annex I parties to meet their emissions reduction commitments in a cost-effective manner through employing its 'flexibility mechanisms', namely Joint Implementation (JI, Article 6), the Clean Development Mechanism (CDM, Article 12), and Emissions Trading (ET, Article 17). The rationale behind all three flexibility mechanisms is 'a process of compensation between a non-reduction in one place and an increased reduction in another'. The mechanisms 'allow reductions to be made where it is economically speaking most efficient'. Thus, their basic idea is 'to achieve the overall reduction target at lower cost'.[61]

Article 6(1) Kyoto Protocol enables Annex I parties under certain conditions to fulfil their emissions reduction commitments under Article 3 in the way that

[60] See below at Section 13.4.3.

[61] Bothe and Rehbinder, above n 47, 6.

> any Party included in Annex I may transfer to, or acquire from, any other such Party emission reduction units resulting from projects aimed at reducing anthropogenic emissions by sources or enhancing anthropogenic removals by sinks of greenhouse gases in any sector of the economy.

However, any such JI must result in an emissions reduction or removal by sinks 'that is additional to any that would otherwise occur', as well as 'supplemental to domestic actions' (Article 6(1)(b) and (d)).

Contrary to JI, the CDM, as defined in Article 12 Kyoto Protocol, allows for interaction between Annex I and non-Annex I parties in the following way: Annex I parties may engage in, and finance, 'project activities resulting in certified emission reductions' that take place in non-Annex I parties which do not have quantified reduction obligations of their own. The beneficial effect of such undertakings is that the Annex I parties concerned 'may use the certified emission reductions accruing from such project activities to contribute to compliance with part of their quantified emission limitation and reduction commitments under Article 3' (Article 12(3)(b)). Again, the emission reductions achieved in the host country must be 'additional to any that would occur in the absence of the certified project activity' (Article 12(5)(c)).

Based on the idea that

> [a] regulator sets a cap on aggregate emissions, distributes the right to emit to regulated facilities (with their emission allowances totalling less than the aggregate emissions), and permits the market to determine the emission price and degree of abatement at individual facilities,[62]

Article 17 Kyoto Protocol allows Annex B parties, a subgroup of the parties listed in Annex I, to 'participate in emissions trading for the purpose of fulfilling their commitments under Article 3'. This cryptic regulation is complemented by the requirement that any such trading must be 'supplemental' to domestic reduction actions. Consciously keeping away from establishing a fully fledged regulatory regime for ET, Article 17 mandates the COP to 'define the relevant principles, modalities, rules and guidelines, in particular for verification, reporting and accountability for emissions trading'.

Articles 5, 7 and 9 Kyoto Protocol impose on Annex I parties detailed reporting obligations which build upon the respective procedures established under the UNFCCC. By contrast, instead of making its own rules on compliance, Article 18 of the Protocol mandates the COP/MOP in a clear-cut way to address this question at its very first session.[63]

Ultimately, many of the above-named rules of the Kyoto Protocol, particularly those on accounting LULUCF activities under Article 3(3) and (4), are rudimentary, fragmentary or ambiguous with the consequence that they are not fully operational in practice. Accordingly, the Kyoto Protocol has been criticised as being 'the most recent in a long series of first steps in international environmental law' that 'do more harm than good by appearing to provide solutions and remedies where none exist'.[64] As a matter of fact, the Protocol does not satisfy the demands of the 'framework convention and protocol approach':[65] rather than fulfilling its role to make the UNFCCC fully applicable in prac-

[62] Birnie, Boyle and Redgwell, above n 5, 364.

[63] For more details *cf* below Chapter 22.

[64] B Pardy, 'The Kyoto Protocol: Bad News for the Global Environment' (2004) 14 *Journal of Environmental Law and Practice* 27, 40, 42.

[65] *Cf* Chapter 18.3.1.

tice, the Protocol itself shows numerous deficiencies and is therefore far from being operational. This is why right from the start the parties to the Protocol were required to provide for its functioning.

13.4.3 From Kyoto to Copenhagen: Building a Post-2012 Climate Protection Regime

Since 1997 a very broad and intensive negotiation process on operationalising the Kyoto Protocol and building a post-2012 climate regime has been running under the UNFCCC and the Kyoto Protocol, especially during the following regular COP/MOP meetings: COP 4, held at Buenos Aires in November 1998; COP 5, held at Bonn in October/November 1999; COP 6, held at The Hague in November 2000; Resumed COP 6 *bis*, held at Bonn in July 2001; COP 7, held at Marrakesh in November 2001; COP 8, held at New Delhi in October/November 2002; COP 9, held at Milan in December 2003; COP 10, held at Buenos Aires in December 2004; COP 11/MOP 1, held at Montreal in November/December 2005; COP 12/MOP 2, held at Nairobi in November 2006; COP 13/MOP 3, held in Bali in December 2007; COP 14/MOP 4, held at Poznán, Poland, in December 2008; and COP 15/MOP 5, held at Copenhagen in December 2009. The negotiations under the aegis of the COP/MOP have been accompanied by several external high-level discussions on climate change, such as at the UN Secretary General's Summit on Climate Change in New York on 22 September 2009, and the talks within the meetings of the 'Group of Eight' ('G 8', 2005–2009) and the 'Group of Twenty' ('G 20', 2008–2009).[66]

A first step towards making the Kyoto Protocol fully applicable and developing an efficient post-2012 climate regime was certainly the 1998 Buenos Aires Plan of Action (BAPA). Adopted by COP 4, it set COP 6 at The Hague (2000) as the deadline for reaching agreement on the operational details of the Kyoto Protocol and on strengthening implementation of the UNFCCC.

However, COP 6 finally failed to reach compromises between the European Union, G-77/China and the 'Umbrella Group'[67] on a number of key issues, such as allowing credits for carbon sinks in forests and agricultural lands, the consequences of non-compliance with Article 3(1) of the Protocol, and financial assistance of developing countries severely suffering from the adverse effects of climate change. COP 6 was suspended without agreement, but resumed at Bonn in July 2001.[68] Termed 'COP 6 *bis*', this meeting was overshadowed by the fact that a few months ago the newly elected US president, George

[66] For a survey of all these negotiations see SC Mazlum *et al* (eds), *Post-2012 Climate Change Negotiations Guidebook*: *Turkey* (co-ordinated by the Turkish Ministry of Environment and Forestry) (Ankara 2009), available at www.undp.org.tr/energEnvirDocs/KyotoSon.pdf.

[67] The Umbrella Group is an informal association of developed countries which was formed in the aftermath of the adoption of the Kyoto Protocol in 1997. It usually consists of Australia, Canada, Iceland, Japan, New Zealand, Norway, the Russian Federation, Ukraine, and the United States (www.sourcewatch.org.index.php?title=Umbrella_Group).

[68] For a detailed discussion on COP 6 see L Rajamani, 'Re-negotiating Kyoto: A Review of the Sixth Conference of Parties to the Framework Convention on Climate Change' (2001) 12 *Colorado Journal of International Environmental Law and Policy* 201, 209 *et seq*; B Buchner, 'The Dynamics of the Climate Negotiations: A Focus on the Development and Outcomes from The Hague to Delhi' in Bothe and Rehbinder (eds), above n 47, 30 *et seq*.

W Bush, had expressed his opposition to the Kyoto Protocol, which he believed to be 'fatally flawed', and refused to submit it to the Congress for ratification.[69] Consequently, the US delegation to COP 6 *bis* did not participate in the negotiations related to the Protocol. This setback notwithstanding, COP 6 *bis* resulted in the Bonn Agreements which contained a political understanding on the following concerns of the BAPA that had not been met at The Hague: establishing detailed accounting rules regarding LULUCF for the first commitment period 2008–2012; laying out the principles, nature and scope of the Kyoto flexibility mechanisms; developing the key issues of a compliance system; recognising the need for 'new and additional funding' and establishing new funds.[70] The positive effect of COP 6 *bis* was that it refuted commentators who had forecast the end of the Protocol and 'a descent into environmental anarchy'.[71]

At COP 7, held at Marrakesh in November 2001, states parties adopted a comprehensive package of draft decisions designated to be adopted by a subsequent COP/MOP 1 after the entry into force of the Kyoto Protocol. Built on the Bonn Agreements, the Marrakesh Accords constitute what the Climate Change Secretariat has called in its 2002 Guide to the UNFCCC and Kyoto Protocol 'a detailed rulebook for the Kyoto Protocol' that marks 'the close of a major negotiating cycle'.[72] The Marrakesh Accords address, *inter alia*, the flexibility mechanisms, compliance control, capacity building and funding.[73]

As indicated above, Article 3(3) and (4) Kyoto Protocol contains rules governing the LULUCF sector. As specified by the Marrakesh Accords, these rules include four main elements: (1) a set of principles to guide LULUCF activities; (2) a list of eligible activities; (3) common definitions; and (4) a four-tier capping system limiting the use of LULUCF activities to meet emissions targets. Most important in this respect is that the Marrakesh Accords designate four eligible activities, namely forest management, cropland management, grazing land management and revegetation, in addition to those already mentioned in Article 3(3) of the Protocol. Consequently, emissions and removals from all these activities shall be now accounted for to help Annex I parties meet their emission reduction commitments.[74]

As regards the flexibility mechanisms, rather than placing a numerical cap on their use to fulfil emissions reduction commitments, the Marrakesh Accords provide that 'the use of the mechanisms shall be supplemental to domestic action and that domestic action shall

[69] See Summary of the Resumed Sixth Session of the Conference of the Parties to the UNFCCC: 16–27 July 2001, Earth Negotiations Bulletin vol 12 no 176 (30 July 2001) 2.

[70] For more detailed information on the outcome of COP 6 *bis* see again Earth Negotiations Bulletin, *ibid*, 3 *et seq*. See also Buchner, above n 68, 32 *et seq*.

[71] See Earth Negotiations Bulletin, *ibid*, 13.

[72] Climate Change Secretariat, *A Guide to the Climate Change Convention and Its Kyoto Protocol* (Bonn 2002) 7, available on the UNFCCC website: www.unfccc.int.

[73] For a survey of the COP 7 decisions taken at Marrakesh see P Sands, *Principles of International Environmental Law* (2nd edn Cambridge 2003) 377 *et seq*.

[74] See Decision 11/CP7, paras 1 and 6; *cf* Climate Change Secretariat, above n 72, 25 *et seq*. For a more detailed discussion see Rajamani, above n 68, 221 *et seq*; SA Kennett, 'Carbon Sinks and the Kyoto Protocol: Legal and Policy Mechanisms for Domestic Implementation' (2003) 21 *Journal of Energy and Natural Resources Law* 252, 254 *et seq*.

thus constitute a significant element of the effort made' by Annex I Parties in meeting their commitments under Article 3(1) of the Protocol.[75]

'Certified emission reductions' (CERs), 'emissions reduction units' (ERUs) and 'assigned amount units' (AAUs) under Articles 6, 12 and 17 of the Protocol, as well as 'removal units' generated by sink activities according to Article 3(3) and (4) of the Protocol, may be used to meet the emissions reduction commitments of Annex I parties under Article 3(1) of the Protocol.[76]

Three new funds relating to combating climate change were established: an adaptation fund under the Kyoto Protocol; a special climate change fund designed to finance projects relating, *inter alia*, to capacity building, adaptation, technology transfer, and climate change mitigation; and a least developed countries (LDCs) fund that will support a special work programme to assist LDCs. All three new funds will be managed by the Global Environment Facility (GEF) which operates as the financial mechanism of the UNFCCC and the Protocol.[77]

Finally, the COP decision on the establishment of the Compliance Committee consisting of a 'facilitative branch' and an 'enforcement branch'[78] will be separately discussed in Chapter 22.3.

The adoption of the Marrakesh Accords raised hopes that they would enable widespread ratification of the Kyoto Protocol and its rapid entry into force, preferably at the 2002 Johannesburg Summit. However, the Protocol's entry into force took another three and a half years to become a reality.

Eventually, in late 2005 at Montreal, the parties to the UNFCCC and the parties to the Protocol convened for the first time together as the Conference of the Parties to the UNFCCC and the Meeting of the Parties to the Kyoto Protocol (COP 11/MOP 1). It was evident to all negotiators at Montreal that the very future of the Kyoto process was at stake. However, they failed to agree on more than a political call to negotiate deeper cuts in future GHG emissions, notably with a view to the period after 2012 when the first commitment period expires. Institutionally, COP 11/MOP 1 decided to establish a new subsidiary body, namely the Ad Hoc Working Group on Further Commitments for Annex I Parties under the Kyoto Protocol (AWG-KP).[79]

In December 2007, at COP 13/MOP 3, held in Bali, the parties agreed upon the Bali Roadmap which proved to be an important stage in the cumbersome efforts to develop a post-2012 climate change regime. Central to this roadmap was a COP/MOP decision, titled the Bali Action Plan (BAP),[80] which made plain that the road from Bali to Copen-

[75] Decision 15/CP7, para 1 in UN Doc FCCC/CP/2001/13/Add2 (21 January 2002) 3.

[76] Decision 15/CP7, para 6, *ibid*, 4. *Cf* Climate Change Secretariat, above n 72, 27 *et seq*.

[77] Decision 7/CP7 (10 November 2001) in UN Doc FCCC/CP/2001/13/Add1 (21 January 2002) 43; Climate Change Secretariat, above n 72, 15. *Cf* below Chapter 23.4.2.

[78] Decision 24/CP7 (10 November 2001) in UN Doc FCCC/CP/2001/13/Add3 (21 January 2002) 64.

[79] For a detailed review of COP 11/MOP 1 see Earth Negotiations Bulletin, vol 12 no 291 (12 December 2005); C Bausch and M Mehling, '"Alive and Kicking": The First Meeting of the Parties to the Kyoto Protocol' (2006) 15 *RECIEL* 193.

[80] Decision 1/CP13 (14–15 December 2007) in UN Doc FCCC/CP/2007/6/Add1 (14 March 2008) 3. For a detailed account of the BAP see Earth Negotiations Bulletin vol 12 no 354 (18 December 2007) particularly 15 *et seq*; Birnie, Boyle and Redgwell, above n 5, 375 *et seq*; MJ Mace, 'The Bali Road Map: Can it Deliver an Equitable post-2012 Climate Agreement for Small Island States?' (2008) 17 *RECIEL* 183; J Depledge,

hagen would involve two fully fledged negotiation tracks, namely the 'Convention track' concerning all parties to the UNFCCC, and the 'Kyoto track' concerning only the parties to the Kyoto Protocol.

As regards the 'Convention track', the BAP contains two important decisions. Firstly, a two-year comprehensive negotiation process was launched

> to enable the full, effective and sustained implementation of the Convention through long-term cooperative action, now, up to and beyond 2012, in order to reach an agreed outcome and adopt a decision at its fifteenth session [in December 2009 at Copenhagen].[81]

Secondly, a new subsidiary body, the 'Ad Hoc Working Group on Long-term Cooperative Action under the Convention' (AWG-LCA), was established with the mandate to 'complete its work in 2009 and present the outcome of its work to the Conference of the Parties for adoption at its fifteenth session'.[82] The new AWG-LCA is the only body where all states, including the United States and developing countries, participate in discussions on quantified emission limitation and reduction objectives. It was decided that the AWG-LCA should address '[a] shared vision for long-term cooperative action, including a long-term global goal for emission reductions, to achieve the ultimate objective of the Convention', as well as '[e]nhanced national/international action on mitigation of climate change'. Parties agreed that such action requires consideration of '[m]easurable, reportable and verifiable nationally appropriate mitigation commitments or actions, including quantified emission limitation and reduction objectives, by all developed country Parties', as well as '[n]ationally appropriate mitigation actions by developing country Parties in the context of sustainable development, supported and enabled by technology, financing and capacity-building, in a measurable, reportable and verifiable manner'.[83]

As regards the 'Kyoto track', the AWG-KP considered in Bali the focus of its future work. It adopted conclusions referring to some key findings of the IPCC that global GHG emissions must peak in the next 10–15 years and that Annex I parties are required to reduce their emissions by 25–40 per cent below 1990 levels by 2020. However, it is important to note that the parties convened in Bali did not agree on these targets.

The next regular meeting of the COP/MOP was held at Poznán, Poland, in December 2008. COP 14/MOP 4 was a classic 'in-between' negotiating event marking the midway point between Bali and Copenhagen. It did not bring about any clarification on substance and form of Copenhagen's prospective outcome. Its only concrete outcome is the operationalisation of the Adaptation Fund. Although the Fund had been already established by COP 7 at Marrakesh in 2001, the respective institutional arrangements were finalised only at the Bali meeting in December 2007. At Poznán, the Fund has been expected to start

'High Politics, High Theatrics in Bali' (2008) 38 *Environmental Policy and Law* 14; C Spence, K Kulovesi, M Gutiérrez and M Muñoz, 'Great Expectations: Understanding Bali and the Climate Change Negotiations Process' (2008) 17 *RECIEL* 142.

[81] Para 1 BAP, Decision 1/CP13, *ibid*, 3.

[82] Para 2 BAP, *ibid*, 5.

[83] Sub-paras 1(b)(i) and 1(b)(ii) BAP, *ibid*, 3.

financing adaption projects and programmes in developing countries in 2009. However, parties were not able to secure additional resources for the Fund.[84]

The AWG-LCA and the AWG-KP, the two key bodies for processing the Bali Roadmap, held, mostly in parallel to each other, four negotiating sessions in 2008: Bangkok (March/April), Bonn (June), Accra (August) and Poznán (December). In 2009 both subsidiary bodies met at Bonn (March/April, June and August), at Bangkok (September/October) and at Barcelona (November). During all its meetings the AWG-LCA was engaged in elaborating a manageable draft negotiating text for long-term co-operative action beyond 2012 with a view to reaching an agreement at Copenhagen in late 2009. The AWG-KP tried to develop a proposal for amendments to the Kyoto Protocol, with a focus on agreeing on further emission reduction commitments for Annex I parties in the post-2012 period. A key issue cutting across the two AWGs was the legal form that the expected outcome at Copenhagen should take. Unfortunately, both bodies did not make significant progress in laying solid ground for an effective post-2012 climate change regime.[85]

The long-awaited Copenhagen Conference (COP 15/MOP 5), attended by around 115 world leaders and more than 40000 registered participants, was one of the largest environmental meetings in history. It took place at Copenhagen from 7 to 19 December 2009.[86] However, the opening statements of major states groups, namely the G-77 and China, the AOSIS, the European Union (EU) and the Umbrella Group (including, *inter alia*, Australia, Canada, Russia and the United States) at COP 15/MOP 5 indicated from the outset that the Copenhagen Conference would have considerable difficulties in meeting the extremely high hopes which the state community and the world public had placed on it.[87] The negotiations to develop a post-2012 climate change regime at Copenhagen suffered seriously from the severe dichotomy of interests between the aforementioned major groups that had already impeded the two-year negotiating process under the BAP.[88] The EU took the position that developed countries should collectively reduce their GHG emissions by 25–40 per cent by 2020, and respectively by 80–95 per cent by 2050, compared to 1990 levels; the Umbrella Group supported a limit of 2°C on global temperature rise and a 50 per cent reduction in global emissions by 2050 (including the developing countries); the AOSIS called for an agreement on emission reductions by all major emitting countries which would limit temperature increases to below 1.5°C and atmospheric GHG concentrations to 350 ppm; and the G-77 and China continued to object to the proposals that developing countries should undertake binding emission

[84] For a review of the 2008 Poznán meeting see Earth Negotiations Bulletin vol 12 no 395 (15 December 2008); J Depledge, 'Poznan: Midway to Copenhagen' (2009) 39 *Environmental Policy and Law* 24; T Santarius, C Arens, U Eichhorst, D Kiyar, F Mersmann, HE Ott, F Rudolph, W Sterk and R Watanabe, 'Pit Stop Poznan. An Analysis of Negotiations on the Bali Action Plan at the Stopover to Copenhagen' (2009) 6 *Journal for European Environmental and Planning Law* 75.

[85] For a survey of the work of both AWGs see Earth Negotiations Bulletin vol 12 no 459 (22 December 2009) 2 *et seq*; J Depledge, 'Spring 2008 Climate Meetings: Bangkok and Bonn' (2008) 38 *Environmental Policy and Law* 194; *id*, 'Bonn Climate Talks: The End of the Beginning' (2009) 39 *Environmental Policy and Law* 136.

[86] See Earth Negotiations Bulletin vol 12 no 459 (22 December 2009) 1.

[87] See *ibid*, 3.

[88] For a review of the run-up process to Copenhagen see *eg* J Depledge, 'Crafting the Copenhagen Consensus: Some Reflections' (2008) 17 *RECIEL* 154; K Kulovesi and M Gutiérrez, 'Climate Change Negotiations Update: Process and Prospects for a Copenhagen Agreed Outcome in December 2009' (2009) 18 *RECIEL* 229.

reduction commitments and to emphasise the need for supporting developing countries via financial resources and technology transfer in the context of mitigation and adaptation.[89]

Accordingly, the final outcome of the Copenhagen Conference was a poor political compromise, the so-called Copenhagen Accord of 18 December 2009,[90] rather than a fully fledged, legally binding international agreement establishing a post-2012 climate change regime.[91]

The Copenhagen Accord, headed by a list of 112 parties (111 states and the EU) indicating their support for it, contains in its preamble the rather doubtful statement that it 'is operational immediately'. In the beginning, the parties stress their 'strong political will to urgently combat climate change in accordance with the principle of common but differentiated responsibilities and respective capabilities' (paragraph 1). They agree that deep cuts in global emissions are required with a view to keeping the increase in temperature below 2°C, and to 'cooperate in achieving the peaking of global and national emissions as soon as possible, recognizing that the time frame for peaking will be longer in developing countries' (paragraph 2). The Accord recognises that '[a]daptation to the adverse effects of climate change and the potential impacts of response measures is a challenge faced by all countries'; in this respect, developed countries 'shall provide adequate, predictable and sustainable financial resources, technology and capacity-building' to support adaptation actions (paragraph 3). Annex I parties 'commit to implement individually or jointly the quantified economy-wide emissions targets for 2020, to be submitted . . . to the Secretariat by 31 January 2010'. Annex I parties that are party to the Kyoto Protocol will thereby further strengthen the emission reductions initiated by the Protocol. Delivery of reductions and financing by developed countries will be measured, reported and verified in accordance with guidelines adopted by the COP (paragraph 4). Non-Annex I parties to the Convention will implement mitigation actions, including those to be submitted to the Secretariat by 31 January 2010. 'Least developed countries and small island developing States may undertake actions voluntarily and on the basis of support'. Developing countries shall submit national GHG inventories every two years; unsupported mitigation action will be subject to domestic monitoring, reporting and verification, with provisions for international consultations and analysis under clearly defined guidelines that will ensure that national sovereignty is respected (paragraph 5). The Accord recognises the crucial role of 'reducing emissions from deforestation and forest degradation' (REDD-plus)[92] and provides the immediate establishment of a mechanism including REDD-plus

[89] See Earth Negotiations Bulletin, above n 86, 3, and especially Mazlum *et al* (eds), above n 66, 46 *et seq*.

[90] Decision 2/CP15 in UN Doc FCCC/CP/2009/11/Add1 (30 March 2010) 5 *et seq*. For its contents see also Earth Negotiations Bulletin, above n 86, 9 *et seq*.

[91] For a first account of the Copenhagen Accord see *eg* D Bodansky, 'The Copenhagen Climate Change Accord' (12 February 2010) 14 *ASIL Insight*, available at www.asil.org/files/insight100212pdf.pdf; T Marauhn and AM Böhringer, 'Klimaschutz nach Kopenhagen—Die Zukunft des völkerrechtlichen Klimaschutzes' in J Gundel and KW Lange (eds), *Klimaschutz nach Kopenhagen—Internationale Instrumente und nationale Umsetzung* (Tübingen 2011) 1–15.

[92] The United Nations Collaborative Programme on REDD characterises 'REDD' as 'an effort to create a financial value for the carbon stored in forests, offering incentives for developing countries to reduce emissions from forested lands and invest in low-carbon paths to sustainable development. "REDD+" goes beyond deforestation and forest degradation, and includes the role of conservation, sustainable management of forests

to help mobilise resources from developed countries (paragraph 6). It envisages, *inter alia*, the opportunity 'to use markets, to enhance the cost-effectiveness of, and to promote mitigation actions' (paragraph 7). It includes the 'collective commitment' by developed countries 'to provide new and additional resources, including forestry and investments through international institutions, approaching US$30 bn for the period 2010–2012 with balanced allocation between adaptation and mitigation'. It sets a longer-term goal of mobilising jointly US$100 bn per year by 2020 from a wide variety of sources, but only in the context of 'meaningful mitigation and transparency on implementation' (paragraph 8). Institutionally, the Accord provides the establishment of a High Level Panel as an advisory body of the COP, the Copenhagen Green Climate Fund 'as an operating entity of the financial mechanism of the Convention', and a Technology Mechanism to accelerate technology development and transfer in support of adaptation and mitigation actions (paragraphs 9–11). The accord ends with a 'call for an assessment of the implementation of this Accord to be completed by 2015', including consideration of limiting temperature rises to 1.5°C (paragraph 12).

Due to objections by a small group of states, including Sudan, Venezuela, Bolivia and Nicaragua,[93] the COP's closing plenary on 19 December 2009 merely 'took note of' rather than adopting the Copenhagen Accord. It was agreed that the names of parties which 'associate themselves' with the Accord would be listed in its chapeau. As of the end of March 2010, 73 states (40 Annex I and 33 non-Annex I parties) have submitted targets or actions to the Climate Change Secretariat. Of these, 64 have explicitly associated themselves with the Accord. An additional 35 states have explicitly associated themselves with the Accord but have not submitted targets or actions. 13 states, including Brazil, China and India, have expressed support for the Accord without 'associating' themselves with it. Nine states have submitted letters to the Climate Change Secretariat neither associating with nor supporting the Accord.[94]

The fact that a broad majority of states has associated itself with the Accord does not change the status of the latter. This has been clearly confirmed by the Climate Change Secretariat which stated:

> Since the Conference of the Parties neither adopted nor endorsed the Accord, but merely took note of it, its provisions do not have any legal standing within the UNFCCC process even if some Parties decide to associate themselves with it. . . . The accord is a political agreement rather than a treaty instrument.[95]

and enhancement of forest carbon stocks' (www.un-redd.org/).

[93] The objecting states mainly criticised that only 25 out of 192 countries took part in the preparation of the Accord, with only 14 developing countries. Venezuela was indignant over 'the lack of respect for sovereign nations', supported by Cuba deploring 'the non-democratic process and imposition of the agreement'. See Earth Negotiations Bulletin, above n 86, 8.

[94] See J Werksman, 'Nearly 100 Countries Formally "Associate" with Copenhagen' in *Daily Climate News and Analysis*, 25 March 2010, available at http://solveclimate.com/blog/20100325/nearly-100-countries-formally-associate-copenhagen-accord. See the UNFCCC website for the latest developments: http://unfccc.int/home/items/5262.php.

[95] Werksman, *ibid*, 2.

Despite its non-legal character and its regulatory shortcomings and gaps, and, at least in part, its weak or ambiguous language, the Accord brings about a political interim solution. Some of its key elements[96] may be used as a starting-point and textual basis for renewed negotiations with the aim of agreeing upon the establishment of a legally sound post-2012 climate change regime. Moreover, states can be expected to learn from the mistakes that they have made in Copenhagen with respect to the negotiating strategy, method and form.[97]

13.5 Outer Space Activities and Environmental Protection

During the past 50 years humankind has launched innumerable objects into outer space. Today, an estimated 19000 man-made objects are in orbit around the earth, among them about 900 satellites. Objects that no longer serve any useful purpose, such as spent rocket stages, defunct satellites, explosion fragments and even the odd wrench dropped by an astronaut, form what is called space debris. How long such fragments persist depends on how high their orbit is: above 600 miles orbits can last for centuries; below 300–400 miles they decay in years. If enough debris accumulates, there is risk of a chain reaction of colliding fragments, finally leading to an orbital 'debris belt', making access to space increasingly dangerous.[98] Most of the objects re-entering the atmosphere will burn up; only larger ones can reach the ground intact.

On a very few occasions satellites falling on earth have raised serious concerns about public safety and environmental integrity. In January 1978 the Cosmos-954, a Soviet nuclear-powered satellite, fell out of orbit and plummeted into the Northern Territories of Canada. In February 2008, USA-193, a US spy satellite, which had failed shortly after its launch, was deliberately intercepted and destroyed by an SM-3 missile rather than being allowed to fall to the earth's surface in an uncontrolled way.[99] In February 2009 the collision of a spent Russian satellite with an US Iridium communications satellite over Siberia left a cloud of debris in orbit that posed the risk of damaging other satellites and the International Space Station.[100] Thus, the environmental problems which may be caused by human activities in outer space are mainly orbital space debris and damage on earth caused by objects plummeting from space.[101]

In the late 1960s and 1970s states entered into three international treaties that, *inter*

[96] This applies *eg* to the commitment by developed countries to provide short-term and long-term finance for adaptation and mitigation actions undertaken by developing countries in para 8 of the Accord. *Cf* the statement of UNFCCC Executive Secretary Y de Boer in UNFCCC Secretariat press release (31 March 2010), available at http://unfccc.int/press/items/2794.php.

[97] Hopes that this would happen at the COP's Cancun meeting in December 2010 were in vain.

[98] See RP Merges and GH Reynolds, 'Rules of the Road for Space? Satellite Collisions and the Inadequacy of Current Space Law' (2010) 40 *Environmental Law Reporter* 10009, 10010.

[99] See L Parks, 'When Satellites Fall: On the Trails of Cosmos 954 and USA 193' (2009), http://flowtv.org/?p=3989.

[100] See Merges and Reynolds, above n 98, 10009.

[101] See Sands, above n 73, 382.

alia, cover environmental aspects of outer space: the 1967 Outer Space Treaty,[102] the 1972 Space Liability Convention[103] and the 1979 Moon Treaty.[104]

The Outer Space Treaty[105] declares outer space to be the 'province of all mankind', and to be 'free for exploration and use by all States without discrimination', on a basis of equality, and that '[t]here shall be free access to all areas of celestial bodies' (Article I). Article II provides that outer space is not subject to national appropriation 'by claim of sovereignty', or 'by means of use or occupation'. Article IV makes plain that nuclear weapons and other weapons of mass destruction must not be placed in orbit around the Earth, installed on celestial bodies or stationed in outer space; the moon and other celestial bodies shall be used by all states parties 'exclusively for peaceful purposes'. Article VII makes each state party liable for damage caused by an object launched into space. Article IX requires that all space activities must be undertaken 'with due regard to the corresponding interests of all other States Parties to the Treaty', but is not directed to protect the space environment 'as an end in itself'.[106]

Under the Space Liability Convention a state that launches a space object is, as a rule, 'absolutely liable to pay compensation for damage caused by its space object on the surface of the Earth or aircraft in flight' (Article II). So far, this rule of 'state liability without fault'[107] has been put to the test only once: In 1979 Canada presented a claim to the former USSR to pay CDN $6 million to cover the cost of restoring its territory damaged by the crash of Cosmos-954. In 1981, the USSR paid CDN $3 million to Canada, and both sides agreed that this payment settled the claim.

The Moon Treaty, whose provisions relating to the moon also apply to other celestial bodies within the solar system (Article 1(1)), is designed to supplement the Outer Space Treaty. It provides that the moon 'shall be used . . . exclusively for peaceful purposes' (Article 3(1)) and declares the moon and its natural resources to be the 'common heritage of mankind' (Article 11(1)). Instead of prohibiting any exploitation of the moon's natural resources, it requires states parties to establish an international regime to govern the exploitation of the respective natural resources (Article 11(5)). Among the main purposes of the aspired international regime are 'orderly and safe development', and 'rational management' of these resources, as well as an 'equitable sharing by all States Parties in the benefits derived from those resources', taking into account the interests and needs of

[102] The Treaty on Principles Governing the Activities of States in the Exploration and Use of Outer Space, including the Moon and Other Celestial Bodies, in force since 10 October 1967, is binding on 100 parties; see UN Doc ST/SPACE/11/Rev2/Add3: 'Status of international agreements relating to activities in outer space as at 1 January 2010'.

[103] The Convention on International Liability for Damage Caused by Space Objects, in force since 1 September 1972, is binding on 90 parties.

[104] The Agreement Governing the Activities of States on the Moon and Other Celestial Bodies, in force since 11 July 1984, is binding on 13 parties.

[105] The Treaty was preceded by the UN General Assembly's Declaration of Legal Principles Governing the Activities of States in the Exploration and Use of Outer Space, adopted on 13 December 1963 (Resolution 1962 (XVIII)).

[106] In this sense Sands, above n 73, 383, and D Tan, 'Towards a New Regime for the Protection of Outer Space as a Province of All Mankind' in C Ku and PF Diehl (eds), *International Law: Classic and Contemporary Readings* (3rd edn Boulder, CO/London 2009) 421, 427.

[107] *Cf* also below Chapter 24.3.

developing countries as well as the contributions made by the developed countries to the moon's exploration (Article 11(7)).

These outer space-related international treaties have been followed by some legally non-binding principles and declarations of the UN General Assembly. Only one of them directly addresses environmental aspects, namely the 1992 Principles Relevant to the Use of Nuclear Power Sources in Outer Space; Principle 3, for example, calls upon states launching space objects with nuclear power sources on board 'to protect individuals, populations and the biosphere against radiological hazards'.[108] Noteworthy is also the General Assembly's 1996 Declaration on International Cooperation in the Exploration and Use of Outer Space for the Benefit and in the Interest of All States, Taking into Particular Account the Needs of Developing Countries.[109]

For the simple reason that as yet the competition to exploit space has fallen far short of expectations, all these instruments, with the exception of the 1972 Liability Convention, still wait to be put to serious practical test.

13.6 Conclusions

While the protection of the space environment is incumbent on future rather than present generations, combating transboundary air pollution, ozone depletion and climate change are tremendous challenges that humankind faces here and now. However, these challenges are so different in kind that the means and methods to be used to meet them are dissimilar. While only a considerable change of human behaviour promises to reduce global warming or keep it within tolerable limits, states succeeded in halting ozone depletion simply through the use of appropriate technological means. Transboundary air pollution can be best combated by a combination of methods and means, namely technologically neutralising the detrimental effects of emitted gases, prescribing clear-cut emission reduction targets and setting incentives for a behavioural change towards avoiding such emissions. While air pollution normally shows clearly perceptible short-term effects to the detriment of the environment and human health, the most serious environmental impacts of ozone depletion and climate change, at least in the northern temperate zones, become evident only in the long term. This is why winning human societies over to behavioural changes in favour of protecting the ozone layer and the global climate has been far from easy.

Accordingly, the track records of states in combating these three types of atmospheric pollution vary considerably. The LRTAP Convention and its related protocols successfully managed to establish clear-cut regional environmental standards for air pollution control. Their rules are applicable to industrialised states in the OECD/UNECE/EU context only. However, the LRTAP Convention may serve as a model for relevant treaty regimes in rapidly industrialising parts of the world where similar regimes are still missing. Based

[108] UNGA Res 47/68 (14 December 1992).
[109] UNGA Res 51/122 (13 December 1996).

on the Ozone Convention and the Montreal Protocol, international action on combating ozone depletion succeeded in a total phase-out of the production and consumption of certain ozone-depleting substances. The high level of compliance with the obligations of the Montreal Protocol has resulted in signs of ozone layer recovery. As indicated above, combating global climate change requires a far-reaching economic restructuring of the industrialised societies in the North, as well as a change in the development path of developing countries in the South. The enormity of this challenge explains why the existing global climate protection regime has not as yet matched the effectiveness of the ozone protection regime. Unfortunately, the Copenhagen Accord reached at COP 15 in December 2009 contains nothing but a vague political understanding of the states convened that the increase in global temperature should be held below 2.0°C with the option of strengthening this goal to 1.5°C by 2015. However, instead of prescribing mandatory emissions cuts to achieve this objective, the Copenhagen Accord merely invites voluntary pledges for emission targets from developed countries and for nationally appropriate mitigation actions from developing countries. It remains to be hoped that subsequent meetings under the UNFCCC and the Kyoto Protocol will succeed in shaping an appropriate legally binding post-2012 climate protection regime.[110]

Further Reading

JE Aldy and RN Stavins (eds), *Architectures for Agreement. Addressing Global Climate Change in the Post-Kyoto World* (Cambridge 2007).

SO Andersen and K Madhava Sarma, *Protecting the Ozone Layer: The United Nations History* (London 2002).

F Biermann, *Saving the Atmosphere. International Law, Developing Countries and Air Pollution* (Frankfurt am Main 1995).

M Bothe and E Rehbinder (eds), *Climate Change Policy* (Utrecht 2005).

Climate Change Secretariat (UNFCCC), *A Guide to the Climate Change Convention and Its Kyoto Protocol* (Bonn 2002).

Climate Change Secretariat (UNFCCC), *Kyoto Protocol Reference Manual: On Accounting of Emissions and Assigned Amount* (Bonn 2008).

C Flinterman, B Kwiatkowska and J Lammers (eds), *Transboundary Air Pollution. International Legal Aspects of the Co-operation of States* (Dordrecht 1986).

A Gillespie, *Climate Change, Ozone Depletion and Air Pollution. Legal Commentaries with Policy and Science Considerations* (Leiden/Boston 2006).

J Gupta, *The Climate Change Convention and Developing Countries. From Conflict to Consensus?* (Dordrecht 1997).

——, 'International Law and Climate Change. The Challenges Facing Developing Countries' (2005) 16 *Yearbook of International Environmental Law* 119–153.

D Helm (ed), *Climate-Change Policy* (Oxford 2005).

D Kaniaru (ed), *The Montreal Protocol: Celebrating 20 Years of Environmental Progress: Ozone Layer and Climate Protection* (London 2007).

[110] *Cf* on the whole U Beyerlin and J Grote Stoutenburg, 'Environment, International Protection' in R Wolfrum (ed), *Max Planck Encyclopedia of Public International Law* (Heidelberg/Oxford 2011), para 37, available at www.mpepil.com.

K Madhava Sarma, SO Andersen, D Zaelke and KN Taddonio, 'Ozone Layer, International Protection' in R Wolfrum (ed), *Max Planck Encyclopedia of Public International Law* (Heidelberg/Oxford 2009), available at www.mpepil.com.

S Oberthür and H Ott, *The Kyoto Protocol: International Climate Policy for the Twenty-first Century* (Berlin 1999).

P Okowa, *State Responsibility for Transboundary Air Pollution in International Law* (Oxford 2000).

HM Osofsky, 'Is Climate Change "International"? Litigation's Diagonal Regulatory Role' (2009) 49 *Virginia Journal of International Law* 585–650.

EA Page, *Climate Change, Justice and Future Generations* (Cheltenham/Northampton 2006).

EA Parson, *Protecting the Ozone Layer: Science and Strategy* (Oxford 2003).

J Peel, 'Climate Change Law: The Emergence of New Legal Discipline' (2008) 32 *Melbourne University Law Review* 922–979.

A Petsonk, '"Docking stations": Designing a More Welcoming Architecture for a post-2012 Framework to Combat Climate Change' (2008/09) 19 *Duke Journal of Comparative & International Law* 433–466.

AL Plein, 'A Story between Success and Challenge: 20th Anniversary of the Montreal Protocol' (2007) 11 *New Zealand Journal of Environmental Law* 67–98.

L Rajamani, 'Re-negotiating Kyoto: A Review of the Sixth Conference of the Parties to the Framework Convention on Climate Change' (2001) 12 *Colorado Journal of International Environmental Law and Policy* 201–238.

IH Rowlands, 'Atmosphere and Outer Space' in D Bodansky *et al* (eds), *The Oxford Handbook of International Environmental Law* (Oxford 2007) 315–336.

L Schenck, 'Climate Change "crisis": Struggling for Worldwide Collective Action' (2008) 19 *Colorado Journal of International Environmental Law and Policy* 319–379.

'Symposium—Climate Justice and International Environmental Law: Rethinking the North-South Divide' (2009) 10 *Melbourne Journal of International Law* 411–595.

D Tan, 'Towards a New Regime for the Protection of Outer Space as a Province of All Mankind' in C Ku and PF Diehl (eds), *International Law: Classic and Contemporary Readings* (3rd edn Boulder, CO/London 2009) 421–453.

P Taylor, *An Ecological Approach to International Law. Responding to the Challenges of Climate Change* (London 1998).

MA Toman and B Sohngen (eds), *Climate Change* (Aldershot/Burlington 2004).

R Verheyen, *Climate Change Damage and International Law. Prevention Duties and State Responsibility* (Leiden/Boston 2005).

R Wolfrum (ed), *Max Planck Encyclopedia of Public International Law* (Heidelberg/Oxford 2009), available at www.mpepil.com.

F Yamin and J Depledge, *The International Climate Change Regime. A Guide to Rules, Institutions and Procedures* (Cambridge 2004).

14

Flora, Fauna and Biological Diversity

14.1 Survey

The protection of flora and fauna in their respective habitats, the conservation of biological diversity, and the sustainable use of forests and soil are interrelated. However, as will be shown, pertinent agreements differ in respect of object and purpose and follow different regulatory approaches, not least in light of the distinctive historical development of each of them.

While international efforts to protect wildlife go back to the nineteenth century,[1] some of the early instruments had very little effect, due to limited coverage of species, their narrow geographical scope or because of the small number of participating states. By way of example, reference may be made to the 1911 Convention for the Preservation and Protection of Fur Seals concluded between the United States, Russia, the United Kingdom and Japan as a result of the preceding *Bering Sea Fur Seals* arbitration.[2] This Convention, limited in scope and in participation, was only supplemented in 1957 by an Interim Convention on the Conservation of North Pacific Fur Seals.

Addressing species exploited for food, commerce or sports, or otherwise useful to humans, early wildlife treaties often emerged from conflicts about the use of certain species, perceived as more valuable than others or at risk because of overexploitation in the territory of another state or on the high seas. The 1900 Convention for the Preservation of Wild Animals, Birds and Fish in Africa and the 1902 Convention for the Protection of Birds Useful to Agriculture are pertinent examples. Both are indifferent to some species while explicitly protecting others. Successor instruments, however, such as the 1933 Convention Relative to the Preservation of Fauna and Flora in their Natural State and

[1] Examples are provided by LK Caldwell, *International Environmental Policy* (3rd edn Durham NC 1996) ch 2.

[2] PH Sand, 'A Century of Green Lessons: The Contribution of Nature Conservation Regimes to Global Governance' (2001) 1 *International Environmental Agreements: Politics, Law and Economics* 33, 34; S Lalonde, 'Bering Sea' in R Wolfrum (ed), *Max Planck Encyclopedia of Public International Law* (Heidelberg/Oxford 2009), paras 24 *et seq*, available at www.mpepil.com.

the 1950 International Convention for the Protection of Birds, moved towards broader protection.[3] It must be noted that the 1950 Birds Convention is binding for nine European states only. A truly broad protection of species could have been achieved with the 1940 Convention on Nature Protection and Wild Life Preservation in the Western Hemisphere; but, as of today, there are only 19 states parties.

Even though a myriad of wildlife treaties have been concluded so far, international law protecting flora and fauna is largely dominated by a small number of regimes, most of which go back to the 1970s. These treaties, namely the 1971 Ramsar Convention on Wetlands, the 1972 UNESCO World Heritage Convention, the 1973 Washington Treaty on International Trade in Endangered Species, the 1979 Bonn Convention on Migratory Species and the 1979 Bern Convention on European Wildlife and Natural Habitats, will be addressed in detail below.

All of these agreements address the conservation of natural resources with a view to their territoriality and are related to the territorial jurisdiction of one or more states. This even applies to migratory species moving between territories, thereby subject to the jurisdiction of one or more states. While under the traditional principle of territorial sovereignty each of the states concerned has absolute sovereignty over the natural resources, including living resources, within its borders, the wildlife agreements addressed aim at balancing the sovereign rights (typically focusing on utilisation) of the host state with the interests of the international community in conserving wildlife. In principle, thus, the agreements protecting flora and fauna limit the exercise of territorial sovereignty of states and make them a kind of trustee for the international community. While such trusteeship obligations have not yet become part of customary international law,[4] the concept of trusteeship is increasingly important in order to understand pertinent international agreements.[5] Furthermore, it is noteworthy that most of the agreements concluded in the 1970s exclusively focus on conservation, not on utilisation, with the important exception of the Ramsar Convention which aims at 'wise use'.[6]

Wildlife agreements have demonstrated their ability to adapt to changed circumstances. All of them have either experienced amendments or subsequent treaty practice which often has contributed to extending the scope of protection far beyond what had originally been envisaged. This applies, among others, to the number of species protected by the Washington Treaty on International Trade in Endangered Species[7] as well as to the number of listed wetlands under the Ramsar Convention.

Even though the UN Convention on Biological Diversity (CBD) has emerged out of

[3] MJ Bowman, 'International Treaties and the Global Protection of Birds (Part I)' (1999) 11 *Journal of Environmental Law* 87, 91–92 and *id*, 'International Treaties and the Global Protection of Birds (Part II)' (1999) 11 *Journal of Environmental Law* 281, 297–299.

[4] See, among others, PH Sand, 'Sovereignty Bounded: Public Trusteeship for Common Pool Resources?' (2004) 4 *Global Environmental Politics* 47.

[5] For an application of the concept to the law of the sea *cf* PH Sand, 'Public Trusteeship for the Oceans' in TM Ndiaye and R Wolfrum (eds), *Law of the Sea, Environmental Law and Settlement of Disputes. Liber amicorum Judge Thomas A Mensah* (Leiden *et al* 2007) 521.

[6] D Farrier and L Tucker, 'Wise Use of Wetlands under the Ramsar Convention: A Challenge for Meaningful Implementation of International Law' (2000) 12 *Journal of Environmental Law* 21, 23 *et seq*.

[7] R Reeve, 'Enhancing the International Regime for Protecting Endangered Species' (2003) 63 *ZaöRV* 333.

the multiplicity of instruments protecting flora and fauna, it categorically differs from these instruments for a variety of reasons. Firstly, the CBD focuses on biological diversity as such, its intrinsic value, and its relevance for the evolution and conservation of life-sustaining biospheric systems. Its focus on genetic resources is much broader than the conservation of particular species of flora and fauna. Secondly, the CBD does not aim at conservation *per se* but at utilisation and conservation, considering conservation as an inherent element of sustainable use; it further complements the interest of the host state in utilising 'its' biodiversity with the interest of other states in having access to these resources.[8]

When negotiations on the CBD began, there were early attempts to exclude biodiversity and genetic resources from the power of disposal of states. However, these attempts failed for political and conceptual reasons.[9] On the one hand, the Convention explicitly confirms the sovereign right of states to exploit their own resources pursuant to their own environmental policies; on the other hand, it includes obligations of conservation and sustainable use. The economic incentive to apply conservation measures is based on the double mechanism of developing states parties allowing the exploitation of their resources by industrialised states parties which in return provide financial and technological support; granting access to genetic resources is matched by an obligation to share the benefits arising out of the use of these resources. As a matter of principle, the CBD thus aims at balancing a variety of objectives and at bringing together developed and developing countries. Consequently, many of the obligations included in the CBD are of a reciprocal nature.

As many other recent multilateral environmental agreements, the CBD is a framework convention and details will have to be agreed upon within implementing protocols (such as the Cartagena Protocol on Biosafety) and as part of supplementing arrangements. This is particularly true for intellectual property rights and the protection of traditional knowledge.[10] Even though the CBD has been further developed on the basis of many decisions of the Conference of the Parties (COP) it is still a rudimentary regime with a number of issues yet unsettled. One of the major problems is that developing countries still have difficulties in attaching significant economic value to biological resources. As long as there is little progress in this respect, international environmental law cannot adequately protect biodiversity since it remains under the jurisdiction of states.

The protection of forests, which may be considered a particularly sensitive part of biological diversity, is strongly influenced by the inherent tension between conserva-

[8] A Smagadi, 'Analysis of the Objectives of the Convention on Biological Diversity: Their Interrelation and Implementation Guidance for Access and Benefit Sharing' (2006) 31 *Columbia Journal of Environmental Law* 243.

[9] See M Bowman and C Redgwell, *International Law and the Conservation of Biological Diversity* (Cambridge, MA/The Hague 1996); see also F MacConnell, *The Biodiversity Convention: A Negotiating History* (London *et al* 1996) and V Koester, 'The Biodiversity Convention: Negotiation Process and Some Comments on the Outcome' (1997) 27 *Environmental Policy and Law* 175.

[10] Traditional knowledge is primarily addressed in Art 8(j); other related provisions are Art 10(c) and Art 17(1) of the Convention. At its fifth meeting in May 2000 the COP adopted its Programme of Work on Art 8(j) and related provisions; see www.cbd.int/decision/cop/?id=7158 and the Art 8(j) website at www.cbd.int/traditional.

tion and utilisation of natural resources.[11] In addition, the protection of forests is at the interface between instruments combating climate change and preserving biodiversity; both issues have not yet been adequately combined.[12] An important practical (and pragmatic) step is the International Tropical Timber Agreement (ITTA 1994 and 2006) which aims at ensuring that exports of tropical timber only originate from sustainably managed sources. To reach this objective, the Agreement establishes a fund to assist tropical timber producers in obtaining the necessary resources. The Rio Forest Principles of 1992, which have remained a purely political instrument, reflect the deep controversies between developing and industrialised countries. Similarly, the 1999 Yaoundé Declaration on the Conservation and Sustainable Management of Tropical Forests does not go beyond a mere political statement of intent. In the absence of binding treaty law, so-called Voluntary Partnership Agreements have been pushed by the European Union (EU) in response to a call for action at the 2002 World Summit on Sustainable Development in Johannesburg. These Voluntary Partnership Agreements are meant to act as a practical mechanism for identifying and excluding illegal timber from the EU market. Under the scheme, timber that is legally harvested and exported to the EU would be identified by means of licences issued in Voluntary Partnership Agreement signatory countries. Timber shipments to the EU from partner countries that do not have a permit would be denied entry under the Agreement. So far, agreements have been signed with Ghana (2009), with the Republic of Congo (2010), with Cameroon (2010) and with the Central African Republic (2010); further negotiations are ongoing, among others, with Indonesia, Liberia and Malaysia.

In light of the scarcity of land, international protection of the soil is increasingly becoming a matter of concern.[13] Soil is indispensable for the conservation of biological diversity; soil degradation reduces the habitat available for flora and fauna and leads to loss of species. The non-binding World Soil Charter adopted by the Council of the Food and Agriculture Organization of the United Nations (FAO) on 25 November 1981 is primarily concerned with the productivity of land. In contrast, the Alpine Convention of 7 November 1991 combines protection of alpine flora and fauna with protection of alpine forests and soils, thus adopting a holistic approach. At the universal level, the 1994 UN Convention to Combat Desertification addresses the issue of land degradation in arid and semi-arid regions. The complexity of soil protection is reflected in Article 1(e) of the Convention which defines land as 'the terrestrial bio-productive system that comprises soil, vegetation, other biota, and the ecological and hydrological processes that operate within the system'. Article 4(2)(c) of the Convention to Combat Desertification obliges states to 'integrate strategies for poverty eradication into efforts to combat desertification and mitigate the effects of drought'. Bearing in mind the differences between these sketched issue areas, there is a need to distinguish carefully between the various matters

[11] See RD Lipschutz, 'Why Is there no International Forestry Law? An Examination of International Forestry Regulation, both Public and Private' (2000/2001) 19 *UCLA Journal of Environmental Law & Policy* 153 and B Boer, 'Developments in International Environmental Law Relating to Forests' (1997) 14 *Environmental and Planning Law Journal* 378.

[12] See A Trouwborst, 'International Nature Conservation Law and the Adaptation of Biodiversity to Climate Change: A Mismatch?' (2009) 21 *Journal of Environmental Law* 419.

[13] For an account of IUCN's regulatory efforts see WJ Futrell, 'The IUCN Sustainable Soil Project and Enforcement Failures' (2007) 24 *Pace Environmental Law Review* 99.

while at the same time looking for convergence. It seems likely that the CBD has the potential to act as a catalyst in the long run.

In the following, the focus will be on the protection of flora and fauna as well as on the sustainable use of biodiversity. It will be shown that agreements on flora and fauna largely follow a preserving and conserving approach. MEAs addressing biodiversity rather focus on sustainable use. International environmental law addressing forests and soil is only of recent origin and still rudimentary. This chapter will conclude with an overall evaluation of all these developments.

14.2 Flora and Fauna

The protection of flora and fauna historically forms the starting point of international efforts in nature conservation. Thus, it is by no means surprising that some of the early multilateral environmental agreements were concluded in this field. Their focus on conservation rather than utilisation will be discussed in the following.

14.2.1 The Protection of Habitat

The first global instrument protecting habitat is the Convention on Wetlands of International Importance especially as Waterfowl Habitat (Ramsar Convention) of 2 February 1971, amended by the Paris Protocol of 3 December 1982 and by the Regina Amendments of 28 May 1987.[14] As defined by the Eighth COP to the Ramsar Convention in 2002, the Convention's mission is

> the conservation and wise use of all wetlands through local, regional and national actions and international cooperation, as a contribution towards achieving sustainable development throughout the world.[15]

The original emphasis of the Convention was upon the conservation and wise use of wetlands primarily as a habitat for waterbirds.[16] However, increasingly the scope of implementation of the Convention has been broadened to include all aspects of wetland conservation and wise use.[17] These developments take into account that wetlands are among the world's most productive environments, being important for biological diversity, and providing the water and primary productivity upon which countless species of plants and animals depend for survival. The Convention was developed in order to address wetland loss and degradation, given that many wetlands are international systems

[14] The Convention entered into force on 21 December 1975 and currently counts 160 contracting parties.

[15] Resolution VIII.25 ('The Ramsar Strategic Plan 2003–2008') (18–26 November 2002) Annex, para 5.

[16] *Cf* the Preamble of the original version of the Convention, www.ramsar.org/cda/ramsar/display/main/main.jsp?zn=ramsar&cp=1-31-38^20708_4000_0__; see also Ramsar Convention Secretariat, *The Ramsar Convention Manual: A Guide to the Convention on Wetlands (Ramsar, Iran, 1971)* (4th edn Gland 2006) 6, available at www.ramsar.org/pdf/lib/lib_manual2006e.pdf.

[17] See Ramsar Information Paper no 2, available at www.ramsar.org/pdf/about/info2007-02-e.pdf; see also Ramsar Convention Secretariat, *ibid*, 6.

lying across the boundaries of two or more states, or are part of river basins that include more than one state. In addition, many of the wetland fauna consist of migratory species whose conservation and management also require international co-operation.

The Ramsar Convention pursues a threefold approach towards wetland protection. Firstly, it establishes a 'List of Wetlands of International Importance' (the Ramsar List); secondly, states parties are responsible for the 'wise use' of wetland fauna; thirdly, states parties co-operate internationally towards better protection of wetlands.

Wetlands are defined in Article 1(1) as 'areas of marsh, fen, peatland or water, whether natural or artificial, permanent or temporary, with water that is static or flowing, fresh, brackish or salt, including areas of marine water the depth of which at low tide does not exceed six metres'. According to Article 2(1), states parties designate wetlands suitable for listing, with the Secretariat (the so-called 'Bureau') of the Convention (Article 8) maintaining this list. While the Convention only stipulates that 'wetlands should be selected for the List on account of their international significance in terms of ecology, botany, zoology, limnology or hydrology' (Article 2(2)), the COP adopted 'Criteria for the Identification of Wetlands of International Importance' from 1980 onwards,[18] without, however, making these criteria legally binding. A state becoming a member of the Ramsar Convention has to designate at least one wetland (Article 2(4)), with options for adding and deleting (only in case of 'urgent national interests') additional areas or restricting their boundaries (Article 2(4)–(6)). Once a wetland has been designated, this does not prejudice the exclusive sovereign rights of the respective party (Article 2(3)).

States parties are under an obligation to develop policies of 'wise use' of wetlands and their flora and fauna (Articles 2(6), 3(1), 6(2) and (3)). While the notion of 'wise use' is not defined in the Convention, the Third COP in 1987 established 'wise use of wetlands' as 'their sustainable utilization for the benefit of humankind in a way compatible with the maintenance of the natural properties of the ecosystem'.[19] This definition was updated in 2005: 'Wise use of wetlands is the maintenance of their ecological character, achieved through the implementation of ecosystem approaches, within the context of sustainable development.'[20] Comparing this with the definition of sustainable use as included in Article 2 CBD, 'wise use' more or less equals 'sustainable use'.[21]

The third pillar of the Convention is the obligation of parties to co-operate among each other with Article 5 explicitly requiring consultations among parties, in particular, in

[18] Criteria were first recommended in 1980 (Recommendation 1.4); they were revised in 1987 (Recommendation 3.1) and in 1990 (Recommendation 4.2). In 1996 new criteria were added, in particular on fish and fishing (Resolution VI.2) with further differentiations in 1999 (Resolution VII.11 on 'Strategic framework and guidelines for the future development of the List of Wetlands of International Importance') and certain criteria were deleted in 2005 (Resolution IX.1, Annex B, 'Revised Strategic Framework and guidelines for the future development of the List of Wetlands of International Importance' and Resolution IX.6). For an overview see www.ramsar.org/cda/ramsar/display/main/main.jsp?zn=ramsar&cp=1-36-37^7726_4000_0__ (FAQs).

[19] Recommendation 3.3. (27 May–5 June 1987). For a general discussion of the 'wise use' concept within Ramsar see Ramsar Convention Secretariat, *Wise Use of Wetlands: A Conceptual Framework for the Wise Use of Wetlands* (3rd edn Gland 2007), available at www.ramsar.org/pdf/lib/lib_handbooks2006_e01.pdf.

[20] Resolution IX.1 Annex A (8–15 November 2005) on 'A Conceptual Framework for the wise use of wetlands and the maintenance of their ecological character'.

[21] Farrier and Tucker, above n 6, 30.

the case of a 'wetland extending over the territories' of several parties or 'where a water system is shared' by several parties.

The Convention provides for two organs, namely the Conference of the Parties (Articles 6 and 7) and the Bureau (Article 8) which is handled by the International Union for the Conservation of Nature and Natural Resources (IUCN). With the 1982 Paris Protocol, Article 10 *bis* was included in the Convention, allowing the adoption of amendments 'by a two-thirds majority of the Contracting Parties present and voting' (Article 10(5)). While the Convention seems to be relatively weak, its practical impact has been impressive, with, currently, some 1900 wetlands included in the list, covering a total surface area of some 185 million hectares.[22] In 1990, the COP decided to set up the Ramsar Small Grants Fund,[23] which is a mechanism to assist developing countries and those with economies in transition to implement the Convention and to support the conservation and wise use of wetland resources. From 1991 to 2008 the Fund has provided a total of SFr 7.5 million to 227 projects from 108 countries.[24]

Another agreement addressing habitat is the Convention Concerning the Protection of the World Cultural and Natural Heritage (World Heritage Convention) as adopted by the General Conference of UNESCO on 16 November 1972, with currently 186 states parties. While the Convention also pursues a 'listing approach', its scope differs substantially from that of the Ramsar Convention. Apart from cultural heritage, the World Heritage Convention covers 'natural heritage' (Article 2), which includes, among others, areas constituting 'the habitat of threatened species of animals and plants of outstanding universal value from the point of view of science or conservation'. At the time of writing, the World Heritage List includes 180 natural properties and 27 mixed properties, though it also covers 704 cultural properties.[25]

The identification and delineation of properties protected by the Convention is the individual responsibility of each state party (Article 3). According to Article 4, a state party, for the purpose of identification, protection, conservation, presentation and transmission to future generations of a site located on its territory, 'will do all it can to this end, to the utmost of its own resources and, where appropriate, with any international assistance and co-operation, in particular, financial, artistic, scientific and technical, which it may be able to obtain', though Article 5 qualifies this 'in so far as possible, and as appropriate for each country'. While Article 6 stipulates that it is the duty of the international community as a whole to co-operate for the protection of world heritage, the Convention explicitly states that the sovereignty of states is respected (Article 6(1)).

Article 8 of the Convention establishes an 'Intergovernmental Committee for the Protection of the Cultural and Natural Heritage of Outstanding Universal Value', the 'World Heritage Committee', apart from the General Assembly, as one of the decisive organs of the heritage regime. This body maintains the Word Heritage List (Article 11). One of the key benefits of the Convention, particularly for developing countries, is access to the World Heritage Fund (Articles 15–18) which was set up to support activities requested

[22] For detailed information on the status of protected wetlands see www.ramsar.org.
[23] Resolution 4.3 (27 June–4 July 1990).
[24] *Cf* the Project Portfolio 2009, available at www.ramsar.org/pdf/sgf/sgf_portfolio_2009.pdf.
[25] *Cf* http://whc.unesco.org/en/list.

by states parties in need of international assistance. However, with an annual budget of about US$4 million, the Fund's volume is relatively small.

Even though it is not treaty-based, the UNESCO Man and the Biosphere Programme (MAB), established in 1977,[26] needs to be mentioned here. Biosphere reserves recognised under this programme are sites used for innovative approaches to conservation and sustainable development. The Programme establishes an international biosphere network providing benefits with regard to the integration of conservation, development and scientific research concerns to sustainably manage ecosystems.[27] Inclusion in the network is based on nominations prepared by national governments with criteria laid down in the Statutory Framework of the World Network of Biosphere Reserves adopted by the UNESCO General Conference in 1995[28] and in the so-called 'Seville Strategy'.[29] The Statutory Framework sets criteria for an area qualified for designation as a biosphere reserve and lays down the designation procedure for biosphere reserves. The Seville Strategy sets out actions recommended for the development of biosphere reserves. It is much more a policy document than the Statutory Framework. The legal relevance of the Seville Strategy derives from its recommendations being the yardstick for decisions of the International Co-ordinating Council (ICC) of the MAB Programme on nominations for designation of a site as a UNESCO Biosphere Reserve.

The Seville Strategy and the CBD with its 'ecosystem approach' are mutually supportive. One might perhaps even argue that the interface between the (soft law) approach taken by UNESCO and the (hard law) approach which parties to the CBD have to consider hardens the biosphere concept of UNESCO, bringing it closer to the sphere of law. At the time of writing there are 564 sites worldwide in 109 countries.[30]

14.2.2 Regulating Trade in Endangered Species: CITES

One of the most important instruments adopted in the 1970s, initiated by IUCN in 1963,[31] seeks to protect flora and fauna by regulating wildlife trade: the Convention on International Trade in Endangered Species of Wild Fauna and Flora (CITES) of 3 March 1973.[32]

Generally speaking, CITES establishes controls for international trade in specimens of listed species. In particular, the Convention requires that all import, export, re-export

[26] See www.unesco.org/mab for details.

[27] See generally JD Brown, 'The Integration of Man and the Biosphere' (2002) 14 *Georgetown International Environmental Law Review* 741.

[28] UNESCO (Res 2.4, adopted by the 28th Session of the General Conference) 'The Seville Strategy on Biosphere Reserves and the Statutory Framework of the World Network of Biosphere Reserves' (14 November 1995) 32 *et seq*.

[29] See for the text UNESCO, *Biosphere Reserves: The Seville Strategy and the Statutory Framework of the World Network* (Paris 1996) 6 *et seq*, available at www.unesco.org/mab/doc/brs/Strategy.pdf.

[30] See http://portal.unesco.org/science/en/ev.php-URL_ID=4801&URL_DO=DO_TOPIC&URL_SECTION=201.html.

[31] For the origins of CITES see PH Sand, 'Whither CITES? The Evolution of a Treaty Regime in the Borderland of Trade and Environment' (1997) 8 *European Journal of International Law* 29, 31 *et seq*.

[32] It entered into force after ten ratifications on 1 July 1975. At the time of writing, 175 states have become parties to the Convention. *Cf* www.cites.org/eng/disc/parties/index.shtml.

and introduction from the sea of species covered by the Convention have to be authorised through a licensing system.

Based upon a broad definition of species in Article I of the Convention,[33] Article II of CITES establishes three different levels of protection. The highest level of protection is to be provided for species threatened with extinction and affected by trade (paragraph 1). Upon inclusion in Appendix I, trade in specimens[34] of such species must be subject to particularly strict regulation in order not to endanger further their survival and must only be authorised in exceptional circumstances. Less stringent rules apply to species 'which although not necessarily now threatened with extinction may become so' unless strictly regulated (paragraph 2). These species shall be included in Appendix II and their regulation shall be designed 'to avoid utilization incompatible with their survival'. The lowest level of protection applies to species listed in Appendix III; these include all species which any party identifies as being subject to regulation within its jurisdiction 'for the purpose of preventing or restricting exploitation, and as needing the co-operation of other parties in the control of trade' (paragraph 3). Article II(4) CITES requires parties not to allow trade in specimens of species included in any of the three Appendices, 'except in accordance with the provisions of the present Convention'.

Currently, roughly 5000 species of animals and 28000 species of plants are protected by CITES against overexploitation through international trade.[35] The decisive question thus must be how species are included in and deleted from any of the Appendices. It is the COP which is competent to 'consider and adopt amendments to Appendices I and II in accordance with Article XV' (Article XI(3)(b) CITES). Proposals for listing (or deletion) may be submitted by any party, irrespective of whether or not the species is usually found within the party's territory, and inclusion may be made despite objections by states the species are natives to, as long as there is sufficient (two-thirds majority) support for the listing (or deletion). It is noteworthy that the Convention itself does not further specify requirements for listing a species in Appendices I or II. The COP has, however, adopted a set of biological and trade criteria to help determine whether a species should be included in Appendices I or II.[36]

The export of any specimen of a species included in Appendix I requires, as stipulated in Article III CITES, the prior grant and presentation of an export permit. Such permit shall only be granted if (i) the export will not be detrimental to the survival of that species; (ii) the specimen was not obtained in contravention of national laws for the protection of fauna and flora; (iii) the risk of injury, damage to health or cruel treatment of any living specimen is minimised; and (iv) an import permit has been granted for the specimen (paragraph 2). Similarly, the import of a species, included in Appendix I, requires the prior grant and presentation of an import permit which may only be granted if (i) the import will be for purposes which are not detrimental to the survival of the species involved; (ii) the proposed recipient of a living specimen is suitably equipped to house and care for it; and (iii) the specimen is not to be used for primarily commercial

[33] 'Species' means any species, subspecies or geographically separate population thereof.
[34] In the first instance 'Specimens' are defined as animals or plants, whether dead or alive.
[35] See www.cites.org/eng/disc/species.shtml.
[36] Resolution Conf 9.24 (Rev CoP15) (24 March 2010).

purposes (paragraph 3). The re-export of any specimen of a species included in Appendix I requires the prior grant and presentation of a re-export certificate (paragraph 4).

Trade in specimens of species included in Appendix II is governed by Article IV CITES. Whereas the export of such species (paragraph 2) necessitates similar requirements as the export of Appendix I species, import only requires prior presentation of either an export permit or a re-export certificate (paragraph 4).

The export of specimens of species included in Appendix III (Article V(2)) necessitates the prior grant and presentation of an export permit which may only be granted if the specimen was not obtained in contravention of national laws for the protection of fauna and flora, and if the risk of injury, damage to health or cruel treatment of any living specimen is minimised. Import of such a specimen only requires prior presentation of a certificate of origin, unless it is exported from a state which has included the species on Appendix III, in which case an export permit is necessary (paragraph 3).

In addition, all permits and certificates required by Articles III–V must meet the requirements stipulated in Article VI CITES. The requirements of Articles III, IV and V do not apply 'to specimens that are personal or household effects' (Article VII(3)). There are also exemptions for exchange between scientists or scientific institutions (Article VII(6)).

Each party to the Convention must designate Management Authorities in charge of administering the licensing system (Article IX CITES).

One of the most important provisions of the Convention is its Article VIII which lays down obligations of states parties to take appropriate measures to enforce the provisions of the Convention and to prohibit trade in specimens in violation thereof. These include obligations to penalise and to provide for confiscation and return. Formalities required for trade have to be performed with a minimum of delay. Furthermore, records of trade in specimens of species have to be kept. Often, however, domestic legislation is either non-existent, or only provides penalties incommensurate with the gravity of the crime and insufficient deterrents to wildlife traders. Indeed, many parties have failed to designate Management Authorities, to adopt laws prohibiting trade in violation of CITES, to impose penalties for such trade, or to enact laws providing for the confiscation of specimens.[37]

Article X ensures that trade with non-parties does not undermine the effectiveness of CITES.

While it cannot be disputed that CITES has regularly seen problems of implementation, it has to a certain extent been successful.[38] Thus, some highly endangered species have been protected from extinction, such as the African elephant, the leopard and the Nile crocodile. In addition, it has been shown that trade in wild birds included in Appendix II has gone down substantially since 1989.[39]

Some examples serve to illustrate the operation of CITES and its impact on species. The African elephant has been on the agenda of CITES since 1976. After an initial inclu-

[37] R Reeve, *Policing International Trade in Endangered Species: The CITES Treaty and Compliance* (London 2002); *id*, above n 7, 344 *et seq*.

[38] Sand, above n 31, 52.

[39] Data on the volume of trade in birds by Appendix for the years 1984–2008 is provided by the CITES Trade Data Dashboards, available at http://cites-dashboards.unep-wcmc.org/global?id=Birds.

sion in Appendix III, the African elephant was placed on Appendix II for several years. Given the global demand for ivory and in light of the income which could be generated from the illegal ivory trade, reliance upon Appendix II proved to be inadequate. Efforts to curb illegal trading failed due to unrestrained corruption and because permits were easily forged, stolen and reused. It was only after the ban of the commercial import of ivory by the United States, Canada, Australia, the European Community and a few other importing countries in May 1989 that the Conference of the Parties in October 1989, after controversial debates, transferred the African elephant from Appendix II to Appendix I. This became effective in January 1990. The elephant population recovered more or less immediately. This, however, in turn caused problems for rural populations in Botswana, Namibia and Zimbabwe: the rigid CITES system meant that these states could not even draw economic benefits from their huge elephant population, and governments were left with tons of ivory resulting from lawful management of the elephant population or from ivory confiscated from poachers. A decision on partial delisting was therefore taken in June 1997. COP 10 decided to rearrange elephant listings, with the African elephant currently being split-listed, with all populations listed in Appendix I, except those of Botswana, Namibia and Zimbabwe, included in Appendix II in 1997, and South Africa joining these three states in 2000.[40] In addition, ivory trade with China and Japan was partly permitted.[41] COP 15 in 2010 rejected requests by Tanzania and Zambia to downlist their elephant populations to Appendix II.[42] A proposal by Congo, Ghana, Kenya, Liberia, Mali, Rwanda and Sierra Leone for a 20-year moratorium was withdrawn.[43] Finally, COP 15 adopted a revised Action Plan for the control of trade in elephant ivory,[44] and agreed on a revised version of Resolution 10.10 on trade in elephant specimens.[45]

Even though the split listing was criticised by some NGOs, it does not only seem plausible but also a matter of law. If the conservation of species is the primary objective of CITES (and related regimes), then the question arises whether or not the rigid approach adopted by CITES serves this objective. The concept of 'sustainable use' probably contributes much better and more effectively to the management of species, providing incentives for the local population and authorities to preserve species which may serve as a source of income. While no obligation of sustainable use may be drawn from CITES, Article 2 CBD explicitly refers to sustainable use as 'the use of components of biological diversity in a way and at a rate that does not lead to the long-term decline of biological diversity, thereby maintaining its potential to meet the needs and aspirations of present and future generations'. As most parties to CITES are also parties to the CBD, it may be argued that the concept of 'sustainable use' overarches the overly rigid system of CITES,

[40] Decisions 10.1 (9–20 June 1997) and 10.2 (Rev COP11) (10–20 April 2000). See JE Carey, 'Improving the Efficacy of CITES by Providing the Proper Incentives to Protect Endangered Species' (1999) 77 *Washington University Law Quarterly* 1291, 1311. See also Resolution Conf10.10 (Rev CoP14) (3–15 June 2007).

[41] See www.cites.org/eng/news/press/2008/080716_ivory.shtml.

[42] CoP15 Prop 4 and 5; see summary record of the fifth plenary session, CoP15 Plen5 (Rev1) (25 March 2010) 4 *et seq*.

[43] CoP15 Prop 6; see summary record of the sixth plenary session, CoP15 Plen6 (Rev1) (25 March 2010) 1.

[44] Decision 13.26 (Rev CoP15) (24 March 2010).

[45] Resolution Conf10.10 (Rev CoP15) (24 March 2010).

since the CBD does not compete with CITES but co-determines the implementation of CITES.[46]

Another example to be considered is the protection of tigers. They are killed for their skins and rugs; parts of their bodies are used in rituals or for Oriental medicine. 'Tigers and other big cats' were first listed in Appendix I in 1975. Of particular concern is the South China Tiger.[47] To address the adverse impact on tiger populations of escalating trade in tiger parts COP 9 (1994) adopted Resolution 9.13 on the Conservation of and Trade in Tigers which urged range states to introduce effective legislation to reduce such activities. COP 11 (2000) aimed at strengthening efforts to conserve populations of tigers and combat illegal trade in live specimens and parts thereof by adopting Resolution 11.5, superseding Resolution 9.13. Resolution 12.5, adopted by COP 12 (2002), extended the scope of Resolution 11.5 to all Asian big cats listed in Appendix I, encouraging increased regional co-operation and improved control of domestic markets. COP 14 adopted a number of pertinent reporting decisions but an assessment of the implementation of Resolution 12.5 showed the degree to which range states had failed in their reporting obligations. These measures notwithstanding, tiger populations obviously continue to decline. To this end, a revised version of Resolution 12.5,[48] as well as several decisions addressing trade in tigers and other Asian big cat species listed in Appendix I, were eventually adopted by the COP.[49]

As far as other species are concerned, currently, only three subspecies of sharks are included in Appendix II (whale shark, basking shark and great white shark).[50] Proposals to include further subspecies were rejected by COP 15 in 2010.[51] The proposal to transfer polar bears from Appendix II to Appendix I was also rejected by COP 15[52] due to, as it was argued, insufficient scientific evidence to support an Appendix I listing.[53]

14.2.3 Protecting Migratory Species

Migratory species are particularly vulnerable, irrespective of whether or not such migration is triggered by a change of seasons, and whether it occurs over land, air or sea.

[46] With regard to co-operation between the two regimes see R Cooney, 'CITES and the CBD: Tensions and Synergies' (2001) 10 *RECIEL* 259; for a review of CITES see U Beyerlin, 'Perspectives on Wildlife Conservation: A Critical Assessment of the Relevant International Treaties and EC Instruments' in T Zhenghua and R Wolfrum (eds), *Implementing International Environmental Law in Germany and China* (London 2001) 41, 51–54.

[47] See, among others, A Tierney, 'Can CITES Prevent the Tiger Being Worshipped to Death in China?' (1998) 3 *Asia Pacific Journal of Environmental Law* 3.

[48] Resolution 12.5 (Rev CoP15) (24 March 2010).

[49] Decisions 15.46 to 15.49, 15.70 and 14.66 (Rev CoP15); all decisions were adopted on 24 March 2010; for a brief summary of COP15 outcomes on tigers and Asian big cats see Earth Negotiations Bulletin, vol 21 no 67 (29 March 2010) 9.

[50] However, Resolution 12.6 on the conservation and management of sharks has been slightly revised (25 March 2010).

[51] CoP15 Prop 15–18; see summary record of the sixth plenary session, above n 43, 1 *et seq*.

[52] CoP15 Prop 3; see summary record of the fifth plenary session, above n 42, 4.

[53] *Cf* the Press Release on the results of COP15, 'CITES Conference ends without new sharks in its net' (25 March 2010), available at www.cites.org/eng/news/press/index.shtml.

These species require hospitable grounds and sustenance along their routes, relying upon the life cycles of other plants and other animals. Apart from the threats inherent in the coverage of long distances, climate change is threatening the existence of some migratory species. Climate change contributes partly to diminishing habitat, disrupting sources for nutrition, affecting nesting and breeding habits, and increasing exposure to disease. In addition, migratory species often cross state boundaries and, consequently, conservation measures require international co-operation. Migratory species may not only fall victim to hazardous weather, or lack of food or water, but many of them are trapped and shot. It is against this background that the Bonn Convention on the Conservation of Migratory Species of Wild Animals (CMS) of 23 June 1979 was developed. Other agreements related to the issue of migratory species, such as the Ramsar Convention and the Agreement relating to the Conservation and Management of Straddling Fish Stocks and Highly Migratory Fish Stocks, have already been addressed elsewhere in this book.[54] By their very nature, migratory species have thus become a symbol of the need for international co-operation in nature conservation; they can only be effectively conserved if all the range states work together.

The CMS, concluded under the auspices of the United Nations Environment Programme, distinguishes between migratory species threatened with extinction (listed in Appendix I of the Convention) and migratory species which need or would significantly benefit from international co-operation (listed in Appendix II). As can be taken from the preamble of the Convention, parties are aware 'that each generation of man holds the resources of the earth for future generations and has an obligation to ensure that this legacy is conserved and, where utilized, is used wisely'. Parties recognise that they 'must be the protectors of the migratory species of wild animals that live within or pass through their national jurisdictional boundaries'. For a migratory species to be included in Appendix I, Article III(2) CMS requires reliable evidence, including the best scientific evidence available, indicating that the species is endangered. Species can be removed from Appendix I if there is scientific evidence that the species is no longer endangered and that it is unlikely that this species will become endangered again due to its removal from Appendix I (Article III(3)). With regard to migratory species included in Appendix I, parties to the Convention are required under Article III(4) to conserve and even restore habitat for and to prevent, remove, compensate for or minimise the adverse effects of activities or obstacles that seriously impede or prevent the migration of these species. Under Article III(5) of the Convention, parties shall prohibit the taking of animals belonging to such species. The conditions for inclusion of species in Appendix II are laid down in Article I(1)(c) of the Convention. This requires, among other things, consideration of population dynamics data, indications that the species is not maintaining itself on a long-term basis as a viable component of its ecosystems, and the availability of sufficient habitat to maintain the population of the species on a long-term basis. As far as the protection of species included in Appendix II is concerned, the Convention invites parties to enter into regional agreements for the protection of these species (Article IV). Article V of the Convention lays down guidelines for such regional agreements. Their

[54] See Chapter 12.4.2.

object 'shall be to restore the migratory species concerned to a favourable conservation status or to maintain it in such a status' (Article V(1)), if possible they should 'deal with more than one migratory species' (Article V(3)) and 'cover the whole of the range of the migratory species concerned' (Article V(2)). Truly detailed minimum standards for such regional agreements are included in Article V(5).[55]

The CMS establishes a fairly detailed organisational setting. According to Article VI, the Secretariat keeps an up-to-date list of range states with regard to all species included in Appendices I and II. Detailed reporting obligations are laid down for all range states. The COP acts as the decision-making organ of the Convention (Article VII(1)); it is in charge of reviewing the implementation of the Convention (Article VII(5)) and enjoys the support of a Scientific Council (Article VIII) and a Secretariat, located in Bonn and 'provided by the Executive Director of the United Nations Environment Programme' (Article IX(2)). The Convention includes treaty-specific mechanisms for the amendment of its text (Article X) and its Appendices (Article XI).[56]

14.2.4 Other Instruments

Firstly, a number of regional agreements have been concluded on the basis of Articles IV(4) and V CMS. Reference may be made, in particular, to the Agreement on the Conservation of Seals in the Wadden Sea of 16 October 1990, concluded in response to a dramatic decline in the common seal population in the Wadden Sea in 1988; the Agreement on the Conservation of Bats in Europe of 10 September 1991; the Agreement on the Conservation of Small Cetaceans of the Baltic and North Seas of 13 September 1991, dealing with marine mammals such as whales, dolphins and porpoises; the African-Eurasian Migratory Waterbird Agreement of 26 June 1995; the Agreement on the Conservation of Cetaceans of the Black Sea, Mediterranean Sea and Contiguous Atlantic Area of 22 November 1996; the Agreement on the Conservation of Albatrosses and Petrels of 19 June 2001; and, finally, the CMS Agreement on the Conservation of Gorillas and their Habitats of 26 October 2007. In light of this multitude of agreements the question has been raised whether a sufficient degree of coherence exists.[57] However, it is plausible to argue that the Bonn Convention acts as a framework of reference and that it has proven its potential as a catalyst by grouping together regional agreements.

The Bern Convention on the Conservation of European Wildlife and Natural Habitats (Bern Convention) of 19 September 1979,[58] concluded within the framework of the Council of Europe, aims at ensuring the conservation and protection of wild plant and animal species and their natural habitats. To this end endangered plants and animals are listed in three Appendices, and a fourth Appendix includes prohibited means and methods

[55] For a discussion of the protection of migratory species see N Matz, 'Chaos or Coherence? Implementing and Enforcing the Conservation of Migratory Species through Various Legal Instruments' (2005) 65 *ZaöRV* 197, 200–202 and 204–207.

[56] See Chapter 18.4.

[57] See, among others, Matz, above n 55.

[58] The Bern Convention is binding on 50 parties.

of killing, capture and other forms of exploitation in relation to listed species. According to Article 2 of the Convention, parties shall take requisite measures to maintain the population of wild flora and fauna at, or adapt it to, a level which corresponds in particular to ecological, scientific and cultural requirements, while taking account of economic and recreational requirements and the needs of subspecies, varieties or forms that are at risk locally. Article 3 requires the development of appropriate national policies, and Article 4 addresses the protection of habitats. The core provisions related to the protection of listed species are included in Articles 5–9. With regard to 'strictly protected flora species' as included in Appendix I, Article 5 requires parties to take appropriate and necessary legislative and administrative measures to ensure their special protection. The Convention specifies that '[d]eliberate picking, collecting, cutting or uprooting of such plants shall be prohibited' and that parties shall as far as appropriate 'prohibit the possession or sale of these species'. Article 6 deals with strictly protected fauna species, as listed in Appendix II, and stipulates that appropriate and necessary legislative and administrative measures have to be taken, prohibiting in particular all forms of deliberate capture and keeping and deliberate killing. Finally, Article 7 requires the development and application of regulatory policies with regard to wild fauna specified in Appendix III in order to keep the populations out of danger.

There are also other (non-regional) agreements addressing flora and fauna. While the Agreement on Conservation of Polar Bears of 15 November 1973[59] is unique, the CMS Secretariat developed drafts to complement existing global shark conservation and management efforts.[60] In the course of deliberations, consensus was reached that the instrument should be a non-legally binding Memorandum of Understanding (MOU). The final text was opened for signature at the Meeting on International Cooperation on Migratory Sharks under the Convention on Migratory Species at Manila on 12 May 2010.[61] Annex 1 defines the species covered by the MOU which include all seven shark species currently in Appendix I and II of CMS. The MOU's objective 'is to achieve and maintain a favourable conservation status for migratory sharks based on the best available scientific information, taking into account the socio-economic and other values of these species for the people of the Signatories' (section 2). Conservation and management of migratory sharks are embodied in the development of a Migratory Sharks Conservation Plan (section 4), its implementing measures applying 'widely both an ecosystem and a precautionary approach' (section 3.9).

[59] For an interesting discussion of the Agreement in light of climate change see N Bankes, 'Climate Change and the Regime for the Conservation of Polar Bears' in T Koivurova *et al* (eds), *Climate Governance in the Arctic* (Berlin 2009) 351.

[60] Consensus could not be reached on the final form that the CMS agreement should take (legally or non-legally binding) until the second meeting on sharks, held in Rome, Italy on 6–8 December 2008; see www.cms.int/bodies/meetings/regional/sharks/Docs_Manila_Mtg/Shk3_Doc_04_Revised_draft_Sharks_MoU_En.pdf, 3.

[61] The official summary sheet on the status of the MOU on migratory sharks is available at www.cms.int/pdf/en/summary_sheets/sharks.pdf.

14.3 Biological Diversity

The importance of protecting the diversity of life forms attracted increased attention in 2010, the International Year of Biodiversity. Biodiversity is often used as an indicator to assess the health of biological systems. This diversity is not distributed evenly across the globe: it is rich in the tropics and less rich in polar regions, where fewer species are found. Since most genetic resources are located in developing countries, while the know-how for their commercial use is found in developed countries, access to these resources and the fair sharing of the benefits arising from their use is a problem that must be addressed.

Although the biodiversity of species is subject to natural variation, rapid environmental modifications may cause extinctions. Today, human impact on the environment is leading to a mass reduction in biodiversity, particularly due to the destruction of plant and animal habitats. In addition, human practices have caused a loss of genetic biodiversity. In light of the global health implications of this biodiversity loss, the relevance of biodiversity to human health has become a major international issue and efforts to strengthen the protection of biodiversity have been stepped up.

14.3.1 The Biodiversity Convention

The most important instrument for the protection of biological diversity is the CBD which was opened for signature in June 1992 after adoption of its text at Nairobi in May 1992. The Convention entered into force on 29 December 1993.[62]

The adoption of the Convention signals a paradigmatic change in the protection of fauna and flora. Instead of protecting particular categories of species or particular ecosystems, it takes a look at biodiversity as a whole, including all its parts and in particular its genetic bases. The Convention's main regulatory efforts focus on genetic resources. In its preamble, it stresses the 'intrinsic value' of biological diversity and declares its conservation a 'common concern of humankind'.[63] The preamble as well as Article 1 of the Convention identify three main objectives of the CBD: (i) the conservation of biological diversity; (ii) the sustainable use of its components; and (iii) the fair and equitable sharing of the benefits arising out of the utilisation of genetic resources. Even though Article 1 seems to focus on conservation as the primary objective of the Convention, the regulatory approach adopted puts a stronger focus on economic aspects, making use of an incentive structure for the benefit of biodiversity protection. This is best reflected in

[62] For a general overview see DR Downes, 'The Convention on Biological Diversity: Seeds of Green Trade?' (1994) 8 *Tulane Environmental Law Journal* 163.

[63] It is noteworthy, however, that the original plan to develop the Convention on the common heritage principle did not materialise; see T Lochen, *Die völkerrechtlichen Regelungen über den Zugang zu genetischen Ressourcen* (Tübingen 2007) 23–40.

the Convention's focus on 'sustainable use',[64] which entails a categorical shift away from the rather strict conservationist approach of the treaties adopted in the 1970s.[65]

It is worth mentioning that during COP 10 the 'Strategic Plan for Biodiversity for the Period 2011–2020' with its 'Aichi Targets',[66] based on the three objectives of the Convention was adopted. It includes 20 headline targets for 2020, organised under five strategic goals. These goals address, *inter alia*, the underlying causes of biodiversity loss, reduce the direct pressures on biodiversity and promote sustainable use, and improve the status of biodiversity by safeguarding ecosystems, species and genetic diversity. The 'Aichi Target' is seen as the 'overarching framework on biodiversity'[67] as it, *inter alia*, provides the basis for the development of national biodiversity strategies and action plans. Furthermore, COP 10 welcomed the 'Multi-Year Plan of Action for South-South Cooperation on Biodiversity for Development' as adopted by the 131 members of the Group of 77 and China.[68] The Plan of Action calls, *inter alia*, for close co-ordination with the Strategic Plan for the period 2011–2020 and for the support and engagement from G-77 members at regional as well as at national levels.

Another innovative feature of the Convention is its explicit recognition of national sovereignty over national resources. The Convention even makes use of national sovereignty as an instrument for the protection of biodiversity.[69] If biological diversity, and in particular its constitutive genetic resources, enjoy an intrinsic economic value and if their sustainable use is protected by international law, then a state on whose territory such resources are located will have an interest to preserve those resources and to benefit from their use. This state will try to prevent the exploitation or even extinction of such resources by others. At the same time this state is under an obligation to apply the sustainability idea with regard to its own treatment of biological resources.

This idea governs not only the conservation of biological resources as such but in particular the system of access and benefit-sharing (ABS). Article 3 CBD affirms 'the sovereign right [of states] to exploit their own resources' subject to their obligation not to 'cause damage to the environment of other States or of areas beyond the limits of

[64] On the various (theoretical and managerial) approaches to conserving biological resources see R Rayfuse, 'Biological Resources' in D Bodansky *et al* (eds), *The Oxford Handbook of International Environmental Law* (Oxford 2007) 362, 367–374; see also M Bowman, 'The Nature, Development and Philosophical Foundations of the Biodiversity Concept in International Law' in M Bowman and C Redgwell (eds), *International Law and the Conservation of Biological Diversity* (Boston 1996) 5.

[65] On the drafting history of the CBD see, among others, M Chandler, 'The Biodiversity Convention: Selected Issues of Interest to the International Lawyer' (1993) 4 *Colorado Journal of International Environmental Law and Policy* 141 and Koester, above n 9.

[66] See Decision X/2 in UNEP/CBD/COP/10/27 (20 January 2011).

[67] See CBD Press Release, 'A New Era of Living in Harmony with Nature is Born at the Nagoya Biodiversity Summit' (29 October 2010), available at www.cbd.int/doc/press/2010/pr-2010-10-29-cop-10-en.pdf.

[68] Decision X/23 in UNEP/CBD/COP/10/27 (20 January 2011), para 1; *cf* also UNEP/CBD/COP/10/18/Add1/Rev1 (17 October 2010) Annex.

[69] See, among others, R Wolfrum, 'The Convention on Biological Diversity: Using State Jurisdiction as a Means of Ensuring Compliance' in *id* (ed), *Enforcing Environmental Standards: Economic Mechanisms as Viable Means?* (Heidelberg 1996) 373 and T Marauhn, 'Die Erhaltung der biologischen Vielfalt und die nachhaltige Nutzung ihrer Bestandteile. Rechtsinstitute der Nachhaltigkeit auf der Grundlage des UN-Übereinkommens über die biologische Vielfalt' in K Lange (ed), *Nachhaltigkeit im Recht. Eine Annäherung* (Baden-Baden 2003) 87.

national jurisdiction'. Article 4 of the Convention defines its jurisdictional scope which includes all activities within the limits of a party's territorial jurisdiction but also extends to activities beyond the territory under its 'jurisdiction or control'.

Articles 5–7 and 10–14 lay down a number of measures to be taken by parties with regard to the conservation of biological diversity. Apart from an obligation to co-operate (Article 5), parties shall, among others, develop national strategies for the conservation and sustainable use of biological diversity. Article 10 ensures the sustainable use of components of biological diversity. Research and training (Article 12), public education and awareness (Article 13), and the adoption of incentives for the conservation and sustainable use of components of biological diversity (Article 11) are encouraged. Article 14 CBD even foresees impact assessments for projects which 'are likely to have significant adverse effects on biological diversity', including purely national projects. All these obligations are softened by the phrase 'as far as possible and as appropriate'.

The Convention includes two strategies for the conservation of biological resources: in-situ (Article 8) and ex-situ (Article 9) conservation.[70] As the conservation of biological diversity necessitates the conservation of ecosystems and natural habitats, in-situ conservation enjoys preference over ex-situ conservation.[71] Article 8 CBD requires parties (again 'as far as possible and as appropriate') to establish protected areas and to develop appropriate legislation.[72] Particular attention deserves the protection of the traditional knowledge of indigenous communities, 'subject to its national legislation' (Article 8(j)) and the obligation to promote the wider application of such knowledge.[73] Finally parties shall co-operate with regard to providing financial and other support for in-situ conservation by developing countries in particular. As far as ex-situ conservation is concerned, appropriate measures are considered complementary to in-situ conservation (Article 9). These measures may include activities of botanic gardens, aquaria, gene banks, seed banks and others.[74]

One of the most important objectives of the Convention concerns balancing the conservation and utilisation of biological diversity. While Article 15 deals with access to genetic resources, Article 16 addresses access to and transfer of technology. The two provisions together lay grounds for the access and benefit-sharing system. Their role in the overall system of the CBD emerges from the principle of national sovereignty over national resources as reflected in Articles 3 and 4 of the Convention. Host countries

[70] For a closer discussion see E Louka, *International Environmental Law. Fairness, Effectiveness and World Order* (Cambridge 2006) 299–302.

[71] L Glowka *et al*, *A Guide to the Convention on Biological Diversity* (Gland/Cambridge 1994) 52.

[72] For an interesting example/case-study see WT King and JG Maki, 'The Convention on Biological Diversity: In-situ Conservation in the Cook Islands' (1997) 6 *RECIEL* 304.

[73] On the protection of traditional knowledge see A von Hahn, *Traditionelles Wissen indigener und lokaler Gemeinschaften zwischen geistigen Eigentumsrechten und der 'public domain'* (Heidelberg 2004). See also CB Graber and D Girsberger, 'Traditional Knowledge at the International Level: Current Approaches and Proposals for a Bigger Picture that Include Cultural Diversity' in J Schmid and H Seiler (eds), *Recht des ländlichen Raums. Festgabe der Rechtswissenschaftlichen Fakultät der Universität Luzern für Paul Richli zum 60. Geburtstag* (Zürich *et al* 2006) 243.

[74] For an overview of ex-situ conservation see Glowka *et al*, above n 71, 52; see also R Wolfrum and T Stoll, *European Workshop on Genetic Resources Issues and Related Aspects: Access and Benefit Sharing, Intellectual Property Rights, Ex-situ collections* (Berlin 2000).

(which in fact predominantly are developing countries) enjoy sovereignty over genetic resources. Host countries are under an obligation to facilitate (to be distinguished from an obligation to grant) access to their genetic resources on the basis of Article 15(2), (4) and (5). These paragraphs focus on agreement between the country which seeks access to resources and the country which enjoys sovereignty over such resources. Terminology refers to 'mutually agreed terms' (Article 15(4)) and to 'prior informed consent' (Article 15(5)). The meaning of these terms has been refined by the so-called Bonn Guidelines[75] and numerous contractual arrangements have been made between institutions and companies involved in bioprospecting and host countries.[76] Granting access, however, is not unconditional. Article 15(7) CBD requires states parties to share 'in a fair and equitable way the results of research and development and the benefits arising from the commercial and other utilization of genetic resources'. This obligation is incumbent upon parties seeking access to those resources. Article 15(7) CBD underlines: 'Such sharing shall be upon mutually agreed terms.'[77]

Host countries (*ie* primarily developing countries) may be compensated for granting access under Article 16 CBD by getting access to technology. Article 16 CBD distinguishes between technologies 'relevant to the conservation and sustainable use of biological diversity' (Article 16(1) and (2) CBD) and technologies which are designed to 'make use of genetic resources' (Article 16(1) and (3) CBD). Paragraph 2, referring to 'fair and most favourable terms', provides a higher protection of intellectual property rights (of industrialised countries) than paragraph 3, which relies upon 'mutually agreed terms'. This allows industrialised states to limit their contribution to the development of biotechnology in developing countries. The overall impact of Article 16 CBD has remained weak because it concentrates on the protection of intellectual property rights rather than ensuring a balanced approach to the sharing of benefits. Comparing the protection of established intellectual property rights such as patents with the protection of traditional knowledge under the CBD, again developing countries are put at a disadvantage, due to a vagueness of wording and to the fact that traditional intellectual property rights draw their protection from other sources than the CBD, whereas traditional knowledge inserts something 'new' into the system of intellectual property rights. Moreover, the vagueness of obligations to share the benefits and to grant access to technology heavily relies on 'bona fide' implementation of these obligations by industrialised countries. Such a bona

[75] Bonn Guidelines on Access to Genetic Resources and Fair and Equitable Sharing of the Benefits Arising out of their Utilization, available at www.cbd.int/doc/publications/cbd-bonn-gdls-en.pdf. For a discussion of the guidelines see S Tully, 'The Bonn Guidelines on Access to Genetic Resources and Benefit Sharing' (2003) 12 *RECIEL* 84; see also MI Jeffery, 'Bioprospecting: Access to Genetic Resources and Benefit-Sharing under the Convention on Biodiversity and the Bonn Guidelines' (2002) 6 *Singapore Journal of International & Comparative Law* 747.

[76] PT Stoll, 'Access to Genetic Resources and Benefit Sharing: Underlying Concepts and the Idea of Justice' in EC Kamau and G Winter (eds), *Genetic Resources, Traditional Knowledge and the Law: Solutions for Access and Benefit Sharing* (London 2009) 3.

[77] For a discussion see G Henne, '"Mutually agreed terms" in the Convention on Biological Diversity: Requirements under Public International Law' in J Mugabe *et al* (eds), *Access to Genetic Resources—Strategies for Sharing Benefits* (Nairobi 1997) 71.

fide approach seems to be still lacking, not only in the context of Article 16 CBD but also with regard to similar obligations under the TRIPS agreement.[78]

14.3.2 Access and Benefit-Sharing: Bonn Guidelines and Nagoya Protocol

In order to meet the obligations laid down in Article 15 CBD, parties set up, during COP 5 in 2000, an Ad Hoc Open-ended Working Group on Access and Benefit-Sharing.[79] Negotiated within two years, COP 6 adopted the so-called Bonn Guidelines in 2002. Without being legally binding, these Guidelines aim at assisting governments in the development of national and regional legislation as well as other mechanisms to ensure fair access to genetic resources and the sharing of benefits from these resources. Notwithstanding progress towards a binding regime,[80] the Bonn Guidelines still represent the current consensus as to what can be achieved in substance.[81] They identify the actors involved (*ie* the country of origin, the provider, the user and the requesting state), their roles and their respective obligations. The Guidelines ensure participation of all relevant stakeholders, including indigenous and local communities. In order to safeguard the rights of all actors, the Bonn Guidelines rely upon the concepts of prior informed consent (PIC)[82] and mutually agreed terms (MATs).[83] These general concepts notwithstanding, the Guidelines largely rely on the conclusion of material transfer agreements (MTAs), offering some elements to be included therein. Criticism of the Bonn Guidelines arises in part from the fact that the various instruments referred to in the Guidelines are not clearly related to each other.[84] After their adoption, parties continued to negotiate within the framework of a Working Group on Access and Benefit-Sharing.[85]

In 2008, COP 9 instructed the Working Group to finalise the negotiation process and to submit an instrument for consideration and adoption by COP 10.[86] Furthermore,[87] the Executive Secretary was requested to commission studies relating to, *inter alia*, the question how an international regime on access and benefit-sharing could be in harmony with and coexist alongside other international instruments and forums that govern the use of genetic resources.[88] In November 2009, parties agreed on a negotiating text, the

[78] See T Cottier, 'Geistiges Eigentum, Handel und nachhaltige Entwicklung. Erfahrungen und Perspektiven im Nord-Süd-Verhältnis' in W Meng *et al*, *Das internationale Recht im Nord-Süd-Verhältnis* (Heidelberg 2005) 237, 256 *et seq*.

[79] Decision V/26 in UNEP/CBD/COP/5/23 (15–26 May 2000) 197.

[80] See Notification Ref SCBD/OMG/NP/74306 'United Nations Secretary General welcomes COP10 Outcomes' (8 November 2010), available at www.cbd.int/doc/notifications/2010/ntf-2010-201-cop10-en.pdf.

[81] Tully, above n 75.

[82] KJ Ni, 'Legal Aspects of Prior Informed Consent on Access to Genetic Resources' (2009) 42 *Vanderbilt Journal of Transnational Law* 227.

[83] Henne, above n 77.

[84] Lochen, above n 63, 165 *et seq*.

[85] See www.cbd.int/abs/regime.shtml.

[86] Decision IX/12 in UNEP/CBD/COP/9/29 (19–30 May 2008) 110; see also UNEP/CBD/WG-ABS/7/7 (6 March 2009), 'International Regime on Access and Benefit-Sharing: Negotiation of Operational Text'.

[87] Decision IX/12 in *ibid*, 111.

[88] See, *eg*, UNEP/CBD/WG-ABS/7/INF/3/Part1 (3 March 2009), 'Study on the Relationship between an International Regime on Access and Benefit-Sharing and Other International Instruments and Forums that Govern the Use of Genetic Resources: The International Treaty on Plant Genetic Resources for Food and

so-called 'Montreal Annex',[89] a single negotiating text incorporating all elements of the international ABS regime, which had been discussed as the Nagoya Protocol on Access to Genetic Resources and the Fair and Equitable Sharing of Benefits Arising from their Utilization to the Convention on Biological Diversity (Nagoya Protocol).[90] In light of the legally non-binding character of the Bonn Guidelines, the binding nature of the envisaged Protocol has become an important question of debate. It is argued that the international character of the ABS process requires more than national legislation and voluntary guidelines.[91]

Finally, after 10 years of negotiation, the Nagoya Protocol was adopted by the Conference of the Parties at its 10th Meeting on the basis of a draft,[92] focusing primarily on procedural aspects.[93] In particular, Article 4 includes provisions regarding benefit-sharing and Article 5 states that access to genetic resources is subject to prior informed consent of the provider country. Appropriate legislative, administrative or policy measures must aim at legal certainty, clarity and transparency; provide for timely written decision by a competent national authority; provide for the issuance of a permit or internationally recognised certificate as evidence of the decision to grant prior informed consent; and set out criteria for indigenous and local communities' prior informed consent and involvement concerning access to their genetic resources in such cases where applicable national law recognises and affirms their rights to genetic resources. Furthermore, the establishment of clear rules and procedures is necessary for requiring and establishing mutually agreed terms at the time of access. Article 9(1) of the Nagoya Protocol stipulates that parties shall give due consideration to indigenous and local community laws, customary laws, community protocols and procedures with respect to traditional knowledge associated with genetic resources. As regards the relationship between the Nagoya Protocol and other international agreements and instruments, Article 3 *bis* Nagoya Protocol includes provisions which deserve closer attention. According to its paragraph 1, its provisions 'shall not affect the rights and obligations of any Party deriving from any existing international agreement, except where the exercise of those rights and obligations would cause a serious damage or threat to biological diversity'. At the same time it is stressed that

Agriculture and the Commission on Genetic Resources for Food and Agriculture of the Food and Agriculture Organization of the United Nations'. See also UNEP/CBD/WG-ABS/7/INF/3/Part2 (3 March 2009), 'Study on the Relationship between an International Regime on Access and Benefit-Sharing and other International Instruments and Forums that Govern the Use of Genetic Resources: WTO; WIPO; and UPOV'.

[89] See www.cbd.int/abs/regime.shtml; Summary of the Ninth Meeting of the Working Group on Access and Benefit-Sharing of the Convention on Biological Diversity, 22–28 March 2010, Earth Negotiations Bulletin, vol 9 no 503 (31 March 2010) 3.

[90] UNEP/CBD/WG-ABS/8/8 (20 November 2009) 21 *et seq*; see also UNEP/CBD/COP/10/5/Add5 (17 October 2010), 'Report of the Third Part of the Ninth Meeting of the Ad Hoc Open-Ended Working Group on Access and Benefit-Sharing', 6 *et seq*.

[91] S Bhatti and TR Young, 'A Contractual View of ABS' in S Bhatti *et al* (eds), *Contracting for ABS: The Legal and Scientific Implications of Bioprospecting Contracts* (Gland 2009) 11, 29, available at http://data.iucn.org/dbtw-wpd/edocs/EPLP-067-4.pdf.

[92] See UNEP/CBD/COP/10/L43/Rev1 (29 October 2010), 'Access to Genetic Resources and the Fair and Equitable Sharing of Benefits Arising from their Utilization: Draft decision submitted by the President of the Conference of the Parties'.

[93] See Decision X/1 on 'Access to Genetic Resources and the Fair and Equitable Sharing of Benefits Arising from their Utilization' in UNEP/CBD/COP/10/27 (20 January 2011).

there is no intention to create a hierarchy between the Protocol and other international instruments. Paragraph 3 provides that '[t]his Protocol shall be implemented in a mutually supportive manner with other international instruments' relevant to it. Although its wording is considered to be rather vague and ambiguous, it nevertheless has the potential to 'become a powerful tool for a more balanced implementation of the CBD's three objectives'.[94]

The Bonn Guidelines and the Nagoya Protocol can be regarded as complementary.[95] The Protocol sets the procedural framework for ABS, and the Bonn Guidelines provide for a set of substantive criteria which can be taken as points of reference whenever parties are negotiating individual agreements on access and benefit-sharing.

14.3.3 The International Treaty on Plant Genetic Resources

Genetic resources have not only been a matter of concern from the perspective of international environmental law, but also in view of their contribution to sustainable agriculture and food security. While farmers maintained, and even increased, genetic diversity over a long period of time in the process of selecting wild plants and thereby altering their genotypes, since World War II, many farmers have become reliant on commercial and industrialised breeders and seed-processors for their supply of quality seeds. With the biotechnological revolution, modern agriculture is increasingly based on genetically uniform high-yielding crop varieties. It has been argued that the 'sustainability of such a system is at stake, owing to the loss of genetic diversity that ensues'.[96] Since hardly more than 150 species are currently cultivated and 'most of mankind now lives off no more than 12 plant species',[97] access to genetic resources is highly important in order to maintain a minimum of genetic variability. Responding to this finding, the FAO, in 1983, adopted the International Undertaking on Plant Genetic Resources (IUPGR).[98] This non-legally binding instrument is based on the assumption that plant genetic resources are the common heritage of mankind. Meanwhile, this instrument has been further developed into the International Treaty on Plant Genetic Resources for Food and Agriculture (ITPGRFA), notwithstanding continued resistance on the part of some industrialised states during the negotiations and the failure of the United States and Japan to sign.[99]

The IUPGR and the CBD follow diametrically opposed regulatory approaches, with the IUPGR relying on the concept of common heritage and the CBD relying on the

[94] Summary of the Tenth Conference of the Parties to the Convention on Biological Diversity: 18–29 October 2010, Earth Negotiations Bulletin, vol 9 no 544 (1 November 2010) 27.

[95] *Cf* in this respect the wording in the 'preamble' of the pertinent COP decision (see n 93 above) which reads as follows: 'Recognizing that the international regime is constituted of the Convention on Biological Diversity, the Protocol on Access to Genetic Resources and the Fair and Equitable Sharing of the Benefits Arising from their Utilization, as well as complementary instruments, including . . . the Bonn Guidelines.'

[96] M Lightbourne, 'The FAO Multilateral System for Plant Genetic Resources for Food and Agriculture' (2009) 30 *Washington University Journal of Law and Policy* 465, 466.

[97] J Esquinas-Alcázar, 'Protecting Crop Genetic Diversity for Food Security: Political, Ethical and Technical Challenges' (2005) 6 *Nature Reviews Genetics* 946, 947.

[98] FAO (Res 8/83, adopted by the 22nd Session of the Conference) (23 November 1983).

[99] The Treaty has been adopted on 3 November 2001; it is binding on 125 parties.

concept of national sovereignty over natural resources. During the negotiations of the ITPGRFA these opposing concepts were imminent and led to differences between the CBD and the ITPGRFA as far as access to genetic resources is concerned.

Covering all plant genetic resources, the ITPGRFA promotes 'an integrated approach to the exploration, conservation and sustainable use of plant genetic resources for food and agriculture' (Article 5(1)) and encourages on-farm and in-situ conservation. The ITPGRFA aims at guaranteeing food security, not only by encouraging sustainable use of plant genetic resources for food and agriculture, but also by establishing a system of fair and equitable benefit sharing arising from the use of such resources. In addition, the ITPGRFA recognises farmers' rights of access to genetic resources and of participation in relevant decision-making processes.

The most important element of the ITPGRFA is its Multilateral System of Access and Benefit-Sharing (Articles 10–13).[100] This includes all plant genetic resources 'listed in Annex I that are under the management and control of the Contracting Parties and in the public domain' as well as those listed in Annex I but held in ex-situ collections of the International Agricultural Research Centers of the Consultative Group of the International Agricultural Research (CGIAR). On a voluntary basis the system can also be applied to plant genetic resources held by natural and legal persons within the jurisdiction of contracting parties as well as by selected international institutions. The Multilateral System is based on the idea that benefits accruing from plant genetic resources 'shall be shared fairly and equitably through the following mechanisms: the exchange of information, access to and transfer of technology, capacity-building, and the sharing of the benefits arising from commercialization' (Article 13(2) ITPGRFA). Contracting parties undertake to 'facilitate access to technologies for the conservation, characterization, evaluation and use of plant genetic resources' (Article 13(2)(b)(i) ITPGRFA) covered by the system but the Treaty ensures that the technology transfer remains 'consistent with the adequate and effective protection of intellectual property rights' (Article 13(2)(b)(ii)–(iii) ITPGRFA). The interpretation of this provision is, however, disputed, in particular as far as the isolation of genetic material and minimal modification of such material are concerned. The commercialisation of products emerging from access to and use of plant genetic resources triggers the payment of a contribution to the Treaty's benefit-sharing system (Article 13(2)(d)(ii) ITPGRFA). The system was further developed by the adoption of a Standard Material Transfer Agreement (SMTA) by the International Treaty Governing Body in June 2006.[101]

While there are different regulatory approaches of the CBD and the ITPGRFA to the protection of genetic materials, in particular with regard to access and benefit-sharing, their relationship to the WTO Agreement on Trade-Related Aspects of Intellectual Property Rights (TRIPS) creates specific problems. Even though all three agreements are independent of each other, their scope partly overlaps and the question arises whether recognition of intellectual property rights by the CBD and the ITPGRFA is adequate to

[100] D Cooper, 'The International Treaty on Plant Genetic Resources for Food and Agriculture' (2002) 11 *RECIEL* 1, 4 *et seq.*

[101] Available at ftp://ftp.fao.org/ag/agp/planttreaty/agreements/smta/SMTAe.pdf.

avoid conflict with the protection of intellectual property rights under the TRIPS agreement. Some have called for a revision of the TRIPS agreement, in order to include an obligation to disclose the origin of genetic resources used when applying for a patent or to provide a certificate about the way these resources were obtained. Patent law could thus develop into a mechanism to remedy the implementation deficit of the CBD and the ITPGRFA with regard to the protection of individuals as well as local and indigenous communities and their rights related to genetic resources held by them.[102]

14.3.4 Trading Genetic Material: The Biosafety Protocol

As important as research and development in biotechnology may be, as beneficial as progress in biotechnology may be for medical and pharmaceutical or for agricultural and nutritional purposes, the risks biotechnology pose to biological diversity as such and to humans must not be underestimated. This is why, according to Article 19(3) CBD, the parties to the Biodiversity Convention undertook to

> consider the need for and modalities of a protocol setting out appropriate procedures, including, in particular, advance informed agreement, in the field of the safe transfer, handling and use of any living modified organism resulting from biotechnology that may have adverse effect on the conservation and sustainable use of biological diversity.

Indeed, after difficult negotiations, on 29 January 2000, the Conference of the Parties to the Convention on Biological Diversity adopted the Cartagena Protocol on Biosafety (Cartagena Protocol).[103] This instrument is designed to protect biological diversity from the potential risks posed by living modified organisms resulting from modern biotechnology.

The Protocol is concerned with living modified organisms; such an organism is defined as ‘any living organism that possesses a novel combination of genetic material obtained through the use of modern biotechnology’ (Article 3(g) Cartagena Protocol). The scope of the Protocol, however, is limited to ‘the transboundary movement, transit, handling and use of all living modified organisms’. These limitations notwithstanding, the Protocol addresses effects that living organisms may have ‘on the conservation and sustainable use of biological diversity, taking also into account risks to human health’ (Article 4). In addressing the dangers of living modified organisms, the Protocol pursues a precautionary approach and affirms Principle 15 of the Rio Declaration on Environment and Devel-

[102] With regard to the discussion on disclosure of the origin of genetic resources used in patented technologies see Lochen, above n 63, 279 *et seq* and J Carr, ‘Agreements that Divide: TRIPS vs. CBD and Proposals for Mandatory Disclosure of Source and Origin of Genetic Resources in Patent Applications’ (2008) 18 *Journal of Transnational Law and Policy* 131–154; on the relationship between TRIPS and CBD see also www.wto.org/english/tratop_e/trips_e/art27_3b_background_e.htm.

[103] UNEP/CBD/ExCOP/1/3 (29 January 2000); see L Boisson de Chazournes, UP Thomas, FX Perrez, F Pythoud, S Shaw, R Schwartz and S Zarrilli, ‘The Biosafety Protocol: Regulatory Innovation and Emerging Trends’ (2000) 10 *Schweizerische Zeitschrift für internationales und europäisches Recht* 513 and R Mackenzie, F Burhenne-Guilmin, AGM La Viña and JD Werksman in cooperation with A Ascencio, J Kinderlerer, K Kummer and R Tapper, *An Explanatory Guide to the Cartagena Protocol on Biosafety* (Gland/Cambridge 2003).

opment (Preamble and Article 1 Cartagena Protocol).[104] The precautionary approach is reflected in a number of other provisions of the Protocol. Thus, Articles 10(6) and 11(8) Cartagena Protocol state that

> [l]ack of scientific certainty due to insufficient relevant scientific information and knowledge regarding the extent of the potential adverse effects of a living modified organism on the conservation and sustainable use of biological diversity in the Party of import, taking also into account risks to human health, shall not prevent that Party from taking a decision, as appropriate, with regard to the import of [the] living modified organism [in question] . . . in order to avoid or minimize such potential adverse effects

and Annex III on risk assessment notes that '[l]ack of scientific knowledge or scientific consensus should not necessarily be interpreted as indicating a particular level of risk, an absence of risk, or an acceptable risk'. In order to meet its objectives, the Protocol establishes a so-called advance informed agreement (AIA) procedure for ensuring that countries are provided with the information necessary to make informed decisions before agreeing to the import of living modified organisms into their territory (Articles 8–10 and 12 Cartagena Protocol).[105] Furthermore, the Protocol establishes a Biosafety Clearing-House to facilitate the exchange of information on living modified organisms and to assist countries in the implementation of the Protocol (Article 20 Cartagena Protocol).

Similar to the CBD and the ITPGRFA, the Protocol raises a number of difficult questions concerning its relationship with WTO law.[106] Among others, the Agreement on the Application of Sanitary and Phytosanitary Measures, the Agreement on Technical Barriers to Trade, and the Agreement on Trade-Related Aspects of Intellectual Property Rights, contain provisions of relevance to the Protocol. The Protocol itself seeks to accommodate some of the conflicts, and in its Preamble states, *inter alia*, that parties recognise that trade and environment agreements should be mutually supportive; that the Protocol should not be interpreted as implying a change in the rights and obligations under any existing agreements; and, finally, that the Protocol is not intended to be subordinated to other international agreements.

14.4 Forests

The main legally binding international agreement for the protection of forests focuses on tropical forests. The International Tropical Timber Agreement (ITTA) is neither a purely conservationist instrument nor a traditional commodity agreement. It seeks to balance concerns about deforestation in tropical countries with recognition of the fact that trade in tropical timber is highly relevant for the economic development of these

[104] See R Hill, S Johnston and C Sendashonga, 'Risk Assessment and Precaution in the Biosafety Protocol' (2004) 13 *RECIEL* 263.

[105] *Cf* Chapter 15 on the prior informed consent procedure which resembles the advance informed agreement procedure.

[106] *Cf* AH Qureshi, 'The Cartagena Protocol on Biosafety and the WTO—Co-existence or Incoherence?' (2000) 49 *ICLQ* 835.

countries.[107] The ITTA thus combines forest conservation and development with trade in tropical timber. After long and protracted negotiations, which had already begun in 1976 within the framework of UNCTAD, the first ITTA was adopted on 18 November 1983. It was superseded by its successor agreement of 26 January 1994, which entered into force on 1 January 1997. Negotiations for a third ITTA were concluded in 2006. It is expected to enter into force in the near future. The ITTA 2006 builds on its predecessors, combining the sustainable management of the resource base and at the same time encouraging timber trade. It operates as the constitutive document of the International Tropical Timber Organization (ITTO) which was first established on the basis of the ITTA 1983 (Article 3(1) ITTA 2006). The ITTO enjoys international legal personality (Article 17(1) ITTA 2006). It includes producing and consuming members (Article 4 ITTA 2006) and functions through the International Tropical Timber Council (Article 6 ITTA 2006), committees and subsidiary bodies (Article 26 ITTA 2006) and a secretariat headed by an Executive Director (Article 14 ITTA 2006). The Council at least meets annually (Article 9(1) ITTA 2006). It is the main decision-making body of the ITTO with weighted voting rights (Article 10 ITTA 2006), based upon trade volume and regionally split. Consensus is favoured, but, if consensus cannot be reached, all decisions are taken by a simple distributed majority vote (Article 12 ITTA 2006). The ITTO provides funding on a project basis ('Special Account', Article 20 ITTA 2006) and, more generally, seeks to enhance the capacity of members to focus on the export of sustainably managed sources ('Bali Partnership Fund', Article 21 ITTA 2006).

Article 1 ITTA 2006 lays down the Agreement's overall objective which is 'to promote the expansion and diversification of international trade in tropical timber from sustainably managed and legally harvested forests and to promote the sustainable management of tropical timber producing forests'. In its implementing activities the ITTO focuses on policy work and on project activities. Policy work necessitates the prior establishment, on a regular basis, of an action plan (Article 24 ITTA 2006) which shall be reflected in the work programme approved by the Council. Further, guidelines, manuals, studies and reports are part of the Organization's policy activities as well as communication and outreach. Proposals for projects may be submitted either by members or by the Executive Director (Article 25 ITTA 2006). The Council is tasked to develop criteria for project approval, taking into account the criteria listed in Article 25 ITTA 2006. These include the environmental and social effects of projects, their relationship to national forest programmes and strategies, their cost effectiveness, technical and regional needs, the need to avoid duplication efforts, and the need to incorporate lessons learned. In order to operate on a sufficiently solid basis of factual knowledge, the Agreement foresees co-operation with other relevant international organisations and NGOs (Article 27(1) ITTA 2006). While parties to the Agreement are under an obligation to 'cooperate to promote the attainment of its objectives and avoid any action contrary thereto' (Article 29(1) ITTA 2006), Article 34 ITTA 2006 clearly states that '[n]othing in this Agreement authorizes the use of measures to restrict or ban international trade in, and in particular as they

[107] See D König, 'New Approaches to Achieve Sustainable Management of Tropical Timber' in Wolfrum (ed), above n 69, 337.

concern imports of, and utilization of, timber and timber products'. The quorum for entry into force (Article 39 ITTA 2006) requires a minimum of producers and consumers with a minimum of trade in topical timber to be 'on board'.

A second international instrument addressing forests as an object of protection is the Non-Legally Binding Authoritative Statement of Principles for a Global Consensus on the Management, Conservation and Sustainable Development of All Types of Forests adopted at the 1992 Rio Conference[108] and informally labelled the 'Forest Principles'. Even though this declaration is not legally binding, it is a useful point of reference because it reflects 'a first global consensus on forests', identifying 15 principles for the management, conservation and sustainable development of all types of forests.[109] However, since the principles are broadly worded, their potential for innovation and their steering capacity have been limited. In line with general international environmental law, the Forest Principles recognise 'the sovereign right' of states 'to exploit their own resources pursuant to their own environmental policies'. At the same time they stress the responsibility of states 'to ensure that activities within their jurisdiction or control do not cause damage to the environment of other States or of areas beyond the limits of national jurisdiction' (Principle 1(a)). This is taken up by Principle 2(a), however, qualified by the recognition that '[a]ppropriate measures should be taken to protect forests against harmful effects of pollution . . . in order to maintain their full multiple value' (Principle 2(b)). *Inter alia*, the Forest Principles encourage all countries to engage in forest planting and conservation; they underline that sustainable use of forests necessitates sustainable patterns of production and consumption; they call for the sharing of profits from biotechnology products and genetic materials taken from forests; they stress that planted forests are environmentally sound sources of renewable energy and industrial raw materials; they call for national plans to protect unique examples of forests, for various reasons, including cultural, spiritual and historical aspects. Planning and implementation of national forest policies should be done on an inclusive basis with broad participation of all concerned.

It is obvious that compliance with and further development of the Forest Principles would substantially enhance the protection of forests. However, given their broad wording and their character as legally non-binding, they cannot replace a treaty establishing a legal framework for the sustainable use and conservation of forests which had been envisaged during the process leading to the Rio Conference. The Principles even fail to call explicitly for negotiations towards a legally binding instrument.

Several universal forest fora were established in the aftermath of the UNCED: the Intergovernmental Panel on Forests (IPF; 1995–1997), transformed into the Intergovernmental Forum on Forests (IFF; 1997–2000); the Interagency Task Force on Forests (ITFF; established 1995); the United Nations Forum on Forests (UNFF; established 2000); and the Collaborative Partnership on Forests (CPF; established 2001).[110] Key outcomes of the

[108] UN Doc A/CONF151/26 (vol III), adopted on 14 August 1992.

[109] For a closer analysis see K Kunzmann, 'The Non-legally Binding Instrument on Sustainable Management of All Types of Forests—Towards a Legal Regime for Sustainable Forest Management?' (2008) 9 *German Law Journal* 981.

[110] M Steiner, 'The Journey from Rio to Johannesburg: Ten Years of Forest Negotiations, Ten Years of Successes and Failures' (2002) 32 *Golden Gate University Law Review* 629.

deliberations under the IPF (established by the UN Commission on Sustainable Development (CSD)) and the IFF (established by the UN ECOSOC) are presented in the final reports of these processes, IPF4[111] and IFF4,[112] in the form of more than 270 proposals for action towards sustainable forest management; they are considered collectively as the IPF/IFF Proposals for Action.[113] In 1995 an informal, high-level ITFF was created, made up of eight international organisations. The UNFF[114] was established by ECOSOC Resolution/2000/35[115] as part of a new international arrangement on forests, with the main objective to promote 'the management, conservation and sustainable development of all types of forests and to strengthen long-term political commitment to this end'.[116] The Forum has universal membership, and is composed of all Member States of the United Nations and specialised agencies. Following nearly three years of intense negotiations, starting from UNFF5 and culminating at UNFF7, the Non-Legally Binding Instrument on All types of Forests[117] was adopted by the UN General Assembly on 17 December 2007.[118] The CPF was established in April 2001, following an ECOSOC recommendation. This innovative partnership of 14 major forest-related international organisations, institutions and convention secretariats is designed to support the work of the UNFF and its member countries and to foster increased co-operation and co-ordination on forests.

Chapter 11 of Agenda 21 not only urges states to develop national forest strategies and appropriate plans but it also calls for the formulation of criteria and guidelines to help sustainably manage, conserve and utilise forests. According to Chapter 11.12(e) of Agenda 21, it is one of the objectives of this programme area to 'consider the need for and the feasibility of all kinds of appropriate internationally agreed arrangements to promote international cooperation on forest management, conservation and sustainable development of all types of forests'. Chapter 11 addresses four programme areas for the protection of forests, namely sustaining the multiple roles and functions of forests; enhancing the conservation and sustainable management of forests and the greening of degraded forest areas through rehabilitative means; promoting efficient resource utilisation and assessment; and strengthening capacities for the planning and assessment of forests and respective activities.

On 3 October 2002, the member states of the Southern African Development Community (SADC) adopted the Protocol on Forestry which provides a policy framework for the management and protection of forests.[119] The Protocol lays down guiding principles (Article 4) and encourages the adoption of sustainable national forest policies and programmes (Articles 8, 9). The Protocol strongly encourages community-based forest management (Article 12), and specifically addresses the management and conservation

[111] Available at www.un.org/documents/ecosoc/cn17/ipf/1997/ecn17ipf1997-12.htm.

[112] Available at www.un.org/documents/ecosoc/cn17/2000/ecn172000-14.htm.

[113] Available at www.un.org/esa/forests/pdf/ipf-iff-proposalsforaction.pdf.

[114] See www.un.org/esa/forests/about.html for details.

[115] Available at www.un.org/esa/forests/pdf/2000_35_E.pdf.

[116] For details on the principle functions of UNFF see www.un.org/esa/forests/about.html.

[117] Available at www.daff.gov.au/__data/assets/pdf_file/0018/1141092/non-legally-binding-instrument.pdf.

[118] UNGA Res 62/98 (17 December 2007), available at www.fao.org/forestry/14717-1-0.pdf.

[119] Signed in October 2002, there is not yet a sufficient number of ratifications. The Protocol will enter into force after ratification by two-thirds of SADC member states.

of transboundary forests (Article 14). Furthermore, the Protocol covers forest genetic resources (Article 17) and traditional forest-related knowledge (Article 16). Its provisions take into account the needs of forest-based industries (Article 18). With regard to implementation, the Protocol establishes a mechanism for reporting and information exchange (Article 21). It even provides for the possibility to make use of the SADC Tribunal for the settlement of disputes (Article 23).

Another regional instrument worth mentioning is the Central American Convention for the Management and Conservation of Natural Forest Ecosystems and the Development of Forest Plantations of 29 October 1993 which entered into force on 15 October 1999.[120] The Convention's objective is to promote national and regional strategies and procedures for the sustainable management of forests, including the establishment of a homogeneous soil classification system and the recovery of deforested areas. To this end, the Convention reaffirms the sovereign right of parties to use, manage and develop their forests (Article 1), reflects agreement of its parties to adopt policies for the sustainable development of forest resources (Article 3), encourages parties to implement financial and related measures (Article 4), and requires parties to take measures to strengthen forestry management institutions and laws at the national level, including mandatory environmental impact assessments (Article 6).

Finally, there is the Forest Stewardship Council (FSC), an independent and not-for-profit NGO that was established in 1993 as a response to concerns over global deforestation. The FSC has developed into a meaningful certification system which provides internationally recognised standard-setting and accreditation services to companies, organisations and communities interested in responsible forestry.[121] While its standards are not legally binding *per se*, reference to FSC standards in national legislation and in decision-making by local or national authorities has provided proof of working public–private co-operation.[122]

14.5 Soil

While soil has always been considered important as a basis for agricultural production and for food supply, its specific environmental vulnerability has only recently become a matter of international concern. As the top layer of the earth's crust, soil is formed by mineral particles, organic matter, water, air and living organisms: it is thus an extremely complex, variable and living medium. It is a non-renewable resource with many vital functions apart from food and biomass production. Soil allows for the storage, filtration and transformation of many substances including water, carbon and nitrogen, and

[120] 'Convenio Regional para el Manejo y Conservación de los Ecosistemas Naturales Forestales y el Desarrollo de Plantaciones Forestales'; the Spanish text of the Convention is available at www.sica.int/busqueda/busqueda_archivo.aspx?Archivo=conv_1232_1_31052005.pdf.

[121] KM Kloven, 'Eco-labeling of Sustainably Harvested Wood under the Forest Stewardship Council: Seeing the Forest for the Trees' (1998) 9 *Colorado Journal of International Environmental Law and Policy* 48.

[122] See below Chapter 21.

provides both a habitat and a gene pool. Soil degradation can be caused by, *inter alia*, erosion, loss of organic matter, salinisation, landslides, contamination and sealing—all of these have negative effects not only on human health but also on economies, ecosystems and the climate.[123]

Early efforts to protect soil can be found in the 1971 Ramsar Convention discussed above, which lays down obligations to preserve and maintain wetlands. The Convention, which was negotiated against the background of increasing loss and degradation of wetland habitat for migratory waterbirds, protects particular sites and their resources.

An important regional instrument which may be considered here is the Convention on the Protection of the Alps (Alpine Convention) of 7 November 1991 with its Protocol on the Implementation of the Alpine Convention of 1991 in the Field of Soil Conservation (Soil Conservation Protocol) of 16 October 1998. The Convention itself is a framework agreement. It only sets out the basic principles of all the activities under the Convention and lays down general measures for sustainable development in alpine regions (Article 2 Alpine Convention). More detailed obligations are laid down in a number of subsequently adopted protocols (Article 11 Alpine Convention). Article 2(1) Alpine Convention requires parties to pursue a comprehensive policy for the preservation and protection of the alpine environment, based upon the concepts of prevention ('no harm'), polluter pays, co-operation, and prudent as well as sustained use of resources. The Convention envisages intensified transborder co-operation to this end.[124]

The object and purpose of the Soil Conservation Protocol is to preserve alpine soil in a sustainable manner to allow it to perform its natural function, its historic function ('as an archive of natural history and the history of civilisation') and a variety of socioeconomic functions, including agricultural use, human settlement and tourism activities, other commercial usages, and its capacity as a source of raw materials (Article 1 Soil Conservation Protocol). Article 1(2) of the Protocol underlines the 'ecological functions of soil' which must be safeguarded and preserved. In addition, the restoration of impaired soils shall be promoted. While the Protocol focuses on utilisation, Article 2(2) thereof clarifies that protection shall be given priority over utilisation if 'there is a risk of serious and sustained damage to the functionality of soils'. The Protocol follows an integrated (Article 3) and a participatory approach (Article 4). Specific measures include the designation of protected areas (Article 6), the development of plans and programmes for the economical and prudent use of soils (Article 7), an obligation towards economical use and prudent extraction of mineral resources (Article 8), particular provisions for wetlands, endangered areas, and for alpine areas threatened by erosion (Articles 9–11). Economic uses of soil and effects of economic activities on soil are also specifically addressed (Articles 12–17).

At the universal level, states have intensified their efforts to stem the negative effects of desertification. To this end the UN Convention to Combat Desertification (UNCCD) was adopted on 17 June 1994 and entered into force on 26 December 1996.[125] Participa-

[123] See AM Wyatt, 'The Dirt on International Environmental Law Regarding Soils: Is the Existing Regime Adequate?' (2008) 19 *Duke Environmental Law and Policy Forum* 165, 169 *et seq*.

[124] MF Price, *Co-operation in the European Mountains 1: The Alps* (Gland/Cambridge 1999) 13 *et seq*.

[125] See U Beyerlin, 'Desertification' in R Wolfrum (ed), *Max Planck Encyclopedia of Public International Law* (Heidelberg/Oxford 2009) paras 7 *et seq*, available at www.mpepil.com, for details on the UNCCD.

tion in this Convention, which goes back to a recommendation of Agenda 21 and is the first binding post-Rio instrument, has become close to universal. In light of the particular problems in Africa, a 'Resolution on urgent action for Africa' was adopted on the same day as the Convention in order to ensure that measures were already taken before entry into force of the Convention. Based on the principles of participation, partnership and decentralisation, the Convention's activities build upon innovative local programmes and supportive international partnerships. The Convention acknowledges that the causes of desertification, defined in Article 1(f) UNCCD as

> reduction or loss . . . of the biological or economic productivity and complexity of rainfed cropland, irrigated cropland, or range, pasture, forest and woodlands resulting from land uses . . . including processes arising from human activities and habitation patterns, such as . . . soil erosion . . . ; . . . deterioration of the physical, chemical and biological or economic properties of soil; and . . . long-term loss of natural vegetation,

are many and complex and that the struggle to protect drylands is not an easy one. According to Article 2(2) UNCCD, combating desertification and mitigating the effects of drought necessitates 'long-term integrated strategies that focus simultaneously . . . on improved productivity of land, and the rehabilitation, conservation and sustainable management of land and water resources . . . in particular at the community level'. In terms of instruments, the Convention focuses on the development and carrying out of national, subregional and regional action programmes (Articles 9–15 UNCCD). Criteria for preparing these programmes are detailed in the Convention's five regional implementation Annexes for Africa, Asia, Latin America and the Caribbean, the Northern Mediterranean, and Central and Eastern Europe. These Annexes form an integral part of the Convention (Article 29(1) UNCCD). The Convention pursues a bottom-up approach with action programmes as its primary instruments. Article 10(2)(f) UNCCD makes it clear that the affected developing country parties shall develop and implement their National Action Programmes through participatory mechanisms ensuring the active involvement of NGOs and local populations, particularly resource users, in relevant policy-planning, decision-making and implementation. Thus, in as much as Article 5 UNCCD may be read as a top-down regulatory approach, the other provisions referred to complement it by an innovative bottom-up approach that provides for real participation of local populations and communities directly affected by desertification. This basically means that higher levels of government must structure their activities along the needs of the lower levels. To this end, governments must take steps towards good governance, including the decentralisation of authority, improvements in land tenure systems, and measures empowering women, farmers and pastoralists. Article 4 UNCCD states that parties are under an obligation to follow an integrated approach, 'addressing the physical, biological and socio-economic aspects of the processes of desertification and drought' and to bear in mind the need for international co-operation. Articles 5 and 6 UNCCD lay down respective obligations for developing and for developed countries, whereby the first have to give 'due priority' to combating desertification and the second undertake to 'provide substantial financial resources and other forms of support' to developing countries. While Article 7 UNCCD gives priority to Africa, Article 8 encourages parties to co-ordinate their activities under other multilateral environmental agreements than those pursued under UNCCD.

Articles 16–21 UNCCD deal with scientific and technical co-operation and address supporting mechanisms, including financial ones. As laid down in Article 20 UNCCD, all parties to the Convention 'shall make every effort to ensure that adequate financial resources are available'. Developed country parties are under a particular obligation to provide funding, including the mobilisation of resources to cover the 'agreed incremental costs' of anti-desertification and drought mitigation programmes through the Global Environment Facility. The need for additional resources notwithstanding, the Convention underlines the need for cost effectiveness and efficiency (Article 20(4) and (5) UNCCD). Article 21 establishes a Global Mechanism in order to 'increase the effectiveness and efficiency of existing financial mechanisms'. The Mechanism basically provides advisory services to UNCCD parties in order to upscale finance for sustainable land management.

With the Conference of Parties (Article 22 UNCCD), the Permanent Secretariat (Article 23 UNCCD) and a Committee on Science and Technology (Article 24 UNCCD) the Convention establishes three permanent organs. The Conference of Parties 'shall make, within its mandate, the decisions necessary to promote [the] effective implementation' of the Convention.

Outlining a strategy for action, the Regional Implementation Annex for Africa is the most detailed of the regional annexes to the Convention, benefiting from the early attention of signatories as documented by the above-mentioned 'Resolution on urgent action for Africa'. Based on this Annex, most African countries have formulated National Action Programmes. Several Subregional Action Programmes have also been adopted, co-ordinated by the Arab Maghreb Union (AMU), the Permanent Interstate Committee for Drought Control in the Sahel (CILSS), the Intergovernmental Authority on Development (IGAD) and the Southern African Development Community (SADC). Finally, a Regional Action Programme (RAP) is under development. According to Article 6 of Annex I UNCCD, action programmes have to be developed through a 'consultative and participatory process'.

The effectiveness of the UNCCD depends upon whether the affected states parties meet their obligation to establish action programmes at the national, sub-regional and regional level. While there are a number of such programmes, their quality is not always convincing. Indeed, more than ten years after its entry into force, the UNCCD is still in a phase of transition from awareness-raising to implementation. In light of the deficiencies in implementation, at COP 7, in 2005, 'The New Alliance to Combat Land Degradation in Africa (TerrAfrica)' was launched. Its aim is to constitute 'a stage for partnership and collective actions in addressing land degradation, and mobilizing financial resources'.[126] COP 8, in 2007, decided to establish a 'Ten-Year Strategic Plan and Framework to Enhance the Implementation of the Convention'.[127]

Apart from the Soil Conservation Protocol adopted under the (sub-regional) Alpine Convention and the UNCCD, at least one other important regional instrument may be referred to: the 2003 African Convention on the Conservation of Nature and Natural

[126] 'Summary of the Seventh Conference of the Parties to the Convention to Combat Desertification', Earth Negotiations Bulletin vol 12 no 186 (31 October 2005) 7.

[127] Decision 3/COP8 (14 September 2007) in ICCD/COP(8)/16/Add1 (23 October 2007).

Resources (Maputo Convention) takes up land and soil protection, including an obligation of parties to 'develop long-term integrated strategies for the conservation and sustainable management of land resources, including soil, vegetation and related hydrological processes' (Article VI(1)). Article VI establishes a link with land tenure policies, taking into account the rights of local communities.

14.6 Conclusions

Flora, fauna, forests, soil and biodiversity are not equally protected by international law. This is not only due to the fact that the primary treaties for each of these areas were negotiated at different times in history or without adequate recognition of the North–South dimension. It is primarily due to different regulatory approaches which range from instruments protecting and conserving individual species, others focusing on habitat, a third category being more of an economic nature (either curbing trade or promoting sustainable development) and a fourth category with only rudimentary regulation for the time being. Broadly speaking, three conclusions can be drawn with regard to regulatory approaches.

Firstly, international legal instruments dealing with fauna and flora primarily focus on conservation. This is particularly true for major treaties originating in the 1970s. These treaties have been developed further and adapted to new challenges but their regulatory approach has remained the same.

Secondly, the CBD and the Biosafety Protocol, in particular, move away from pure conservation towards sustainable use. While conservation is not ignored by these instruments, they are much more economy-oriented, taking into account and building upon economic incentives and economic rationales of governmental and other (non-state) actors. Whether or not this approach is successful is still an open question. However, building upon national precedents in sustainable forest management, there is at least a degree of plausibility that economic instruments may be viable means to achieve sustainable management of natural resources.

Thirdly, international protection of forests and soil is still in its infancy. There are major deficits in this field even though the international community has at least started to address the issues systematically. Instruments addressing habitat seem to be most promising in this context since they pursue an integrated approach.

Further Reading

DM Bodansky, 'International Law and the Protection of Biological Diversity' (1995) 28 *Vanderbilt Journal of Transnational Law* 623–634.

M Bowman (ed), *International Law and the Conservation of Biological Diversity* (London 1996).

L Glowka, 'Complementarities between the Convention on Migratory Species and the Convention on Biological Diversity' (2000) 3 *Journal of International Wildlife Law and Policy* 205–252.

J Hutton and B Dickson (eds), *Endangered Species: Threatened Convention: The Past, Present and*

Future of CITES, the Convention on International Trade in Endangered Species of Wild Fauna and Flora (London 2000).

V Koester, 'The Nature of the Convention on Biological Diversity and its Application of Components of the Concept of Sustainable Development' (2006) 16 *Italian Yearbook of International Law* 57–84.

F McConnell, *The Biodiversity Convention: A Negotiating History* (London 1996).

C Muffet, 'International Protection of Wildlife' in FL Morrison *et al* (eds), *International, Regional and National Environmental Law* (The Hague *et al* 2000) 343–354.

R Reeve, *Policing International Trade in Endangered Species: The CITES Treaty and Compliance* (London 2002).

PH Sand, 'Whither CITES? The Evolution of a Treaty Regime in the Borderland of Trade and Environment' (1997) 8 *EJIL* 29–58.

——, 'A Century of Green Lessons: The Contribution of Nature Conservation Regimes to Global Governance' (2001) 1 *International Environmental Agreements: Politics, Law & Economics* 33–72.

——, 'Sovereignty Bounded: Public Trusteeship for Common Pool Resources?' (2004) 4 *Global Environmental Politics* 47–71.

C Shine, 'Selected Agreements Concluded Pursuant to the Convention on the Conservation of Migratory Species of Wild Animals' in D Shelton (ed), *Commitment and Compliance: The Role of Non-Binding Norms in the International Legal System* (Oxford 2000) 196–223.

A von Hahn, 'Implementation and Further Development of the Biodiversity Convention: Access to Genetic Resources, Benefit Sharing and Traditional Knowledge of Indigenous and Local Communities' (2003) 63 *Heidelberg Journal of International Law (ZaöRV)* 295–312.

R Wolfrum, 'The Convention on Biological Diversity: Using State Jurisdiction as a Means of Ensuring Compliance' in R Wolfrum (ed), *Enforcing Environmental Standards: Economic Mechanisms as Viable Means?* (Berlin 1996) 373–393.

R Wolfrum and PT Stoll, *Access and Benefit Sharing, Intellectual Property Rights, Ex-situ Collections* (Berlin 2000).

15

Wastes and Hazardous Substances

15.1 Survey

Due to economic growth, urbanisation and industrialisation there has been a dramatic increase in the volume and types of waste and hazardous substances with severe consequences for the environment and natural resources at both the global and local level. It is estimated that more than 2 billion tonnes of waste are generated each year in Organisation for Economic Co-operation and Development (OECD) states alone;[1] figures on the global volume of hazardous waste range from 300 to 500 million tonnes.[2] It is assumed that about 10 per cent of this amount is shipped across international borders.[3] There are estimates that, in 2006, the total amount of municipal solid waste generated globally reached 2.02 billion tonnes[4] and that between 2007 and 2011, global generation of municipal waste has increased by 37.3 per cent.[5] The World Bank estimates that in developing countries it is common for municipalities to spend up to 50 per cent of their available budget on solid waste management.[6] This is not only due to locally generated waste but also to imported waste and hazardous substances. UNEP is even expecting an 'e-waste' crisis in developing countries within the next decade.[7] However, given that there are

[1] OECD Environmental Data Compendium 2006-2008, available at www.oecd.org/document/49/0,3343,en_2649_34395_39011377_1_1_1_1,00.html.

[2] See AL Parrish, 'Sovereignty's Continuing Importance: Traces of *Trail Smelter* in the International Law Governing Hazardous Waste Transport' in RM Bratspies and RA Miller (eds), *Transboundary Harm in International Law: Lessons from the* Trail Smelter *Arbitration* (Cambridge *et al* 2006) 181, 187 with further references.

[3] J Krueger, 'The Basel Convention and the International Trade in Hazardous Wastes' in OS Stokke and ØB Thommessen (eds), *Yearbook of International Co-operation on Environment and Development* (London 2001/2002) 43, 44.

[4] Global Waste Management Market Report, Executive Summary (2007), available at www.keynote.co.uk/market-intelligence/view/product/1903/global-waste-management/chapter/1/executive_summary.

[5] UNEP, *Developing Integrated Solid Waste Management Plan: Training Manual: Volume 2: Assessment of Current Waste Management System and Gaps therein* (Nairobi 2009) 2.

[6] *Cf* the information at the website of the World Bank on urban solid waste management at www.worldbank.org/solidwaste/.

[7] UNEP Press Release, 'Urgent Need to Prepare Developing Countries for Surge in E-Wastes: Rocketing

various methods for classifying and defining waste categories, *eg* with regard to their origin, composition and level of risk, and that statistical definitions can vary from country to country, data on waste should be treated with caution.[8]

Wastes and hazardous substances are primarily dealt with at the local and at the national level. In light of the potential long-range effects caused by persistent pollutants and with a view to the international trade in wastes and hazardous substances, however, these substances have increasingly been addressed by international law. Among the various hazardous substances, chemicals and nuclear materials stand out as being particularly dangerous. Currently, more than 55 million organic and inorganic chemical substances are used on a global scale[9] and the chemical industry is economically vital to many states. However, the risk potential of about 99 per cent of all marketed substances has not yet been assessed comprehensively.[10] The environmental effects resulting from the use of chemicals are broad and range from ecosystem effects to eutrophication of water and stratospheric ozone depletion. Chemical contamination is widespread. According to estimates, more than approximately two million sites across Europe are contaminated.[11] Use of chemicals has grown fast due to the growth of the chemical industry in developing countries and emerging market economies. The 1986 Chernobyl accident and the debate about the future of nuclear energy have vividly demonstrated that nuclear materials and nuclear waste entail a distinct risk potential. The main risks associated with the use of nuclear power result from unsolved issues in relation to the transport and storage of radioactive waste and to possible accidents which could be caused by mechanical failure or human error as well as by natural disasters. So-called high-level waste[12] consists, *inter alia*, of highly radioactive elements such as plutonium, which remains hazardous for about 240000 years.[13] It is estimated that about 10000 m^3 of such waste is produced annually by nuclear power generation facilities around the world.[14] Given that underground water could transport contaminated substances into the environment, safe storage options have yet to be found.

As far as national treatment of waste is concerned, appropriate legislation seeks to avoid, recycle or dispose of waste in an environmentally sound manner. International environmental law has so far rarely addressed the national treatment of waste. Apart from the 1997 Joint Convention on the Safety of Spent Fuel Management and on the Safety of Radioactive Waste Management, there are only a few relevant soft law instruments,

Sales of Cell Phones, Gadgets, Appliances in China, India, Elsewhere Forecast' (22 February 2010), available at www.unep.org/Documents.Multilingual/Default.print.asp?DocumentID=612&ArticleID=6471&l=en&t=long.

[8] UNEP, *Vital Waste Graphics 2* (Geneva 2006) 39.

[9] *Cf* the registry database of the Chemical Abstracts Service (CAS), a division of the American Chemical Society, available at www.cas.org/expertise/cascontent/registry/regsys.html.

[10] Commission (EC), 'Strategy for a future Chemicals Policy' (White Paper) COM(2001) final, 27 February 2001, 6.

[11] UNEP, *Global Environment Outlook (GEO) 4: Environment for Development* (Nairobi 2007) 95.

[12] The categorisation of nuclear waste is based on its level of radioactivity and on how long it retains its hazardous nature.

[13] See Greenpeace, 'Nuclear Power: A Dangerous Waste of Time' (January 2009) 4, available at www.greenpeace.org/international/Global/international/planet-2/report/2009/4/nuclear-power-a-dangerous-was.pdf.

[14] IAEA Factsheet, 'Managing Radioactive Waste' (1998), available at www.iaea.org/Publications/Factsheets/English/manradwa.html.

including an early OECD recommendation of 1976,[15] UNEP's Cairo Guidelines and Principles for the Environmentally Sound Management of Hazardous Wastes of 1987,[16] and Chapter 20 of Agenda 21.

International rules related to waste have largely been developed since the 1980s in light of increasing transboundary movements of waste, in particular with a view to illegal exportation of waste from developed to developing countries. In 1984 the European Community adopted Council Directive 84/631/EEC on the Supervision and Control within the European Community of the Transfrontier Shipment of Hazardous Wastes. The Directive was replaced by Council Regulation (EEC) 259/93 of 1 February 1993 on the Supervision and Control of Shipments of Waste within, into and out of the European Community, and the Regulation was replaced by Regulation (EC) 1013/2006 of the European Parliament and of the Council of 14 June 2006 on Shipments of Waste. Apart from the EU's activities, the OECD has also addressed the problem of imports and exports of waste since 1984. These measures were consolidated in 2001 and subsequently revised in 2005 and 2008 on the basis of an OECD Council Decision[17] which establishes a control system and permits trade in recyclable materials in an environmentally safe manner.

The Basel Convention on the Control of Transboundary Movements of Hazardous Wastes and their Disposal, negotiated under the auspices of UNEP and adopted on 22 March 1989, is the first legally binding international instrument adopted at the universal level which incorporates the idea of a common responsibility of exporting and importing states for the environmentally sound disposal of wastes. With its entry into force on 5 May 1992, the Convention established a limited prohibition of the transboundary movement of waste, in particular to developing countries. To this end, it required prior informed consent of importing states, subject to carefully balanced controls. On 22 September 1995, COP 3 adopted an amendment to the Convention, banning all exports to non-OECD countries. However, this Amendment has not yet entered into force.[18]

On 30 January 1991 the Bamako Convention on the Ban of the Import into Africa and the Control of Transboundary Movement and Management of Hazardous Wastes within Africa was adopted. It prohibits all imports of hazardous wastes into Africa from non-African Union (AU)[19] countries but allows certain transboundary movements within Africa. The Convention entered into force on 22 April 1998.

Another instrument built along the model of the Basel Convention is the Waigani Convention to Ban the Importation into Forum Island Countries of Hazardous and Radioactive Wastes and to Control the Transboundary Movement and Management of Hazardous Wastes within the South Pacific Region which was adopted on 16 September

[15] OECD C(76)155 final (28 September 1976) on 'A Comprehensive Waste Management Policy'.

[16] UNEP GC Dec 14/30 on 'Environmentally Sound Management of Hazardous Wastes' (17 June 1987).

[17] OECD C(2001)107/final (14 June 2001); this Decision was amended in 2005 (OECD C(2005)141) in light of COP 7 of the Basel Convention and the amendments of Annexes VIII and IX thereto; it was further amended in 2008 (OECD C(2008)156).

[18] There is an ongoing controversy as to the amendment's entry into force; see below at Section 15.2.1 for details.

[19] The AU has replaced the Organisation of African Unity (OAU) in 2002. For further details on the AU see M Killander, 'Regional Co-operation and Organization: African States' in R Wolfrum (ed), *Max Planck Encyclopedia of Public International Law* (Heidelberg/Oxford 2009), para 6, available at www.mpepil.com.

1995. The Convention, which entered into force on 21 October 2001, goes beyond the Basel Convention since it covers radioactive wastes and its territorial scope extends beyond the territorial sea to the exclusive economic zone.[20]

International trade in hazardous substances has drastically increased in light of the economic uses of toxic chemicals, pesticides and nuclear materials. Given the dangers and risks involved, it is surprising that effective control of hazardous substances is a relatively new development in international environmental law. To some extent this is due to limited scientific knowledge about the toxicity of a wide range of tradable hazardous substances and the complexity of the problems to be addressed. However, business actors and governments have long been unwilling to reach agreement on these issues, objecting to disclosure of the properties of certain products containing hazardous substances.

Nevertheless, initial steps were taken in the 1980s with the adoption of a number of soft law instruments. In 1985 the FAO adopted an International Code of Conduct on the Distribution and Use of Pesticides.[21] This legally non-binding instrument promotes a number of behavioural standards for public and private entities in respect of the use of and trade in pesticides. It was amended in 1989 to include the prior informed consent procedure. A fully revised version was adopted in 2002.[22]

In 1987 UNEP adopted its London Guidelines for the Exchange of Information on Chemicals in International Trade,[23] which were amended in 1989.[24] They recommend that exporting and importing states apply the prior informed consent procedure with the International Register of Potentially Toxic Chemicals as the central contact point. It is noteworthy that the voluntary prior informed consent procedure as established by FAO and UNEP was firstly changed to a voluntary 'interim prior informed consent procedure' by the Conference of Plenipotentiaries on the Rotterdam Convention,[25] which was repealed after entry into force of the Rotterdam Convention in 2006.[26]

The Rotterdam Convention on the Prior Informed Consent Procedure for Certain Hazardous Chemicals and Pesticides in International Trade, adopted on 10 September 1988 and amended by COP 1 (2004) and by COP 4 (2008), was the first multilateral treaty on hazardous substances. It establishes the prior informed consent procedure as the primary

[20] D van Hoogstraten and P Lawrence, 'Protecting the South Pacific from Hazardous and Nuclear Waste Dumping: The Waigani Convention' (1998) 7 *RECIEL* 268.

[21] FAO Res 10/85, adopted by the 23rd Session of the Conference (9–28 November 1985).

[22] FAO Res 1/123, adopted by the 123rd Session of the Governing Council (28 October–1 November 2002). Its text is available at ftp://ftp.fao.org/docrep/fao/009/a0220e/a0220e00.pdf.

[23] UNEP GC Dec 14/27 on 'Environmentally Safe Management of Chemicals, in Particular those that are Banned and Severely Restricted in International Trade' (17 June 1987).

[24] UNEP GC Dec 15/30 on 'Environmentally Safe Management of Chemicals, in Particular those that are Banned and Severely Restricted, in International Trade' (25 May 1989).

[25] Resolution on Interim Arrangements, see Final Act of the Conference of Plenipotentiaries on the Convention on the Prior Informed Consent Procedure for Certain Hazardous Chemicals and Pesticides in International Trade (UNEP/FAO/PIC/CONF/5) (17 September 1998) 8 *et seq*.

[26] Decision RC-1/13 on Transitional Arrangements, see Report of the Conference of the Parties to the Rotterdam Convention on the Prior Informed Consent Procedure for Certain Hazardous Chemicals and Pesticides in International Trade on the work of its first meeting (UNEP/FAO/RC/COP1/33) (22 October 2004) 48 *et seq*. *Cf* for some background information especially concerning the interim prior informed consent procedure under the Convention TL McDorman, 'The Rotterdam Convention on the Prior Informed Consent Procedure for Certain Hazardous Chemicals and Pesticides in International Trade: Some Legal Notes' (2004) 13 *RECIEL* 187.

means to better protect human health and the environment when trading in hazardous substances. The Convention, which builds on the model of the Basel and the Bamako Convention, entered into force on 24 February 2004.

Closely related is the Stockholm Convention on Persistent Organic Pollutants (POPs) which was adopted on 22 May 2001 and entered into force on 17 May 2004. This Convention builds upon the fact that certain organic compounds are resistant to natural decomposition through chemical, biological and photolytic processes. Thus persisting in the environment, they can be transported over long distances and accumulated in humans and in animals, they can negatively impact the nutrition chain and have significant effects on human health and the environment. Early examples of POPs are pesticides; others are used in industrial processes, including solvents and pharmaceuticals.

Nuclear materials have long raised concerns. While early codes of practice and nuclear safety standards had already been adopted by the IAEA in the 1960s, legally binding international instruments were only developed in the 1990s. These include the Convention on Nuclear Safety of 17 June 1994, which entered into force on 24 October 1996, and the Joint Convention on the Safety of Spent Fuel Management and on the Safety of Radioactive Waste Management of 5 September 1997, which became effective on 18 June 2001.

In addition, many other minimum requirements for the transboundary transportation of dangerous goods can be found in legally non-binding instruments as well as in treaties focusing on transportation as such. They deal with reliable identification and packing of such goods as well as with safety standards for individual modes of transportation. Road,[27] rail,[28] ship[29] and air[30] transport are each covered by instruments set up by specialised international organisations.

15.2 Control of Transboundary Movements of Wastes

15.2.1 The Basel Convention

Currently, there are 174 parties to the Basel Convention on the Control of Transboundary Movements of Hazardous Wastes and their Disposal. Recognising, in its preamble, the sovereign right of states to ban the entry or disposal of foreign hazardous wastes and sub-

[27] *Cf* the European Agreement Concerning the International Carriage of Dangerous Goods by Road of 30 September 1957 (negotiated under the auspices of UNECE) which entered into force on 29 January 1968. Since its entry into force Annexes A and B have been regularly amended.

[28] Regulations concerning the International Carriage of Dangerous Goods by Rail (which are contained in Appendix C to the Convention Concerning International Carriage by Rail of 9 May 1980 in the version of the Protocol of Modification of 3 June 1999); they are updated regularly. The Regulations form Annex I of the Uniform Rules concerning the Contract for International Carriage of Goods by Rail (CIM), which are attached as Appendix B to the Convention concerning International Carriage by Rail (COTIF).

[29] International Maritime Dangerous Goods Code (developed by the International Maritime Organization (IMO)); they are also updated on a regular basis. See also the European Agreement Concerning the International Carriage of Dangerous Goods by Inland Waterways of 26 May 2000 which entered into force on 29 February 2008 and includes annexed regulations which are regularly updated.

[30] ICAO Technical Instructions for the Safe Transport of Dangerous Goods by Air (regularly updated).

stances, prioritising the environmentally sound disposal of wastes in the state where they were generated, recognising the need for stringent control of transboundary movement of hazardous wastes and other wastes, and expressing concern about illegal transboundary transportation of wastes and hazardous substances, it can be argued that since the entry into force of the Basel Convention waste disposals in other states are only permissible if not harmful.[31]

Hazardous wastes, according to Article 1 Basel Convention, include particularly dangerous wastes listed in Annex I (*lit* a) as well as wastes defined as hazardous by the domestic legislation of the party of export, import or transit (*lit* b). Such national definitions of hazardous wastes must be communicated through the Secretariat of the Convention (Article 3).[32]

The most important obligations of parties to the Convention are laid down in Article 4 thereof. According to its paragraph 1, each contracting party is entitled to prohibit the import of hazardous wastes or other wastes for disposal. In such a case, the other parties have to be informed of that decision (*lit* a). Upon such notification, every party to the Convention has to prohibit exportation of such wastes to the party which prohibits the import (*lit* b). If there is no notification, exporting parties must obtain consent in writing from the importing party or prohibit the export of hazardous wastes. According to Article 4(2), each party is responsible to 'ensure that the generation of hazardous wastes and other wastes within its territory is reduced to a minimum'; that adequate disposal facilities are available; 'that the transboundary movement of hazardous wastes and other wastes is reduced to the minimum'; and that such movement (if performed) 'is conducted in a manner which will protect human health and the environment'. In addition, the state of origin must prohibit the export, *inter alia*, 'if it has reason to believe that the wastes in question will not be managed in an environmentally sound manner' by the importing state; similarly, the target state must prevent the import 'if it has reason to believe that the wastes in question will not be managed in an environmentally sound manner'. As stipulated by Article 4(3), the parties to the Convention 'consider that illegal traffic in hazardous wastes or other wastes is criminal', and, as may be taken from Article 9(5), they have to introduce appropriate domestic legislation to prevent and punish such illegal traffic. Exportation to and importation from non-parties is not permissible (Article 4(5)). In no case can the conventional obligation of states parties generating waste to require the environmentally sound management of hazardous wastes and other wastes be transferred to states parties of import or transit (Article 4(10)).

While Article 4 establishes a partial prohibition of the transboundary movement of waste, Article 6 focuses on obligations to notify. Only after notifications by the exporting party (to all states concerned, including, according to Article 7, non-parties) and an appropriate response (consent with or without conditions or denial) by the party of import may the exporting party allow the transboundary movement of such wastes (Article 6(1)–(3)). Parties of transit may waive their right of prior written consent. In such a case, the exporting party may permit the export if there is no response from the party of transit

[31] P Birnie, A Boyle and C Redgwell, *International Law and the Environment* (3rd edn Oxford 2009) 473.

[32] A Daniel, 'Transboundary Movements of Hazardous Waste' (2007) 18 *Yearbook of International Environmental Law* 258.

'within 60 days of the receipt of a given notification by the State of transit' (Article 6(4)). Article 8 of the Convention provides for a duty of reimport if a transboundary movement of wastes cannot be completed in accordance with the terms of the contract. This applies to the exporting party as well as to the party of transit. If the Convention is violated, the transboundary movement of wastes is considered as illegal traffic according to Article 9(1) of the Convention. If the exporter's behaviour has caused the movement to be considered as illegal, the exporting party itself must, if necessary, take back the waste; if the importer's behaviour has caused the illegality of the movement, the importing party itself must, if necessary, dispose of the waste in an environmentally sound manner (Article 9(2) and (3)).

According to Article 10(1) of the Convention, '[p]arties shall co-operate with each other to improve and achieve environmentally sound [waste] management.' As provided by Article 12, parties have negotiated a protocol addressing 'liability and compensation for damage resulting from the transboundary movement and disposal of . . . wastes' which has, however, not yet entered into force. The Secretariat, which is located in Geneva, is charged, *inter alia*, with ensuring compliance with the Convention and promoting co-ordination and information exchange between the parties (*cf* Article 16(1)).

As already indicated, the Basel Convention only partially bans transboundary movement of waste. Indeed, African countries, together with other developing countries and NGOs, such as Greenpeace, criticised the Convention from the start as legitimising trade with hazardous waste rather than preventing it. Eventually, in 1994, a coalition of developing countries and some European countries, supported by Greenpeace, managed to convince COP 2 to adopt by consensus Decision II/12 whereby all transboundary movements of hazardous waste from OECD to non-OECD states, destined for final disposal, were immediately prohibited and other transboundary movements of hazardous wastes, destined for recycling or recovery operations, from OECD to non-OECD states were phased out by 31 December 1993.[33] After the adoption of this decision, it was argued, however, that the decision was not as such legally binding unless the Convention was formally amended.[34] Despite continued opposition from, among others, the United States, South Korea, Australia and Canada, an amendment was adopted, by consensus, at COP 3, inserting a new preambular paragraph, a new Article 4A (which basically takes up Decision II/12) and a new Annex VII.[35] According to Article 17(5) of the Convention, amendments adopted by the COP shall enter into force between parties that have accepted them 90 days after ratification, approval, formal confirmation or acceptance by at least three-quarters of the accepting parties.[36] With 82 parties present at COP 3 this requires 62 ratifications out of these; the fact that there are altogether 69 ratifications of the amendment[37] does not allow for a different conclusion, even though legal debate about the

[33] See the text of Decision II/12 in Report of the Second Meeting of the Conference of the Parties to the Basel Convention on the Control of Transboundary Movements of Hazardous Wastes and their Disposal (UNEP/CHW.2/30) (25 March 1994) 19 *et seq*.

[34] On the amendments of treaties and protocols see Chapter 18.4.1.

[35] Decision III/1, see Decisions Adopted by the Third Meeting of the Conference of the Parties to the Basel Convention (UNEP/CHW.3/35) (28 November 1995) 1 *et seq*.

[36] For general information concerning the treaty amendment procedure see Chapter 18.4.1.

[37] See www.basel.int/ratif/ban-alpha.htm.

interpretation of Article 17(5) of the Convention is ongoing.[38] In light of the distinction between hazardous and other wastes included in Decision III/1 there is a need to clarify the meaning of 'hazardous'. Work to this end has been performed by the Technical Working Group and taken up by the Conference of the Parties.[39]

While the first decade of the Convention's operation focused on establishing a framework for the transboundary movement of wastes, specifying the prior informed consent procedure and elaborating criteria for the environmentally sound management of wastes, recent work has concentrated on issues of implementation and enforcement. To this end, COP 6 adopted a compliance mechanism and a Strategic Plan for the Implementation of the Convention.[40] During COP 7, a Ministerial Statement on Partnerships for Meeting the Global Waste Challenge was adopted, recognising the environmentally sound management of hazardous wastes as part of the wider issues of water protection, improved sanitation, solid waste management, and economic and social development.[41] This is very much in line with the encouragement included in Article 11 of the Convention to make use of regional agreements and arrangements aimed at controlling transboundary movements of wastes. In 1999 a Protocol on Liability and Compensation was adopted, laying down rules on liability and compensation for damages caused by accidental spills of hazardous wastes during export, import or during disposal.[42] Entry into force of the Protocol requires ratification by 20 parties. With a total of 13 signatories and 10 ratifications,[43] there still is a long way to go, as has been acknowledged also by Decision IX/24 calling upon parties 'to continue to consult at the national and regional levels with a view to determining possible means of overcoming perceived obstacles to ratification of the Protocol'.

15.2.2 The Bamako Convention

The Bamako Convention partly builds upon the text of the Basel Convention. This is not only true for the definitions included in Article 1 but also for the provisions on scope (Article 2).[44]

[38] Information on ongoing consultations on the interpretation of Article 17(5) can be found at www.basel.int/legalmatters/article17%285%29/Decision%20VI/comments%20oewg6.html.

[39] During COP 4, held in Kuching, Malaysia, 23–27 February 1998, Annexes VIII and IX were added to the Basel Convention (Decision IV/9). Annex VIII contains a list of wastes characterized as hazardous under Article 1(1)(a) of the Convention ('List A'), whereas wastes listed in Annex IX ('List B') will not be wastes covered by Article 1(1)(a) 'unless they contain Annex I material to an extent causing them to exhibit an Annex III characteristic'. Both lists were amended by decisions VI/35 and VII/19, respectively.

[40] Decision VI/1 and Decision VI/12, see Report of the Conference of the Parties to the Basel Convention on the Control of Transboundary Movements of Hazardous Wastes and their Disposal (UNEP/CHW.6/40) (10 February 2003) 34 *et seq* and 45 *et seq*.

[41] See its text in Report of the Conference of the Parties to the Basel Convention on the Control of Transboundary Movements of Hazardous Wastes and their Disposal (UNEP/CHW.7/33) (25 January 2005) Annex V, 99 *et seq*.

[42] Decision V/29, see Report of the Fifth Meeting of the Conference of the Parties to the Basel Convention (UNEP/CHW.5/29) (10 December 1999) 56.

[43] *Cf* www.basel.int/ratif/protocol.htm.

[44] CN Eze, 'The Bamako Convention on the Ban on the Import into Africa and the Control of the Transboundary Movement and Management of Hazardous Wastes Within Africa: A Milestone in Environmental Protection?' (2007) 15 *African Journal of International and Comparative Law* 208.

However, the Bamako Convention goes beyond the Basel Convention by establishing a ban on imports of hazardous wastes from non-parties into the AU. According to Article 4(1) of the Convention, parties 'shall take appropriate legal, administrative and other measures to prohibit the import of all hazardous wastes' from outside Africa by non-parties. The Convention considers such imports as illegal and as criminal acts. Article 4(2) bans the dumping of hazardous wastes at sea, including internal waters, territorial seas, exclusive economic zones and the high seas. Article 4(3) emphasises measures to reduce the generation of hazardous wastes and to prevent pollution resulting from such wastes within Africa (*lit* a–h); in addition, the provision lays down a number of requirements for the transportation and the transboundary movement of hazardous wastes within Africa (*lit* i–u). Parties shall, among other things, prevent the export of hazardous wastes to states which have prohibited such imports (*lit* r). Parties may only allow exports to states which have the facilities for disposing of hazardous wastes in an environmentally sound manner (*lit* j). Furthermore, parties are required to 'ensure that hazardous wastes to be exported are managed in an environmentally sound manner in the State of import and transit'.

In addition to these rules, the Convention includes the prior informed consent procedure. Article 6 requires notification by the exporting state (para 1) and a response by the importing state (para 2) and specifies that exports shall not be allowed until there is a written consent of the importing state, and a 'written confirmation of the existence of a contract between the exporter and the disposer specifying an environmentally sound management of the wastes in question' (paragraph 3(a) and (b)). Even if all states concerned have expressed their consent to the transboundary movement of hazardous wastes, Article 8 provides for a duty to reimport the waste if the movement 'cannot be completed in accordance with the terms of the contract'. In the case of 'illegal traffic as the result of conduct on the part of the exporter', the exporting state shall ensure that the wastes in question are taken back, if necessary by itself, within 30 days of having been informed about the illegal traffic (Article 9(3)). If the illegality of the movement is the result of conduct on the part of the importer the importing state is required to 'ensure that the wastes . . . are returned to the exporter' (Article 9(4)).

Article 10 stipulates that African states shall co-operate 'to improve and achieve the environmentally sound management of hazardous wastes'. Should an accident occur during the transboundary movement of hazardous wastes or their disposal with the risk of damage to human health or the environment of other states, parties are under an obligation immediately to inform the states concerned (Article 13(1)).

15.3 International Regulation of Hazardous Substances

15.3.1 The Rotterdam Convention

The Rotterdam Convention on the Prior Informed Consent Procedure for Certain Hazardous Chemicals and Pesticides in International Trade implements the prior informed consent procedure for trade in hazardous substances. At present, there are 138 parties to the Convention.

According to its Article 1, the Convention seeks 'to promote shared responsibility and cooperative efforts among Parties in the international trade of certain hazardous chemicals in order to protect human health and the environment from potential harm' and to contribute to the environmentally sound use of those hazardous chemicals, not only by facilitating information exchange but also by providing for a national decision-making process on their import and export.[45]

The Convention is applicable to 'banned or severely restricted chemicals' (Article 3) as well as to 'severely hazardous pesticide formulations'. These are defined in detail in Article 2 of the Convention. The Rotterdam Convention does not apply to narcotic drugs and psychotropic substances; radioactive materials; wastes; chemical weapons; pharmaceuticals, including human and veterinary drugs; chemicals used as food additives; food; and chemicals in quantities not likely to affect human health or the environment provided they are imported for the purpose of research or analysis or by an individual for his or her own personal use in quantities reasonable for such use (Article 3(2)).

In order to achieve the necessary transparency, each party, according to Article 5(1) of the Convention, must notify the Secretariat of any 'final regulatory action'[46] towards banning or limiting chemicals no later than 90 days after it becomes effective. Data required as part of this notification are specified in Annex I to the Convention. In accordance with Article 5(3) Rotterdam Convention, summaries and synopses of the information received are made available to the parties by the Secretariat within a fixed time frame. Should a banned or severely restricted substance be exported from the territory of a party, the party concerned must notify the importing party of its export (Article 12(1)). The export notification must include the information specified in Annex V. Such notifications must be submitted before the first export after a ban or a limitation takes place, and thereafter annually preceding the first export (Article 12(2)). The requirement of prior notification can be waived by the authorities of the importing party.[47]

Articles 10 and 11 can be considered as the core provisions of the Convention. They lay down the prior informed consent procedure which applies to all chemicals listed in Annex III. Each party, at the time of entry into force of the Convention at the latest, undertakes to inform the Secretariat whether or not (and possibly to what extent and according to specified conditions) it agrees to imports of substances listed in Annex III (Article 10(7)). If a party does not allow imports or if it only allows imports subject to certain conditions, these must apply to all imports irrespective of the origin of the substance and its production (Article 10(9)). Parties will be informed by the Secretariat of the responses it has received on a semi-annual basis. According to Article 11(1)(b), each party takes 'appropriate legislative or administrative measures to ensure that exporters

[45] P Barrios, 'The Rotterdam Convention on Hazardous Chemicals: A Meaningful Step Toward Environmental Protection?' (2004) 16 *Georgetown International Environmental Law Review* 679.

[46] According to Art 2(e) Rotterdam Convention a 'final regulatory action' is defined as 'an action taken by a Party, that does not require subsequent regulatory action by that Party, the purpose of which is to ban or severely restrict a chemical'.

[47] *Cf* McDorman, above n 26.

within its jurisdiction comply with decisions in each response' of importing states no later than six months after the date on which the Secretariat first informs the parties thereof according to Article 10(10) of the Convention. Should any importing party, in exceptional circumstances, fail to transmit a response, other parties shall ensure that a chemical listed in Annex III is not exported from their territories to that importing party (Article 11(2)).

In order to facilitate the implementation of the Convention, the Conference of the Parties, as stipulated by Article 13(1), 'shall encourage the World Customs Organization to assign specific Harmonized System customs codes to the individual chemicals or groups of chemicals listed in Annex III'. Article 16 provides for technical assistance to developing countries and countries in transition.

So far, the implementation of the Rotterdam Convention has been fairly successful. COP 1 decided to establish a transition period from 24 February 2004 onwards (the date of entry into force) and to operate the prior informed consent procedure on a provisional basis.[48] Furthermore, a Chemical Review Committee was established by COP 1,[49] among others, in order to make recommendations on the inclusion of chemicals notified as banned and severely restricted and to prepare guiding documents. It is noteworthy that COP 4 decided to continue discussions about a non-compliance system.[50]

15.3.2 The Stockholm Convention

The Stockholm Convention on Persistent Organic Pollutants is based on the fact that exposure to persistent organic pollutants (POPs) can have serious health effects, including certain cancers, birth defects, dysfunctional immune and reproductive systems, greater susceptibility to disease and even diminished intelligence. The Convention recognises that no government can respond to these threats alone. As can be taken from its Article 1, the Convention's objective is to protect human health and the environment from POPs. It explicitly refers to the precautionary approach and to Principle 15 of the Rio Declaration.[51]

To this end, the Convention requires parties to adopt measures to reduce or eliminate the release of POPs into the environment from intentional production and use. These measures, as specified in Article 3(1)(a) of the Convention, include prohibitions as well as legal and administrative measures to eliminate the production, use, import and export of specified chemicals listed in Annex A. According to Article 3(1)(b), chemicals listed in Annex B are subject to several restrictions rather than to elimination. In addition, Article 3(3) requires parties to 'take measures to regulate with the aim of preventing the production and use of new pesticides or new industrial chemicals which . . . exhibit the characteristics of persistent organic pollutants' (as specified in Annex D).

Apart from prohibiting and severely restricting production and use of intentionally

[48] Decision RC-1/13 on Transitional Arrangements, above n 26, 48 *et seq*.

[49] Decision RC-1/6, *ibid*, 34 *et seq*.

[50] Decision RC-4/7, Report of the Conference of the Parties to the Rotterdam Convention on the Prior Informed Consent Procedure for Certain Hazardous Chemicals and Pesticides in International Trade on the work of its fourth meeting (UNEP/FAO/RC/COP.4/24) (31 October 2008) 26.

[51] PL Lallas, 'The Stockholm Convention on Persistent Organic Pollutants' (2001) 95 *AJIL* 692. *Cf* Chapter 7.

produced POPs and of placing restrictions on exports and imports of such POPs, the Convention also includes provisions on the safe handling of existing stockpiles (Article 6). To this end, stockpiles must be identified (paragraph 1(a) and (b)), and managed (paragraph 1(c)) in an environmentally sound way. According to Article 6(2), the COP shall co-operate with the appropriate bodies of the Basel Convention in order, *inter alia*, to address the problem of an environmentally sound disposal of stockpiles.

In addition to curbing intentionally produced POPs, the Convention also includes provisions on the reduction of emissions of unintentionally produced POPs such as dioxins and furans (*cf* Article 5 and Annex C). Article 5 follows the precautionary approach and requires parties to develop an appropriate action plan and to promote the use of best available techniques and best environmental practices, avoiding the unintentional production of POPs.[52]

Controversies about the lists have arisen from the very beginning of the Stockholm Convention implementation process. These primarily concern the use of certain pesticides, including DDT, the use of which has been limited to malaria control. One of the problems related to the implementation of the Convention is the lack of data and information about the sources, releases and environmental levels of POPs in developing countries. This hampers negotiations on specific compounds.[53] Nevertheless, new substances were added to the Stockholm Convention in May 2009.[54]

15.3.3 Conventions on Nuclear Materials

The two conventions relating to nuclear safety to be discussed here are the 1994 Convention on Nuclear Safety[55] and the 1997 Joint Convention on the Safety of Spent Fuel Management and on the Safety of Radioactive Waste Management.[56]

The objectives of the Convention on Nuclear Safety may be taken from its Article 1. They include the achievement and maintenance of a high level of nuclear safety based on national measures and international co-operation alike; the establishment and maintenance of effective defences in nuclear installations against potential radiological hazards for the protection of individuals as well as the environment; and the prevention of accidents with radiological consequences as well as the mitigation of such consequences. Nuclear installations to which the Convention, according to its Article 3, applies are defined in Article 2(i) as 'any land-based civil nuclear power plant under its jurisdiction including such storage, handling and treatment facilities for radioactive materials as are on the same site and are directly related to the operation of the nuclear power plant'.

[52] C vanden Bilcke, 'The Stockholm Convention on Persistent Organic Pollutants' (2002) 11 *RECIEL* 328.

[53] H Bouwman, 'South Africa and the Stockholm Convention on Persistent Organic Pollutants' (2004) 100 *South African Journal of Science* 323.

[54] Decisions SC-4/10 to SC-4/18, see Report of the Conference of the Parties of the Stockholm Convention on Persistent Organic Pollutants (UNEP/POPS/COP4/38) (8 May 2009) 63 *et seq.*

[55] K McMillan, 'Strengthening the International Legal Framework for Nuclear Energy' (2001) 13 *Georgetown International Environmental Law Review* 983, 993 *et seq*.

[56] P Cameron, 'Joint Convention on the Safety of Spent Fuel Management and on the Safety of Radioactive Waste Management' in NLJT Horbach (ed), *Contemporary Developments in Nuclear Energy Law: Harmonising Legislation in CEEC/NIS* (The Hague 1999) 117–128.

The Convention primarily commits the parties to adopt national measures 'to ensure that the safety of nuclear installations . . . is reviewed as soon as possible' (Article 6). These include legislation and regulation (Articles 7–9) and general safety considerations (Articles 10–16) as well as provisions on the safety of installations (Articles 17–19). Even though the preamble and Article 1 refer to international co-operation, only Article 17 includes an explicit reference to such co-operation by stipulating that parties shall take appropriate steps

> for consulting Contracting Parties in the vicinity of a proposed nuclear installation, insofar as they are likely to be affected by that installation and, upon request providing the necessary information to such Contracting Parties, in order to enable them to evaluate and make their own assessment of the likely safety impact on their own territory of the nuclear installation.

While Organizational Meetings of Contracting Parties have been held regularly (with the latest on 29 September 2009), an extraordinary meeting was held on 28 September 2009 in order to discuss a revised version of Guidelines Regarding National Reports.[57]

The Joint Convention on the Safety of Spent Fuel Management and on the Safety of Radioactive Waste Management is the first legally binding treaty to address spent fuel management and radioactive waste management at the universal level. Its Article 1 lays down the following objectives which are similar to those of the Convention on Nuclear Safety: to achieve and maintain a high level of safety worldwide in spent fuel and radioactive waste management; to ensure that during all stages of spent fuel and radioactive waste management there are effective defences against potential hazards in order to protect human health and the environment; to prevent accidents with radiological consequences and to mitigate their consequences should they occur during any stage of spent fuel or radioactive waste management.[58]

Parties are under an obligation primarily to develop national safety measures (Articles 18–26). In addition, the Convention includes procedural obligations requiring parties to consider issues affecting the safety of neighbouring parties. Parties must, among other things, carefully select the sites for treatment of spent fuel and disposal of radioactive waste and consult neighbouring states (Article 13(1)(iv)). Furthermore, emergency plans must be made available before beginning the operation of any facility covered by the Convention (Article 25(1)). Article 25(2) provides that each party

> shall take the appropriate steps for the preparation and testing of emergency plans for its territory insofar as it is likely to be affected in the event of a radiological emergency at a spent fuel or radioactive waste management facility in the vicinity of its territory.

Notification and response are required for the transboundary movement of radioactive waste and spent fuel (Article 27). Article 27(2) explicitly prohibits the licensing of any

[57] This is already the third version of the guidelines (INFCIRC/572/Rev3, see www-ns.iaea.org/downloads/ni/safety_convention/infcicr_572_rev3.pdf), with the first edition adopted in 1998 (INFCIRC/572, see www.iaea.org/Publications/Documents/Infcircs/1998/infcirc572.shtml). The second edition was approved in 2002 (INFCIRC/572/Rev2, www.iaea.org/Publications/Documents/Infcircs/2002/infcirc572r2.pdf).

[58] W Tonhauser, 'The Peer Review Process under the Joint Convention on the Safety of Spent Fuel Management and on the Safety of Radioactive Waste Management' (2006) 4 *Zeitschrift für Europäisches Umwelt- und Planungsrecht* 131.

shipment of spent fuel or radioactive waste to a destination south of latitude 60°S for storage or disposal. According to Article 27(1)(iii), transboundary movements of spent fuel or radioactive waste are only permissible if the recipient state 'has the administrative and technical capacity, as well as the regulatory structure, needed to manage the spent fuel or the radioactive waste in a manner consistent with this Convention'.

15.4 Conclusions

Even though the transboundary movement of wastes and hazardous substances is still a fairly novel subject of international environmental law, it is possible to identify a number of common elements in pertinent instruments. The most important thereof is the prior informed consent procedure which resembles the advance informed agreement procedure adopted under the Biosafety Protocol.[59]

The main problem of the transboundary movement of wastes and hazardous substances seems currently to be the implementation of existing agreements. A statistical comparison of global trends analysing a concrete situation before and after the entry into force of a convention is the most appropriate method of assessment of the implementation of the respective instrument. However, especially as far as data on hazardous wastes under the Basel Convention are concerned, it is quite difficult to obtain sufficient information on volumes and types of such wastes at all. In 2006, for example, only 86 parties to the Basel Convention out of then 168 transmitted national reports including relevant data.[60] Therefore, COP 9 decided to apply a new strategic framework for the implementation of the Basel Convention for the period of 2012–2021 which is currently being prepared by the Convention's Open-ended Working Group for adoption by COP 10 in 2012.[61] The situation under the Stockholm Convention is quite similar, taking into account that a global monitoring plan for the identification of global trends relating to the presence of POPs and the assessment of the effectiveness of the Convention was only adopted in 2007 and has yet to be implemented.[62] Whereas substantive and procedural elements have been agreed upon successfully, the main problem, in particular with regard to the transfer of hazardous substances from developing to developed countries, is the lack of an effective ban on such transfers. As long as the amendment to the Basel Convention has not entered into force, wastes and hazardous substances will continue to be disposed in places where there is least objection and lowest protection of the environment.[63] Some

[59] *Cf* Chapter 14.3.4.

[60] See the table at the website of the Basel Convention www.basel.int/natreporting/stat-report/graphical.html. *Cf* also the Report of the seventh session of the Basel Convention Implementation and Compliance Committee (UNEP/CHW/CC/7/10) (3 August 2009) 5, taking 'note of the decreasing trend in reporting'.

[61] *Cf* Decision IX/3 in Report of the Conference of the Parties to the Basel Convention on the Control of Transboundary Movements of Hazardous Wastes and their Disposal on its ninth meeting (UNEP/CHW9/39) (27 June 2008) 19 *et seq*.

[62] See http://chm.pops.int/Programmes/Global%20Monitoring%20Plan/Overview/tabid/83/language/en-US/Default.aspx.

[63] A Andrews, 'Beyond the Ban—Can the Basel Convention Adequately Safeguard the Interests of the World's Poor in the International Trade of Hazardous Waste?' (2009) 5 *Law, Environment and Development*

recent incidents, like the 2006 Abidjan disaster, show that the Basel Convention is still far from being a 'success story'.[64]

It is possible that it will be necessary to develop international standards for the national treatment of waste in order to overcome negative economic incentives for the environmentally sound treatment of waste at the place where it originates.

Further Reading

A Andrews, 'Beyond the Ban—Can the Basel Convention Adequately Safeguard the Interests of the World's Poor in the International Trade of Hazardous Waste?' (2009) 5 *Law, Environment and Development Journal* 167–184.

P Barrios, 'The Rotterdam Convention on Hazardous Chemicals: A Meaningful Step Toward Environmental Protection?' (2004) 16 *Georgetown International Environmental Law Review* 679–762.

S Choksi, 'The Basel Convention on the Control of Transboundary Movements of Hazardous Wastes and their Disposal: 1999 Protocol on Liability and Compensation' (2001) 28 *Ecology Law Quarterly* 509–539.

A Daniel, 'Hazardous Substances, Transboundary Impacts' in R Wolfrum (ed), *Max Planck Encyclopedia of Public International Law* (Heidelberg/Oxford 2009), available at www.mpepil.com.

——, 'Transboundary Movements of Hazardous Waste' (2007) 18 *Yearbook of International Environmental Law* 258–266.

S Dawson, 'A Proposal for an International Framework Convention to Assess the Environmental Risks of Commercially Available Nanomaterials' (2008) 15 *University of Baltimore Journal of Environmental Law* 129–150.

CN Eze, 'The Bamako Convention on the Ban on the Import into Africa and the Control of the Transboundary Movement and Management of Hazardous Wastes Within Africa: A Milestone in Environmental Protection?' (2007) 15 *African Journal of International and Comparative Law* 208–229.

CU Gwam, 'Travaux Preparatoires of the Basel Convention on the Control of Transboundary Movements of Hazardous Wastes and their Disposal' (2003–2004) 18 *Journal of Natural Resources and Environmental Law* 1–78.

A Kiss, 'State Responsibility and Liability for Nuclear Damage' (2006) 35 *Denver Journal of International Law and Policy* 67–83.

PL Lallas, 'The Stockholm Convention on Persistent Organic Pollutants' (2001) 95 *AJIL* 692–708.

TL McDorman, 'The Rotterdam Convention on the Prior Informed Consent Procedure for Certain Hazardous Chemicals and Pesticides in International Trade: Some Legal Notes' (2004) 13 *RECIEL* 187–200.

K McMillan, 'Strengthening the International Legal Framework for Nuclear Energy' (2001) 13 *Georgetown International Environmental Law Review* 983–1012.

Journal 167; *cf* also Z Lipman, 'Trade in Hazardous Waste: Environmental Justice Versus Economic Growth', available at www.ban.org/Library/lipman.html and Basel Action Network Briefing Paper 1, 'The Basel Ban: A Triumph for Global Environmental Justice' (May 2010), available at www.ban.org/Library/BP1_10_05.pdf.

[64] For more information on the 'Abidjan Disaster' see Greenpeace International, 'Toxic Waste in Abidjan: Greenpeace Evaluation' (15 September 2006), available at www.greenpeace.org/international/en/news/features/toxic-waste-in-abidjan-green/.

JF St Cyr, 'The International Jurisprudence and Politics of Hazardous Substances: Managing a Global Dilemma' (2004) 12 *Buffalo Environmental Law Journal* 91–121.

TR Subramanya, 'The Basel Convention on the Control of Transboundary Movements of Hazardous Wastes and their Disposal of 1989 and Related Developments' (2006) 46 *The Indian Journal of International Law* 406–428.

16

Procedural Environmental Obligations

16.1 Basic Observations

Basically, two types of procedural environmental obligations can be distinguished, namely (i) the duty to pay mutual respect in interstate relations, and (ii) the duty to ensure intra-state public participation.

The duty to pay mutual respect in interstate relations governs in particular relations between neighbouring states. It includes the substantive duty to inflict no environmental harm on each other,[1] accompanied by the procedural obligations to notify all activities and events likely to be harmful, to engage in the exchange of information and consultation, and to carry out environmental impact assessments (to be dealt with in more detail in sections 16.2 and 16.3).

The duty to ensure intra-state public participation includes three forms of active involvement in governmental affairs: access to governmental information; participation in governmental decision-making; and access to judicial remedies (to be discussed in section 16.4).

16.2 Information, Notification and Consultation in Interstate Relations

The obligation of states to exchange information is of particular relevance in two situations: (i) between neighbouring states when an activity planned on the territory of one of the neighbouring states is likely to cause transboundary environmental harm (situations of likely transboundary environmental harm); (ii) where a state at risk of becoming the victim of a transboundary environmental accident has no chance to escape from, or

[1] For the 'no harm' rule see above Chapter 6.

minimise, its detrimental effects, unless it has been informed in a timely manner about this event by the state of origin (situations of transboundary environmental emergency).

16.2.1 Situations of Likely Transboundary Environmental Harm

A state on whose territory an environmentally sensitive activity is planned must give timely and sufficient information on that activity to any state whose environment or rights and interests are likely to be significantly affected by it. Particularly in bilateral or trilateral environmental agreements between neighbouring states, this obligation to exchange information is often interlinked with the commitment to engage in consultation with each other in the spirit of good neighbourliness. Thus, there are good reasons to argue that in the relationship between neighbouring states, both obligations are part of today's customary international environmental law.[2] Accordingly, Principle 19 of the Rio Declaration calls upon states to

> provide prior and timely notification and relevant information to potentially affected states on activities that may have a significant adverse transboundary environmental effect and shall consult with those states at an early stage and in good faith.[3]

Today, international environmental agreements of all kind, including the multilateral ones, contain standard obligations to exchange information and to report on a regular basis. As a rule, these duties are rather unspectacular in legal terms.[4]

16.2.2 Situations of Transboundary Environmental Emergency

Many MEAs provide interstate co-operation in the management of environmental emergencies. Among them are the IAEA Vienna Convention on Early Notification of a Nuclear Accident (IAEA Notification Convention) of 26 September 1986,[5] accompanied by the Convention on Assistance in the Case of a Nuclear Accident or Radiological Emergency of the same date;[6] the London International Convention on Oil Pollution Preparedness, Response and Co-operation (OPRC Convention) of 30 November 1990;[7] the Madrid Protocol on Environmental Protection to the Antarctic Treaty (Madrid Protocol) of 4 October 1991;[8] and the UNECE Helsinki Convention on the Transboundary Effects of Industrial Accidents (Industrial Accidents Convention) of 17 March 1992.[9]

[2] For a brief general discussion see E Louka, *International Environmental Law. Fairness, Effectiveness and World Order* (Cambridge 2006) 120.

[3] Similar Arts 8 and 9 of the ILC's Draft Articles on Prevention of Transboundary Harm from Hazardous Activities (2001). For the text see ILC, 'Report of the International Law Commission on the Work of its 53rd Session' (23 April–1 June and 2 July–10 August 2001) UN Doc A/56/10, 146 *et seq*, available at http://untreaty.un.org/ilc/texts/instruments/english/draft%20articles/9_7_2001.pdf. *Cf* also Chapter 6.

[4] For a thorough discussion on information provision and reporting see P Sands, *Principles of International Environmental Law* (2nd edn Cambridge 2003) 832 *et seq*.

[5] In force since 27 October 1986; it is binding on 108 parties.

[6] In force since 26 February 1987; it is binding on 105 parties.

[7] In force since 13 May 1995; it is binding on 102 parties.

[8] In force since 14 January 1998; it is binding on 27 parties.

[9] In force since 19 April 2000; it is binding on 40 parties.

In reaction to the USSR's failure to provide timely information on the Chernobyl nuclear plant accident in 1986, the IAEA Notification Convention was established. It provides that in the event of a nuclear accident that results or may result in a transboundary release of radioactive material 'that could be of radiological safety significance for another State' (Article 1(1)), the state of origin must notify potentially affected states and the IAEA of 'the nuclear accident, its nature, the time of its occurrence and its exact location where appropriate', and provide them 'with such available information relevant to minimizing the radiological consequences in those States, as specified in article 5' (Article 2(a) and (b)). Each state party must make known to the IAEA and to other states parties its 'competent authorities and point of contact responsible for issuing and receiving the notification and information referred to in article 2' (Article 7(1)).[10]

The 1990 OPRC Convention[11] imposes on states parties the duty 'to take all appropriate measures . . . to prepare for and respond to an oil pollution incident' (Article 1(1)), and to ensure that all ships flying their flag have on board a 'shipboard oil pollution emergency plan' (Article 3(1)(a)). Moreover, each state party must ensure that persons having charge of ships flying its flag 'report without delay any event on their ship . . . involving a discharge . . . of oil' (Article 4(1)(a)). Each party receiving such a report is obliged to take appropriate control actions and to pass all relevant information to all states whose interests are likely to be affected (Articles 5, 6 and 7).

Under the 1991 Madrid Protocol, each party is required to 'provide for prompt and effective response action' to environmental emergencies 'which might arise in the performance of scientific research programs, tourism and all other . . . activities in the Antarctic Treaty area for which advance notice is required' and to 'establish contingency plans for response to incidents with potential adverse effects on the Antarctic environment or dependent and associated ecosystems' (Article 15(1)(a) and (b)).[12]

The 1992 Industrial Accidents Convention applies to industrial accidents from activities involving (non-nuclear) hazardous substances (Article 1(a) and (b) and Annex I). For purposes of prevention, 'the Party of origin shall take measures, as appropriate, to identify hazardous activities within its jurisdiction and to ensure that affected Parties are notified of any such proposed or existing activity' (Article 4(1)). The parties are required to 'enter into discussions on the identification of those hazardous activities that are, reasonably, capable of causing transboundary effects'. In case of disagreement among the parties as to whether an activity is hazardous, any party may 'submit that question to an inquiry commission in accordance with the provisions of Annex II . . . for advice' (Article 4(2)).[13]

The above treaty practice appears to be uniform enough to argue that, today, the obli-

[10] In 2002 the IAEA Board of Governors approved the legally non-binding document 'Preparedness and Response for a Nuclear or Radiological Emergency'. It establishes requirements for international notification and information exchange in the case of a 'transnational emergency', *ie* an emergency of actual, potential or perceived radiological significance for more than one state (*Cf* IAEA Safety Standards Series No GS-R-2, available at www-pub.iaea.org/MTCD/publications/PDF/Pub1133_scr.pdf).

[11] *Cf* also Chapter 12.3.7.

[12] In Addition, Annex VI of the Protocol stipulates rules for 'Liability Arising From Environmental Emergencies'.

[13] This provision is very similar to Art 3(7) of the 1991 Espoo Convention on Environmental Impact Assessment in a Transboundary Context (to be dealt with in more detail below at Section 16.3).

gation of states to notify each other in a timely fashion of any environmental emergency that has caused or is likely to cause significant transboundary harm so as to enable the affected state to avert that harm or to minimise its consequences is close to becoming, if it has not already become, part of customary international law.[14]

16.3 Environmental Impact Assessment (EIA)

EIA, as defined in Article 1(vi) of the Espoo Convention on Environmental Impact Assessment in a Transboundary Context of 25 February 1991,[15] means 'a national procedure for evaluating the likely impact of a proposed activity on the environment'. It is a tool which enables the relevant public authority to take a final decision on granting a permit to the respective project. Thus, the authority must balance the information on the environmental consequences of the project and its alternatives provided by the EIA against any other considerations, including those of economic development, which it deems to be decisive in the given case.

EIAs were first established in the domestic law of the United States, namely in the US National Environmental Policy Act of 1969, and a number of other states, including Canada (1992)[16] and China (2002).[17] With the adoption of a series of EC directives in 1985, 1997, 2001, 2003 and 2009, EIA became an important tool of the European Union's environmental policy.[18] Notwithstanding the 'differences in the frequency and sophistication with which EIA is used across this range of jurisdictions, there has been a worldwide sharing of methodology and the basic features of most schemes are very similar'.[19]

Internationally, Principle 17 of the 1992 Rio Declaration stating that '[e]nvironmental impact assessment, as a national instrument, shall be undertaken for proposed activities that are likely to have a significant adverse impact on the environment and are subject to a decision of a competent national authority'[20] reflects the worldwide acceptance of EIA. The formulation 'impact on the environment' in Principle 17 is broad enough to encom-

[14] Similar Article 17 of the ILC's Draft Articles (above n 3): 'The State of origin shall, without delay and by the most expeditious means, at its disposal, notify the State likely to be affected of an emergency concerning an activity within the scope of the present articles and provide it with all relevant and available information.' *Cf* also Principle 18 of the Rio Declaration: 'States shall immediately notify other states of any natural disasters or other emergencies that are likely to produce sudden harmful effects on the environment of those states.' For more detailed information see Sands, above n 4, 841 *et seq*.

[15] In force since 10 September 1997, it is binding on 43 states and the EU.

[16] Canadian Environmental Assessment Act, assented to 23 June 1992.

[17] Environmental Impact Assessment Law of the People's Republic of China, adopted on 28 October 2002.

[18] Council Directive 85/337/EEC of 27 June 1985 on the Assessment of the Effects of Certain Public and Private Projects on the Environment ([1985] OJ L/175/40) as amended by Council Directive 97/11/EC of 14 March 1997 ([1997] OJ L/73/5), Council Directive 2003/35/EC of 25 June 2003 ([2003] OJ L/156/17) and Directive 2009/31/EC of the European Parliament and of the Council of 23 April 2009 ([2009] OJ L/140/14); Directive 2001/42/EC of the European Parliament and of the Council of 27 June 2001 on the Assessment of the Effects of Certain Plans and Programmes on the Environment ([2001] OJ L197/30).

[19] P Birnie, A Boyle and C Redgwell, *International Law and the Environment* (3rd edn Oxford 2009) 166.

[20] See its text in Report of the UN Conference on Environment and Development, Rio de Janeiro, UN Doc A/CONF151/26/Rev1 (vol I) 3 *et seq*; (1992) 31 ILM 874.

pass the environment in its domestic, transboundary and global dimension.[21] However, relevant international state practice reveals that at present customary international law neither requires states to assess possible global environmental impacts nor impacts on the domestic environment.[22]

While initially, national EIAs may have been conceived as tools designed to protect only domestic environments, since the late 1970s states have become increasingly aware of the need to identify and assess the possible transboundary environmental impacts of a proposed activity in the same way as domestic ones, *ie* on the basis of non-discrimination.

The earliest support for transboundary EIAs can be found in a series of legally non-binding recommendations adopted by the OECD Council[23] and UNEP[24] in the late 1970s. These 'soft law' instruments provided a model for the subsequent conclusion of a number of MEAs containing provisions on transboundary EIA. Among them are the UNCLOS (Article 206);[25] the 1991 Espoo Convention; the 1991 Antarctic Environmental Protocol (Article 8 with Annex);[26] the 1991 US–Canada Air Quality Agreement (Article V);[27] the 1993 North American Agreement on Environmental Cooperation (Article 2(1)(e));[28] and the 1997 EC Directive 97/11 which amended the 1985 EC Directive on EIA not least in order to bring it in line with the Espoo Convention.[29] Thus, Article 7 of the ILC's 2001 Draft Articles on Transboundary Harm, which states that

> [a]ny decision in respect of the authorization of an activity within the scope of the present articles shall, in particular, be based on an assessment of the possible transboundary harm caused by that activity, including any environmental impact assessment

only summarises the main features of relevant MEAs existing today.

[21] Birnie, Boyle and Redgwell, above n 19, 166.

[22] See *ibid*, 167.

[23] See the following OECD Recommendations: C (74)224 (14 November 1974) on 'Principles Concerning Transfrontier Pollution'; C (77)28 (17 May 1977) on the 'Implementation of a Regime of Equal Right of Access and Non-Discrimination in Relation to Transfrontier Pollution', paras 8–10; C (78)77 (21 September 1978) on 'Strengthening International Co-operation on Environmental Protection in Frontier Regions', para 3. Their texts are available at http://webnet.oecd.org/oecdacts/Instruments/ListByTypeView.aspx.

[24] 1978 UNEP Draft Principles of Conduct in the Field of the Environment for the Guidance of States in the Conservation and Harmonious Utilization of Natural Resources Shared by Two or More States (Principle 4); see their text in (1978) 17 ILM 1097 *et seq*.

[25] It reads as follows: 'When States have reasonable grounds for believing that planned activities under their jurisdiction or control may cause substantial pollution of or significant and harmful changes to the marine environment, they shall, as far as practical, assess the potential effects of such activities on the marine environment and shall communicate reports of the results of such assessments in the manner provided in article 205.'

[26] Art 8 provides: '(1) Proposed activities referred to in paragraph 2 below shall be subject to the procedures set out in Annex I for prior assessment of the impacts of those activities on the Antarctic environment or on dependent or associated ecosystems according to whether those activities are identified as having: (a) less than a minor or transitory impact; (b) a minor or transitory impact; or (c) more than a minor or transitory impact.'

[27] Art V(1) provides: 'Each Party shall, as appropriate and as required by its laws, regulations and policies, assess those proposed actions, activities and projects within the area under its jurisdiction that, if carried out, would be likely to cause significant transboundary air pollution, including consideration of appropriate mitigation measures.'

[28] Art 2(1)(e) provides that '[e]ach Party shall, with respect to its territory . . . assess, as appropriate, environmental impacts'.

[29] For a survey of relevant MEAs see A Epiney, 'Environmental Impact Assessment' in R Wolfrum (ed), *Max Planck Encyclopedia of Public International Law* (Heidelberg/Oxford 2009), paras 5 and 6, available at www.mpepil.com.

Of particular relevance in international state practice is the 1991 Espoo Convention. Its core elements are laid down in Article 2, according to which

- all parties are required to 'take all appropriate and effective measures to prevent, reduce and control significant adverse transboundary environmental impact from proposed activities' (paragraph 1);
- each party of origin must 'ensure that affected Parties are notified of a proposed activity listed in Appendix I that is likely to cause a significant adverse transboundary impact' (paragraph 4);
- the parties concerned are required to 'enter into discussions on whether one or more proposed activities not listed in Appendix I is or are likely to cause a significant adverse transboundary impact and thus should be treated as if it or they were so listed' (paragraph 5); and
- each party of origin 'shall provide . . . an opportunity to the public in the areas likely to be affected to participate in relevant environmental impact assessment procedures regarding proposed activities and shall ensure that the opportunity provided to the public of the affected Party is equivalent to that provided to the public of the Party of origin' (paragraph 6).[30]

These obligations under Article 2 of the Espoo Convention are specified and complemented by, *inter alia*, the following procedural provisions.

Article 3(7) provides that where a party considers that it is likely to be 'affected by a significant adverse transboundary impact of a proposed activity listed in Appendix I', and it has not been notified according to Article 3(1), an exchange of 'sufficient information' must take place 'for the purposes of holding discussions on whether there is likely to be a significant adverse transboundary impact'; if the parties concerned cannot agree whether such an impact is likely, any such party 'may submit that question to an inquiry commission in accordance with the provisions of Appendix IV to advise on the likelihood of significant adverse transboundary impact'. To date, such an enquiry procedure under Article 3(7) has been initiated only once, namely in July 2006 when the governments of Romania and the Ukraine disagreed upon the likely significant transboundary impact of the planned Ukrainian deep-water navigation canal from the Danube to the Black Sea.[31] It remains to be seen whether this method of seeking advice from an independent enquiry commission will in practice prove to be a promising means to settle a conflict between states parties as to whether the adverse environmental impact of a proposed activity in a given case exceeds the thresholds of 'significance' and 'foreseeability'.

Article 4(1) provides for the preparation of an 'environmental impact assessment documentation' which must meet the minimum standards of information laid down in

[30] *Cf* below at Section 16.4.2.

[31] On 16 July 2006 the Espoo Inquiry Commission (consisting of three scientific or technical experts and an independent chairperson) presented its Final Report 'On the Likely Significant Adverse Transboundary Impacts of the Danube–Black Sea Navigation Route at the Border of Romania and the Ukraine' issuing a number of (legally non-binding) recommendations. It came to the conclusion that in the case at hand a significant adverse transboundary impact was likely; accordingly, the Ukraine was expected to send a notification about the Canal to Romania in accordance with the Espoo Convention (Final Report, at 7). The report is available at www.unece.org/env/eia/documents/inquiry/Final%20Report%2010%20July%202006.pdf.

Appendix II. According to Article 4(2), the party of origin must ensure that this documentation is sent to the affected party and distributed to its authorities and the public in the areas likely to be affected, and that the comments of those authorities and that public are submitted to the competent authority of the party of origin 'within a reasonable time before the final decision is taken on the proposed activity'.

Article 5 requires the party of origin and the affected parties, 'without undue delay' to 'enter into consultations' concerning the potential transboundary impact and measures to reduce or eliminate the impact. Under Article 6, each party of origin must ensure that in the final decision on the proposed activity 'due account is taken' of the outcome of the EIA, including the EIA documentation, the comments thereon received, and the outcome of the consultations. Finally, under Article 7 the concerned parties 'shall determine whether, and if so to what extent, a post-project analysis shall be carried out'; any such analysis shall include 'the surveillance of the activity and the determination of any adverse transboundary impact' (*cf* Appendix V).

The Kiev Protocol on Strategic Environmental Assessment to the Convention on Environmental Impact Assessment in a Transboundary Context of 21 May 2003[32] is aimed at extending EIAs from the few 'proposed activities' listed in Appendix I of the Espoo Convention to a broader number of 'plans and programmes'.[33] The Protocol provides for the establishment of 'clear, transparent and effective procedures for strategic environmental assessment', *ie*, according to Article 1(c) and Article 2(6),

> the evaluation of the likely environmental, including health, effects, which comprises the determination of the scope of an environmental report and its preparation, the carrying-out of public participation and consultations, and the taking into account of the environmental report and the results of the public participation and consultations in a plan or programme.

As regards EIAs concerning 'policies and legislation', it imposes on states parties only a weakly formulated duty (Article 13(1): 'shall endeavour to ensure'; 'to the extent appropriate').

National legislation in Europe and North America, many international environmental agreements, including the Espoo Convention, relevant EU directives,[34] as well as the alleged failures by certain states to undertake transboundary EIAs in a number of ICJ and ITLOS cases[35] support the conclusion that the obligation to undertake transboundary EIAs has become part of customary international law.[36] The ICJ in its 2010 judgment

[32] In force since 11 July 2010, it is binding on 18 parties, including the EU.

[33] This means 'plans and programmes . . . [r]equired by legislative, regulatory or administrative provisions; and . . . [s]ubject to preparation and/or adoption by an authority for adoption, through a formal procedure, by a parliament or a government' (Art 2(5) of the Kiev Protocol).

[34] For references see Epiney, above n 29, para 5 *et seq*.

[35] *Request for an Examination of the Situation in Accordance with Paragraph 63 of the Court's Judgment of 20 December 1974 in the Nuclear Tests (New Zealand v France)* case (1995) ICJ Reports 288; *Gabčíkovo-Nagymaros* case *(Hungary v Slovakia)* (1997) ICJ Reports 7; *MOX Plant* case *(Ireland v United Kingdom)* (Provisional Measures, Order of 3 December 2001) ITLOS Case No 10; *Land Reclamation* case (Provisional Measures, Order of 8 October 2003) ITLOS Case No 12. For a more detailed discussion on relevant case law see Birnie, Boyle and Redgwell, above n 19, 169 *et seq*.

[36] In this sense also Birnie, Boyle and Redgwell, *ibid*; Sands, above n 4, 824; and Epiney, above n 29, para 47.

in the case concerning *Pulp Mills on the River Uruguay* asserted 'a requirement under general international law to undertake an environmental impact assessment where there is a risk that the proposed industrial activity may have a significant adverse impact in a transboundary context, in particular, on a shared resource'.[37] At the same time, the ICJ rejected the Argentine argument that a state undertaking a transboundary EIA is legally obliged 'to consult the affected populations'.[38]

16.4 Participatory Rights of Non-Governmental Actors

16.4.1 'Public Participation' in General

The term of 'public participation'[39] is tantamount to that of 'participation of the public'. It means 'participation of non-governmental actors' in governmental affairs.

Public participation claims practical importance primarily in the domestic sphere of states, but also at the international level.[40] International treaty norms granting 'public participation' in domestic decision-making processes are conceptually linked to procedural human rights guarantees in international human rights treaties.[41] Non-governmental actors exercising these participatory rights help ensure that their states comply with their obligations under international environmental law. As regards international decision-making processes, there is a general move towards expanding the involvement of non-governmental actors in decision-making. Consequently, at present governments increasingly waive their accustomed prerogative to represent the public. On the other hand, public participation 'helps to make governmental decisions more effective by enhancing the legitimacy and, thus, the acceptance level of decisions taken'.[42]

'Public participation', with its three pillars 'access to information', 'participation in decision-making' and 'access to justice', emerged from the idea of guaranteeing all non-state actors equal participation on the basis of 'non-discrimination', a concept which traces back to the then highly innovative OECD Council's Recommendations 'Principles Concerning Transfrontier Pollution' of 14 November 1974[43] and 'Equal Right of Access

[37] *Argentina v Uruguay*, Judgment of 20 April 2010, para 204, available at www.icj-cij.org/docket/index.php?p1=3&p2=3&k=88&case=135&code=au&p3=4.

[38] *Ibid*, paras 215, 216.

[39] *Cf* J Ebbesson, 'Public Participation' in D Bodansky *et al* (eds), *The Oxford Handbook of International Environmental Law* (Oxford 2007) 681, 685.

[40] Principle 10 of the Rio Declaration reflects the state of law in 1992 regarding public participation in domestic environmental decision-making by stating: 'Environmental issues are best handled with the participation of all concerned citizens, at the relevant level. At the national level, each individual shall have appropriate access to information concerning the environment that is held by public authorities, including information on hazardous materials and activities in their communities, and the opportunity to participate in decision-making processes. States shall facilitate and encourage public awareness and participation by making information widely available. Effective access to judicial and administrative proceedings, including redress and remedy, shall be provided.'

[41] *Cf* Ebbesson, above n 39, 686 and 687.

[42] *Ibid*, 688.

[43] See para 4 of Recommendation C (74)224; its text is available at http://webnet.oecd.org/oecdacts/Instruments/ListByTypeView.aspx.

in Relation to Transfrontier Pollution' of 11 May 1976. The latter recommendation states in its Annex, paragraph 2:

> [T]he rights accorded to 'persons affected by transfrontier pollution' should be equivalent to those accorded to persons whose . . . interests within the territory of the country where the transfrontier pollution originates are or may be affected under similar conditions by a same pollution, as regards: [a] Information concerning projects, new activities and courses of conduct which may give rise to a significant risk of pollution; [b] Access to information which the competent authorities make available to persons concerned; [c] The participation in hearings and preliminary enquiries and the making of objections in respect of proposed decisions by the public authorities which could directly or indirectly lead to pollution; [d] Recourse to and standing in administrative and judicial procedures (including emergency procedures).[44]

Instruments granting transboundary participatory rights to non-state actors on the basis of non-discrimination have the merit of being indifferent to national borders.[45] Each state which decides on the permit for an activity with transboundary effects must ensure equal access to its decision-making procedures to those potentially affected in other states. However, the quality of participation of non-state actors on the other side of the border depends on the domestic law of the state of origin.[46] As '[e]qual access guarantees no substantive standard of environmental protection, and no procedural rights of any kind save to the extent that these are already available for domestic claimants',[47] states must be otherwise legally obliged to meet certain minimum standards of transboundary public participation.

The Nordic Convention on the Protection of the Environment of 19 February 1974[48] was the first legally binding instrument which provided individuals with equal access to justice, *ie* the third pillar of 'public participation'.[49] As shown above,[50] the 1991 Espoo Convention includes in its Article 2(6) all three pillars of public participation, namely access to information, participation in decision-making, and access to justice. The 1992 Industrial Accidents Convention follows the Espoo Convention by requiring the parties

[44] Recommendation C (76)55; for its text see *ibid.*

[45] Art 15 ('Non-discrimination') of the ILC's Draft Articles (above n 3), provides that '[u]nless the States concerned have agreed otherwise for the protection of the interests of persons, natural or juridical, who may be exposed to the risk of significant transboundary harm as a result of an activity within the scope of the present articles, a State shall not discriminate on the basis of nationality or residence or place where the injury might occur, in granting to such persons, in accordance with its legal system, access to judicial or other procedures to seek protection or other appropriate redress'.

[46] See Ebbesson, above n 39, 696 *et seq.*

[47] Birnie, Boyle and Redgwell, above n 19, 310.

[48] In force since 5 October 1976; it is binding on Denmark, Finland, Norway and Sweden.

[49] Art 3 of the Nordic Convention reads as follows: 'Any person who is affected or may be affected by a nuisance caused by environmentally harmful activities in another Contracting State shall have the right to bring before the appropriate Court or Administrative Authority of that State the question of the permissibility of such activities including the question of measures to prevent damage, and to appeal against the decision of the Court or the Administrative Authority to the same extent and on the same terms as a legal entity of the State in which the activities are being carried out.' *Cf* also Art 6(2) of the 1993 North American Agreement on Environmental Cooperation: 'Each Party shall ensure that persons with a legally recognized interest under its law in a particular matter have appropriate access to administrative, quasi-judicial or judicial proceedings for the enforcement of the Party's environmental laws and regulations'; the text is available in (1993) 4 *Yearbook of International Environmental Law* 169.

[50] *Cf* at Section 16.3.

concerned to ensure that adequate information is given to the public in the areas likely to be affected by an industrial accident, and obliging the party of origin to give this public, whenever possible and appropriate, the opportunity to participate in relevant procedures equivalent to that accorded to the public of the party of origin (Article 9(1) and (2)).[51]

With the 1998 Aarhus Convention on Access to Information, Public Participation and Decision-Making and Access to Justice in Environmental Matters (Aarhus Convention) and the Revised 2003 Maputo African Convention on the Conservation of Nature and Natural Resources (Maputo Convention), there are currently two legally binding instruments which, in rather broad terms, oblige parties to grant participatory rights to non-governmental actors in domestic environmental affairs, including those entailing transboundary effects.

The innovative approach of the Aarhus Convention is interesting enough to deserve our closer attention and will be discussed in more detail in the following section.

The Revised Maputo Convention commits its parties to 'ensure timely and appropriate . . . access of the public to environmental information; . . . participation of the public in decision-making with a potentially significant environmental impact; and . . . access to justice in matters related to protection of environment and natural resources' (Article XVI). With this provision, the Maputo Convention evidently borrows from the aforementioned Aarhus Convention. However, it is still some way from entering into force.[52]

16.4.2 The Aarhus Convention

The Aarhus Convention was signed on 25 June 1998 and came into force on 30 October 2001. Established within the framework of the UNECE, the Aarhus Convention is currently binding on 43 states, including most of the former Soviet states, the United States and Canada, and the European Union. However, any state that is a member of the United Nations may accede to it (Article 19(3)).

Praised as 'the most ambitious venture in the area of "environmental democracy" so far undertaken under the auspices of the United Nations', and considered to have the 'potential to serve as a global framework for strengthening citizens' environmental rights',[53] the Convention is designed 'to contribute to the protection of the right of every person of present and future generations to live in an environment adequate to his or her health and well-being'. To this effect 'each Party shall guarantee the rights of access to information, public participation in decision-making, and access to justice in environmental matters' (Article 1).

Under Article 3(1) of the Convention

> [e]ach Party shall take the necessary legislative, regulatory and other measure, including measures to achieve compatibility between the provisions implementing the information, public

[51] *Cf* Annex VIII. See www.unece.org/env/documents/2006/teia/Convention%20E%20no%20annex%20I.pdf.

[52] To date, the Maputo Convention has obtained only eight ratifications, out of the quorum of fifteen ratifications required by its Article XXXVIII.

[53] K Annan, 'Foreword' in S Steg, S Casey-Lefkowitz and J Jendroska, *The Aarhus Convention: An Implementation Guide* (New York 2000) v.

> participation and access-to-justice provisions in this Convention, as well as proper enforcement measures, to establish and maintain a clear, transparent and consistent framework to implement the provisions of this Convention.

In fact, all three conventional participatory rights are closely interdependent: '[A]ccess to information is a prerequisite for meaningful public participation in environmental decision-making, access to justice is a means to having acts, decisions, decision-making processes, and omissions reviewed'.[54]

Article 4 of the Aarhus Convention guarantees access to information to 'the public', *ie* to 'anyone'.[55] Thus, public authorities are required to make available to the public environmental information as broadly defined by Article 2(3), 'without an interest having to be stated', and without an unreasonable charge for supplying information, 'at the latest within one month after the request has been submitted' (Article 4(1) and (2)). A request may be refused only for a number of exceptional grounds, such as confidentiality of public proceedings, commercial and industrial secrets, intellectual property rights, and confidentiality of personal data and files (listed in Article 4(3) and (4)). These exceptions must be interpreted in a restrictive way. Any refusal to disclose information is to be subject to the Convention's provisions on access to judicial review (Article 9). Under Article 5, parties are required to ensure that public authorities collect and update environmental information relevant to their functions, and to establish mandatory systems necessary to guarantee an adequate flow of information on activities which may significantly affect the environment (paragraph 1). This obligation to make all relevant information available in transparent and accessible ways is supplemented and endorsed by Article 5(6), which is aimed at the private sector and requires each party to

> encourage operators whose activities have a significant impact on the environment to inform the public regularly of the environmental impact of their activities and products, where appropriate within the framework of voluntary eco-labelling or eco-auditing schemes or by other means.

Unlike access to information, participatory rights under Article 6 of the Aarhus Convention, *ie* participation in decision-making, is available only to 'the public concerned', as defined in Article 2(5) as 'the public affected or likely to be affected by, or having an interest in, the environmental decision-making' with the proviso that 'non-governmental organizations promoting environmental protection and meeting any requirements under national law shall be deemed to have [such] an interest'.

Article 6 applies to making decisions on proposed activities listed in Annex I and other activities that may have a significant effect on the environment. Public participation in relevant decision-making includes early access to information and the right to submit comments, information, analyses or opinions considered relevant. Procedures for public participation shall allow the public to submit, in writing or at a public hearing, 'any comments, information, analyses or opinions' considered relevant (Article 6(7)). Moreover, parties must ensure that in the decision 'due account is taken of the outcome

[54] J Ebbesson, 'Public Participation in Environmental Matters' in R Wolfrum (ed), *Max Planck Encyclopedia of Public International Law* (Heidelberg/Oxford 2009), para 3, available at www.mpepil.com.

[55] According to Art 2(4) 'the public' means 'one or more natural or legal persons, and, in accordance with national legislation or practice, their associations, organizations or groups'.

of the public participation' (Article 6(8)). Parties must enable the public to participate during the preparation of environmental plans and programmes 'within a transparent and fair framework' (Article 7) and 'strive to promote effective public participation' during the preparation of 'executive regulations and other generally applicable legally binding rules that may have a significant effect on the environment' (Article 8).

With providing access to justice, Article 9 establishes the third pillar of the Aarhus Convention. It requires each party not only to provide judicial review for any denial of requested information (paragraph 1), but also to ensure that in respect of any decision, act or omission subject to Article 6 'members of the public concerned' that have a 'sufficient interest' or maintain 'impairment of a right' have access to a 'review procedure before a court of law and/or another independent and impartial body established by law' to challenge its substantive and procedural legality (paragraph 2).

Article 9 further provides that 'sufficient interest' and 'impairment of a right' 'shall be determined in accordance with the requirements of national law and consistently with the objective of giving the public concerned wide access to justice' (*ibid*). Moreover, according to paragraph 3, each party

> shall ensure that, where they meet the criteria, if any, laid down in its national law, members of the public have access to administrative or judicial procedures to challenge acts and omissions by private persons and public authorities which contravene provisions of its national law relating to the environment.

These procedures 'shall provide adequate and effective remedies, including injunctive relief as appropriate'; moreover, they must be 'fair, equitable, timely and not prohibitively expensive' (paragraph 4).

Institutionally, the Aarhus Convention provides for the establishment of a Meeting of the Parties (Article 10) and an Executive Secretariat (Article 12). Fulfilling its mandate in Article 15 to 'establish, on a consensual basis, optional arrangements of a non-confrontational, non-judicial and consultative nature for reviewing compliance with the provisions of this Convention', the Meeting of the Parties established the Aarhus Convention Compliance Committee in 2002.[56]

With the legally non-binding 2005 Almaty Guidelines in Promoting the Application of the Principles of the Aarhus Convention in International Forums,[57] there has been an innovative initiative by parties to extend the 'Aarhus standards' to international negotiating and decision-making processes.[58]

The Kiev Protocol on Pollutant Release and Transfer Registers (PRTRs) to the Aarhus Convention of 21 May 2003 is open to accession by all states, including those that did not ratify the Aarhus Convention and those that are not members of the UNECE.[59] Its objective is 'to enhance public access to information through the establishment of coherent,

[56] This body will be discussed in more detail below in Chapter 22.3.5.

[57] Decision II/4 of the Meeting of the Parties to the Aarhus Convention; UN Doc ECE/MP.PP/2005/2/Add5 (20 June 2005).

[58] *Cf* Ebbesson, above n 39, 691 *et seq*.

[59] In force since 8 October 2009; it is binding on 26 parties, including the EU.

integrated, nationwide [PRTRs] . . ., which could facilitate public participation in environmental decision-making as well as contribute to the prevention and reduction of pollution of the environment' (Article 1).

16.5 Conclusions

As a rule, MEAs establish mutually agreed substantive and/or procedural obligations which states parties are obliged to comply with. It is the states parties themselves rather than other natural or legal persons, such as individuals or NGOs, which directly benefit from treaty compliance. All procedural environmental obligations that have been addressed under 16.2 and 16.3 result from MEAs of this type. With the 1998 Aarhus Convention, a different type of MEA has newly emerged in international environmental practice. Like the aforementioned MEAs it establishes mutually agreed international obligations which the parties concerned have promised each other to meet. What makes the Aarhus Convention clearly distinguishable from these MEAs is the fact that individuals and NGOs rather than the committed parties benefit from the parties' treaty compliance. Interestingly, the Espoo Convention combines both types of interstate commitments in Article 2(6) which integrates elements of 'public participation' in states' national EIA procedures. This helps to improve the informational basis of decision-making and strengthens the participatory rights of potentially affected individuals.

The Aarhus standards, *ie* access to environmental information, public participation in decision-making and access to justice, constitute procedural rights which each state party is obliged to assign to 'the public' or likely affected individuals. The Aarhus standards come close to those guarantees in international human rights treaties that have been 'greened' by international human rights judicial and non-judicial bodies such as the European Court of Human Rights and the UN Human Rights Committees.[60] The fact that individuals lack the opportunity under the Aarhus Convention to submit complaints to an independent international body distinguishes the Aarhus standards from procedural human rights guarantees. Nonetheless, the parties to the Aarhus Convention, including the European Union, must pay due regard to the three pillars of public participation in their decision-making processes.[61]

[60] *Cf* below at Chapter 26.2.

[61] The first pillar of the Aarhus Convention was implemented at EU level by Directive 2003/04/EC of the European Parliament and of the Council of 28 January 2003 ([2003] OJ L/41/26), the second one by Directive 2003/35/EC of the European Parliament and of the Council of 26 May 2003 ([2003] OJ L/156/17). As regards the third pillar, there is a Proposal for a directive of 24 October 2003 (COM [2003] 624 final). In addition, Regulation (EC) No 1367/2006 of the European Parliament and of the Council of 6 September 2006 provides the application of the Aarhus standards to Community institutions and bodies ([2006] OJ L/264/13).

Further Reading

K Bastmeijer and T Koivurova (eds), *Theory and Practice of Transboundary Environmental Impact Assessment* (Leiden 2007).

N Craik, *The International Law of Environmental Impact Assessment: Process, Substance and Integration* (Cambridge 2008).

J Ebbesson, 'Public Participation' in D Bodansky *et al* (eds), *The Oxford Handbook of International Environmental Law* (Oxford 2007) 681–703.

——, 'Access to Information on Environmental Matters' in R Wolfrum (ed), *Max Planck Encyclopedia of Public International Law* (Heidelberg/Oxford 2009), available at www.mpepil.com.

——, 'Access to Justice in Environmental Matters' in R Wolfrum (ed), *Max Planck Encyclopedia of Public International Law* (Heidelberg/Oxford 2009), available at www.mpepil.com.

——, 'Public Participation in Environmental Matters' in R Wolfrum (ed), *Max Planck Encyclopedia of Public International Law* (Heidelberg/Oxford 2009), available at www.mpepil.com.

Ecologic and FIELD, *Participation of Non-Governmental Organisations in International Environmental Co-operation: Legal Basis and Practical Experience* (Berlin 2002).

A Epiney, 'Environmental Impact Assessment' in R Wolfrum (ed), *Max Planck Encyclopedia of Public International Law* (Heidelberg/Oxford 2009), available at www.mpepil.com.

KS Hanna (ed), *Environmental Impact Assessment: Practice and Participation* (Oxford 2006).

JH Knox, 'The Myth and Reality of Transboundary Environmental Impact Assessment' (2002) 96 *AJIL* 291–319.

T Koivurova, 'The Convention on Environmental Impact Assessment in a Transboundary Context (Espoo Convention)' in G Ulfstein *et al* (eds), *Making Treaties Work: Human Rights, Environment and Arms Control* (Cambridge 2007) 218–239.

RK Morgan, *Environmental Impact Assessment: A Methodological Perspective* (Dordrecht 2002).

G Papadimitriou and P Patronos (eds), *The Implementation of the Espoo Convention, A Hellenic Approach* (Athens/Brussels 2002).

C Redgwell, 'Access to Environmental Justice' in F Francioni (ed), *Access to Justice as a Human Right* (Oxford 2007) 153–175.

BJ Richardson and J Razzaque, 'Public Participation in Environmental Decision-making' in BJ Richardson and S Wood (eds), *Environmental Law for Sustainability* (Oxford 2006) 165–194.

N de Sadeleer, G Roller and M Dross, *Access to Justice in Environmental Matters and the Role of NGOs: Empirical Findings and Legal Appraisal* (Groningen 2005).

S Steg, S Casey-Lefkowitz and J Jendroska, *The Aarhus Convention: An Implementation Guide* (New York 2000).

Part IV

International Environmental Governance I: ‘Setting the Rules of the Game’

17

International Environmental Governance

17.1 Theoretical Premises and Policy Framework

'International environmental governance' is a frequently used term which has primarily been developed in disciplines other than law, in particular in international relations theory. The rise of the term is closely related to the debate about the 'new institutionalism' in international relations which was first heard in the late 1980s.[1] This debate takes up existing scholarship on international organisations and international law but broadens it by treating international governance systems as social institutions. These are described as

> sets of rules of the game or codes of conduct that serve to define social practices, assign roles to the participants in these practices, and guide the interactions among occupants of these roles.[2]

'Rules of the game' refers to the evolving normative framework of international policy regimes, in particular, international environmental policy regimes.[3] What is important about debating 'new institutionalism' is the examination of the roles that international organisations play in creating and administering international governance systems and the question what is meant by describing certain governance systems as legal regimes. The specific interest in 'new institutionalism' and the notion of international (environmental) governance thus results from bringing together the 'cultures of law and the social sciences in the study of international governance'.[4]

In the following, we will use the term 'international environmental governance' for the purpose of addressing the making of and compliance with international environmental law. Focusing on actors and forms of action, our governance approach may be best understood

[1] See OR Young, *International Governance: Protecting the Environment in a Stateless Society* (Ithaca, NY *et al* 1994) 1–10.

[2] *Ibid*, 3.

[3] For a similar use of the term see LE Preston and D Windsor, *The Rules of the Game in the Global Economy: Policy Regimes for International Business* (2nd edn Boston *et al* 1997) 4.

[4] Young, above n 1, 11.

as an action-oriented model. Governance thus refers to processes and systems that make an organisation or a society work. Global governance consequently may be described as

> a continuing process through which conflicting or diverse interests may be accommodated and co-operative action may be taken. It includes formal institutions and regimes empowered to enforce compliance, as well as informal arrangements.[5]

Institutions as defined above are complemented by regimes which may be understood as a set of explicit or implicit 'principles, norms, rules, and decision making procedures around which actor expectations converge in a given issue-area'.[6]

These regimes are normally treaty-based and often emerge from the development of common interests of states and related institutions.[7] The effective steering capacity of international environmental law largely depends on the proper combination of various levels and techniques of governance. It requires international, regional, national and also subnational or local governance, in other words: multilevel governance.

In recent years, there have been many discussions about the concept of global environmental governance.[8] Although there is no clear definition of global governance, three broad usages of the term may be identified:[9] some use the term to illustrate current sociopolitical transformation, others see it as a political programme which is aimed at regaining steering capacity for problem-solving, and yet others refer to the concept in a critical way, focusing on threats to national sovereignty. With regard to an action-oriented approach, authors[10] have characterised global environmental governance as a multi-actor governance system which extends beyond traditional actors (such as states and international organisations) and includes non-governmental organisations, in particular, activist groups, networks of scientists, business associations and policy research institutions. While states, at least formally, are still the primary actors within this framework, there is a growing number of non-governmental organisations (NGOs), societal movements and other private actors which are transforming the character of the whole system.[11] It has also been pointed out that global governance is characterised by new forms of co-operation beyond the traditional intergovernmental negotiation of international law as non-state actors increasingly become part of norm-setting and norm-implementing institutions and mechanisms.[12] It is possible, thus, to describe global (environmental)

[5] Commission on Global Governance, *Our Global Neighbourhood* (Oxford 1995) 2–3. See also M Koskenniemi, 'Global Governance and Public International Law' (2004) 37 *Kritische Justiz* 241.

[6] SD Krasner, 'Structural Causes and Regime Consequences: Regimes as Intervening Variables' in SD Krasner (ed), *International Regimes* (Ithaca, NY 1983) 1, 2.

[7] U Beyerlin, 'State Community Interests and Institution-Building in International Environmental Law' (1996) 56 *ZaöRV* 602.

[8] See, among others, F Biermann and P Pattberg, 'Global Environmental Governance: Taking Stock, Moving Forward' (2008) 33 *Annual Review of Environment and Resources* 277–294.

[9] *Ibid*, 279 *et seq*.

[10] F Biermann, 'Global Environmental Governance: Conceptualization and Examples' (2004) Global Governance Working Paper no 12, November 2004, 10–11, available at www.glogov.org/images/doc/WP12.pdf.

[11] J Hierlmeier, 'UNEP: Retrospect and Prospect—Options for Reforming the Global Environmental Governance Regime' (2002) 14 *Georgetown International Environmental Law Review* 767, 770.

[12] Biermann, above n 10, 10–11.

governance as non-hierarchical.[13] This has led to more segmentation, overlapping and increasing complexity of international environmental law through fragmentation.[14]

While such differentiation, segmentation or fragmentation may have its problems, it reflects the fact that governance is a broad concept which encompasses decision- and policy-making processes as well as the institutional structure for implementing these decisions and policies. It is similar to, but not synonymous with, government; governance differs from government in particular in so far as it relies less on formal authority than on shared goals.[15] How can social science based (often empirical) findings about modern forms of (global) governance be brought together with the often formal and sometimes even narrow approach of public international law to such complex governance issues? Is it really possible conceptually to link norm-based governance as it is often perceived by lawyers (with its reliance on formal authority) to much broader notions of governance which take into account that there are many other techniques to arrive at environmental protection and sustainable development alike?

This chapter seeks to illustrate how it is possible to bridge the gap between positivist approaches firmly rooted in international legal discourse with findings from international relations about the complexities of global governance. Our illustration of international environmental governance will begin with an identification of and a differentiation among actors involved (section 17.2). We will then turn to forms of action (section 17.3) which will be addressed in detail in the following chapters before taking a closer look at the complexities of fragmented and multilevel governance (section 17.4). Thus, we hope to illustrate the role of international environmental law in international environmental governance.

17.2 Actors

As is true for public international law in general, states are not only important actors, but have remained the primary actors in international environmental governance. However, changes that the international legal system in general underwent in the second half of the twentieth century also prompted changes in the role of states in international environmental law. This transformation of the international legal system occurred over a period of years with a broad variety of inputs.

Until the early 1970s, states could be considered not only the primary but almost the sole actors in international environmental law. They were the authors, addressees and guardians of the few rules of international environmental law that existed at that time. However, some international environmental regimes had already been established, which, over time, led to a progressive institutionalisation of international environmental law and thus to the gradual rise in importance of a new type of international actor, namely international organisations. The first attempts at institutionalising treaties addressing natural

[13] Hierlmeier, above n 11, 771.
[14] Biermann, above n 10, 11.
[15] Hierlmeier, above n 11, 769.

resources can be traced back to the European River Commissions of the nineteenth century. Notwithstanding few prominent examples of the first half of the twentieth century, such as the International Whaling Commission (IWC) set up under the International Convention for the Regulation of Whaling of 1946, the impressive rise of an organisational infrastructure of international environmental law only began in the 1970s. Until then few international organisations were mandated to address environmental issues. Not even Articles 1(3) and 55 of the UN Charter include the environment. The major impetus for developments in the field arose from the 1972 United Nations Conference on the Human Environment and the existing infrastructure, extending from treaty-based institutions across UN specialised agencies and UN General Assembly bodies to institutions based on co-operative agreements between other international organisations. However, even today there is no world environment organisation with a mandate to address all environmental issues at the global level. Most international environmental institutions established to date have highly specialised mandates. Today, we may even speak of a proliferation of international environmental regimes and institutions in such a way that it is difficult to identify a coherent system of international environmental organisations. While there have been attempts to cluster such regimes and institutions around either the UN Environment Programme (UNEP) or the Commission on Sustainable Development (CSD), these efforts have so far been unsuccessful.[16] Indeed, as in international law in general, there are tendencies towards a fragmentation of international environmental law.

It is not only international organisations that have contributed to the broadening spectrum of actors in international environmental law. NGOs have also played an increasingly prominent role. Indeed, international environmental law has not only taken note of NGOs, but has granted them varying degrees of legal status. Moreover, in light of their considerable impact—both positive and negative—on environmental protection, commercial actors, in particular transnational corporations, must also be borne in mind.

Last but not least, the individual has become increasingly involved as an actor in international environmental law, as is reflected in, *inter alia*, the 1998 UNECE Convention on Access to Information, Public Participation in Decision-Making and Access to Justice in Environmental Matters (Aarhus Convention). Nevertheless, there is still much scepticism *vis-à-vis* a human right to a healthy environment,[17] notwithstanding the tremendous amount of literature that has been published in this regard. Whether or not such a right exists needs not be resolved here, because international human rights institutions have drawn upon other, well-established, human rights to address environmental considerations. For instance, the European Court of Human Rights has built upon the protection of one's home and privacy in order to establish a human rights basis for protection against at least certain activities detrimental to the human environment.[18]

The complexity of international environmental relations arising out of the plurality

[16] See U Beyerlin and T Marauhn, *Law-Making and Law-Enforcement in International Environmental Law after the 1992 Rio Conference* (Berlin 1997) 46–50 and 62–63.

[17] *Cf* AE Boyle and M Anderson (eds), *Human Rights Approaches to Environmental Protection* (Oxford 1996).

[18] H Post, 'Hatton and Others: Further Clarification of the "Indirect" Individual Right to a Healthy Environment' (2002) 2 *Non-State Actors and International Law* 259; see Chapter 26.2.5 for details.

of actors is thus of a dual nature, which can be described by reference to the notions of internationalisation and privatisation. Internationalisation, as understood here, refers to the increasing number of government-based actors beyond the state, such as regional and universal intergovernmental organisations; privatisation refers to the increasing number of non-governmental actors at the local, national, regional and international levels, reflecting to a certain extent the environmental concerns of civil society but also of the business community. While international organisations as well as private actors are non-state actors, they differ, however, in that intergovernmental organisations can be more easily considered to be instrumental for state or public interests, whereas non-governmental actors rather focus on individual and particulate interests, notwithstanding the fact that they often claim to be representing public interests.

17.2.1 States

Contemporary statehood and its relevance for international environmental law can best be illuminated by focusing on the roles assumed by states in this context, namely as authors, addressees and guardians of the law.[19]

Within the decentralised system of international law, states still are the primary authors thereof. This assessment also applies to international environmental law: treaties are normally adopted and ratified by states; customary international environmental law is based on state practice and *opinio iuris* as derived from official statements; and even general principles of international environmental law are developed on the basis of principles of national environmental law, which means that they ultimately are state-authored norms.[20] The role of states as authors of the law has, however, changed over time. While the final decision within law-making processes still rests with states, they have lost in relative importance in the process of law-making. Many multilateral environmental agreements (MEAs) have been drafted under the auspices of international organisations,[21] and participation of NGOs in international environmental conferences can influence the substance of the law. In addition, resolutions of international organisations and declarations adopted by global conferences have changed the law-making process. While none of these types of documents are binding *per se*, they have contributed to the development of international environmental law. Quite a few of them have invited states to act on the basis of the objectives agreed upon, thus developing a significant law-making effect without, however, depriving states of their final say in the law-making process.

The continued relevance of states as authors of international environmental law remains legitimate for several reasons.[22] Firstly, states enjoy a comprehensive legitimacy

[19] On the following see T Marauhn, 'Changing Role of the State' in D Bodansky *et al* (eds), *The Oxford Handbook of International Environmental Law* (Oxford 2007) 727, 732 *et seq*.

[20] For a discussion of the continued relevance of state consent in law-making see DB Hollis, 'Why State Consent Still Matters: Non-State Actors, Treaties, and the Changing Sources of International Law' (2005) 23 *Berkeley Journal of International Law* 137.

[21] See J Sommer, 'Environmental Law-Making by International Organisations' (1996) 56 *ZaöRV* 628.

[22] D Bodansky, 'The Legitimacy of International Governance: A Coming Challenge for International Environmental Law?' (1999) 93 *AJIL* 596.

as actors in public international law. Secondly, states still bear primary responsibility also as addressees of those norms and—insofar as the behaviour of private actors is concerned—they remain the primary implementing agents of such rules. Thirdly, comprehensive democratic legitimacy and accountability can be best safeguarded within states. Thus, states legitimately are and remain the primary authors of international environmental law.

States are not only authors but also addressees of international environmental law. Even though international environmental governance eventually has an impact on private actors, those are hardly ever directly addressed by international law. Consequently, states are faced with at least three different types of obligations: obligations to refrain, obligations to prevent and obligations to preserve. While obligations to refrain from certain conduct harmful to the environment are a typical feature of municipal environmental law, addressed to private entities, similar obligations are included in international agreements although they are directed towards states: international environmental law includes obligations to refrain from transboundary environmental harm, from polluting transboundary watercourses, from dumping hazardous wastes on land or sea, from releasing particular substances into the atmosphere, from destroying ecosystems or biodiversity, and so forth, even though these obligations must be implemented domestically to have an impact on the behaviour of non-state actors. In light of this fact, the most important type of obligations addressed towards states are obligations to prevent environmentally harmful conduct of non-state actors. Such obligations include the adoption of legislation, the establishment of an administrative infrastructure (such as licensing systems and supervisory bodies), and sometimes even the enforcement by criminal law, thus always necessitating governmental activities. As a third category of obligations addressed towards states, the obligation to preserve may require more than merely preventing further degradation of the environment either by the state's own conduct or by activities of non-state actors under its jurisdiction and control. The obligation to preserve ecosystems may include state action towards improvements with regard to a particular environmental resource. Thus, the preservation of the marine environment may necessitate improvements of water quality in coastal areas, and protecting the earth's climate may include reforestation measures under the Clean Development Mechanism of the climate change regime.

Finally, states act as guardians of international environmental law, traditionally in the context of law enforcement, with an initiating and often decisive role in the context of compliance-control procedures. Traditional law enforcement still focuses on state responsibility for breaches of international law and on secondary obligations (normally an obligation to make reparations) resulting therefrom. There seems to be widespread agreement on the limited effectiveness of the state responsibility regime in environmental matters.[23] As the examples of the Chernobyl accident, the Sandoz chemical spill, and the salination of the Rhine illustrate, even when the facts are clear, there may be no recourse to the law of state responsibility. Retorsions and reprisals are not really an option in

[23] M Bothe, 'The Evaluation of Enforcement Mechanisms in International Environmental Law. An Overview' in R Wolfrum (ed), *Enforcing Environmental Standards: Economic Mechanisms as Viable Means?* (Berlin *et al* 1996) 13, 27–29.

case of threats to common goods and thus largely fail to meet the needs of international environmental law. It may thus be argued that the role of states has changed to the most significant extent where they act as guardians of the law. In light of the ineffectiveness of traditional law enforcement, new compliance-control systems have been developed, with a less dominant role for individual states.[24] Since collective rather than unilateral enforcement, co-operation rather than confrontation, prevention rather than repression and compliance assistance rather than sanctions have become the characteristics of the 'enforcement' of international environmental law, the contribution of states to this system has become largely, though not exclusively, procedural: they may initiate the procedure, provide relevant data for the assessment of their own or another party's compliance, and participate in decision-making about responses to non-compliance.[25]

In the context of modern international environmental law, contemporary statehood can thus be best understood as an element of a global system of (environmental) governance with states assuming particular roles within such a system. The specifics of these roles are changing over time as the international legal system is also under ongoing processes of transformation.

17.2.2 International Organisations

International law recognises that international organisations enjoy legal personality within the system of international law. Normally, these organisations, which are set up by states, are treaty based. They achieve their purposes and perform their functions through organs. Decision-making by these organs is distinct from related processes at the municipal level. Most international organisations were established after World War II, with the United Nations being the focal point and the model for many of them. Notwithstanding the lack of a specific environmental mandate of the United Nations, its subsidiary organs and UN specialised agencies have become important actors in international environmental relations. Whereas their mandate often is primarily political, institutions based on MEAs—whether or not they amount to international organisations *stricto sensu*—undertake meaningful activities at a more technical level, even though these treaty-based institutions contribute to both the implementation and further development of their constitutive treaties.[26]

UN specialised agencies are international organisations established by separate treaties but they enjoy a special relationship with the United Nations on the basis of agreements concluded with the Economic and Social Council (ECOSOC) pursuant to Articles 57 and 63 of the UN Charter. While there is no such agency with primary responsibility for the protection of the global environment, quite a few of them address environmental issues at a subordinate level. These include the International Maritime Organization (IMO), the Food and Agriculture Organization, the World Health Organization (WHO),

[24] See Chapter 22 for more details.

[25] T Marauhn, 'Towards a Procedural Law of Compliance Control in International Environmental Relations' (1996) 56 *ZaöRV* 696.

[26] On the distinction between various types of international environmental organisations see E Hey, 'International Institutions' in Bodansky *et al* (eds), above n 19, 749, 752.

the International Atomic Energy Agency, the International Bank for Reconstruction and Development (IBRD or World Bank) and some others. The extent to which they may have an impact on international environmental law-making depends on their capacities as laid down in their constitutive instruments. This is not limited to powers expressly stated but includes so-called implied powers. According to the International Court of Justice (ICJ) in the *Reparation for Injuries* case, an international organisation 'must be deemed to have those powers which, though not expressly provided . . ., are conferred upon it by necessary implication as being essential to the performance of its duties'.[27]

These powers notwithstanding, the contribution of specialised agencies to international environmental treaty-making has been limited. They have had an impact on the development of international environmental law primarily on the basis of secondary acts, binding upon the organisation's members only. Thus, the WHO enjoys the power of secondary law-making. Article 21 WHO Constitution authorises the Health Assembly of the WHO to adopt relevant regulations. Such norms are directly binding upon those members which have not opted out. In general, however, the capacity of UN specialised agencies is limited to the adoption of non-binding declarations and resolutions, which at most indirectly contribute to international environmental law-making. Some of these indirect contributions may, nevertheless, have an important impact on global environmental governance, as can be exemplified by the World Bank Inspection Panel, established by the Executive Directors of the IBRD and the International Development Association (IDA) in September 1993.[28] The three-member Panel aims to increase the accountability of the World Bank and to improve compliance with its social and environmental policies. It is available as a forum for local people who may be adversely affected by Bank projects as a result of violations of the Bank's policies.

Notwithstanding the lack of reference to environmental protection in the UN Charter, the United Nations has developed a significant environmental profile of its own. The most prominent features thereof have been the three global UN Conferences at Stockholm (1972), Rio de Janeiro (1992) and Johannesburg (2002). However, the United Nations has not limited itself to conference diplomacy. It has diversified its own organisational infrastructure in environmental matters on the basis of UN Charter provisions providing for the establishment of subsidiary organs. Thus, UNEP has been established pursuant to Article 22 of the UN Charter as a UN General Assembly body. Similarly, the UN Development Programme and the UN Institute for Training and Research have also contributed to international environmental governance, although rather marginally.

UNEP was established in accordance with General Assembly Resolution 2997 (XXVII) (Institutional and financial arrangements for international environmental co-operation) of 15 December 1972. Its Governing Council, which consists of 58 members elected by the UN General Assembly for four-year terms, reports to the General Assembly through the Economic and Social Council. The original mandate and objectives of UNEP were

[27] *Reparation for Injuries Suffered in the Service of the United Nations (Advisory Opinion)* (1949) ICJ Reports 174, 182.

[28] *Cf* A Gowlland Gualtieri, 'The Environmental Accountability of the World Bank to Non-State Actors' (2001) 72 *British Yearbook of International Law* 213.

included in UN General Assembly Resolution 2997. According to its mandate, UNEP has been established, *inter alia*,

> (a) [t]o promote international cooperation in the field of the environment and to recommend, as appropriate, policies to this end;
> (b) [t]o provide general policy guidance for the direction and coordination of environmental programmes within the United Nations system.

Since its establishment, several decisions have been taken with regard to UNEP's mandate. Among others, Chapter 38, paragraph 21 of Agenda 21, adopted at the UN Conference on Environment and Development (UNCED), reaffirms UNEP's co-ordinating role, stating that,

> in the follow-up to the Conference, there will be a need for an enhanced role for UNEP and its Governing Council. The Governing Council should, within its mandate, continue to play its role with regard to policy guidance and coordination in the field of the environment, taking into account the development perspective.

Further decisions include the 1997 Nairobi Declaration on the Role and Mandate of UNEP,[29] adopted at the Nineteenth Session of the UNEP Governing Council, redefining and strengthening UNEP's mandate, and the Malmö Ministerial Declaration of 31 May 2000,[30] adopted by the first so-called Global Ministerial Environment Forum (GMEF). The purpose of the Forum was to institute a process for regaining policy coherence in international environmental relations, responding to a call for such action in the 1998 report of the UN Secretary-General on environment and human settlements. While one of the reasons for establishing GMEF was to ensure broader participation of UN Member States in UNEP's work, the modalities of interaction between the Governing Council and the GMEF do not seem to be sufficiently clear.[31] Apart from its sponsorship role in the establishment of several MEAs concerning biodiversity, chemicals and atmosphere, UNEP has served as a co-ordinator and has strengthened its capacities in the field by establishing a Division for Environmental Law and Conventions in order to co-ordinate MEAs and track inconsistencies in the decisions of the Conferences of the Parties to such agreements. In addition, UNEP has convened co-ordination meetings for secretariats; since 1998, the UN office in Nairobi has offered administrative services to the secretariats.[32]

Another subsidiary organ established within the UN and highly relevant to international environmental governance is the CSD. The CSD was established by the UN General Assembly in December 1992 to ensure effective follow-up of the UNCED. Its mandate differs from UNEP's mandate in that its focus is not international environmental governance as such but sustainable development. The Commission is tasked

[29] UNEP GC Dec 19/1 (7 February 1997).

[30] Available at www.unep.org/malmo/malmo2.pdf.

[31] See U Beyerlin, 'Strengthening International Governance for Sustainable Development: Expectations for the 2002 Johannesburg World Summit' (2002) 5 *Potchefstroom Electronic Law Journal* 17.

[32] On UNEP's contribution to international environmental law *cf*, among others, D Kaniaru, 'Development and Implementation of Environmental Law—A Contribution by UNEP' (2000) 30 *Environmental Policy and Law* 234.

with reviewing progress in the implementation of Agenda 21 and the Rio Declaration on Environment and Development. Furthermore, it provides policy guidance to follow up the Johannesburg Plan of Implementation at the local, national, regional and international levels. The CSD operates as a functional commission of ECOSOC. The sessions during its annual meetings have been opened to broad participation from both governmental and non-governmental actors.[33]

Treaty-based institutions have become the third institutional layer of international environmental governance. Conferences or Meetings of the Parties (COPs or MOPs) and secretariats to MEAs and their protocols today figure prominently as actors and effectively contribute to the development of international environmental governance. Worth mentioning are also subsidiary bodies such as those on scientific and technical co-operation and on compliance. In light of their growing importance and their specific characteristics they will be addressed separately below.

Institutions based on co-operative agreements between international organisations are still a relatively innovative feature of international governance. Their development is due to several practical necessities in the implementation and further development of MEAs. The Intergovernmental Panel on Climate Change (IPCC) was set up in 1989 as agreed between UNEP and the World Meteorological Organization (WMO).[34] It is an intergovernmental body with a scientific mandate to assess the current state of climate change and its potential environmental and socioeconomic consequences. The Global Environment Facility (GEF) is an international financial institution, set up as a global partnership between states, international organisations, NGOs and the private sector. Originally, GEF had been established as a pilot programme in the World Bank in 1991 to assist in the protection of the global environment and to promote environmental sustainable development. In 1994 it was restructured and moved out of the World Bank system to become a separate institution.[35] It provides financial resources, originating from donor countries, for projects related to six focal areas: biodiversity, climate change, international waters, land degradation, the ozone layer and persistent organic pollutants. GEF also operates as the designated financial mechanism for a number of MEAs, including the Climate Change Convention (UNFCCC) and the Biodiversity Convention (CBD).[36]

In light of the fragmented organisational framework for international environmental governance, there has been, since the 1970s, an ongoing debate about the establishment of a World Organisation for the Environment (WEO), in order to unify UN efforts. Originally, states had envisaged UNEP developing into an 'environmental conscience' within the UN system; however,

> UNEP was—and continues to be—a long way from an international organization commensurable with other sectoral bodies, such as the International Labour Organization.[37]

[33] On the CSD see J Tornberg, 'The United Nations Commission on Sustainable Development' (2001) 17 *New York Law School Journal of Human Rights* 957.

[34] UNGA Res 43/53 (6 December 1988).

[35] 'Instrument for the Establishment of the Restructured Global Environment Facility', available at www.thegef.org/gef/sites/thegef.org/files/publication/GEF_Instrument_March08.pdf.

[36] On the GEF see L Boisson de Chazournes, 'The Global Environment Facility (GEF)' (2005) 14 *RECIEL* 193.

[37] F Biermann and S Bauer, 'The Debate on a World Environment Organization: An Introduction' in

The debate was revived in 1989 when 24 states adopted the Declaration of The Hague which called for an authoritative international body on the atmosphere. Part of the debate was stimulated by doubts about the effectiveness of UNEP. A third round of proposals for a WEO was made in the late 1990s in the context of UN reform but not limited to it. Over the years, the debate has become more refined, and it is now possible not only to distinguish various models of a WEO, but also to consider carefully any arguments against the establishment of a WEO.[38]

Moderate proposals for a WEO simply suggest an upgrade of UNEP to a specialised UN agency with a comprehensive organisational status, modelled along the lines of WHO or the International Labour Organization. More far-reaching proposals advocate an integration of environmental regimes similar to the World Trade Organization which has integrated diverse multilateral trade agreements under one umbrella. This entails a more streamlined architecture. The most radical models aim at a hierarchical intergovernmental organisation with majority decision-making and enforcement powers building on the European Union and the UN Security Council.

Critics of these proposals are not only sceptical but fear that the debate about a WEO diverts attention from more pressing problems of environmental governance. Furthermore, they argue that centralisation is an anachronistic paradigm. Decentralised institutional clusters, it is argued, may be better suited to deal with diverse sets of environmental issues rather than one central organisation which would also be very costly. Subsidiarity and tailor-made responses to environmental problems are considered as alternatives to a WEO.

17.2.3 Treaty Bodies

Most MEAs today have an organisational backbone of their own: treaty bodies. These have been described as 'a new form of international cooperation'.[39]

These treaty bodies go beyond mere intergovernmental conferences since their 'conferences of the parties' are permanent, and they have subsidiary bodies as well as secretariats; at the same time they are less autonomous than traditional intergovernmental organisations.

There may be various reasons for states to prefer treaty bodies *vis-à-vis* traditional international organisations. Firstly, treaty bodies are limited to those states which have accepted obligations agreed upon in the respective treaty; making use of an existing international organisation would include states which are not parties to the agreement. Secondly, if states do not want to use an existing international organisation, the establish-

F Biermann and S Bauer (eds), *A World Environment Organization: Solution or Threat for Effective International Environmental Governance?* (Aldershot 2005) 1, 4.

[38] For arguments in favour of a World Environment Organisation see, among others, S Charnovitz, 'Toward a World Environment Organization: Reflections upon a Vital Debate' in Biermann and Bauer (eds), *ibid*, 87; for arguments against *cf* S Oberthür and T Gehring, 'Reforming International Environmental Governance: An Institutional Perspective on Proposals for a World Environment Organization' in Biermann and Bauer (eds), *ibid*, 205.

[39] G Ulfstein, 'Treaty Bodies' in Bodansky *et al* (eds), above n 19, 877, 878.

ment of a new one may be more costly and bureaucratic than just developing the slim infrastructure of a treaty body. Finally, treaty bodies may be more flexible as they do not require a permanent seat but their COPs may meet in different countries.

The supreme organ of an MEA typically is the COP, which is composed of representatives of all treaty parties and meets regularly (typically on an annual or biannual basis).[40] Its powers can be taken from the constitutive MEA and normally include the establishment of subsidiary bodies, the adoption of rules of procedure, and the provision of guidance to subsidiary bodies and the secretariat. Some COPs are authorised to adopt legally binding or non-binding decisions, in particular for the further development of the treaty regime concerned, and they may even enter into arrangements with states, international organisations or organs of other MEAs. COPs may also have implied powers.

Secretariats are another common feature of treaty bodies. Sometimes the MEA itself designates a permanent secretariat, sometimes the final decision is left to the COP. An increasing number of MEAs locate their secretariats with existing international bodies, including UNEP, the UN Economic Commission for Europe and the IMO. Besides the performance of mere administrative tasks, functions exercised by secretariats cover conducting studies, preparing draft decisions for the COP and subsidiary bodies, providing technical assistance to the parties, and receiving and circulating reports on the implementation of commitments. Sometimes secretariats are intensely involved in the co-operation with other MEAs and international organisations.

Treaty bodies often include subsidiary organs established on the basis of provisions of the constitutive MEA or a decision of the COP. Their functions may include financial assistance, technology transfer, compliance or scientific advice. Whereas most of them are composed of treaty parties, some consist of persons acting in their individual capacity.

Overall, treaty bodies reflect the general trend towards institutionalising co-operation between states in order to address specific problems.[41] However, whereas treaty bodies also play an important role in international human rights law and in arms control law, the extent to which treaty bodies are involved in governance and the powers granted to those bodies are unique to international environmental law.

Over the last three or four decades, the community of states has increasingly demonstrated its fundamental interest in resolving global environmental problems, to which the individual interests of its members must give way. Accordingly, the parties to many MEAs such as the UNFCCC and the CBD referred in varying formulations to the existence of a 'common interest' of states in reaching certain jointly defined goals. How this specific 'common interest' character usually becomes manifest in an MEA is hard to define. However, what can be said is that MEAs providing for the establishment of certain treaty-specific institutions that are entrusted with decision-making functions belong to such type of agreements. Thus, qualified institution-building within a treaty is a clear signal for, if not a logical consequence of, the parties' understanding of the 'common interest' character of their treaty.[42]

[40] On the following see Ulfstein, *ibid*, 879–880.

[41] *Cf* Beyerlin, above n 7, 613 *et seq*; see also T Marauhn and M Ehrmann, 'Workshop on "Institution-Building in International Environmental Law". Summary of the Discussion' (1996) 56 *ZaöRV* 820.

[42] For further details *cf* Beyerlin, above n 7, 611 *et seq*.

Today, a multitude of MEAs showing such a 'qualified' institutional setting provides for the dynamic evolution and continuing growth of international environmental treaty law. Gehring has rightly observed that environmental treaty systems

> constitute hybrid structures somewhere between traditional international treaties . . . and international organizations. . . . In addition to substantive obligations, they include institutional components of varying design, which are, compared to multilateral agreements in other policy fields, remarkably strong.[43]

As already indicated, every modern MEA has its own institutional apparatus. The role which these treaty organs normally play within MEAs has been summed up by Kiss and Shelton as follows:

> Treaty organs . . . serve as compliance monitoring bodies, but also act in a quasi-legislative capacity, making decisions, interpreting the principal agreement, and adopting recommendations, plans of action, amendments and protocols to achieve the goals of the instrument. They set the policy for most treaty regimes, act as information clearing-houses, and promote scientific research. It is these bodies that maintain the flexibility and responsiveness of international environmental treaties and they are thus of crucial importance to the effectiveness of the agreements.[44]

17.2.4 Private Actors

The involvement of private actors in the development of international environmental law has increased significantly since the 1970s. Comparing the Stockholm and the Rio Conferences, the number of participating NGOs rose from about 300 to approximately 1400.[45] Private actors in general include for-profit and non-profit entities, a distinction which is more often addressed in international relations than in international law. Non-profit actors are usually identified with NGOs and civil society in general, whereas for-profit actors are mostly labelled as business—a terminological distinction which will also be used in this chapter. The growing importance of private actors in international environmental relations cannot be separated from the general 'meteoric rise' of NGOs 'on the world stage'.[46] However, their contribution to and integration into MEAs and the regimes emerging therefrom have been particularly significant. The growth of international environmental NGOs can best be illustrated by referring to Greenpeace International. The organisation, originally known as the Greenpeace Foundation, was established in Canada in 1971, and today, now based in Amsterdam, has national and regional offices in more than 45 countries. It is estimated to have more than 3 million financial supporters.

[43] T Gehring, 'Treaty-Making and Treaty Evolution' in Bodansky *et al* (eds), above n 19, 467, 468.

[44] AC Kiss and D Shelton, *International Environmental Law* (3rd edn Ardsley 2004) 149.

[45] See R Khan, 'The Development of International Law: Alternatives to Treaty-Making? International Organizations and Non-State Actors' in R Wolfrum and V Röben (eds), *Developments of International Law in Treaty Making* (Berlin *et al* 2005) 331, 332.

[46] PJ Spiro, 'Non-Governmental Organizations and Civil Society' in Bodansky *et al* (eds), above n 19, 770, 771.

From the perspective of international environmental governance, civil society and business are actors contributing to such governance, and they may be involved in various forms of action, from law-making, across national and international implementation, to ensuring compliance. Taking up the concept of private environmental governance, this chapter aims at demonstrating that private actors have moved far beyond being merely tolerated within traditional forms of international environmental governance. They have begun to make their own rules and standards, which may acquire authority outside formal political structures.[47] This has long been accepted among international relations scholars. However, it is not clear how private authority and private regulatory institutionalisation can be integrated into international environmental law.

17.3 Forms of Action

17.3.1 Law-Making, Implementation and Ways to Ensure Compliance

On the basis of our action-oriented model of international environmental governance, the following chapters will focus on various forms of action. In general, these include law-making, implementation and ways to ensure compliance with international environmental norms.

International environmental law-making extends across all the major sources of public international law as they are referred to in Article 38(1) of the Statute of the ICJ, namely treaty law, customary international law and general principles of law. These will be addressed separately in Chapters 18, 19 and 20. The contribution of private actors to the development of international environmental law must also be considered (Chapter 21).

As far as the implementation of international environmental law is concerned, it is necessary to distinguish international and national implementation.

National implementation has been identified as 'a key element in ensuring compliance with international environmental law'.[48] Nevertheless, it is only rarely addressed in international environmental law textbooks, and national treatises often isolate the discussion of international environmental law from the analysis of national environmental law. In the following we will at least provide some basic information about the important elements of national implementation of international environmental law and about the requirements imposed by international environmental law in respect of national implementation. National implementation has been defined as 'measures parties take to make international agreements operative in their domestic law'.[49]

There are basically three types of hard or legal implementation mechanisms by gov-

[47] See PH Pattberg, 'Private Environmental Governance and the Changing Nature of Authority'. Paper presented at the annual meeting of the International Studies Association, Le Centre Sheraton Hotel, Montreal, Quebec, Canada, 17 March, 2004; available at www.allacademic.com/meta/p72515_index.html.

[48] C Redgwell, 'National Implementation' in Bodansky *et al* (eds), above n 19, 922, 923.

[49] R Reeve, *Policing Trade in Endangered Species: The CITES Treaty and Compliance* (London 2002) 16.

ernmental actors, namely legislative, administrative and judicial.[50] In addition, private actors may contribute to national implementation by softer mechanisms, though these will not be addressed here. With regard to national implementation by governmental actors, the impact of domestic constitutional legal orders on implementation has to be borne in mind. Obviously, there are not only differences as to the position of international law within municipal law in general but also different systems for the distribution of legislative competences with regard to environmental matters, particularly in federal states.

Legislative implementation of international environmental law firstly gives rise to the question of whether such legislation is necessary at all. This can only be ascertained on the basis of an analysis of whether or not domestic law already fulfils the international obligations undertaken. It also raises the question whether or not the treaty permits non-legislative implementation by circular or other methods. States must also develop an administrative infrastructure which allows for transnational administrative implementation and enforcement, goes beyond issuing permits and mutual recognition of permits, but includes information gathering and appropriate mechanisms. Judicial implementation tends to be increasingly important in light of the fact that the human rights dimension of international environmental law enables private actors to bring matters related to international environmental law to the attention of courts. Treaties such as the Aarhus Convention not only ensure public participation in environmental decision-making but facilitate access to courts in transboundary environmental matters.[51]

Many MEAs spell out requirements of national implementation, though with varying degrees of specificity. These obligations include, but are not limited to, the development of policies and strategies for implementation (Article 6 CBD), the adoption of laws, regulations and other measures, the designation of an authority responsible for issuing permits, maintaining records and monitoring the environment (Article VI of the 1972 London Dumping Convention), the taking of appropriate steps to prevent and punish contraventions to the treaty (Article 4 MARPOL Convention), and the monitoring and surveillance, in particular with regard to living resources (Article IV of the 1946 International Convention for the Regulation of Whaling).

In contrast to national implementation, which is concerned with making international agreements operative in domestic law, international implementation can be characterised as the administration of international environmental law at the international level.[52] The norms governing international implementation are increasingly referred to as a distinctive type of law, namely global administrative law.[53] International implementation of international environmental law, thus understood, includes a broad variety of activities short of international dispute settlement and enforcement. They comprise the concretion, specification and co-ordination of obligations, monitoring and verification, technical and financial assistance, compliance procedures, and may also extend to international respon-

[50] *Cf* Redgwell, above n 48, 929–938.

[51] For further details see Chapter 16.

[52] *Cf* D Bodansky, J Brunnée and E Hey, 'International Environmental Law: Mapping the Field' in Bodansky *et al* (eds), above n 19, 1, 19.

[53] *Cf* B Kingsbury, 'Global Environmental Governance as Administration. Implications for International Law' in Bodansky *et al* (eds), above n 19, 63.

sibility and liability. Above all, international implementation deals with the organisational infrastructure and the institutional design of the above-mentioned procedures which aim at supervising the conduct of states (and sometimes other actors) at the international level.

The following chapters will address all relevant forms of action in detail, firstly those related to law-making (Chapters 18–21), then those related to implementation, compliance and enforcement (Chapters 22–25). However, in light of their conceptual importance for the development of international environmental law, this chapter will take a closer look at legislative and administrative environmental governance within MEAs before addressing the multilevel character of international environmental governance. The difference between legislative and administrative environmental governance as discussed in the following can be best explained by defining legislative governance as law-making, whereas administrative governance deals with the application of the law. While there are linkages between the making and the application of the law, it is important to distinguish the two, not the least in the interest of the international rule of law and of legal certainty.[54]

17.3.2 Treaty-Based Legislative Environmental Governance

Particularly important is the role of the COP in further developing the substantive commitments of the parties to an MEA.[55] For instance, according to Article 23(4) CBD, the COP is empowered to consider and adopt implementing protocols, amendments to the CBD and its annexes, amendments to any protocol, as well as to any annexes thereto, and additional annexes to the CBD. Under some MEAs the COPs can employ simplified procedures for the adoption of amendments or adjustments of treaty annexes.[56] Thus, *prima facie* it appears that COPs provide for the dynamics of the MEA regimes by means of engaging in a sort of treaty-specific law-making. However, there is ongoing debate on whether COPs are actually able to play a genuine legislative role.

To argue that the law-making decisions of COPs remain legally meaningless, unless they are followed by formal acceptance by states parties, would certainly mean to underestimate the 'legislative' role COPs are able to play within MEAs. In the view of Brunnée, COPs can be seen as 'issue-specific global legislatures', a sort of international organisation, or simply as a forum in which law-making by states takes place. Notwithstanding these distinctions, she discerns three types of COP law-making: (i) law-making involving formal consent (*eg* the adoption or amendment of a protocol); (ii) law-making through 'other means' to express consent (*eg* the adoption or amendment of an annex which becomes legally effective unless states opt out); and (iii) law-making through binding COP decisions or 'de facto law-making' (*eg* adjustment decisions according to Article

[54] See generally JK Cogan, 'Noncompliance and the International Rule of Law' (2006) 31 *Yale Journal of International Law* 189.

[55] In this sense Ulfstein, above n 39, 881 *et seq*; RR Churchill and G Ulfstein, 'Autonomous Institutional Arrangements in Multilateral Environmental Agreements: A Little-Noticed Phenomenon in International Law' (2000) 94 *AJIL* 623, 636 *et seq*.

[56] Among the other functions assigned to COPs under many MEAs are those of making decisions on implementation and non-compliance issues, as for instance according to Arts 17 and 18 Kyoto Protocol (see Chapter 22.4.), as well as authoritative treaty interpretation.

2(9) of the Montreal Protocol, and COP decisions on emissions trading under Article 17 of the Kyoto Protocol.[57] Similarly, Gehring argues that the COPs are fulfilling *de facto*, if not *de jure* law-making functions that have been delegated to them by the states parties concerned, even if dissenting parties normally are entitled to opt out.[58] Brunnée is right to stress that 'the explicit lawmaking authority provided under the Montreal Protocol is the exception rather than the rule', as well as to indicate that in other cases

> the underlying treaty simply assigns the development and adoption of a decision to the COP, without explicit provision for the legal status of that decision or subsequent consent by individual parties.[59]

Thus, there is still considerable uncertainty as to whether the said COP decisions produce legal effects, and if so, of what kind the latter are.

It is far from clear what *de facto* law, compared to *de jure* law, means in practice. Therefore, it is perhaps more suitable to argue that COP decisions, with the exception of those that might be taken someday under Article 2(9) Montreal Protocol, are merely quasi-legislative acts. Normally a COP decision does not immediately produce primary legal effects. It can be seen as a first procedural step in the process of, for example, amending a treaty, a protocol related thereto, or an annex. It furthermore defines the essential contents of the respective amendment. It imposes on the states parties concerned certain secondary treaty obligations, *eg* to strive mutually in good faith towards reaching the COP decision's purpose. It creates what may be called an imperfect obligation similar to that in Article 18 Vienna Convention on the Law of Treaties (VCLT) which obliges a state 'to refrain from acts which would defeat the object and purpose of a treaty' it has signed. However, even those COP decisions which have been unanimously adopted by the states parties concerned do not bring about any primary legal obligations for the latter on their own unless they are followed by their formal acceptance.

17.3.3 Treaty-Based Administrative Environmental Governance

Leaving aside the multiple administrative tasks which the secretariats to MEAs normally perform,[60] in the following the focus will be on the administrative decision-making activities of COPs within MEAs. Gehring has found that

> [v]irtually all modern environmental treaty systems provide the institutional framework for the adoption of administrative decisions of various kinds for the filling of gaps in the treaty law or for its formal or informal adjustment to changed circumstances.[61]

He has developed a scheme of treaty-specific administrative decision-making which dif-

[57] See for a thorough discussion of this question J Brunnée, 'Reweaving the Fabric of International Law? Patterns of Consent in Environmental Framework Agreements' in Wolfrum and Röben (eds), above n 45, 101, 106 *et seq*; *cf id*, 'COPing with Consent: Law-Making under Multilateral Environmental Agreements' (2002) 15 *Leiden Journal of International Law* 1, 15 *et seq*.

[58] *Cf* Gehring, above n 43, 490.

[59] *Cf* Brunnée (2005), above n 57, 110.

[60] *Cf* Ulfstein, above n 39, 880.

[61] *Cf* Gehring, above n 43, 480.

ferentiates between COP decisions aimed at (i) renewing normative expectations and bridging unexpected gaps of treaty law; (ii) relieving treaty-making negotiations from numerous tasks that could in principle also have been dealt with earlier in this process; (iii) rapidly developing the environmental treaty system concerned through the adoption of decisions that are not expressly provided for in the respective treaties; and (iv) creating 'soft law instruments, if the adoption of hard law proves to be impossible'.[62] With respect to the latter type of decision-making, COPs work at the interface between administrative and legislative environmental governance.

Gehring has also found that COPs are able to delegate their administrative decision-making competences to committees or to more complex decision-making arrangements,[63] a capability which COPs quite often make use of in practice. Thus, for instance, the administration of the Clean Development Mechanism (CDM) under the Kyoto Protocol has been delegated to the Executive Board of the CDM; and under the Montreal Protocol decision-making on funding has been delegated to an Executive Board which consists of a limited number of representatives of developing and developed countries.[64]

Ulfstein has rightly observed that the COPs and also the secretariats are engaged in various forms of administrative decision-making at the external level, such as collaboration with (i) the international organisation hosting the respective secretariat, (ii) the state hosting the secretariat and meetings of the parties, (iii) international financial institutions, and (iv) the treaty bodies of other MEAs.[65] The question whether MEAs can organise this kind of 'foreign policy' in the form of international treaties or mere 'soft law' arrangements depends on whether the COPs and secretariats possess the necessary international legal personality.

After all, administrative decision-making within MEAs appears to be gaining increasing importance. There is an implicit trade-off between the complexity of substantive regulation in the original MEA and the relevance of secondary (legislative and administrative) decision-making. Gehring is right to conclude:

> The more detailed the substantive regulations of the treaty are, the less room exists for subsequent decision-making. . . . The less elaborate the substantive treaty rules are and the more actors resort to postponing decisions to later stages of the governance process, the more important the institutional component of the arrangement will be from which such later decisions emerge and the more flexibly will the environmental law governing the issue area in question develop.[66]

Thus, secondary decision-making within MEAs results in perpetuating the treaty system concerned, and, at the same time, making it more flexible and dynamic.

[62] See *ibid*, 481 *et seq*.
[63] See *ibid*, 482.
[64] *Cf* again *ibid*, with references.
[65] See for more details Ulfstein, above n 39, 885 *et seq*.
[66] *Cf* Gehring, above n 43, 481.

17.4 Multilevel Governance

With regard to international environmental law, the complexity of international environmental governance can be reduced by introducing a variety of analytical perspectives. However, in order to grasp a full picture of such governance all levels have to be brought together.[67]

As this chapter has shown, international environmental governance involves a broad variety of actors, some of them enjoying legal personality as traditional subjects of public international law, while others still have to be accommodated within the international law framework. A second level of analysis which has been taken up pertains to the forms of action: it has been demonstrated that new forms of legislative governance have been developed within the framework of MEAs; furthermore, the development of new forms of administrative governance on the basis of MEAs has been explained above. The details of ordinary law-making will be addressed in the following chapters; the broad variety of means to ensure compliance with international environmental law will be addressed in detail in subsequent chapters.

Furthermore, international environmental governance is multilevel in character in light of national and international implementation of international environmental law. Increasingly, this is no longer limited to the interface between the international and the national level, but with growing regionalisation it includes regional environmental law (most obviously within Europe, but increasingly also in other regional forums) and local (or subnational) issues. Participation of public as well as private actors in international environmental governance as well as varying degrees of normativity (from soft law to treaty law, from principles to customary international law, etc) further complicate multilevel governance.

Generally speaking, legally binding international commitments as well as politically binding instruments can be framed at the universal, the regional and the subregional or bilateral level. Which of these levels is best suited to address a particular environmental problem first of all depends on the geographical reach of the subject-matter concerned. Thus, neighbouring states will seek to accommodate their conflicting interests in the use of natural resources at the subregional or bilateral level. The protection of the marine environment and of certain marine resources will often be addressed best at the regional level, whereas climate change and other global environmental issues necessitate governance at the universal level.

Selecting the best level of governance, however, will not only depend on the spatial range of the environmental issues in question, but may also depend on the suitability of pertinent political forums and the feasibility of reaching a meaningful (both effective and efficient) normative solution, preferably a treaty. The more the regulatory level moves towards universality, the more heterogeneous is the group of actors involved. This may lead to lower levels of protection. On the other hand, the more local the normative

[67] For a broad perspective *cf* G Winter, *Multilevel Governance of Global Environmental Change* (Cambridge *et al* 2006).

approach, the more diverse international environmental law will be in the end, and the less environmental solidarity will be around.

International environmental practice has shown that universal, regional and subregional norms addressing one and the same environmental problem can be complementary and may even reinforce each other. This means that none of the normative levels will enjoy absolute preference *vis-à-vis* the others but that there is a need carefully to co-ordinate activities at all levels.

This may be illustrated by reference to Part XII of the 1982 UN Convention on the Law of the Sea (UNCLOS) which lays down a framework for marine environmental protection and allows the needs of specific regions to be accommodated via appropriate regional agreements that complement the Convention. Accordingly, the preamble of the 1992 Convention for the Protection of the Marine Environment of the North-East Atlantic (OSPAR Convention) recalls the

> relevant provisions of customary international law reflected in Part XII of the United Nations Law of the Sea Convention and, in particular, Article 197 on global and regional cooperation for the protection and preservation of the marine environment.

A different approach to addressing multilevel governance has been included in the 1994 UN Convention to Combat Desertification. The Convention itself sets a normative framework and includes five Annexes for five different regions (Africa, Asia, Latin America and the Caribbean, the Northern Mediterranean, and Central and Eastern Europe). Furthermore, the Convention requires the implementation of action programmes at the national, subregional and regional level (Articles 5, 9–15). As can be taken from Article 15, the '[g]uidelines for the preparation of action programmes and their exact focus and content for particular subregions and regions' are laid down in the five Annexes.

Finally, universal agreements sometimes include dynamic or static references to regional norms which substantiate some of the provisions of the universal agreement. This approach is made use of in UNCLOS. Among others, Article 207 UNCLOS requires states to

> adopt laws and regulations to prevent, reduce and control pollution of the marine environment . . . taking into account internationally agreed rules, standards and recommended practices and procedures.

In particular, states

> shall endeavour to establish global and regional rules, standards and recommended practices and procedures to prevent, reduce and control pollution of the marine environment from land-based sources.

Another feature of multilevel governance is the diversified (positive), but sometimes unduly fragmented (negative) nature of international environmental law.[68] This may not

[68] On fragmentation in general *cf* M Koskenniemi and P Leino, 'Fragmentation of International Law? Postmodern Anxieties' (2002) 15 *Leiden Journal of International Law* 553; for a discussion of fragmentation in the context of climate change *cf* M Doelle, 'Linking the Kyoto Protocol and other Multilateral Environmental Agreements: From Fragmentation to Integration?' (2004) 14 *Journal of Environmental Law and Practice* (Special Issue) 75.

only lead to complexities but also to conflicts in international environmental law. Some of these conflicts are due to ecological interdependences. By way of example, some chemicals that substitute ozone-depleting substances are known to be greenhouse gases. Whereas use of these substitutes would be in conformity with the Montreal Protocol it would be contrary to the objectives of the UN Climate Change Convention and its Kyoto Protocol. In order to avoid such regulatory tensions, it is necessary to link the approaches taken by instruments which are intended to protect the ozone layer with those aimed at preventing or mitigating climate change.[69] Multilevel governance necessitates approaches to manage these conflicts either at the substantive or the procedural level. The co-ordination of conflicting obligations is thus not limited to the relationship between international environmental law and other branches of the law (which will be addressed in Chapters 26–28) but must also be addressed as between various MEAs.

Further Reading

S Andresen, 'The Effectiveness of UN Environmental Institutions' (2007) 7 *International Environmental Agreements: Politics, Law and Economics* 317–336.

S Bernstein, 'Legitimacy in Global Environmental Governance' (2005) 1 *Journal of International Law & International Relations* 139–166.

F Biermann and P Pattberg, 'Global Environmental Governance: Taking Stock, Moving Forward' (2008) 33 *Annual Review of Environment and Resources* 277–294.

D Bodansky, 'The Legitimacy of International Governance: A Coming Challenge for International Environmental Law?' (1999) 93 *AJIL* 596–624.

RR Churchill and G Ulfstein, 'Autonomous Institutional Arrangements in Multilateral Environmental Agreements: A Little-Noticed Phenomenon in International Law' (2000) 94 *AJIL* 623–659.

D French, 'Finding Autonomy in International Environmental Law and Governance' (2009) 21 *Journal of Environmental Law* 255–289.

J Hierlmeier, 'UNEP: Retrospect and Prospect—Options for Reforming the Global Environmental Governance Regime' (2002) 14 *Georgetown International Environmental Law Review* 767–805.

M Jahnke, 'International Environmental Governance' (2001) 31 *Environmental Policy and Law* 124–127.

A Najam, M Papa and N Taiyab, *Global Environmental Governance: A Reform Agenda* (Winnipeg, Manitoba 2006).

S Oberthür and T Gehring, 'Reforming International Environmental Governance: An Institutionalist Critique of the Proposal for a World Environment Organisation' (2004) 4 *International Environmental Agreements: Politics, Law and Economics* 359–381.

A Wiersema, 'The New International Law-Makers? Conferences of the Parties to Multilateral Environmental Agreements' (2009) 31 *Michigan Journal of International Law* 231–287.

NB Winchester, 'Emerging Global Environmental Governance' (2009) 16 *Indiana Journal of Global Legal Studies* 7–23.

G Winter, *Multilevel Governance of Global Environmental Change: Perspectives from Science, Sociology and the Law* (Cambridge *et al* 2006).

[69] R Wolfrum and N Matz, *Conflicts in International Environmental Law* (Berlin *et al* 2003) 4.

OR Young, *International Governance: Protecting the Environment in a Stateless Society* (Ithaca, NY *et al* 1994).

——, The Institutional Dimensions of Environmental Change: Fit, Interplay, and Scale (Cambridge, MA 2002).

18

International Environmental Treaty-Making and Treaty Regime-Building

18.1 Treaty Negotiation and Treaty Conclusion in General

International treaties are the most frequently used source of international law in international environmental relations. Due to their capacity to solve a given environmental problem as definitely and thoroughly as possible, international treaties are by far superior to customary international law which, by its very nature, remains rather abstract in substance.

Before 1972, international environmental treaties were mainly concluded by neighbouring states with the aim of settling conflicts over environmental utilisation. In the post-Stockholm era states increasingly became confronted with serious global environmental threats. This is why in the last three decades an immense body of MEAs emerged. While industrialised states, especially European ones, had clearly dominated international environmental treaty-making up to the second half of the twentieth century, the decolonisation process that started in the 1960s opened up a new era of international environmental treaty-making. The so-called Third World states increasingly became integrated into all important global environmental negotiation and treaty-making processes. The ongoing divide between the environmental and the developmental interests of the North and South continues to make international environmental negotiation and treaty-making a difficult task.

18.1.1 Procedural Aspects

The success or failure of negotiation processes depends greatly on whether the North and South, *ie* the groups of industrialised states and developing countries, each of which is far from being homogeneous, meet each other in an atmosphere of partnership rather than rivalry. As to possible strategies for optimising the processes of international environmental negotiation, it may suffice here to point to some essentials all negotiating actors should observe. Successful treaty negotiations should begin with setting the course in the preliminary talks phase, *ie* before the states' formal treaty negotiations commence. At this early stage a few 'leading states' ought to assume an informal 'stewardship' role. A precondition for successfully playing this role is that the group of 'leading states' is sufficiently representative and legitimised to act on behalf of all potential treaty partners, be they industrialised states or developing countries. States wishing to conclude an MEA usually convene an international conference where they enter into extensive formal negotiations. Even in this formal phase the substantive negotiations should not be held in the plenary sessions of the conference, but in smaller negotiating committees, although this practice risks disadvantaging smaller developing countries. Here again it is most important that the various groups of states are best represented by persons of integrity who have high leadership skills and sufficient authority to influence the political decision-making process of those states which are not present in the respective negotiating bodies. Leaving enough leeway for the building of coalitions over and above the different groups of states should contribute significantly to the success of the negotiations.

In principle, the procedures for the conclusion of international environmental agreements are the same as those employed in other areas of international treaty law. As a rule, an international treaty, be it bilateral or multilateral, enters into force and thereby becomes effective in international relations after its text has been negotiated, signed and finally—following the usually necessary domestic approval by national parliaments or other internal processes—ratified.[1] This composite treaty-making procedure has long been recognised in customary international law, as confirmed and specified in Articles 9 *et seq* VCLT. This process generally takes a great deal of time and therefore quite often prevents international treaty law from coming swiftly into operation. Even worse, it notoriously entails the risk of failure for any number of reasons even at the very end. While some less important, especially technical, international agreements can be made in a simplified and shortened procedure, all other international treaties, including the important MEAs, have to go through these procedural stages.

The opportunities to simplify and speed up the lengthy and cumbersome process of international treaty-making are very limited. The more important a treaty is, the more prolonged the procedure between negotiation and entry into force will be. This will continue to be so as long as states stick to their traditional sovereignty-based thinking. The only way to avoid the imponderability and troubles which treaty-making procedures notoriously involve is to resort to a 'soft law' arrangement which entails political-moral rather than legally binding effects and is therefore not subject to any procedural restrictions.[2]

In principle, the amendment of a treaty must go through the same procedure as its conclusion. Thus, it has to be signed and—following domestic approval—ratified. Article 40 VCLT provides that any amendment to a multilateral treaty only becomes binding on the consenting parties. For those parties who have not ratified the amendment in question,

[1] Art 18 Vienna Convention on the Law of Treaties (VCLT) provides that a state which has signed a treaty is obliged to refrain from any acts defeating the purpose of that treaty. This was probably the reason why in 2001 the Bush Administration withdrew the US signature of the Kyoto Protocol. *Cf* Chapter 13.4.

[2] See for a more thorough discussion below Chapter 20.2.

the original treaty remains valid. In order to avoid such an unfortunate splitting of an originally unified treaty regime into diverging part regimes, many modern MEAs contain their own revision clauses which give the parties some leeway for solving the amendment problem. The various concrete options treaty partners may have for easing the process of amendments to MEAs, as well as related protocols and annexes, will be the subject of closer scrutiny in section 18.4. However, it seems likely that as long as sovereign states remain the dominant actors in international environmental relations, they will be bound neither by a treaty nor by its amendment against their will.

18.1.2 Substantive Aspects

Every treaty is only worth what is subsequently done to comply with it in practice. The soundness of treaty-making depends on structuring the treaty content in such a way that the co-operation benefits gained by the contracting parties are finely and accurately balanced with the costs inevitably arising out of the fulfilment of their contractual obligations. As most modern MEAs have been made in the North–South context, striking a sound balance between contractual costs and benefits is most difficult. Accordingly, the particular art of treaty design lies in giving sufficient positive incentives for all state groups involved, *ie* for the industrialised states as much as for the developing countries. This is all the more difficult as in most cases the 'short-term' costs caused by the compliance with a contractual environmental obligation must be measured against 'long-term' benefits the parties can expect to derive from co-operation.

Another important prerequisite for the acceptance of treaty contents is drafting the latter as clearly and precisely as possible. The less effort contracting parties put into reaching this ideal, the more they will encounter failures to comply with the treaty in question. Thus, the first step necessary for ensuring treaty compliance is sound treaty-making, which requires in particular textual precision and lack of ambiguity. However, quite often the contracting parties consciously resort to vague formulations in order to conceal a lack of political accord or to evade a concrete commitment.

Finally, a method commonly used to attract as many states as possible to sign an MEA, and coincidentally to reduce the risk of subsequent non-compliance, is to reduce the burden of the treaty content. This can be achieved by removing those regulatory elements on which a consensus cannot be achieved at that time. Thus, it is typical for modern MEAs, especially the so-called framework conventions, that they hardly ever contain a meaningful body of legally binding environmental standards, but are mostly restricted to laying down the main goals and imposing significant procedural obligations on their parties (see section 18.3.1). Another technique for unburdening the content of an MEA is to remove certain regulatory segments to secondary rule-making through COP decisions. This method may be used in two opposite situations: firstly, when the parties agree upon postponing the regulation of some less important details to a later date; and secondly, when an issue is so sensitive or complex in nature that it needs further examination by experts and is therefore transferred to a secondary rule-setting level within that treaty to be regulated at a later stage (see Chapter 17.3.2 above and section 18.3.2 below).

18.2 Levels of Treaty-Making

International treaties can be concluded at a universal, regional, subregional or bilateral level. Which of these levels is best suited to the solution of a particular environmental problem depends on various factors, particularly the geographical range of the environmental problem in question. For instance, an environmental utilisation conflict between two or more neighbouring states typically does not affect a greater circle of states. Accordingly, it should be solved at the bilateral or subregional level. In contrast, in cases where global environmental threats, such as climate change or ozone depletion, concern the state community as a whole, then in order to be effective, remedial action by way of treaty-making at the universal level is called for. Once a global instrument has been established, it is often followed by supporting treaties to be concluded at lower levels.

In broad environmental fields, such as the protection of the marine environment and the conservation of marine living resources, states generally pursue a strategy of combining the effects of treaty-making at various levels. With UNCLOS, a comprehensive rules system for the management and protection of the oceans and their living resources exists at the universal level. However, as UNCLOS's legal framework is rather broad and abstract, it must be substantiated and further developed by way of regional-level treaties. Due to the fact that the geographical, ecological and socioeconomic realities in states' coastal waters or exclusive economic zones differ considerably from one ocean to another, each regional sea should be subject to a specific legal regime adapted to its particularities. Thus, there is ample need for treaty-making at the regional and/or subregional level. Accordingly, the role of UNCLOS is generally limited to giving some guidance for shaping the pertinent regional treaty regimes on the marine environment.

In the field of nature protection, choosing the 'right' treaty-making level entails peculiar difficulties. Nature degradation, such as the loss of valuable species of flora and fauna and the deterioration of their habitats, does not only have negative local effects, but is also to the detriment of humankind as a whole. The protection of important natural goods is of common concern for all states. It should therefore be the object of multilevel treaty-making. A universal 'umbrella' treaty should empower states owning valuable natural resources on their territories to conclude more concrete agreements on nature conservation at regional, subregional or even local levels, and give them respective guidance.[3] Thus, the cumulative use of different levels is a suitable means of optimising the regulatory effects of treaty-making. This strategy proves to be the more promising the better the specific advantages of one level of treaty-making are used to compensate for possible deficits in effectiveness at another level.

The paramount consideration of states in choosing the 'right' treaty-making level must be how to achieve the most substantial solution. Two (coinciding or conflicting) aspects should determine this choice: (i) the treaty-making level should correspond as best as possible to the range of the subject matter; (ii) the group of states willing to enter into

[3] A striking example of such hierarchical international treaty-making is Art IV of the 1979 Bonn Convention on Migratory Species of Wild Animals (CMS). *Cf* above Chapter 14.2.3.

a given treaty should be as homogeneous as possible. In the latter respect it is almost a truism that the higher the treaty-making level, the more heterogeneous the contracting parties will be. Thus, treaties made at the universal level typically suffer much more from the lack of normative strength and regulatory density than those concluded at lower levels. The greater the number of states parties to a universal treaty, the more likely it is that they merely agree upon the 'lowest common denominator'. Therefore, in individual cases treaty-making at a lower level than indicated by the subject matter may appear preferable because greater homogeneity of states allows a more substantial solution, although this might induce other states to benefit from these efforts as 'free riders'. On the other hand, it should also have become clear that any unnecessary treaty-making at a lower level entails the risk of producing an undue proliferation and fragmentation of treaties showing at least in part overlaps and even inconsistencies or contradictions between their respective contents.

18.3 Regulatory Approaches to Treaty-Making

With the draft of the International Covenant on Environment and Development, first published in 1995, the International Union for Conservation of Nature (IUCN) made a respectable attempt to create a universal environmental treaty[4] destined to help consolidate or even integrate the disparate environmental law-making efforts of states into a closer and more effective partnership of states. However, it would be illusory to expect that there will ever be a broad majority of states willing to accept such a high-level treaty on integrated environmental protection. Any centralisation of international environmental treaty-making entails the risk of bureaucratisation. It would ultimately slow down the norm-setting process rather than accelerate it, and deprive states of their flexibility in treaty-shaping. Thus, diversification of environmental treaty-making may better help than its centralisation to balance the heterogeneous interests of states in a still highly divided world, or even to make these interests converge in the longer term. However, this plea in favour of diversifying the process of international environmental treaty-making does not mean to argue for its fragmentation, because any uncontrolled emergence of individual MEAs undermines the effectiveness of the international environmental treaty system.

Attempts to concentrate international environmental treaty-making at the highest level, such as the IUCN draft for a global environmental 'umbrella treaty', sharply contrast with the so-called 'piecemeal approach'. This method of treaty-making that has long been used in practice is aimed at singling out particular environmental problems for isolated treatment in separate treaties.[5] Such a policy may be helpful in specific, rather narrow regulatory situations, *eg* when a small, more or less homogeneous group of states situated in a narrower geographic area agrees that a particular segment of an environmental

[4] The third and revised edition of this Draft Convention of 2004 is available at www.i-c-e-l.org/english/EPLP31EN_rev2.pdf.

[5] *Cf* G Sjöstedt, 'Critical Attributes of International Environmental Negotiations' in O Höll (ed), *Environmental Cooperation in Europe: The Political Dimension* (Boulder, CO *et al* 1994) 103, 119.

problem needs to be dealt with as promptly and substantively as possible.[6] In such a case, regulating 'a piece of the whole' might be better than trying in vain to solve the whole set of problems in one go. However, the more multifaceted and complex a particular environmental problem is, the less advisable such a selective strategy will be. On the other hand, states confronted with such a problem would be ill-advised to make the attempt of solving it *uno actu*. In such regulatory situations a strategy called 'framework convention and protocol approach' may prove to be a useful alternative.

18.3.1 'Framework Convention and Protocol Approach'

Particularly at the universal level, states with rather heterogeneous interests and needs often feel urged to master an environmental problem as comprehensively as possible. However, the more complicated and delicate this problem is, the less states will be able to solve it at once. In such a case there is no other option for them but to pursue a step-by-step approach. In the last three decades, states have established tailor-made solutions for various environmental problem areas, such as the reduction of transboundary air pollution,[7] the protection of the ozone layer,[8] combating climate change[9] and the conservation of biological diversity,[10] by means of a number of consecutive consensual acts.

The task of persuading states with heterogeneous interests to enter into an international treaty that deals with the above-mentioned problem areas as perfectly as possible is a very arduous undertaking for two reasons. Firstly, the more effective the environmental protection mechanisms in an international agreement are, especially if combined with the establishment of treaty bodies entrusted with functions in this respect, the more states will hesitate to join this agreement for reasons of sovereignty. Secondly, the more intense the contractual environmental commitments entered into are, the greater the financial burdens their fulfilment will entail for the treaty parties. This is why hitherto the negotiation processes initiated by states with the aim of establishing effective treaty regimes for the protection of global environmental goods mostly took a very long time.

Pursuing a 'framework convention approach' necessarily implies that states willing to enter into an international treaty take two steps. Firstly, as indicated by its name,

[6] An example of the piecemeal approach is the 1989 Convention for the Prohibition of Fishing with Long Driftnets in the South Pacific which prompted the UN General Assembly to adopt Resolution 46/215 (20 December 1991) ((1992) 31 ILM 241) requesting compliance with a moratorium on this fishing method in all oceans.

[7] The 1979 Geneva Convention on Long-Range Transboundary Air Pollution has been followed (as yet) by eight implementing protocols (1984–1999) which provide for strict limit values or emissions reductions within specific deadlines. *Cf* Chapter 13.2.1.

[8] The largely empty framework of the 1985 Vienna Convention for the Protection of the Ozone Layer was rapidly filled by the 1987 Montreal Protocol on Substances that Deplete the Ozone Layer, which in turn has been amended several times. *Cf* Chapter 13.3.

[9] The 1992 United Nations Framework Convention on Climate Change (UNFCCC) was brought to life by the 1997 Kyoto Protocol. *Cf* Chapter 13.4.

[10] The 1992 United Nations Convention on Biological Diversity (CBD), which provides a global framework for the development of measures to conserve the earth's biodiversity, also relies on being implemented by subsequent protocols. However, so far, with the 2000 Cartagena Protocol on Biosafety, this happened only with respect to Art 19(3) of the Convention. *Cf* Chapter 14.3.4.

this approach requires the conclusion of an international framework convention which is broadly worded. This type of MEA establishes only a rudimentary treaty relationship, mostly by stipulating certain mutually agreed treaty aims, defining some more or less indefinite obligations to act in a certain way, and, most importantly, establishing a procedural framework of concerted action. It leaves, however, all regulatory details which eventually bring the treaty to life unregulated because there is no consensus on them for the time being. Thus, the treaty regime established by the framework convention is imperfect as long as its lacunae have not been filled by the parties' subsequent course of action. Taken alone, the conventional rules are hardly operational. The convention's legal and practical value essentially lies in the fact that it commits its parties to a procedural framework which ensures that they will enter into negotiations with a view to agreeing in due course upon a more substantial instrument with concrete commitments. This will best be achieved by a framework convention which legally predetermines the subsequent course of action of the parties as clearly and definitely as possible.[11]

The second step consists of elaborating one or more subsequent protocols. However, quite frequently both the framework convention and the protocol, or one of them, are preceded by a respective 'soft law' instrument. This occurs particularly in the following two situations.

Firstly, treaty partners who are not yet ready to compromise about the contents of an environmental framework convention politically commit themselves in a legally non-binding understanding to enter into a negotiation process in view of making such a convention. Rather than seeking a legally binding solution, they only agree upon a 'road map' that might help them conclude such a convention and give them some guidance in this respect.[12]

Secondly, state parties to a framework convention sometimes feel politically hindered to implement this convention in due time by way of adopting one or more legally binding protocols. In this case, they can provisionally resort to an implementing 'soft law' instrument. Normally, the latter is only an intermediate step towards agreeing upon a legally binding protocol.[13] However, if the partners expect to be permanently hindered from obtaining a legally binding consensus on a particular implementation issue, the 'soft law' instrument in question may *ex post* become permanent.

If the implementing protocol consciously leaves a certain issue unsolved and postpones its further regulation to a later date, this issue will sometimes be addressed by a

[11] This may be best ensured by a framework convention which, in the form of a *pactum de negotiando*, requires the contracting parties to enter into negotiations with the mutual will to agree upon an implementing protocol.

[12] An example is the Hague Declaration on the Environment of 1989, which was a first step towards the conclusion of the 1992 UNFCCC. However, this technique is not an exclusive one for initiating a framework convention. It can also be used in the context of other agreement categories. *Cf* Chapter 20.2.

[13] An illustrious example of this sort of procedure is the so-called Berlin Mandate, a political declaration of intent adopted by COP 1 of the UNFCCC in spring 1995, which provided the appointment of an 'open-ended *ad hoc* group of Parties' to be entrusted with the mandate to elaborate a protocol or a different legal instrument for the purpose of implementing the abstract framework rules of the UNFCCC; a final outcome of the Berlin Mandate is the Kyoto Protocol which was adopted in 1997.

subsequent 'soft law' instrument. Thus, 'soft law' can serve as a tool for filling lacunae which the implementing protocol has left.[14]

18.3.2 'Convention and Annexes Approach'

A traditional strategy of unburdening the contents of international treaties is to divide them into separate parts. Usually, all core elements of an international treaty, such as the aims and fundamental principles, the obligations of the parties to act in a certain way, and the treaty's procedural and institutional setting relating to implementation, compliance and dispute settlement, form part of the treaty's main body. However, quite often the treaty partners prefer to bring the more specific contractual regulations, particularly those of a scientific-technical nature, into one or more separate annexes. The parties regularly sign and ratify these annexes together with the treaty concerned, and declare them to be an integral part of the latter.[15]

The 'convention and annexes approach', long used in many fields of international law, is of primary importance in environmental treaty-making practice. Interestingly, it is typical of the recent practice of MEAs that their parties agree to leave the adoption of (additional) technical annexes to the COPs concerned which are, *inter alia*, competent for further developing the respective treaty regimes.[16] Examples of this type of shaping MEA are the London Convention for the Prevention of Pollution from Ships of 2 November 1973, as modified by Protocol of 17 February 1978 (MARPOL 73/78); the Washington Convention on International Trade in Endangered Species of Wild Fauna and Flora (CITES) of 3 March 1973; the Bonn Convention on the Conservation of Migratory Species of Wild Animals (CMS) of 23 June 1979; the United Nations Economic Commission for Europe (UNECE) Helsinki Convention on the Transboundary Effects of Industrial Accidents of 17 March 1992; and the Kyoto Protocol of 11 December 1997.

The annexes to these MEAs differ from each other. While some of them are of a mere technical-scientific character, others regulate, at least in part, important substantive issues and are therefore politically much more sensitive. For example, the annexes related to the Kyoto Protocol evidently vary in character. Consequently, the procedures to be employed for their adoption and amendment considerably differ from each other. Those annexes that are of a scientific, technical, procedural or administrative character can be adopted and amended in a simplified procedure, namely by a decision of the COP (Article 20(1) Kyoto Protocol).[17] In contrast, all existing annexes, especially the substantive Annexes A

[14] For example, Art 18 of the 1997 Kyoto Protocol calls for the development of 'appropriate and effective procedures and mechanisms to determine and address cases of non-compliance'. So far this provision has been implemented by the respective procedures and mechanisms in the so-called Marrakech Accords (Decision 24/CP7 (10 November 2001)), as first agreed upon by COP 7 of the UNFCCC in November 2001 and finally adopted by COP/MOP 1 at its Montreal Meeting in 2005 (Decision 27/CMP1 (9–10 December 2005)). It is the MOP's prerogative 'to decide on the legal form' of the Kyoto compliance regime. However, to date no such decision has been taken. See J Brunnée, 'The Kyoto Protocol: Testing Ground for Compliance Theories?' (2003) 63 *ZaöRV* 255, 272 *et seq*.

[15] Sometimes the annexes are complemented by related appendices.

[16] See also above at Chapter 17.3.2.

[17] As already shown above (Chapter 17.2.3), the taking of decisions on the adoption and amendment of treaty annexes is among the functions which COPs under the respective MEAs typically fulfil.

and B to the Kyoto Protocol, are subject to the standard procedure of treaty-making and treaty-amendment that requires the parties' express consent to be bound, *ie* the deposit of instruments of acceptance by parties (Article 19 Kyoto Protocol).[18]

18.4 Simplified Amendment Procedures Regarding Treaties, Protocols and Annexes

18.4.1 Amendments of Treaties and Protocols

Generally, amendments of treaties and protocols follow the same procedure as treaty conclusions (*cf* Article 39 VCLT). They only become binding on those states which have signed and ratified the respective amendment treaty.[19] This does not necessarily mean that it is always up to states parties to elaborate and adopt the amendment's text themselves. It has become typical of modern MEAs (and protocols related thereto) to include clauses expressly authorising the COPs concerned to adopt if necessary treaty amendments, new protocols, as well as amendments to existing protocols.[20] Thus, today states parties to an MEA regularly delegate the task of adopting a treaty (or protocol) amendment to the respective COP in which they all are represented. There is common understanding in legal doctrine that the COP cannot fulfil this function unless it has been clearly authorised by states parties to do so. This is in line with today's treaty practice. Almost all MEAs contain respective authorisation clauses. Consequently, classic negotiations between states parties on treaty amendments have meanwhile become rather obsolete. Another question is whether the amendment gains legal effectiveness in international law by mere COP decision or whether it needs subsequent formal acceptance by parties. This question is the subject of ongoing controversy.

Prototypical in this respect is Decision II/12 which the COP to the 1989 Basel Convention on the Control of Transboundary Movements of Hazardous Wastes and their Disposal adopted by consensus on 25 March 1994 at its Second Meeting. Decision II/12 banned the export of hazardous wastes from Organisation for Economic Co-operation and Development (OECD) to non-OECD countries as of 31 December 1997.[21] Thereby, the COP considerably modified the Convention's original control regime. While the COP was undoubtedly authorised under Article 17(2) of the Convention to adopt the treaty amendment concerned, this adoption immediately initiated heated debate among the delegations of states parties as to whether or not the extended ban of waste exports could be rendered effective in international law by mere COP decision.[22] Aware that this act alone could

[18] See also below at Section 18.4.2.

[19] *Cf eg* Art 15(3) UNFCCC and Art 29(3) CBD.

[20] See *eg* Art 15 UNFCCC and Article 23(4)(d) and (e) CBD.

[21] See the text of Decision II/12 in UNEP/CHW2/30 (25 March 1994) 19.

[22] The Basel Convention Secretariat's website itself acknowledges that 'because Decision II/12 was not incorporated in the text of the Convention itself, the question as to whether it was legally binding or not arose'; see www.basel.int/pub/baselban.html.

not meet the procedural requirements of Article 17(3) of the Convention,[23] the COP at its Third Meeting formally adopted the extended ban on the export of wastes as an amendment to the Convention (Decision III/1 of 22 September 1995). The entry into force of the Ban Amendment depends on its ratification by at least three-quarters of the parties who accepted it (Article 17(5) of the Convention). To date, the Amendment has been ratified by 63 states. However, at its Ninth Meeting in June 2008 the COP still disagreed about the question of whether these 63 ratifications met the requirement of three-quarters of parties.[24]

18.4.2 Amendments and Adjustments of Annexes

While efforts to ease the process of making treaty and protocol amendments have so far met with little success, hindered as they are by states persisting to think in strict terms of sovereignty, we will see that the procedure of amending annexes to MEAs is much more susceptible to simplification.

With regard to amendments, in numerous cases, the states parties to MEAs have agreed upon simplified procedures for the initial adoption of annexes and their potential subsequent amendment. For instance, the Vienna Convention for the Protection of the Ozone Layer of 22 March 1985, the UNFCCC of 9 May 1992, the CBD of 22 May 1992, the United Nations Convention to Combat Desertification (UNCCD) of 17 June 1994, and the Basel Convention all provide that the existing annexes to these MEAs can be amended by consensus, and if consensus cannot be attained by qualified majority decision, with an immediate legally binding effect for all those parties which have not expressly objected these amendments within a specified time-limit ('opting-out').[25]

The parties to MEAs can choose between various voting procedures for amending treaty annexes. Firstly, the qualified majority that is needed to take a positive amendment decision varies from two-thirds,[26] to three-quarters,[27] to nine-tenths.[28] Secondly, the requirement for a qualified majority vote can be combined with that of reaching a certain quorum of 'opting-in' or 'opting-out' declarations. Thus, states parties can agree that the adopted amendment to a treaty annex cannot become binding in international law if the opting-out declarations reach a specified 'prohibitive quorum'. However, they can also proceed exactly the other way around by agreeing that an amendment to the annex concerned only becomes binding for those parties who voted in favour of it if their votes reach the predetermined 'positive quorum' within a year. Both the prohibitive and positive quorum have one and the same purpose, namely to moderate the limitations imposed

[23] Art 17(3) of the Basel Convention requires that an amendment, once it has been adopted, if not by consensus, by a three-quarters majority vote of the Parties present and voting at the meeting, must be submitted to all Parties for ratification, approval, formal confirmation or acceptance.

[24] See Summary of the Ninth Conference of the Parties to the Basel Convention, 23–27 June 2008, Earth Negotiations Bulletin, vol 20 no 31 (30 June 2008) 2, 14.

[25] See Art 10(3) Ozone Convention; Art 16(4) UNFCCC; Art 30(3) CBD; Art 18(3) Basel Convention; Art 31(2) UNCCD.

[26] *Eg* Art XV CITES; Art XVI CMS; Art 31(1) UNCCD.

[27] *Eg* Art 10(3) Ozone Convention.

[28] *Eg* Art 26(4) UNECE Convention on the Transboundary Effects of Industrial Accidents (1992).

on states' sovereignty by allowing for qualified majority decisions. Both types of quorum can also be linked to requirements such as, for example, that the group of objecting, respectively non-objecting, states parties must include a fixed number of states which meet certain qualitative criteria.[29]

Practice reveals that 'opting-out' clauses, particularly if linked to prohibitive or positive quorums, sometimes have the consequence that amendments to the annexes of MEAs by qualified majority decisions with a direct legally binding effect in international law for all contracting parties are not crowned with success. This was reason enough to consider the adjustment of annexes to MEAs (without the possibility of opting-out) as an alternative to the above-described simplified annex amendment procedure.

The method of merely adjusting a treaty annex instead of amending it has been first provided by the Protocol on Further Reduction of Sulphur Emissions of 1994, destined to implement the 1979 Geneva Convention on Long-Range Transboundary Air Pollution, by stipulating in Article 11(6) that 'adjustments to [the Protocol's] Annex II shall be adopted by consensus of the Parties present at a session of the Executive Body and shall become effective for all Parties to the present Protocol [at a specified date].'

The 1987 Montreal Protocol relating to the Ozone Convention goes much further. It entitles, in its Article 2(9)(a), the parties to decide on certain adjustments to the ozone-depleting potentials specified in Annexes A, B, C and/or E, as well as on certain further adjustments and reductions of production or consumption of the controlled substances. The decision on these alterations of the Montreal Protocol's central substantive commitments should be taken whenever possible by consensus, and if this cannot be attained, by a two-thirds majority vote that is carried by simple majorities of both developing and developed countries (*lit* c). Article 2(9)(d) states that the adjustment decided on is legally binding on all parties without exception; it will enter into force (within a specified period of time) without having been ratified by the parties. As the opportunity of opting-out is not available to the parties, the majority of the latter can bind the minority against its will. However, so far all adjustments of these annexes to the Montreal Protocol have been made by consensus.[30]

18.4.3 COPs' Decision-Making Procedures

With regard to the amendment of treaties and protocols as well as the amendment or adjustment of treaty annexes, it has become practice in recent years that the states parties to an MEA expressly authorise the COP as the treaty organ to consider and adopt the relevant amendments or adjustments.

The fact that Decision II/12 of the COP to the Basel Convention was followed by a

[29] *Eg* Art 16(2)(f)(ii) MARPOL 73/78 provides that 'an amendment to an Annex to the Convention shall be deemed to have been accepted . . . on the date on which it is accepted by two-thirds of the Parties, the combined merchant fleet of which constitute not less than fifty percent of the gross tonnage of the World's merchant fleet '.

[30] See RR Churchill and G Ulfstein, 'Autonomous Institutional Arrangements in Multilateral Environmental Agreements: A Little-Noticed Phenomenon in International Law' (2000) 94 AJIL 623, 638 *et seq*; T Gehring, 'Treaty-Making and Treaty Evolution' in D Bodansky *et al* (eds), *The Oxford Handbook of International Environmental Law* (Oxford 2007) 467, 489 *et seq*.

formal ban amendment to the Convention (see section 18.4.1 above) is reason enough to argue that amendments of MEAs and protocols cannot become legally binding in international law by mere COP decision but only after they have passed the ordinary amendment procedure of formal acceptance by parties. Thus, in such cases the COPs' role is confined to taking the relevant adoption decision, while it is up to the parties to ensure that the adopted amendments become legally binding.[31]

The legal situation is different in cases where treaty annexes are to be amended or adjusted. In both cases the COPs are entitled to take qualified majority decisions with the immediate effect that the amendments or adjustments become legally binding on the parties without having gone through the ordinary procedures of acceptance. In the case where the COP has taken a qualified majority decision on amending an annex, individual states parties are generally able to expressly object this decision and thus abscond from its legally binding effect. By contrast, in a case where an annex is to be merely adjusted, a qualified majority of the parties may be allowed, at least on paper, to do so against the minority's will.

Thus, treaty annexes can be modified with immediate legal effect in a simplified procedure, namely by decisions taken by the COP at a secondary level of treaty-making. However, in order to benefit from this procedural simplification in practice, the parties to the MEA concerned must have agreed upon the voting rules which a COP must respect in the relevant decision-making process. In view of the paramount decision-making role which COPs usually play within the framework of modern MEAs, the question as to how to conceive the voting conditions in the COP's rules of procedure is important. Thus, it is hardly a surprise that this question gave rise to ongoing controversies among states parties to MEAs, particularly in the North–South dimension.

A closer look at today's relevant treaty practice reveals how difficult it is to shape the rules of procedure of COPs in such a way that all states parties involved in secondary decision-making processes can participate in voting on equitable terms. As yet, neither the COP to the UNFCCC, nor the Meeting of the Parties (MOP) to the related Kyoto Protocol, nor the COP to the CBD can rely on formally adopted voting rules. The COPs and MOPs to the UNFCCC and the Kyoto Protocol, respectively, still apply the Draft Rules of Procedure proposed at the COP's First Meeting in 1995. However, they do not apply Draft Rule 42 on voting because there is still controversy regarding the majorities required for decisions the COP/MOP takes on matters of substance. The COP to the CBD formally adopted its Rules of Procedure at its First Meeting in 1994 with the exception of the rule on voting, Rule 40(1), which provides that in the event that the parties are unable to reach agreement by consensus, decisions on matters of substance shall be made by a two-thirds majority vote of the parties present and voting. Due to the parties' ongoing disagreement on voting, COP/MOP decisions under the UNFCCC and the Kyoto Protocol, as well as those under the CBD, can still only be taken by consensus.[32]

[31] This is not to say that a treaty amendment that has been solely adopted by COP's decision necessarily remains legally meaningless, as long as it has not passed the ordinary procedure of acceptance by parties. As Chapter 17.3.2 has shown, such acts of secondary rule-making arguably produce quasi-legal or *de facto* binding effects.

[32] *Cf* U Beyerlin, 'Bridging the North–South Divide in International Environmental Law' (2006) 66 *ZaöRV* 259, 283 *et seq*.

The COPs acting under other MEAs, namely the Ozone Convention, the Montreal Protocol, the Basel Convention, the OSPAR Convention and the 1998 Rotterdam Convention on the Prior Informed Consent Procedure for Certain Hazardous Chemicals and Pesticides in International Trade, dispose of formally adopted voting rules. These rules[33] show a certain trend towards requiring either a two-thirds or three-quarters majority vote of the parties present and voting for decision-making on matters of substance, including the amendment of the treaties and treaty annexes concerned. Most promising with respect to an equitable participation of developing and developed states in international decision-making processes is, as already shown above, the voting procedure for taking decisions on the adjustment of annexes in Article 2(9)(c) Montreal Protocol that requires double majorities of both groups of states. However, relevant treaty practice has not yet followed the example of the Montreal Protocol's annex adjustment procedure. For the time being, this procedure remains unique.

18.5 Conflicts between Different MEAs and Their Settlement

18.5.1 Parallel, Overlapping and Conflicting MEAs

During the last 40 years the number of MEAs has grown enormously: in the two decades between the Stockholm and Rio Conferences the number more than doubled compared to the pre-Stockholm era. At the beginning of the twenty-first century there were about a thousand international agreements dealing with aspects of environmental protection. This ever-growing proliferation of interstate treaties has had a number of deleterious effects on international environmental treaty practice which can be subsumed under the catchword of 'treaty congestion'. As most current international environmental agreements fail to pursue an integrative and holistic approach, there are often serious divergences, if not contradictions between them, particularly with regard to their subject areas and their objectives, as well as the regulatory approaches pursued by the respective parties to the conflicting agreements. Some of them address global environmental threats, others regulate just one or a few selected environmental problems of a regional, or even local, scope. Some deal with a given issue as thoroughly and extensively as possible, others deliberately address it in rather broad terms. Even the states parties to MEAs mostly do not make explicit reference to conflicting environmental matters, although they should have been aware of their interfaces from the outset. An exception in this respect is the UNCCD which stresses its close interlinkage with other global threats and the respective MEAs, such as the UNFCCC and CBD.[34] Wolfrum and Matz have rightly summed up these drawbacks by stating that:

> most international treaties exist parallel to one another and are further developed without the benefit of consideration being given to potential conflict with other agreements either during

[33] For a more detailed description of these rules on voting see again *ibid*, 284.
[34] See the Preamble and Art 8(1) UNCCD.

> their negotiation or at a later stage of their existence. Insofar as these agreements overlap, this overlap can either take the form of a doubling of efforts concerning a particular problem or as [*sic*] a contradiction or conflict between the objectives, programs or means of the respective agreements.[35]

There is urgent need of remedying these defects in the current system of international environmental agreements. Theoretically, there are various methods for settling treaty conflicts, thereby providing for greater coherence of MEAs. Firstly, the parties to the conflicting agreements can resort to Article 30 VCLT, the *lex posterior* or *lex specialis* rules; alternatively they can attempt a harmonising treaty interpretation. Secondly, they can endeavour to co-ordinate the conflicting agreements by means of interinstitutional co-operation.

18.5.2 Article 30 VCLT; *Lex Posterior* and *Lex Specialis*; Harmonising Treaty Interpretation

Article 30 VCLT and the rules on *lex posterior* and *lex specialis*, both based upon customary international law, are rules for resolving incompatibilities in the contents of rival agreements. They are designed to remedy this kind of conflict by giving one agreement priority over the other. Article 30 VCLT addresses a number of special situations where a later treaty that deals exactly with the same subject matter as an earlier treaty enjoys priority. However, as far as MEAs are concerned, this provision offers little help, because there are hardly any two MEAs that deal with fully indentical subject matters. The same holds true for the customary *lex posterior* rule. Although its applicability is broader than that of Article 30 VCLT, it functions as a rule of derogation that gives one agreement preference over the other, provided that the parties to both agreements are identical.[36] However, *lex posterior* is of little help in case of conflicting MEAs for two reasons: firstly, there are hardly any two MEAs having identical states parties; secondly, most of the conflicts between MEAs should not result in one MEA superseding (overriding) the other, but lead to a solution that brings the MEAs concerned into line with each other as much as possible, for instance by means of a harmonising interpretation of their conflicting rules. *Lex specialis* is another rule destined for fulfilling a derogative function. It gives the more specific treaty priority over the more general treaty. However, it hardly helps in a case where MEAs, *eg* two framework conventions that are equally vague in content, come into conflict with each other.[37]

A more promising method for resolving incompatibilities between two agreements is harmonising their contradictory contents by means of interpretation. The aim of this approach is to bring the rival agreements into line with each other rather than abrogating or suspending one of them. However, any such attempt must fail unless the parties to these agreements are mutually willing to respect their coexistence and the relevance of

[35] R Wolfrum and N Matz, *Conflicts in International Environmental Law* (Berlin *et al* 2003) 2.

[36] *Eg* in the case of two bilateral agreements successively concluded by the same two states the customary *lex posterior* rule determines that the later agreement in time can claim priority.

[37] *Cf* again Wolfrum and Matz, above n 35, 147 *et seq*.

their commitments that have been made under each of them. For instance, the parties to two MEAs that are both destined to serve an overarching interest of the whole state community, but use different ways and means for reaching this aim, may feel morally urged to interpret the respective MEAs in a way that best helps to serve this fundamental common interest.[38] Quite often the parties to MEAs will have sufficient leeway to harmonise successfully interpretation of the treaties. However, this method of solving treaty conflicts will be of little help in cases where the contradictory treaty notions are so clearly and unambiguously worded that they are not open to being harmonised by dynamic interpretation.[39]

18.5.3 Treaty Co-ordination by Means of Interinstitutional Co-operation

The above-mentioned methods available for solving treaty conflicts (Article 30 VCLT; rules of *lex posterior* and *lex specialis*; and harmonising treaty interpretation) cannot be expected to settle all conflicts arising from the collision of international environmental agreements. Especially in cases where a conflict between two rival agreements cannot be remedied by means of a harmonising norm interpretation, the states parties concerned must consider alternative ways and means for bridging the clashes between the respective agreements.

Most promising in this respect is that the treaty organs to many MEAs have entered into well-ordered forms of interinstitutional co-operation with the aim of co-ordinating the activities they are individually mandated to undertake within the MEAs concerned, with the inclusion of concerted, if not joint, measures for smooth treaty implementation. This can best be achieved by legally non-binding arrangements made between the treaty organs concerned. As will be shown below in more detail,[40] the COPs and/or secretariats to many MEAs have entered into 'memoranda of understanding' that are, *inter alia,* aimed at enhancing interinstitutional treaty co-ordination. By doing so, they mitigate the negative consequences of undue proliferation and diversification of relevant agreements; moreover, they produce a maximum degree of synergy between the latter. Thus, treaty co-ordination by means of interinstitutional co-operation is key to any sound interplay of competing MEAs: it either complements the harmonising treaty interpretation reached by the parties concerned and reinforces its positive effects, or it substitutes the latter in case of its failure.[41]

Further Reading

AO Adede, 'Towards New Approaches to Treaty-Making in the Field of Environment' (1993) 1 *African Yearbook of International Law* 81–121.

[38] In this sense CM Pontecorvo, 'Interdependence between Global Environmental Regimes: The Kyoto Protocol on Climate Change and Forest Protection' (1999) 59 ZaöRV 709, 742.

[39] *Cf* Wolfrum and Matz, above n 35, 133 *et seq*, particularly 146 *et seq*.

[40] See Chapter 20.3.

[41] *Cf* Wolfrum and Matz, above n 35, 159 *et seq*, and Pontecorvo, above n 38, 745 *et seq*.

M Betsill, 'Environmental NGOs Meet the Sovereign State: The Kyoto Protocol Negotiations on Global Climate Change' (2002) 13 *Colorado Journal of International Environmental Law and Policy* 49–64.

U Beyerlin, 'Bridging the North–South Divide in International Environmental Law' (2006) 66 *Heidelberg Journal of International Law (ZaöRV)* 259–296.

R Blair, 'Addressing North–South Power Asymmetry in International Environmental Negotiations' in K Gallagher *et al* (eds), *Reforming the International Environmental Treaty-Making System* (Cambridge 2001) 207–238.

PS Chasek, 'Margins of Power: Coalition Building and Coalition Maintenance of the South Pacific Island States and the Alliance of Small Island States' (2005) 14 *RECIEL* 125–137.

RR Churchill and G Ulfstein, 'Autonomous Institutional Arrangements in Multilateral Environmental Agreements: A Little-Noticed Phenomenon in International Law' (2000) 94 *AJIL* 623–659.

T Gehring, 'Treaty-Making and Treaty Evolution' in D Bodansky *et al* (eds), *The Oxford Handbook of International Environmental Law* (Oxford 2007) 467–497.

G Handl, 'International "Lawmaking" by Conferences of the Parties and Other Politically Mandated Bodies' in R Wolfrum and V Röben (eds), *Developments of International Law in Treaty Making* (Berlin *et al* 2005) 127–143.

G Loibl, 'The Role of International Organisations in International Law-Making—An Empirical Study' (2001) 1 *Non-State Actors and International Law* 41–66.

N Matz, *Wege zur Koordinierung völkerrechtlicher Verträge* (Berlin *et al* 2005).

G Palmer, 'New Ways to Make International Environmental Law' (1992) 86 *AJIL* 259–283.

CM Pontecorvo, 'Interdependence between Global Environmental Regimes: The Kyoto Protocol on Climate Change and Forest Protection' (1999) 59 *Heidelberg Journal of International Law (ZaöRV)* 709–748.

C Redgwell, 'Multilateral Environmental Treaty-Making' in V Gowlland-Debbas (ed), *Multilateral Treaty-Making* (The Hague *et al* 2000) 89–107.

V Röben, 'Institutional Developments under Modern International Environmental Agreements' (2000) 4 *Max Planck Yearbook of United Nations Law* 363–443.

G Sjöstedt (ed), *International Environmental Negotiation* (Newbury Park *et al* 1993).

R Wolfrum and N Matz, *Conflicts in International Environmental Law* (Berlin *et al* 2003).

19

Customary International Environmental Law; Environmental *Jus Cogens* and Obligations *Erga Omnes*

19.1 Customary International Law in General

19.1.1 Meaning and Function of Customary International Law

Customary international law (CIL), one of three sources of international law recognised in Article 38(1) of the Statute of the ICJ, is defined in *lit* b of this provision as 'international custom, as evidence of a general practice accepted as law'. Together with the source of 'general principles of law recognized by civilized nations' (*ibid*, *lit* c), CIL constitutes what is often referred to in legal doctrine as 'general international law'. Compared to CIL, the 'general principles of law', understood as principles which are uniformly applied in all or most municipal legal systems,[1] have gained little weight in international state practice as yet. This is why in the following our discussion will concentrate on CIL.

Broadly speaking, the significance of CIL rules decreases in practice the denser the network of international treaties becomes. Yet this does not mean that new international treaty law necessarily supplants existing CIL. Rather, international treaties and CIL rules, which have always been the supporting pillars of the international legal order, can exist side by side. However, as they often regulate the same issues, they run the risk of coming into conflict. This risk is attenuated by the fact that the regulatory effects of a CIL rule and a treaty norm differ considerably. While CIL rules are necessarily rather abstract, treaty norms are usually much more precise and detailed, provided that the parties to the

[1] A minority of scholars takes the position that 'general principles' also include 'principles recognized by international law itself', see *eg* PW Birnie, AE Boyle and C Redgwell, *International Law and the Environment* (3rd edn Oxford 2009) 26 *et seq*.

treaty are politically willing to solve the respective problem. Accordingly, treaties and custom tend to complement rather than conflict with each other.

Therefore, CIL rules primarily have the function of filling lacunae which often arise in situations where a certain question has been left unsolved by the treaty regulation concerned or in the relationship between states which are partly bound, partly not bound by a certain treaty. In the latter case, CIL has the function of catching non-contracting 'outsiders'.

19.1.2 Formation of Customary International Law

As indicated in Article 38(1) of the ICJ Statute, a CIL rule at the universal or regional level is constituted by a combination of two elements, namely 'a general practice' of states (objective element) and what is usually designated as *opinio iuris* (*sive necessitatis*) of states (subjective element). With regard to both elements there are still several uncertainties. As far as the objective element is concerned, it appears to be widely accepted in doctrine that state practice must be widespread and repetitive, but there is little consensus as to which and how many states must take part in that practice for it to be considered 'general'. There is also ongoing disagreement on how long a particular practice must have been established. In this respect, the judgment of the ICJ in the *North Sea Continental Shelf* cases (1969) may help to find a solution when it concludes:

> Although the passage of only a short period of time is not necessarily, or of itself, a bar to the formation of a new rule of customary international law . . ., an indispensable requirement would be that within the period in question, short though it might be, State practice, including that of States whose interests are specifically affected, should have been both extensive and virtually uniform.[2]

As to the question of what kind of state acts are capable of constituting 'general practice', the scope of such acts should be determined rather broadly. It should range from authoritative governmental statements made in the domestic sphere and declarations issued in the international arena, to national legislative acts and court decisions, to the various forms of state conduct or actions in international organisations and other international bodies.

There is common understanding that individual 'persistent objectors' cannot prevent the establishment of a particular CIL rule; they can only avoid being bound by this rule.

International treaties can be evidence of CIL provided that a particular environmental problem has been uniformly regulated in a number of treaties. However, here again there is uncertainty as to the quantity of individual treaties, the number of states involved in them, and the duration of such uniform treaty practice to be required. It is again the ICJ, in its judgment in the *North Sea Continental Shelf* cases, which offers valuable guidance for decision-making by stating that

[2] *North Sea Continental Shelf* (*Federal Republic of Germany/Denmark; Federal Republic of Germany/ Netherlands)* (1969) ICJ Reports 3, 43.

> it might be that, even without the passage of any considerable period of time, a very widespread and representative participation in the convention might suffice of itself, provided it included states whose interests were specifically affected.[3]

State practice alone does not suffice as evidence of a newly existing rule of CIL. It must rather be accompanied by the psychological element of *opinio iuris* (*sive necessitatis*), namely the states' conviction that the form of conduct followed and the respective actions taken by them are required by international law. There must be evidence 'that a state has acted in a particular way because it believes that it is required to do so by law'.[4] It is debatable whether state practice and *opinio iuris* must always and necessarily be separate, or whether *opinio iuris* can be implied in state practice. It appears that the better arguments speak in favour of answering this question in the latter sense, if the ICJ, once again in its judgment in the *North Sea Continental Shelf* cases, was right in concluding that practice must be such

> as to be the evidence of a belief that this practice is rendered obligatory by the existence of a rule of law requiring it. . . . The States concerned must therefore feel that they are conforming to what amounts to a legal obligation.[5]

International state practice shows that CIL can be generated in four different ways: (i) in exceptional cases it originates from former 'comity' or 'courtoisie'; (ii) it emanates from a (more or less) uniform international treaty practice; (iii) it emerges from a non-legal source in the way that 'soft law' turns to 'hard law';[6] and (iv) it can accrue from 'general principles of law'. Whether these different forms of CIL generation, together with the ongoing controversy on the concept of 'instant customary law', are of particular relevance in international environmental law shall be discussed in the following.

19.2 Customary International Environmental Law

In the view of Dupuy, the process of customary law-making in the field of international environmental protection 'is analogous to the process in general international law'. A closer look at relevant international practice reveals that Dupuy is right to speak of the 'banality of the customary law-making process'[7] in this particular branch of international law.

19.2.1 The Dynamics of Customary International Environmental Law

Like the other branches of international law which are influenced by and respond to

[3] *Ibid*, 42.

[4] P Sands, *Principles of International Environmental Law* (2nd edn Cambridge 2003) 146, referring to the Judgment of the ICJ in the *North Sea Continental Shelf* cases, above n 2, 44.

[5] *North Sea Continental Shelf* cases, above n 2, 41. *Cf* A Orakhelashvili, 'Natural Law and Customary Law' (2008) 68 *ZaöRV* 69, 89.

[6] *Cf* below Chapter 20.

[7] PM Dupuy, 'Formation of Customary International Law and General Principles' in D Bodansky *et al* (eds), *The Oxford Handbook of International Environmental Law* (Oxford 2007) 449, 454.

rapid technical and technological progress, such as the law of interstate communication or economic and trade law, international environmental law develops quite dynamically. This is why the requirements concerning the duration of the 'general practice' of states in international environmental law are possibly less strict than those in other fields of international law. However, this does not amount to an acceptance in international environmental law of 'instant customary law'.

It was in the middle of the twentieth century that Roberto Ago and Bin Cheng first advocated the concept of 'instant customary law' ('diritto spontaneo').[8] They claimed that CIL can spontaneously emerge solely on the basis of the *opinio iuris* of states, as expressed for instance in their approval of legally non-binding acts of an international organisation, such as UN General Assembly resolutions, without the need of showing that these resolutions were confirmed by states' subsequent 'general practice'. Even today controversy exists as to whether the concept of 'instant customary law' conforms to the requirements of international law-making. This question is of considerable concern for international environmental law, because a number of declarations adopted at universal state conferences, such as the ground-breaking declarations of Stockholm (1972) and Rio (1992), have exercised considerable influence on the further development of international environmental law. However, there are serious doubts whether the mere fact of a state's consent to a legally non-binding recommendation of an international organisation can be taken as evidence of *opinio iuris*, because this particular state might have refrained from consenting to this resolution if it were known for its capability to produce legal effects. Therefore, any attempts to conclude from the 'soft law' documents issued at the Rio Conference in 1992 that concepts such as intergenerational responsibility, sustainable development and precautionary action have become customary international environmental law (CIEL) shortly after the closure of this conference[9] do not convince.

As indicated above, rules of CIEL can emanate from various sources, including 'general principles of law', 'soft law' and international treaties.

One of the rare examples of 'general principles of law' which subsequently grew into CIEL rules is *sic utere tuo ut alienum non laedas*. This principle common to all or most national legal systems developed, via the *Trail Smelter* arbitration (1941) and the Declarations of Stockholm (1972) and Rio (1992), to what today is understood to be a universally recognised rule of CIL, namely the obligation of states not to cause transboundary environmental harm.[10] This is testimony for the process of silent conversion of one source of international law into another one.

An example of a CIEL rule which originates from two concurrent sources, namely 'soft law' and international treaties, is the obligation of states bordering an international watercourse to use this shared natural resource in an equitable manner. It can be traced back to the legally non-binding 1978 UNEP Draft Principles of Conduct in the Field of

[8] R Ago, 'Science juridique et droit international' (1956-II) 90 *Recueil des cours* 849 *et seq*; B Cheng, 'United Nations Resolutions on Outer Space: "Instant" International Customary Law?' (1965) 5 *Indian Journal of International Law* 23 *et seq*.

[9] See *eg* H Hohmann, 'Ergebnisse des Erdgipfels von Rio—Weiterentwicklung des Umweltvölkerrechts durch die UN-Umweltkonferenz von 1992' (1993) 12 *Neue Zeitschrift für Verwaltungsrecht* 311, 318.

[10] *Cf* Dupuy, above n 7, 461. Compare Chapter 6.

the Environment for the Guidance of States in the Conservation and Harmonious Utilization of Natural Resources Shared by Two or More States,[11] as well as to several bilateral and multilateral international treaties on the use of shared international watercourses, especially the two multilateral watercourses conventions of 1992 and 1997.[12]

'Precautionary action' is perhaps one of the very few examples of CIEL generation flowing from 'soft law'. Expressly articulated for the first time in the mid-1980s, 'precautionary action' was enshrined in the 1992 Rio Declaration as Principle 15 and has since arguably grown to a principle or rule of CIEL.[13]

19.2.2 Examples of Existing or Emerging Rules of Customary International Environmental Law

Brownlie's early statement in 1973 that custom 'provides limited means of social engineering' in international environmental law[14] is still valid in modern international environmental law. The rules of CIL almost always show such a degree of abstractness and indefiniteness that their capacity to exert a steering effect on states' behaviour is limited. Consequently, there is little hope that lacunae left in an international environmental treaty will be sufficiently filled by subsequent rules of CIEL. This is why the contracting parties should feel compelled to provide for the best possible clarity and precision of all treaty norms from the outset. CIEL will hardly ever be capable of repairing what has gone wrong in a treaty. It is rather predestined to substitute deficient interstate environmental treaty relations. However, in this respect CIEL hardly differs from CIL in other fields of international law.

As any attempt to take reliable stock of all existing or emerging rules of CIEL must fail, it may suffice here to point to the few examples of those rules whose customary legal status appears to be widely accepted in legal doctrine. Among existing CIEL rules are, for instance

- the duty of a state not to allow or tolerate any activity within its jurisdiction that may cause damage to the environment of other states or of areas beyond its national jurisdiction, unless the transboundary environmental impacts of this activity prove to be insignificant;[15]
- the obligation of a state not to allow activities within its jurisdiction which might

[11] Text in (1978) 17 ILM 1097.

[12] Convention on the Protection and Use of Transboundary Watercourses and International Lakes of 17 March 1992 and United Nations Convention on the Law of the Non-Navigational Uses of International Watercourses of 21 May 1997.

[13] For a more detailed discussion see Chapter 7 and Section 19.2.2. Considerably bigger is the number of international environmental treaties tracing back to 'soft law' instruments. For instance, the 1989 Hague Declaration on the Environment ((1989) 28 ILM 1308), which called for the protection of the atmosphere against global warming, can be seen as the catalyst for the 1992 UNFCCC and the thereto related 1997 Kyoto Protocol. *Cf* Chapter 13.4.2.

[14] I Brownlie, 'A Survey of International Customary Rules of Environmental Protection' (1973) 13 *Natural Resources Journal* 179, 180.

[15] See Chapter 6.

prove to be environmentally harmful until an environmental impact assessment has been undertaken that shows that the activity in question is unobjectionable;[16] and
- the obligation of a state to give all neighbouring states prior notice of any activities planned on its territory that might affect the environment beyond its jurisdiction, and to give early warnings to them in case of an ecological disaster.[17]

Other concepts appear to have the potential to become CIEL rules, but are not yet beyond all reasonable doubt as to whether they have already reached this status. Among them is the concept of 'precautionary action'. As defined in Principle 15 of the legally non-binding Rio Declaration of 1992, such action is designed to command early international action to address environmental threats in cases where there is ongoing scientific uncertainty with regard to the causes of these threats. Thus, 'precautionary action' certainly meets the normative requirements of a rule, albeit one with uncertain contours. The bigger the number of MEAs which integrate this concept into their operative norms, the better are the reasons to argue that it has become part of CIEL. Emerging CIEL rules contrast with concepts such as 'sustainable development' in so far as the latter already lacks the normative quality that is an indispensable prerequisite for ascribing to it the quality of a CIEL rule.[18]

19.3 Environmental *Jus Cogens* and Obligations *Erga Omnes*

While traditionally there was no hierarchy of norms in international law, today the existence of a small layer of 'peremptory norms of international law', commonly known as *jus cogens*, at the top of the international legal system is recognised by state practice, codified in treaty law and confirmed by doctrine.[19] These norms, which are said to reflect fundamental values accepted by the international community of states as a whole, deserve absolute respect in the sense that they cannot be abrogated by lower-ranking norms in international treaties or CIL (the so-called *jus dispositivum*). Article 53 VCLT makes plain that a treaty which 'conflicts with a peremptory norm of general international law' is 'void', but gives no examples of *jus cogens*. Accordingly, individual norms of *jus cogens* are hard to ascertain.

While there is ongoing controversy in doctrine on many norms suggested as candidates for *jus cogens*, it appears to be widely accepted to classify a few fundamental norms, such as those prohibiting the use of force, slavery, piracy, genocide, torture, as well as the right of people to self-determination and basic human rights, as peremptory norms. As

[16] See Chapter 16.

[17] The question of whether in such a case neighbouring states are bound by CIEL to enter into consultations with each other has not yet been settled; see *eg* VP Nanda and G Pring, *International Environmental Law & Policy for the 21st Century* (Ardsley 2003) 11.

[18] See for a more thorough discussion of such type of concepts Part II of this book. Compare also U Beyerlin, 'Different Types of Norms in International Environmental Law. Policies, Principles, and Rules' in Bodansky *et al* (eds), above n 7, 425, 438 *et seq*.

[19] See in place of many other scholars JA Frowein, 'Jus Cogens' in R Wolfrum (ed), *Max Planck Encyclopedia of Public International Law* (Heidelberg/Oxford 2009), para 5, available at www.mpepil.com.

evidence for this assumption the *obiter dictum* in the judgment of the ICJ in the *Barcelona Traction* case of 1970[20] and Article 19 of the 'Draft Articles on State Responsibility' of the International Law Commission (ILC) as originally adopted in 1980 are mostly referred to.[21] Draft Article 19 introduced the notion of 'international crime' which is seen as a violation of *jus cogens*.[22] This Article, in its paragraph 3, gives some examples of 'international crimes' to which other states may respond by recourse to reprisals; it refers, *inter alia*, to 'a serious breach of an international obligation of essential importance for the safeguarding and preservation of the human environment, such as those prohibiting massive pollution of the atmosphere or of the seas' (Article 19(3)(d)). What militates against taking this clause as evidence for the existence of *jus cogens* in current international environmental law is scepticism as to whether *jus cogens* is the appropriate concept to get a grip on environmental pollution, which normally remains, in terms of quality, clearly behind the other offences enumerated in Article 19(3) (aggression, colonial domination, slavery, genocide and apartheid). The fact that the entire Article 19 with its distinction between 'international delicts' and 'international crimes' was dropped when the ILC adopted its 'Draft Articles on the Responsibility of States for Internationally Wrongful Acts'[23] in the third and final reading in August 2001 confirms these doubts.[24] Article 40 of the ILC's Final Draft confines itself to defining a separate category of 'serious breaches of obligations under peremptory norms of general international law'. However, the possible consequences of such a serious breach are rather limited (Draft Article 41). The commentary on Article 40 suggests that the prohibition of aggression, colonial domination, slavery, genocide and apartheid can be allocated to the category of peremptory norms. Tellingly, it makes no mention of a 'serious breach' of obligations arising under international environmental law.

A concept which comes close to that of *jus cogens* is 'obligations *erga omnes*'. According to the ICJ's *obiter dictum* in the *Barcelona Traction* judgment, this concept recognises the existence of 'obligations of a State towards the international community as a whole' which are 'the concern of all States' and in whose protection all states could be held to have a 'legal interest'.[25] Thus, the norms producing obligations *erga omnes* are about the same as those which fall under the category of *jus cogens*. Albeit closely intertwined, both types of norms are not identical with each other. While in most cases violations of *jus cogens* are also violations of obligations *erga omnes*,[26] this proves not

[20] Case concerning *The Barcelona Traction, Light and Power Company, Limited (New Application: 1962) (Belgium v Spain) Second Phase* (1970) ICJ Reports 3.

[21] ILC, 'Report of the International Law Commission on the Work of its 32nd Session' (5 May–25 July 1980) UN Doc A/35/10, 32.

[22] *Cf* again Frowein, above n 19, para 6.

[23] ILC, 'Report of the International Law Commission on the Work of its 53rd Session' (23 April–1 June and 2 July–10 August 2001) UN Doc A/56/10, 43.

[24] EM Kornicker, 'State Community Interests, *Jus Cogens* and Protection of the Global Environment: Developing Criteria for Peremptory Norms' (1998) 11 *Georgetown International Environmental Law Review* 101, has thoroughly discussed three '*jus cogens* candidates', namely 'the prohibition of willful serious damage to the environment during armed conflicts', 'the general prohibition of causing or not preventing environmental damage that threatens the international community as a whole', and 'the human right to a sound environment'. However, her conclusions are far from compelling.

[25] *Barcelona Traction* case, above n 20, 32.

[26] *Cf eg* Frowein, above n 19, para 10.

always true vice versa. The acknowledgement that the international legal system includes a layer of norms which are 'the concern of all states', namely norms which constitute obligations *erga omnes*, in essence corresponds to what is typical of all norms of international environmental law whose fulfilment is in the interest of the state community. Examples of such a type of norms are particularly those which are aimed at protecting certain global environmental goods, such as atmosphere, climate and biological diversity. This is why Article 48 of the ILC's Draft Articles on State Responsibility of 2001 provides that whenever the obligation breached 'is owed to the international community as a whole' not only the injured state, but also any other state is entitled to invoke the responsibility of the infringer state.[27]

Further Reading

U Beyerlin, 'Different Types of Norms in International Environmental Law. Policies, Principles, and Rules' in D Bodansky *et al* (eds), *The Oxford Handbook of International Environmental Law* (Oxford 2007) 425–448.

D Bodansky, 'Customary (and Not So Customary) International Environmental Law' (1995) 3 *Indiana Journal of Global Legal Studies* 105–119.

I Brownlie, 'A Survey of International Customary Rules of Environmental Protection' (1973) 13 *Natural Resources Journal* 179–189.

B Cheng, 'United Nations Resolutions on Outer Space: "Instant" International Customary Law?' (1965) 5 *Indian Journal of International Law* 23–48.

GM Danilenko, *Law-Making in the International Community* (Dordrecht *et al* 1993).

PM Dupuy, 'Formation of Customary International Law and General Principles' in D Bodansky *et al* (eds), *The Oxford Handbook of International Environmental Law* (Oxford 2007) 449–466.

JA Frowein, 'Jus Cogens' in R Wolfrum (ed), *Max Planck Encyclopedia of Public International Law* (Heidelberg/Oxford 2009), available at www.mpepil.com.

L Hannikainen, *Peremptory Norms (Jus Cogens) in International Law. Historical Development, Criteria, Present Status* (Helsinki 1988).

C Hinds, 'Das Prinzip "Sic utere tuo ut alienum non laedas" und seine Bedeutung im internationalen Umweltrecht' (1992) 30 *Archiv des Völkerrechts* 298–325.

S Kadelbach, '*Jus Cogens*, Obligations *Erga Omnes* and Other Rules—The Identification of Fundamental Norms' in C Tomuschat and JM Thouvenin (eds), *The Fundamental Rules of the International Legal Order* (Leiden 2006) 21–40.

EM Kornicker, 'State Community Interests, *Jus Cogens* and Protection of the Global Environment: Developing Criteria for Peremptory Norms' (1998) 11 *Georgetown International Environmental Law Review* 101–135.

O McIntyre, 'The Role of Customary Rules and Principles of International Environmental Law in the Protection of Shared International Freshwater Resources' (2006) 46 *Natural Resources Journal* 157–210.

M Mendelson, 'The Formation of Customary International Law' (1998) 272 *Recueil des cours* 155–410.

A Orakhelashvili, 'Natural Law and Customary Law' (2008) 68 *Heidelberg Journal of International Law (ZaöRV)* 69–110.

[27] We will return to this particular aspect of state responsibility in Chapter 24.2.

20

International Environmental 'Soft Law'

20.1 Theoretical Premises

International law is characterised by close interaction between the sources of law listed in Article 38 of the ICJ Statute, namely international treaties, international custom and general principles of law.[1] The first two sources are the main pillars of the international legal system. Although mostly composed of co-equal norms, this system shows some elements of hierarchy. While at its top there are rather few peremptory norms (*jus cogens*) and obligations *erga omnes*, which are of a higher legal quality than the mass of ordinary norms, at its bottom there is an ever-growing number of norms with dubious normative quality and ambiguous (legal or non-legal) status.

In current international environmental relations, this grey area of norms with amorphous contents, blurred contours and unclear provenance is particularly broad and diffuse. While some of these 'twilight' norms ultimately prove to be part of international environmental law, others are not able to pass the threshold of becoming law. Norms of the latter sort fall in the category of what is mostly named 'soft law'. This term is unfortunate, if not to say misleading, because it suggests that there is a layer of law of lesser quality than 'hard law'. Essentially, 'soft law' proves to be non-legal in character rather than of an inferior legal quality. Even so, internationally the term 'soft law' has been in common usage for a long time; it will therefore also be used here.

What are the criteria for distinguishing 'soft law' from 'hard law' in international relations? Are there any characteristics which 'hard law' necessarily exhibits and 'soft law' does not?

The subject matter of an interstate accord hardly provides a reliable criterion for differentiating between 'hard law' and 'soft law'. States which are willing to deal with each other usually have the free choice between concluding an international treaty and entering

[1] The list of sources of international law in Art 38 of the ICJ Statute is not exhaustive in the sense that it precludes possible new sources of international law from emerging. Thus, there is no *numerus clausus* of sources due to which 'soft law' could be forever prevented from becoming part of international law.

into a non-legal arrangement. However, there are specific situations where the states concerned typically make a non-legal arrangement rather than an international treaty. For instance, states which feel urged to address a certain problem as quickly as possible naturally prefer a legally non-binding arrangement to a legally binding agreement because the latter is much slower to negotiate and often faces difficulties in overcoming the hurdles of national parliamentary approval or other domestic processes. Moreover, the 'soft law' approach allows states to take action at a time when they do not (yet) want to enter into a legally binding commitment. Finally, states which are willing to reach a transitory solution to a given problem normally decide to establish a mere 'soft law' instrument that might be easily withdrawn if needed.

'Hard law' and 'soft law' instruments can, with respect to their possible functions, complement each other in shaping interstate (environmental) relations. It may occur that interstate 'hard law' differs from interstate 'soft law' in functional terms, but this is not necessarily so. Thus, the function which an accord is destined to fulfil does not reliably indicate its nature.

What 'hard law' and 'soft law' have in common is their normative quality, understood as the capacity to steer directly or indirectly the conduct of their addressees. While it is beyond doubt that this specific quality is typical of legally binding international rules, it is also a criterion 'soft law' must meet. It is exactly its normativity that makes 'soft law' distinguishable from mere political or moral ideals.

After all, both 'hard law' and 'soft law' norms bring about binding effects in the sense that their addressees are bound to behave or act in the way prescribed. However, what separates both types of norms is the nature of their binding effect. While 'hard law' is legally binding in character, with the consequence that non-compliance with its norms provokes legal responses, 'soft law' gains its strength from an international political-moral order.[2] Consequently, reactions to breaches of 'soft law' norms are political rather than legal in nature; however, compliance with 'soft law' obligations might be subject to some sort of international supervision.

Due to its non-legal nature, 'soft law' is part of an international order based on political-moral values which is a categorically differing counterpart to the international legal order. Both normative systems are on a par. They complement one another. What separates international 'soft law' from international 'hard law' is their divergent grounds of validity (*Geltungsgrund*).

'Soft law' instruments differ significantly among each other in respect of provenance, form and function. International practice evidences that it is not only states that make use of 'soft law' instruments as tools for protecting the environment; international organisations and other international institutions do so too. Several international organisations are

[2] For a similar view see AE Boyle, 'Some Reflections on the Relationship of Treaties and Soft Law' (1999) 48 *ICLQ* 901; *id,* 'Soft Law in International Law-Making' in MD Evans (ed), *International Law* (Oxford 2006) 141, 142 *et seq*. This understanding of 'soft law' is in sharp contrast to the view of J Klabbers, 'The Redundancy of Soft Law' (1996) 65 *Nordic Journal of International Law* 167–182, according to which 'soft law does not include political or moral commitments; these are . . . commitments of a political or moral nature, and are thus on their own terms . . . not legal at all. And if they are not legal at all, it follows that they cannot be softly legal either' (*ibid*, 168).

actively involved in tackling a broad spectrum of mostly global environmental problems, especially in the way that their plenary organs adopt a large number of resolutions and declarations on environmental matters. These documents are altogether legally non-binding in character. There is also a growing practice of international arrangements made between the treaty bodies belonging to different MEAs. For instance, the COPs and secretariats to various treaties make non-legal arrangements (so-called Memoranda of Understanding) with the aim of co-ordinating their individual efforts or even undertaking joint actions.

In the following, non-legal interstate arrangements, non-legal interinstitutional arrangements, and recommendations of international organisations will be discussed in more detail.

20.2 Legally Non-Binding Agreements between States

States have long been prepared to make non-legal arrangements whenever they felt urged to reach understanding between them as quickly as possible without entering into a legal commitment. In former times, such interstate arrangements were designated as 'gentlemen's agreements'. They were mostly concluded between statesmen or diplomats.[3] As the personal element in international relations over time considerably lost importance, the notion of the 'gentlemen's agreement' has eventually become outdated. It has been replaced by the more objective notion of 'legally non-binding agreement'.

It is exactly this subtype of 'soft law' that has gained particular importance in today's international environmental practice. According to the varying functions they can fulfil, legally non-binding agreements between states can be subdivided into (i) political action programmes; (ii) political declarations on existing or emerging environmental principles and rules; (iii) codes of conduct replacing international legally binding rules; and (iv) accords on provisional treaty implementation. All four subtypes deserve greater attention.

(i) Typically, political environmental action programmes are adopted by states convened to international conferences on international environmental and developmental matters, such as those of Stockholm, Rio and Johannesburg.[4] The Action Plan for the Human Environment, adopted by the Stockholm Conference in 1972, as well as Agenda 21, adopted by the Rio Conference in 1992, and the Plan of Implementation, adopted by the Johannesburg Summit in 2002, are the most prominent examples of relevant action programmes. Each of them constitutes a bundle of recommendations which are together destined to induce the diverse actors operating in international environmental relations to behave in a certain way or to take certain actions. In this respect, Agenda 21, with its broad catalogue of targets, instructions and guidelines, has deployed and continues to deploy considerable normative force, although it is merely political in character.

[3] See W Fiedler, 'Gentlemen's Agreement' in R Bernhardt (ed), *Encyclopedia of Public International Law*, vol II (Amsterdam *et al* 1995) 546 *et seq*.

[4] For details see above Chapters 2.1, 3.2, and 4.2.1.

Moreover, Agenda 21 has been, and in many respects still is, an important catalyst for initiating subsequent international treaty-making and/or the formation of CIEL.

(ii) Prime examples of political declarations bearing witness to existing or emerging environmental principles and rules are the 1972 Stockholm Declaration and the 1992 Rio Declaration. They both contain an impressive corpus of existing or emerging norms of CIEL. Notwithstanding their non-legal character, they can claim remarkable authority in current international environmental law. A minority of scholars even considers these declarations to be authoritative indicators for the *opinio juris* of states as the subjective element of CIEL formation.[5] However, this view ignores the fact that the states convened to the conferences of Stockholm and Rio consciously renounced to make the said principles part of legally binding instruments. Moreover, at the time when the Stockholm and Rio Declarations were adopted, only some of the principles listed in these documents clearly formed part of the then existing norms of CIEL, while many others could at best be expected to gain that status in future. Thus, even if these principles were indicators for the evolution of CIEL, they could hardly be lumped together.

(iii) Non-legal codes of conduct in international environmental relations are destined to produce steering effects on states' behaviour. Most of them remain silent as to whether they are destined to substitute relevant legally binding rules only transitionally or for an indefinite time. Such codes of 'soft law' type can be distinguished from each other particularly according to their authorship. Some of them have been adopted by states assembled at important international conferences, while others originate from international organisations, such as the FAO and the IAEA, or international institutions lacking international legal personality of their own, such as UNEP. Examples of this subtype of 'soft law' are the 1985 FAO International Code of Conduct on the Distribution and Use of Pesticides, as revised in 2002;[6] the 1987 UNEP London Guidelines for the Exchange of Information on Chemicals in International Trade;[7] the 1990 IAEA Code of Practice on the International Transboundary Movement of Radioactive Waste;[8] the 1992 Non-Legally Binding Authoritative Statement of Principles for a Global Consensus on the Management, Conservation and Sustainable Development of All Types of Forests adopted by the Rio Conference;[9] the 1995 FAO Code of Conduct for Responsible Fisheries;[10] and the

[5] *Cf* Chapter 19.1.2.

[6] FAO (Res 1/123, adopted by the 123rd Session of the Governing Council) 'International Code of Conduct on the Distribution and Use of Pesticides (Revised Version)' (28 October–1 November 2002) available at ftp://ftp.fao.org/docrep/fao/009/a0220e/a0220e00.pdf.

[7] UNEP GC Dec 14/27 on 'Environmentally safe management of chemicals, in particular those that are banned and severely restricted in international trade' (17 June 1987). Together with the FAO Code of Conduct, the UNEP Guidelines ultimately led to the 1998 Convention on Prior Informed Consent Procedure for Certain Hazardous Chemicals and Pesticides in International Trade.

[8] IAEA (General Conference Res GC [XXXIV]/RES/530) 'Code of Practice on the International Transboundary Movement of Radioactive Waste' (21 September 1990), Doc INFCIRC/386 (13 November 1990). The Code of Conduct can be accessed at www.iaea.org/Publications/Documents/Infcircs/Others/inf386.shtml.

[9] Based on these 'Principles on Forests', the UN General Assembly adopted the 'Non-legally binding instrument on all types of forests'; see UNGA Res 62/98 (17 December 2007).

[10] FAO (Res 4/95, adopted by the 28th Session of the Conference) 'The Code of Conduct for Responsible Fisheries' (31 October 1995).

2002 Bonn Guidelines on Access to Genetic Resources and Fair and Equitable Sharing of Benefits Arising out of their Utilization.[11]

As clearly evidenced in international environmental and developmental practice, non-legal codes of states' conduct often function as catalysts for relevant international treaty-making.[12] Testimonies of this role 'soft law' can play are the following examples: the 1983 FAO International Undertaking on Plant Genetic Resources[13] was transformed into the 2001 Treaty on Plant Genetic Resources for Food and Agriculture;[14] the 1985 IAEA Guidelines on Reportable Events, Integrated Planning and Information Exchange in a Transboundary Release of Radioactive Materials[15] formed the basis for the rapid adoption of the 1986 IAEA Convention on Early Notification of Nuclear Accidents;[16] the 1985 UNEP Montreal Guidelines for the Protection of the Marine Environment against Pollution from Land-Based Activities[17] served as a model for regional agreements on the subject, *eg* the 1990 Kuwait Protocol for the Protection of the Marine Environment against Marine Pollution from Land-Based Sources;[18] and the 1987 UNEP Goals and Principles of Environmental Impact Assessment[19] found their way into the 1991 UNECE Espoo Convention on Environmental Impact Assessment in a Transboundary Context.

(iv) States can also resort to non-legal accords as a means directed towards further developing or implementing MEAs. Such accords can, at least on a transitional basis, substitute legally binding forms of treaty amendment and implementation, respectively. An example of this particular type of 'soft law' is the 1985 Resolution of the Consultative Meeting of the 1972 London Dumping Convention which imposed a provisional moratorium on radioactive waste dumping at sea.[20]

As practice has shown, such non-legal accords hold some potential for further developing MEAs in a simplified way. In 1990, the Second MOP to the Montreal Protocol, in its Decision II/8, established the Multilateral Fund as an interim financial mechanism with effect as of 1 January 1991. In 1993, this fund was put on a permanent footing.[21] In 1994, the Second COP to the 1989 Basel Convention approved in its Decision II/12 the

[11] The Bonn Guidelines were adopted by the 6th Meeting of the COP to the CBD, *cf* Decision VI/24 in UNEP/CBD/COP/6/20 (7–19 April 2002) 262.

[12] Regarding the relationship of 'soft law' to international treaties compare generally *eg* Boyle (2006), above n 2, 145 *et seq*; TA Mensah, 'Soft Law: A Fresh Look at an Old Mechanism' (2008) 38 *Environmental Policy and Law* 50, 51 *et seq*.

[13] FAO (Res 8/83, adopted by the 22nd Session of the Conference) (23 November 1983).

[14] The text of the International Treaty on Plant Genetic Resources for Food and Agriculture can be found at ftp://ftp.fao.org/ag/cgrfa/it/ITPGRe.pdf.

[15] IAEA Doc INFCIRC/321 (January 1985).

[16] See P Sands, *Principles of International Environmental Law* (2nd edn Cambridge 2003) 647, note 213.

[17] UNEP GC Dec 13/18 on 'Environmental Law' (24 May 1985).

[18] See Mensah, above n 13, 51 and Boyle (2006), above n 2, 146.

[19] UNEP GC Dec 14/25 on 'Environmental Impact Assessment' (17 June 1987).

[20] Resolution LDC 21(9) of the 9th Consultative Meeting of the States Parties to the London Convention. This resolution was strictly speaking not legally binding. The moratorium was later formally incorporated into the Convention by means of a (legally binding) amendment to the London Convention (Resolution LDC 51(16) of the 16th Consultative Meeting of the States Parties to the London Convention). *Cf* Mensah, above n 13, 53.

[21] Decision IV/18 of the 4th MOP to the Montreal Protocol in UNEP/OzLPro4/15 (25 November 1992) 18.

so-called 'Basel Ban'; one year later this ban has been adopted by the Third COP as a formal amendment to the Convention.[22]

20.3 Interinstitutional Non-Legal Arrangements

With the advent of Memoranda of Understanding (MOUs), a new phenomenon of non-legal interinstitutional arrangements emerged in international environmental relations. One of the main reasons for the growing number of MOUs today is the fact that international institutions willing to co-operate on a consensual basis quite often do not possess the international legal personality which is required for international treaty-making. Consequently, these institutions are forced to resort to non-legal interinstitutional arrangements. However, even in cases where the actors concerned have the free choice between international treaty-making and entering into an MOU, the latter form of arrangement sometimes proves to be more attractive because it is much more flexible than an international treaty, which normally needs to be approved by national parliaments and ratified in a lengthy procedure.

Accordingly, interinstitutional co-operation in the form of MOUs has gained increasing importance in the international processes of MEA implementation. A closer look at these processes shows a very broad and multifaceted use of MOUs. This holds particularly true for the field of protection of biological diversity and nature conservation, areas where the various MEAs are significantly interrelated in substance. For instance, both the secretariats to the 1971 Ramsar Convention on Wetlands of International Importance Especially as Waterfowl Habitat and CITES entered into a multitude of MOUs with the treaty bodies of other MEAs, international (specialised) organisations, and NGOs.[23] The same applies to the Convention on Migratory Species.[24] The objectives which these MOUs are destined to achieve include the avoidance of undue overlaps and discrepancies of the work done individually by the treaty organs of the MEAs concerned, and the undertaking of joint action with the aim of treaty implementation. For instance, the secretariats to the Convention on Biodiversity and the Ramsar Convention repeatedly established Joint Work Plans (JWPs) for better co-ordination of their respective activities.[25] In 2001, the secretariats to the CBD, the Climate Change Convention and the Convention to Combat Desertification agreed to form the Joint Liaison Group (JLG) as an informal forum for exchanging information, facilitating co-operation at the national and international level, and identifying

[22] See for a more detailed discussion Chapter 18.4.1.

[23] For an overview of the MOUs concluded by the Bureau of the Ramsar Convention see www.ramsar.org/index_mou.htm. Concerning the MOUs concluded by the Secretariat of CITES see www.cites.org/eng/disc/sec/index.shtml.

[24] For an overview of the MOUs concluded by the CMS Secretariat see UNEP/CMS/Conf7.11 (21 August 2002), available at www.cms.int/bodies/COP/cop7/list_of_docs/pdf/en/CP7CF7_11_Cooperation_Other_Bodies.pdf.

[25] The first JWP was adopted in May 1998. It has been superseded by the following JWP. The current fourth JWP (2007-2010) was endorsed by the 35th Meeting of the Ramsar Standing Committee (Decision SC35-30). See also www.ramsar.org/index_mou.htm.

possible areas of joint activities. Since 2004 the JLG has been exploring options for enhancing co-ordination.[26] Other examples are the MOUs which the COPs to the CBD and UNFCCC, on the one side, and the Council of the Global Environment Facility (GEF), on the other side, concluded in 1996 in order to give effect to the respective roles and responsibilities of the COPs and GEF and to provide for the required interaction between them under the said conventions.[27] The COPs can be seen as autonomous MEA institutions endowed with international legal personality, including treaty-making power, of their own.[28] In contrast, the GEF still lacks this legal capacity, although it has been restructured by the World Bank, UNDP and UNEP in 1994. This is why the two COPs concerned had no other choice than to enter into an MOU with the GEF Council.

On the other hand, those international institutions which are endowed with international legal personality are certainly free to make their choice between entering into an MOU or concluding an international treaty when they make an arrangement amongst themselves. Once an interinstitutional arrangement has been made, only a closer look at its text can reveal whether the arrangement concerned is legal or non-legal in character. Ultimately, it depends on whether its text reflects the firm and unequivocal will of the parties to be legally bound or not. In this respect, the strictness or softness of the respective obligation clauses is certainly more telling than the mere fact that the arrangement contains clauses on its 'entry into force' and 'termination'.

20.4 Recommendations of International Organisations

It is typical of the plenary organs of international organisations to express their will in form of resolutions or declarations which are non-legal in character and can therefore be classified as a subtype of international 'soft law'.[29] Acts of this kind certainly do not constitute a new source of international law in the sense of Article 38(2) of the ICJ Statute. However, it cannot be denied that recommendations issued by important international organisations can have a significant impact on the further development of international environmental law. This is all the more noteworthy as 'the multiplication of

[26] See UN Doc FCCC/SBSTA/2002/3. For more information, compare www.cbd.int/cooperation/liaison.shtml.

[27] Under both Conventions the GEF is the international entity entrusted with the operation of this mechanism (Art 21(1) and (3) CBD and Art 11(1) and (3) UNFCCC, respectively). For the MOU between the COP of the CBD and the Council of the GEF see UNEP/CBD/COP/3/10 (11 October 1996). For the MOU between the COP of the UNFCCC and the Council of the GEF see FCCC/CP/1996/15/Add1 (19 July 1996).

[28] See RR Churchill and G Ulfstein, 'Autonomous Institutional Arrangements in Multilateral Environmental Agreements: A Little-Noticed Phenomenon in International Law' (2000) 94 *AJIL* 623, 655. However, the status of COPs is still in dispute. For a more thorough discussion see Chapter 17.2.3.

[29] It is only by way of exception that international organisations are empowered to take legally binding decisions. For instance, Arts 21(a) and 22 of the WHO Constitution confer the authority upon the WHO Assembly to adopt legally binding regulations which enter into force for all WHO Member States that do not opt out them within a specified period of time.

inter-governmental organisations has considerably augmented the number and diversity of non-binding texts'.[30]

Among the resolutions on environmental and developmental matters which deserve greater attention are certainly many resolutions and declarations of the UN General Assembly, especially those that have been adopted by consensus or unanimous vote. These resolutions, which are altogether recommendatory in character, can be subdivided into resolutions stipulating broad environmental and developmental policy goals, and 'directive recommendations' containing guidelines which are destined to steer the behaviour of states.[31]

Examples of the first category of resolutions are the World Charter for Nature, annexed to General Assembly Resolution 37/7 of 28 October 1982, and more recently the United Nations Millennium Declaration, adopted in form of Resolution 55/2 of 18 September 2000. Resolutions of this kind have been clearly outnumbered by the UN General Assembly's 'directive resolutions'. Among the latter are broadly worded resolutions, such as those on the protection of the marine environment, the relationship between environment and development, and co-operation on shared natural resources. Others are conceived as instruments for steering the environmental conduct of states more definitely and directly. Prototypical in this respect are Recommendation 44/225 of 1989 by which the General Assembly called for the imposition of moratoria on all large-scale pelagic drift-net fishing on the high seas by the end of 1993,[32] and Recommendation 56/13 of 2001 by which the Assembly supported the precautionary approach to the conservation, management and exploitation of straddling and highly migratory fish stocks.[33] More recently, on 17 December 2007, the UN General Assembly adopted Resolution 62/98, entitled 'Non-Legal Binding Instrument on All Types of Forests',[34] which was negotiated in April 2007 within the UN Forum on Forests and transmitted to the Assembly following its approval by the UN Economic and Social Council.

Akin to political declarations on environmental principles,[35] recommendations of international organisations might have the potential to facilitate the progressive evolution of CIEL. However, even recommendations adopted by consensus or unanimous vote can hardly be taken as evidence for the *opinio juris* of states, unless they have been observed by states in subsequent practice.[36]

Further Reading

JE Alvarez, *International Organizations as Law-makers* (Oxford 2005).

[30] AC Kiss and D Shelton, *International Environmental Law* (3rd edn Ardsley 2004) 91.

[31] Kiss and Shelton, above n 31, distinguish 'directive recommendations' from 'declarations of principles'; see *ibid*, 92 *et seq*. However, most of the texts of the latter type have been adopted by interstate conferences rather than international organisations. This is why declarations such as those of Stockholm and Rio have been dealt with above in Chapter 20.2.

[32] UNGA Res 44/225 (22 December 1989).

[33] UNGA Res 56/13 (28 November 2001).

[34] UNGA Res 62/98 (17 December 2007).

[35] See above Section 20.2.

[36] In this sense also Boyle (2006), above n 2, 153 *et seq*.

U Beyerlin, 'Different Types of Norms in International Environmental Law. Policies, Principles, and Rules' in D Bodansky *et al* (eds), *The Oxford Handbook of International Environmental Law* (Oxford 2007) 425–448.

M Bothe, 'Legal and Non-Legal Norms—A Meaningful Distinction in International Relations?' (1980) 11 *NYIL* 65–95.

AE Boyle, 'Some Reflections on the Relationship of Treaties and Soft Law' (1999) 48 *ICLQ* 901–913.

——, 'Soft Law in International Law-Making' in MD Evans (ed), *International Law* (Oxford 2006) 141–158.

RR Churchill and G Ulfstein, 'Autonomous Institutional Arrangements in Multilateral Environmental Agreements: A Little-Noticed Phenomenon in International Law' (2000) 94 *AJIL* 623–659.

PM Dupuy, 'Soft Law and the International Law of the Environment' (1990–1991) 21 *Michigan Journal of International Law* 420–435.

MA Fitzmaurice, 'International Environmental Law as a Special Field' (1994) 15 *NYIL* 181–226.

H Hillgenberg, 'A Fresh Look at Soft Law' (1999) 10 *EJIL* 499–515.

J Klabbers, 'The Redundancy of Soft Law' (1996) 65 *Nordic Journal of International Law* 167–182.

TA Mensah, 'Soft Law: A Fresh Look at an Old Mechanism' (2008) 38 *Environmental Policy and Law* 50–56.

G Palmer, 'New Ways to Make International Environmental Law' (1992) 86 *AJIL* 259–283.

K Raustiala, 'Form and Substance in International Agreements' (2005) 99 *AJIL* 581–614.

PH Sand, *Lessons Learned in Global Environmental Governance* (New York 1990).

O Schachter, 'The Twilight Existence of Nonbinding International Agreements' (1977) 71 *AJIL* 296–304.

D Shelton (ed), *Commitment and Compliance: The Role of Non-Binding Norms in the International Legal System* (Oxford 2000).

——, 'Normative Hierarchy in International Law' (2006) 100 *AJIL* 291–323.

21

Private Environmental Governance

21.1 Introduction

We will first discuss the contribution of private actors to international environmental law-making, both in the context of treaty-making and with regard to the development of non-treaty norms. Environmental standard-setting will be addressed as an area which, from the perspective of law, is probably the best example of private environmental governance because it means the exercise of private regulatory authority. Private standards may fill in gaps, they may provide the technical foundation for existing rules, and they may be precursors to international agreements. Eventually, we will take up international public–private partnerships (PPPs) as the most visible interface of public and private environmental governance.

21.2 Contribution of Private Actors to International Environmental Law-Making

In just a few decades, private entities have become actors in international environmental governance both among elite and popular audiences. From a legal perspective, this extends across various stages from law-making to implementation and ensuring compliance with the law. Whereas the formal aspects of treaty-making, such as the capacity to conclude treaties, the designation of negotiators (including conferral of full powers), the adoption and authentication of the text, and the expression to be bound by the treaty typically remain in the hands of the state and pertinent governmental organs, the substance of a treaty very often results from contributions of civil society, business, and existing or emerging epistemic communities.[1] Legal analysis tends to ignore the contribution

[1] P Haas, 'Epistemic Communities' in D Bodansky *et al* (eds), *The Oxford Handbook of International Environmental Law* (Oxford 2007) 791, 798–802 explains how the ecological epistemic community has contributed to the evolution of ecological sustainability and governance.

of private actors and networks to the final outcome of multilateral negotiations, since public international law is primarily concerned with the formal aspects of law-making and the results thereof. Not surprisingly, there are hardly any explicit rules on participation of private actors in the making of international environmental law,[2] even though their involvement gives rise to a number of legal questions, in particular with regard to issues of legitimacy and accountability.[3]

21.2.1 NGO Involvement in Environmental Treaty-Making

Since 1972 a large number of multilateral treaty negotiations have been initiated by international bodies.[4] The most prominent of them has been the UNEP, calling for, *inter alia*, conferences leading to the Ozone Convention and to the Basel Convention. Numerous treaty-making efforts have further been stimulated by IUCN, which unites both states and NGOs. The primary focus of IUCN has been on nature conservation, including CITES and the Convention on Migratory Species. IUCN has also prepared drafts contributing to the CBD. While not formally initiating negotiations, NGOs have often been constructively involved in a variety of pre-normative processes and have taken the opportunity of agenda-setting during state conferences where negotiations were held.[5] The 1979 UN Convention on Long-Range Transboundary Air Pollution is but one example. However, hardly any MEA has truly emerged from NGO activities as such. This contrasts with recent developments in international humanitarian law where the origins of the 1997 Ottawa Convention on the Prohibition of the Use, Stockpiling, Production and Transfer of Anti-Personnel Mines and on their Destruction and of the 2008 Oslo Convention on Cluster Munitions can be clearly traced back to civil society initiatives.

While not necessarily initiating treaty negotiations, environmental NGOs have become important actors in negotiating processes, with some rules on their participation existing at the UN level at least.[6] It has become common to permit participation of NGO representatives and of business. Although normally neither can participate in any formal decision-making process, such as voting or formulating a consensus, they not only attend many meetings of state representatives (sometimes including expert organs), but may

[2] In contrast, the principle of public participation through NGOs in environmental law processes at the domestic level is not only well established but has been imposed upon states as an obligation by binding and non-binding international instruments: see A Tanzi, 'Controversial Developments in the Field of Public Participation in the International Environmental Law Process' in PM Dupuy and L Vierucci (eds), *NGOs in International Law: Efficiency in Flexibility?* (Cheltenham *et al* 2008) 135, 137–148.

[3] *Cf* E Meidinger, 'Competitive Supragovernmental Regulation: How Could It Be Democratic?' (2008) 8 *Chicago Journal of International Law* 513.

[4] L Susskind, *Environmental Diplomacy: Negotiating More Effective Global Agreements* (New York *et al* 1994) 24–25.

[5] See S Hobe, 'The Role of Non-State Actors, in Particular of NGOs, in Non-Contractual Law-Making and the Development of Customary International Law' in R Wolfrum and V Röben (eds), *Developments of International Law in Treaty Making* (Berlin *et al* 2005) 319, 321–322.

[6] According to Art 71 of the UN Charter, the 'Economic and Social Council may make suitable arrangements for consultation with non-governmental organizations which are concerned with matters within its competence.' For a broader legal and empirical survey see AK Lindblom, *Non-Governmental Organizations in International Law* (Cambridge 2005) 446 *et seq*.

also submit observations and proposals, and sometimes even address negotiating forums orally. This means that civil society contributes to and participates in the international legislative process. While such participation can be considered as generally inclusive, it is important to note that some of the well-financed and particularly knowledgeable private actors have strongly influenced the course and outcome of negotiations. Both, NGOs and business have developed campaign strategies to further their objectives in multilateral environmental negotiations.[7]

The question of representativeness and accountability poses a challenge to the credibility of private actors in international environmental relations and to their potential impact on the development of international environmental law. The problem exacerbates if any of these private actors collaborates its activities with some of the governmental actors involved. Formally, this does not affect sovereign equality of states; however, it has an impact on and causes shifts in the balance of power within multilateral forums. As can be illustrated by reference to the negotiations on the Biosafety Protocol to the CBD, such 'coalitions' may be perceived by some as detrimental to their interests, and may on occasions also impede the development of international environmental law.[8] Another downside of private actors participating in international environmental law-making may be that this blurs lines of accountability and responsibility because it cuts across traditional categories of actors.

However, overall participation of private actors in multilateral environmental negotiations can be useful in a number of respects. They provide sources of information that would otherwise not be available to states, they facilitate communication between various types of actors, and finally, co-operation between public and private actors has the potential to provide synergies when implementing international environmental agreements at the municipal level. This by far outweighs the above-mentioned criticisms. As has rightly been pointed out, participation of private actors in international environmental law-making does not simply mean privatisation. Rather, 'these private actors are integrated into the lawmaking process and as such are imbued with public authority'.[9]

21.2.2 Private Actor Contributions to the Development of Non-Treaty Norms

Notwithstanding the impressive numbers of environmental treaties, non-treaty norms in international environmental law have proliferated. While the role of private actors in treaty negotiations seems to be fairly clear, their contribution to the development of non-treaty norms is less obvious.

With regard to customary international law, state practice cannot be established on the basis of the activities of private actors. However, states will often respond to NGO or business activities.[10] Thus, private actors sometimes indirectly contribute to the establish-

[7] See EI Manolas, 'Campaign Strategies by Environmental NGOs in the Negotiations on Climate Change' in W Leal Filho and F Mannke (eds), *Interdisciplinary Aspects of Climate Change* (Frankfurt aM 2009) 169 *et seq*.

[8] See A Thomson, 'The Dangers of Secret Treaty-Making. The Biosafety Protocol as a Case Study' (2000) 52(2) *Institute of Public Affairs Review* 21, 21.

[9] V Röben, 'Proliferation of Actors' in Wolfrum and Röben, above n 5, 511, 536.

[10] Even though states agreed upon a treaty amendment in response to the Brent Spar campaign of Greenpeace,

ment of customary international law. As far as general principles of law are concerned, they cannot be deduced from the statements or actions of private actors.

In addition, private actors induce three categories of non-contractual law-making: law-making by international organisations, the development of soft law, and restatements of international law.[11] In respect of the development of soft law and with regard to restatements of international law, IUCN, the Institut de Droit International (IDI), and the International Law Association (ILA) have all contributed to the identification, to the making and, indirectly, to the further development of non-contractual international environmental law. ILA has drafted many instruments related to the protection of the environment, IDI has broadly addressed the environment in one of its sessions (1997), and some activities of IUCN have already been mentioned.

Private persons and organisations have come to play an increasingly important role as participants in law-making. The question arising from the involvement of private actors in international environmental relations is whether their contribution to the development of non-treaty norms necessitates a departure from the traditional view that this has not changed the traditional paradigm with private participation normally channelled through governmental action. Some authors suggest that customary international law is not resistant to the influences of non-governmental action, calling for a reconsideration of the formation of modern customary international law, referring to the increasing importance of transnational co-operation among both governments and private actors.[12] For the time being, however, private actor involvement in the development of international environmental law as based on traditional sources does not imply a paradigm shift. This can also be illustrated by contrasting it with more direct forms of private environmental governance such as the codification of standards.

21.3 Environmental Standard-Setting

21.3.1 Distinguishing Environmental Standards from Environmental Law-Making

Unfortunately, in most of the literature on public international law little attention is paid to the distinction between the adoption of standards and the making of law. Quite often environmental standard-setting is understood as the adoption of substantive provisions in international environmental law, and thus equated with law-making.[13] A different

this case is illustrative of the interaction between NGO campaigning and government response: see E Kirk, 'The 1996 Protocol to the London Dumping Convention and the Brent Spar' (1997) 46 *ICLQ* 957.

[11] As to participation of NGOs in law-making, UNEP has drafted a manual for NGOs on the negotiation and implementation of MEAs: see United Nations Environment Programme, *Negotiating and Implementing Multilateral Environmental Agreements (MEAs)* (Nairobi 2007).

[12] See T Mueller, 'Customary Transnational Law. Attacking the Last Resort of State Sovereignty' (2008) 15 *Indiana Journal of Global Legal Studies* 19.

[13] To give but one example, the following phrase may serve to illustrate this: 'International standards have been formulated in bilateral and multilateral treaties at the regional and international levels' (C Chinkin, 'International Environmental Law in Evolution' in T Jewell and J Steele (eds), *Law in Environmental Decision-Making: National, European and International Perspectives* (Oxford 1998) 229, 243).

approach can, however, be identified in literature whenever the dichotomy between public and private is taken up:[14] several authors have distinguished between (private) standards and (public) rules—or, in a broader sense, they distinguish the concept of 'law' from contractual relations between private actors, reserving 'law' for state-authored rules. While this approach has been categorically opposed by commentators arguing in favour of a broader concept of non-hierarchical global or universal law,[15] a terminological distinction may serve to highlight the specifics of non-state 'standards' *vis-à-vis* state-based law. Thus, this chapter—for the purpose of clarity—will reserve the term 'standards' for private regulation and the term 'law' for state-authored rules, without thereby preferring one or the other approach to a legal analysis of international private governance.

Private standards neither originate from intergovernmental agreements nor do they directly address states. They are market-oriented and make use of a broad variety of incentives. They are not necessarily regulatory.[16] Understanding private environmental standard-setting in the context of public international environmental law necessitates a brief discussion of the reasons for their increasingly prominent role in international environmental relations. Firstly, international private environmental standard-setting counters the proliferation of national or regional technical instructions and helps globalised business enterprises to reduce transaction costs.[17] Secondly, private standards help suppliers to establish a positive social and environmental track record and to meet consumer and societal expectations which tend to prefer such suppliers.[18] Thirdly, due to dissatisfaction with 'command and control' approaches to environmental regulation, private actors pursue incentive- and information-based approaches to supplement traditional regulation.[19]

International private environmental standards have meanwhile been adopted by a broad variety of agencies. While the adoption of these standards by private agencies, such as the International Organization for Standardization (ISO), or by transnational corporations, such as oil companies adopting best-practice standards,[20] seem to fit best into our analytical framework of private governance, quite a few environmental standards have been adopted by international organisations, including not only environmental programmes (such as UNEP) but also international financial institutions,[21] either to be directly applied by private entities or to serve as models for the development of standards by business. The latter standards include, among others, the Industrial Pollution Prevention and Abate-

[14] See AG Heyes and JW Maxwell, 'Private vs Public Regulation: Political Economy of the International Environment' (2004) 48 *Journal of Environmental Economics and Management* 978.

[15] See G Teubner, 'Breaking Frames: Economic Globalisation and the Emergence of Lex Mercatoria' (2002) 5 *European Journal of Social Theory* 199.

[16] J Morrison and N Roht-Arriaza, 'Private and Quasi-Private Standard Setting' in Bodansky *et al* (eds), above n 1, 498, 499.

[17] On the methodology of transaction costs see PK Rao, *The Economics of Transaction Costs: Theory, Methods and Applications* (Basingstoke 2003).

[18] Morrison and Roht-Arriaza, above n 16, 516 *et seq*.

[19] For an evaluation of command and control versus incentive-based regulation at the national level see R O'Ryan and JM Sánchez, 'Comparison of Net Benefits of Incentive-Based and Command and Control Environmental Regulations: The Case of Santiago, Chile' (2008) 22 *World Bank Economic Review* 249.

[20] See AS Wawryk, 'Adoption of International Environmental Standards by Transnational Oil Companies' (2002) 20 *Journal of Energy and Natural Resources Law* 402.

[21] See DB Hunter, 'Civil Society Networks and the Development of Environmental Standards at International Financial Institutions' (2008) 8 *Chicago Journal of International Law* 437.

ment Guidelines adopted by the World Bank, UNEP's Code of Ethics on International Trade in Chemicals, and the UN Global Compact which contains three principles for the protection of the environment.

ISO, founded in 1946 as a federation of national standards bodies,[22] is probably the best-known standard-setting agency. While ISO allows only one member per country, those members can be governmental or private representatives, thus leading to an unusual public–private blend. ISO's primary focus is not environmental but trade-related, aiming at facilitating the international exchange of goods and services. With more than 14000 standards adopted since the mid-1940s, ISO's influence has been strengthened by recognition and inclusion of its standards in major international agreements. Thus, the Technical Barriers to Trade Agreement (TBT) within the framework of the WTO not only alludes to but requires parties to adopt 'relevant international standards', thereby implicitly referring to ISO.[23] While originally focusing on product specification standards, ISO moved into the environmental, and thus public, policy area with the creation of its first environmental management standard (ISO/TC 207) in 1993.

While ISO has increasingly been integrated into public policy-making, normative performance or management standards initiated by environmental NGOs are exclusively civil-society based. They are intended to help consumers identify sustainable products in the marketplace. Typically, relevant NGOs offer logos that can be placed on products, promotional material or facilities of actors which comply with pertinent standards. Among the most prominent initiatives to this end is the 1993 Forest Stewardship Council (FSC),[24] which served as a model for the 1997 Marine Stewardship Council (MSC), the latter originally created by the World Wildlife Fund and the Unilever Corporation. In contrast to these resource-specific standards, business has primarily developed sector-specific codes.[25]

21.3.2 Categorising Standards

Standards, in general, can be defined as:

> documented agreements containing technical specifications or other precise criteria to be used consistently as rules, guidelines, or definitions of characteristics, to ensure that materials, products, processes and services are fit for their purpose.[26]

Based on their distinct approaches to environmental protection, they may be categorised

[22] On the ISO in general see CN Murphy and J Yates, *The International Organization for Standardization (ISO). Global Governance through Voluntary Consensus* (London 2009); on ISO's role in international environmental law-making see N Roht-Arriaza, 'Shifting the Point of Regulation: The International Organization for Standardization and Global Lawmaking on Trade and the Environment' (1995) 22 *Ecology Law Quarterly* 479.

[23] See Art 2.4 of the TBT Agreement, available at www.wto.org/english/docs_e/legal_e/17-tbt.pdf.

[24] See KM Kloven, 'Eco-labeling of Sustainably Harvested Wood under the Forest Stewardship Council: Seeing the Forest for the Trees' (1998) *Colorado Journal of International Environmental Law and Policy* 48.

[25] Morrison and Roht-Arriaza, above n 16, 501.

[26] *Ibid*, 506.

as (i) technical specifications and performance standards; (ii) process and management system standards; and (iii) measurement and reporting standards.[27]

Environmental technical specification and performance standards have primarily established minimum levels for energy use or air and water emissions. They can be qualitative or quantitative, depending on whether they generally reduce the use or pollution of natural resources or whether they focus on emissions per product. So-called 'best-in-class' standards, which are not absolute but comparative, have recently gained prominence for eco-labelling schemes.[28] They benchmark one producer's performance against another's.

Focusing on the process rather than on the product itself, environmental process and management system standards have become well known through the ISO 9000 series on quality management.[29] Standards focusing on a company's production process have contributed to the development of harmonised environmental management practices, as may be illustrated by the International Chamber of Commerce Business Charter for Sustainable Development[30] and the 1989 principles of the Coalition for Environmentally Responsible Economies (CERES).[31] Environmental management system (EMS) standards are much wider in scope than process standards alone. They include, *inter alia*, policy-setting, planning, management programmes, internal auditing and operational controls of undertakings. At the international level, ISO 14001 has become the primary EMS standard,[32] based to some extent on the EU Eco-Management and Audit Scheme (EMAS).[33] Since management standards do not include prescriptive environmental performance levels, commentators have questioned the credibility of management standards and criticised ISO 14001 as only demonstrating 'that a management system is in place'.[34] Obviously, the environmental impact of such management system standards is hard to prove.

A third category of standards are measurement and reporting standards. They can provide a credible template for reporting which may not only help business to measure and disclose environmental effects of their activities but will also assist various audiences to use the information for benchmarking and comparing results. The ISO air and water quality measurement standards (TC 146/147), various greenhouse gas emissions standards such as the ISO 14064 standard or the WBCSD/WRI Greenhouse Gas Protocol,[35] and the much broader framework of the Global Reporting Initiative (GRI) may serve

[27] *Ibid*, 506–511.

[28] *Cf* T Cooper, 'Picture This: Promoting Sustainable Fisheries through Eco-labeling and Product Certification' (2004/2005) 10 *Ocean and Coastal Law Journal* 1.

[29] For the essentials of ISO 9000 see www.iso.org/iso/iso_catalogue/management_standards/iso_9000_iso_14000/iso_9000_essentials.htm.

[30] See www.iccwbo.org/policy/environment/id1309/index.html.

[31] For further details see JA Smith, 'The CERES Principles. Model for Public Environmental Accountability' (1995) 4 *RECIEL* 116.

[32] *Cf* PS Evers, 'ISO 14000 and Environmental Protection' (1997) 67 *Mississippi Law Journal* 463.

[33] For an assessment of EMAS after its first decade see T Kiel, 'Ten Years of European Environmental Management and Audit Scheme (EMAS)' (2006) 6 *Yearbook of European Environmental Law* 61.

[34] Morrison and Roht-Arriaza, above n 16, 508.

[35] World Business Council for Sustainable Development and World Resources Institute; for the text of the Protocol see www.ghgprotocol.org/files/ghg_project_protocol.pdf.

as examples. Among the principles on which GRI is based, transparency, auditability, accuracy and comparability figure prominently.

21.3.3 Ensuring Compliance with Private Standards

Whereas it is obvious that state-authored rules can in principle be enforced (subject to the specifics of public international law), compliance with private standards, which are perceived as voluntary, is not a matter of course. However, quite often private standards are much more consequential than the pertinent terminology suggests.

Assessing the ways in which private standards work necessitates a broad perspective which does not distinguish between standard-setting and compliance therewith. Such a broad perspective extends from incentives to develop such standards to external (and often regulatory) incentives to comply with these standards.

As for market dynamics, it has already been mentioned that private environmental standards can first of all be adopted for internal purposes: for business this can mean improving eco-efficiency as well as avoiding liability; labelling schemes or procurement standards often result from demands of business partners and customers;[36] and, finally, reputational incentives are relevant.[37] Market dynamics are largely based on the perception of business that private standards can make them more attractive to other market participants.

There are also regulatory incentives for compliance with private standards. This is not only true for disclosure initiatives which establish a right to know for consumers and others concerned; it also applies to positive incentives (streamlined procedures and shorter licensing times) whereby governments encourage companies to go beyond regulatory minimum standards. Sometimes, private standards are integrated in governmental regulation; this is particularly true for environmental impact assessments and related audit policies.[38]

For the time being there are no meaningful international mechanisms for ensuring compliance with international private environmental standards. Measures to redress non-compliance with management or certification schemes are extremely limited. The loss of ISO certification seems to be more a theoretical option than a real one. Typically, the effectiveness of such private standards depends upon their application within a national framework. This notwithstanding, there is a trend towards interlinking public and private standards not only at the national but also at the international level. In the period leading up to the 2002 World Summit on Sustainable Development (WSSD) in Johannesburg, Friends of the Earth International promoted a multilateral treaty on corporate accountability.[39] The proposal did not materialise but the Plan of Implementation encouraged

[36] See Kloven, above n 24, 48.

[37] Morrison and Roht-Arriaza, above n 16, 516–517.

[38] See J Glasson, 'Principles and Purposes of Standards and Thresholds in the EIA Process' in M Schmidt *et al* (eds), *Standards and Thresholds for Impact Assessment* (Berlin *et al* 2008) 3, 7 *et seq*; see also A Cherp, 'The Role of Environmental Management Systems in Enforcing Standards and Thresholds in the Context of EIA Follow-Up' in *ibid*, 433, 443 *et seq*.

[39] J Clapp, 'Global Environmental Governance for Corporate Responsibility and Accountability' (2005) 5 *Global Environmental Politics* 23, 29–31.

> industry to improve social and environmental performance through voluntary initiatives, including environmental management systems, codes of conduct, certification and public reporting on environmental and social issues, taking into account such initiatives as the International Organization for Standardization standards and Global Reporting Initiative guidelines on sustainability reporting.[40]

There is, however, a new development in the field of human rights protection to improve adherence to private standards by strengthening their relationship with public standards. The former UN Commission on Human Rights elaborated Draft Norms and Guidelines on the Responsibilities of Transnational Corporations and Other Business Enterprises with Regard to Human Rights.[41] The Office of the High Commissioner for Human Rights took up the issue and the new UN Human Rights Council extended the mandate of the Special Representative of the Secretary-General on the issue of human rights and transnational corporations and other business enterprises. Perspectives for strengthening the interrelationship between human rights, environmental policy and private standards appear to be a promising option for ensuring compliance with private environmental standards.[42]

21.3.4 Inherent Limitations of Private Standard-Setting

Private standards have a number of advantages, including their flexibility, their precise tailoring to the needs of a particular undertaking, and their acceptance by business. However, these strengths at the same time tend to be their weaknesses, including limited enforcement and credibility thereof. Some additional inherent limitations of international private environmental governance have to be borne in mind.

Firstly, the legitimacy of the authors of private environmental standards and the inclusiveness of appropriate forums can be questioned. It is notable that developing countries and small businesses are underrepresented.[43] Secondly, due to the proliferation of standardisation initiatives, private actors may choose the standards most convenient for them; thus, in the forestry sector, companies may prefer ISO 14001 certification over more rigorous FSC certification.[44] Thirdly, the comparability of standards may also be at issue, leading to growing confusion about certification and labelling systems. This makes standards less reliable than perceived at first sight. Fourthly, the interrelationship between private standards and overall principles of good governance[45] (including demo-

[40] Plan of Implementation of the World Summit on Sustainable Development (4 September 2002), UN Doc A/CONF199/20, para 18(a), available at www.un.org/esa/sustdev/documents/WSSD_POI_PD/English/WSSD_PlanImpl.pdf.

[41] UNCHR (26 August 2003) UN Doc E/CN4/Sub2/2003/12/Rev2; environmental issues are referred to in para 14, available at www.unhchr.ch/huridocda/huridoca.nsf/%28Symbol%29/E.CN.4.Sub.2.2003.12.Rev.2.En.

[42] S Deva, 'UN's Human Rights Norms for Transnational Corporations and Other Business Enterprises—An Imperfect Step in the Right Direction?' (2004) 10 *ILSA Journal of International & Comparative Law* 493; *cf* also Chapter 26.

[43] Morrison and Roht-Arriaza, above n 16, 502–503.

[44] *Ibid*, 511; see also B Cashore, G Auld, S Bernstein and C McDermott, 'Can Non-state Governance "Ratchet Up" Global Environmental Standards? Lessons from the Forest Sector' (2007) 16 *RECIEL* 158.

[45] S Deva, 'Sustainable Good Governance and Corporations: An Analysis of Asymmetries' (2006) 18 *Georgetown International Environmental Law Review* 707.

cratic legitimacy and human rights standards) will only remain balanced if they pursue the same objectives. Otherwise, tensions may arise which will be to the detriment of either or both.

21.4 International Environmental Partnerships

Different types of international partnerships have emerged since the 1990s. While some partnerships can be termed public–private partnerships (PPPs) (bearing in mind such forms of co-operation between business and government at the national level), many other partnerships established bring together governments and a broad variety of public or private institutions, often from different countries, such as research institutions. Addressing the latter as PPPs may be misleading. Therefore, identifying them as 'multi-stakeholder partnerships' seems to be more appropriate. We will first address the reasons for the rise of partnerships, followed by a separate discussion of partnerships in practice, including multi-stakeholder partnerships and PPPs, respectively. Finally, their contribution to international environmental governance will be assessed.

21.4.1 The Emergence of Partnerships in International Environmental Law

Several reasons can be identified for partnerships becoming instrumental in international environmental governance since the 1990s.[46]

Firstly, the implementation of international environmental agreements does not exclusively depend on traditional governmental actors. Private actors often are the final, though not explicit, addressees of environmental agreements. Even though they are neither affected immediately nor directly by these agreements, the impact of changes in the law, in particular if necessitating behavioural change, is felt most closely by them. It is against this background that national environmental governance has long recognised the need to involve private actors at various levels and across several areas, including legislation. With a growing number of transnational business activities and pertinent economic globalisation, the need to ensure participation of private actors in international environmental law has become a matter of concern.

Secondly, policies for sustainable development with their 'interdependent and mutually reinforcing pillars' of economic development, social development and environmental protection cannot be implemented by regulatory approaches alone.[47] By their very nature these policies raise new challenges which cannot be addressed from an exclusively state-centred perspective. They require the participation of economic (and thus predominantly private) actors. Linking international environmental policies to international

[46] SJ Scherr and RJ Gregg, 'Johannesburg and Beyond: The 2002 World Summit on Sustainable Development and the Rise of Partnerships' (2006) 18 *Georgetown International Environmental Law Review* 425, 435–439.

[47] See the 2005 World Summit Outcome, UNGA Res 60/1 (24 October 2005) 12.

socioeconomic policies leads to increased participation of private actors in international environmental law.[48]

Thirdly, the complex nature of global environmental challenges, with an increasing impact on the availability of resources necessary for the survival of humankind, cannot be handled by governmental actors alone. Some of the resources, including financial assets, are not at the disposal of governments and many of the challenges go beyond their capacities. This necessitates the inclusion of all actors capable of addressing international environmental matters.

Fourthly, in light of the human and financial resources necessary for the further development and implementation of international environmental law it is noteworthy that partnerships, in particular in the context of international investments and infrastructure, have become an instrument to acquire substantial funds.

The Millennium Declaration of 2000 and the eight Millennium Development Goals (MDGs) considerably predetermined the bargaining process and the outcomes of the Johannesburg Summit. Rather than turning towards new MEAs, the Johannesburg Summit addressed the implementation gap with regard to existing agreements. This was not limited to improving compliance and enforcement mechanisms but covered general aspects of facilitating implementation. This broad approach was considered to enhance the effectiveness of appropriate international instruments. In the following, the focus will be on the Summit's 'type 2 outcome' which deals with partnerships in general and with PPPs in particular.[49]

In 2001, the UN General Assembly acknowledged the emergence of PPPs as appropriate tools to achieve sustainable development.[50] On the occasion of the 2002 World Summit in Johannesburg, PPPs were recognised as a new type of environmental instrument, taking into account the need for effective implementation much more than the traditional law-making and guidelines-setting processes on which the conferences in Stockholm and Rio had focused. States taking part in the Summit came to affirm that implementation of the WSSD outcomes

> should involve all relevant actors through partnerships, especially between Governments of the North and South, on the one hand, and between Governments and major groups, on the other, to achieve the widely shared goals of sustainable development [and that] such partnerships are key to pursuing sustainable development in a globalizing world.[51]

Two documents have contributed to shaping the further development of partnerships: the 2002 Bali Guiding Principles[52] and the 2003 UN Commission on Sustainable Development

[48] A Alkoby, 'Non-State Actors and the Legitimacy of International Environmental Law' (2003) 3 *Non-State Actors and International Law* 23.

[49] See Chapter 4.2 for further details on the Johannesburg outcomes.

[50] UNGA Res 56/76 (24 January 2002), *cf*, *inter alia,* para 16.

[51] Plan of Implementation of the World Summit on Sustainable Development, above n 40, para 3.

[52] 'Guiding Principles for Partnerships for Sustainable Development ("type 2 outcomes") to be Elaborated by Interested Parties in the Context of the World Summit on Sustainable Development (WSSD)'. See the text in UN Doc A/CONF199/4, Report of the Commission on Sustainable Development acting as the preparatory committee for the World Summit on Sustainable Development (Fourth Session), Annex III Appendix, 34–35.

(CSD) Guidelines on Partnerships for Sustainable Development.[53] The Guiding Principles, which had been developed by two Vice-Chairs of the fourth preparatory committee meeting (PrepCom IV) for the Johannesburg Summit, were used by the CSD Secretariat to review partnerships for sustainable development proposals submitted between the Bali meeting and the 11th Meeting of the CSD (April/May 2003) when governments agreed that partnerships should be developed and implemented in accordance with a set of new criteria and guidelines, the CSD Guidelines. The Summit had before assigned to the CSD the role of serving as 'a focal point for the discussion of partnerships that promote sustainable development, including sharing lessons learned, progress made and best practices'.[54]

The main provisions of the CSD Guidelines are the following:

- Partnerships should contribute to the implementation of Agenda 21, the Programme for the Further Implementation of Agenda 21 and the Johannesburg Plan of Implementation.
- Partnerships are not intended to substitute commitments made by governments.
- Partnerships should be designed and implemented in a transparent and accountable manner.
- Partnerships should be publicly announced with the intention of sharing the specific contribution that they make.
- The leading partner of a partnership initiative should inform the national focal point for sustainable development of the involved country/countries about the initiation and progress of the partnership, and all partners should bear in mind the guidance provided by governments.
- The CSD is competent to register partnerships, to receive and publicise their reports and to foster their creation, implementation and operation.

21.4.2 Partnerships in Practice

In practice, the notion of 'partnership' covers a broad variety of forms of co-operation. In the field of international environmental governance, it is noteworthy that most partnerships can be considered as multi-stakeholder partnerships.

Originally, some 220 multi-stakeholder partnerships had been officially announced at the Johannesburg Summit, allowing public and private stakeholders alike to join forces in order to achieve common objectives relating to sustainable development. Eventually, participating states adopted a 'Consolidated List of Partnerships for Sustainable Development', which as of 3 February 2003 numbered 255 of such partnerships.[55] In 2004, a Partnerships Database, administrated by the CSD as the institution designated to promote

[53] CSD-11 Decision on the future programme and organisation of work of the Commission on Sustainable Development, paras 22 *et seq*.

[54] Plan of Implementation of the World Summit on Sustainable Development, above n 40, para 148(b).

[55] See www.un.org/jsummit/html/sustainable_dev/consolidated_*list*_091202.pdf.

and facilitate partnerships, was established.[56] Today, the CSD Partnerships Database lists around 350 partnerships.

It is noteworthy that these partnerships are not labelled 'partnerships for the environment' but 'partnerships for sustainable development'. This illustrates that they do not exclusively focus on environmental protection but that they include the other two pillars of sustainable development, namely social and economic development. Nevertheless, they constitute a 'vision of a new and innovative type of environmental governance'.[57]

Public–private partnerships *stricto sensu* must be distinguished from multi-stakeholder partnerships. Public–private partnerships were first developed at the national level and may still be considered to be exceptional at the international level. At the national level PPPs are agreements between government and the private sector regarding the provision of public services or infrastructure. International PPPs are institutionalised co-operative relationships between public and private actors beyond the nation-state for governance purposes.[58] They involve governments and intergovernmental organisations on the one hand, and corporate and civil society actors on the other. Sometimes they are named transnational rather than international PPPs, a distinction which is not relevant for the purposes of this chapter. While PPPs have become a common feature of national policy frameworks, international PPPs are still a relatively new, though growing, phenomenon with little legal analysis thereof. In the following we will explain the legal basis of international PPPs and their contribution to the development of international environmental law.

Public–private partnerships normally come into existence on the basis of contractual arrangements between the participating entities. The applicable law is determined by those arrangements and relevant conflict-of-law rules. In the present context, these arrangements are of secondary importance only. While PPPs are neither hard nor soft law instruments, lacking normative force as such, they are action-oriented tools which contribute to filling the implementation gap in international environmental law. They do not replace but complement legally binding interstate instruments.

Some PPPs may acquire the status as a partnership for sustainable development. In order to reach such a status, the PPPs in question must comply with the above-mentioned CSD Guidelines. Thus, the Guidelines not only consolidate the format and substance of PPPs but they also better integrate PPPs into other policy measures aiming at sustainable development. The Bali Principles and the CSD Guidelines have thus performed a co-ordinating function.[59] Today, however, it is not yet clear whether the guidelines will contribute to shaping international PPPs beyond the particular context of the Johannesburg Summit and its follow-up process.

[56] See http://webapps01.un.org/dsd/partnerships/public/browse.do.

[57] JM Witte and C Streck, 'Introduction' in T Benner *et al* (eds), *Progress or Peril? Partnerships and Networks in Global Environmental Governance. The Post-Johannesburg Agenda* (Berlin/Washington DC 2003) 1, 2.

[58] K Bäckstrand, 'Accountability of Networked Climate Governance. The Rise of Transnational Climate Partnerships' (2008) 8 *Global Environmental Politics* 74, 77–78; see also T Börzel and T Risse, 'Public Private Partnerships. Effective and Legitimate Tools for Transnational Governance?' in E Grande and L Pauly (eds), *Complex Sovereignty. Reconstituting Political Authority in the Twentyfirst Century* (Toronto 2005) 195, 198.

[59] See C Streck, 'The World Summit on Sustainable Development. Partnerships as New Tools in Environmental Governance' (2002) 13 *Yearbook of International Environmental Law* 63.

Numerous PPPs have been developed outside the formal CSD framework. By way of example, Articles 10 and 16 CBD as well as numerous decisions of the COPs explicitly refer to business, and many of the CBD's Programmes of Work are directly relevant for business activities.[60] The primary purpose of these provisions and programmes is to facilitate the implementation and further development of the Convention, in particular, to provide financial assistance or know-how needed to this end. This is, to a certain extent, similar to the contribution of PPPs at the national level, facilitating public services or developing infrastructure. With regard to the preservation of biodiversity, the Sustainable Tree Crops Program (STCP), which started in 2000, may be mentioned. It was established as a PPP and innovation platform in order to generate growth in rural income among tree crop farmers in an environmentally and socially responsible manner in West and Central Africa.[61] The programme is managed by the International Institute of Tropical Agriculture (IITA) and—according to its website—provides a framework for collaboration between farmers, the global cocoa industry, the local private sector, national governments, NGOs, research institutes and development investors. With regard to climate change, PPPs played an important role in getting the Clean Development Mechanism (CDM) and the carbon market off the ground. It has recently been argued, however, that the more the carbon market matures, the more business will replace PPPs since technical and economic risks are reduced in light of the many lessons learned by public and private actors.[62] To provide an example for a climate change-related international PPP, Senegal, in 2006, launched a biofuels programme, with direct support from Brazil, carried out by entrepreneurs from India. While Senegal offers land and human resources, Brazil contributes scientific and technological know-how, and Indian business provides capital—a PPP mitigating climate change.[63]

As has already been indicated, PPPs have also become a common feature of implementing the CBD and the UNFCCC. With regard to the CBD, the COP at its Eighth Meeting in 2006 took a decision noting that PPPs 'may be of use in facilitating contributions from business and industry towards the implementation of the Convention'.[64] Similarly, various decisions on PPPs have been adopted within the UNFCCC framework,[65] in particular at the Bali Summit in 2007.[66] While these partnerships are treaty-linked, there are also other

[60] On the occasion of COP 9, participants intensely discussed the involvement of business in the implementation of the Convention; see www.cbd.int/business/.

[61] It is surprising that the programme is not listed in the CSD Partnerships Database. Donors, among others, include US-American, Canadian, Danish, and German development agencies as well as the World Bank and the International Cocoa Initiative.

[62] See G Benecke, L Friberg, M Lederer and M Schröder, 'From Public–Private Partnership to Market. The Clean Development Mechanism (CDM) as a New Form of Governance in Climate Protection', SFB-Governance Working Paper Series, no 10, Research Center (SFB) 700, Berlin, April 2008, available at www.sfb-governance.de/publikationen/sfbgov_wp/wp10_en/index.html.

[63] See the following press release: www.scidev.net/en/news/brazil-and-india-join-senegal-for-biofuel-producti.html.

[64] UNEP/CBD/COP/DEC/VIII/17 (15 June 2006); see also UNEP/CBD/COP/8/INF/21 (20 January 2006).

[65] For a pertinent analysis of the CDM see R Stewart and D Anderson, *The Clean Development Mechanism: Building International Public–Private Partnerships under the Kyoto Protocol. Technical, Financial and Institutional Issues* (New York/Geneva 2000).

[66] Report of the Conference of the Parties on its 13th Session, held in Bali from 3 to 15 December 2007 (FCCC/CP/2007/6/Add1 (14 March 2008)).

'levitating' PPPs, the development of which has been strongly promoted on the occasion of the Johannesburg Summit.[67]

21.4.3 Assessing the Contribution of Partnerships to International Environmental Governance

Firstly, considering the partnerships included in the CSD database it must be noted that many of these are not international PPPs; quite a few are government–government or private–private partnerships, and even if public and private actors co-operate, some lack a transboundary element. This eventually means that international environmental PPPs cannot easily be equated with partnerships for sustainable development. As a consequence, legal analysis lacks a sufficiently coherent empirical base of international environmental PPPs.

Secondly, the very existence of international PPPs testifies that private actors are continuously gaining importance in the law on sustainable development and in international environmental law. Their contribution, however, still seems to be rather modest. Thus, it seems to be appropriate to consider this involvement of private actors just as broadening international governance, not as a paradigm shift.

Thirdly, notwithstanding the short history of international environmental PPPs, their contribution to the conceptual debate and their practical relevance in the implementation of environmental regimes supports the assumption that they are fairly important instruments contributing to the further development of international environmental governance and making this a reality of international relations and the daily life of people, not least because they help to acquire the necessary funds for applying pertinent rules.[68]

Fourthly, while their contribution to the further development of international environmental governance should not be underestimated, there are also reasons to be cautious in placing too much emphasis on PPPs as an instrument for international environmental governance. Not only may states start to advocate these informal tools as a substitute for legal or political commitments such as treaty regimes and plans of action, but partnership action may also be ineffective by virtue of (irreconcilable) differences among the interests of the public- and private-sector entities engaged in the partnerships. In addition, notwithstanding the CSD's supervisory role with regard to such partnerships, they lack accountability in face of the absence of adequate mechanisms to supervise compliance with sustainable development goals.[69]

[67] N Matz, 'New Strategies for Environmental Financing?' (2003) 63 *ZaöRV* 503, 513–514.

[68] On the role of PPPs in providing funding for public policy issues see J Bennett, 'Public Private Partnerships. The Role of the Private Sector in Preventing Funding Conflict' (2002) 35 *Vanderbilt Journal of Transnational Law* 711.

[69] For an analysis of the pros and cons of type II partnerships *cf* M Wilson, 'The New Frontier in Sustainable Development: World Summit on Sustainable Development—Type II Partnerships' (2005) 36 *Victoria University of Wellington Law Review* 389–426; on the continued need for further law-making notwithstanding the rise of partnership arrangements see CE Bruch and J Pendergrass, 'Type II Partnerships, International Law, and the Commons' (2003) 15 *Georgetown International Environmental Law Review* 855–886.

Further Reading

T Benner *et al* (eds), *Progress or Peril? Networks and Partnerships in Global Environmental Governance. The Post-Johannesburg Agenda* (Berlin/Washington, DC 2003).

B Cashore, G Auld, S Bernstein and C McDermott, 'Can Non-state Governance "Ratchet Up" Global Environmental Standards? Lessons from the Forest Sector' (2007) 16 *RECIEL* 158–172.

J Gupta, 'The Role of Non-State Actors in International Environmental Affairs' (2003) 63 *Heidelberg Journal of International Law (ZaöRV)* 459–486.

J Morrison and N Roht-Arriaza, 'Private and Quasi-Private Standard Setting' in D Bodansky *et al* (eds), *The Oxford Handbook of International Environmental Law* (Oxford 2007) 498–527.

N Roht-Arriaza, 'Shifting the Point of Regulation: The International Organization for Standardization and Global Lawmaking on Trade and the Environment' (1995) 22 *Ecology Law Quarterly* 479–539.

SJ Scherr and RJ Gregg, 'Johannesburg and Beyond: The 2002 World Summit on Sustainable Development and the Rise of Partnerships' (2006) 18 *Georgetown International Environmental Law Review* 425–463.

Part V

International Environmental Governance II: Ensuring Compliance

22

Compliance Control

22.1 Compliance Control and Assistance as 'Active Treaty Management'

The number of multilateral environmental agreements (MEAs) concluded since the 1970s is impressive. The question must be raised, however, whether all these MEAs have had any effect. International relations scholars answer this question in terms of the behavioural or environmental changes which can be attributed to specific MEAs.[1] In contrast, international lawyers and legal scholars will examine the effectiveness of MEAs in terms of the extent to which parties comply with their commitments. Accordingly, ensuring compliance with MEAs is a major concern of international environmental law.

Traditionally, confrontational methods were considered as the primary strategy for ensuring compliance with international agreements. In light of little normative and administrative hierarchy in public international law, and with states being the authors, addressees and guardians of the law, this largely meant reliance upon measures taken by one state against another state in order to prevent or respond to violations of the law. The means at hand were countermeasures adopted in response to non-compliance, such as reprisals, retorsions[2] and perhaps even sanctions, as well as state responsibility and dispute-settlement procedures[3] as a means to establish and perhaps enforce claims.

Reprisals are acts which, if taken in isolation, are illegal under international law, if, however, adopted by one state in response to the commission of an earlier illegal act by another state they become lawful.[4] They are subject to certain limitations, including non-use of force and proportionality. Retorsions, such as breaking diplomatic relations, are lawful *per se* but unfriendly, acting in the same way as reprisals.

[1] *Cf* RB Mitchell, 'Compliance Theory' in D Bodansky *et al* (eds), *The Oxford Handbook of International Environmental Law* (Oxford 2007) 893, 894–895.

[2] W Fiedler, 'Gegenmaßnahmen' in W Fiedler *et al* (eds), *Gegenmaßnahmen: mit Diskussion; with English Summaries of the Reports (Counter Measures)* (Heidelberg 1998) 9 *et seq* and E Klein, 'Gegenmaßnahmen' in *ibid*, 39 *et seq*.

[3] *Cf* JR Crawford, 'State Responsibility' in R Wolfrum (ed), *Max Planck Encyclopedia of Public International Law* (Heidelberg/Oxford 2006), available at www.mpepil.com.

[4] M Ruffert, 'Reprisals' in R Wolfrum (ed), *Max Planck Encyclopedia of Public International Law* (Heidelberg/Oxford 2009), available at www.mpepil.com.

Reprisals and retorsions are not only confrontational but also bilateral in essence. Since a reprisal requires the infringement of particular rights of a state, it is doubtful whether it facilitates the enforcement of international obligations in the interest of the international community as a whole. This is only the case in so far as these obligations constitute obligations *erga omnes*.[5] Even though a retorsion can be applied without a prior violation of international law and may thus display a preventive and perhaps even a precautionary effect, it must be noted that states will not easily undertake unfriendly acts against each other merely for the sake of environmental policy. Furthermore, in light of the increasing juridification of international relations, there are only limited means available for acts of retorsion which do not themselves contravene international law.[6]

As far as other traditional means to ensure compliance are concerned, states have only rarely made use of sanctions in response to non-compliance with international environmental law; sanctions, being often expensive and of delayed effectiveness only, are perceived as unsuitable by their very nature.[7] Even if imposed collectively, as provided for in the Montreal Protocol,[8] they are not without problems, as the pertinent debate about the Protocol's compatibility with the General Agreement on Tariffs and Trade (GATT) has shown.[9]

Enforcement in national as well as international law has largely been associated with traditional coercive methods. International relations scholars, addressing the reasons why, if at all, states change their behaviour, have shown that these methods are not really adequate in many fields. Providing positive incentives and replacing repressive sanctions with co-operative means of 'active treaty management'[10] seems to have a more significant impact on state behaviour.

What can be taken from a closer analysis of compliance with environmental legislation at the national level is that the relationship between government and citizen has shifted from command and control to negotiations between the authors and the addressees of the law.[11] Co-operative solutions serve to overcome motivations impeding implementation, or at least change them into interests compatible with the objectives pursued by pertinent

[5] JA Frowein, 'Obligations Erga Omnes' in R Wolfrum (ed), *Max Planck Encyclopedia of Public International Law* (Heidelberg/Oxford 2008), available at www.mpepil.com.

[6] For a discussion of enforcement strategies in international environmental law see J Brunnée, 'Enforcement Mechanisms in International Law and International Environmental Law' in U Beyerlin *et al* (eds), *Ensuring Compliance with Multilateral Environmental Agreements: A Dialogue Between Practitioners and Academia* (Leiden/Boston 2006) 1.

[7] AH Chayes, A Chayes and RB Mitchell, 'Active Compliance Management in Environmental Treaties' in W Lang (ed), *Sustainable Development and International Law* (London *et al* 1995) 75, 77; for details see A Chayes and AH Chayes, *The New Sovereignty: Compliance with International Regulatory Agreements* (Cambridge, MA 1995) 29–108.

[8] *Cf* Arts 4 and 4A Montreal Protocol ('Control of trade with non-Parties' and 'Control of trade with Parties').

[9] See R Twum-Barima and LB Campbell, *Protecting the Ozone Layer Through Trade Measures: Reconciling the Trade Provisions of the Montreal Protocol and the Rules of the GATT* (Geneva 1994); see also W Lang, 'Trade Restrictions as a Means of Enforcing Compliance with International Environmental Law: Montreal Protocol on Substances that Deplete the Ozone Layer' in R Wolfrum (ed), *Enforcing Environmental Standards: Economic Mechanisms as Viable Means?* (Berlin *et al* 1996) 265, 274 *et seq*, and in general EU Petersmann, 'Trade and the Protection of the Environment after the Uruguay Round' in Wolfrum (ed), *ibid*, 165.

[10] Chayes, Chayes and Mitchell, above n 7, 83 *et seq*.

[11] See M Bothe, 'Vollzugsdefizit im Völkerrecht—Überlegungen zu 30 Jahren Umweltrecht' in HJ Cremer *et al* (eds), *Tradition und Weltoffenheit des Rechts: Festschrift für Helmut Steinberger* (Berlin *et al* 2002) 83.

legislation. These developments have also been adapted to international environmental law, developing collective rather than unilateral and co-operative rather than authoritative strategies to promote compliance. Ensuring compliance in a co-operative way means convincing states and other subjects of international law to observe the law, not according to the 'all or nothing' principle, but with the aim of attaining a 'reasonable level of compliance'.[12]

The employment of partnership methods is intended to respond to deficient compliance not by addressing the symptoms but by removing the causes. In their research, AH Chayes and A Chayes come to the conclusion that in international environmental law wilful non-compliance with a treaty is the exception.[13] They point out that states normally enter into treaty commitments with the intent of complying with them. Since they have already brought in their own interests in the course of negotiations, the implementation and observation of these obligations is in their own interests. Admittedly, treaties are frequently the result of a compromise; but they will hardly ever be completely contrary to the interests of one or the other party.

So if states mostly intend to comply with their obligations, what are the reasons for non-compliance? It has been shown that a major cause is often a deficient administrative, economic and technical infrastructure of the parties.[14] These deficiencies are all the more important since states, under MEAs, will often have to monitor and control private conduct. Administrative deficits in monitoring such conduct are often caused by problems such as inadequate human resources of the authorities and insufficient training of the personnel responsible for monitoring. In addition, developing countries often do not have the financial means, not just for the personnel, but also for the infrastructure needed for monitoring (from computers for electronic data-gathering to major technological apparatus).

It is against this background that the concepts of compliance control and compliance assistance have been developed.[15] They reflect that meaningful approaches to compliance cannot be couched in 'black and white' terms; they must deal justly with the diverse reasons for non-compliance. Both models should be regarded as differentiated approaches to the elimination of compliance deficits; they are prototypes for a system of 'active treaty management'. Compliance control and compliance assistance are based on the premise that (i) collective and institutionalised approaches towards compliance are more convincing than unilateral ones; (ii) co-operation is better than confrontation; (iii) prevention enjoys preference over repression; and (iv) assistance is superior to sanctions.[16]

The decentralised structure of traditional enforcement mechanisms in international law has already been mentioned. To effect the observance of multilateral obligations,

[12] Chayes, Chayes and Mitchell, above n 7, 80: 'We believe that there are acceptable levels of compliance—not an invariant standard, but one which changes over time with the capacities of the parties and the urgency of the problem.'

[13] Chayes and Chayes, above n 7, 8–10.

[14] *Ibid*, 13 *et seq.*

[15] See J Brunnée, 'Compliance Control' in G Ulfstein *et al* (eds), *Making Treaties Work: Human Rights, Environment and Arms Control* (Cambridge *et al* 2007) 373, 373–374; EM Mrema, 'Cross-cutting Issues Related to Ensuring Compliance with MEAs' in Beyerlin *et al* (eds), above n 6, 201.

[16] On the following see U Beyerlin and T Marauhn, *Law-Making and Law-Enforcement in International Environmental Law after the 1992 Rio Conference* (Berlin 1997) 83–87.

and even more so, of those serving the common interest of the international community as a whole, it is plausible to entrust international institutions with a stronger role in ensuring compliance. This promises a number of benefits,[17] including collective compliance mechanisms, less relevance of political considerations of expediency, openness to participants other than states, and the destigmatisation of compliance mechanisms by dissociating them from specific conflicts and making 'control' a matter of routine. Such institutionalisation can build on experiences with international monitoring which is nothing fundamentally new.[18] Reference may be made to the Rhine Commission of 1815, the International Labour Organization (ILO) and the mandates system of the League of Nations, as well as to the corresponding academic and political debate between the two world wars. After 1945, monitoring was developed in a number of fields, from human rights law across trade law to arms control and disarmament. Monitoring is a common feature of modern MEAs. Early examples are included in the 1946 Convention for the Regulation of Whaling, the 1959 Antarctic Treaty, the 1973 Convention on International Trade in Endangered Species of Wild Fauna and Flora (CITES), as well as in the agreements on the protection of the marine environment of Oslo (1972 Oslo Convention) and Paris (1974 Paris Convention). More recent ones have been developed under the 1979 LRTAP Convention and its Protocols, the 1987 Montreal Protocol, the 1989 Basel Convention on the Control of Transboundary Movements of Hazardous Wastes and Their Disposal, the 1992 OSPAR Convention, the 1992 Convention on Biological Diversity (CBD) and the 1992 UN Framework Convention on Climate Change (UNFCCC) with its 1997 Kyoto Protocol.

In contrast to the traditional means of enforcement in international law which often are confrontational, compliance control and compliance assistance bear the hallmarks of co-operation and partnership. They are designed to convince participating parties that the benefits of treaty compliance at least equal the costs associated with it. Co-operative mechanisms seek to establish transparency among parties. Such transparency generates two important effects: (i) it builds confidence in relations among the parties; and (ii) it creates pressure to observe the treaty. As to the first of these effects, transparency can overcome misperceptions over the extent to which other parties comply with their obligations, and it can equip *bona fide* parties with the means of demonstrating their own compliance. On the other hand transparency will also discourage parties from violating a treaty, as they must expect their default to be discovered. Transparency, apart from information exchange, may also include fact finding, including inspections. Of course, fact finding is nothing new in international law, referring to the enquiry as a traditional means of peaceful dispute settlement according to Article 33 of the UN Charter. However, modern MEAs include much more refined systems of fact finding.

Prevention is indispensable for meaningful MEAs. It is not the substantive content of rules alone which is important, but also the utilisation of preventive procedural measures, which ensure that MEAs are indeed complied with and breaches of pertinent treaties

[17] PW Birnie, AE Boyle and C Redgwell, *International Law and the Environment* (3rd edn Oxford 2009) 239 *et seq*.

[18] See W Lang, 'Verhinderung von Erfüllungsdefiziten im Völkerrecht. Beispiele aus Abrüstung und Umweltschutz' in J Hengstschläger *et al* (eds), *Für Staat und Recht: Festschrift für Herbert Schambeck* (Berlin 1994) 817.

do not normally occur. This is what 'active treaty management' means. The following components are central to such an approach: (i) the continuous (routine) monitoring of the conduct of the parties; (ii) mechanisms for dispute avoidance and settlement; (iii) compliance assistance; and (iv) flexible methods for treaty amendments and adjustments.[19] The incorporation of positive and negative incentives towards compliance within the treaty itself is not a prerequisite for such treaty management, but a useful support.[20] Routine monitoring is without doubt the most important element in active treaty management. The aim of such monitoring should not be the detection of treaty violations, but the identification and overcoming of problems with treaty compliance, and improvements in future compliance with these rules. Apart from informal mediation procedures, an authoritative interpretation by treaty bodies can be of significance in the context of dispute settlement. This can contribute to a more flexible handling of treaty obligations, *inter alia*, in that obligations are 'adjusted' in content, within the limits of the treaty text. Compliance assistance enhances the ability of states to comply with their obligations under MEAs. Finally, the adjustment of treaties to changed circumstances also prevents deficient compliance.[21] This may be best achieved by way of simplified treaty amendments or by following the 'framework convention and protocol approach'.[22]

In addition, it is important to include incentives for the promotion of intrinsic compliance with MEAs. Assistance provided within the framework of an MEA can thus be a response to identified non-compliance or a preventive means to steer the behaviour of parties if integrated into the MEA from the outset. While these two approaches cannot be strictly separated, one must be aware of their different functions: on the one hand the removal of material deficits which impair the ability to comply, on the other incentives to observe normative standards. In respect of the latter, market-based and other economic mechanisms have proved to be important. They have been included in the Kyoto Protocol, labelled 'flexibility mechanisms'.

22.2 The Legal Basis of Compliance-Control Procedures

Hardly any of the existing MEAs include comprehensive provisions on the introduction of a compliance-control procedure. Indeed, the design of such a procedure is largely based on an academic analysis of a broad variety of treaty provisions and decisions taken by treaty organs. These provisions and decisions have been brought together to explain the approach to bring about compliance on the basis of reporting, monitoring, verification and evaluation. As will be explained in the following, procedures of compliance

[19] See Chapter 25 on environmental dispute settlement and Chapter 23 on compliance assistance; for more information on 'Simplified Amendment Procedures Regarding Treaties, Protocols and Annexes' see Chapter 18.4.

[20] *Cf* M Bothe, 'The Evaluation of Enforcement Mechanisms in International Environmental Law: An Overview' in Wolfrum (ed), above n 9, 13, 17–22.

[21] On the interaction between law-making and law-enforcement see, among others, U Beyerlin, PT Stoll and R Wolfrum, 'Conclusions drawn from the Conference on Ensuring Compliance with MEAs' in Beyerlin *et al* (eds), above n 6, 359, 360 *et seq.*

[22] See above Chapters 18.3.1 and 18.4.

control vary between MEAs. However, it is possible to identify a number of common elements. They include procedural steps ranging from the 'triggering' of the mechanism to reporting and other means of ascertaining facts up to factual and legal evaluation in order to provide for a sufficiently sound basis for treaty organs to take decisions in light of deficient compliance. Not all of the MEAs discussed here include all procedural steps. Some of them are limited to a few steps only. A similar word of caution applies to the procedural principles to be discussed.[23]

A first attempt to provide an overview of existing compliance-control procedures is to look at the legal basis on which pertinent mechanisms are based. The starting point is the text of the respective treaties.

To begin with, Articles XI, XII and XIII of CITES may be discussed: Article XI CITES is the legal basis for the establishment of the Conference of the Parties (COP); Article XII CITES deals with the Secretariat; and Article XIII addresses 'international measures'. Reporting obligations of parties are included in Article VIII(7) CITES. There is no explicit reference to compliance issues. This may be due to the fact that CITES is one of the earlier agreements. However, the term 'implementation' is used,[24] and the Secretariat (Article XII(2)(d) CITES) and the COP (Article XI(3)(d) CITES) are entrusted with functions related to reports submitted by the parties. Article XIII CITES looks at international measures and may be considered to come closest to a compliance-control mechanism. According to Article XIII CITES, the Secretariat may contact individual parties in case of information about adverse effects on species by trade therein or in case of information about deficient implementation. The process thus triggered may lead to an inquiry and to recommendations adopted by the next COP. Article XIII CITES thus can be considered to form the legal basis of compliance control under CITES. An additional provision which may be mentioned here is Article XII(2)(i) CITES. This provision can be read as a catch-all clause, tasking the Secretariat with performing 'any other function as may be entrusted to it by the Parties'.[25]

In the case of the Montreal Protocol there is not only an explicit provision on reporting obligations of parties to the Protocol (Article 7), but there is also an explicit provision on compliance control. Article 8 requires the Protocol's parties to 'consider and approve procedures and institutional mechanisms for determining non-compliance with the provisions of this Protocol and for treatment of Parties found to be in non-compliance'. This is a provision empowering an organ established by the Protocol to draft and implement compliance-control procedures. The Protocol refrains from laying down any details.[26]

Another example can be taken from the 1994 Sulphur Protocol under the LRTAP Convention. This Protocol—in contrast to earlier Protocols—for the first time under the

[23] For a comparative analysis see, among others, Beyerlin *et al* (eds), above n 6, and T Treves *et al* (eds), *Non-Compliance Procedures and Mechanisms and the Effectiveness of International Environmental Agreements* (The Hague 2009).

[24] *Cf* Art VIII(7) CITES: 'Each Party shall prepare periodic reports on its implementation of the present Convention'.

[25] On compliance control under CITES see S Biniaz, 'Remarks about the Cites Compliance Regime' in Beyerlin *et al* (eds), above n 6, 89 and R Reeve, 'The Convention on International Trade in Endangered Species of Wild Fauna and Flora (CITES)' in Ulfstein *et al* (eds), above n 15, 134, 136–148.

[26] On compliance control under the Montreal Protocol *cf* K Madhava Sarma, 'Compliance with the Multilateral Environmental Agreements to Protect the Ozone Layer' in Beyerlin *et al* (eds), above n 6, 25.

LRTAP regime includes an explicit provision on compliance procedures. Article 7(1) of the Protocol establishes an 'Implementation Committee' with the mandate 'to review the implementation of the present Protocol and compliance by the Parties with their obligations'. Thus, the body in charge of the procedure is directly established by treaty law, whereas the details of the procedure to be applied are entrusted to the parties at the first session of the Executive Body: 'The Parties shall . . . adopt a decision that sets out the structure and functions of the Implementation Committee as well as procedures for its review of compliance' (*cf* Article 7(3) of the Protocol). While the Committee is labelled 'Implementation Committee', the heading of Article 7 as such refers to 'Compliance'.[27]

Article 10 of the 1992 Paris Convention for the Protection of the Marine Environment of the North-East Atlantic (OSPAR Convention) establishes a Commission made up of representatives of the parties. Among the duties to be fulfilled by the Commission is the supervision of 'the implementation of the Convention' (Article 10(2)(a) OSPAR Convention). There is no explicit reference to the term 'compliance' but the Commission has indeed adopted procedures to that end.[28]

The multitude of provisions under the UNFCCC and the Kyoto Protocol which address compliance issues deserves interest. While no compliance committee was established under the UNFCCC, its Articles 3(1) and 4(1) and (2) are relevant with regard to the mandate of the Committee established under the Kyoto Protocol. Of primary importance in this context is Article 18 Kyoto Protocol which requires the parties to the Protocol (convened as the MOP) to 'approve appropriate and effective procedures and mechanisms to determine and to address cases of non-compliance with the provisions of this Protocol'. Thereby the parties are obliged and empowered to establish a compliance-control mechanism. However, Article 18 Kyoto Protocol also provides for an amendment of the Protocol if the parties wish to adopt 'procedures and mechanisms . . . entailing binding consequences'. Further details are partly governed by the Protocol itself (Articles 2, 3(1), 4, 5(1) and (2), 6, 7(1) and (4), 8, 12, and 17 Kyoto Protocol), partly by decisions adopted by the MOP.[29]

Similar to the UNFCCC and the Kyoto Protocol, the CBD itself does not include a comprehensive compliance-control mechanism. The CBD only deals with identification and monitoring (Article 7 CBD) and reports of the parties (Article 26 CBD).[30] However, the Cartagena Biosafety Protocol establishes a compliance committee, based upon its Article 34. With Article 33 of this Protocol laying down reporting obligations of the parties, Article 34 of the Cartagena Protocol stipulates that the MOP 'shall, at its first meeting, consider and approve cooperative procedures and institutional mechanisms to

[27] For further details see T Kuokkanen, 'The Convention on Long-Range Transboundary Air Pollution' in Ulfstein *et al* (eds), above n 15, 161, 166–172; *id*, 'Practice of the Implementation Committee under the Convention on Long-Range Transboundary Air Pollution' in Beyerlin *et al* (eds), above n 6, 39.

[28] See A Simcock, 'OSPAR Convention on the Protection of the Marine Environment of the North-East Atlantic' in Beyerlin *et al* (eds), above n 6, 97.

[29] See R Wolfrum and J Friedrich, 'The Framework Convention on Climate Change and the Kyoto Protocol' in Beyerlin *et al* (eds), above n 6, 53; see also J Brunnée, 'The Kyoto Protocol: Testing Ground for Compliance Theories?' (2003) 63 *ZaöRV* 255 and M Fitzmaurice, 'The Kyoto Protocol Compliance Regime and Treaty Law' (2004) 8 *Singapore Journal of International & Comparative Law* 23.

[30] UNEP, *Compliance Mechanisms Under Selected Multilateral Environmental Agreements* (Nairobi 2007) 47.

promote compliance with the provisions of this Protocol and to address cases of non-compliance'.[31]

Similarly, Article 27 UNCCD, Article 17 of the Rotterdam Convention on the Prior Informed Consent Procedure for Certain Hazardous Chemicals and Pesticides in International Trade, and Article 17 of the Stockholm Convention on Persistent Organic Pollutants provide for a treaty-based compliance mechanism of, however, varying density.[32]

Having had a brief look at the treaty basis for compliance-control procedures in a variety of MEAs it can be concluded that, as a rule, treaties, if they include precise obligations and if they are not merely framework instruments, include an obligation and an authorisation of the parties thereof to develop and establish a compliance-control mechanism. Even though there are MEAs which do not include such mechanisms it can be argued that such treaty provisions are a common feature of pertinent agreements. While there is indeed a treaty basis for such procedures, the details are obviously considered as being more technical than political and thus are left to the plenary organs established by the respective MEAs. Only in some cases is the delegation of decision-making to organs established by the MEA limited. The most prominent example thereof is Article 18 Kyoto Protocol which in the case of entrusting the compliance body with the power to take binding decisions requires an amendment of the Protocol.[33] Other agreements are essentially tacit but the language used suggests that the powers of the subsidiary organs established for the purpose of compliance control are limited.

Nevertheless, the second layer of provisions forming the legal basis of compliance-control procedures is important. This secondary law has to be assessed and interpreted in light of international institutional law.[34] Even though it is debatable whether the institutional structure of MEAs themselves allows us to consider these as a kind of international organisation, the delegation of power included in the respective treaty provisions necessitates the application of the same principles which apply to law-making powers of international organisations. Such law-making must remain within the limits of the delegating provision. This is particularly important with regard to the binding effect of such secondary law-making. Compliance-control procedures will generally be internal law of international organisations or the institutional backbone of MEAs. However, if in response to deficient compliance or non-compliance treaty bodies adopt binding decisions *vis-à-vis* parties, these measures necessitate separate legal authority. Normally, there will be explicit treaty provisions authorising measures to redress such a situation. This seems to be the assumption also of Article 18 Kyoto Protocol in the absence of an explicit authorisation of the Protocol's organs to respond to such situations with binding

[31] See V Koester, 'The Compliance Mechanism of the Cartagena Protocol on Biosafety' (2009) 18 *RECIEL* 77.

[32] *Cf* also, *eg*, Art 15(5)(e) of the Basel Convention dealing with the establishment of subsidiary bodies deemed necessary for the implementation of the Convention, Art 16 of the 1992 Convention on the Protection of the Environment of the Baltic Sea Area (Helsinki Convention) relating to reporting and exchange of information and Art 15 of the 1998 Aarhus Convention on review of compliance.

[33] Fitzmaurice, above n 29, 28.

[34] J Klabbers, *An Introduction to International Institutional Law* (2nd edn Cambridge 2009) 163–228.

decisions.[35] In addition, interpretation of secondary rules must be done in light of the authorising treaty, its wording, its context and its object and purpose.

In the following, most of the details of the compliance-control procedures discussed will be traced back to secondary law established under the respective MEAs. Treaty provisions will be taken into account in so far as they are relevant to the interpretation of the pertinent decisions of treaty bodies.

22.3 The Procedural Framework

Compliance control is the main strategy to counter deficient or non-compliance in international environmental law. While compliance assistance focuses on specific administrative, technical and financial measures, compliance control's primary objective is transparency which underscores its co-operative character. In essence, compliance control can be considered as institutionalised and formal monitoring of parties in respect of meeting their treaty obligations.

There are two procedural variants of compliance-control mechanisms: (i) 'routine procedures' which are continuously applied; and (ii) '*ad hoc* procedures' which are initiated only if a party encounters difficulties in meeting its treaty obligations. The first variant has developed into a common feature of MEAs in the form of obligations to submit declarations and to report, sometimes followed by verification, building largely upon reporting procedures in international human rights law. The second variant is labelled 'non-compliance procedure' in MEAs and builds upon experiences with *ad hoc* procedures in international arms control law. The second variant, typically as an option to be decided upon by the pertinent COP or MOP, has been included, among others, in the Montreal Protocol (Article 8),[36] the LRTAP Convention (beginning with the Oslo Protocol),[37] the UNCCD (Article 27, with a slightly more open wording than in the other cases),[38] the UNFCCC (Article 13), the Kyoto Protocol (Article 18),[39] the Basel Convention (Article 19),[40] the Rotterdam Convention (Article 17),[41] the Cartagena Protocol (Article 34)[42] and the Stockholm Convention (Article 17).[43]

[35] Fitzmaurice, above n 29, 28.

[36] See MOP 4 Decision IV/5 in UNEP/OzLPro4/15 (25 November 1992); *cf* also Decision IX/10 in UNEP/OzLPro10/9 (23–24 November 1998).

[37] Decision 1997/2 of the Executive Body in ECE/EB.AIR/53 (7 January 1998), Decision 1998/6 'Concerning the Application of the Compliance Procedure to the Oslo Protocol' in ECE/EB.AIR/59 (8 January 1999) and Decision 2006/2 in ECE/EB.AIR/2006/2.

[38] In this respect see Decision 28/COP9 (2 October 2009) in ICCD/COP(9)/18/Add1 (18 November 2009).

[39] Decision 24/CP7 (10 November 2001) in UN Doc FCCC/CP/2001/13/Add3 (21 January 2002), Decision 27/CMP1 (9–10 December 2005) in UN Doc FCCC/KP/CMP/2005/8/Add3 (30 March 2006), Decision 4/CMP2 (17 November 2006) in UN Doc FCCC/KP/CMP/2006/10/Add1 (2 March 2007) and Decision 4/CMP4 (12 December 2008) in UN Doc FCCC/KP/CMP/2008/11/Add1 (19 March 2009).

[40] *Cf* Decision V/16 in UNEP/CHW5/29 (10 December 1999) and Decision VI/12 in UNEP/CHW6/40 (10 February 2003).

[41] Decision RC-4/7 in UNEP/FAO/RC/COP4/24 (31 October 2008).

[42] See BS-I/7 in UNEP/CBD/BS/COP-MOP/1/15 (14 April 2004) and BS-II/1 in UNEP/CBD/BS/COP-MOP/2/15 (6 June 2005).

[43] SC-4/33 in UNEP/POPS/COP4/38 (8 May 2009).

In legal terms, compliance control is implemented on the basis of procedural law providing procedural steps and procedural principles. In the following, four procedural steps will be discussed separately: (i) trigger mechanisms (routine or *ad hoc*); (ii) verification; (iii) evaluation; and (iv) measures to redress a situation. An analysis of pertinent treaty law and practice will be followed by a discussion of procedural principles and safeguards.

22.3.1 Trigger Mechanisms

In the case of routine compliance control, the mechanism is typically triggered on the basis of regularly submitted declarations and appropriate reporting. This reflects the vital importance of properly establishing the facts for compliance control. Factual uncertainty carries considerable potential for conflict. On the basis of ascertained relevant facts, each party to an MEA is able to assess the degree of treaty compliance by any other party. This builds confidence among parties. The first and foremost technique of fact finding in modern multilateral agreements is reporting, which normally takes the form of submitting initial declarations about national implementation and thereafter further declarations at regular intervals.[44]

Although reporting and declaration obligations as part of routine compliance control are comparable to the obligations to exchange (environmentally relevant) information as between states, there is a qualitative distinction. Information exchange between states typically focuses on scientific and technical data. These obligations must be distinguished from information gathering for the purpose of reporting. As may be taken from Article 5 of the 1985 Vienna Ozone Convention, reporting for the purpose of compliance control focuses on 'information on the measures adopted by them [*ie* the parties] in implementation of this Convention'. Reporting obligations vary considerably, ranging from general obligations to transmit to the responsible organs information of measures taken to implement the agreement, to detailed reporting duties on production, emission and other data.[45] In some cases, Secretariats[46] or COPs[47] have been empowered to specify the details,

[44] A Kiss, 'Reporting Obligations and Assessment of Reports' in Beyerlin *et al* (eds), above n 6, 229.

[45] See Art 26 CBD, Art 33 Biosafety Protocol, Arts 4, 7(2)(f), 8(2)(b) and 12 UNFCCC and Art 15 Stockholm Convention. Under the Rotterdam Convention, there is no self-reporting obligation but some provisions include operational information exchanges which allow for the assessment of performance (*cf eg* Art 5 which foresees that each party shall inform the Secretariat of its final regulatory action within 90 days).

[46] *Cf* para 2 of the decisions adopted by COP 1 to the Vienna Ozone Convention in UNEP/OzLConv1/5 (28 April 1989) 9; see also Art 5 of the Oslo Protocol.

[47] MOP 1 to the Montreal Protocol decided to modify the 'Harmonised Commodity Description and Coding System' (UNEP/OzLPro1/5 (6 May 1989) 13 and Annex VII, 1 *et seq*); *cf* Decision XVII/16 in UNEP/OzLConv7/7–UNEP/OzLPro17/11 (25 January 2006) where MOP 17 to the Montreal Protocol decided to request the Ozone Secretariat to revise the reporting format. See also the guidelines for parties to the Climate Change Convention: for reports according to Art 12 (UN Doc FCCC/CP/1996, L13, paras 4–11) and for Annex I countries (UN Doc FCCC/CP/1996/L12). In regard to the first reports the Secretariat criticised a lack of comparability (UN Doc FCCC/CP/1996/12, paras 29, 34, 45), a matter which is stressed in the guidelines: 'to encourage the presentation of information in ways that are, to the extent possible, consistent, transparent and *comparable* as well as flexible' (UN Doc FCCC/CP/1996/L12, Annex, para 1(b); author's italics); 'to facilitate the process of considering the national communications . . . by encouraging the presentation of information in ways that are consistent, transparent and *comparable*' (UN Doc FCCC/CP/1996/Add1, para 1(b); author's italics). See also some of the later decisions of the COP: Decision 14/CP11 (9–10 December 2005) in FCCC/

establishing formats for reporting, thereby guaranteeing a degree of uniformity and comparability.[48] Some MEAs provide for Secretariats 'to request such further information' with respect to reports submitted 'as it deems necessary to ensure implementation of the present Convention' (Article XII(2)(d) CITES).[49]

As important as reporting is for meaningful routine compliance control, states increasingly face problems in meeting the numerous reporting obligations.[50] Obtaining relevant data from private actors, including business, requires national legislation and administrative capacities, eventually involving high financial burdens for the parties. It is important to preserve cost-efficiency by carefully selecting which information is important for assessing compliance and how often such information needs to be updated as well as by building upon synergies among different regimes as far as possible.[51]

Normally, reports must be conveyed to the relevant treaty Secretariats which often act not only as 'switchboards' but process information and draft reports for other treaty bodies.[52] Communication of the reports of parties in their entirety to the plenary organ of the respective MEA is rare in light of its limited effectiveness. Reference can be made to Article 12(c) of the Montreal Protocol providing for the Secretariat to produce and make available to the parties reports on the basis of information received in accordance with Articles 7 and 9 of the Protocol. The Protocol's COP does not scrutinise the information channelled according to Articles 7 and 9 of the Protocol, but only the reports drafted by the Secretariat.[53]

The initiation of *ad hoc* or non-compliance procedures depends upon the trigger mech-

CP/2005/5/Add2 (30 March 2006) relating to the common reporting format for land use, land-use change and forestry, Decision 6/CP5 (4 November 1999) in FCCC/CP/1999/6/Add1 (2 February 2000) relating to the guidelines for the technical review of greenhouse gas inventories from Annex I countries and Decision 10/CP13 (14–15 December 2007) in FCCC/CP/2007/6/Add1 (14 March 2008) referring to the submission of the fifth national communication (in this respect see also FCCC/CP/1999/7 (16 February 2000) containing revised guidelines adopted by the COP). *Cf* also the Decision of COP 1 to the Stockholm Convention SC-1/22 in UNEP/POPS/COP1/31 (6 May 2005) according to which the parties are requested to use the format attached to that decision.

[48] See K Sachariew, 'Promoting Compliance with International Environmental Legal Standards: Reflection on Monitoring and Reporting Mechanisms' (1991) 2 *Yearbook of International Environmental Law* 31, 44.

[49] See also the Basel Convention which provides a similar example in its Art 16(1)(b) foreseeing that the Secretariat may also use information provided by relevant intergovernmental and non-governmental entities.

[50] On this *cf* the 'Report of the Expert Group Meeting on Identification of Principles of International Law for Sustainable Development' (Geneva, 26–28 September 1995) para 158, available at www.un.org/documents/ecosoc/cn17/1996/background/ecn171996-bp3.htm; in addition see the deliberations of the 4th Session of the CSD in UN Doc E/CN17/1996/17 (28 February 1996) para 13 and Add 1, para 23. Compare in this respect the issue paper of the High-Level Meeting on Compliance with and Enforcement of Multilateral Environmental Agreements, 'Envisioning the Next Steps for Compliance with and Enforcement of MEAs', 21–22 January 2006, available at www.unep.org/DEC/docs/Issue.paper.doc.

[51] See G Loibl, 'Reporting and Information Systems in International Environmental Agreements as a Means for Dispute Prevention' (2005) 5 *Non-State Actors and International Law* 1, 15 *et seq*; see also Kiss, above n 44, 243 *et seq*.

[52] See Kiss, *ibid*, 242.

[53] Similarly, under the Kyoto Protocol, the reporting obligations of the Annex I parties (developed country parties and country parties undergoing the process of transition to a market economy) as contained in Art 7 Kyoto Protocol are reviewed by expert review teams under the co-ordination of the Secretariat (Art 8 Kyoto Protocol), The report summarising the outcome of the review process is circulated by the Secretariat to the Protocol's COP/MOP in order to assess 'the implementation of the commitments of the Party and identifying any potential problems in, and factors influencing, the fulfilment of commitments' (Art 8(3) Kyoto Protocol).

anisms provided for in pertinent instruments. This will normally be an application by a party prompting action by the Secretariat.[54] While most applications may be made in the form of traditional 'inter-state applications', some non-compliance procedures allow for self-incrimination. In order to avoid abuse, some procedures require that the application is accompanied by corroborating information. NGOs are normally not entitled to initiate non-compliance procedures.[55] Treaty bodies can only act *ex officio* in a very limited number of cases.[56]

22.3.2 Verification

Information provided by the parties on the basis of reporting obligations must be verifiable in respect of their relevance to compliance and also as to their veracity. It is obvious that the effectiveness of compliance control is essentially governed by the leeway given to treaty bodies for verification and related additional fact finding. Indeed, it is important that treaty bodies are not limited to requests for clarification with a view to ambivalent data, but also have access to other sources of information, whether obtained from third parties, NGOs or by their own means, including on-site inspections.[57]

The following means have been applied by various MEAs and will be discussed accordingly: (i) information provided by other parties; (ii) information obtained from NGOs or private individuals; (iii) information gathered through on-site inspections; and (iv) technical monitoring.

As far as information provided by other parties is concerned, there is a general reluctance of one party to comment on the conduct of other parties. Nevertheless, some treaties allow for such information to be included. Most important is the power of parties to initiate non-compliance procedures, as provided for under the Montreal Protocol (paragraph 1) and the Oslo Protocol (paragraph 3).[58] Such applications must be accompanied by 'corroborating information', thus providing for third-party input. The compliance procedure under the Cartagena Protocol also allows for the initiation of the procedure by a party 'which is affected or likely to be affected'.[59] Similarly, under the Kyoto Protocol compliance mechanism 'any Party with respect to another Party, supported by corroborating information' is able to submit questions of implementation to the Committee.[60]

[54] *Cf* Decision BS-I/7, above n 42, 99 at IV for the Biosafety Protocol, Decision 27/CMP.1, above n 39, 96 at VI for the Kyoto Protocol and Decision I/7 in ECE/MP.PP/2/Add8 (2 April 2004), 4 part IV for the Aarhus Convention.

[55] A Epiney, 'The Role of NGOs in the Process of Ensuring Compliance with MEAs' in Beyerlin (eds), above n 6, 319, 330. In the case of the Kyoto Protocol competent NGOs are allowed to submit relevant technical or factual information to the pertinent branch.

[56] *Eg* in the case of the Aarhus Convention the Secretariat may bring a case of possible non-compliance by a party to the attention of the Committee, see Decision I/7, above n 54, 4 para 17.

[57] For a discussion of pertinent regimes *cf* M Bothe, 'Ensuring Compliance with Multilateral Environmental Agreements – Systems of Inspection and External Monitoring' in Beyerlin (eds), above n 6, 247.

[58] See Decision IV/5, above n 36, 44 para 1 (Montreal Protocol) and Decision 2006/2, above n 37, 2 para 4 (Oslo Protocol).

[59] See BS-I/7, above n 42, 98 *et seq.*

[60] See Decision 27/ CMP1, above n 39, Annex, s VI, para 1.

Obtaining additional information from NGOs or private individuals is particularly interesting for two reasons. Firstly, such information can function as 'counter-statement' *vis-à-vis* information provided by parties or as a 'substitute' for data parties have failed to provide. Secondly, this capacity directly affects the legal status of NGOs within the institutional structure, with regard to the procedural rights granted to them, and in public international law as a whole. Indeed, MEAs have increasingly included NGOs as relevant actors, principally by granting them observer status. Initially, their status was determined by the appropriate COP on the basis of its rules of procedures. Increasingly, it is today the text of the MEA itself which grants a particular status to NGOs.[61]

According to Article 11 of the 1992 Paris Convention for the Protection of the Marine Environment of the North-East Atlantic, the Commission (as the Convention's plenary organ) 'may, by unanimous vote of the Contracting Parties, decide to admit as an observer: . . . any international governmental or any non-governmental organisation, the activities of which are related to the Convention'. Similarly, Article XI(7) CITES, Article 11(5) of the Montreal Protocol and Article 7(6) UNFCCC include a legal basis for NGO involvement. Whereas procedural rights are specified in rules of procedures of pertinent treaty bodies, Article 11(2) of the 1992 Paris Convention itself provides that 'such observers may participate in meetings of the Commission, but without the right to vote and may present to the Commission any information or reports relevant to the objectives of the Convention'. The criteria for admission and participation are, however, left with the Commission (Article 11(3) of the 1992 Paris Convention). In some cases, NGOs have even obtained access to treaty bodies with limited membership, such as the LRTAP Executive Body.

In general, if their functions are specified at all, NGOs are limited to providing information.[62] Their role will remain limited 'as long as their standing with respect to the reporting procedure is not expressly defined'.[63] A stronger and more formalised role for NGOs is desirable if, as has been argued with regard to CITES, they act as 'guardians of the spirit and purpose of [a treaty] by monitoring both compliance and enforcement'.[64] Nevertheless, parties will remain the 'masters of the proceedings'.

On-site inspections, due to their visible effects on state sovereignty, are not the most common means to ascertain facts under MEAs. Nevertheless, they have been taken up by some MEAs, however, subject to several procedural safeguards. Article XIII(2) CITES refers to an 'inquiry' which is only permissible with the consent of the party in question. However, no further details can be taken from the treaty text itself or from any decision of a treaty organ adopted on that basis. Under the 1971 Ramsar Convention a so-called

[61] For further details see Epiney, above n 55.

[62] *Cf eg* Rule 7 para 1 of the rules of procedure of the Meeting of the Parties of the Montreal Protocol for their role at meetings, Decision I/1, above n 47, Annex I.

[63] Sachariew, above n 48, 49. For the role of NGOs in the prevention of compliance deficits, see also J Cameron, 'Compliance, Citizens and NGOs' in J Cameron *et al* (eds), *Improving Compliance with International Environmental Law* (London 1996) 29, 36 *et seq*; and Epiney, above n 55, 333.

[64] P Sands and AP Bedecarre, 'Convention on International Trade in Endangered Species: The Role of Public Interest Non-Governmental Organizations in Ensuring the Enforcement of the Ivory Trade Ban' (1989/1990) 17 *Boston College Environmental Affairs Law Review* 799, 800.

'monitoring' procedure was instituted by COP 4.[65] The Montreal[66] and Oslo[67] non-compliance procedures provide for information-gathering on the territory of a party 'upon the invitation of the Party concerned', to be carried out by the Implementation Committee.[68] None of the procedures is specified beyond establishing the requirement to obtain the consent of the party concerned. This may be due to the complex legal framework which must be established if on-site inspections are implemented, as can be taken from experiences in the field of arms control.[69] Legal matters to be addressed include the diplomatic status of the personnel involved, questions of liability, the protection of confidential data (government and business), and the protection of individual rights of persons affected by such on-site inspections.

Technical monitoring (*stricto sensu*) in spite of its immediate plausibility has only rarely been used in MEA-based compliance control. Such monitoring focuses on the collection of scientific and technical data. It aims at providing information on the situation of the environment, without directly taking up issues of compliance. Typically, the primary use of such data has been the preparation of normative standards which does not exclude their use in compliance control.[70] However, comprehensive technical monitoring is being further developed, not only at the national level but also by international bodies, including UNEP. Noteworthy is the EMEP Programme, a monitoring system established for the LRTAP Convention.[71]

22.3.3 Evaluation

As far as evaluation of the findings is concerned, it is important to distinguish between factual and legal evaluation. Factual evaluation means the way in which decisions as to whether certain facts exist or do not exist are taken.[72] The question to be addressed here is whether there are specific rules for factual evaluation. When addressing this issue it has to be kept in mind that most MEAs are neither clear nor comprehensive on these matters. If

[65] This procedure is used in cases where, due to human influence, changes in the ecological character of certain areas included in the 'List of Wetland of International Importance' are likely, or have actually occurred. In such instances, on-site visits and discussions with the affected state are provided for. See C de Klemm, 'The Year in Review (Nature Conservancy: Natural Lands and Biological Diversity)' (1990) 1 *Yearbook of International Environmental Law* 187, 189.

[66] See Decision X/10, above n 36, Annex II para 7(e).

[67] Decision 2006/2, above n 37, para 6(b) .

[68] On the Implementation Committee, see W Lang, 'Compliance Control in International Environmental Law: Institutional Necessities' (1996) 56 *ZaöRV* 685, 689.

[69] *Cf* for example W Lang, above n 18, 825 *et seq*; see also Bothe, above n 6, 256.

[70] Under the Oslo Protocol, state reports in accordance with Art 5, para 1, are also evaluated by the Cooperative Programme for Monitoring and Evaluation of the Long-Range Transmission of Air Pollutants in Europe (EMEP). On the programme see UN Economic Commission for Europe, *Strategy for EMEP 2000–2009: Convention On Long-Range Transboundary Air Pollution: Cooperative Programme for Monitoring and Evaluation of the Long-Range Transmission of Air Pollutants in Europe (EMEP)* (Geneva 2001). See also T Schneider and J Schneider, 'EMEP—Backbone of the Convention' in J Sliggers and W Kakebeeke (eds), *Cleaning the Air: 25 Years of the Convention on Long-Range Transboundary Air Pollution* (Geneva 2004) 31.

[71] See Art 9 of the Convention on Long-range Transboundary Air Pollution.

[72] Kiss, above n 44, 234 *et seq.*

compliance control is to be effective, reporting and verification must be complemented by a binding statement of facts. This is important in the case of any type of legal assessment to be made whether by the parties or by any treaty organ.

Article XII(2)(d) CITES entrusts the Secretariat with more than 'switchboard services' between parties: the Secretariat is tasked 'to study the reports' submitted by the parties. In addition, the Secretariat may request additional information if necessary which indicates that the Secretariat is empowered to examine the reports closely. This may also be considered a prerequisite for the preparation of its annual reports to the parties according to Article XII(2)(g) CITES, covering, *inter alia*, problems of enforcement. Article XIII CITES supports the reading that the Secretariat enjoys powers of factual evaluation ('in the light of information received'). Similarly, under the Vienna Ozone Convention, the Secretariat, according to Article 7(1)(b), has '[t]o prepare and transmit reports based upon information received' from the parties. As may be taken from Article 5 of the Convention, which reads that these reports are submitted to the COP 'through the secretariat', the powers of the Secretariat are broad enough to cover factual evaluation, including the filtering of such reports and the extracting of relevant information. The Montreal Protocol requires parties to transmit to the Secretariat statistical information (Article 7) initially and on an annual basis. The Secretariat 'receive[s]' (Article 12(a)) such data and 'prepare[s] and distribute[s] reports based on information received' (Article 12(c)). Again, similarly to the provisions of the Ozone Convention, this may include elements of factual evaluation before submitting information to the Protocol's MOP.[73]

Legal evaluation understood as assessing the facts in light of the obligations undertaken by the parties to an MEA is not normally included in the administrative part of compliance control but left to a 'political' body. Thus, the resulting evaluation rather is political in nature and leaves room for the co-operative settlement of compliance problems.[74] This avoids conclusions on whether or not there has been a breach of treaty, but by restricting the administrative part of compliance control to 'pure' fact finding, fosters 'soft' approaches to deficient or non-compliance. It is not surprising that even non-compliance (*ie ad hoc*) procedures have been described as 'the middle way between diplomacy and law'.[75]

To illustrate this briefly, CITES is unclear in respect of the legal evaluation since Article XII CITES does not suffice as a legal basis. On the other hand, Article XIII CITES ('[i]s satisfied that any species . . . is being affected adversely . . . or that the provisions . . . are not being effectively implemented') suggests that the Secretariat is not prevented from undertaking a legal evaluation of the facts established. While the parties have been reluctant to provide further powers to the Secretariat according to Article

[73] See Sarma, above n 26, 32.

[74] Comparing enforcement and compliance control, *cf* Brunnée, above n 6, 1 *et seq*; for a discussion of the relationship between non-compliance and breach of treaty see M Koskenniemi, 'Breach of Treaty or Non-Compliance? Reflections on the Enforcement of the Montreal Protocol' (1992) 3 *Yearbook of International Environmental Law* 123; see also PH Sand, 'Sanctions in Case of Non-Compliance and State Responsibility: Pacta Sunt Servanda—Or Else?' in Beyerlin *et al* (eds), above n 6, 259.

[75] MM Goote, 'Non-Compliance Procedures in International Environmental Law: The Middle Way between Diplomacy and Law' (1999) 1 *International Law Forum* 82.

XII(2)(i) CITES, the Secretariat's reports on deficient compliance have always been taken seriously by the parties.[76]

As can be taken from Article 11(4)(a) of the Montreal Protocol, the evaluation of facts in light of the obligations undertaken is within the purview of the Protocol's MOP and also of the Implementation Committee.[77] Apart from its early involvement in the implementation of reporting obligations,[78] the Committee is of primary significance for the non-compliance procedure, including factual[79] and legal evaluation.[80] In particular, the authority of the Committee to include recommendations to the MOP makes apparent that it must legally evaluate the information it receives.

22.3.4 Measures in Response to Non-Compliance

If non-compliance is established, competent treaty bodies must assess how to respond. While some MEAs contain general stipulations on available measures, others provide detailed catalogues. MEAs tend to allocate pertinent powers with the COP without providing further details of content. According to Article XIII CITES, the COP 'may make whatever recommendations it deems appropriate'. Whether 'recommendations' alone are adequate means in response to non-compliance has rightly been questioned.[81] In particular, Article XIII CITES seems to block recourse to other, equally effective measures such as warnings that if reporting obligations are not met measures will be taken on the basis of estimations or unofficial data.[82]

The non-compliance procedure developed under the Montreal Protocol is much more refined. The Protocol's Implementation Committee, unless finding a consensual solution with the party concerned, may submit non-binding recommendations to the MOP which will 'decide upon and call for steps to bring about full compliance with the Protocol, including measures to assist the Party's compliance with the Protocol, and to further the Protocols objectives' (paragraph 9). As laid down in the (non-exhaustive) 'Indicative List of Measures that might be taken by the Meeting of the Parties in respect of non-compliance with the Protocol',[83] agreed upon by the MOP, there are carrots and sticks

[76] DS Favre, *International Trade in Endangered Species: A Guide to CITES* (Dordrecht *et al* 1989) 295, with further references.

[77] On the details, see Lang, above n 68, 689 *et seq* as well as *id,* 'Compliance-Control in Respect of the Montreal Protocol' (1995) 89 *Proceedings of the American Society of International Law at its 89th Annual Meeting* 206.

[78] Lang (1995), *ibid*, 209. See also P Szell, 'Implementation Control: Non-compliance Procedure and Dispute Settlement in the Ozone Regime' in W Lang (ed), *The Ozone Treaties and their Influence on the Building of International Environmental Regimes* (Wien 1996) 43, 47. On the details, see the protocols of the 1st–45th Meetings of the Implementation Committee, UNEP/OzLPro/ImpCom/1/2-45/4.

[79] *Cf* para 7 of the Montreal non-compliance procedure: '[r]eceive, consider and report on any submission; . . . receive, consider and report on any information or observations forwarded by the Secretariat in connection with the preparation of the reports referred to in Article 12(c) of the Protocol and on any other information received and forwarded by the Secretariat'.

[80] *Cf ibid,* paras 8 and 9: '[s]ecuring an amicable solution of the matter on the basis of respect for the provisions of the Protocol' and '[t]o report to the Meeting of the Parties, including any recommendations'.

[81] Favre, above n 76, 297: 'A more "toothless" provision would be hard to imagine.'

[82] For details see Sachariew, above n 48, 43.

[83] UNEP/OzLPro4/15 (25 November 1992) Annex V, 48.

available. These include appropriate assistance, issuing cautions, and the suspension of specific rights and privileges.

More broadly worded are the powers entrusted to the plenary organ under the 1992 Paris Convention:[84] The Commission may '[w]hen appropriate, decide upon and call for steps to bring about full compliance with the Convention, and decisions adopted thereunder, and promote the implementation of recommendations, including measures to assist a Contracting Party to carry out its obligations' (*cf* Article 23). No further specification is included in the Paris Convention.

The stringent rules for fact finding contrast sharply with the flexibility for measures to redress non-compliance. This is not without problems as it is difficult to distinguish between breach of treaty and non-compliance.[85] However, legal precision is not an end in itself and co-operative dispute avoidance reflects new approaches. On the occasion of the third meeting of the Ad Hoc Working Group of Legal Experts on Non-Compliance with the Montreal Protocol[86] the following situations were considered as 'non-compliance': (i) failure to meet the control requirements of Article 2 of the Protocol; (ii) failure to comply with restrictions imposed on trade with non-parties; (iii) non-compliance with time schedules and failure to meet reporting obligations; (iv) lack of co-operation, as defined in Article 9 of the Protocol; (v) non-payment of contributions under Article 10; (vi) non-observance of the provisions on the transfer of technology; and (vii) disregard of MOP decisions. The parties could not agree on whether payments in accordance with Article 10 of the Protocol are voluntary, and to what extent MOP decisions are binding. Thus, the list was not formally adopted.[87]

22.3.5 Procedural Principles and Safeguards

In order to maintain both the co-operative and 'quasi-judicial'[88] character of compliance-control mechanisms, factual and legal evaluation are normally kept apart from each other. Ascertaining facts remains within the purview of procedural law, whereas reactions to non-compliance are dealt with in a much more flexible way. Indeed, increasingly, the procedure follows a clear-cut legal and administrative design. There are many reasons for a solid procedural framework: compliance-control impacts on sovereignty; private individuals and business actors may be affected by data collection and reporting; and politically sound decision-making requires a solid factual basis. Pertinent procedural law deals with sequencing elements of compliance control (procedural steps) and procedural principles; most of them are indeed principles, some even enjoy the status of rules, according to R Dworkin's legal theory.[89]

[84] *Cf* Simcock, above n 28, 105 *et seq.*

[85] Koskenniemi, above n 74, 155 *et seq.*

[86] UNEP/OzLPro/WG.3/3/3 (9 November 1991) Annex II.

[87] P Szell, 'The Development of Multilateral Mechanisms for Monitoring Compliance' in Lang (ed), above n 7, 97, 101 note 13.

[88] DG Victor, 'The Montreal Protocol's Non-Compliance Procedure: Lessons for Making Other Environmental Regimes More Effective' in Lang, above n 78, 58, 62–63.

[89] Principles are norms that are first and foremost designed to give guidance to their addressees for future conduct and to shape the interpretation and application of rules already in existence; see Chapter 5.

Basically compliance-control mechanisms provide the following procedural steps:[90] (i) opening of the procedure; (ii) verification; (iii) evaluation; and (iv) taking of measures in response to non-compliance. The opening of the procedure, as already shown, depends on whether the procedure is routine (*ie* declarations and reporting) or *ad hoc* (non-compliance procedure). Some of the opening steps involve the determination of the mandate and the specification of the standards applicable; this is equivalent to the establishment of jurisdiction for compliance control. The scope of the procedure regularly depends on the substantive provisions of the MEA concerned; the more specific their wording, the clearer are the standards of compliance control.[91] CITES and the Montreal Protocol include fairly precise stipulations; compliance can be assessed easily and in a largely cost-efficient manner. Other MEAs are more broadly worded and compliance with them is more difficult to ascertain. This is true for the CBD as well as for the UNFCCC and the Kyoto Protocol, even though the latter includes rather precise obligations imposed upon developed country parties. Inasmuch as the applicable standards cannot be directly taken from the provisions of the MEA concerned, they are set by competent treaty bodies, primarily the COP, sometimes the Secretariat. As regards the other steps, reference can be made to the above discussion of the main procedural elements of compliance-control mechanisms.

To date, compliance-control mechanisms do not explicitly include comprehensive sets of procedural principles. However, the following principles, serving the protection of the rights and interests of entities affected by compliance control, can be derived from pertinent procedural arrangements: (i) the principle of procedural co-operation; (ii) the right to be heard; (iii) the principle of equal treatment; (iv) the principle of proportionality; and (v) the protection of confidential information, whether governmental or business.[92]

The principle of procedural co-operation requires parties and treaty bodies to deploy a degree of co-operation in implementing compliance-control mechanisms. Parties and treaty bodies must be considerate of each other's interests. As concerns the parties to an MEA, procedural co-operation is rooted in the obligation of *bona fide* compliance with substantive and procedural treaty law as included in Article 26 VCLT and its customary law equivalent. Self-incrimination as provided for in some non-compliance procedures also reflects this principle. The obligation imposed on treaty bodies to search for 'amicable' (Montreal Protocol) or 'constructive' (Oslo Protocol) solutions also is an expression of the procedural co-operation principle.[93] This principle is also referred to in the non-compliance procedures under the Cartagena Biosafety Protocol,[94] the Kyoto Protocol[95] and the Aarhus Convention.[96]

[90] See T Marauhn, 'Towards a Procedural Law of Compliance Control in International Environmental Relations' (1996) 56 *ZaöRV* 696, 699 *et seq.*

[91] *Cf* E Brown Weiss and HK Jacobsen, 'Strengthening Compliance with International Environmental Accords: Preliminary Observations from a Collaborative Project'(1995) 1 *Global Governance* 119, 139.

[92] See Marauhn, above n 90, 722 *et seq.*

[93] *Cf* para 8 of the Montreal and para 3(b) of the Oslo non-compliance procedures.

[94] Part I para 2 of the non-compliance procedure states that the procedures and mechanisms shall be simple, facilitative, non-adversarial and co-operative in nature.

[95] Part V para 6 of the non-compliance procedure states that the consequences to be applied by the Enforcement Branch shall be, *inter alia*, aimed at providing an incentive to comply.

[96] According to part III para 13(c) of the non-compliance procedure the Committee shall facilitate the

The right to be heard emanates from the principle of procedural co-operation. It forms part of what is today known as the 'international rule of law'.[97] Thus, before responding to deficient or non-compliance, the CITES Secretariat (for example) must draw the attention of the national Management Authority to implementation problems of the party concerned (Article XIII CITES). Non-compliance procedures go beyond notification requirements and seek to ensure the participation of a representative of the party under scrutiny in the deliberations of the competent treaty body, such as the Implementation Committee under the Montreal and Oslo Protocols.[98] This does not include the party's participation in decision-making on measures in response to non-compliance. The right to be heard is included in the non-compliance procedure adopted under the Cartagena Biosafety Protocol[99] as well as in the procedures under the Kyoto Protocol[100] and the Aarhus Convention.[101]

The principle of equal treatment emerges from the principle of sovereign equality as included in the UN Charter.[102] It requires that all parties to an MEA must be equally subjected to compliance control.[103] This does not exclude non-compliance procedures on particular parties as long as there is a plausible reason for differential treatment of the parties.

The principle of proportionality has by now developed into a standard element of international compliance procedures.[104] It is reflected in various procedural provisions, including the obligation of Secretariats to restrict data acquisition to 'necessary' infor-

implementation of and compliance with the reporting obligations and may in accordance with part XI para 36(a) in consultation with the party concerned take measures listed in the procedure. On compliance control under the Aarhus Convention see V Koester, 'The Convention on Access to Information, Public Participation in Decision-Making and Access to Justice in Environmental Matters (Aarhus Convention)', in Ulfstein *et al* (eds), above n 15, 179, 197–202.

[97] *Cf* A Watts, 'The International Rule of Law' (1993) 36 *German Yearbook of International Law* 15; see also S Chesterman, 'Rule of Law' in R Wolfrum (ed), *Max Planck Encyclopedia of Public International Law* (Heidelberg/Oxford 2007), available at www.mpepil.com.

[98] According to the non-compliance procedure of the Montreal Protocol, a party whose compliance has been made the object of a submission by another state party, or has made a submission of self-incrimination to the Secretariat, can 'participate in the consideration by the Committee of that submission' (para 10). However, it is granted no right of participation 'in the elaboration and adoption of recommendations on that matter' (para 11). Similar provisions are made in the Oslo non-compliance procedure (paras 9 and 10).

[99] According to part IV para 4 '[a] Party, in respect of which a submission is made or which makes a submission, is entitled to participate in the deliberations of the Committee' and in accordance with part V para 1(a) '[t]he Committee shall consider relevant information from the Party concerned'.

[100] Part VII para 7 allows the party concerned to comment in writing on all information relevant to the question of implementation and the decision to proceed. According to part IX para 2 'the enforcement branch shall hold a hearing at which the Party concerned shall have the opportunity to present its views'.

[101] According to part IX para 34 the Committee shall take into account any comments made by the party concerned.

[102] Art 2(1) of the Charter.

[103] It is doubtful, however, whether this principle has been modified by the concept of 'common but differentiated responsibilities' in Art 3(1) UNFCCC, so that within this Convention developed parties can be subject to stricter controls than developing nations.

[104] See especially JA Green, 'Self-Preservation' in R Wolfrum (ed), *Max Planck Encyclopedia of Public International Law* (Heidelberg/Oxford 2007), available at www.mpepil.com; M Ruffert, 'Reprisals' in R Wolfrum (ed), *Max Planck Encyclopedia of Public International Law* (Heidelberg/Oxford 2009), available at www.mpepil.com and H Fujita, 'Proportionality' in R Wolfrum (ed), *Max Planck Encyclopedia of Public International Law* (Heidelberg/Oxford—forthcoming), available at www.mpepil.com.

mation.[105] Admittedly, explicit stipulations in treaties and decisions adopted by treaty organs are as yet rudimentary and piecemeal. The Cartagena Biosafety Protocol and the Kyoto Protocol both include a '*de minimis* rule' as an expression of the principle of proportionality.[106]

The protection of confidential information extends to confidential business information as well as to sensitive government data. Some instruments have detailed the substance thereof, *eg* Article VIII(8) CITES, Article 12(9) UNFCCC and paragraph 15 of the Montreal non-compliance procedure. So far, no disputes have arisen in respect of any of the above provisions. Due to the economic sensitivity of pertinent data, the non-compliance procedures under the Cartagena Biosafety Protocol,[107] the Kyoto Protocol[108] and the Aarhus Convention[109] all include provisions on the protection of confidential information.

22.4 Institutional Setting

Compliance control in MEAs is entrusted to international organs, which ensure that control mechanisms are implemented in the interests, and to the benefit, of the respective treaty community.[110] Whereas earlier agreements apply an adversarial trilateral structure, with the participation of an (active) third party, and sometimes an impartial international body, more recent MEAs favour an asymmetrical bilateral structure, in which an international organ actively monitors the conduct of a party. The Ozone regime reflects both types of institutional arrangements. The earlier type is exemplified in the parties exchanging information through the Secretariat which exercises a 'switchboard' function. The regime includes traditional dispute settlement within the non-compliance procedure. Similarly, reporting obligations in most MEAs today take place via the Secretariat, which 'filters' data and subsequently makes available the processed information to other contracting parties.

The type of bodies chosen for administering the compliance-control procedures is of utmost importance. Ideally, it should be possible to distinguish between specialised international bureaucracies, expert committees, judicial or quasi-judicial institutions and 'political' bodies, such as the COPs.

Specialised international bureaucracies, usually Secretariats, are composed of inter-

[105] Para 7(c) of the Montreal non-compliance procedure, according to which the Implementation Committee '[m]ay request, where it considers *necessary*, . . . further information ' (authors' italics); there is no corresponding insertion in para 7(c) of the Oslo non-compliance procedure. Para 9 of the Montreal Procedure contains the wording 'appropriate'.

[106] *Cf* part IV para 1 of the non-compliance procedure of the Cartagena Protocol according to which the Committee may reject to consider any submission that is *de minimis* and part VII para 2(b) of the non-compliance procedure of the Kyoto Protocol according to which a preliminary examination shall ensure that the question is not *de minimis.*

[107] *Cf* part V para 4 of the non-compliance procedure: 'The Committee . . . shall maintain the confidentiality of any information that is confidential under Article 21 of the Protocol.'

[108] See part VIII para 6 and part IX para 2 of the non-compliance procedure.

[109] *Cf* part VIII of the non-compliance procedure.

[110] See Birnie, Boyle and Redgwell, above n 17, 239 *et seq.*

national civil servants committed to the objectives of the MEA in question, but not dependent on their home government financially or in any other way.[111] Their impartiality is similar to that of the members of expert committees chosen *ad personam*. Judicial and quasi-judicial institutions are also characterised by specialised knowledge, as well as by the independence and impartiality of their members. Such bodies may be operational either on a continuous basis or else made use of on an *ad hoc* basis. Unlike the bodies just mentioned, political organs exclusively consist of governmental representatives of the parties. The fewer members such political bodies have, the less they will merely be forums for diplomatic negotiations. Form follows function: the type of organ opted for primarily depends on the function assigned to it. Sometimes these are even mixed bodies, composed of so-called government experts. This is the case with the Subsidiary Body for Implementation of the Climate Change Convention.[112] The same applies to expert committees which fulfil quasi-judicial functions. In practice a blend of different types and levels of bodies are made use of within procedures of compliance control.

In addition to such specialised bodies, Secretariats are important actors throughout the whole procedure of compliance control: not only do they receive important information and submissions, but they also process data for the parties in different ways. In addition, they often perform, similar to appropriate expert committees, a tentative evaluation of data, ask additional questions and even collect their own information by, for example, on-site inspections. The further evaluation of this material, including the elaboration of recommendations, is, however, not normally entrusted to Secretariats but rather to specialised bodies, due to their neutrality and impartiality. Decision-making in response to non-compliance is left to political organs. Overall, therefore, a mixture of different types and levels of organs within a system can be discerned. Accordingly, an interaction of political and non-political bodies is operative, distantly suggestive of a 'separation of power'.

There are dispositions of such a division of labour, *inter alia*, in the Montreal Protocol and the UNFCCC, but not, however, in the 1992 Paris Convention.[113] Under the Montreal Protocol, the Secretariat receives information, processes it and may then initiate the non-compliance procedure. The Implementation Committee, which consists of government representatives, may gather data, make suggestions for the resolution of compliance problems and even make recommendations to the plenary organ. The Committee can only successfully fulfil these functions because, with only ten members, very few parties are represented on it.[114] The Meeting of the Parties, the political plenary organ, ultimately decides on reactions in the event of non-compliance, ranging from compliance assistance to sanctions.

Under the 1992 Paris Convention, the primary body is the so-called Commission, which—contrary to what is suggested by its name—is a plenary organ composed of

[111] See Y Beigbeder, 'Civil Service, International' in R Wolfrum (ed), *Max Planck Encyclopedia of Public International Law* (Heidelberg/Oxford 2007), available at www.mpepil.com.

[112] See Art 10(1) UNFCCC.

[113] In the 1992 Paris Convention (Art 23) all functions are centralised in the Commission.

[114] Compare para 5, 2nd sentence of the non-compliance procedure.

government representatives.[115] It evaluates the reports submitted to it by the parties, and information from other sources. On this basis, it decides on the measures to be taken. It is surprising that the institutional structure of this Convention is scarcely developed and that a political body carries the main burden of compliance control. This is justifiable, however, in the light of the relatively small and homogeneous group of parties.

Effective compliance control must be oriented as far as possible towards the substantive obligations to be implemented; this necessitates a largely treaty-specific procedural architecture, which is a separate 'tailor-made' regime for every MEA. The merger of existing institutions or the establishment of a centralised institution would run counter to these considerations. On the other hand, cost-efficiency factors can militate against a proliferation of international bodies and institutions. It is with good reasons, therefore, that Agenda 21 recommends that states, within the bounds of feasibility, should rely on existing institutions.[116]

Whereas procedural law can be made treaty-specific without disproportionate costs, the same does not apply to the international bodies charged with compliance control. It does not appear necessary that new bodies are always established. States can rather fall back on existing bodies. Indeed, UNEP structures have been used for secretariat services under the Ozone regime and the Basel Convention.[117] The same does not, however, apply to political bodies such as the COPs. The heterogeneous membership of the various MEAs alone necessitates their creation anew for each MEA. In addition, these bodies must take into account the specific peculiarities of the given treaties when deciding on measures to be taken in response to deficient or non-compliance.

The question arises to what extent existing treaty bodies can co-operate with each other. Closer co-operation will promote learning capacities and bring to light facts about similar compliance problems of individual parties, thus contributing to overcome deficient or non-compliance. Recognition that one party has implementation problems in relation to several MEAs may signify that a targeted support or improvement of that party's administrative and possibly also legislative infrastructure is indicated. Beyond this, an appropriate exchange of information between the various Secretariats will lead to a more targeted use of financial support for certain developing countries. A co-ordinated establishment of facts may also have a positive influence. For example, the exchange of certain biological/technical data is conceivable to avoid duplicated monitoring. Finally, practicing joint on-site inspections may also be considered, so that the associated costs are kept to a minimum.[118]

[115] *Cf* Art 10(1).

[116] Agenda 21, Chap 38.8(i).

[117] UNEP fulfils Secretariat functions in accordance with Art 16(2)–(3), in conjunction with a decision of the first Conference of the Parties of the Basel Convention, as well as in accordance with Art 2(7) of the Vienna Ozone Convention in conjunction with Decision 8 of the first Meeting of the Parties (UNEP/OzLConv1/5 (28 April 1989) 11 'to designate UNEP as the Secretariat of the Convention') for the Montreal Protocol (according to Art 1(3) of the Protocol the Secretariat of the Vienna Ozone Convention is also the Secretariat of the Protocol).

[118] On the foregoing, compare the developments within the UNECE, where a joint 'Interim Implementation Committee' for the Oslo Protocol and the forthcoming second NO*x* Protocol is being suggested (UN Doc ECE/EB.AIR/R95).

'Memoranda of Understanding' have become the basis for co-ordination and co-operation, agreed between the respective COPs and sometimes between the respective Secretariats. Such interinstitutional agreements are not new as such.[119] Interinstitutional exchange of information was implemented early, within the framework of the Basel Convention and the UNFCCC. In both cases, documents were produced, as a basis for discussion, which summarised experiences with already existing procedures.[120]

The extent to which the Commission on Sustainable Development (CSD) can be made use of for these purposes is rather small. Even though, as provided in Agenda 21 itself, the CSD was primarily tasked to '[e]nsure the effective follow-up of the [Rio] Conference' and to 'monitor progress in the implementation of Agenda 21', Chapter 38.13 of Agenda 21 states that the CSD shall 'consider, where appropriate, information regarding the progress made in the implementation of environmental conventions, which could be made available by the relevant Conferences of the Parties'. As useful as it may be in practical terms, this is not to be understood as a kind of supervisory institution for existing COPs.

22.5 Conclusions

The traditional means of ensuring compliance with MEAs have hitherto only been of limited efficacy in international practice. Therefore, new ways and means have been developed. Although the employment of a collective, non-confrontational method to this end appears to be promising, this is as yet far from being perfect.

Not only have the reporting requirements established under the various MEAs been met, but the non-compliance procedures have in a number of cases also been applied successfully in practice. One of the early positive examples concerns Russia's self-incrimination under the LRTAP Convention. Greece was subject to the non-compliance procedure established under the Kyoto Protocol,[121] and Kazakhstan,[122] Ukraine[123] and Turkmenistan[124] gave rise to cases dealt with under the non-compliance procedure of the Aarhus Convention. This demonstrates that even the *ad hoc* non-compliance procedures have won the support of the parties and have emerged as accepted instruments to ensure compliance with pertinent MEAs.

Compliance-control mechanisms are often treaty-specific and hence diverse. However, there are a number of common features: (i) fact finding is ultimately important, preferably as a routine mechanism; (ii) a non-compliance procedure facilitates the handling of cases of deficient or non-compliance and helps to determine adequate responses; (iii) institutional requirements necessitate the establishment of treaty bodies or the use of existing

[119] For further details on this issue see Chapter 20.3.
[120] UNEP/CHW3/Int5 as well as UN Doc FCCC/CP/1995/Misc2.
[121] *Cf* the final decision adopted by the Enforcement Branch in CC-2007-1-8/Greece/EB (17 April 2008).
[122] See Decision III/6c in ECE/MP.PP/2008/2/Add11 (26 September 2008).
[123] *Cf* Decision III/6f in ECE/MP.PP/2008/2/Add14 (26 September 2008).
[124] Compare Decision III/6e in ECE/MP.PP/2008/2/Add13 (26 September 2008).

organisations. In addition, NGOs may increasingly play a role in compliance-control procedures.

The fact that a broad number of MEAs include compliance-control mechanisms necessitates consideration of the possibility of clustering the proceedings of compliance control in such a way as to achieve synergies while preserving the specific characteristics of each MEA. It is unlikely that synergies are best reached if responsibilities are entrusted with a single body.

With the advent of compliance-control procedures in the 1990s it is important today to consolidate these mechanisms and to optimise their operational capabilities. This necessitates a critical stock-taking of the positive and negative experiences to date in order to determine how to make MEAs more effective and improve cost-efficiency in the future.

Further Reading

H Adsett *et al*, 'Compliance Committees and Recent Multilateral Environmental Agreements: The Canadian Experience with Their Negotiation and Operation' (2004) 42 *The Canadian Yearbook of International Law* 91–142.

NE Bafundo, 'Compliance with the Ozone Treaty: Weak States and the Principle of Common but Differentiated Responsibility' (2006) 21 *American University International Law Review* 461–495.

U Beyerlin *et al* (eds), *Ensuring Compliance with Multilateral Environmental Agreements: A Dialogue between Practitioners and Academia* (Leiden/Boston 2006).

J Brunnée, 'The Kyoto Protocol: Testing Ground for Compliance Theories?' (2003) 63 *Heidelberg Journal of International Law (ZaöRV)* 255–280.

T Crossen, 'Multilateral Environmental Agreements and the Compliance Continuum' (2004) 16 *Georgetown International Environmental Law Review* 473–500.

MA Fitzmaurice, 'The Kyoto Protocol Compliance Regime and Treaty Law' (2004) 8 *Singapore Year Book of International Law and Contributors* 23–40.

A Gillespie, 'Implementation and Compliance Concerns in International Environmental Law: The State of the Art within Three International Regimes' (2003) 7 *New Zealand Journal of Environmental Law* 53–84.

——, 'The Search for a New Compliance Mechanism within the International Whaling Commission' (2003) 34 *Ocean Development & International Law* 349–367.

D Hanschel, 'Environment and Human Rights—Cooperative Means of Regime Implementation' (2003) 3 *Yearbook of Human Rights & Environment* 189–243.

V Koester, 'Review of Compliance under the Aarhus Convention: A Rather Unique Compliance Mechanism' (2005) 2 *Journal for European Environmental & Planning Law* 31–44.

PTB Kohona, 'The International Rule of Law and Encouraging Compliance: Treaties on Sustainable Development' (2003) 9 *Romanian Journal of International Affairs* 30–49.

T Kolari, 'Constructing Non-Compliance Systems into International Environmental Agreements–A Rise of Enforcement Doctrine with Credible Sanctions Needed?' (2003) 14 *Finnish Yearbook of International Law* 205–231.

N Matz, 'Chaos or Coherence?—Implementing and Enforcing the Conservation of Migratory Species through Various Legal Instruments' (2005) *65 Heidelberg Journal of International Law (ZaöRV)* 197–215.

EM McOmber, 'Problems in Enforcement of the Convention on International Trade in Endangered Species' (2002) 27 *Brooklyn Journal of International Law* 673–701.

MG Nigoff, 'The Clean Development Mechanism: Does the Current Structure Facilitate Kyoto Protocol Compliance?' (2006) 18 *Georgetown International Environmental Law Review* 249–276.

A Nollkaemper, 'Compliance Control in International Environmental Law: Traversing the Limits of the National Legal Order' (2002) 13 *Yearbook of International Environmental Law* 165–186.

R Reeve, 'Enhancing the International Regime for Protecting Endangered Species: The Example of CITES' (2003) 63 *Heidelberg Journal of International Law (ZaöRV)* 333–353.

M Rodi, M Mehling, J Rechel and E Zelljadt, 'Implementing the Kyoto Protocol in a Multidimensional Legal System: Lessons from a Comparative Assessment' (2005) 16 *Yearbook of International Environmental Law* 3–79.

I Sagemueller, 'Non-Compliance Procedures Under the Cartagena Protocol: A Wise Decision for a "Soft" Approach?' (2005) 9 *New Zealand Journal of Environmental Law* 163–208.

A Shibata, 'The Basel Compliance Mechanism' (2003) 12 *RECIEL* 183–198.

G Ulfstein and J Werksman, 'The Kyoto Compliance System: Towards Hard Enforcement' in OS Stokke *et al* (eds), *Implementing The Climate Regime: International Compliance* (London/Sterling, VA 2005) 39–62.

S Urbinati, 'Non-Compliance Procedure under the Kyoto Protocol' (2003) 3 *Baltic Yearbook of International Law* 229–251.

T Usuki, 'Measures to Ensure Compliance with the Montreal Ozone Protocol—New Institutionalized Reaction to Non-Compliance' (2000) 43 *The Japanese Annual of International Law* 19–44.

X Wang and G Wiser, 'The Implementation and Compliance Regimes under the Climate Change Convention and its Kyoto Protocol' (2002) 11 *RECIEL* 181–198.

23

Compliance Assistance

23.1 The Concept of Compliance Assistance

The awareness that poor compliance or non-compliance with international environmental law is not normally deliberate but has other causes has led since the early 1980s to the development of a number of treaty provisions in MEAs seeking to address these causes. It has already been pointed out that, in addition to often broadly worded substantive obligations and to the difficulties of adapting treaty obligations to changed circumstances, deficient or even defunct administrative, economic or technical national governance structures are often the main reasons for inadequate or non-compliance with MEAs.[1] Since most environmentally relevant activities are performed by private actors, whether individual or corporate, parties to MEAs have to invest in monitoring mechanisms in order to ensure the surveillance of the activities of such actors. Normally, this entails profound challenges for states, not only in technological terms, but also with a view to financial, administrative and human resources. In addition, compliance with MEAs often, at least implicitly, necessitates socioeconomic changes at the national level, creating a strain on the economy of parties, with benefits being global rather than local.[2]

There is broad consensus that compliance control alone does not guarantee the effectiveness of international environmental law. Rather, there is a need to assist states in the implementation of and compliance with MEAs to which they are parties. This is the object and purpose of compliance assistance. Such assistance may take various forms: capacity-building, transfer of technology and financial assistance.

In many instances, the recipients of compliance assistance are developing countries, whereas developed countries act as donors. This necessitates a few words of caution on the relationship between compliance assistance and development co-operation. The two are distinct, but interrelated. Similar to compliance assistance, development co-operation may be implemented bilaterally or at the multilateral level. The United Nations Development Programme (UNDP) and the World Bank Group are just two examples of multilateral institutions providing a framework for such development co-operation which, in the

[1] *Cf* A Chayes and AH Chayes, 'On Compliance' (1993) 47 *International Organization* 175, 188.

[2] See L Boisson de Chazournes, 'Technical and Financial Assistance' in D Bodansky *et al* (eds), *The Oxford Handbook of International Environmental Law* (Oxford 2007) 947, 948–950.

first place, aims at strengthening the socioeconomic infrastructure of recipient countries. Sometimes this includes the planning and implementation of environmental projects. The main factor to distinguish development co-operation from compliance assistance is the latter's indispensable relationship to treaty obligations resulting from MEAs. Whereas in the case of development co-operation there is no direct link to obligations arising out of a recipient country's treaty obligations under an MEA, compliance assistance is directly related to compliance with such obligations. Whether such assistance prevents or remedies cases of poor or non-compliance is only of secondary importance. It furthers treaty compliance. This is reminiscent of Indira Gandhi's statement at the Stockholm Conference in 1972:

> The rich countries may look upon development as the cause of environmental destruction, but to us it is one of the primary means of improving the environment of living, of providing food, water, sanitation and shelter. . . . We cannot forget the grim poverty of large numbers of people. . . . How can we speak to those who live in villages and in slums about keeping the oceans, rivers and the air clean when their own lives are contaminated at the source? Environment cannot be improved in conditions of poverty. Nor can poverty be eradicated without the use of science and technology.[3]

Compliance assistance is anchored in the concept of 'common but differentiated responsibilities' as included in Principle 7 of the 1992 Rio Declaration,[4] which can be understood as a manifestation of equity and as an application of the concept of sustainable development. It builds upon a common responsibility of developing and developed countries to address current global environmental threats but takes into account that both groups enjoy very different financial, technological and other capacities and means to counter prevailing environmental threats. The concept of common but differentiated responsibilities reflects considerations of distributive justice which legitimise differentiated treatment of the parties even though they enjoy sovereign equality.[5] It may thus be argued that the recognition of the concept of compliance assistance was a qualitative leap in the consideration given to the needs and interests of developing countries in international environmental relations. Their specific interests were not only considered as contextual background, as a reason for the different interpretation of one and the same provision, or as the basis for differing obligations, but gave rise to specific obligations for compliance assistance to developing countries.[6]

An early example for a contextual norm[7] can be taken from the 1946 International Convention for the Regulation of Whaling, Article VIII(2) of which stipulates that '[a]ny whales taken under these special permits shall so far as practicable be processed'. The clause 'so far as practicable' allows the different needs of different countries to be taken into account without specifically referring to developing countries. In contrast, Article

[3] See MK Tolba (ed), *Evolving Environmental Perceptions*: *From Stockholm to Nairobi* (London 1988) 96 *et seq;* see also RP Anand, *Legal Regime of the Sea-Bed and the Developing Countries* (Leyden 1976) 256 *et seq.*

[4] For further information on 'Common but Differentiated Responsibilities' *cf* Chapter 9.

[5] *Cf* E Brown Weiss, 'Environmental Equity: The Imperative for the Twenty-First Century' in W Lang (ed), *Sustainable Development and International Law* (London *et al* 1995) 17, 19.

[6] On these categories see DB Magraw, 'Legal Treatment of Developing Countries: Differential, Contextual, and Absolute Norms' (1990) 1 *Colorado Journal of International Environmental Law and Policy* 69.

[7] See Chapter 9.4.1 for references to 'Common but Differentiated Responsibilities' in single MEAs.

11(3) of the 1976 Barcelona Convention for the Protection of the Mediterranean Sea against Pollution requires the 'provision of technical and other possible assistance . . . with priority to be given to the special needs of developing countries'. Even stronger is Article 202 of the UN Convention on the Law of the Sea (UNCLOS), which provides for differential treatment for developing states:

> Developing States shall, for the purposes of prevention, reduction and control of pollution of the marine environment or minimization of its effects, be granted preference by international organizations in: (a) the allocation of appropriate funds and technical assistance; and (b) the utilization of their specialized services.

Hence, not only is priority given to their needs but preference granted to them. Modern MEAs even go one step further in explicitly imposing an obligation upon developed countries to provide compliance assistance to developing countries. Pertinent examples are Articles 5 and 10 of the Montreal Protocol; Articles 10 and 14 of the Basel Convention; Articles 4, 11 and 21 of the UN Framework Convention on Climate Change (UNFCCC); Articles 16, 20, 21 and 39 of the Convention on Biological Diversity (CBD); and Articles 6 and 19–21 of the UN Convention to Combat Desertification (UNCCD).[8]

Notwithstanding the concept of common but differentiated responsibilities, an obligation under customary international law to provide compliance assistance cannot currently be ascertained.[9] However, developed countries will continue to be under political pressure to include provisions for compliance assistance in future MEAs since it can hardly be assumed that developing countries will join MEAs without appropriate provisions. Whereas transfer of technology and finance will be of particular interest for developing countries, developed countries will increasingly be faced with budgetary concerns and thus be less willing to take on financial assistance obligations. This has been amply demonstrated by the effects of the financial crisis on the occasion of the 14th Conference of the Parties (COP 14) under the UNFCCC and the fourth Conference of the Parties serving as the Meeting of the Parties (MOP 4) under the Kyoto Protocol and the subsequent failure of the Copenhagen Summit (COP 15/MOP 5).[10] It may be presumed that new financial obligations of developed countries are feasible only at the expense of clear-cut obligations and on the basis of voluntary transfers.

23.2 Typology

23.2.1 Capacity-Building

Capacity-building has become increasingly important in many fields of international relations, whether in human rights law, in international trade law or in international envi-

[8] See L Gündling, 'Compliance Assistance in International Environmental Law: Capacity-Building, Transfer of Finance and Technology' (1996) 56 *ZaöRV* 796.

[9] *Ibid*, 802–804.

[10] *Cf* D Bodansky, 'The Copenhagen Climate Change Conference. A Postmortem' (2010) 104 *AJIL* 230.

ronmental law.[11] It is debatable whether there is a general definition of capacity-building in international law. At least, in international environmental law, reference can be made to the definition of the term in Chapter 37 of Agenda 21, which states that '[s]pecifically, capacity-building encompasses the country's human, scientific, technological, organizational, institutional and resource capabilities'. While such outside support would once have been considered as an intervention into the internal affairs of a state, today this is one of the standard approaches contributing to the effective implementation of MEAs by developing countries. A telling example is Article 4(2) of the Vienna Ozone Convention which does not call for 'assistance' but for 'co-operation':

> The Parties shall co-operate . . . in promoting . . . the development and transfer of technology and knowledge. Such co-operation shall be carried out particularly through . . . (c) The supply of necessary equipment and facilities for research and systematic observations; (d) Appropriate training of scientific and technical personnel.

Similar provisions are included in Article 6 UNFCCC and in Article 12 CBD. Capacity-building may also take the form of providing personnel for advisory, administrative and legislative purposes. Model laws may be developed by international organisations and environmental education may also be part of capacity-building. Last, but not least, there are some positive examples of capacity-building by organs established under MEAs, such as the World Heritage Convention and the Ramsar Convention.[12]

23.2.2 Transfer of Technology

The transfer of technology is closely linked to capacity-building. It is often understood as a part of capacity-building. Demands that the transfer of technology between industrialised and developing countries should be eased for the first time became the subject of international political and legal debates in the context of discussions on the so-called 'New International Economic Order'[13] in the 1970s. These discussions emerged from the recognition of development co-operation as resulting from a political obligation of the international community and from the need to integrate the new states emerging from decolonisation into the world economy. The developing countries' claim to a share in technology was perceived as a prerequisite of economic autonomy over their natural resources. In 1973, along the same lines, during the Third UN Conference on the Law of the Sea, developing countries pushed for a share in the exploitation of deep sea-bed resources, labelled as 'common heritage of mankind', which were thereby removed from the exclusive disposition of developed countries. Even though their strategy was largely unsuccessful, various provisions of the 1982 UNCLOS now in force along with the so-called 'Implementation Agreement', have served as models for the transfer of technology, namely Articles 202 and 203 as well as Articles 266 and 267 of the Convention, none of

[11] AM Drumbl, 'Does Sharing Know its Limits? Thoughts on Implementing International Environmental Agreements' (1999) 18 *Virginia Environmental Law Journal* 281.

[12] See, among others, D Navid, 'Compliance Assistance in International Environmental Law: Capacity-Building, Transfer of Finance and Technology' (1996) 56 *ZaöRV* 810, 811.

[13] A Boyle, 'A Comment on the Paper by Diana Ponce-Nava' in Lang, above n 5, 137.

them being affected by the changes in respect of Part XI. Article 202 takes account of the particular needs of developing countries in marine environmental protection[14] in accordance with Article 192, and obliges parties to assist developing parties in scientific and technical matters. The Convention not only includes the training and further education of scientific and technical personnel, scientific research, the gathering of biological-technical data and other programmes, but also specific assistance by 'supplying them with necessary equipment and facilities' and 'enhancing their capacity to manufacture such equipment'.[15] Article 266(2) UNCLOS includes a general obligation to transfer marine technology, also for the purposes of marine environmental protection. The development and transfer of appropriate technology should be 'on fair and reasonable terms and conditions' (*cf* Article 266(1) UNCLOS). The parties should 'endeavour to foster favourable economic and legal conditions . . . for the benefit of all parties concerned on an equitable basis' (*cf* Article 266(3) UNCLOS). Article 267 ensures that '*inter alia*, the rights and duties of holders, suppliers and recipients of marine technology' will be safeguarded.

Another provision explicitly providing for the transfer of technology to developing countries is Article 10A of the Montreal Protocol. According to this provision, parties 'shall take every practicable step' on the basis of the financial mechanism 'to ensure: that the best available, environmentally safe substitutes and related technologies are expeditiously transferred' to developing countries (as specified in Article 5(1) of the Protocol) 'under fair and most favourable conditions'.

Slightly weaker is the obligation to transfer technology under the UNFCCC. Article 4(5) UNFCCC stipulates that developed parties

> shall take all practicable steps to promote, facilitate and finance, as appropriate, the transfer of, or access to, environmentally sound technologies and know-how to other Parties, particularly developing country Parties, to enable them to implement the provisions of the Convention.

In addition, the industrialised countries shall 'support the development and enhancement of endogenous capacities and technologies of developing country Parties'.[16]

The situation is different again in the case of the CBD. The Convention not only reflects the interest of developed countries in the conservation of biodiversity but also in accessing genetic material located in developing countries.[17] Thus, the CBD's provisions on the transfer of technology are much more favourable to developing countries than in the UNFCCC. This can be explained by the fact that developing countries enjoyed a better negotiating position in the CBD negotiation process. The CBD, however, distin-

[14] See R Wolfrum, 'The Protection of the Marine Environment after the Rio Conference: Progress or Stalemate?' in U Beyerlin *et al* (eds), *Recht zwischen Umbruch und Bewahrung. Festschrift für Rudolf Bernhardt* (Berlin *et al* 1995) 1003 and U Beyerlin, 'New Developments in the Protection of the Marine Environment: Potential Effects of the Rio Process' (1995) 55 *ZaöRV* 544.

[15] This provision is noteworthy because of its details, see AO Adede, *International Environmental Law Digest: Instruments of International Responses to Problems of Environment and Development 1972–1992* (Amsterdam *et al* 1993).

[16] X Wang and G Wiser, 'The Implementation and Compliance Regimes under the Climate Change Convention and its Kyoto Protocol' (2002) 11 *RECIEL* 181.

[17] *Cf* R Wolfrum, 'The Convention on the Protection of Biological Diversity: Using State Jurisdiction as a Means of Enforcing Compliance' in R Wolfrum (ed), *Enforcing Environmental Standards: Economic Mechanisms as Viable Means* (Berlin *et al* 1996) 373.

guishes between technologies assisting in the preservation and sustainable use of biological diversity, and those facilitating the utilisation of genetic resources. Article 16(2) CBD stipulates that technology transfer aimed at the maintenance and sustainable use of biological diversity 'shall be provided and/or facilitated under fair and most favourable terms, including on concessional and preferential terms where mutually agreed'. The following paragraph requires the parties to take legislative, administrative and political measures in favour of developing countries for the access to and transfer of 'technology which makes use of those resources on mutually agreed terms'. In contrast, the obligation in Article 16(1) CBD is weakly worded. As far as the protection of intellectual property rights is concerned, Article 16(2) CBD states that, so far as patents and other intellectual property rights are concerned, access to and transfer of technology must be under conditions which 'recognise and are consistent with the adequate and effective protection of intellectual property rights'. The following paragraphs 3, 4 and 5, however, demonstrate that the protection of intellectual property rights must not be an insurmountable obstacle to the transfer of technology: Article 16(5) CBD commits developed countries (even though not explicitly named) to co-operate with developing countries ensuring that these property rights 'are supportive of, and do not run counter to [the Convention's] objectives'. The Convention relies on the phrase 'mutually agreed terms' in a number of provisions, including Articles 15(4) and 16(2). It has been rightly characterised as a 'fall-back' in the interests of developed countries.[18]

23.2.3 Financial Mechanisms

Financial assistance does not focus on the specific problems of specific countries under specific treaty regimes to the same extent as this is done by capacity-building and the transfer of technology. Making use of financial assistance for the purpose of enhancing compliance with MEAs necessitates means to control the utilisation of financial resources made available. Calls for financial assistance by developing countries may accordingly be perceived as negotiating tools when substantive commitments to combat global environmental threats are at issue: 'Finance can lubricate the process of international diplomacy.'[19]

The inclusion of provisions on the transfer of finance in MEAs resulted from the recognition that the implementation of these agreements entails costs for national economies, which some states cannot, or are not prepared to, bear. In order to integrate these states into the fight against global environmental dangers, it is necessary to provide financial resources. Legally, the question is not whether but how financial mechanisms should be organised.[20]

[18] M Chandler, 'The Biodiversity Convention: Selected Issues of Interest to the International Lawyer' (1993) 4 *Colorado Journal of International Environmental Law and Policy* 141, 164.

[19] A Jordan and J Werksman, 'Additional Funds, Incremental Costs and the Global Environment' (1994) 3 *RECIEL* 81, 82.

[20] Boisson de Chazournes, above n 2, 947.

Financial mechanisms have become a common feature of MEAs since the creation of the Multilateral Fund under the Montreal Protocol. Financial obligations are also included in Article 4(3) UNFCCC, Articles 20 and 21 CBD, as well as Articles 20 and 21 UNCCD which impose clear-cut legal obligations on parties. Article 10(6) of the Montreal Protocol reads: 'The Multilateral Fund shall be financed by contributions from Parties not operating under paragraph 1 of Article 5.' Similarly, Article 4(3) UNFCCC and Article 20(4) CBD stipulate: 'The developed country Parties . . . shall provide.' According to Article 20(2) UNCCD, 'developed country Parties . . . undertake to: (a) mobilize substantial financial resources' rather than making specific payments. Article 20(2) UNCCD also requires developed countries to 'promote the mobilization of adequate, timely and predictable financial resources, including new and additional funding from the Global Environment Facility'.

Unfortunately, it is difficult to determine precisely the substance of all these obligations, in particular, as far as the amount of required financial assistance is concerned.[21] Article 10(1) of the Montreal Protocol, Article 4(3) UNFCCC, Article 20(2) CBD and Article 20(2)(b) UNCCD refer to 'agreed full costs' or 'agreed (full) incremental costs'. Arguably this is a compromise formula which acquiesces to the demands of both the developed ('agreed'), and the developing countries ('full').[22] Nevertheless, it may be argued that the costs incurred by developing countries in implementing these MEAs can be assigned to the respective financial mechanisms. Also, these financial transfers must not be at the expense of previously agreed or implemented development co-operation; according to Article 10(1) of the Montreal Protocol, the funds must be 'additional to other financial transfers'.[23]

23.3 Conditionality of Assistance

Reflecting upon the above treaty provisions the question arises whether compliance of developing countries with these MEAs is conditioned upon receipt of adequate resources or whether these can be truly characterised as assistance. Indeed, developing country parties are interested in ensuring that developed country parties meet their obligations in the transfer of technology and finance as well as in capacity-building. To this end MEAs include provisions on the relationship between environmental obligations and the various forms of compliance assistance. These provisions may be subject to different interpretations. It is important not to interpret these provisions to the detriment of the environment, while at the same time ensuring developed country compliance with these obligations.

Article 5(5) of the Montreal Protocol stipulates that implementation of the Protocol

[21] L Boisson de Chazournes, 'Technical and Financial Assistance and Compliance: The Interplay' in U Beyerlin *et al* (eds), *Ensuring Compliance with Multilateral Environmental Agreements: A Dialogue between Practitioners and Academia* (Leiden/Boston 2006) 273.

[22] *Cf* D Bodansky, 'The United Nations Framework Convention on Climate Change' (1993) 18 *Yale Journal of International Law* 492, 524.

[23] NE Bafundo, 'Compliance with the Ozone Treaty: Weak States and the Principle of Common but Differentiated Responsibility' (2006) 21 *American University International Law Review* 461.

by developing country parties 'will depend upon the effective implementation of the financial co-operation as provided by Article 10A'. Similarly, Article 4(7) UNFCCC states that '[t]he extent to which developing country Parties will effectively implement their commitments under the Convention will depend on the effective implementation by developed country Parties of their commitments under the Convention related to financial resources and transfer of technology'. Article 20(4) CBD, which corresponds to Article 4(3) UNFCCC, may be interpreted as a plain statement of fact, or else as a legal recognition of the reciprocal relationship between the environmental obligations of developing countries and the financial obligations of the developed countries.[24] The reading of these provisions as a treaty-based, genuinely reciprocal relationship is doubtful, at least when assuming that an affected developing country can decide for itself whether or not to meet its primary obligations under the respective MEA. It may be argued that a reading like this would not only generally run counter to the aims and purpose of the MEA in question, but beyond this, it would bilateralise the enforcement of the obligations, contrary to the idea of institutionalised compliance control.

An alternative interpretation of the provisions in question is to allow developing countries a defence if the industrialised countries do not meet their obligations, of which they can make use only when being accused of not meeting their environmental commitments. Such an interpretation presupposes validation by a formal procedure and a link to the requirement that the developing country in question has actually made a *bona fide* attempt to meet its commitments, and then failed due to its technical, financial or personnel deficiencies. The assumption of such a requirement has a precedent in compliance control, namely Article 4 of the non-compliance procedure under the Montreal Protocol. This provision allows self-incrimination of a party after 'having made its best, bona fide efforts . . . to comply fully with its obligations under the protocol'. If the relevant treaty norms were set accordingly, then the developing countries' interest in the actual implementation of financial and technology transfers would be safeguarded along with the developed countries' interest in the involvement of the developing countries in the common battle against global environmental threats. This avoids interpreting pertinent provisions as a mere subsidy for compliance with treaty obligations.

Article 5(1) of the Montreal Protocol supports such a reading.[25] Whether a country can actually rely on this provision is to be determined in a formalised procedure. Article 5(8) of the Protocol requires that states parties must reconsider the status under Article 5(1) in the light of the transfer of resources and technology that have already taken place.[26] Article 5(6) also includes other procedural safeguards beyond this as a developing country which has not complied with its control obligations under Article 2A–2E, or Article 2F–2H together with Article 5(1 *bis*), can 'exculpate' itself after notification of the

[24] D Ponce-Nava, 'Capacity-Building in Environmental Law and Sustainable Development' in Lang, above n 5, 136; see also Wolfrum, above n 17, 390 referring to the 'clear link between the conservation of biological diversity and additional funding'.

[25] See also Art 3(1) UNFCCC which refers to the 'common but differentiated responsibilities and respective capabilities' of the parties and Art 4(2) UNFCCC which includes special obligations for developed country parties and other parties included in Annex I to the Convention.

[26] In this respect see UNEP/OzLPro7/12 (27 December 1995) Annex II and Annex III.

Secretariat of lacking finance and technology transfers. In accordance with Article 5(7) of the Protocol, this will even preclude the initiation of the non-compliance procedure against this party.

23.4 Institutional Setting

23.4.1 Tailor-Made Institutions

In light of the parallels between compliance control and compliance assistance it is plausible to rely upon tailor-made, treaty-specific organs for the implementation of compliance assistance. There are various options which have been followed in recent treaty practice.

As an early example, the World Heritage Committee, instituted under the World Heritage Convention, was established, *inter alia*, for the purpose of compliance assistance in the context of this treaty.[27] The Committee is empowered to develop a procedure for handling requests for compliance assistance. Article 21 states:

> The World Heritage Committee shall define the procedure by which requests to it for international assistance shall be considered and shall specify the content of the request, which should define the operation contemplated, the work that is necessary, the expected cost thereof, the degree of urgency and the reasons why the resources of the State requesting assistance do not allow it to meet all the expenses.

Before making a decision on the request, the Committee is to 'carry out such studies and consultations as it deems necessary'. Financial resources are provided by the World Heritage Fund, established in accordance with Article 15 of the Convention, administered by the World Heritage Committee, and sustained by fixed voluntary payments from parties. In addition to the stipulations in Article 22 of the Convention, the so-called Operational Guidelines for the Implementation of the Convention particularise the criteria for assistance and the procedure to be followed.[28] Experiences with compliance assistance under this Convention are positive, even if the annual amount of about US$4 million is actually fairly modest. The advantages of compliance assistance being handled by treaty-specific institutions are manifested here in the rapid availability (due to a non-bureaucratic structure) of resources to the recipient countries for the preservation of specific, gravely threatened 'natural sites', and in the targeted utilisation of resources.[29] Positive experiences have been made in particular with training measures.[30]

The parties to the Ramsar Convention oriented themselves on the model of the World Heritage Convention. On the basis of a resolution adopted by the parties in Montreux in

[27] Navid, above n 12, 812–813.

[28] For the latest version see UNESCO—Intergovernmental Committee for the Protection of the World Cultural and Natural Heritage, Doc WHC08/01 (January 2008), available at http://whc.unesco.org/archive/opguide08-en.pdf.

[29] Navid, above n 12, 813–814.

[30] *Cf* the strategy agreed by the World Heritage Committee in December 1995 at its 19th Session for the targeted use of resources for education purposes; see also the report WHC-95/CONF203/16 (31 January 1996).

1990, a financial mechanism[31] which was not originally foreseen in the treaty was established, namely the Ramsar Small Grants Fund for Wetland Conservation and Wise Use.[32] This fund is totally maintained by voluntary contributions of parties, and in the past has had a little over US$400000 at its disposal annually.[33] It is administered by the Ramsar Standing Committee, which is responsible for the implementation of the treaty between Conferences of the Parties. Even with this relatively small fund, experiences have been positive: it enables quick and unbureaucratic support of actual projects in developing countries with technical (compliance) assistance.[34]

For treaties addressing global problems, such as the Montreal Protocol, the UNFCCC and the CBD, there are good reasons for entrusting important parts of the procedure to the hands of treaty-specific institutions. Decisions on compliance assistance relating to the provision of financial resources, even if the actual objective is capacity-building, should largely be made by the respective parties themselves. This is especially so because pertinent MEAs are frequently the end-result of compromises tailored to the various specific interests. These compromises must be taken into account when implementing compliance assistance.

The Multilateral Fund of the Montreal Protocol, initially established on a provisional basis at the second Meeting of the Parties, with contributions amounting to US$490 million,[35] became a permanent financial mechanism at the fourth Meeting of the Parties. It is treaty-specific and under the direct control of the parties.[36] At this Meeting of the Parties, further contributions were agreed upon. An executive committee, appointed directly by the parties, and consisting of seven representatives each from developing and industrialised countries is responsible for the Multilateral Fund.[37] The composition of the Multilateral Fund is quite unusual as only the industrialised countries are obliged to make financial contributions while control over the Fund's financial resources is equally distributed in the hands of the donors and the potential recipients.[38] At the Rio Conference, this approach was favoured by developing countries, and also by environmental protection groups as a model for financial mechanisms for the treaties on the agenda at that time. Its advantages—particularly from the point of view of developing countries—are the clear commitments of the industrialised countries, and the use of the one state/one vote principle in decision-making procedures concerning financial compliance assistance.[39]

[31] Resolution 4.3 ('A Wetland Conservation Fund') (27 June-4 July 1990).

[32] Originally the 'Wetland Conservation Fund', renamed at the Conference of the Parties in Brisbane, 19–27 March 1996, *cf* Resolution VI.6 ('The Wetland Conservation Fund') para 8.

[33] The Conference of the Parties at its 7th Meeting requested that States make at least US$1 million available, *cf* Resolution VII.28 ('Financial and Budgetary Matters') para 17.

[34] Navid, above n 12, 816.

[35] This is the total budget for the 2009–2011 triennium.

[36] The parties to the Montreal Protocol decide on its budget every three years with contributions calculated on the basis of the UN assessments scale.

[37] *Cf* for the Terms of Reference of the Executive Committee Decision IX/16 in UNEP/OzLPro9/12 (25 September 1997) 31 and Annex V and Decision XVI/38 in UNEP/OzLPro16/17 (16 December 2004) 68.

[38] See Decision IX/16 in UNEP/OzLPro9/12 (25 September 1997) Annex V para 10.

[39] *Cf* also Art 10(10) of the Montreal Protocol.

23.4.2 The Global Environment Facility

As an alternative to the model of treaty-specific financial mechanisms or funds, developed countries had already proposed the so-called Global Environment Facility (GEF) in the run-up to the Rio Conference. This trust fund, initially established on a provisional basis by the World Bank, the United Nations Environment Programme (UNEP) and UNDP, was conceived by developed countries as a general financial mechanism for future environmental agreements. Unlike compliance assistance in the form of capacity-building and the transfer of technology, where the expertise of treaty-specific institutions is needed, financial compliance assistance offers a much better opportunity to make use of other specialised institutions, such as the World Bank Group.

The legal bases for the GEF's pilot phase (1991–1994) were (i) a resolution by the Executive Directors of the World Bank;[40] (ii) an 'interagency agreement' between the World Bank, UNDP and UNEP; (iii) parallel resolutions of the Governing Councils of UNEP and UNDP and (iv) so-called 'instruments of contribution' signed by the contributing governments. It was, however, the World Bank Resolution which actually established the GEF, creating a global environment trust fund and regulating the conditions for contributions to the fund. All decisions were within the competence of the Bank, notwithstanding the already mentioned interagency agreement 'Procedural Arrangements for Operational Cooperation under the Global Environment Facility'[41] between the World Bank, UNDP and UNEP. This agreement was primarily a co-operation commitment between the institutions involved and the recipient countries. A prerequisite for participation in the GEF, but not for the receipt of assistance, was the payment of a specified minimum amount.

Criticism of the institutional structure of the GEF pilot phase particularly focused on the allegation that it took insufficient account of the difficulties in North–South relations coming to the surface anew in the course of negotiations on the UNFCCC and the CBD, and was oriented more on the traditional relations between donor and recipient countries. As a consequence, the GEF was rejected by the developing countries as a (provisional) financial mechanism for the Rio Conventions. Instead, the G-77 in particular advocated a 'Green Fund', which should no longer be dominated by the donor countries.[42] On the basis of a compromise, the developing countries eventually accepted the GEF as a provisional financial mechanism, though with the qualification that it should be institutionally adapted to the decision-making process of the pertinent COPs.

Accordingly, Articles 11 and 21(3) UNFCCC and Articles 21 and 39 CBD provide that the GEF should first be restructured before finally regulating its relationship with the Conferences of the Parties.[43] Agenda 21 also emphasised the need to restructure the GEF. In this context, the developed countries were concerned that the principles previously

[40] IBRD Res No 91-5; (1991) 30 ILM 1758 *et seq*.

[41] See Annex C to IBRD Res No 91-5; (1991) 30 ILM 1766 *et seq*.

[42] *Cf* P Haas, M Levy and T Parson, 'Appraising the Earth Summit: How Should We Judge UNCED's Success?' (1992) 34 *Environment* 6.

[43] The wording of Art 11 UNFCCC as well as of Art 21 CBD both suggest that an alternative financial mechanism would be permissible.

applied within multilateral financing institutions, especially those relating to raising and use of financial resources, as well as the safeguarding of donors' interests in the pertinent governing councils, should also be applied in the new GEF in such a way that increased resources would be made acceptable. The developing countries' concerns, however, were issues regarding equal rights and representation in the governing councils, transparency in the decision-making process, and universal membership.

In 1994 the Instrument for the Establishment of the Restructured GEF[44] was adopted by the three Implementing Agencies, *ie* UNDP, UNEP and the World Bank. The GEF Instrument represents a compromise between the interests of donor and recipient countries. It provides for the establishment of a Council (with an 'elected chairperson' chosen from the members), a Secretariat (whose head is chairperson of the GEF), and an Assembly meeting every three years. The interests of the developing countries are reflected in the following:

- membership is no longer tied to financial contributions;[45]
- the 16 votes of the developing countries equal those of the industrialised states (14) and the 'economies in transition' (2) together;[46]
- the Secretariat is independent, at least functionally, from the World Bank and the Implementing Agencies;[47]
- the Implementing Agencies are 'accountable to the Council for their GEF-financed activities';[48] and
- amendments to the Instrument can in future only be agreed by consensus in the Assembly upon recommendation of the Council.[49]

With the new voting system, based on a double-weighted majority, where a decision can only be taken when 60 per cent of the countries represented in the Council concur, and this majority simultaneously represents 60 per cent of the contributions to the trust fund, the interests of the industrialised countries are also taken into consideration. They cannot be outvoted by the developing countries.[50] It is also in the interest of the industrialised countries that (i) the Council adopts guidelines for the utilisation of resources; (ii) the areas of activity of the GEF (prevention of climate change, maintenance of biodiversity, protection of international waters, protection of the ozone layer, measures to combat desertification and deforestation in so far as related to the other four activities and operation in the field of persistent organic pollutants)[51] remain unchanged; and (iii) no new institution has been established.

[44] Henceforth referred to as the GEF Instrument. For the original text see (1994) 33 ILM 1273 *et seq*. The GEF Instrument was amended in 2002 and in 2006 by the 2nd and 3rd GEF Assemblies. For the latest text including the amendments *cf* www.thegef.org/gef/sites/thegef.org/files/publication/GEF_Instrument_March08.pdf.

[45] GEF Instrument, para I.7.

[46] GEF Instrument, para III.16.

[47] GEF Instrument, para III.21.

[48] GEF Instrument, para III.22.

[49] GEF Instrument, para IX.34; amendments only enter into force with the agreement of the Governing Bodies of the three Implementing Agencies: the World Bank, UNDP and UNEP.

[50] GEF Instrument, para IV.25(c).

[51] GEF Instrument, para I.2.

Despite the continuing criticisms expressed by developing countries, the restructuring of the GEF represents a substantial step forward and is highly beneficial, particularly to the developing countries themselves. That does not mean that all outstanding issues have been settled. Unresolved questions will need to be answered soon, if a permanent and constructive relationship between the COPs and the GEF is to be achieved.

First, the legal qualification of the Instrument presents some problems. Paragraph I.1 of the Instrument states that the GEF was 'accepted by representatives of the States participating in the GEF' and 'adopted by the Implementing Agencies in accordance with their respective rules and procedural requirements'. The GEF Trust Fund, in accordance with paragraph I.8, 'shall be established, and the World Bank shall be invited to serve as the Trustee of the Fund'. These wordings, and also the provisions on amendment and termination of the Instrument,[52] may be taken to qualify the GEF Instrument as a legal rather than a policy document. However, it is doubtful whether it can be considered as a formal agreement concluded between the participating states.[53] Rather than emphasising their concurrence by the use of the words 'agreed' or 'consented', it was simply the term 'accepted' which was chosen. In addition, the use of 'adopted' points towards an act of the implementing agencies (in particular the World Bank). Further, paragraph I.8 in particular suggests a leading role for the World Bank. If the GEF Instrument therefore cannot ultimately be considered as an agreement under international law (neither between the participating states nor between the World Bank, UNEP and UNDP), it may be argued that the Facility is based on an act of only one of the Implementing Agencies, namely the World Bank.

The second question is whether the GEF should be considered a subject of international law. This was the topic of a report by the Legal Advisor to the United Nations.[54] In the report, the following point was made on the matter:

> [T]he restructured GEF constitutes an entity, established by the World Bank and the United Nations, acting through UNDP and UNEP, as defined in the Instrument. As such, the restructured GEF is a new entity which is distinct from the former GEF, which . . . was established as pilot programme of the World Bank by resolution 91-5 of its Executive Directors.[55]

Regarding this statement, it should be noted that the GEF has a Council of its own, empowered to make decisions concerning the Fund's resources; it can also request additional reports regarding the use of these resources from the World Bank, UNEP and UNDP. However, the Secretariat is hosted by the World Bank, and the Trust Fund was also established within the framework of the World Bank. On the other hand, the Secre-

[52] GEF Instrument, para IX.34.

[53] *Cf* in this respect P Sands and P Klein, *Bowett's Law of International Institutions* (6th edn London 2009) 130, stating that 'the GEF is not established by direct treaty, but rather is the progeny of three distinct institutions'.

[54] Note by the Interim Secretariat, 'Modalities for the Functioning of Operational Linkages Between the Conference of the Parties and the Operating Entity or Entities of the Financial Mechanism: Legal Opinion of the United Nations Office of Legal Affairs' UN Doc A/AC237/74 (23 August 1994) Annex.

[55] *Ibid,* Annex, para 6, 5th sentence. At the request of the World Bank, this report replaces an earlier version communicated to the Secretariat of the Climate Change Convention, in which the Legal Advisor had described GEF as a 'joint subsidiary body' of the World Bank and the United Nations.

tariat is functionally independent and an independent Scientific and Technical Advisory Panel (STAP) supports the GEF in its work. Thus, ultimately the GEF may have more of the characteristics of an international law subject than its precursor in the pilot phase. The World Bank itself, though, is of the opinion that the restructured GEF is neither a joint organ of the Bank and the United Nations, nor is it able to enter into treaties binding under international law.

These findings are of relevance for answering the (third) open question, namely the legal character of the respective Memoranda of Understanding between the COPs and the Environment Facility.[56] If the Facility already lacks international legal personality, then these Memoranda cannot in any way be considered as agreements under international law. Neither the international legal personality of the COPs, nor the empowerment of the Facility in its Instrument to conclude agreements changes this. Currently, the following Memoranda have been negotiated and are applied: the Memorandum of Understanding between the Conference of the Parties to the UNFCCC and the GEF Council,[57] between the Conference of the Parties to the CBD and the GEF Council,[58] between the Conference of the Parties to the UNCCD and the GEF Council,[59] and between the Conference of the Parties to the Stockholm Convention on Persistent Organic Pollutants and the GEF Council.[60] According to these Memoranda, the COPs will determine the general political guidelines for the distribution of funds, which the GEF will be obliged to observe. The Council of the Facility has to decide on specific projects, whose implementation, according to the subject-matter, will be put into the hands of the World Bank, UNEP or UNDP. If a state is not satisfied with a decision of the Council, it may appeal to the COP concerned. In general, the GEF will be obliged to report to the COP. This obligation is not, however, legally enforceable. At most, it can be said that the parties are already committed to further compliance with this obligation on the basis of the treaties agreed upon and the Articles of the Agreement of the World Bank, but this only has an indirect effect on the relations between the GEF and the COPs.

The determination of the quantity of the financial commitments of the industrialised countries in the Memoranda is especially difficult.[61] Article 11(3)(d) UNFCCC and Article 21(1) CBD both make an understanding on this matter obligatory. The distribution of resources between the Facility's six main areas of involvement, and the financial assistance required by the two conventions mentioned, has remained a matter of debate which gives rise not only to discussions between North and South but also within the respective groupings of developed and developing countries.

Despite all the caveats, the division of labour between the COPs and the GEF in matters of compliance assistance has proven to be useful. Similarly, a division of labour between the World Bank, UNDP and UNEP would also be useful. In this respect, it

[56] *Cf eg* the consultations on Draft Memoranda in UN Doc FCCC/CP/1996/9 (21 May 1996) and UNEP/CBD/COP/2/11 (21 August 1995).

[57] For its text see Decision 12/CP2 in UN Doc FCCC/CP/1996/15/Add1 (19 July 1996) 56 *et seq*. See also the Annex to this Memorandum in Decision 12/CP3 in UN Doc FCCC/CP/1997/7/Add1 (1 December 1997).

[58] Decision III/8 in UNEP/CBD/COP/3/38 (November 1996) 61 *et seq*.

[59] Decision 6/COP7 (28 October 2005) in ICCD//COP(7)/16/Add1 (25 November 2005) 16 *et seq*.

[60] SC-1/11 in UNEP/POPS/COP1/31 (6 May 2005) 58 *et seq*.

[61] See UN Doc FCCC/CP/1996/9 (21 May 1996) Annex.

remains to be clarified to what extent treaty-specific bodies continue to be active in the area of capacity-building and technology transfer, in parallel with the parties themselves, UNEP and UNDP. Certainly Chapter 38.24 of Agenda 21 assigns responsibilities in compliance assistance to both UNDP and UNEP. An expansion of the environmental programmes within the UNDP has remained an option. The role of the UN Institute for Training and Research (UNITAR) in capacity-building measures may also be mentioned, such as the Joint Training Programme ('CC: TRAIN')[62], established by UNDP, financed by the GEF, and jointly supported by UNITAR and the UNFCCC Secretariat.

23.5 Conclusions

Compliance assistance has proven to be a useful instrument in ensuring compliance with MEAs. In particular, developing countries have benefited from the various instruments which were developed both within MEAs and outside these agreements.[63] The role played by the GEF has been much more positive than originally expected.

The legal arrangements adopted as a basis for compliance assistance and for the facilitation of its implementation have been innovative and have posed a variety of challenges with impacts on the law of international institutions, in particular. Their continued application and further development will enhance not only the effectiveness of MEAs but also their efficiency.

Further Reading

H Adsett, A Daniel, M Husain and TL McDorman, 'Compliance Committees and Recent Multilateral Environmental Agreements: The Canadian Experience with Their Negotiation and Operation' (2004) 42 *The Canadian Yearbook of International Law* 91–142.

NE Bafundo, 'Compliance with the Ozone Treaty: Weak States and the Principle of Common but Differentiated Responsibility' (2006) 21 *American University International Law Review* 461–495.

F Bloch, *Technologietransfer zum internationalen Umweltschutz: Eine völkerrechtliche Untersuchung unter besonderer Berücksichtigung des Schutzes der Ozonschicht und des Weltklimas* (Bern *et al* 2007).

L Boisson de Chazournes, 'Technical and Financial Assistance and Compliance: the Interplay' in U Beyerlin *et al* (eds), *Ensuring Compliance with Multilateral Environmental Agreements: A Dialogue between Practitioners and Academia* (Leiden/Boston 2006) 273–300.

——, 'Technical and Financial Assistance' in D Bodansky *et al* (eds), *The Oxford Handbook of International Environmental Law* (Oxford 2007) 947–973.

J Brunnée, 'The Kyoto Protocol: Testing Ground for Compliance Theories?' (2003) 63 *Heidelberg Journal of International Law (ZaöRV)* 255–280.

[62] *Cf* UN Doc FCCC/SBI/1996/4 (30 January 1996) paras 11–13; see also FCCC/SBI/1996/10 (14 June 1996); in addition, there are further programmes: 'CC: INFO', 'CC: FORUM', 'CC: SUPPORT'.

[63] Boisson de Chazournes, above n 21, 274 *et seq.*

P Clarke, I Millar and K Sollberger, *Capacity Building for Environmental Law in the South Pacific: South Pacific Regional Environmental Law Capacity Building Project: Scoping Report* (Gland 2008).

A Epiney, 'Durchsetzungsmechanismen im Umweltvölkerrecht: ausgewählte Aspekte und Perspektiven' (2005) 15 *Schweizerische Zeitschrift für internationales und europäisches Recht (Revue suisse de droit international et de droit européen)* 429–443.

L Gündling, 'Compliance Assistance in International Environmental Law: Capacity-Building through Financial and Technology Transfer' (1996) 56 *Heidelberg Journal of International Law (ZaöRV)* 796–809.

PTB Kohona, 'The International Rule of Law and Encouraging Compliance: Treaties on Sustainable Development' (2003) 9 *Romanian Journal of International Affairs* 30–49.

C Kreuter-Kirchhof, 'Dynamisierung des internationalen Klimaschutzregimes durch Institutionalisierung' (2005) 65 *Heidelberg Journal of International Law* (*ZaöRV*) 967–1014.

N Matz, 'Chaos or Coherence? Implementing and Enforcing the Conservation of Migratory Species through Various Legal Instruments' (2005) 65 *Heidelberg Journal of International Law* (*ZaöRV*) 197–215.

K Nussbaumer, *Durchsetzungsmechanismen im Umweltvölkerrecht: Wahl und Ausgestaltung im Hinblick auf unterschiedliche Vertragsziele* (Bern 2003).

I Sagemueller, 'Non-Compliance Procedures Under the Cartagena Protocol: A Wise Decision for a "Soft" Approach?' (2005) 9 *New Zealand Journal of Environmental Law* 163–208.

X Wang and G Wiser, 'The Implementation and Compliance Regimes under the Climate Change Convention and its Kyoto Protocol' (2002) 11 *RECIEL* 181–198.

24

Responsibility and Liability

24.1 Introduction

The breach of an international obligation arising from treaty law, customary law or any other source of international law by a state creates a responsibility with respect to any other state whose rights have thereby been violated provided that such violation is attributable to the acting state. The establishment of responsibility normally gives rise to an obligation of restitution in kind.[1] This is an accepted rule of customary international law and also applies to international environmental law. State responsibility was at the origin of modern international environmental law as can be taken from the *Trail Smelter* arbitration.[2] In light of the absence of provisions on state responsibility in most recent MEAs this is most important.

However, state responsibility for wrongful activities is not encountered frequently in international environmental law. This may be due to a number of factors, including broad exceptions and derogations in many MEAs, the lack of specific standards the breach of which could clearly be considered an internationally wrongful act, and the preference of states for co-operation rather than confrontation in the management of disputes. Nevertheless, the notion of state responsibility often figures prominently in international environmental debates; one might even describe it as providing a bottom line for what is permissible and what is not.

Even though the Stockholm Declaration[3] called upon states to further develop responsibility regimes in order to ensure compensation for those suffering from environmental wrongs,[4] only a limited number of bilateral and multilateral environmental agreements

[1] JR Crawford, 'State Responsibility' in R Wolfrum (ed), *Max Planck Encyclopedia of Public International Law* (Heidelberg/Oxford 2006), available at www.mpepil.com; TA Benvick, 'Responsibility and Liability for Environmental Damage: A Roadmap for International Regimes' (1998) 10 *Georgetown International Environmental Law Review* 257.

[2] *Cf* Chapter 1.1.

[3] *Cf* Chapter 2.1.

[4] Principle 22; see also Principle 13 Rio Declaration.

have taken up the idea and included an explicit provision on state responsibility. Thus, building upon Article 7 of the 1967 Outer Space Treaty,[5] which establishes the international liability of a party that launches or procures the launching of an object into outer space for damage to another party on the earth, in the air or in outer space, the 1972 Convention on International Liability for Damage Caused by Space Objects[6] lays down absolute liability for damage caused by a 'space object on the surface of the earth or to aircraft flight' (Article II) and fault-based liability for damage caused elsewhere (Article III). Article 235 UNCLOS refers to general international law on responsibility and liability. According to Article 12 of the 1982 Basel Convention on the Control of Transboundary Movements of Hazardous Wastes and Their Disposal, parties 'shall co-operate with a view to adopting . . . a protocol setting out appropriate rules and procedures in the field of liability and compensation for damage resulting from the transboundary movement and disposal of hazardous wastes and other wastes'. The Basel Protocol on Liability and Compensation was adopted on 10 December 1999, focusing on the question of who is financially responsible in the event of an incident; it has, however, not yet entered into force. Article 13 of the 1992 Convention on the Transboundary Effects of Industrial Accidents calls upon parties to 'support appropriate international efforts to elaborate rules, criteria and procedures in the field of responsibility and liability'. In response, a Protocol on Civil Liability for Damage and Compensation for Damage Caused by Transboundary Effects of Industrial Accidents on Transboundary Waters was adopted on 21 May 2003, as a joint instrument to the above Convention and to the Convention on the Protection and Use of Transboundary Watercourses and International Lakes. In 2005, Annex VI to the Protocol on Environmental Protection to the Antarctic Treaty on Liability Arising from Environmental Emergencies was adopted.[7]

In the absence of treaty-based provisions on state responsibility, states are left with pertinent rules of customary international law. These rules only apply in cases of an internationally wrongful act. This means that for a state to be held responsible for pollution, such pollution must be wrongful under international law. If such pollution is legal, a state will not be held responsible for environmental damage caused.

Since most pollution does not constitute a wrongful act and since the concept of state responsibility is thus of limited application, states have sought to develop a concept of 'International Liability for Injurious Consequences Arising out of Acts not Prohibited by International Law'.[8] The idea behind such a concept is to open up liability for states for certain ultra-hazardous activities taking place within their borders or even performed by

[5] The Treaty on Principles Governing the Activities of States in the Exploration and Use of Outer Space, including the Moon and Other Celestial Bodies, in force since 10 October 1967.

[6] This Treaty is in force since 1 September 1972.

[7] See M Johnson, 'Liability for Environmental Damage in Antarctica' (2006) 19 *Georgetown International Environmental Law Review* 33; see also DJ Bederman and SP Keskar, 'Antarctic Environmental Liability' (2005) 19 *Emory International Law Review* 1383.

[8] For a historical overview regarding the work of the International Law Commission (ILC) on this concept and for the text of the Draft Articles see ILC, 'Report of the International Law Commission on the work of its 48th Session' (6 May–26 July 1996) UN Doc A/51/10, 77 *et seq* and 101 *et seq*; for an analysis see M Fitzmaurice, 'International Liability for Injurious Consequences of Acts not Prohibited by International Law (the "Liability Draft")' (1999/2000) 24 *The Polish Yearbook of International Law* 47.

themselves. For purposes of clarity, this chapter will distinguish between responsibility (entailing an internationally wrongful act) and liability of states (referring to cases of lawful environmental damage).

Civil liability is not normally covered by international law. However, in light of the transboundary environmental effects of many activities performed by business actors, states have adopted a number of international instruments implementing and further developing the polluter-pays concept.[9] These instruments channel liability to the person in control of a dangerous activity and ensure that private actors do not escape such liability simply because they are beyond the reach of the victim of any damage caused. Some international regimes provide for additional compensatory mechanisms funded by entities benefiting from the activity concerned. Thus, the 1992 Oil Pollution Convention is supplemented by a Fund Convention from the same year. In case civil liability does not cover the damage, some treaties provide for state liability as a subsidiary means.

24.2 State Responsibility

24.2.1 2001 ILC Draft Articles

After many years of studies and deliberations the International Law Commission (ILC) eventually adopted draft rules in 2001, consisting of 59 Articles as well as commentaries thereto.[10] Since these rules have not been formally adopted by states, they do not have legally binding force. However, they provide authoritative guidance for the development of international law. The Draft Articles are divided into four parts, addressing the internationally wrongful act of a state (Articles 1–27), the content of the international responsibility of a state (Articles 28–41), the implementation of the international responsibility of a state (Articles 42–54) and general provisions (Articles 55–59). The Draft Articles largely reflect customary international law.[11]

Basically, a state is responsible for 'internationally wrongful acts' that can be attributed to it. While, in principle, it is not disputed that the conduct of state organs is attributable to a state (Article 4), the following Articles further specify what else is to be considered as conduct of a state. What can be taken from these Articles is the rule that the conduct of private persons is not as such attributable to the state. In contrast to the 1996 Draft, it is relatively difficult on the basis of the 2001 Draft Articles to conclude that a state may, nevertheless, be responsible for the effects of the conduct of private parties, if it failed to take the necessary measures to prevent those effects. It is only possible to draw such a conclusion on the basis of Article 10(3) and a cumulative reading of Articles 4–11 of

[9] For further information on 'polluter pays' *cf* Chapter 8.

[10] See the Draft Articles on Responsibility of States for Internationally Wrongful Acts in ILC, 'Report of the International Law Commission on the work of its 53rd Session' (23 April–1 June and 2 July–10 August 2001) UN Doc A/56/10, 26 *et seq.*

[11] D Bodansky and JR Crook (eds), 'Symposium: the ILC's State Responsibility Articles' (2002) 96 *AJIL* 773.

the current Draft. However, without such an extended responsibility states could easily escape responsibility since environmentally relevant activities are often performed by private entities and not by the state itself.

A difficult question is whether or not there is an element of fault in the establishment of state responsibility. Draft Article 2 can be read as to establish responsibility without fault.[12] In principle, this seems to reflect customary international law. However, the Draft includes at least one reference which may be read as a subjective element. According to Article 23 wrongfulness of an act is precluded 'if the act is due to force majeure, that is . . . an unforeseen event, beyond the control of the State'. Whether Article 14(3) of the Draft Articles can be read as another subjective element seems doubtful since the earlier version of Article 23 of the 1996 Draft Articles was not taken up again in the finally adopted draft.[13] It seems that the draft still reflects a compromise between fault-based responsibility and responsibility without fault. The following excerpt from the commentary on Article 2 of the Draft Articles is highly illustrative to this end:

> Whether responsibility is 'objective' or 'subjective' in this sense depends on the circumstances, including the content of the primary obligation in question. The articles lay down no general rule in that regard. The same is true of other standards, whether they involve some degree of fault, culpability, negligence or want of due diligence. Such standards vary from one context to another for reasons which essentially relate to the object and purpose of the treaty provision or other rule giving rise to the primary obligation.[14]

It is noteworthy that the notion of 'international crimes'[15] which was included in earlier drafts has been replaced by the notion of 'serious breaches of obligations under peremptory norms of general international law' (Articles 40 and 41). Article 41 contains the legal consequences of such 'serious breaches', namely the obligation to co-operate to bring such breaches to an end, to refrain from recognising a situation created by a serious breach as lawful and from rendering assistance in maintaining that situation. Peremptory norms are not defined in the draft articles but the term must be read in conjunction with Articles 53 and 64 of the Vienna Convention on the Law of Treaties. It seems that only very few rules can actually be considered as peremptory norms and that hardly any of them is part of international environmental law.[16] In addition, Article 40 of the Draft Articles includes a further limitation by requiring a 'serious' breach. This is defined in Article 40(2) as one that involves 'a gross or systematic failure by the responsible State to fulfil the obligation' in question. As the ILC commentary on Article 40 points out, this 'signifies that a certain order of magnitude of violation is necessary in order not to trivialize the breach and it is not intended to suggest that any violation of these obligations is not

[12] For a closer analysis *cf* O Diggelmann, 'Fault in the Law of State Responsibility—Pragmatism ad Infinitum?' (2006) 49 *German Yearbook of International Law* 293.

[13] Art 14(3) reads as follows: 'The breach of an international obligation requiring a State to prevent a given event occurs when the event occurs and extends over the entire period during which the event continues and remains not in conformity with that obligation.'

[14] *Cf* ILC, 'Report of the International Law Commission on the work of its 53rd Session', above n 10, 34.

[15] The 1996 drafts included in Art 19 a definition of 'international crimes' and provided in Art 53 the consequences of international crimes.

[16] *Cf* Chapter 19.3.

serious or is somehow excusable'.[17] It is thus relatively unlikely that an internationally wrongful act in the field of international environmental law qualifies as a serious breach according to Article 40.

Articles 20–27 of the ILC Draft address circumstances precluding wrongfulness. These include consent (Article 20), self-defence (Article 21), countermeasures (Article 22), *force majeure* (Article 23), distress (Article 24) and necessity (Article 25).

What are the legal consequences of state responsibility? Part II of the Draft Articles includes several chapters addressing these consequences. General principles are laid down in Chapter I (Articles 28–33), followed by Chapter II focusing on 'reparation for injury' (Articles 34–39) and by Chapter III (Articles 40 and 41) on 'serious breaches' as discussed above. According to Article 34 of the Draft, there are three forms of reparation for injury: restitution, compensation and satisfaction. Unless materially impossible or involving a disproportionate burden, restitution in kind is considered to be the regular consequence of an internationally wrongful act (*cf* Article 35). According to Article 36(1) compensation, *ie* the payment of damages, may be an additional obligation if restitution does not make good the damage.[18] Article 37(2) provides that 'satisfaction may consist in an acknowledgement of the breach, an expression of regret, a formal apology or another appropriate modality'. It is important to note that the Draft Articles underline a continued duty of performance (*cf* Article 29) and make it clear that damage is not limited to material damage (*cf* Article 31(2)).

A matter that is not addressed by the Draft[19] is the question of who is entitled to claim state responsibility in case of damage to global environmental goods such as the climate. If a global environmental good is affected by an activity attributable to a state, and if this environmental good is of 'common concern' for all states, then it is not an individual state that has become victim of an internationally wrongful act but the international community as a whole. In such a case a single state might be interested in claiming reparation representing the state community as a whole; this is only possible, however, if the international obligation breached is an obligation *erga omnes*. This cannot be simply taken from reference to 'common concern' in the treaty in question or related to the customary law obligation under consideration. As the notion of 'international crime' has been replaced by the concept of 'serious breach' it has become more difficult to single out particular obligations as being applicable *erga omnes*.[20] As pointed out above, Articles 40 and 41 of the Draft Articles refer to peremptory norms rather than to obligations *erga omnes*. Should, however, an *erga omnes* obligation be established, it is possible for a state to bring a claim as a representative of the international community.

[17] ILC, 'Report of the International Law Commission on the work of its 53rd Session', above n 10, 113.

[18] *Cf* S Wittich, 'Compensation' in R Wolfrum (ed), *Max Planck Encyclopedia of Public International Law* (Heidelberg/Oxford 2008), available at www.mpepil.com.

[19] It is important to note that the debate about the legal basis for state responsibility is ongoing; in this respect *cf* J Crawford and S Olleson, 'The Continuing Debate on a UN Convention on State Responsibility' (2005) 54 *ICLQ* 959.

[20] *Cf* Chapter 19.3.

24.2.2 Case Law

Given that the 2001 Draft Articles are legally non-binding as such and that few treaties include provisions on state responsibility, it is worthwhile to take into account some cases which illustrate that, notwithstanding the general reluctance of states to seek recourse to the rules of state responsibility, these rules have shown relevance in practice.[21]

The earliest case to refer to is the international arbitral award of 11 March 1941 in the *Trail Smelter* case.[22] Emerging from a dispute between the USA and Canada concerning damages suffered by the USA following the discharge of sulphur dioxide emissions from a lead and zinc smelting plant in Canada, the arbitral tribunal not only established the rule of 'no harm' but also held Canada responsible for the damages already inflicted and for possible further adverse transboundary effects on the environment in the neighbouring state. The tribunal, however, introduced a difficult criterion to be met if responsibility is to apply: according to the tribunal, the polluting acts must be 'of serious consequence' and the injury must be established with 'clear and convincing evidence'. Both the question of whether the pollution is considered of serious consequence and increasing the evidentiary threshold to this height are prohibitive for bringing environmental claims, not least because the effects of pollution on humans and nature are often inconclusive and scientific certainty is difficult to reach. Nevertheless, the arbitral award rendered in the *Trail Smelter* case has become an important precedent both for the principle of limited territorial sovereignty and integrity,[23] and for the application of state responsibility in the field of international environmental law.

The second case relevant to state responsibility is the *Corfu Channel* case,[24] which deserves mentioning here even though it is not directly related to international environmental law. The case arose out of an incident in the Corfu Strait where, on 22 October 1946, two British destroyers were hit by mines in Albanian waters and suffered serious damage. The UK government filed an application with the International Court of Justice (ICJ) arguing that Albania was internationally responsible for the consequences of the incident. The UK sought reparation or compensation. Irrespective of whether the mines had been laid by Albania or not, the Court, on 9 April 1949, held Albania responsible for the explosions and for the resulting damage and loss of human life. The Court argued that Albania should have observed any such action given that the minefield was so close to the coast and that Albania had failed to inform the UK about any resulting danger. The Court, in December 1949, ordered Albania to pay compensation.[25]

A more recent case related to state responsibility and international environmental law alike is the *Certain Phosphate Lands in Nauru* case.[26] Nauru, an island in Micronesia in

[21] See J Brunnée, 'Sic Utere Tuo ut Alienum non Laedas' in R Wolfrum (ed*), Max Planck Encyclopedia of Public International Law* (Heidelberg/Oxford 2007), available at www.mpepil.com and *id*, 'Of Sense and Sensibility. Reflections on International Liability Regimes as Tools for Environmental Protection' (2004) 53 *ICLQ* 351.

[22] (1949) 3 RIAA 1903 *et seq*.

[23] See in detail Chapter 6.

[24] *UK and Northern Ireland v Albania* (1949) ICJ Reports 4 *et seq*.

[25] *Ibid*, 23.

[26] *Nauru v Australia* (1992) ICJ Reports 240 *et seq*.

the South Pacific, had first been exploited for phosphates when the Germans took control in 1908. Administered by, *inter alia*, Australia, under a League of Nation's mandate and later under a UN trusteeship agreement, the island obtained independence in 1968. As a result of extensive mining, large parts of the island are today a wasteland and essentially inaccessible on environmental grounds.[27] In 1989 Nauru filed a claim with the ICJ against Australia claiming compensation for the damage caused by phosphate mining before independence. Nauru argued that Australia had violated its basic responsibility as an administering power not to cause irreparable damage to or substantially prejudice the interests of the administered territory and its population and that, by exporting phosphates to Australia, it had also violated Nauru's sovereignty over its natural resources. The ICJ rejected Australia's preliminary objections and declared Nauru's claim to be admissible. The case was eventually settled by agreement in 1993 with an Australian payment in compensation for environmental damage, and a further agreement aiming at rehabilitation and development, signed in 1994.[28]

It is noteworthy that the UN Compensation Commission, established in 1991 as a subsidiary organ of the UN Security Council to deal with claims for losses and damage suffered as a direct result of Iraq's invasion and occupation of Kuwait,[29] was entitled to assess Iraq's responsibility with a view to 'any direct loss, damage—including environmental damage and the depletion of natural resources'.[30] In one of its decisions the Governing Council of the Commission specified various categories of damage encompassed by the above clause. These include, *inter alia*, expenses for abatement and prevention of environmental damage, including expenses directly relating to fighting oil fires and stemming the flow of oil in coastal and international waters; reasonable measures already taken to clean and restore the environment; reasonable monitoring and assessment of the environmental damage for the purposes of evaluating and abating the harm and restoring the environment; and depletion of or damage to natural resources.[31]

The issue of nuclear testing was also brought before the ICJ when Australia and New Zealand claimed that France had committed a wrongful act by conducting nuclear atmospheric tests that caused nuclear fallout. Australia, in the second *Nuclear Test* case,[32] argued that the effects of nuclear tests on the environment would be irremediable. However, it was difficult to prove damages since the case involved hazardous and radioactive substances, the effect of which on human health and the environment is cumulative and does not necessarily occur immediately. Thus, France could easily respond that in the absence of damage definitively attributable to its nuclear experiments, there was no

[27] JM Gowdy and CM McDaniel, 'The Physical Destruction of Nauru: An Example of Weak Sustainability' (1999) 75 *Land Economics* 333, 334.

[28] For a discussion of the case in full see NJ Schrijver, 'Certain Phosphate Lands in Nauru Case (Nauru v Australia)' in R Wolfrum (ed), *Max Planck Encyclopedia of Public International Law* (Heidelberg/Oxford 2008), available at www.mpepil.com.

[29] In Security Council Resolution 687 (1991) UN Doc S/RES/687 Iraq's responsibility was reaffirmed (section E para 16) and it was decided to create a compensation fund and a commission to administer the fund (section E para 18). The UNCC was established by Security Council Resolution 692 (1991).

[30] *Ibid*, para 16.

[31] Decision 7 'Criteria for Additional Categories of Claims' (17 March 1992) S/AC26/1991/7/Rev1.

[32] *Request for an Examination of the Situation in Accordance with Paragraph 63 of the Court's Judgment of 20 December 1974 in the Nuclear Tests (New Zealand v France) Case* (1995) ICJ Reports 288.

violation of any rule of international law. Unfortunately, the case was not decided on the merits. France not only challenged the jurisdiction of the ICJ but renounced further atmospheric testing, and the Court eventually held, in light of these circumstances, that the dispute no longer existed.[33]

The *Rainbow Warrior* case emerged out of an act of sabotage by French secret service agents, who sank a vessel belonging to Greenpeace International, an action that also resulted in the death of one of the crew members. At that time Greenpeace was campaigning against French nuclear testing in the Pacific and its ship, the *Rainbow Warrior*, was berthed in a New Zealand harbour. The two agents responsible for the sabotage were arrested and sentenced by a New Zealand court. Following mediation of the UN Secretary-General, France and New Zealand signed an agreement[34] which was not fully respected by France. New Zealand then initiated arbitration proceedings. The arbitral tribunal stressed that 'any violation by a State of any obligation, of whatever origin, gives rise to State responsibility'.[35] In its reasoning, the tribunal also dealt with *force majeure*, necessity and distress, all claimed by France. However, finally the tribunal held France responsible and ordered compensation to be paid.[36]

As can be taken from this case law, state responsibility is neither irrelevant nor obsolete in international environmental law.[37] However, it is rather difficult successfully to present a case exclusively based upon state responsibility. It is much easier to refer to state responsibility as a political argument within international environmental negotiations.

24.3 State Liability

Many usages of the environment are today considered indispensable and thus lawful in principle even though they include risk of damage to the environment, whether at the national or at the transboundary level. If such damage materialises, state responsibility does not apply as far as such pollution does not constitute a wrongful act. Since this is unacceptable in cases of serious damage, the idea of state liability for certain ultra-hazardous activities has been promoted. So far, however, few agreements have taken up the idea, among them Article 7 of the 1967 Outer Space Treaty, the 1972 Convention on International Liability for Damage Caused by Space Objects, and Article 14 of the 1979

[33] For a closer analysis see CG Weeramantry, 'Judicial Decisions and Awards International—ICJ's Order Dated 22 September 1995' (1996) 36 *Indian Journal of International Law* 77.

[34] *Rainbow Warrior (New Zealand v France)* ILR 74 (1987) 241.

[35] *Case concerning the difference between New Zealand and France concerning the interpretation or application of two agreements, concluded on 9 July 1986 between the two States and which related to the problems arising from the Rainbow Warrior Affair (New Zealand v France)* ILR 82 (1990) 499, 551.

[36] C Harding, 'Vingt Ans Après: Rainbow Warrior, Legal Ordering, and Legal Complexity' (2006) 10 *Singapore Yearbook of International Law* 99; M Pugh, 'Legal Aspects of the Rainbow Warrior Affair' (1987) 36 *ICLQ* 655.

[37] A Mori, 'State Responsibility: A Green Law View' (2000) 11 *Finnish Yearbook of International Law* 359; J Brunnée, 'International Legal Accountability Through the Lens of the Law of State Responsibility' (2007) 36 *Netherlands Yearbook of International Law* 21.

Agreement Governing the Activities of States on the Moon and Other Celestial Bodies.[38] Liability in these agreements is related to lawful activities in outer space which, however, entail serious risks; if damage results from such lawful activities, states can be held liable. Unfortunately, there is very limited treaty practice beyond these examples. In most cases involving ultra-hazardous transboundary activities, states prefer to resort to instruments establishing civil liability of the operator in charge, as will be exemplified by reference to the oil pollution regime and treaties dealing with nuclear liability.

In light of these findings it is very difficult to argue that state liability for (lawful) ultra-hazardous activities is part of customary international law. In 1978, the ILC established a working group to consider, in a preliminary manner, the scope and nature of international liability for injurious consequences arising out of acts not prohibited by international law. The Commission continued its work on the topic as a whole until 1997 when the Commission decided to divide it into two parts, one dealing with preventive rules, the other with liability rules.[39] The original focus of the Commission's work on direct state liability for lawful activities posed a number of problems, some of them related to different perceptions of responsibility and liability, others related to whether or not to address the notion of due diligence, and finally, an increasing scholarly opposition to the development of a distinct set of rules, separate from the rules on state responsibility. In 2001, the ILC adopted the final text of Draft Articles on Prevention of Transboundary Harm from Hazardous Activities and submitted the text to the General Assembly, consisting of a preamble and 19 Articles, with commentaries thereto.[40]

These Draft Articles require a state of origin prepared to authorise a hazardous activity to perform a risk assessment that also covers the transboundary harm that might be caused by the activity. Should the state conclude that the activity is likely to cause 'significant transboundary harm', procedural obligations to notify and to inform have to be met. States even are under an obligation to consult (Draft Article 9) to find acceptable solutions within a reasonable timeframe. Draft Article 10 requires a balancing of interests, which must take into account, *inter alia*, the degree of risk, the availability of means to prevent, minimise or repair harm, and the importance of the activity to the state of origin. It is surprising that there is no reference to the concept of strict liability in the Draft.

In 2006, the ILC adopted its 'Draft Principles on the Allocation of Loss in the Case of Transboundary Harm Arising out of Hazardous Activities'.[41] These Draft Principles reflect the general attitude of states to shift liability to the operator rather than being held liable themselves. In their comments on an earlier draft, states noted that hazardous activities are undertaken primarily for the benefit of the operator and that state liability should be

[38] See Chapter 13.5 on 'Outer Space Activities and Environmental Protection'.

[39] UNGA Res 52/156 (15 December 1997) 7; F Orrego Vicuña, 'Current Trends in Responsibility and Liability for Environmental Harm under International Law' in K Koufa (ed), *Protection of the Environment for the New Millennium—2000 International Law Session* (Athens *et al* 2002) 127.

[40] See the Draft Articles in ILC 'Prevention of Transboundary Harm from Hazardous Activities—Draft Preamble and Draft Articles adopted by the Drafting Committee on second reading', 53rd Session (23 April–1 June and 2 July–10 August 2001) UN Doc A/CN4/L601.

[41] See the Draft Articles in ILC, 'Title and texts of the Preamble and the Draft Principles on the Allocation of Loss arising out of Hazardous Activities adopted by the Drafting Committee on second reading' 58th Session (1 May–9 June and 3 July–10 August 2001) UN Doc A/CN4/L686.

supplementary only. This position is reflected in Draft Principle 4 which requires states to 'take all necessary measures to ensure that prompt and adequate compensation is available for victims of transboundary damage caused by hazardous activities located within its territory or otherwise under its jurisdiction or control', but adds that '[t]hese measures should include the imposition of liability on the operator or, where appropriate, other person or entity'. Principle 3(3) and (4) even envisages that operators should have insurance or other financial guarantees and that industry-wide funds be established. State liability thus largely is subsidiary: 'In the event that the measures under the preceding paragraphs are insufficient to provide adequate compensation, the State of origin should also ensure that additional financial resources are made available' (Principle 3(5)). It has rightly been argued that

> [t]he debates that are shaping the regime of allocation of costs in the case of transboundary harm resulting from hazardous activities demonstrate the lack of willingness of states to subscribe to an international liability regime that would hold them primarily responsible for transboundary harm.[42]

One might even conclude that the original intentions pursued by the ILC with regard to a regime of state liability complementing the responsibility regime have largely been given up in favour of civil liability regimes. Even though some of the changes in the direction of the work of the ILC on both state responsibility and state liability in the 1990s and in the early years of the twenty-first century seem to have been motivated by the desire to conclude these long-lasting drafting projects, their impact on the overall direction of international law on state responsibility and liability has been to limit governmental responsibilities in this regard. It is all the more important to consider what international law contributes to civil liability of private entities in this regard.

24.4 Civil Liability

As already pointed out, transboundary environmental damage calling for reparation or compensation more often results from the activities of private entities than from those of state organs. It is thus not surprising that liability regimes in international environmental law have increasingly turned to private entities. As will be shown, however, most of the more recent international agreements combine civil liability and subsidiary state liability. The majority of instruments are issue-specific, focusing on oil pollution, nuclear energy and the transboundary movement of wastes. The instrument on liability for damage to the Antarctic environment is the only one focusing on the vulnerability of a particular region. In 2005, the parties to the 1991 Protocol on Environmental Protection to the Antarctic Treaty, meeting their obligation to 'elaborate rules and procedures relating to liability for damage arising from activities taking place in the Antarctic Treaty area', adopted an

[42] E Louka, *International Environmental Law. Fairness, Effectiveness and World Order* (Cambridge 2006) 481.

annex on 'Liability Arising from Environmental Emergencies'. Annex VI to the Protocol creates a regime which ensures prompt and effective response when significant harm is caused to the Antarctic environment. It includes rules on jurisdiction and standing, provides for compulsory arbitration and lays down limits for liability.[43] The only general instrument in this respect is the Convention on Liability for Damage Resulting from Activities Dangerous to the Environment adopted by the Council of Europe in 1993.

24.4.1 Oil Pollution and Other Hazardous Substances

The anti-oil pollution regime has evolved in response to a number of oil spills, beginning with the 1969 *Torrey Canyon* incident, followed by the *Amoco Cadiz* disaster of 1978, the *Exxon Valdez* oil spill of 1989, to the more recent incidents of the *Erika* (1999) and the *Prestige* (2000). It can thus be characterised as reactive rather than anticipatory. The anti-oil pollution regime focuses on pollution by ships and does not cover spills related to accidents on oil platforms. The *Deepwater Horizon* catastrophe (2010) might accelerate action in this respect on the international level. Today, the regime is primarily comprised of the 1969 Convention on Civil Liability for Oil Pollution Damage, the 1971 Fund Convention, the 1992 Convention on Civil Liability for Oil Pollution Damage and the 1992 Fund Convention, amending the 1969/1971 instruments, as well as the 2003 Protocol to the International Convention on the Establishment of an International Fund for Compensation for Oil Pollution Damage. A state can only join the Fund Convention if it is a party to the respective Liability Convention. In addition to these oil pollution-related instruments, the 1996 International Convention on Liability and Compensation for Damage in Connection with the Carriage of Hazardous and Noxious Substances (HNS Convention) deserves closer scrutiny.

The 1992 Civil Liability Convention and the 1992 Fund Convention establish a liability regime consisting of two layers.[44] Firstly, there is strict liability of the owner of a ship carrying bulk oil for pollution damage caused by that ship in the territory, territorial sea or exclusive economic zone of a party to the 1992 Civil Liability Convention. Secondly, if compensation from the owner is insufficient to cover the damage, the international fund established by the 1992 Fund Convention will supplement the compensation to be paid under the Liability Convention up to a defined maximum amount. At present there are 123 parties to the 1992 Liability Convention representing 96.7 per cent of world tonnage. One hundred and four parties have ratified both the 1992 Liability Convention and the 1992 Fund Convention. Due to an increasing number of states ratifying the 1992 instruments and denouncing the 1969/1971 instruments, the latter are no longer of major importance. The 1971 Fund Convention even ceased to be in force on 24 May 2002 when its number of members fell below 25. The 1971 Fund thus is in the process of being wound up, but will operate until all pending claims have been settled.

The Civil Liability Convention only covers

[43] See Johnson, above n 7, for details on Annex VI to the Antarctic Environment Protocol.
[44] M Mason, 'Civil Liability for Oil Pollution Damage' (2003) 27 *Marine Policy* 1.

> loss or damage caused outside the ship by contamination resulting from the escape or discharge of oil from the ship, wherever such escape or discharge may occur, provided that compensation for impairment of the environment other than loss of profit from such impairment shall be limited to costs of reasonable measures of reinstatement actually undertaken or to be undertaken

as well as 'the costs of preventive measures and further loss or damage caused by preventive measures' (Article I(6)). In the Convention, the definition of damage to the environment is limited in scope. It only covers the costs of reasonable reinstatement measures aimed at accelerating natural recovery. The Fund is administered by an intergovernmental organisation consisting of all parties to the 1992 Fund Convention and financed by contributions levied by parties, calculated on the basis of the amount of oil received in one calendar year by any person, whether government, public or private, if the amount is more than 150000 tonnes of oil.

In 2000, amendments to the 1992 Fund Convention were adopted, increasing the maximum amount of compensation payable from the fund from 135 million Special Drawing Rights (SDR) (US$173 million) to 203 million SDR (US$260 million). However, the maximum payment goes beyond this if three parties receive more than 600 million tonnes of oil per year.

In 2003, another Protocol to the International Convention on the Establishment of an International Fund for Compensation for Oil Pollution Damage was adopted in order to establish a third tier of compensation,[45] the so-called International Oil Pollution Compensation Supplementary Fund. The Supplementary Fund is applicable in cases where the damage surpasses the amount available under the 1992 Conventions. Its territorial scope is in conformity with that of the 1992 Conventions, and the compensation payable is limited to a combined total of 750 million SDR. At present, there are 27 parties to the Supplementary Fund Protocol.

Reference may also be made to the 2001 International Convention on Civil Liability for Bunker Oil Damages[46] which entered into force in 2008 and currently has 54 parties representing 84.66 per cent of world tonnage.[47] Modelled on the 1992 Liability Convention, the 2001 Convention aims at closing the gap left by previous oil pollution conventions.[48] In particular, it applies to fuel spills from ships' bunkers, while the other conventions cover oil spills from tankers. The definition of pollution damage corresponds to that of the 1992 Liability Convention. The Convention applies to damages and preventive measures, wherever taken to prevent or minimise such damage, caused in the territory, including the territorial sea, or the exclusive economic zone of a party. The definition of the owner of a ship is slightly broader than that included in the 1992 Convention. Similar to all the other liability conventions, the 2001 Convention, in Article 6, provides for a limitation

[45] P Sands, *Principles of International Environmental Law* (2nd edn Cambridge 2003) 915.

[46] For an introduction see NJ Gaskell and CJS Forrest, 'Marine Pollution Damage in Australia: Implementing the Bunker Oil Convention 2001 and the Supplementary Fund Protocol 2003' (2008) 27 *The University of Queensland Law Journal* 103, 125 *et seq*.

[47] More than a third of the parties are European states, *eg* Germany, United Kingdom, Norway, Denmark or Spain, but also land-locked states such as Hungary or Poland. The Convention has also been ratified by Canada, the Russian Federation, China, some other Asian states, Australia, some Pacific island states, Panama, some Caribbean states, a few Arabic states, and some African states, *eg* Egypt, Sierra Leone and Liberia.

[48] Gaskell and Forrest, above n 48, 130.

of liability in accordance with national and international regimes, such as the Convention on Limitation of Liability for Maritime Claims of 1976. The Convention requires ships with a gross tonnage of over 1000 tonnes to maintain insurance or other financial security equal to the limitation under the applicable national or international regime. The Convention allows a claim for compensation to be brought directly against the insurer.

The 1996 HNS Convention is built on the above oil pollution regime and establishes strict but limited liability of the owners of ships supplemented by the International Hazardous and Noxious Substances Fund (HNS Fund).[49] According to Article 1(6) HNS Convention, it covers loss of life or personal injury on board or outside the ship, loss of or damage to property outside the ship, loss or damage by contamination of the environment caused by the hazardous and noxious substances, and the cost of preventive measures and further loss or damage caused by preventive measures. If the owner of the ship is not available or if the owner covers the damage inadequately, the HNS Fund will supplement the liability. The maximum amount is 250 million SDR. The contributions to the HNS Fund will come from the receivers of HNS cargo. The HNS Convention has not yet entered into force: it currently has 14 ratifications, representing 13.61 per cent of world tonnage.[50] In 2010, a Protocol to the HNS Convention was adopted in order to bring the Convention into effect by addressing some practical problems which have prevented further ratifications so far. Most important are the rules upon limitation of damages to be paid. In addition, the rules for the Convention's entry into force have been amended.

24.4.2 Nuclear Energy

In light of the fact that nuclear accidents might cause damage of extreme magnitude often not confined to the territory of one individual state, it is important to have an international regime which provides for compensation for nuclear damage in a transboundary context. The nuclear civil liability regime is based on a set of different international agreements:[51] the 1960 Convention on Third Party Liability in the Field of Nuclear Energy (Paris Convention), as amended in 2004; the 1963 Convention Supplementary to the Paris Convention (Brussels Convention), also amended in 2004; and the 1963 Vienna Convention on Civil Liability for Nuclear Damage, revised in 1997, together with the 1997 Convention on Supplementary Compensation for Nuclear Damage and the 1988 Joint Protocol Relating to the Application of the Vienna Convention and the Paris Convention.

The Paris Convention is a regional instrument, with currently 12 parties, which has been sponsored by the OECD. It includes rules on civil liability and compensation for damage caused by accidents occurring while producing nuclear energy. The Convention channels liability exclusively to the operator of the nuclear installation. It imposes strict,

[49] For a closer analysis see P Wetterstein, 'Carriage of Hazardous Cargoes by Sea—The HNS Convention' (1997) 26 *Georgia Journal of International & Comparative Law* 595.

[50] The following States have ratified the Convention: Angola, Russian Federation, Cyprus, Saint Kitts and Nevis, Ethiopia, Samoa, Hungary, Sierra Leone, Liberia, Slovenia, Lithuania, Syrian Arab Republic, Morocco and Tonga.

[51] For a brief introduction see JG Lammers, 'Compensation for Nuclear Damage under the Paris, Brussels and Vienna Conventions' (2003) 16 *Hague Yearbook of International Law* 46.

but limited (both in terms of amount and with regard to the period for making claims) liability on the operator of such an installation. In addition, the Convention requires insurance without, however, specifying the amount, type and terms of such insurance. Furthermore, the Convention provides for exclusive jurisdiction of the courts of one country, which normally is the country where the incident occurs. The 2004 amendment has not yet entered into force. Increasing the operator's liability to no less than €700 million and the minimum liability applicable to low-risk installations and transport activities to €70 million and €80 million, respectively, the amendment also broadens the scope of the Convention. In addition to personal injury and property damage, the cost of measures to reinstate an impaired environment, the loss of income resulting from that impaired environment and the costs of preventive measures are covered by the revised Convention. It does not only apply to operative nuclear installations but also to those being decommissioned and all installations for the disposal of nuclear substances (Article 1 of the revised Convention). Subject to certain conditions, including reciprocity, the Convention will also apply to nuclear damage suffered in a non-party (Article 2 of the revised Convention). Furthermore, prescription and extinction periods are extended (Article 8 of the revised Convention).

The Brussels Convention supplements the Paris Convention by providing additional funds to compensate damage as a result of a nuclear incident where Paris Convention funds prove to be insufficient. It requires that public funds be provided for this purpose, not only from the operator's state but from all parties to the Convention. The 2004 amendment to the Brussels Convention has not yet entered into force. It improves the three-tier liability regime as follows: the operator's financial security is increased to a minimum of €700 million; the public funds provided by the home state are increased to €500 million; and the additional public funds provided by all parties are increased to €300 million. In addition, the amendment modifies the calculation of the contributions, giving more weight to installed nuclear capacity than to the gross domestic product of the parties (65 per cent/35 per cent compared to 50 per cent/50 per cent under the original Brussels Convention).

The Vienna regime is similar to the Paris/Brussels regime. Originally, it adopted the same definition of damage, allowing, however, for other types of damage included should the law of the competent court so provide. After the 1986 Chernobyl incident a Protocol was adopted in 1997 to include further damages such as economic loss arising from loss of life or personal injury, or loss of, or damage to, property, the cost of measures of reinstatement of impaired environment, loss of income deriving from an economic interest in any use or enjoyment of the environment, and the cost of preventive measures (Article 2(2) of the 1997 Protocol). In order to avoid parallel recourse to both regimes, the 1988 Protocol establishes a link between the Vienna Convention (with 36 parties at present) and the Paris Convention. Moreover, in 1997 members of the IAEA adopted the Convention on Supplementary Compensation for Nuclear Damage in order to supplement the Paris and Vienna Conventions. This Convention, which has not yet entered into force, aims at establishing a worldwide fund consisting of contributions by all parties.

24.4.3 Wastes

The 1999 Basel Protocol on Liability and Compensation for Damage Resulting from Transboundary Movements of Hazardous Wastes and their Disposal has not yet entered into force. At present, 10 parties have ratified, pending another 10 ratifications for entry into force (Article 29 of the Protocol).[52]

The Protocol aims at 'a compensation regime for liability and for adequate and prompt compensation for damage' resulting from the transboundary movement and disposal of wastes. Damage as defined in Article 2(2)(c) of the Protocol includes loss of life or personal injury, loss or damage to property, loss of income deriving from an economic interest in use of the impaired environment, and costs of certain measures taken to prevent, minimise or mitigate damage, or to effect an environmental clean-up. The Protocol provides for strict liability of the person notifying the designated state of the transboundary movement of wastes but transfers this liability to the disposer once in possession of the wastes transferred (Article 4). Liability will not only be incurred by these two parties but may include many others which, however, are only subject to fault-based liability (Article 5) caused by non-compliance with Convention requirements. The amount is limited according to Article 12 and Annex B to the notifying person, exporter, importer and disposer. Time limits for claims are laid down in Article 13 (10 and 5 years after the incident or knowledge, respectively). Article 15 refers to existing mechanisms when compensation under the Protocol is inadequate.

24.4.4 The 1993 Liability Convention

The 1993 Convention on Liability for Damage Resulting from Activities Dangerous to the Environment adopted by the Council of Europe establishes a liability regime for potentially environmentally harmful activities aiming at adequate compensation and restitution (Article 1). Holding the operator strictly[53] liable for incidents as defined by Article 2(11), the Convention does not provide for limitations on liability. It protects the environment, which is defined as 'natural resources both abiotic and biotic, such as air, water, soil, fauna and flora and the interaction between the same factors; property which forms part of the cultural heritage; and the characteristic aspects of the landscape' (*cf* Article 2(10)). This means that the Convention also applies to so-called ecological damage. According to Article 3, it also covers transboundary activities. The Convention has a broad scope of application in this respect. It encompasses incidents occurring in the territory of a party 'regardless to where the damage is suffered' and also incidents outside the territory of a party if conflict-of-law rules lead to the application of the law of a contracting state. The Convention does not apply to tolerable levels of pollution under locally relevant circumstances (*cf* Article 8(d)).

[52] See A Daniel, 'Hazardous Wastes, Transboundary Impacts' in R Wolfrum (ed), *Max Planck Encyclopedia of Public International Law* (Heidelberg/Oxford 2009), available at www.mpepil.com.

[53] Arts 5–7, but see exemptions in Art 8.

24.5 Conclusions

The current state of international environmental law related to responsibility and liability for environmental damage is ambivalent. On the one hand, there is an increasing trend to conclude international agreements ensuring civil liability of operators for any damage caused. This ensures that international environmental obligations are channelled to the final addressees, which are not normally states or public entities, but individuals or private entities typically causing environmental damage. If international environmental law is to have an impact on the behaviour, not only of states and other subjects of international law, but also of individual persons and businesses, then this is a trend which deserves recognition and support. On the other hand, the scope of existing instruments available in this field still is very limited. This is best reflected in the fact that most agreements only deal with particular environmental hazards, and only one of them is generally applicable. The expansion of civil liability regimes has to some extent been at the expense of state responsibility and state liability. While the ILC has largely given up the distinction between internationally wrongful acts and lawful acts in its work on responsibility and liability, it has at the same time narrowed down the applicability of state responsibility. The adoption of pertinent draft articles and principles with regard to both state responsibility and liability, at the beginning of the twenty-first century has brought these projects to a conclusion, but seemingly at the expense of a very limited scope of application. Notwithstanding the case law on state responsibility, this supports the conclusion that state responsibility and liability are of political rather than legal relevance to international environmental protection.

Further Reading

AH Ansari, 'Trends in Shipowners' Liability for Marine Environmental Impairment' (2006) 1 *Asian Journal of International Law* 157–207.

TA Berwick, 'Responsibility and Liability for Environmental Damage: A Roadmap for International Regimes' (1998) 10 *Georgetown International Environmental Law Review* 257–267.

D Bodansky and JR Crook (eds), 'Symposium: the ILC's State Responsibility Articles' (2002) 96 *AJIL* 773–874.

A Boyle and J Harrison, 'Environmental Accidents' in R Wolfrum (ed), *Max Planck Encyclopedia of Public International Law* (Heidelberg/Oxford 2007), available at www.mpepil.com.

J Brunnée, 'Of Sense and Sensibility. Reflections on International Liability Regimes as Tools for Environmental Protection' (2004) 53 *ICLQ* 351–368.

——, 'International Legal Accountability Through the Lens of the Law of State Responsibility' (2007) 36 *Netherlands Yearbook of International Law* 21–56.

JR Crawford, 'State Responsibility' in R Wolfrum (ed), *Max Planck Encyclopedia of Public International Law* (Heidelberg/Oxford 2006), available at www.mpepil.com.

J Crawford and S Olleson, 'The Continuing Debate on a UN Convention on State Responsibility' (2005) 54 *ICLQ* 959–971.

A Daniel, 'Hazardous Wastes, Transboundary Impacts' in R Wolfrum (ed), *Max Planck Encyclopedia of Public International Law* (Heidelberg/Oxford 2009), available at www.mpepil.com.

O Diggelmann, 'Fault in the Law of State Responsibility—Pragmatism Ad Infinitum?' (2006) 49 *German Yearbook of International Law* 293–306.

MM Esquivel de Cocca, 'International Liability for Damages Caused by Persons or Space Objects in Outer Space or on Celestial Bodies to Persons, Properties or Environment in Outer Space or Celestial Bodies' (2000) *Proceedings of the Forty-Second Colloquium on the Law of Outer Space* 50–59.

C Harding, 'Vingt Ans Après: Rainbow Warrior, Legal Ordering, and Legal Complexity' (2006) 10 *Singapore Yearbook of International Law* 99–116.

AC Kiss, 'Strict Liability in International Environmental Law' in M Führ (ed), *Umweltrecht und Umweltwissenschaft. Festschrift für Eckard Rehbinder* (Berlin 2007) 213–221.

T Koivoruva, 'Due Diligence' in R Wolfrum (ed), *Max Planck Encyclopedia of Public International Law* (Heidelberg/Oxford 2007), available at www.mpepil.com.

JG Lammers, 'New Developments Concerning International Responsibility and Liability for Damage Caused by Environmental Interferences' (2007) 19 *Hague Yearbook of International Law* 87–112.

M Mason, 'Civil Liability for Oil Pollution Damage' (2003) 27 *Marine Policy* 1–12.

A Mori, 'State Responsibility: A Green Law View' (2000) 11 *Finnish Yearbook of International Law* 359–413.

F Orrego Vicuña, 'Current Trends in Responsibility and Liability for Environmental Harm under International Law' in K Koufa (ed), *Protection of the Environment for the New Millennium—2000 International Law Session* (Athens *et al* 2002) 127–182.

M Pedrazzi, 'Outer Space, Liability for Damage' in R Wolfrum (ed), *Max Planck Encyclopedia of Public International Law* (Heidelberg/Oxford 2008), available at www.mpepil.com.

NJ Schrijver, 'Certain Phosphate Lands in Nauru Case (Nauru v Australia)' in R Wolfrum (ed), *Max Planck Encyclopedia of Public International Law* (Heidelberg/Oxford 2008), available at www.mpepil.com.

S Wittich, 'Compensation' in R Wolfrum (ed), *Max Planck Encyclopedia of Public International Law* (Heidelberg/Oxford 2008), available at www.mpepil.com.

25

Environmental Dispute Settlement

25.1 Survey

Article 33 of the UN Charter obliges states parties to settle international disputes peacefully by means of their own choice, such as negotiation, enquiry, mediation, conciliation, arbitration and judicial settlement. States can resort to these means in all areas of international law, including international environmental relations. Modern MEAs often contain dispute-settlement clauses which enable states parties to have recourse to said means. Even if an MEA lacks such a clause, as some early MEAs in fact did,[1] the states parties concerned were bound by customary international law to settle their disputes peacefully by choosing between non-judicial (diplomatic) means (*ie* negotiation, enquiry, mediation and conciliation) and judicial means (arbitration and judicial settlement). There is no hierarchy of dispute-settlement means under general international law, either between the two categories or within the latter. However, following an intrinsic logic, many MEAs provide that the parties to a dispute can only resort to judicial means after having tried in vain to settle the dispute by way of negotiation.

The procedures of enquiry, mediation and conciliation have in common that the parties to a dispute request an independent third party to help them settle their dispute. These bodies confine themselves to making legally non-binding recommendations to the adversary parties rather than force them to accept a dictated solution. Thus, compared to judicial dispute settlement, non-judicial means interfere to a lesser extent with traditional perceptions of state sovereignty. By contrast, parties will not submit a dispute to an international court or tribunal unless they accept the decision of the court or tribunal as legally binding. Consequently, states seeking judicial dispute settlement waive part of their sovereignty.

Like compliance control, dispute settlement is aimed at ensuring observance of international law. While the former takes place in the context of treaty-based partnership, it is

[1] *Eg* the 1946 International Convention for the Regulation of Whaling.

typical of the latter that it is adversarial in character and involves only a limited number of parties.

There has been a considerable increase in international litigation on environmental matters in international courts of general jurisdiction (*eg* the ICJ and the Court of Justice of the European Union, consisting of the European Court of Justice, the General Court (formerly the Court of First Instance) and the Civil Service Tribunal), in courts and tribunals specialised in non-environmental issues (*eg* the International Tribunal for the Law of the Sea (ITLOS), the European Court of Human Rights (ECtHR) and the WTO dispute-settlement system), and in environment-focused judicial bodies (*eg* the proposed International Court for the Environment).[2] In addition, in a number of important international environmental disputes *ad hoc* or institutional arbitration has been quite successfully utilised. The case law of all these courts and tribunals will be discussed below in more detail. Notwithstanding the growing proliferation of international adjudicative bodies engaged in international environmental disputes, for more than 20 years there have been proposals to establish a specialist international environmental court. However, as yet such proposals have not found sufficient support in the international environmental arena.

25.2 Non-Judicial Dispute Settlement

Most modern MEAs refer only to negotiation as a means of non-judicial dispute settlement. States are obliged to make all good-faith efforts to reach a just and fair solution. However, due to the non-formality of negotiation and openness regarding its final outcome, negotiation hardly curtails states' freedom of decision.

While MEAs mostly refer to negotiation as a dispute-settlement means, consultation is a means that treaty partners normally use to resolve disagreements at a stage prior to a proper dispute on treaty compliance. Thus, treaty clauses requiring parties to enter into consultations are aimed at dispute avoidance rather than dispute settlement.

Quite often disputes between states parties to an MEA arise from their disagreement regarding the existence or non-existence of certain legally relevant facts. Treaty parties that have been unable to solve a factual difference on their own may request an impartial and independent body to undertake an enquiry about the disputed facts. Among the few MEAs that provide for a formal enquiry as a means of dispute settlement is the 1991 Espoo Convention which provides in Article 3(7) that in cases where the states parties concerned cannot agree on the question whether one of them is likely to be affected by a significant adverse transboundary impact of a proposed activity of the other, any such party may submit that question to an enquiry commission 'to advise on the likelihood of significant adverse transboundary impact'. Thus, a commission acting under the Espoo Convention is charged with both 'fact-finding' and legal evaluation of the ascertained facts.[3]

[2] See T Stephens, *International Courts and Environmental Protection* (Cambridge 2009) 9, referring to P Sands, *Principles of International Environmental Law* (2nd edn Cambridge 2003) 65.

[3] For more details see above Chapter 16.3.

States involved in an environmental dispute that have failed to settle their dispute by way of negotiation or consultation are allowed under many MEAs to seek the mediation or good offices of a third party. In both cases a neutral state, an international organisation or an international institution offers its advisory services for the promotion of dispute settlement. Thus, it facilitates the negotiations between the parties concerned, without acting as a formal adjudicative body.

While an enquiry normally only comprises fact finding, conciliation may include findings on matters of law and of fact. As a rule, conciliation procedures go beyond mediation procedures insofar as they include elements of enquiry procedures. As alternatives to judicial settlement and arbitration, enquiry and conciliation both attract states parties as a helpful third-party intervention that ensures that 'whatever the outcome of the proceedings, the parties remain free to negotiate a politically acceptable settlement of their differences without being bound to adhere strictly to treaty provisions or rules of international law'.[4]

The technique of sequencing various non-judicial dispute-settlement means and combining them with judicial ones is exemplified by Article 33 of the 1997 UNECE Convention on the Law of the Non-navigational Uses of International Watercourses which stipulates that where an agreement cannot be reached by negotiation, the parties 'may jointly seek the good offices of, or request mediation or conciliation by, a third party, or . . . agree to submit the dispute to arbitration or to the International Court of Justice' (paragraph 2). A dispute that has not been settled within six months through the means referred to in paragraph 2, 'shall be submitted, at the request of any of the parties to the dispute, to impartial fact-finding' (paragraph 3), a task to be assigned to a special Fact-finding Commission (paragraph 4).

25.3 Judicial Dispute Settlement

International judicial settlement and arbitration have in common that they are based on the consent of the parties to each dispute. In principle, both judicial settlement and arbitration rely on the genuine independence of the judicial body that offers its expertise in dispute settlement. However, there are also some core features that distinguish judicial settlement and arbitration. International arbitration 'is highly adaptable, allowing the parties to agree on a process that matches their needs in resolving disputes as they arise' as well as 'to agree upon the composition of the arbitral tribunal, the rules for making submissions on law and fact, the applicable law, and modalities for implementing the award'.[5] Thus, it leaves to the parties concerned a considerable leeway of decision. By contrast, permanent

[4] *Cf* P Birnie, A Boyle and C Redgwell, *International Law and the Environment* (3rd edn Oxford 2009) 265; see also Sands, above n 2, 204. Conciliation in particular is provided for in a number of MEAs (*eg* Art 11(4) and (5) of the Vienna Convention for the Protection of the Ozone Layer, Art 27(4) of the Convention on Biological Diversity, Art 22(4) of the International Treaty on Plant Genetic Resources for Food and Agriculture, and Art 284 and Annex V of UN Convention on the Law of the Sea).

[5] Stephens, above n 2, 34.

courts and tribunals composed of long-time appointed impartial judges 'have the capacity to adopt a more independent stance, oriented towards public interest considerations'. Due to these attributes they may develop 'a more self-directed approach to the settlement of environmental disputes'. Thus, their decisions appear to be better suited than those of arbitral tribunals to contribute to the further development of international environmental law beyond the solely *inter partes* dispute-settlement process.[6]

25.3.1 The ICJ and Other Permanent International Courts

The ICJ and its predecessor, the Permanent Court of International Justice (PCIJ) are the only two international courts with general subject matter jurisdiction and global reach. The ICJ's contentious jurisdiction can arise in two ways. Firstly, the ICJ can have jurisdiction by agreement between the parties to a dispute, either by a special agreement in view of a particular dispute, or by a compromissory clause in an international treaty (Article 36(1) ICJ Statute), as it can be found in many MEAs. Secondly, parties to the ICJ Statute may declare that they accept the ICJ's jurisdiction either unconditionally, or on condition of reciprocity, or for a limited period of time (Article 36(2) ICJ Statute).

Among the 60 cases submitted to the PCIJ, only the judgment in the *River Oder* case of 1929[7] deserves attention from an environmental perspective. Due to its broad contentious and advisory jurisdiction the ICJ is well suited to dealing with major interstate environmental disputes. However, to date the ICJ has delivered only a limited number of relevant judgments and advisory opinions. Among them are the advisory opinion on the *Legality of the Threat or Use of Nuclear Weapons* (1996),[8] as well as the judgments in the *Gabčíkovo-Nagymaros Project* case (1997)[9] and in the *Pulp Mills on the River Uruguay* case (2010).[10] Although clearly focusing on the interpretation of environmental obligations flowing from bilateral treaties between neighbouring states, the latter judgments also comment on the customary law status of the 'no harm' rule (*Gabčíkovo-Nagymaros* case) and the obligation to undertake a transboundary environmental impact assessment (*Pulp Mills* case).[11] However, the ICJ's overall contribution to the further development of international environmental law has so far been marginal. The scarcity of its relevant case law clearly reflects the ongoing reluctance of states to make use of the contentious jurisdiction of the ICJ for settling transboundary environmental disputes. Aware of its lack of attractiveness, in 1993 the ICJ established under Article 26(1) of its Statute a permanent Chamber for Environmental Matters composed of seven judges in order to enhance its environmental credentials. However, as it became evident that the Chamber would not meet the hopes placed on it, the Court stopped the annual elections for a bench of the said Chamber in 2006.

[6] See *ibid*, 36.

[7] *Case Relating to the Territorial Jurisdiction of the International Commission of the River Oder (United Kingdom v Poland)* PCIJ Report Series A No 23.

[8] (1996) ICJ Reports 226.

[9] *Hungary v Slovakia* (1997) ICJ Reports 7.

[10] *Argentina v Uruguay*, Judgment of 20 April 2010, available at www.icj-cij.org/docket/index.php?p1=3&p2=3&k=88&case=135&code=au&p3=4.

[11] See Chapters 6.3.5 and 16.3.

Part XV UNCLOS provides for a sophisticated dispute-settlement system which is 'highly distinctive in international environmental law by virtue of its comprehensive coverage and its compulsory character'.[12] Article 287 UNCLOS outlines the available dispute-settlement procedures. Under this provision states are at any time free to declare a preference for one or more of four judicial bodies: (i) the International Tribunal for the Law of the Sea (ITLOS) as the pre-eminent institution in the UNCLOS dispute-settlement system; (ii) the ICJ with its general jurisdiction; (iii) an Annex VII arbitral tribunal; and (iv) an Annex VIII special arbitral tribunal. Each of the four bodies referred to in Article 287 has broad jurisdiction under Article 288 to address any dispute arising from the application of UNCLOS.

In operation since 1996, ITLOS[13] has to date dealt with 14 cases, delivered seven judgments, and made a large number of substantive and procedural orders. Although nine of the cases dealt with raised significant environmental issues, none of them proceeded to a full hearing on the merits.

Under Article 290(1) UNCLOS and Article 31 of the 1995 Fish Stocks Agreement,[14] ITLOS is allowed to prescribe provisional measures 'to prevent serious harm to the marine environment'. Making use of this power, ITLOS, on 27 August 1999, issued its Order prescribing provisional measures in the *Southern Bluefin Tuna* cases.[15] In this order parties were, *inter alia*, required to keep catches to the levels last agreed, to refrain from conducting an experimental fishing programme, to resume negotiations and to seek agreement with others engaged in fishing for southern bluefin tuna. The Order has been considered to be 'one of the most important judicial decisions in international environmental law, demonstrating a sensitivity both to the gravity of the problem of overfishing and the interplay between "living resources" issues and marine environmental questions more generally'.[16] On 4 August 2000 an Annex VII arbitral tribunal delivered its Award on Jurisdiction and Admissibility in the *Southern Bluefin Tuna* case.[17] In finding that it did not have jurisdiction to rule on the merits of the case, the arbitral tribunal revoked the 1999 ITLOS Order for provisional measures and encouraged the parties to continue to seek to resolve their dispute under the peaceful means provided for in the 1993 Convention for the Conservation of Southern Bluefin Tuna. The downside effect of the award is 'to allow unsustainable high seas fishing to continue while precluding direct enforcement of the duty of all states to conserve and manage living resources'.[18]

In the *MOX Plant* case between Ireland and the United Kingdom, ITLOS prescribed

[12] Stephens, above n 2, 41.

[13] Like the ICJ, ITLOS disposes of an environmental chamber, which, however, has also as yet remained unused.

[14] United Nations Agreement for the Implementation of the Provisions of the United Nations Convention on the Law of the Sea of 10 December 1982 relating to the Conservation and Management of Straddling Fish Stocks and Highly Migratory Fish Stocks of 4 December 1995, in force since 11 December 2001.

[15] *Australia v Japan; New Zealand v Japan* (Provisional Measures, Order of 27 August 1999) ITLOS Cases Nos 3 and 4; ITLOS Press Release, 'Southern Bluefin Tuna Cases/Tribunal prescribes provisional measures' (27 August 1999) ITLOS/Press 28. *Cf* A Boyle, 'Environmental Dispute Settlement' in R Wolfrum (ed), *Max Planck Encyclopedia of Public International Law* (Heidelberg/Oxford 2009) para 16, available at www.mpepil.com.

[16] Stephens, above n 2, 227.

[17] *Australia and New Zealand v Japan* (2000) 39 ILM 1359.

[18] Stephens, above n 2, 228.

in its Order of 3 December 2001 a provisional measure under Article 290(5) UNCLOS, 'pending a decision by the Annex VII arbitral tribunal'.[19] With its award of 24 June 2003[20] the Annex VII Arbitral Tribunal constituted for the dispute concerning the MOX plant called upon the parties to comply with the ITLOS order and to engage in meaningful co-operation and consultation at a suitable intergovernmental level.[21]

Other permanent international courts already in existence with potential jurisdiction to adjudicate on environmental disputes are the Court of Justice of the European Union, and few courts established under regional human rights treaties, such as the European Court of Human Rights.[22]

Notwithstanding the existence of various international courts and tribunals well able to deal with international environmental problems, endeavours for the establishment of a new international environmental court started in 1988 and culminated in the propagation of a Draft Treaty for the Establishment of an International Court for the Environment (ICE) by experts convened for the Conference at the Accademia Nazionale dei Lincei in Rome.[23] However, this proposal and others met with resistance in doctrine and practice based on reasonable fears that the establishment of the ICE 'will lead to inconsistent judgments among the many courts able to adjudicate the same environmental problems, as well as a fragmentation of international environmental law, and exacerbate the problem of forum shopping'.[24] As 'settling disputes involving environmental issues requires a wide-ranging grasp of international law as a whole', Boyle is right to stress that '[i]t is difficult to see how an environmental court could either monopolize the field, or avoid the risk of over-specialization and distorted focus for which the WTO disputes system has been criticized'.[25]

25.3.2 International Arbitration

Notwithstanding the fact that arbitrational procedures are organised in a way that respects state sovereignty, dispute settlement by arbitration has not yet found broader acceptance in international environmental relations. Most prominent among the early awards of international arbitral tribunals are those in the 1893 *Bering Sea Fur Seals* case,[26] in the 1941 *Trail Smelter* case,[27] and in the 1957 *Lac Lanoux* case.[28] Over the years, arbitration also became the preferred forum for dispute settlement under the 1982 UNCLOS, as shown

[19] (Provisional Measures, Order) ITLOS Case No 10, (2002) 41 ILM 405, para 89.

[20] *MOX Plant* case *(Ireland v United Kingdom)* (Suspension of Proceedings on Jurisdiction and Merits, and Request for Further Provisional Measures, Order No 3), (2003) 42 ILM 1187, 1196 *et seq,* particularly paras 52 *et seq.*

[21] See Stephens, above n 2, 232 *et seq*, particularly 238.

[22] See below Chapter 26.2.

[23] See SM Hinde, 'The International Environmental Court: Its Broad Jurisdiction as a Possible Fatal Flaw' (2003) 32 *Hofstra Law Review* 727.

[24] *Ibid*, 728.

[25] Boyle, above n 15, para 10.

[26] See Chapter 12.4.2.

[27] See Chapter 1.1.

[28] See Chapter 11.2.

by the *Southern Bluefin Tuna Award* of 4 August 2000,[29] the *MOX Plant Award* of 24 June 2003,[30] and the award of an Annex VII arbitral tribunal in the case concerning *Land Reclamation by Singapore in and around the Straits of Johor* of 1 September 2005.[31]

The 1991 Antarctic Environmental Protocol also provides in its Article 18–20 for compulsory arbitration as a means to solve disputes concerning its interpretation or application, once attempts at negotiation and conciliation have failed.[32]

The Permanent Court of Arbitration (PCA), established under the 1899 Hague Convention for the Pacific Settlement of International Disputes, is most prominent among the arbitral tribunals. In 2001 PCA Member States tried to promote the PCA as a forum for environmental litigation by adopting the Optional Rules for Conciliation of Disputes Relating to Natural Resources and/or the Environment.[33] These Optional Rules are widely and flexibly applicable not only in interstate disputes but also in litigation involving international organisations, NGOs and corporations. Effective as of April 2002, they have not as yet been used by the PCA or any other arbitral tribunal.

To date, only five environment-related disputes have been brought before the PCA. The early award in the *North Atlantic Coast Fisheries* case of 7 September 1910[34] was followed by two awards of the PCA in the MOX Plant dispute only more than 90 years later, namely by the final award in the *Dispute Concerning Access to Information under Article 9 of the OSPAR Convention* (*'OSPAR'* arbitration) of 2 July 2003,[35] and by the award under UNCLOS (*MOX Plant* award) of 24 June 2003,[36] which was preceded by provisional measures proceedings before the ITLOS as indicated above. With the award in a dispute concerning the auditing of accounts relating to the reduction of chloride discharges into the Rhine (*Rhine Chlorides* arbitration) of 12 March 2004[37] and the *Arbitration Regarding the Iron Rhine ('Ijzeren Rijn') Railway* of 24 May 2005 in a dispute concerning the reactivation of a historical railway linking the port of Antwerp to the Rhine basin in Germany[38] another two environment-related arbitrations took place under the aegis of the PCA.

25.3.3 Quasi-Judicial Dispute Settlement

Those states that are still in the grip of traditional sovereignty thinking appear reluctant to get involved in judicial dispute-settlement proceedings which result in legally binding

[29] See *Australia and New Zealand v Japan*, above n 17.

[30] *MOX Plant* case, above n 20.

[31] *Malaysia v Singapore* (Award on Agreed Terms of 1 September 2005) (2008) 27 RIAA 136 *et seq*.

[32] For more details see Boyle, above n 15, para 17.

[33] Available at www.pca-cpa.org/upload/files/ENV%20CONC.pdf.

[34] *Great Britain v United States* (1961) 11 RIAA 167 *et seq*.

[35] *Ireland v United Kingdom* (2003) 42 ILM 1118.

[36] *MOX Plant* case, above n 20.

[37] *Affaire Concernant l'Apurement des Comptes entre le Royaume des Pays-Bas et la République Française en Application du Protocole du 25 Septembre 1991 Additionnel à la Convention Relative à la Protection du Rhin Contre la Pollution par les Chlorures du 3 Décembre 1976 (Netherlands v France)* (2006) 25 RIAA 267 *et seq*.

[38] *Belgium v Netherlands* (2008) 27 RIAA 35 *et seq*.

judicial decisions. This is why states may seek less intrusive forms of dispute settlement by international bodies other than courts or tribunals which are 'quasi-judicial' or 'semi-judicial' in character although they differ from each other as to the grade of authority which they can claim. The scale of quasi-judicial dispute settlement ranges from the WTO dispute-settlement system across various forms of self-contained dispute settlement by authoritative treaty bodies to the World Bank Inspection Panel which provides for an in-house control of Bank-financed projects.

While under the 1947 General Agreement on Tariffs and Trade (GATT)[39] there were dispute-settlement panels with the power to adopt reports that contain legally non-binding recommendations, this dispute-settlement system has been completely restructured by the Understanding on Rules and Procedures Governing the Settlement of Disputes[40] (Dispute Settlement Understanding (DSU)) in Annex 2 to the 1994 Agreement Establishing the World Trade Organization (WTO).[41] Institutionally, the new WTO dispute-settlement system is made up by the Dispute Settlement Body (DSB) which administers the dispute-settlement process, *ad hoc* panels and the standing Appellate Body. Procedurally, disputes between members of the WTO arising under the WTO Agreement and related instruments are settled in the following way. First, they are referred to consultation (Article 4 DSU) or, alternatively, good offices, conciliation and mediation (Article 5 DSU). Where no settlement is reached, the applicant party may request the establishment of an *ad hoc* panel composed of 'well-qualified governmental and/or non-governmental individuals' (Article 8(1) DSU) to deal with the matter referred to the DSB by that party. Once established, the 'panel should make an objective assessment of the matter before it' (Article 11 DSU) and eventually 'issue an interim report to the parties, including both the descriptive sections and the panel's findings and conclusions' that is considered the 'final panel report', if no comments are received from any party within the comment period (Article 15(2) DSU). The panel report addresses certain recommendations to the parties concerned. It becomes legally binding only after its adoption by the DSB which is automatic 'unless a party to the dispute formally notifies the DSB of its decision to appeal or the DSB decides by consensus not to adopt the report' (Article 16(4) DSU). Thus, panel reports can only be prevented from having legal effect by an unanimous decision of the DSB against it. If the panel report is appealed on legal grounds to the Appellate Body, the latter may issue its own report which upholds, modifies or reverses the legal findings and conclusions of the panel. Like a panel report, '[a]n Appellate Body report shall be adopted by the DSB and unconditionally accepted by the parties to the dispute unless the DSB decides by consensus not to adopt [it]' (Article 17(14) DSU). Thus, the WTO dispute-settlement system is still 'quasi-judicial' in character.[42] The ample case law of the WTO Appellate Body concerning the environment/trade interface and the possibilities to accommodate MEAs with the WTO/GATT system will be discussed in detail in Chapter 28.

[39] 55 UNTS 194 and 55 UNTS 308.

[40] Available at www.wto.org/english/tratop_e/dispu_e/dsu_e.htm.

[41] (1994) 33 ILM 13.

[42] See Sands, above n 2, 220 *et seq*; Birnie, Boyle and Redgwell, above n 4, 763 *et seq*; Stephens, above n 2, 47 *et seq*.

There is a number of international environmental agreements under which specific treaty bodies are entrusted with exercising 'quasi-judicial' dispute-settlement functions.[43]

An early example is the US-Canadian International Joint Commission (IJC). It can either make use of its power of fact-finding or act as an arbitrator under Articles 9 and 10 of the 1909 Treaty Relating to Boundary Waters.[44] However, over the years parties preferred to address it as a fact-finding body, because they have not been obliged to follow its recommendations.

Heading the dispute-settlement mechanism available under the 1995 Agreement on the Cooperation for the Sustainable Development of the Mekong River Basin[45] the Mekong River Commission, which consists of Council, Joint Committee and Secretariat, is mandated to address and resolve disputes arising under the Agreement (Articles 18(c), 24(f), 34 and 35). However, in doing so it is essentially acting as a non-judicial body. By contrast, the power given to the Council of the International Tropical Timber Organization (ITTO) under Article 31 of the 1994 International Tropical Timber Agreement (ITTA) equates to that of an international judicial body.[46]

Being part of the NAFTA accords, the North American Agreement on Environmental Cooperation (NAAEC) between Canada, Mexico and the United States provides access to the North American Commission for Environmental Cooperation (NACEC) for NGOs and private individuals asserting 'that a Party is failing to effectively enforce its environmental law' (Article 14(1) NAAEC). The Secretariat of the NAAEC may even be instructed by the Council, by a two-thirds vote, to prepare a factual record which may be made public by the Council (Article 15 NAAEC). This treaty-specific independent fact-finding mechanism is highly innovative as it enables the citizens of states parties to play a direct role in domestic environmental law enforcement.[47]

Finally, in September 1993 the World Bank Inspection Panel was established.[48] It provides a forum for people directly affected by a World Bank project to complain about the detrimental social and environmental impacts of the Bank's non-compliance with its own policy commitments. Having evaluated the claim, the Panel makes a recommendation to the Board of Executive Directors of the Bank as to whether the matter should be investigated. If the Executive Directors so decide, the Panel investigates, prepares a report summarising the results of the investigation and submits it to the Board which eventually will make recommendations in response to the Panel's findings and determine the remedies to be taken in response to the complaint. Relevant practice[49] reveals that the

[43] See Boyle, above n 15, paras 18–20.

[44] For details on the Treaty Relating to Boundary Waters and the IJC see Chapter 11.4.2.

[45] See Chapter 11.4.3 for details on the Agreement.

[46] Art 31 ITTA provides that '[a]ny complaint that a member has failed to fulfil its obligations under this Agreement and any dispute concerning the interpretation or application of this Agreement shall be referred to the Council for decision. Decisions of the Council on these matters shall be final and binding'.

[47] *Cf* Sands, above n 2, 211 *et seq*.

[48] The Panel was established by two resolutions of the International Bank for Reconstruction and Development (IBRD) and the International Development Association (IDA) which were both adopted by the Executive Directors of the pertinent institutions on 22 September 1993 (IBRD Res No 93-10 and the identical IDA Res No 93-6). See (1995) 34 ILM 520 *et seq* for the text of the resolutions.

[49] To date, 71 claims by adversely affected individuals have been brought to the Panel since it started operations in August 1994.

Inspection Panel provides substantial independent review of the Bank's activities, thereby bringing greater public accountability and transparency to the World Bank's lending policies.[50]

25.4 Dispute Settlement and Compliance Control

Dispute-settlement proceedings differ from compliance-control mechanisms in terms of process and outcome. As far as the process is concerned, compliance control combines supervisory powers of international institutions with a co-operative approach between the parties to an MEA. Dispute-settlement proceedings typically are adversarial and confrontational in nature. In respect of the outcome, compliance control focuses on a political response, whereas dispute-settlement mechanisms tend to favour legally binding solutions. In light of these differences the question arises whether compliance control and dispute settlement exist in parallel and, if so, how they are interrelated. Assuming that there is alleged non-compliance of a party with its obligations under the Kyoto Protocol, may the case be brought under the Protocol's non-compliance procedure (based upon Article 18 Kyoto Protocol) as well as under a dispute-settlement mechanism at the same time, including proceedings before the ICJ? If this is possible, how do the different procedures influence each other?

The answers to these questions would be easy if compliance-control mechanisms were so-called self-contained regimes.[51] If this notion exists at all in public international law, it means a closed subsystem which either in procedural terms or in substance excludes the applicability of other (dispute-settlement) mechanisms or even the applicability of external substantive rules. However, compliance-control mechanisms neither explicitly exclude the applicability of other mechanisms nor implicitly allow for such a conclusion. Rather, the opposite seems to be true with most procedures stating that they apply 'without prejudice' to the operation of other dispute-settlement and enforcement mechanisms.[52] Some MEAs, such as the 1992 OSPAR Convention, suggest, however, a graduated system, proposing that parties first settle conflicts 'by means of inquiry or conciliation' (Article 32(1)).

The parallel inclusion of compliance control and dispute settlement in many MEAs results from a compromise which was reached in the course of the negotiations over the Montreal Protocol non-compliance procedure. In the absence of an agreement on whether dispute settlement or compliance control should be given priority, paragraph 12 of the Montreal Protocol non-compliance procedure[53] was phrased so as to include an obliga-

[50] For more information see Sands, above n 2, 210 *et seq*; IFI Shihata, *The World Bank Inspection Panel: In Practice* (2nd edn Oxford 2000).

[51] For further details see E Klein 'Self-Contained Regime', in R Wolfrum (ed), *Max Planck Encyclopedia of Public International Law* (Heidelberg/Oxford 2006), available at www.mpepil.com.

[52] See, among others, the introductory paragraph of the Montreal Protocol non-compliance procedure; Art 7(4) Oslo Protocol; and Art 18 Kyoto Protocol.

[53] See the Report of the Tenth Meeting of the Parties to the Montreal Protocol on Substances that Deplete the Ozone Layer (23–24 November 1998) in UNEP/OzLPro10/9/Corr1 (5 March 1999).

tion '[t]o inform . . . the Meeting of the Parties of the results of proceedings taken under Article 11 of the Convention regarding possible non-compliance, about implementation of those results and about implementation of any decision of the Parties'.[54] It is noteworthy that the Montreal Implementation Committee attempted to concern the Meeting of the Parties with the relationship between compliance control and dispute settlement, though without much success.[55]

No further clarification has been achieved since then, with the Kyoto Protocol and other current mechanisms following the same approach. It has been argued, however, that the wording suggests a 'one-way flow of traffic',[56] only stating that compliance control operates without prejudice to dispute-settlement mechanisms but not vice versa. This may be convincing in light of the difference in outcome between the two: dispute settlement always has the potential to produce legally binding outcomes, whereas compliance control aims at political solutions. Additional support for such an argument can be taken from the broader international legal issues of *res judicata* and/or *lis pendens* in order to prevent the re-litigation of one and the same dispute before other bodies.[57] Both doctrines only apply to judicial proceedings, not to administrative proceedings with legally non-binding outcomes. *Res judicata* means that a final adjudication by a court or arbitral tribunal is conclusive; *lis pendens* seeks to prevent contradictory findings if a case is pending before a tribunal or similar institution by barring re-litigation of claims already submitted to another procedure. Both, however, suggest that the procedural differences between dispute settlement and compliance control must be treated in a way as to prevent recourse to compliance control in the case of completed dispute-settlement proceedings but not to prevent recourse to dispute settlement after completion of compliance-control procedures. This basically means that a party preparing submissions in the context of a non-compliance procedure must be aware that arguments on fact or on law made in the context of compliance control will re-emerge in a subsequent dispute-settlement process.[58]

Further Reading

A Boyle, 'Environmental Dispute Settlement' in R Wolfrum (ed), *Max Planck Encyclopedia of Public International Law* (Heidelberg/Oxford 2009), available at www.mpepil.com.

A Bree, *Harmonization of the Dispute Settlement Mechanisms of the Multilateral Environmental Agreements and the World Trade Agreements* (Berlin 2003).

M Fitzmaurice, 'The International Court of Justice and the Environment' (2004) 4 *Non-State Actors and International Law* 173–197.

[54] *Cf* Art 11 of the Vienna Ozone Convention which, *inter alia*, includes negotiation, mediation by a third party, arbitration and submission of the dispute to the ICJ.

[55] UNEP/OzLProWG3/2/2.

[56] P Sands, 'Non-compliance and Dispute Settlement' in U Beyerlin *et al* (eds), *Ensuring Compliance with Multilateral Environmental Agreements: A Dialogue between Practitioners and Academia* (Leiden/Boston 2006) 353, 354.

[57] *Cf* WS Dodge, 'Res Judicata' in R Wolfrum (ed), *Max Planck Encyclopedia of Public International Law* (Heidelberg/Oxford 2006), available at www.mpepil.com.

[58] *Cf* Sands, above n 56, 358.

SM Hinde, 'The International Environmental Court: Its Broad Jurisdiction as a Possible Fatal Flaw' (2003) 32 *Hofstra Law Review* 727–757.

P Okowa, 'Environmental Dispute Settlement: Some Reflections on Recent Developments' in MD Evans (ed), *Remedies in International Law: The Institutional Dilemma* (Oxford 1998) 157–172.

J Pauwelyn, 'Judicial Mechanisms: Is There a Need for a World Environment Court?' in WB Chambers and JF Green (eds), *Reforming International Environmental Governance: From Institutional Limits to Innovative Reforms* (Tokyo 2005) 150–177.

CPR Romano, *The Peaceful Settlement of International Environmental Disputes: A Pragmatic Approach* (The Hague 2000).

——, 'International Dispute Settlement' in D Bodansky *et al* (eds), *The Oxford Handbook of International Environmental Law* (Oxford 2007) 1036–1056.

A Postiglione, 'An International Court for the Environment?' (1993) 23 *Environmental Policy and Law* 73–78.

T Stephens, *International Courts and Environmental Protection* (Cambridge 2009).

G Ulfstein, 'Dispute Resolution, Compliance Control and Enforcement in International Environmental Law' in G Ulfstein *et al* (eds), *Making Treaties Work: Human Rights, Environment and Arms Control* (Cambridge 2007) 115–133.

PM Vernet, 'Pulp Mills on the River Uruguay (Argentina v Uruguay)' in R Wolfrum (ed), *Max Planck Encyclopedia of Public International Law* (Heidelberg/Oxford 2010), available at www.mpepil.com.

JE Vinuales, 'The Contribution of the International Court of Justice to the Development of International Environmental Law: A Contemporary Assessment' (2008) 32 *Fordham International Law Journal* 232–258.

R Wolfrum, 'Means of Ensuring Compliance with and Enforcement of International Environmental Law' (1998) 272 *Recueil des Cours* 9–154.

Part VI

Relationship between International Environmental Law and Other Areas of International Law

26

Environmental Protection and Human Rights

Due to the acknowledgement that law will never be enforced unless there is a plaintiff, the effectiveness of international environmental law depends on the preparedness of relevant actors to bring serious cases of non-compliance to international courts. Unfortunately, states, as the main actors in the field of international environmental law, have as yet shown considerable reluctance to do so. It may be asked whether single individuals or groups of individuals, including NGOs, could substitute states in their role as plaintiffs before international judicial and non-judicial bodies that hear them with the argument that certain breaches of international environmental obligations constitute human rights violations.

The following enquiry will focus on the questions of whether (i) existing universal and/or regional human rights treaties contain environment-related human rights guarantees, and (ii) human rights organs provide in their case law for protection of ecological human rights. This analysis will be followed by considerations of whether indigenous peoples have distinctive ecological human rights. Finally, it will be shown that the specific forms of protection and assistance accorded to persons internally displaced or forced to flee from their home state for environmental reasons share some features of human rights protection.

26.1 Environmental Human Rights Protection in General

At the universal level a specific human right to environment is included in neither the International Covenant on Civil and Political Rights (ICCPR) nor the International Covenant on Economic, Social and Cultural Rights (ICESCR) which were both adopted in 1966.[1] By contrast, a number of universal soft law instruments explicitly refer to such a human right. Most prominent is Principle 1 of the 1972 UN Stockholm Declaration which stresses that

[1] The International Covenant on Civil and Political Rights, in force since 23 March 1976, is binding on 167 states. The International Covenant on Economic, Social and Cultural Rights, in force since 3 January 1976, has obtained 160 ratifications.

> [m]an has the fundamental right to freedom, equality and adequate conditions of life, in an environment of a quality that permits a life of dignity and well-being, and he bears a solemn responsibility to protect and improve the environment for present and future generations.

Principle 1 of the 1992 UN Rio Declaration shows more restraint by referring only to human beings who are 'entitled to a healthy and productive life in harmony with nature'. However, what both 'principles' have in common is their strong anthropocentric approach.

At the regional level, only two legally binding instruments explicitly provide for a human right to a sound or satisfactory environment. Firstly, Article 24 of the African Charter on Human and Peoples' Rights of 1981 establishes a collective human right to environment by stating that '[a]ll peoples shall have the right to a generally satisfactory environment favourable to their development'. It is complemented by Article 21 which states: 'All peoples shall freely dispose of their wealth and natural resources. This right be exercised in the exclusive interest of the people. In no case shall a people be deprived of it.' Secondly, Article 11 of the Inter-American 'Protocol of San Salvador'[2] of 17 November 1988 affirms that '[e]veryone shall have the right to live in a healthy environment and to have access to basic public services'. The 1998 UNECE Aarhus Convention may be considered to be another international treaty that makes specific provision for individual environmental rights. However, the lack of opportunity for individuals to submit complaints about alleged violations of the Aarhus guarantees (*ie* access to information, public participation in decision-making and access to justice) to an independent international body distinguishes this Convention from genuine human rights treaties.[3]

It has long been advocated that the human right to a sound or satisfactory environment should belong within universal human rights law. In fact, such a right would neatly fit into the catalogue of guarantees contained in the ICESCR, even though a political agreement upon its insertion is more than unlikely. Such a right would be conditioned by Article 2(1) in the same way as the existing ones. Each state party would be required to undertake steps 'to the maximum of its available resources, with a view to achieving progressively the full realization of the rights recognized in the present Covenant by all appropriate means'. Consequently, it would be difficult to enforce any such environmental human right, particularly since states parties to most international human rights treaties, including the ICESCR, have been satisfied with 'greening' the guarantees already existing in these treaties via the case law of the controlling human rights bodies. As will be shown below, this strategy has proved to be particularly successful in the context of the ICESCR and ECHR.

Just as the international legal system governing today's environmental interstate relations primarily relies on substantive norms, the emerging system of environmental human rights protection consists first and foremost of substantive guarantees that individuals can claim against their state. However, in both systems the protection imparted by relevant substantive norms is far from perfect. As it is neither substantial enough nor all-encompassing, substantive principles and rules must necessarily be complemented

[2] The Additional Protocol to the American Convention on Human Rights in the Area of Economic, Social and Cultural Rights entered into force on 16 November 1999. It is binding on 15 states.

[3] *Cf* Chapter 16.4.2.

by procedural ones. The lesser the level of substantive human rights protection is and the bigger its gaps, the more there is need of complementary procedural guarantees. This insight is clearly witnessed in Principle 10 of the Rio Declaration and the 1998 Aarhus Convention, which both propagate three specific procedural guarantees: access to environmental information, the right to participate in environmental decision-making, and access to environmental justice.[4] As will now be shown, this insight has also impacted the legal opinion of the UN Committee on Economic, Social and Cultural Rights (UNCESCR) and the case law of the European Court of Human Rights (ECtHR).

26.2 Environmental Human Rights Protection in Practice

26.2.1 United Nations

As the two International Covenants on Human Rights remain silent about environmental rights, the only possibility for the two UN Human Rights Committees to develop ecological human rights protection within the UN was the attempt to 'green' those existing human rights that do not *per se* deal with environmental protection, but show a certain closeness to conservation of nature or use of natural resources such as land, soil, water, flora and fauna. This holds true for two human rights guarantees in the ICESCR, namely 'the right of everyone to an adequate standard of living for himself and his family, including adequate food, clothing and housing, and to the continuous improvement of living conditions' (Article 11(1)), and 'the right of everyone to the enjoyment of the highest attainable standard of physical and mental health' (Article 12(1)). However, due to the weak clause on 'progressive realization' in Article 2(1) ICESCR, the effect of these guarantees on environmental protection is rather limited.

For many years the international discussion on developing universally applicable resource-related human rights, particularly a right to water, has mainly centred on Article 11(1) ICESCR.[5] In late 2002 the Committee on Economic, Social and Cultural Rights (UNCESCR) took the lead in this debate by issuing its General Comment 15 with ground-breaking observations regarding the right to water, based on Articles 11 and 12 ICESCR.[6] Starting with the succinct statement that '[t]he right to water clearly

[4] Principle 10 reads as follows: 'Environmental issues are best handled with the participation of all concerned citizens, at the relevant level. At the national level, each individual shall have appropriate access to information concerning the environment that is held by public authorities . . ., and the opportunity to participate in decision-making processes. States shall facilitate and encourage public awareness and participation by making information widely available. Effective access to judicial and administrative proceedings, including redress and remedy, shall be provided.'

[5] Other human rights provisions on which human rights of such type may be based are Art 14(2) of the 1979 UN Convention on the Elimination of All Forms of Discrimination against Women and Art 24 of the 1989 UN Convention on the Rights of the Child. *Cf* E Benvenisti, 'Water, Right to, International Protection' in R Wolfrum (ed), *Max Planck Encyclopedia of Public International Law* (Heidelberg/Oxford 2010) para 8, available at www.mpepil.com.

[6] UNCESCR, UN Doc E/C12/2002/11 (20 January 2003); see K Bourquain, *Freshwater Access from a Human Rights Perspective: A Challenge to International Water and Human Rights Law* (Leiden *et al* 2008),

falls within the category of guarantees essential for securing an adequate standard of living, particularly since it is one of the most fundamental conditions for survival',[7] the UNCESCR assumes that Articles 11 and 12 include the right to water.[8] It concludes that '[t]he right to water, like any human right, imposes three types of obligations on States parties: obligations to respect, obligations to protect and obligations to fulfil'.[9] As these obligations are subject to the limitations in Article 2(1) ICESCR, the UNCESCR considered some of them to be 'core obligations' entailing 'immediate effects'.[10] In the Committee's view, these 'core obligations' are, *inter alia*, directed '[t]o ensure the right of access to water and water facilities and services on a non-discriminatory basis, especially for disadvantaged or marginalized groups' and '[t]o ensure equitable distribution of all available water facilities and services'.[11] Finally, the Committee took from Articles 11 and 12 ICESCR some procedural obligations of states, such as the duty to grant individuals and groups of individuals full access to information, participation in all water-related decision-making processes, and 'effective judicial or other appropriate remedies at both national and international levels', albeit resorting to rather soft obligation formulas.[12]

Only recently, in a resolution of 26 July 2010, the UN General Assembly declared 'the right to safe and clean drinking water and sanitation as a human right that is essential for the full enjoyment of life and all human rights'.[13] However, this political declaration does not provide for any further specification of this right in substance.

Apart from this remarkable attempt of the UNCESCR to lay theoretical grounds for a human right to water, there is a small but interesting environment-related case law of the Human Rights Committee of the ICCPR. In *EHP v Canada* (1982) the Committee dealt with the question of whether the storage of radioactive waste threatens the right to life of present and future generations;[14] in *Bordes and Temeharo v France* (1996) the Committee dismissed a complaint about French nuclear tests in the South Pacific alleged to interfere, *inter alia*, with the right to life;[15] and in *Brun v France* (2006) the Committee had to consider the question whether the use of genetically modified crops violates the right of the complainants to live in a healthy environment.[16]

The majority of cases submitted to the ICCPR Committee concern the land rights of indigenous peoples and their access to natural resources. In *Ominayak and Lubicon*

219 *et seq*. *Cf* also Art 4(2) of the UNECE Protocol on Water and Health to the 1992 Convention on the Protection and Use of Transboundary Watercourses and International Lakes stipulating, *inter alia,* that '[t]he Parties shall . . . take all appropriate measures for the purpose of ensuring: (a) Adequate supplies of wholesome drinking water'. On this Protocol see Chapter 11.3.2.

[7] UNCESCR, above n 6, para 3.

[8] Bourquain, above n 6, 135 *et seq* and 156 *et seq*.

[9] UNCECSR, above n 6, para 20.

[10] *Ibid*, paras 37 *et seq*.

[11] *Ibid*, para 37(b) and (c).

[12] *Ibid*, paras 48 and 55.

[13] UN Doc A/64/L63/Rev1 (26 July 2010).

[14] Decision on admissibility of 27 October 1982, Communication No 67/1980; UN Doc CCPR/C/OP/1 (1984).

[15] Decision on admissibility of 22 July 1996, Communication No 645/1995; UN Doc CCPR/C/57/D/645/1995 (1996).

[16] Decision on admissibility of 18 October 2006, Communication No 1453/2006; UN Doc CCPR/C/88/D/1453/2006 (2006).

Lake Band v Canada (1990) the Committee had to judge whether the provincial government of Alberta had deprived the complainants of their means of subsistence and their right of self-determination by granting leases for oil and gas exploration.[17] In *Länsman and Others v Finland* (1994) the Committee found no violation of Article 27 ICCPR[18] because Finland had taken adequate measures to minimise the impact of stone-quarrying activities on reindeer herding in the traditional lands of the Sami people.[19] In *Apirana Mahuika and Others v New Zealand* (2000) the Committee had to deal with the problem of balancing indigenous rights to fishing resources with governmental efforts to conserve these resources. The Committee found that relevant governmental actions neither interfered with the rights of the Maori people to self-determination under Article 1 ICCPR nor were in violation of Article 27 ICCPR.[20] Recently, in *Poma Poma v Peru* (2009) the Committee endorsed the members of a Peruvian indigenous community in their view that governmental water diversion operations seriously affected the community's only means of subsistence and were therefore in violation of Article 27 ICCPR and that the claimants were deprived of their right to an effective remedy under Article 2(3)(a) ICCPR.[21]

26.2.2 Africa

The African Commission on Human and Peoples' Rights (African Commission) is charged with the protection and promotion of human and peoples' rights laid down in the 1981 African Charter on Human and Peoples' Rights (Banjul Charter). In 1998 a protocol to the Banjul Charter envisaging the establishment of the African Court of Human and Peoples' Rights was adopted. Upon its ratification by 15 African states the protocol entered into force on 1 January 2004. So far the Court has not been operational, leaving the African Commission as the only body to ensure compliance with the Banjul Charter. In 2008, a protocol was adopted to establish the African Court of Justice and Human Rights, replacing the 1998 Protocol on the Establishment of the African Court of Human and Peoples' Rights, which, however, will remain in force for a transitional period.[22] Thus, the African Commission is still the only body that has become active in ensuring compliance of African states parties with their obligations under the Banjul Charter.

To date, the African Commission has dealt with only one human rights case involving specific environmental questions, namely in its highly praised decision of 27 May 2002 in the *Ogoni Land* case.[23] The Commission decided in favour of the Ogoni people who had suffered severely from contamination of their environment by numerous oil spills,

[17] Views of 26 March 1990, Communication No 167/1984; UN Doc CCPR/C/38/D/167/1984 (1990).

[18] Art 27 ICCPR provides that '[i]n those States in which ethnic, religious or linguistic minorities exist, persons belonging to such minorities shall not be denied the right, in community with the other members of their group, to enjoy their own culture, to profess and practise their own religion, or to use their own language'.

[19] Views of 8 November 1994, Communication No 511/1992; UN Doc CCPR/C/52/D/511/1992 (1994).

[20] Views of 27 October 2000, Communication No 547/1993; UN Doc CCPR/C/70/D/547/1993 (2000).

[21] Views of 27 March 2009, Communication No 1457/2006; UN Doc CCPR/C/95/D/1457/2006 (2009).

[22] For further details see FZ Ntoubandi, 'The African Court of Justice and Human Rights' (2009) 12 *Law in Africa* 197.

[23] *Social and Economic Rights Action Center and the Center for Economic and Social Rights v Nigeria,* Decision of 27 May 2002, Communication No 155/96.

avoidably caused by the Nigerian National Petroleum Company. The Commission found that the Federal Republic of Nigeria had committed violations of Articles 2, 4, 14, 16, 18(1), 21 and 24 of the Banjul Charter.

The African Commission unequivocally stated that '(t)he right to a general satisfactory environment, as guaranteed under Article 24 of the African Charter . . . imposes clear obligations upon a government'.[24] In its view the right to health and the right to environment under Articles 16 and 24 of the Banjul Charter

> obligate governments to desist from directly threatening the health and environment of their citizens. The State is under an obligation to respect the just noted rights and this entails largely non-interventionist conduct from the State for example, not from carrying out, sponsoring or tolerating any practice, policy or legal measures violating the integrity of the individual.[25]

Moreover, it found that under Article 21(1) Banjul Charter

> [g]overnments have a duty to protect their citizens, not only through appropriate legislation and effective enforcement but also by protecting them from damaging acts that may be perpetrated by private parties. . . . This duty calls for positive action on part of governments.[26]

Finally, the African Commission appealed to the Nigerian government to ensure that 'appropriate environmental and social impact assessments are prepared for any future oil development' and to provide 'information on health and environmental risks and meaningful access to regulatory and decision-making bodies to communities likely to be affected by oil operations'.[27] It is exactly this deduction of these positive state obligations from the said guarantees of the Banjul Charter that makes the *Ogoni Land* decision of the African Commission highly remarkable, although it must be noted that any decision taken by the African Commission remains legally non-binding.[28]

26.2.3 Americas

The two main institutions for the protection of human rights throughout the Americas are the Inter-American Commission on Human Rights and the Inter-American Court of Human Rights.[29] Their case law is mainly based on the 1948 American Declaration of the Rights and Duties of Man and the 1969 American Convention on Human Rights. Part of it is environment-related with a certain focus on relevant indigenous rights.

The Inter-American Commission on Human Rights has published two country studies paying particular attention to environmental rights of indigenous peoples in Ecuador[30] and Brazil.[31] In *Yanomani Indians v Brazil* (1985) the Commission decided that the

[24] *Ibid*, para 52.
[25] *Ibid*.
[26] *Ibid*, para 57.
[27] *Ibid*, para 14.
[28] This follows from Arts 52 and 53 Banjul Charter.
[29] States not party to the 1969 American Convention on Human Rights are subject to the jurisdiction of the Commission only but not to the jurisdiction of the Court.
[30] IACommHR, Report on the Situation of Human Rights in Ecuador, OEA/SerL/V/II96, doc 10, rev 1 (1997).
[31] IACommHR, Report on the Situation of Human Rights in Brazil, OEA/SerL/V/II97, doc 29, rev 1 (1997).

government had violated Articles I, VIII and XI of the 1948 American Declaration by constructing a highway through Yanomani territory and authorising the exploitation of the territory's resources.[32] In *Mary and Carrie Dann v United States* (2002)[33] the Commission concluded that the United Stated had failed to ensure the claimants' right to property under conditions of equality contrary to Articles II, XVIII and XXIII of the American Declaration in connection with their claims to property rights in the Western Shoshone ancestral lands. In *Maya Indigenous Community of the Toledo District v Belize* (2004)[34] the Commission found that

> the State's failure to respect the communal right of the Maya people to property in the lands that they have traditionally used and occupied has been exacerbated by environmental damage occasioned by certain logging concessions granted in respect to those lands, which in turn has affected the members of those communities.[35]

Furthermore, the Commission acknowledged the importance of economic development for the prosperity of the populations in the Americas, but emphasised that

> at the same time, development activities must be accompanied by appropriate and effective measures to ensure that they do not proceed at the expense of the fundamental rights of persons who may be particularly and negatively affected, including indigenous communities and the environment upon which they depend for their physical, cultural and spiritual well-being.[36]

It should be added that in late 2005 the Inter-American Commission had to deal with the so-called 'Inuit petition' against the United States; the petition alleged that the impact of climate change caused by acts and omissions of the United States was violating the Inuit's fundamental human rights.[37] In November 2006, the Commission rejected this petition by stating that the information provided was not sufficient to determine whether the alleged facts suggest a human rights violation. Interestingly, in March 2007 the Commission held a hearing to investigate the relationship between global warming and human rights.[38]

The environment-related case law of the Inter-American Court of Human Rights includes judgments in *Mayagna (Sumo) Awas Tigni Community v Nicaragua* (2001);[39] *Claude Reyes and Others v Chile* (2006);[40] and *Saramaka People v Suriname* (2007).[41] Two of these deserve closer attention.

In the *Awas Tigni* case the Inter-American Court had to decide on an action of the

[32] IACommHR, Case 7615, Decision of 5 March 1985, Resolution 12/85, Annual Report 1984–1985.

[33] IACommHR, Case 11.140, Report No 75/02, Doc 5 rev 1 (2002) 860.

[34] IACommHR, Case 12.053, Report No 40/04, OEA/SerL/V/II122 Doc 5 rev 1 (2004) 727.

[35] *Ibid*, para 148.

[36] *Ibid*, para 150.

[37] Petition 'Violations Resulting from Global Warming Caused by the United States', 7 December 2005, by Sheila Watt-Cloutier *et al* with support of the Inuit Circumpolar Conference, available at www.inuitcircumpolar.com/files/uploads/icc-files/FINALPetitionICC.pdf.

[38] For a more detailed discussion on the matter see L Heinämäki, 'Rethinking the Status of Indigenous Peoples in International Environmental Decision-Making: Pondering the Role of Arctic Indigenous Peoples and the Challenge of Climate Change' in T Koivurova *et al* (eds) *Climate Governance in the Arctic* (Berlin *et al* 2009) 207, 210 *et seq*.

[39] IACtHR, Case 11.577, Judgment of 31 August 2000, Series C No 79.

[40] IACtHR, Case 12.108, Judgment of 19 September 2006, Series C No 151.

[41] IACtHR, Case 12.338, Judgment of 28 November 2007, Series C No 172.

said indigenous community against government-sponsored logging of timber in the Awas Tigni lands. In its judgment of 31 August 2001 the Court found that Nicaragua had violated the right to property (Article 21 of the American Convention) and the right to judicial protection (Article 25). It declared that the state was obliged to create effective demarcating and title mechanisms for the properties of the indigenous communities, in accordance with customary law and indigenous values, uses and customs.

In the *Saramaka People* case the Court had to deal with an action of a community alleging that Suriname, in violation of Articles 21 and 25 of the American Convention, had failed to recognise the rights of this community to use and enjoy traditional lands. It was clear from the outset that the Saramaka people are not indigenous to the region which they inhabit, because they are descendants of African slaves who had been brought to Suriname during the seventeenth century. However, this people argued that they constitute a tribal community entitled to similar rights and protection under international law. In a landmark judgment of 28 November 2007 the Court declared that the Saramaka people are to be considered a tribal community to which the jurisprudence regarding indigenous land and resource rights applies, requiring special measures under international human rights law. Building upon its *Awas Tigni* judgment, the Court concluded that the community's land rights are included in the right to property guaranteed by Article 21 of the American Convention. It emphasised that while Article 21 should not be interpreted in a way that absolutely precludes the state from acting with respect to natural resource exploration and exploitation within Saramaka territory, the restrictions on property rights of indigenous and tribal peoples must not amount to a denial of the traditions and customs in a way that endangers the very survival of the group.[42] To ensure that development is consistent with human rights and environmental protection, the Court set forth three safeguards, namely effective participation of the members of the Saramaka people regarding any development, investment, exploration or extraction plan within tribal territory; a guarantee that the Saramakas will receive a reasonable benefit from any such plan or project; and the performance of a prior environmental and social impact assessment.[43] Finally, the Court awarded compensation, including US$600,000 for damage to the environment and destruction of lands and resources traditionally used by the Saramakas.[44]

26.2.4 Asia

The Charter of the Association of Southeast Asian Nations (ASEAN), adopted on 20 November 2007, commits itself in Article 2(i), *inter alia*, to the promotion and protection of human rights, and requires ASEAN in Article 14(1) to establish an 'ASEAN human rights body'. However, at the time of writing, a regional human rights mechanism for Asia has still not been created.

[42] *Ibid,* paras 126–128.
[43] *Ibid*, para 129.
[44] *Ibid*, para 201.

26.2.5 Europe

Compared to Africa, the Americas and Asia, Europe possesses a progressive system of ecological human rights protection. This holds first of all[45] true for the European Convention on Human Rights (ECHR) of 4 November 1950 and its Additional Protocols. The ECHR contains a broad catalogue of 'classic' civil and political rights to the exclusion of economic and social rights. Only the First Additional Protocol to the ECHR of 1952 provided for a guarantee of the right to property under the Convention. The reasons why the founders of the ECHR refrained from including economic and social rights in its regime may be found in the deeper insight that only claims concerning human rights deemed to be 'self-executing'[46] could have a real chance of success.

The ECHR lacks any specific guarantee for a decent environment. However, as 'a living instrument which must be interpreted in light of present-day conditions',[47] it is flexible enough to be interpreted in such a way that its guarantees accommodate environmental protection. Over the last 30 years the European Commission of Human Rights (EComHR) and the European Court of Human Rights (ECtHR) have developed an ecological jurisprudence unsurpassed in other regional human rights systems.[48] They both developed a 'green' case law that has from the very outset primarily been based on the right to private life as guaranteed in Article 8(1) ECHR, which assigns to everyone 'the right to respect for his private and family life, his home and his correspondence', while the right to life in Article 2 and the right to property (First Protocol, Article 1) were for a long time almost ignored in the context of environmental protection.

Since the 1990s the ECtHR has developed an ample case law on greening human rights which comprises the following judgments: *Powell and Rayner v United Kingdom* (1990);[49] *Fredin v Sweden* (1991);[50] *Zander v Sweden* (1993);[51] *López Ostra v Spain* (1994);[52] *Balmer-Schafroth and others v Switzerland* (1997);[53] *Guerra and others v Italy* (1998);[54] *McGinley and Egan v United Kingdom* (1998);[55] *Bladet Tromso and Stensaas*

[45] The Charter of Fundamental Rights of the European Union ([2010] OJ C 83/389) merely provides in its Art 37: 'A high level of environmental protection and the improvement of the quality of the environment must be integrated into the policies of the Union and ensured in accordance with the principle of sustainable development.' The European Social Charter of 18 October 1961 and the Protocols of 1985, 1988 and 1991 thereto are totally silent about environmental protection.

[46] 'Self-executing' are only those norms which can take immediate effects without the need of taking any prior implementing action. *Eg* it is due to the limitations laid down in Art 2(1) ICESCR that the total of economic and social rights guaranteed in the ICESCR are not 'self-executing'.

[47] *Tyrer v United Kingdom*, judgment of 25 April 1978; Series A, no 26, para 31.

[48] Protocol No 11 to the Convention has been adopted in May 1994 to restructure the control mechanism which was originally headed by two controlling organs, namely the EComHR and the ECtHR. Upon the Protocol's entry into force in July 1996, a new ECtHR has been established. It has jurisdiction to receive applications from any person, NGO or group of individuals claiming to be the victim of a violation of the Convention by one of the states parties.

[49] Judgment of 21 February 1990, Series A, No 172.

[50] Judgment of 18 February 1991, Series A, No 192.

[51] Judgment of 25 November 1993, Series A, No 279-B.

[52] Judgment of 9 December 1994, Series A, No 303-C.

[53] Judgment of 26 August 1997, ECtHR Reports 1997-IV 1346.

[54] Judgment (Grand Chamber) of 19 February 1998, ECtHR Reports 1998-I 210, see also Report of the EComHR of 29 June 1996, 26 EHRR 357.

[55] Judgment of 9 June 1998, ECtHR Reports 1998-III 1334.

v Norway (1999);[56] *Chapman v United Kingdom* (2001);[57] *Kyrtatos v Greece* (2003);[58] *Hatton and others v United Kingdom* (2003);[59] *Taskin and others v Turkey* (2004);[60] *Gomez v Spain* (2004);[61] *Öneryildiz v Turkey* (2004);[62] *Fadeyeva v Russia* (2005);[63] *Katsoulis and others v Greece* (2005);[64] *Giacomelli v Italy* (2006);[65] *Budayeva and others v Russia* (2008);[66] and *Tatar v Romania* (2009).[67]

In cases where highly important economic state interests and the rights of individuals to private or family life compete with each other, the ECtHR has shown from the outset a rather low ecological profile. In *Powell and Rayner* (1990) the ECtHR found that aircraft noise from Heathrow Airport constituted a violation of Article 8 ECHR, but was justified as 'necessary in a democratic society' for the economic well-being of the United Kingdom. Thirteen years later, in *Hatton*, the Grand Chamber of the ECtHR reached a very similar decision: it gave precedence to economic considerations over the sensitivity to noise of a small minority of people living close to Heathrow Airport, arguing that it is 'reasonable, in determining the impact of a general policy on individuals in a particular area, to take into account the individuals' ability to leave the area'.[68] *López Ostra* (1994) was the Court's first genuinely 'green' decision which clearly recognised that severe environmental pollution, although not reaching the level of injuring health, may affect the 'well-being' of individuals to such an extent that it constitutes a violation of Article 8 ECHR. From an ecological perspective the decision of the EComHR of 4 December 1995 in *Narvii Tauira and Others v France* may appear as a step backwards. The Commission rejected the claim of some residents of French Polynesia that the decision of the French government to resume nuclear testing in the South Pacific entailed a real, substantial and immediate risk to life, arguing that only in highly exceptional circumstances could an applicant claim to be victim of a possible future violation of Article 2 ECHR.[69]

In a series of judgments—*Guerra*, *López Ostra*, *Öneryildiz*, *Taskin*, *Fadeyeva*, *Budeyeva* and *Tatar*—the ECtHR developed a straightforward strategy of greening human rights guarantees. Its consistently used legal reasoning was that states have a positive obligation to take adequate preventive measures to control industrial pollution sources that pose a serious risk to life, health, private life or property such as chemical plants, smelters, mines or waste disposal sites. Any failure by the state to regulate environmental problems, enforce environmental laws or disclose information concerning serious environ-

[56] Judgment of 20 May 1999, ECtHR Reports 1999-III 289.
[57] Judgment of 18 January 2001, ECtHR Reports 2001-I 41.
[58] Judgment of 22 May 2003, ECtHR Reports 2003-VI 257.
[59] Judgment (Grand Chamber) of 8 July 2003, ECtHR Reports 2003-VIII 189.
[60] Judgment of 10 November 2004, ECtHR Reports 2004-X 179.
[61] Judgment of 16 November 2004, ECtHR Reports 2004-X 327.
[62] Judgment of 30 November 2004, ECtHR Reports 2004-XII 79.
[63] Judgment of 9 June 2005, ECtHR Reports 2005-IV 255 (see T Stephens, *International Courts and Environmental Protection* (Cambridge 2009) 317).
[64] Judgment of 24 November 2005, Application No 66742/01.
[65] Judgment of 2 November 2006; Application No 59909/00.
[66] Judgment of 20 March 2008; Applications Nos 15339/02; 21166/02; 20058/02; 11673/02; 15343/02.
[67] Judgment of 27 January 2009; Application No 67021/01.
[68] Judgment (Grand Chamber) of 8 July 2003, above n 59, para 127.
[69] Petition No 28204/95, DR 83, 112. For similar reason the ICCPR Committee in *Bordes, Tauira and Temeharo v France* rejected a parallel petition; UN Doc CCPR/C/57/D/645/1995 (1995).

mental risks may interfere with the respective individual rights. However, because among the rights and freedoms guaranteed by the ECHR there is no right to nature preservation, the adverse effects of environmental pollution must attain a certain minimum level if they are to fall within the scope of Article 8.[70] In the *Budayeva* case, a mudslide swept through a town in the central Caucasus, killing several people and destroying many buildings. The ECtHR for the first time found in an environmental case that a state (in this case Russia) had violated Article 2 ECHR, arguing that a state becomes liable for deaths if they have occurred because the authorities neglected their duty to take preventive measures when a natural hazard had been clearly identifiable and effective measures to mitigate the risk were available to them.[71] Thus, the ECtHR extended its concept that states have a positive duty to protect life from a case involving serious environmental risks created by industrial activities (*Öneryildiz*) to a case involving natural disasters (*Budayeva*).[72] In *Tatar* (2009) the ECtHR found that Romania was responsible under Article 8 for the severe environmental and health risks resulting from an ecological disaster at a gold mine in Romania that had occurred in 2000. Interestingly, it referred to Romanian's substantive obligations under various international norms, including Principle 21 of the Stockholm Declaration, Principle 14 of the Rio Declaration and the 'precautionary principle', which in the Court's view 'has moved, on the European level, from a philosophical concept to a juridical norm with content to be applied'.[73]

Another characteristic feature of the ECtHR's 'green' case law is that the ECHR requires states parties to respect its rights and freedoms and to guarantee their free exercise against private and state actors. Accordingly, states have the positive obligation to impose substantive environmental quality standards on private actors to prevent them from interfering with individuals' health, private life or property. In addition, states are also obliged to ensure that private individuals may exercise certain procedural rights for enabling them to assess the environmental risks to which they are likely to be exposed. Central among these procedural guarantees is the individuals' right to environmental information. Aware of the weakness of the freedom 'to receive and impart information' in Article 10 ECHR,[74] today the ECtHR reads a state obligation to provide adequate environmental information into substantive human rights guarantees such as the right to

[70] *Fadeyeva v Russia*, above n 63. Similarly, in *Kyrtatos v Greece* (above n 58), the ECtHR argued that '[n]either Article 8 nor any of the other Articles of the Convention are specifically designed to provide general protection of the environment as such'; however, in the Court's view the applicants in this case failed to show 'that the alleged damage to the birds and other protected species living in the swamp was of such a nature as to directly affect their own rights under Article 8' (paras 52 and 53).

[71] *Budayeva and others v Russia*, above n 66, 146 *et seq*.

[72] See W Kälin and CH Dale, 'Disaster Risk Mitigation—Why Human Rights Matter' (2008) 31 *Forced Migration Review* 38.

[73] *Tatar v Romania*, above n 67, para 69, cited with D Shelton, 'Human Rights and Environment: Past, Present and Future Linkages and the Value of a Declaration', Draft Paper prepared for the High Level Expert Meeting on the New Future of Human Rights and Environment: Moving the Global Agenda Forward, Nairobi, 30 November–1 December 2009, 11, available at www.unep.org/environmentalgovernance/LinkClick.aspx?fileticket=vmj6UL3O5Ho%3d&tabid=2046&language=en-US.

[74] In *Guerra v Italy* (above n 54) the ECtHR found that whilst Art 10 ECHR 'cannot be construed as imposing on a State . . . positive obligations to collect and disseminate information of its own motion', the right to private life in Art 8 has been violated by Italy's failure to provide essential environmental information (paras 53 and 60).

life and to privacy, thereby placing particular emphasis on the public's right to information concerning the risks to life and the duty to investigate when loss of life occurs.[75] The remarkable statement of the ECtHR in *Taskin v Turkey* (2006) that

> whilst Article 8 contains no explicit procedural requirements, the decision-making process leading to measures of interference must be fair and such as to afford due respect for the interests of the individual as safeguarded by Article 8[76]

may indicate that the ECtHR—inspired by Principle 10 of the Rio Declaration and the 1998 Aarhus Convention—accepts that the individuals' participation in environmental decision-making processes is essential for compliance with Article 8.[77] The ECtHR's recent judgment in *Tatar* (2009) also focused in large part on the procedural obligations of Romania to information, public participation and redress.[78]

Finally, it follows from the case law of the ECtHR that environmental protection cannot only be used by individuals as a vehicle for defending their rights under Articles 2, 8, 10 and Protocol 1, Article 1, but also as a legitimate objective that can justify the limitation of individual rights and freedoms. In an early judgment, in *Fredin v Sweden* (1991), the ECtHR declared the protection of the environment to be an increasingly important consideration that can justify a state order that the applicants must cease the commercial exploitation of gravel pit on their land. In several cases states have been allowed a wide margin of appreciation to pursue important environmental objectives provided they maintain a fair balance between the general interests of the community and the protection of the individual's fundamental rights.[79]

26.3 Environmental Rights of Indigenous Peoples

Even though there are a number of international instruments protecting indigenous peoples, the term 'indigenous peoples' has not yet been defined authoritatively. Literature suggests that this term historically and geographically encompasses 'distinct groups seeking greater control over traditionally used lands and living resources in order to protect or achieve good human-ecological relationships (rather than mere cultural distinctiveness)', while other 'groups may find it easier to claim rights as minorities . . . or as non-self-governing territories'.[80]

Initially 'reluctant to associate their claims with the individualistic framework of human rights law', in the 1980s indigenous peoples' organisations began to participate

[75] *Öneryildiz v Turkey*, above n 62, para 90.

[76] *Taskin and others v Turkey*, above n 60, para 118.

[77] Also in this sense PW Birnie, A Boyle and C Redgwell, *International Law and the Environment* (3rd edn Oxford 2009) 295.

[78] *Tatar v Romania*, above n 67.

[79] See only *Katsoulis and others v Greece*, above n 64. See A Boyle, 'Human Rights and the Environment: A Reassessment', UNEP paper (2009) 14, 20 *et seq*, available at www.unep.org/environmentalgovernance/LinkClick.aspx?fileticket=GccCLN-brmg%3D&tabid=2046&language=en-US.

[80] RL Barsh, 'Indigenous Peoples' in D Bodansky *et al* (eds), *The Oxford Handbook of International Environmental Law* (Oxford 2007) 829, 835 *et seq*.

in UN human rights bodies and to claim their collective or community rights, including property rights.[81]

There is no doubt that 'indigenous peoples' share the right of 'all peoples' under Article 1(2) of the two international human rights covenants to dispose freely of their natural wealth and resources as part of self-determination.[82] Accordingly, the ICCPR Committee, in its 1999 Concluding Observations regarding Canada, acknowledged the conclusion of the Canadian Royal Commission on Aboriginal Peoples (RCAP) that 'without a greater share of lands and resources institutions of aboriginal self-government will fail', and recommended that 'decisive and urgent action be taken towards the full implementation of the RCAP recommendations on land and resource allocation' and that 'the practice of extinguishing inherent aboriginal rights be abandoned as incompatible with article 1 of the Covenant'.[83] In line with that the Committee on the Elimination of Racial Discrimination, in its General Recommendation 23 (1997), called upon states parties

> to recognize and protect the rights of indigenous peoples to own, develop, control and use their communal lands, territories and resources and, where they have been deprived of their lands and territories traditionally owned or otherwise inhabited or used without their free and informed consent, to take steps to return those lands and territories.[84]

Indigenous peoples' organisations quickly became aware that their protection under the generally applicable norms of the two international human rights covenants and respective regional instruments[85] needed to be complemented by a more targeted protection of their specific interests. In this respect, the first important international instrument was the ILO Convention Concerning the Protection and Integration of Indigenous Populations and Other Tribal and Semi-Populations in the Independent Countries (Convention No 107) of 2 June 1959. Thirty years later, on 27 June 1989, the ILO adopted its Convention Concerning Indigenous and Tribal Peoples in Independent Countries (Convention No 169).[86] Recognising 'self-identification as indigenous or tribal . . . as a fundamental criterion for determining the groups to which [its] provisions . . . apply' (Article 1(2)), Convention No 169, in Article 7(1), confers on indigenous peoples

> the right to decide their own priorities for the process of development as it affects their lives, beliefs, institutions and spiritual well-being and the lands they occupy or otherwise use, and to exercise control, to the extent possible, over their own economic, social and cultural development.

[81] See again Barsh, *ibid*, 838.

[82] Art 1(2) reads in full: 'All peoples may, for their own ends, freely dispose of their natural wealth and resources without prejudice to any obligations arising out of international economic co-operation, based upon the principle of mutual benefit, and international law. In no case may a people be deprived of its own means of subsistence.'

[83] UN Doc CCPR/C/79/Add105, 7 April 1999, para 8

[84] General Recommendation 23, UN Doc A/52/18, annex V (1997) 122, para 5. *Cf* also the 1994 General Comment No 23, 'The rights of minorities (Article 27)' of the ICCPR Committee; CCPR/C/21/Rev1/Add5 (1994). See E-I A Daes, 'Indigenous Peoples Permanent Sovereignty over Natural Resources', lecture held at the National Native Title Conference, Adelaide, 3 June 2004, available at www.hreoc.gov.au/about/media/speeches/social_justice/natural_resources.html.

[85] The relevant case law of the ICCPR Committee and the two Inter-American human rights bodies has already been presented in Sections 26.2.1 and 26.2.3.

[86] In force since 5 September 1991, it is currently binding on 22 states.

It requires that '[t]he rights of ownership and possession of the peoples concerned over the lands which they traditionally occupy shall be recognised' (Article 14(1)) and that '[t]he rights of the peoples concerned to the natural resources pertaining to their lands shall be specially safeguarded', with the inclusion of 'the right . . . to participate in the use, management and conservation of these resources' (Article 15(1)). According to Article 13(2) of Convention No 169, the use of the term 'lands' in Articles 15 and 16 includes 'the concept of territories, which covers the total environment of the areas which the peoples concerned occupy or otherwise use'. In the view of Barsh, this clause 'extends the rights of indigenous peoples to living resources such as wildlife and fish, and to water, whether located on lands they permanently "occupy" or lands that they traverse seasonally to "use"'.[87]

In 1992 the Rio Conference acknowledged in Agenda 21 that indigenous peoples 'have developed over many generations a holistic traditional scientific knowledge of their lands, natural resources and environment'. This finding was followed by the following recommendation:

> In view of the interrelationship between the natural environment and its sustainable development and the cultural, social, economic and physical well-being of indigenous people, national and international efforts to implement environmentally sound and sustainable development should recognize, accommodate, promote and strengthen the role of indigenous people and their communities.[88]

On 26 August 1994, the Sub-Commission on Prevention of Discrimination and Protection of Minorities adopted the Draft United Nations Declaration on the Rights of Indigenous Peoples.[89] In 1995 a new predominantly governmental Working Group was mandated by the UN Commission on Human Rights to achieve a consensus on the 1994 Draft Declaration. In late June 2006, the UN Human Rights Council, the successor of the Commission on Human Rights, approved a compromise text of the Draft Declaration. Following final changes made in the course of 2007, on 13 September 2007 the United Nations Declaration on the Rights of Indigenous Peoples (UNDRIP) was adopted by UN General Assembly Resolution 61/295 with 143 states voting in favour of and four against it (United States, Canada, Australia and New Zealand), while 11 states abstained.[90] Articles 26 and 29 UNDRIP explicitly deal with indigenous peoples' rights to lands, territories and resources, as well as environmental protection.

Article 26 UNDRIP recognises that indigenous peoples have 'the right to the lands, territories and resources which they have traditionally owned, occupied or otherwise used or acquired', as well as 'the right to own, use, develop and control the lands, territories and resources that they possess'. Article 29 UNDRIP confers on indigenous peoples 'the right to the conservation and protection of the environment and the productive capacity of their lands or territories and resources'. Moreover it ensures that 'no storage or disposal

[87] In this sense Barsh, above n 80, 845 *et seq*.

[88] Agenda 21, para 26.1.

[89] Report of the Sub-Commission on Prevention of Discrimination and Protection of Minorities, UN ESCOR, 46th Session, UN Doc E/CN4/Sub2/1994/45 (1994).

[90] Azerbaijan, Bangladesh, Bhutan, Burundi, Colombia, Georgia, Kenya, Nigeria, Russian Federation, Samoa, Ukraine; another 34 states were absent.

of hazardous materials shall take place in the lands or territories of indigenous peoples without their free, prior and informed consent'.

Article 42 UNDRIP requires the United Nations, its bodies and specialised agencies, and states to 'promote respect for and full application of the provisions of this Declaration and follow up the effectiveness of this Declaration'. Accordingly, Special Rapporteur Anaya characterised UNDRIP as 'an authoritative common understanding, at the global level, of the minimum content of the rights of indigenous peoples, upon a foundation of various sources of international human rights law'.[91]

Only three months after the adoption of this UN Declaration the Inter-American Court of Human Rights issued its landmark decision in the *Saramaka People* case which clearly reflects the rationale behind Article 26(2) and (3) of the Declaration.[92]

26.4 Rights of Environmental Migrants

Academics, policymakers and the media are giving increasing attention to the phenomenon of 'environmental refugees'. Their major concern has been whether environmental change will displace large numbers of vulnerable people in the developing world. In 1995 it was estimated that more than 25 million people were displaced by environmental factors.[93] For the last two decades there have been predictions that the number of environmental refugees could grow to 50 million by 2010.[94] As well-documented cases of environmentally induced migration are largely limited to dramatic events, such as Hurricane Katrina in the Gulf of Mexico in 2005 and the 2010 flood in Pakistan, the consequences of smaller-scale but more pervasive forms of environmental change, such as droughts and soil degradation, are still unclear. However, new research seems to show that 'environmentally induced migration can be temporary and involve relatively short distances, in contrast to fears of large numbers of environmental refugees moving across international borders'.[95]

The current discussion on ways and means to legally solve the problems of environment-related migration is still impeded by controversies about terminology.[96] It should be observed that the term 'refugee' virtually invites association with Article 1A(2) of the

[91] Report of the Special Rapporteur on the situation of human rights and fundamental freedoms of indigenous people, UN Doc A/HRC/9/9 (11 August 2008) para 85.

[92] *Cf* L Brunner, 'The Rise of Peoples' Rights in the Americas: The Saramaka People Decision of the Inter-American Court of Human Rights' (2008) 7 *Chinese Journal of International Law* 699, para 18.

[93] N Myers, 'Environmental Refugees: A Growing Phenomenon of the 21st Century' (2002) 357 *Philosophical Transactions of the Royal Society* 609 *et seq*.

[94] See S Lovgren, 'Climate Change Creating Millions of "Eco Refugees", UN Warns', National Geographic News, 18 November 2005, http://news.nationalgeographic.com/news/2005/11/1118_051118_disaster_refugee.html.

[95] CL Gray, 'Environmental Refugees or Economic Migrants?' (2010), Population Reference Bureau, www.prb.org/Articles/2010/environmentalmigrants.aspx?p=1.

[96] For a comprehensive survey of this discussion with amble references see Umweltbundesamt (Federal Environment Agency) (ed), 'Rechtsstellung und rechtliche Behandlung von Umweltflüchtlingen' [Legal Status and Legal Treatment of Environmental Refugees] (Dessau-Roßlau 2010) www.uba.de/uba-info-medien-e/4035.html.

1951 Convention relating to the Status of Refugees designed to protect any person who is

> owing to well-founded fear of being persecuted for reasons of race, religion, nationality, membership of a particular social group or political opinion, . . . outside the country of his nationality and is unable or, owing to such fear, is unwilling to avail himself of the protection of that country.

Persons expelled from their home state for environmental reasons cannot claim to be victims of this type of persecution. Thus, political refugees and environmental migrants should be clearly distinguished from each other.[97] Therefore, persons forced to leave their home state for compelling environmental reasons should be addressed as 'environmental emigrants' rather than 'environmental refugees'. However, environmental emigrants are clearly outnumbered by persons who, also for environmental reasons, feel forced to leave their homeland and take refuge in other parts of their home state's territory. Legally speaking, these are 'internally displaced persons' (IDPs).

Admittedly, isolating environmental degradation as the only cause for migration is difficult, because 'flight situations' mostly arise out of a conglomeration of various ecological and socioeconomic factors. Furthermore, flight situations can be the result of man-made environmental change as well as natural hazards.

Sometimes people who are innocent victims of serious and widespread environmental degradation have no other choice than leaving their home state and taking refuge abroad. However, it is often the case that only part of the home state's territory is environmentally damaged, and affected citizens flee from their homelands but keep within state borders. In both cases affected citizens are likely in the first instance to try to obtain help from their home state.

There has been much recent discussion on low-lying Pacific small island states, which are threatened by rising sea levels and thus may cease to exist in the not too distant future.[98] Naturally, states should first take all necessary measures to prevent global climate change from posing an immediate threat to their citizens. However, the island states in question are not the main causers of global climate change and are consequently unable themselves to prevent sea levels from rising further. At best, they can take measures to adapt to climate change, such as improving land use, installing early warning systems, etc. In the event that such efforts fail and their territories face being swamped by the sea, these island states can request third states to render assistance to their threatened citizens, *eg* by supporting their safe evacuation or admitting them as 'environmental refugees'.

A primary means to cope with environmental flight situations described above is interstate co-operation. However, *de lege lata*, the African Union Convention for the Protection and Assistance of Internally Displaced Persons in Africa (Kampala Conven-

[97] The UNHCR has been quoted with the observation that '[l]umping both groups together under the same heading would further cloud the issues and could undermine efforts to help and protect either group and to address the root causes of either type of displacement'; see R Wilkinson, 'A Critical Time for Refugees and their Environment' (2002) 127 *Refugees* 4, 13.

[98] Among the states most threatened by permanent flooding are the Maldives in the Indian Ocean and Tuvalu and Kiribati in the South Pacific. For details see C Jakobeit and C Methmann, 'Klimaflüchtlinge—Die verleugnete Katastrophe', study commissioned by Greenpeace (Hamburg 2007) 16 *et seq*, www.greenpeace.de/fileadmin/gpd/user_upload/themen/klima/klimmafluechtlinge_endv.PDF.

tion) of 22 October 2009 is the only legally binding instrument which responds to the problems of IDPs. Clearly inspired by the 1998 UN Guiding Principles on Internally Displaced Persons,[99] it requires states parties, *inter alia*, to 'take measures to protect and assist persons who have been internally displaced due to natural or human made disasters, including climate change' (Article 5(4)). Stories propagated in the media in 2009, according to which the government of Tuvalu, a small, low-lying Pacific island state, had reached an agreement with New Zealand to accept its 11600 citizens in the event that rising sea levels swamp the country, have been formally repudiated by the New Zealand Ministry of Foreign Affairs.[100]

De lege ferenda, there is ongoing discussion on possible ways and means to enhance the precarious situation of environmental migrants. The array of proposals made in this respect is wide, ranging from an additional protocol related to the UNFCCC on 'climate refugees', a framework convention on environmental migrants, integration of environmental refugees in the existing Geneva Refugees Convention, a new convention on environmental refugees or a cross-sectoral convention on environmental migration to a specific convention on climate change refugees.[101] Whether any of these proposals has a chance of success is an open question. The environmental flight situations, the needs of peoples forced to flee and the conditions of protection and help vary significantly from one case to the other. This is why it is extremely difficult to reach a political consensus among states on an international agreement that is broad enough to cover all these situations. As regards the worst-case scenario of peoples living in small island states threatened by rising sea levels, parties to the UNFCCC and/or the Kyoto Protocol should feel prompted to reach an understanding on adequate evacuation and resettlement programmes; to this end a special environmental migration fund could be established into which each state must pay according to its contribution to global warming and its economic capacity.[102]

Another option to help environmental migrants is through international human rights protection. While there is little doubt that environmental IDPs and emigrants could ground their claims for protection and help on the human rights guarantees referred to above, it is not entirely clear as to whom such human rights claims should be addressed. Naturally, it is the home state which owes to its citizens the fulfilment of its obligations to respect, protect and fulfil flowing from human rights guarantees. Accordingly, in cases where severe environmental degradation results in widespread internal displacement of citizens, their home state is obliged to render them adequate human rights protection.

In principle, this also applies to environmental flight situations where the affected citizens feel forced to leave the territory of their state to take permanent refuge abroad. Usually, the home state is debarred from taking any positive action in favour of its emi-

[99] See the text of these Guiding Principles in UN Doc E/CN4/1998/53/Add2, www.unhchr.ch/Huridocda/Huridoca.nsf/0/d2e008c61b70263ec125661e0036f36e?Opendocument.

[100] L West, 'Scholars Predict 50 Million "Environmental Refugees" by 2010', see http://environment.about.com/od/globalwarming/a/envirorefugees.htm?p=1.

[101] For a survey of relevant proposals see again Umweltbundesamt, above n 96, 150 *et seq*.

[102] *Cf* the report of the German Advisory Council on Global Change (Wissenschaftlicher Beirat der Bundesregierung Globale Umweltveränderungen [WBGU]), 'World in Transition—Climate Change as a Security Risk' (London/Sterling, VA 2007) 12 *et seq*.

grant citizens. In a worst-case scenario of a small island state threatened with being swamped by the sea, a potential emigrant therefrom may feel justified in making a human rights complaint against third states suspected of having contributed significantly to global warming and thus eventually to the emigrant's environmental flight. Let us suppose that a citizen of a Pacific small island state who has been forced to emigrate brings a human rights application against one of the states parties to the 1950 ECHR before the ECtHR with the argument that the state concerned, by its greenhouse gas emissions, has essentially contributed to rising sea levels and eventually to the disappearance of the island in question, thereby acting in violation of Article 2 or Article 8 of the ECHR. Is it imaginable that the ECtHR might decide the case in favour of the applicant?

The ECtHR, in light of its 2001 judgment in the case of *Banković and others v Belgium*,[103] most likely would declare such an application inadmissible. As is well known, in 1999, during the Kosovo crisis, NATO forces in which Belgium and nine other states participated launched massive air strikes against the Federal Republic of Yugoslavia. In the bombing of Belgrade several Serbian people were killed or seriously injured. The applicants before the ECtHR were close relatives of these victims. They complained about this bombing by invoking, in particular, Article 2 ECHR. In its *Banković* judgment the Grand Chamber of the ECtHR declared the complaint against the respondent states inadmissible, since there had been no jurisdictional link between the persons who were victims of the act complained of and the respondent states, as required by Article 1 ECHR.[104] It made plain that 'recognition of the exercise of extra-territorial jurisdiction by a Contracting state is exceptional'; it requires that

> the respondent State, through the effective control of the relevant territory and its inhabitants abroad as a consequence of military occupation or through the consent, invitation or acquiescence of the government of that territory, exercises all or some of the public powers normally to be exercised by that Government.[105]

The Grand Chamber rejected the applicants' argument that the bombing of Belgrade by the respondent states constituted an example of an extra-territorial act that could be accommodated by the notion of 'jurisdiction' in Article 1 ECHR.[106] There is no doubt that this reasoning of the *Banković* judgment can be transposed to the worst-case scenario of a doomed small island state whose citizens feel forced to emigrate. Consequently, the latter would be unlikely to succeed with their application before the ECtHR. This finding also applies to international human rights treaty regimes other than the ECHR, such as the 1966 ICCPR or the 1978 American Convention on Human Rights, which contain jurisdictional clauses that are almost identical to that in Article 1 ECHR.

Thus, environmental emigrants will have little chance to win human rights cases. Aware of that, the international community of states should feel morally obliged to substitute for any home state that is barred from acting as human rights protector of its emigrant citizens. Driven by solidarity,[107] it should mandate existing international institutions, such

[103] Judgment of 12 December 2001, ECtHR Reports 2001-XII 333.
[104] *Ibid*, para 82.
[105] *Ibid*, para 71.
[106] *Ibid*, para 74.
[107] *Cf* above Chapter 5.2.1.

as UNEP, UNDP, the International Organization for Migration (IOM) and the UNHCR, to co-ordinate their efforts to prevent environmental degradation, to improve early warning and monitoring systems with the aim of better preparing vulnerable communities for environmental disasters, to mitigate the detrimental effects of displacement, to rehabilitate affected areas in order to return displaced persons to their homes, and, where such a return is impossible, to permanently resettle the displaced persons in new host areas abroad.[108]

Further Reading

SJ Anaya and RA Williams, Jr, 'The Protection of Indigenous Peoples' Rights over Lands and Natural Resources under the Inter-American Human Rights System' (2001) 14 *Harvard Human Rights Journal* 33–86.

SA Atapattu, 'The Right to a Healthy Life or the Right to Die Polluted?: The Emergence of a Human Right to a Healthy Environment Under International Law ' (2002) 16 *Tulane Environmental Law Journal* 65–126.

RL Barsh, 'Indigenous Peoples' in D Bodansky *et al* (eds), *The Oxford Handbook of International Environmental Law* (Oxford 2007) 829–852.

E Benvenisti, 'Water, Right to, International Protection' in R Wolfrum (ed), *Max Planck Encyclopedia of Public International Law* (Heidelberg/Oxford 2010), available at www.mpepil.com.

U Beyerlin, 'Umweltschutz und Menschenrechte' (2005) 65 *Heidelberg Journal of International Law (ZaöRV)* 525–542.

——, 'Environmental Migration and International Law', in D König *et al* (eds), *Coexistence, Cooperation and Solidarity—Liber Amicorum Rüdiger Wolfrum* (Leiden forthcoming).

A Boyle, 'Environment and Human Rights' in R Wolfrum (ed), *Max Planck Encyclopedia of Public International Law* (Heidelberg/Oxford 2009), available at www.mpepil.com.

AE Boyle and MR Anderson (eds), *Human Rights Approaches to Environmental Protection* (Oxford 1996).

F Coomans, 'The Ogoni Case before the African Commission on Human Rights and Peoples' Rights' (2003) 52 *ICLQ* 749–760.

Council of Europe, *Manual on Human Rights and the Environment: Principles Emerging from the Case-Law of the European Court of Human Rights* (Strasbourg 2006).

R Desgagné, 'Integrating Environmental Values into the European Convention on Human Rights' (1995) 89 *AJIL* 263–294.

J Ebbesson and P Okowa (eds), *Environmental Law and Justice in Context* (Cambridge *et al* 2009).

A Fabra, 'The Intersection of Human Rights and Environmental Issues: A Review of Institutional Developments at the International Level' in (2008) 8 *Yearbook of Human Rights & Environment* 195–238.

M Fitzmaurice, 'The Human Right to Water' (2007) 18 *Fordham Environmental Law Review* 537–586.

M Fitzmaurice and J Marshall, 'The Human Right to a Clean Environment—Phantom or Reality? The European Court of Human Rights and English Courts Perspective on Balancing Rights in Environmental Cases' (2007) 76 *Nordic Journal of International Law* 103–151.

[108] For more details see T King, 'Environmental Displacement: Coordinating Efforts to Find Solutions' (2006) 18 *Georgetown International Environmental Law Review* 543, 559 *et seq.*

DI García San José, *Enforcing the Human Right to Environment in Europe: A Critical Overview of the European Court of Human Rights Case Law* (Sevilla 2004).

——, *Environmental Protection and the European Convention on Human Rights: Interpretation and Discretion under the European Convention on Human Rights* (Strasbourg 2005).

G Handl, 'Human Rights and the Protection of the Environment' in A Eide *et al* (eds), *Economic, Social and Cultural Rights: A Textbook* (2nd edn Dordrecht *et al* 2001) 303–328.

T King, 'Environmental Displacement: Coordinating Efforts to Find Solutions' (2006) 18 *Georgetown International Environmental Law Review* 543–565.

PG Kirchschläger, *Menschenrechte und Umwelt / 5. Internationales Menschenrechtsforum Luzern (IHRF)* (Bern 2008).

S Kravchenko and JE Bonine, *Human Rights and the Environment: Cases, Law, and Policy* (Durham, NC 2008).

L Loucaides, 'Environmental Protection through the Jurisprudence of the European Convention on Human Rights' (2004) 75 *The British Yearbook of International Law* 249–267.

T Marauhn, 'Menschenrecht auf eine gesunde Umwelt—Trugbild oder Wirklichkeit' in T Giegerich and A Proelß (eds), *Bewahrung des ökologischen Gleichgewichts durch Völker- und Europarecht* (Berlin 2010) 11–47.

SC McCaffrey, 'The Human Right to Water' in E Brown Weiss *et al* (eds), *Fresh Water and International Economic Law* (Oxford 2005) 93–115.

JG Merrills, 'Environmental Rights' in D Bodansky *et al* (eds), *The Oxford Handbook of International Environmental Law* (Oxford 2007) 663–680.

MJ Oliva, 'Promoting Human Rights and the Environment in Trade and Finance Rules' (2008) 8 *Yearbook of Human Rights & Environment* 1–87.

R Picolotti and JD Taillant (eds), *Linking Human Rights and the Environment* (Tucson 2003).

LE Rodriguez-Rivera, 'Is the Human Right to Environment Recognized under International Law? It Depends on the Source' (2001) 12 *Colorado Journal of International Environmental Law and Policy* 1–45.

C Schall, 'Public Interest Litigation Concerning Environmental Matters before Human Rights Courts: A Promising Future Concept?' (2008) 20 *Journal of Environmental Law* 417–453.

R Schmidt-Radefeldt, *Ökologische Menschenrechte. Ökologische Menschenrechtsinterpretation der EMRK und ihre Bedeutung für die umweltschützenden Grundrechte des Grundgesetze*s (Baden-Baden 2000).

SMA Salman and SA McInerney-Lankford, *The Human Right to Water—Legal and Policy Dimensions* (Washington, DC 2004).

J Scanlon, A Cassar and N Nemes, *Water as a Human Right?* IUCN Environmental Policy and Law Paper No 51 (Gland/Cambridge 2004) Appendix I, 37–42.

D Shelton, 'Human Rights and the Environment: Jurisprudence of Human Rights Bodies' (2002) 32 *Environmental Policy and Law* 158–167.

SR Tully, 'The Contribution of Human Rights to Freshwater Resource Management' (2003) 14 *Yearbook of International Environmental Law* 101–137.

UNEP, 'High Level Expert Meeting on the New Future of Human Rights and Environment: Moving the Global Agenda Forward', Nairobi, 30 November–1 December 2009 (various contributions), available at www.unep.org/environmentalgovernance/Events/HumanRightsandEnvironment/tabid/2046/language/en-US/Default.aspx.

JW von Doussa, A Corkery and R Chartres, 'Human Rights and Climate Change' (2008) 8 *Yearbook of Human Rights & Environment* 89–140.

L Zarsky, *Human Rights and the Environment: Conflicts and Norms in a Globalizing World* (London 2002).

27

Environmental Protection and International Peace and Security

27.1 Peace, Security and the Environment: A Multifaceted Relationship

Chapter 11 of the Brundtland Report, 'Our Common Future', deals with 'Peace, Security, Development, and the Environment'.[1] It addresses environmental stress as a cause of conflict, and conflict as a cause of unsustainable development, and it seeks to provide guidance towards security and sustainable development. This illustrates that the interrelationship between international environmental law and the law related to international peace and security is multifaceted and complex.

There is an obvious tension between the protection of the environment and armed conflict. The parties to an armed conflict are typically guided by their military objectives rather than by environmental considerations. Indeed, their activities normally will have a negative impact on the environment whether intentionally or accidentally. Some parties to an armed conflict even use damage to or modifications of the environment as a means of warfare. While this occurs less often, its consequences are serious.

History is full of examples of the devastating environmental effects of armed conflict. The use of chemical weapons during World War I, area bombardments during World War II, and the atomic bombings of Hiroshima and Nagasaki are telling examples of collateral damage to the environment, and illustrate that the environmental risks of armed conflict have become even more serious with the advent of so-called 'weapons of mass destruction'.[2] Abuse and modification of the environment for military purposes also has

[1] See its text in UNGA 'Development and International Economic Co-operation: Environment: Report of the World Commission on Environment and Development: Note by the Secretary-General'; UN Doc A/42/427 (4 August 1987) 286 *et seq.*

[2] For an analysis of the term see HA Strydom, 'Weapons of Mass Destruction' in R Wolfrum (ed) *Encyclopedia of Public International Law* (Heidelberg/Oxford 2009), available at www.mpepil.com.

a long history. The scorched-earth policy has been used since ancient times, from the poisoning of wells and other freshwater resources to the destruction of dams and dykes in order to flood lands, and the burning of agricultural land.[3]

Serious environmental damage resulted from military operations during the war in Vietnam (1955/1964–1975). Chemical defoliants were used by US armed forces between 1961 and 1971 to counter the enemy strategy of hiding in the jungle. At least one of these defoliants, named Agent Orange, included dioxin as a by-product.[4] Some chemicals were used to destroy rice and other food crops. The Vietnamese landscape, food chain and human health continue to be affected to the present day. Grave environmental problems also arose during the Gulf War of 1990/1991. Iraq dumped crude oil into the Persian Gulf, causing the largest offshore oil spill in history at that time. In addition, Iraqi military forces retreating from Kuwait set fire to Kuwaiti oil wells as part of a scorched-earth policy, causing widespread pollution. In the Kosovo conflict (1999), the use of depleted uranium ammunition[5] and cluster bombs was highly controversial; similarly, environmental effects resulted from the bombing of oil refineries and chemical plants. Most recently, since 2001, the use of air fuel explosives during the war in Afghanistan has given rise to environmental concerns.

The environment is, however, not only affected by actual fighting. Increasingly, the effects of land mines, cluster munitions and remnants of war[6] have become a matter of concern. In addition, the very destruction of existing stockpiles of weapons of mass destruction and of other munitions poses its own environmental problems.

First and foremost, the above-mentioned questions should be addressed from the perspective of the law of armed conflict. In addition, the question of the applicability of multilateral environmental agreements (MEAs) in times of armed conflict must be considered. Furthermore, arms control and disarmament agreements have to be reviewed with a view to their environmental soundness.

27.2 The Law of Armed Conflict

The law of armed conflict (*ius in bello*) has to be clearly distinguished from all rules related to the prohibition of armed force (*ius contra bellum*). Its rules are applicable only in times of armed conflict. They regulate the conduct of hostilities and arise from a desire to prevent unnecessary suffering and destruction without impeding the effective

[3] K Hulme, 'Armed Conflict, Wanton Ecological Devastation and Scorched Earth Policies: How the 1990–91 Gulf Conflict Revealed the Inadequacies of the Current Laws to Ensure Effective Protection and Preservation of the Natural Environment' (1997) 2 *Journal of Conflict and Security Law* 45.

[4] The use of Agent Orange during the Vietnam war has even given rise to claims for damages against the industry involved in producing the agent: see A Roberts, 'The Agent Orange Case: Vietnam ass'n for Victims of Agent Orange/Dioxin v Dow Chemical Co' (2005) 99 *Proceedings of the American Society of International Law at its 99th Annual Meeting* 380.

[5] T Marauhn, 'Environmental Damage in Times of Armed Conflict—Not "Really" a Matter of Criminal Responsibility?' (2000) 840 *International Review of the Red Cross* 1029.

[6] *Cf* Chapter 12.3.1.

waging of war. The law of armed conflict also aims to protect civilians, prisoners of war, the wounded, the sick and the shipwrecked. Pertinent rules distinguish between international and non-international armed conflicts. Most relevant with regard to protecting the environment during times of armed conflict are rules on the means and methods of warfare.

27.2.1 Treaty Law Applicable to International Armed Conflicts

Article 22 of the 1907 Convention (IV) Respecting the Laws and Customs of War on Land[7] establishes, in very general terms, the basic rules that '[t]he right of belligerents to adopt means of injuring the enemy is not unlimited'. While this provision does not include any specific reference to the environment, Article 23 of the Hague Regulations includes some prohibitions which can be made use of for the protection of the environment. This is particularly true for paragraph (a) which prohibits the employment of 'poison or poisoned weapons', and for paragraph (g) which prohibits destruction or seizure of 'the enemy's property', which may include environmental goods, 'unless such destruction or seizure be imperatively demanded by the necessities of war'.[8]

The 1925 Geneva Gas Protocol,[9] which prohibits 'the use in war of asphyxiating, poisonous or other gases, and of all analogous liquids, materials or devices', protects humans not only but also fauna and flora. Its effectiveness has long been limited by reservations which partly reduced its scope to a prohibition of first use of chemical weapons.[10] However, the 1993 Chemical Weapons Convention[11] (CWC) has now established a comprehensive prohibition by stipulating that '[e]ach State Party to this Convention undertakes never under any circumstances . . . [t]o use chemical weapons' (Article I(1)(b)). Including the phrase 'never under any circumstances', the CWC outlaws reservations to the Geneva Protocol of 1925 which consider the use of chemical weapons as lawful in response to an attack with chemical weapons.[12]

Article 53(4) of the 1949 Geneva Convention IV Relative to the Protection of Civilian Persons in Time of War[13] can be read as a confirmation of Article 23(g) of the Hague

[7] The Convention (IV) Respecting the Laws and Customs of War on Land and its Annex: Regulations Concerning the Laws and Customs of War on Land was adopted on 18 October 1907 and entered into force on 26 January 1910. See 205 CTS 277; (1908) 2 *AJIL Supplement* 117.

[8] See S Witteler, *Die Regelungen der neuen Verträge des humanitären Völkerrechts und des Rechts der Rüstungsbegrenzung mit direktem Umweltbezug* (Bochum 1993) 161–162.

[9] The Protocol for the Prohibition of the Use of Asphyxiating, Poisonous or Other Gases, and of Bacteriological Methods of Warfare was adopted on 17 June 1925 and entered into force on 8 February 1928; 94 LNTS 65.

[10] For a differentiated analysis see M Bothe, Das völkerrechtliche *Verbot des Einsatzes chemischer und bakteriologischer* Waffen*: Kritische Würdigung und Dokumentation der Rechtsgrundlagen* (Köln/Bonn 1973) 66–70; see also W Krutzsch, '"Never Under Any Circumstances": The CWC Three Years After its First Review Conference' (2005) 68 *CBW Conventions Bulletin* 1.

[11] The Convention on the Prohibition of the Development, Production, Stockpiling and Use of Chemical Weapons and on Their Destruction was adopted on 13 January 1993 and entered into force on 29 April 1997; (1993) 32 ILM 804 *et seq.*

[12] On the scope of Art I see W Krutzsch and R Trapp, *A Commentary on the Chemical Weapons Convention* (Dordrecht *et al* 1994) 12 *et seq.* .

[13] The Convention was adopted on 12 August 1949 and entered into force on 21 October 1950; 75 UNTS 287.

Regulations, prohibiting any destruction by an occupying power of real or personal property 'except where such destruction is rendered absolutely necessary by military operation'.

As the provisions of the four Geneva Conventions of 1949 were increasingly perceived as inadequate, states entered into intense negotiations in the 1970s on the further development of international humanitarian law. After long and protracted negotiations, two Protocols were adopted in 1977. The First Additional Protocol[14] (AP I) is applicable to international armed conflicts; the Second Additional Protocol[15] (AP II) deals with non-international armed conflicts. While many provisions included in AP I reflect customary international law, others must be considered as innovative, and arguably have kept important military powers away from signing the Protocol.[16] Most relevant are the provisions on the conduct of hostilities (Articles 35–60 AP I).

Article 35(3) AP I states: 'It is prohibited to employ methods or means of warfare which are intended, or may be expected, to cause widespread, long-term and severe damage to the natural environment.' This is confirmed by Article 55(1) AP I which goes, however, beyond Article 35(3) AP I in specifying that '[t]his protection includes a prohibition of the use of methods or means of warfare which are intended or may be expected to cause such damage to the natural environment and thereby to prejudice the health or survival of the population'. Article 55(2) AP I expressly prohibits attacks against the natural environment by way of reprisals. Most commentators consider the prohibition included in these two Articles as being not applicable to nuclear weapons.[17] While the Articles do not distinguish between collateral and intentional damage to the environment, it may be argued that the decisive improvement compared to earlier rules is the lack of any reference to 'military necessity'. The thresholds to be met are, however, high and relatively difficult to interpret and apply. Articles 35 and 55 AP I only prohibit environmental damage which is widespread, long-term and severe. This requires the cumulative presence of all three criteria. The criteria are largely understood as encompassing an area of about several hundred square kilometres, lasting for a period of months, or approximately a season, and involving serious or significant disruption or harm to human life, natural economic resources or other assets.[18] It would be fairly difficult to consider conventional warfare as unlawful on this basis. Additional protection of the environment may be derived from the prohibition of indiscriminate attacks according to Article 51(4) AP I and the limitation of attacks to military objectives under Article 52(1) and (2) AP I.

In response to the US use of defoliants during the war in Vietnam, the Convention

[14] The Protocol Additional to the Geneva Conventions of 12 August 1949, and relating to the Protection of Victims of International Armed Conflicts was adopted on 8 June 1977 and entered into force on 7 December 1978; (1977) 16 ILM 1391.

[15] The Protocol Additional to the Geneva Conventions of 12 August 1949, and relating to the Protection of Victims of Non-International Armed Conflicts was adopted on 8 June 1977 and entered into force on 7 December 1978; (1977) 16 ILM 1442.

[16] AP I has been ratified by 170 states; AP II has been ratified by 165 states. Among the world's major military powers, Iran and the United States have not ratified AP I.

[17] On the applicability of AP I to nuclear weapons and the related disputes see WH Boothby, *Weapons and the Law of Armed Conflict* (Oxford *et al* 2009) 97–98.

[18] *Cf* Witteler, above n 8, 253 *et seq*; see also RA Falk, 'Environmental Disruption by Military Means and International Law' in AH Westing (ed), *Environmental Warfare: A Technical, Legal and Policy Appraisal* (London/Philadelphia 1984) 40 *et seq*.

on the Prohibition of Military or Any Other Hostile Use of Environmental Modification Techniques[19] (ENMOD Convention) was adopted in 1976.[20] Article 1 thereof prohibits engaging in 'military or any other hostile use of environmental modification techniques having widespread, long-lasting or severe effects as a means of destruction, damage or injury to any other State Party'. Thus, the object and purpose of the ENMOD Convention differ from those of AP I, which primarily addresses environmental effects of combat operations, whereas the provisions of the ENMOD Convention aim at preventing the use and modification of the environment as a means of warfare. Article 1 ENMOD applies the same criteria as Article 35(3) AP I; however, it only requires that one of the criteria is met. Nevertheless, most uses of the environment as a means of warfare will be below the thresholds envisaged.[21]

The 1980 UN Convention on Certain Conventional Weapons[22] (CCW) seeks to prohibit or restrict the use of particular conventional weapons that are considered excessively injurious or whose effects are indiscriminate. While the CCW, which is a framework convention, does not expressly address the environment, some of its five Protocols[23] contribute to the protection of the environment in times of armed conflict (Protocols I–IV) and thereafter (Protocol V). Most important in respect of armed conflict situations is Protocol III on Prohibitions or Restrictions on the Use of Incendiary Weapons. It prohibits making the civilian population—civilians themselves as well as civilian objects—the object of attack by any weapon or munition which is primarily designed to set fire to objects or to cause burn injury to persons through the action of flame, heat or a combination thereof, produced by a chemical reaction of a substance delivered on the target. In particular, Article 2(4) of this Protocol prohibits 'to make forests or other kinds of plant cover the object of attack by incendiary weapons except when such natural elements are used to cover, conceal or camouflage combatants or other military objectives, or are themselves military objectives'. This prohibition partly goes beyond the prohibition included in the ENMOD Convention since it may also cover local damage to the environment.[24]

The 2003 Protocol V on Explosive Remnants of War requires the clearance of unexploded ordnance and establishes a responsibility on parties to a conflict at the cessation of active hostilities. This at least offers indirect protective effects for the benefit of the environment which has been affected by such weapons. The same basically applies to the 1997 Convention on the Prohibition of the Use, Stockpiling, Production and Transfer

[19] It entered into force on 5 October 1978; (1977) 16 ILM 88.

[20] The ENMOD Convention was adopted in 1976 by UNGA Res 31/72 (10 December 1976) and was opened for signature at Geneva on 18 May 1977.

[21] S Oeter, 'Methods and Means of Combat' in D Fleck (ed), *The Handbook of International Humanitarian Law* (2nd edn Oxford 2008) para 403.

[22] The Convention on Prohibitions or Restrictions on the Use of Certain Conventional Weapons Which May be Deemed to be Excessively Injurious or to Have Indiscriminate Effects was adopted on 10 October 1980 and entered into force on 2 December 1983; (1980) 19 ILM 1523.

[23] 1980 Protocol on Non-Detectable Fragments (Protocol I) ((1980) 19 ILM 1529), 1980 Protocol on Prohibitions or Restrictions on the Use of Mines, Booby-Traps and Other Devices (Protocol II) ((1980) 19 ILM 1529), amended in 1996 ((1996) 35 ILM 1209), 1980 Protocol on Prohibitions or Restrictions on the Use of Incendiary Weapons (Protocol III) ((1980) 19 ILM 1534), 1995 Protocol on Blinding Laser Weapons (Protocol IV) ((1996) 35 ILM 1218) and the 2003 Protocol on Explosive Remnants of War (Protocol V) ((2006) 45 ILM 1348).

[24] See *ibid*, paras 420–421.

of Anti-Personnel Mines and on their Destruction, and to the 2008 Convention on Cluster Munitions.[25]

It has already been mentioned that the CWC expressly prohibits the use of chemical weapons 'under any circumstances'. The Convention, however, does not include herbicides, even though these are referred to in its preamble. Article II(2) CWC is further limited by including only chemicals 'which through [their] chemical action on life processes can cause death, temporary incapacitation or permanent harm to humans or animals'. Effects on flora do not seem to be covered. Hence, the scope of application of the CWC is limited compared with the 1925 Geneva Protocol.

27.2.2 Customary Law Applicable to International Armed Conflicts

Customary international law is particularly relevant for those states which have not ratified any of the above conventions. It is thus important to assess whether the environment is protected in times of armed conflict not only by treaty law but also by customary international law. Whereas Articles 35(3) and 55 AP I can be considered to have established new law at the time of the adoption of AP I in 1977, a recent study on customary international humanitarian law, commissioned by the International Committee of the Red Cross (ICRC), has shown that the essence of these two provisions has now become part of customary international law.[26]

Rules 43–45 of the customary law study even seem to specify the substance of treaty law. First, Rule 43 confirms that the general principles on the conduct of hostilities apply to the natural environment and goes on to clarify that no part of the natural environment may be attacked, unless it is a military objective. It confirms that destruction of any part of the natural environment is prohibited, unless required by imperative military necessity. Finally, it affirms that attacks against military objectives with disproportionate collateral damage to the environment are prohibited. It is noteworthy that Rule 44 requires states to take all feasible precautions in the conduct of military operations to avoid and minimise incidental damage to the environment; it specifies that lack of scientific certainty as to the effects on the environment does not absolve a party to the conflict from taking such precautions. Finally, Rule 45 affirms the customary character of Articles 35(3) AP I and of Article 1 of the ENMOD Convention.

While this seems to suggest that customary international law has moved forward quite a lot in the protection of the environment during international armed conflict, it must be pointed out that the customary nature of the three rules phrased by the ICRC study is not undisputed.[27]

[25] T Marauhn, 'The Silent Threat: Explosive Remnants of War' in A Fischer-Lescano *et al* (eds), *Frieden in Freiheit: Festschrift für Michael Bothe zum 70. Geburtstag* (Baden-Baden 2008) 193.

[26] JM Henckaerts and L Doswald-Beck (eds), *Customary International Humanitarian Law*. Vol II: *Practice* (Cambridge 2005); see also JM Henckaerts, 'The ICRC Study on Customary International Humanitarian Law: Characteristics, Conclusions and Practical Relevance' (2009) 6 *Slovenian Law Review* 225.

[27] Y Dinstein, 'The ICRC Customary International Humanitarian Law Study' (2006) 36 *Israel Yearbook on Human Rights* 1; H Krieger, 'A Conflict of Norms: The Relationship between Humanitarian Law and Human Rights Law in the ICRC Customary Law Study' (2006) 11 *Journal of Conflict and Security Law* 265.

27.2.3 The Law Applicable to Non-International Armed Conflicts

The rules included in AP II applicable to non-international armed conflicts are less extensive and less precise than those agreed upon in AP I. In 1977, states did not agree upon the inclusion of particular provisions relating to the protection of the international environment in AP II. Furthermore, AP II has not been as widely ratified as AP I.[28] Nevertheless, the Protocol is relevant and reference may be made to some of its provisions.

Articles 13–16 AP II, which are aimed at protecting the civilian population and particular objects from attack, indirectly contribute to the protection of the environment in non-international armed conflicts. While common Article 3 of the Geneva Conventions does not contribute any further to the protection of the environment, the ICRC's study of customary international law suggests that at least the basic rules for the protection of the environment in international armed conflicts, such as the obligation to pay due regard to the environment and the principle that precautions have to be taken, also apply to non-international armed conflicts.[29]

In addition, governments involved in a non-international armed conflict will at least have to respect peacetime rules on the international protection of the environment, in particular the prohibition of the use of means and methods of warfare in non-international armed conflicts which have serious transboundary effects. This can easily be established on the basis of the no-harm rule[30] which undisputedly applies in peacetime international environmental law. Furthermore, in principle, MEAs continue to apply during non-international armed conflicts between the parties unless one party can argue that the armed conflict can be considered as *force majeure*.

27.3 The Applicability of MEAs in Times of Armed Conflict

In light of the relatively weak protection of the environment in times of armed conflict afforded by the law of armed conflict, the question must be raised whether and possibly to what extent states have to continue to respect MEAs in times of armed conflict.

Quite a few arguments can be made in support of the hypothesis that MEAs will not generally be superseded by the law of armed conflict in times of such conflicts. An important hint is provided by Principle 24 of the Rio Declaration which stipulates that 'States shall . . . respect international law providing protection for the environment in times of armed conflict and cooperate in its further development, as necessary.' Even though this is not a provision of treaty law, the ICJ in its advisory opinion on the *Legality of the Threat or Use of Nuclear Weapons* of 8 July 1996 seems to support the Rio Declaration in this respect. Acknowledging that '[t]he existence of the general obligation of States to ensure that activities within their jurisdiction and control respect the environment of

[28] *Cf* above n 16.

[29] JM Henckaerts and L Doswald-Beck, *Customary International Humanitarian Law*. Vol I: *Rules* (Cambridge *et al* 2005) 148–150.

[30] *Cf* Chapter 6.

other States or of areas beyond national control is now part of the corpus of international law relating to the environment',[31] the Court addresses the question of whether peacetime MEAs continue to apply in times of armed conflict, though using much more careful language. It underlines that the question of continued applicability is less relevant than the position of the parties to the treaty 'whether the obligations stemming from these treaties were intended to be obligations of total restraint during military conflict'. According to the Court, MEAs do not hamper the right of self-defence, but in defending itself a state must bear in mind 'what is necessary and proportionate in the pursuit of legitimate military objectives. Respect for the environment is one of the elements that go to assessing whether an action is in conformity with the principles of necessity and proportionality.'[32] Thus, the Court takes the position that protection of the environment as embodied in peacetime MEAs will have to be considered in decision-making processes related to means and methods of warfare.

The ICJ's hesitance in going any further is no surprise. Firstly, there still is a lack of clarity as to which peacetime treaties generally continue to apply during an armed conflict. This is not only true for academic writings on the issue but even more so in terms of state practice and *opinio iuris*. Secondly, most MEAs do not include provisions on their applicability in times of armed conflict. It would, however, be too simple to conclude on the basis of this finding that MEAs continue to apply. General treaty law on the suspension and the denunciation of treaties suggesting a much more hesitant approach must be borne in mind (*cf* Articles 54–64 VCLT). There may be more rules applicable in times of armed conflict than only *erga omnes* or *jus cogens* obligations; however, even their identification is disputed.[33] In conclusion, it appears that at least the object and purpose of many MEAs continue to be relevant in times of armed conflict.

27.4 Environmental Impact of Arms Control and Disarmament Obligations

If there is an inherent tension between armed conflict and protection of the environment, it seems likely that arms control and disarmament promotes environmental protection. However, this is not self-evident. Indeed, it is no surprise that some authors have even identified potential conflicts between 'green' and 'peace'.[34]

By way of example the destruction of existing stockpiles of chemical weapons under the CWC will be discussed here. The primary object and purpose of the CWC is a comprehensive ban on chemical weapons—not only on their use, but primarily the destruction of all stockpiles and the supervision of states in their peaceful use of chemical processes

[31] (1996) ICJ Reports 226, 242.

[32] (1996) ICJ Reports 226, *ibid.*

[33] S Vöneky, *Die Fortgeltung des Umweltvölkerrechts in internationalen bewaffneten Konflikten* (Berlin *et al* 2001) 469 *et seq.*

[34] See T Findlay, 'Green vs Peace? The Johnston Atoll Controversy' (1990) Working Paper no 81, Research School of Pacific Studies, Australian National University, Peace Research Centre.

in order to prevent the abuse of such capacities for military purposes. In order to eliminate entirely this category of weapons, parties to the Convention are under an obligation to destroy existing stockpiles within a rather strict timeframe (Articles IV and V CWC). In light of practical problems, the schedule originally foreseen has been extended by the Organisation for the Prohibition of Chemical Weapons (OPCW). Pertinent provisions of the CWC include an obligation to 'assign the highest priority to ensuring the safety of people and to protecting the environment' (Articles IV(10) and V(11) CWC). Dealing with national implementation of the Convention, Article VII(3) CWC expressly stipulates that each party 'during the implementation of its obligations under this Convention, shall assign the highest priority to ensuring the safety of people and to protecting the environment, and shall cooperate as appropriate with other States Parties in this regard'.[35] These obligations are further specified by the pertinent provisions of the CWC's Annexes.[36] In addition, the OPCW has to this end provided assistance to parties.[37]

The destruction of chemical weapons poses particularly severe threats to the environment. Other arms control and disarmament treaties also raise environmental problems. To this end, states have entered into bilateral agreements aiming at mutual assistance in the environmentally sound implementation of arms control and disarmament obligations.[38]

27.5 Conclusions

While problems related to the environmental impact of armed conflicts are not new, detailed international rules in this field have only recently been developed. Pertinent obligations can be drawn from the general rules of the law of armed conflict. In addition, specific obligations have only been included in the 1977 Additional Protocol I and the 1977 ENMOD Convention as well as subsequent treaty law. Pertinent treaty obligations are relatively weak. All the more surprising are the conclusions drawn by the ICRC study on customary international humanitarian law which is much more specific than some of

[35] *Cf* Krutzsch and Trapp, above n 12, 119; U Beyerlin and T Marauhn, 'The Protection of the Environment in the Context of Chemical Weapons Destruction' in Hague Academy of International Law (ed), *La Convention sur l'Interdiction et l'Élimination des Armes Chimiques: Une Percée dans l'Entreprise Multilatérale du Désarmement* [*The Convention on the Prohibition and Elimination of Chemical Weapons: A Breakthrough in Multilateral Disarmament*] (Dordrecht 1995) 187.

[36] *Cf* the Verification Annex, Part V, paras 11–42.

[37] *Cf* for the extension of the initial deadline (29 April 2007) by five years (29 April 2012) the Decision of the Conference of the States Parties on the 'Request by the United States of America for Establishment of a Revised Date for the Final Deadline for Destroying all of its Category 1 Chemical Weapons' in C-11/DEC17 (8 December 2006) 2; see also the 'Report of the Eleventh Session of the Conference of the States Parties' (5–8 December 2006) in C-11/5 (8 December 2006) 5–6 for further extension decisions concerning the Russian Federation, India, the Libyan Arab Jamahiriya, Albania and another state party. For an analysis of this Session see A Lele, 'CWC's First Decade' (2007) 1 *CBW Magazine: Journal on Chemical and Biological Weapons* 8, 10.

[38] *Cf* Beyerlin and Marauhn, above n 35, 207; I Anthony, 'The Role of the European Union in WMD Nonproliferation' in NE Busch and DH Joyner (eds), *Combating Weapons of Mass Destruction* (Athens, GA 2009) 197, 213. See also T Marauhn, 'Bilaterale Abkommen über Abrüstungshilfe'(1993) 35 *Neue Zeitschrift für Wehrrecht* 221.

the treaty obligations as regards envrionmental protection. Whether or not peacetime MEAs continue to apply in times of armed conflict is still subject to dispute, even though plausible arguments can be made in favour of their continued application.[39] A relatively new field is respect for environmental standards in the context of arms control and disarmament obligations.

What can be taken from the interface between environmental concerns and international security is that there is an increasing recognition of the need to protect the environment not only in peacetime but also in situations which entail enormous risks for the future of individual states or mankind as a whole, namely during armed conflict. Agreement on basic rules on the protection of the environment in times of armed conflict must be considered as a success in the context of general developments in international environmental law. However, progress in this field should not be overestimated. What is indeed positive is that the law has contributed to accommodate different regulatory objectives in the two fields of international security and environmental protection which at first sight seem to be indifferent towards each other.

Further Reading

M Bothe, 'Criminal Responsibility for Environmental Damage in Times of Armed Conflict' in RJ Grunawalt (ed), *Protection of the Environment During Armed Conflict* (Newport, RI 1996) 473–478.

AL Bunker, 'Protection of the Environment During Armed Conflict' (2004) 13 *RECIEL* 201–213.

Y Dinstein, 'Protection of the Environment in International Armed Conflict' (2001) 5 *Max Planck Yearbook of United Nations Law* 523–549.

D Fleck, 'Protection of the Environment During Armed Conflict and other Military Operations: The Way Ahead' in RJ Grunawalt (ed), *Protection of the Environment During Armed Conflict* (Newport, RI 1996) 529–535.

JM Henckaerts, 'Armed Conflict and the Environment' (1999) 10 *Yearbook of International Environmental Law* 188–193.

——, 'Towards Better Protection for the Environment in Armed Conflict' (2000) 9 *RECIEL* 13–19.

——, 'General Developments—Armed Conflict and the Environment' (2002) 13 *Yearbook of International Environmental Law* 241–249.

LY Huang, 'The 2006 Israeli-Lebanese conflict' (2008) 20 *Florida Journal of International Law* 103–113.

K Hulme, 'Armed Conflict, Wanton Ecological Devastation and Scorched Earth Policies' (1997) 2 *Journal of Armed Conflict Law* 45–81.

M Kuhn, 'Aktuelle Entwicklungen zum Schutz der Umwelt in bewaffneten Konflikten' (1996) 9 *Humanitäres Völkerrecht* 42–50.

JH MacNeill, 'Protection of the Environment in Time of Armed Conflict: Environmental Protection in Military Practice' in RJ Grunawalt (ed), *Protection of the Environment During Armed Conflict* (Newport, RI 1996) 536–545.

I Peterson, 'The Natural Environment in Times of Armed Conflict' (2009) 22 *Leiden Journal of International Law* 325–344.

[39] *Cf* in this regard UNEP, *Protecting the Environment During Armed Conflict: An Inventory and Analysis of International Law* (Nairobi 2009) 43 *et seq*.

PK Rakate, 'Desparate measures' (2001) 26 *South African Yearbook of International Law* 132–143.

PJ Richards, 'Mars Meets Mother Nature: Protecting the Environment During Armed Conflict' (1999) 28 *Stetson Law Review* 1047–1090.

H Spieker, 'The Conduct of Hostilities and the Protection of the Environment' in A Fischer-Lescano *et al* (eds), *Frieden in Freiheit: Festschrift für Michael Bothe zum 70. Geburtstag* (Baden-Baden 2008) 741–768.

UNEP, *Protecting the Environment During Armed Conflict: An Inventory and Analysis of International Law* (Nairobi 2009).

JD Van der Vyver, 'The Environment' (2009) 23 *Emory International Law Review* 85–112.

WD Verwey, 'Observations on the Legal Protection of the Environment in Times of International Armed Conflict' (1994) 7 *Hague Yearbook of International Law* 35–52.

28

Environmental Protection and International Economic Law

28.1 Conflict or Complementarity?

Debates on the implementation and on possible obstacles to the further development of international environmental law suggest that there is an inherent conflict between economic development on the one hand and environmental protection on the other.[1] Frequently, developing countries perceive international environmental obligations as an impediment to economic development. However, stronger opposition against strengthening multilateral environmental regimes seems to come from emerging market countries. The Copenhagen Summit failed to bring about a post-Kyoto instrument not least because of fast-developing countries refusing to take on obligations to reduce greenhouse gas emissions. The so-called BRIC countries—a acronym that refers to the countries of Brazil, Russia, India and China, which are deemed to be at a similar level of economic development—seem to take critical positions if they perceive that environmental obligations reduce their perspectives for economic growth. It is not self-evident to consider economic development and environmental protection as antinomies.

Agenda 21 calls upon economic actors to contribute to sustainable development by liberalising trade and strengthening trade and environment as mutually supportive policies.[2] Apart from its support for the liberalisation of trade, Agenda 21 calls upon states to avoid distortion of competition, to protect foreign investments, to ensure the stability of the international financial system, and to strengthen development assistance. This entails addressing the problem of debts in developing countries as well as the transfer of financial and other means. It is assumed that all states will be in a position to develop in an environmentally sound manner and to promote integrated and sustainable development.

Since economic theories and empirical studies have not supported only one of the

[1] See, among others, M Bothe, 'Environment, Development, Resources' (2007) 318 *Recueil des cours* 333, 410 *et seq*.

[2] Agenda 21, Chapter 2.3 lit a and b.

two perspectives, it can be presumed that there is both conflict and complementarity between environmental protection and economic development.[3] In legal terms it is important that the two perceived opposing objectives—international trade and environmental protection—are often brought together as rule and exception, be it within the WTO arrangements (where the focus is on the liberalisation of trade in goods and services and where environmental considerations are construed as an exception to such liberalisation) or within multilateral environmental agreements (MEAs) which tend to oppose the free movement of certain goods (be it protected species under the Convention on International Trade in Endangered Species of Wild Fauna and Flora (CITES) or chlorofluorocarbons under the Montreal Protocol).

As a matter of principle, liberalised international trade does not allow states to partition markets by any other means than customs and duties. In the following it will be shown, however, that unilateral trade restrictions may be permissible under certain circumstances, including for the protection of the transboundary or global environment. Whether such measures are permissible depends on whether or not the state concerned takes on a stewardship role for the environment. This can easily be shown in the case of common goods but it will be much more difficult if the protective measure relates to natural resources in the territory of another state.

28.2 WTO Law

The main body of international economic law today is part of the rules developed, implemented and supervised by the World Trade Organization (WTO). While other instruments, including regional agreements and bilateral investment treaties, may in total outnumber the WTO agreements, the latter serve as a normative model both in terms of substance and in terms of procedure, in particular as regards the settlement of disputes. This will be illustrated by taking a look at the development of WTO law, and the treaty framework of the General Agreement on Tariffs and Trade (GATT) in particular. The GATT provision on general exemptions to liberalised trade (Article XX) will be discussed, as will the Agreement on Sanitary and Phytosanitary Measures. The impact of the WTO Committee on Trade and Environment will be critically reviewed.

28.2.1 The Development of WTO Law

The fact that environmental protection was not explicitly addressed in the text of the GATT 1947 [4] is telling of the then perceived relationship between trade and environment. However, since the 1970s the Secretariat and Council of the GATT have considered the

[3] *Cf* W Beckerman, 'Economic Development and the Environment: Conflict or Complementarity?' (Washington 1992) Policy Research Working Papers/World Development Report (WPS 961), August 1992, available at www-wds.worldbank.org/external/default/WDSContentServer/IW3P/IB/1992/08/01/000009265_3961003070505/Rendered/PDF/multi0page.pdf.

[4] General Agreement on Tariffs and Trade of 30 October 1947; see 55 UNTS 194 and 55 UNTS 308.

ecological aspects of trade. While some environment-related instruments were agreed upon during the Tokyo Round (1973–1979), in particular those on non-tariff barriers, the Uruguay Round (1986–1994) only took up environmental issues in the run-up to the 1992 Rio Conference, eventually leading to the agreements establishing the WTO as adopted at Marrakesh in 1994.[5]

The Final Act of Marrakesh, apart from a number of decisions and declarations adopted by the Ministerial Conference, includes the WTO Agreement[6] which in itself consists of a bundle of instruments. The WTO Agreement, which entered into force on 1 January 1995, serves as an umbrella agreement. Annexed are the agreements on goods (Annex 1A, including the GATT 1994[7] which must be read together with the GATT 1947 as the original agreement dealing with trade in goods, but also agreements on agriculture, sanitary and phytosanitary measures, technical barriers to trade, and others), services (Annex 1B, General Agreement on Trade in Services[8]) and intellectual property (Annex 1C, Agreement on Trade-Related Aspects of Intellectual Property Rights[9]), dispute settlement (Annex 2, Dispute Settlement Understanding (DSU)[10]), and trade policy review mechanism (Annex 3), all of which are 'integral parts of this Agreement, binding on all Members' (Article II(2) WTO). Also annexed are so-called plurilateral agreements which form 'part of this Agreement for those Members that have accepted them, and are binding on those Members' (Article II(3) WTO).

The establishment of the WTO in 1995 meant a paradigm shift in international economic law. With its three principal organs, the Ministerial Conference, the General Council and the Secretariat, it provides a common institutional framework for the conduct of trade relations (*cf* Article II(1) WTO). With its 153 Member States (plus the European Union alongside its members) it perceives itself as a rules-based and member-driven organisation.

The quasi-judicial dispute settlement mechanism that had been developed under the GATT was continued under the WTO Agreement but with decisive improvements.[11] Whereas previously recommendations adopted by GATT panels had to be approved unanimously, the DSU provides that the Dispute Settlement Board (DSB) decides by 'reverse' or 'negative' consensus. In effect this means that the approval is virtually automatic, because recommendations will only be rejected if the DSB unanimously decides to do so (Articles 6.1, 16.4, 17.14 and 22.6 DSU). In addition, there are tight time limits and there is an appellate procedure which allows each party to a dispute to have the case reconsidered by an Appellate Body (Article 17 DSU). The Appellate Body can uphold, modify or reverse the legal findings and conclusions of a panel. Meanwhile the DSB has

[5] For an introduction to the WTO's history, organisational and legal structure see PT Stoll and F Schorkopf, *WTO—World Economic Order, World Trade Law* (Leiden 2006) 11–29 and 31–68.

[6] (1994) 33 ILM 13.

[7] (1994) 33 ILM 28.

[8] (1994) 33 ILM 44.

[9] (1994) 33 ILM 81.

[10] (1994) 33 ILM 112.

[11] On the dispute-settlement mechanism see RE Hudec, 'The New WTO Dispute Settlement Procedure—An Overview of the First Three Years' (1999) 8 *Minnesota Journal of Global Trade* 1.

addressed several disputes emerging from conflicts between trade and environment. They will be discussed below.

28.2.2 The GATT Treaty Framework

The starting point of an analysis of the GATT (meaning the GATT 1947 unless indicated otherwise) must be the provisions aiming at trade liberalisation. Constitutive are the most-favoured nation principle (Article I GATT)[12], the principle of national treatment (Article III GATT)[13] and the prohibition of quantitative restrictions (Article XI GATT).[14] According to the most-favoured nation principle, parties must not normally discriminate between their trading partners. If they grant one of their trading partners a favour (such as reducing duties for one of their products) they will have to do the same for all other WTO members. National treatment means that imported and locally produced goods should be treated equally after having entered the market. Article XI GATT clearly states that no prohibitions or restrictions other than duties, taxes or other charges, whether made effective through quotas, import or export licences or other measures, shall be instituted or maintained in international trade, providing only for few exceptions.

The GATT itself allows for a number of exceptions to these principles. Firstly, Article XI(2) GATT includes three exceptions which may be potentially relevant with a view to environmental protection: export prohibitions or restrictions to prevent or relieve critical shortages of foodstuffs or other products essential to the exporting party; import and export restrictions necessary for the application of standards or regulations for the classification, grading or marketing of commodities in international trade; and import restrictions to preserve the competitiveness of the party's agricultural or fishing industry.

The most important general exception applicable to all GATT provisions is laid down in Article XX GATT.[15] This Article includes two cumulative requirements. Firstly, the measure in question must fall under at least one of the ten exceptions expressly included, with two of them related to environmental considerations. Secondly, the measure in question must satisfy the requirements of the introductory paragraph of Article XX GATT which is often called the 'chapeau'.[16] The 'chapeau' requires that the measure is not applied in a manner which would constitute 'a means of arbitrary or unjustifiable discrimination between countries where the same conditions prevail', and is not 'a disguised restriction on international trade'. Looking at the exceptions listed in Article XX GATT, paragraphs (b) and (g) are of particular relevance to the protection of the environment. Paragraph (b)

[12] WF Schwartz and AO Sykes, 'Toward a Positive Theory of the Most Favored Nation Obligation and its Exceptions in the WTO/GATT System' (1996) 16 *International Review of Law and Economics* 27.

[13] R Pillai, 'National Treatment and WTO Dispute Settlement' (2002) 1 *World Trade Review* 321.

[14] R Schaffer, F Agusti and B Earle, *International Business Law and its Environment* (7th edn Mason, OH 2009) 312 *et seq*.

[15] M Irish, 'GATT Article XX and Global Public Policy' (2004) 33 *Legitimacy and Accountability in International Law* 57.

[16] AE Appleton, 'GATT Article XX's Chapeau: A Disguised "Necessary" Test?' (1997) 6 *RECIEL* 131.

refers to measures necessary to protect human, animal or plant life or health; paragraph (g) concerns measures relating to the conservation of exhaustible natural resources.[17]

A few comments may illustrate the interpretative challenges of these exceptions. Firstly, paragraph (b) only protects fauna and flora as well as the bodily integrity of humans; it does not cover the environment as such. However, the environment may be included in so far as natural resources are indispensable for human livelihood. Secondly, uncertainties are linked to the interpretation of what is 'necessary' to protect human, animal or plant life or health (paragraph (b)). Thirdly, questions may arise as to whether a natural resource is 'exhaustible' within the meaning of paragraph (g). Fourthly, the qualification of paragraph (g) is difficult to interpret since it requires that the measures in question 'are made effective in conjunction with restrictions on domestic production or consumption'. Fifthly, none of the two exceptions specifies the geographical location of the resource to be protected. There is no dispute as to the application of both paragraphs to natural resources located in the territory of the member adopting the measure; however, the treaty text is unclear with regard to the inclusion of environmental resources in the territory of another member or resources of a transboundary or global nature.

It is obvious that the interpretation of Article XX GATT has thus given rise to an extensive case law under the earlier GATT dispute-settlement mechanism as well as under the new WTO mechanism.

28.2.3 Case Law Related to Article XX GATT

An early case related to ecological issues arose out of a dispute between Canada and the United States.[18] The US had introduced an import prohibition on Canadian tuna and tuna products after Canada had seized fishing vessels and arrested US fishermen fishing for albacore tuna in water considered by Canada to be under its jurisdiction. Canada brought a case against the US, arguing that the ban violated Articles I, XI and XIII GATT. In response, the US relied on Article XX(g) GATT. Both parties agreed that tuna was an 'exhaustible resource' according to Article XX(g) GATT. However, Canada contested that the US import ban actually served the protection of this resource. The panel, on 22 February 1982, approved Canada's position arguing that the US import ban had not been adopted 'in conjunction with restrictions on domestic production or consumption' as required by paragraph (g).

Another case between Canada and the US arose out of Canada's prohibitions on the export of unprocessed herring and salmon.[19] While Canada conceded that such prohibition was covered by Article XI(1) GATT, it argued that it could be justified both under Article XI(2) and Article XX(g) GATT. The panel, in 1988, rejected Canada's arguments,

[17] P Bentley, 'A Re-assessment of Article XX, Paragraphs (b) and (g) of GATT 1994 in the Light of Growing Consumer and Environmental Concern About Biotechnology' (2000) 24 *Fordham International Law Journal* 107.

[18] *United States—Prohibition of Tuna and Tuna Products from Canada*, Panel Report (1983) BISD (29th Supp) 91, adopted 22 February 1982.

[19] *Canada—Measures Affecting Exports of Unprocessed Herring and Salmon*, Panel Report (1989) BISD (35th Supp) 98, adopted 22 March 1988.

finding that the prohibitions applied to all unprocessed herring and salmon, not just substandard specimens, and concluding that the export prohibitions could not be considered as 'necessary' to the application of standards according to Article XI(2)(b) GATT. In respect of Article XX(g) GATT the panel found that Canada's export prohibitions were neither primarily aimed at the conservation of salmon and herring stocks nor primarily aimed at rendering effective the restrictions on the harvesting of salmon and herring.

In 1990, a panel report was adopted in relation to a dispute that had arisen between the US and Thailand.[20] Thailand had prohibited the import of cigarettes and similar products, but authorised the sale of domestic cigarettes, arguing that chemicals and other additives contained in, among others, US cigarettes might make them more harmful than Thai cigarettes, thus relying upon Article XX(b) GATT. In the resulting case brought by the US, the panel confirmed that Thailand may adopt non-discriminatory protective measures to contain health risks; however, the panel found that the import ban on foreign cigarettes was not 'necessary' according to Article XX(b) GATT since there were no parallel limitations on the production and marketing of tobacco within Thailand. The panel established that

> the import restrictions imposed by Thailand could be considered to be 'necessary' in terms of Article XX(b) only if there were no alternative measure consistent with the General Agreement, or less inconsistent with it, which Thailand could reasonably be expected to employ to achieve its health policy objectives.

Even though the panel report was never adopted under the old GATT, the tuna–dolphin case brought by Mexico and others against the US still attracts a lot of attention.[21] The facts of the case are related to a biological phenomenon, namely the fact that in certain parts of the Pacific Ocean, schools of yellow fin tuna often swim beneath schools of dolphins. If purse seine nets are used to harvest tuna, dolphins are often trapped in the nets and die unless released. US legislation set protective standards for the domestic fleet but also for countries whose fishing boats catch tuna in these parts of the Pacific. If such a country cannot prove to US authorities that it complies with US standards for the protection of dolphins, the US government must embargo all imports of the fish from that country. The embargo was also addressed against intermediaries handling the tuna en route from Mexico to the United States. When Mexico's exports of tuna to the US were banned, it complained under the GATT in 1991. While Mexico focused on Article III(1) GATT, the panel considered the case under Article XI(1) GATT and discussed whether or not the import ban could be justified under Article XX GATT. Eventually, the panel stated that the US could not embargo imports of tuna products from Mexico simply because Mexican regulations on the way tuna was produced did not satisfy US regulations; the panel established that the US could only rely on the properties of the 'product', not on the 'process' of production. Secondly, the panel objected to extra-territorial enforcement of environmental considerations under Article XX(b) GATT. It argued that GATT rules

[20] *Thailand—Restrictions on Importation of and National Taxes on Cigarettes*, Panel Report (1990) BISD (37th Supp) 200, adopted 7 November 1990.

[21] *United States—Restriction on Imports of Tuna*, Panel Report (1992) BISD (39th Supp) 155, 3 September 1991 (unadopted).

did not allow one country to take measures for the purpose of enforcing its own domestic laws for the animal health or exhaustible natural resources in another country. Had the US arguments been accepted, any country would have been in a position to apply trade restrictions unilaterally. It is important to note that the panel did not assess whether any of the policies were environmentally correct, but argued in favour of making US policy compatible with GATT rules.

A second tuna–dolphin report was presented in 1994 but not, however, adopted.[22] This time, the report was the outcome of a case brought by the EU against the US. Even though the panel followed the recommendations of the panel in the first tuna–dolphin case, it took a different position on a number of important issues. In particular with regard to unilateral extraterritorial measures, the panel argued differently. Referring to two earlier panel reports which had applied Article XX(g) GATT to straddling fish stocks without distinguishing whether the fish were caught within or outside the country's jurisdiction, the panel relied upon Article XX(e) GATT to argue that Article XX GATT does not generally outlaw extraterritorial measures. Subsequently, the panel, as a matter of principle, stated that Article XX GATT must, on the basis of Articles 31 and 32 of the Vienna Convention on the Law of Treaties, be interpreted in light of new MEAs. However, in the case at issue these agreements did not allow for a different conclusion than in the first tuna–dolphin case. The panel rejected reliance upon Article XX(g) GATT and confirmed the first panel's view on the interpretation of 'necessary' measures under Article XX(b) GATT.[23]

Another dispute to be discussed here is the gasoline case, which was brought by Venezuela and Brazil against the US.[24] This was actually one of the first cases under the new DSU established as part of the WTO. It is noteworthy that the case did not challenge a member's right to set environmental standards but focused on the question of whether the US measure discriminated against imported gasoline and in favour of domestic refineries. At issue was the US applying stricter rules on the chemical characteristics of imported gasoline than it did for domestically refined gasoline. Venezuela and Brazil claimed that the Gasoline Rule was inconsistent with Article III GATT and was not covered by Article XX GATT. The US argued that the Gasoline Rule was consistent with Article III, and was at least justified under Article XX(b), (g) and (d). The panel established that the Gasoline Rule was inconsistent with Article III and could not be justified under Article XX GATT. On appeal of the panel's findings on Article XX(g), the Appellate Body found the US measure to be covered by Article XX(g) GATT but failed to meet the requirements of the 'chapeau'.[25]

Finally, the so-called shrimps–turtle case brought by India, Pakistan, Malaysia and

[22] (1994) 33 ILM 839.

[23] For a comment *cf* TH Strom, 'Another Kick at the Can' (1995) 33 *Canadian Yearbook of International Law* 149 and RW Parker, 'The Use and Abuse of Trade Leverage to Protect the Global Commons' (1999) 12 *Georgetown International Environmental Law Review* 1.

[24] *United States—Standards for Reformulated and Conventional Gasoline*, Appellate Body Report and Panel Report, WT/DS2/9 (20 May 1996).

[25] For a comment see MA MacCrory and EL Richards, 'Clearing the Air: the Clean Air Act, GATT and the WTO's Reformulated Gasoline Decision' (1998/99) 17 *UCLA Journal of Environmental Law & Policy* 1.

Thailand against the US deserves to be discussed here.[26] The case arose out of the application of US legislation on endangered species. The US Endangered Species Act of 1973 listed as endangered or threatened five species of sea turtles that occur in US waters, and prohibited their capture or killing within the US, in its territorial sea and the high seas. Legislation required US shrimp trawlers to use so-called 'turtle excluder devices' in their nets when fishing in areas where there is a significant likelihood of encountering sea turtles. Another piece of legislation, enacted in 1989, prohibited imports of shrimps harvested with technology that may adversely affect certain sea turtles—unless the harvesting state could demonstrate that it had protected sea turtles by other measures. The panel considered that the ban was inconsistent with Article XI GATT and could not be justified under Article XX GATT. Upon appeal, the Appellate Body accepted the measure to be provisionally justified under Article XX(g) GATT but not meeting the requirements of the 'chapeau'.[27]

28.2.4 The TBT and the SPS Agreements

Even though the Uruguay Round did not lead to the conclusion of an overall agreement on trade-related environmental protection measures, some of the new WTO instruments include clauses which carefully take into account environmental considerations of world trade.

To begin with, the WTO agreement itself in its preamble includes references which indicate that environmental considerations are taken into account. Thus, there is a list of non-trade issues included in the preamble, such as living standards and full employment, but also 'optimal use of the world's resources in accordance with the objective of sustainable development, seeking both to protect and preserve the environment'.

The General Agreement on Trade in Services (GATS) includes a provision resembling Article XX GATT. Article XIV GATS follows a similar structure to Article XX GATT, with a similarly worded chapeau and an exception provided for in paragraph (b): 'necessary to protect human, animal or plant life or health'. There is no exception related to exhaustible natural resources.

The Agreement on Trade-Related Aspects of Intellectual Property Rights (TRIPS) in its patent-related provisions includes a reference to environmental concerns. Article 27(2) TRIPS allows parties to exclude inventions from patentability if this is necessary 'to protect human, animal or plant life or health or to avoid serious prejudice to the environment'.

Very limited references to environmental considerations are included in the Agreement on Agriculture with its Article 6(1) allowing domestic subsidies if associated with infrastructural environmental programmes (read together with Annex 2 to the Agreement) and the Agreement on Subsidies and Countervailing Measures, Article 8(2) of which permits

[26] *United States—Import Prohibition of Certain Shrimp and Shrimp Products*, Appelate Body Report and Panel Report, WT/DS58/14 (9 April 1999).

[27] *Cf* PC Mavroidis, 'Trade and Environment after the Shrimps-Turtles Litigation' (2000) 34 *Journal of World Trade* 73.

subsidies 'to promote adaptation of existing facilities to new environmental requirements imposed by law and/or regulations'.

Most important, however, from the perspective of environmental protection is the Agreement on Sanitary and Phytosanitary Measures (SPS Agreement).[28] Together with the Agreement on Technical Barriers to Trade (TBT Agreement),[29] the SPS Agreement tries to identify how to meet the need to apply standards and at the same time avoid disguised protectionism. The SPS Agreement deals with food safety and animal and plant health and safety, while the TBT Agreement deals with product standards in general. These two agreements are complementary to Article XX GATT and are of increasing importance for the balancing of trade and environmental concerns. Basically, the SPS Agreement allows members to set their own standards (Articles 2–4), which must, however, be based on science. Such standards should only be applied to the extent necessary for the protection of human, animal or plant life or health. They should not arbitrarily or unjustifiably discriminate between countries with identical or similar conditions. Parties are encouraged to use international standards, guidelines and recommendations where they exist. When they do, they are unlikely to be challenged legally in a WTO dispute. Under certain conditions parties may use measures resulting in higher standards, either on the basis of scientific justification, in light of appropriate risk assessments, or in applying a precautionary approach in light of scientific uncertainty. Precautionary measures are permissible only on a temporary basis (Article 5.7 SPS). The preamble of the TBT Agreement as well as its Article 2(2) and (4) also can be used to take into consideration environmental concerns when applying technical standards.

Two disputes may be referred to here because they illustrate the potential of both agreements with a view to the trade-environment interface: the hormones case brought by Canada against the European Community[30] and the biotechnology disputes based on complaints by the US, Canada and Argentina again against the European Community.[31]

In response to 'mad cow disease', the European Community, in the 1990s, banned the import of meat containing artificial beef hormones. Canada and the US brought the case before the WTO DSB. At issue was the interpretation of Articles 3 and 5 SPS. With regard to Article 3, the panel, in August 1997, took the position that the requirement that SPS measures must be 'based on' international standards, guidelines or recommendations means that SPS measures must 'conform to' such standards. Furthermore, the panel interpreted Article 3.3 SPS as an exception to Articles 3.1 and 3.2 SPS, arguing that the burden of proof for the violation under Article 3.3 SPS shifts to the responding party. In respect of the risk assessment, the panel concluded that the EC measure violated Article 5.1 SPS and Article 3.1 SPS since the Community had not assessed the risks arising from the failure of observance of good veterinary practice combined with problems of control

[28] J Pauwelyn, 'The WTO Agreement on Sanitary and Phytosanitary (SPS) Measures as Applied in the First Three SPS Disputes' (1999) 2 *Journal of International Economic Law* 641.

[29] R Muñoz, 'The "TBT Agreement"' (2001) 4 *Cambridge Yearbook of European Legal Studies* 273.

[30] *EC Measures Concerning Meat and Meat Products*, Appellate Body Report, WT/DS26/AB/R, WT/DS48/AB/R, adopted 16 January 1998.

[31] *European Communities—Measures Affecting the Approval and Marketing of Biotech Products*, Panel Report, WT/DS291/AB/R, WT/DS292/AB/R and WT/DS293/AB/R, adopted 29 September 2006.

of the use of hormones for growth promotion purposes. The scientific evidence presented was not considered conclusive to justify the prohibition. In addition, the panel found that the EC measure resulted in 'discrimination or a disguised restriction of international trade' in violation of Article 5.5 SPS. When the EC appealed, the Appellate Body, in January 1998, upheld the panel's ultimate conclusion that the EC had violated Articles 5.1 and 3.3 SPS. However, it rejected the panel's broad interpretation of Article 3.1 SPS and argued that Articles 3.1, 3.2 and 3.3 SPS each addressed a separate situation. Furthermore, the Appellate Body rejected the panel's reading of Article 5.1 SPS, considering that this provision requires a 'rational relationship' between the measure at issue and the risk assessment. Finally, the Appellate Body did not agree with the panel on Article 5.5 SPS in light of the evidence that there were genuine anxieties concerning the safety of hormones.[32]

In November 2006 the DSB adopted the report on a dispute between the US, Canada and Argentina on the one hand and the European Community on the other concerning approval and marketing of biotechnological products. The dispute concerned a general moratorium of the EC on approvals of biotechnological products and safeguard measures adopted by some EC Member States prohibiting the import and marketing of specific biotechnological products within the territories of these states. The panel found that the decision on the moratorium was a procedural decision to delay final substantive approval. It was thus not applied to achieve sanitary or phytosanitary protection and consequently not an SPS measure subject to Articles 5.1 or 2.2 SPS. The panel, however, held that the EC acted in violation of Annex C(1)(a) and Article 8 SPS because the moratorium amounted to undue delay in the completion of the approval procedure. With regard to the safeguard measures, the panel was not convinced that there had been sufficient evidence to conduct a risk assessment according to Article 5.1 SPS. In the absence of such an assessment, maintaining the measures was contrary to Article 5.1 SPS and to Article 2.2 SPS.[33]

28.2.5 The WTO Committee on Trade and Environment

In 1994, the Ministerial Conference decided to establish a Committee on Trade and Environment (CTE);[34] this came into being on 1 January 1995. The CTE is open to the entire WTO membership, with some international organisations as observers. It is intended to explore the links between international trade and environment within the framework of the WTO Agreement and its annexed agreements. Its mandate includes the identification of the relationship between trade and environmental measures in order to promote sustainable development. The CTE shall make appropriate recommendations on whether any

[32] WT Douma and M Jacobs, 'The Beef Hormones Dispute and the Use of National Standards under WTO Law' (1999) 8 *European Environmental Law Review* 137.

[33] J Peel, 'A GMO by Any Other Name . . . Might be an SPS!: Implications of Expanding the Scope of the WTO Sanitary and Phytosanitary Measures Agreement' (2006) 17 *European Journal of International Law* 1009.

[34] Decision on Trade and Environment, adopted by ministers at the meeting of the Uruguay Round Trade Negotiations Committee in Marrakesh on 14 April 1994, www.wto.org/english/docs_e/legal_e/56-dtenv.pdf.

modifications of the provisions of the multilateral trading system are required. If so, these must be compatible with the open, equitable and non-discriminatory nature of the system.

In fulfilling its mandate the CTE makes use of four parameters: (i) the CTE, confirms that the WTO is 'not an environmental protection agency' and considers that the WTO has only a limited policy co-ordination role with regard to trade and environment; (ii) it stresses that the WTO agreements already provide for significant scope for members to pursue national environmental policies; (iii) it supports co-ordinated policy-making but stresses that this must not be trade-restrictive or discriminatory; (iv) it underlines that 'secure market access opportunities are essential to help developing countries work towards sustainable development'.[35]

The CTE's first work programme goes back to its establishment[36] and covers a range of issues, from trade and environment to individual sectors, and relations with environmental organisations. Paragraphs 31(i) and (ii) and 32 of the Doha Ministerial Declaration of 2001 address the CTE's regular work. It focuses on, but is not limited to, effects of environmental measures on market access, the TRIPS agreement, labelling requirements for environmental purposes as well as the sharing of expertise for national environmental reviews and environmental aspects of the Doha negotiations. The 2002 work programme includes negotiations on clarifying the relationship between existing WTO rules and specific trade obligations in MEAs and procedures for information exchange between MEA Secretariats and the WTO.

Looking at the overall performance of the CTE, the following can be pointed out. Firstly, the CTE prefers environmental multilateralism over unilateralism; secondly, it is not very clear on its position related to trade restrictions in MEAs and their relationship to WTO obligations; nevertheless, there seems to be a tendency to consider trade-related rules in MEAs as specific rules governing trade in specific areas; thirdly, it stresses the contribution of the dispute-settlement system of the WTO to addressing conflicts between trade and environment; fourthly, it seems to have no major problems with labelling for products but it objects to labelling for process and production methods; fifthly, there have been fruitful discussions on the interrelationship between TRIPS and the Convention on Biological Diversity, though without clear findings; sixthly, it is critical of NGOs.

28.2.6 The Relationship between WTO Agreements and MEAs

Notwithstanding the activities of the CTE and the findings of the GATT and WTO panels, the interrelationship between WTO agreements and MEAs has not yet been satisfactorily resolved. In principle, MEAs and WTO agreements are co-equal. There is no hierarchy between them. Conflicting obligations have to be addressed on the basis of the rules of *lex posteriori derogat legi priori* and *lex specialis derogat legi generali*. These rules,

[35] *Cf* VP Yu, 'Briefing Paper on the WTO Committee on Trade and Environment', available at www.iatp.org/tradeobservatory/library.cfm?refID=25583; on the Committee in general see RG Tarasofsky, 'The WTO Committee on Trade and Environment—Is it Making a Difference?' (1999) 3 *Max Planck Yearbook of United Nations Law* 471.

[36] See for its text the Decision on Trade and Environment, above n 34.

however, only apply if the subject matter of the treaties and the parties are one and the same, and the conflict cannot be resolved by harmonising interpretation.

CITES is the only MEA seeking protection of fauna and flora by way of import and export limitations. Its subject matter thus directly affects the GATT. If there is a dispute between two parties of CITES which are members of the WTO on whether or not a measure adopted under CITES is compatible with applicable WTO law, firstly, Article XX GATT has to be considered, and secondly, other means of harmonising the two obligations have to be assessed. Only then can the rules of *lex posterior* and *lex specialis* be applied. In principle, Article XX(b) and (g) GATT can accommodate export limitations adopted under CITES. Taking into account the second tuna–dolphin panel report,[37] import limitations, which serve to protect fauna and flora of the exporting state, are only permissible if Article XX GATT is read to apply to extraterritorial environmental goods. While it will be relatively easy for a state to demonstrate that CITES measures are covered by the objectives included in Article XX(b) and (g) GATT, it may be much more difficult to demonstrate their proportionality under the chapeau of Article XX GATT. However, so far CITES measures have not been challenged under WTO law, either by parties to CITES, or by non-parties. There seems to be tacit approval of the WTO compatibility of CITES measures.[38]

Should, however, a conflict between WTO law and an MEA not be resolved as indicated above, Article 30 of the Vienna Convention on the Law of Treaties (VCLT) and its *lex posterior* rule comes into play. The GATT 1994 might thus easily prevail with regard to earlier MEAs. However, as the GATT 1994 largely leaves the GATT 1947 unchanged, in particular Articles I, III, XI and XX, it may be argued that pertinent MEAs, concluded after 1947, prevail on the basis of the *lex posterior* rule. The MEA concerned would then lead to an *inter se* modification of the GATT according to Article 41 VCLT: 'Two or more of the parties to a multilateral treaty may conclude an agreement to modify the treaty as between themselves alone', subject to certain conditions laid down in Article 41(1) and (2) VCLT. In addition, it may be easily argued that an MEA enjoys preference over the GATT by virtue of the rule of *lex specialis*. Thus, parties implementing and applying such MEAs do not run the risk of being held responsible for violating WTO agreements.

Apart from CITES, some other MEAs make use of trade restrictions as a means to pursue environmental objectives.[39] These include, among others, the 1985 Vienna Ozone Convention and the 1987 Montreal Protocol, and the 1989 Basel Convention on the Control of Transboundary Movements of Hazardous Wastes and their Disposal. Problems arise if a party to one of these MEAs adopts trade restrictions *vis-à-vis* a WTO member who is not a party to the relevant MEA. In such a case, Article 30(4) VCLT provides that 'as between a State party to both treaties and a State party to only one of the treaties, the treaty to which both States are parties governs their mutual rights and obligations',

[37] (1994) 33 ILM 839.

[38] M Yeater and J Vasquez, 'Demystifying the Relationship between CITES and the WTO' (2001) 10 *RECIEL* 271.

[39] See TP Stewart and DS Johanson, 'A Nexus of Trade and the Environment: The Relationship Between the Cartagena Protocol on Biosafety and the SPS Agreement of the World Trade Organization' (2003) 14 *Colorado Journal of International Environmental Law and Policy* 1.

meaning that it is only WTO law which applies as between these parties, unless the activities adopted under the relevant MEA can be justified under Article XX GATT. Another, intermediate means to reach a compromise solution may be the adoption of a waiver under WTO law.

Briefly considering the prohibition of imports or exports under the Basel Convention, an import ban amounts to a non-tariff barrier as prohibited by Article XI(1) GATT. If the import ban concerns hazardous wastes harmful to human health it can easily be justified under Article XX(b) GATT. In the case of an export ban it may be argued that, assuming that extraterritorial goods can be protected, hazardous wastes typically affect human, animal or plant life or health and that the export ban thus is 'necessary' within the meaning of Article XX(b) GATT. The situation may be much more difficult in the case of non-hazardous wastes. It may be argued, however, that such an export ban serves to prevent the construction of landfills, which affects landscape as an 'exhaustible natural resource' according to Article XX(g) GATT.

In the case of the Montreal Protocol, Article 4 includes trade restrictions *vis-à-vis* non-parties. The ozone layer is part of the global commons. Nevertheless, trade restrictions can be justified both by reference to Article XX(b) GATT and by reference to Article XX(g) GATT since measures equally effective for the protection of the ozone layer will hardly be available. In view of the Montreal Protocol's near-universality, the problem is, however, no longer topical even though it may serve as an interesting precedent for future arrangements.[40]

28.3 Trade Issues beyond the WTO

The interface between environment and economics does not only arise at the universal level. It also is relevant at the regional level. Free trade agreements and customs unions have become important instruments for regional economic development. To name but a few, the EU, the North American Free Trade Agreement (NAFTA), the Andean Community of Nations, the Mercado Común del Sur (MERCOSUR), the Southern African Development Community (SADC), the Caribbean Community, the Economic Community of West African States, the ASEAN Free Trade Area and the free trade arrangements within the Asia Pacific Economic Cooperation may be mentioned. While none of them can be addressed in detail here, it is noteworthy that quite a few of them are seeking to balance economic and environmental considerations by adopting environmental provisions, protocols or side agreements.

NAFTA was signed in 1992 and entered into force on 1 January 1994. Its provisions include a number of references to the environment.[41] Thus, Article 904(1) NAFTA, included in Part III of the agreement which deals with technical barriers to trade, allows

[40] A Rutgeerts, 'Trade and Environment—Reconciling the Montreal Protocol and the GATT' (1999) 33 *Journal of World Trade* 61.

[41] BJ Condon, 'NAFTA and the Environment' (1994) 14 *Northwestern Journal of International Law & Business* 528.

each party to 'adopt, maintain or apply any standards-related measure, including any such measure relating to safety, the protection of human, animal or plant life or health, the environment or consumers, and any measure to ensure its enforcement or implementation', as long as the measure does not create unnecessary obstacles to trade within the meaning of Article 904(4) NAFTA. Articles 905 and 906 NAFTA include obligations to harmonise standards in light of existing international standards. The final clause of Article 905 NAFTA explicitly states that

> [n]othing in paragraph 1 shall be construed to prevent a Party, in pursuing its legitimate objectives, from adopting, maintaining or applying any standards-related measure that results in a higher level of protection than would be achieved if the measure were based on the relevant international standard.

In addition, Article 2101(1) NAFTA refers to the GATT and thus makes the general exception of Article XX GATT available to NAFTA parties. Apart from the NAFTA itself, the three parties, in 1994, adopted the North American Agreement on Environmental Cooperation (NAAEC), which is the legal basis for the Commission for Environmental Cooperation (CEC). The Commission primarily looks into the state of the environment rather than protecting natural resources as such.[42]

As far as MERCOSUR is concerned, its constitutive treaty refers to the environment only in passing, with its preamble stating that market integration must be achieved by, *inter alia*, 'making optimum use of available resources, [and] preserving the environment'. However, in 2001, the members of MERCOSUR adopted the 'Framework Agreement on the Environment of MERCOSUR'.[43] It provides, *inter alia*, for the harmonisation of environmental management systems and increased co-operation on shared ecosystems, in addition to participatory mechanisms. It includes provisions on standards, a section on protected areas, one on conservation and sustainable use of natural resources, and provisions for protecting health and quality of life.[44]

The constitutive treaty of SADC in its Article 5 stipulates that the objectives of SADC shall include the achievement of 'sustainable utilisation of natural resources and effective protection of the environment'. In addition, Article 21 states that members agree to co-operate in the area of 'natural resources and environment'. While SADC has not yet developed a comprehensive environmental policy, its work on specific issues of environmental protection, including a number of protocols concluded on specific issues, such as transboundary waters and mining, is impressive.[45]

[42] C Wold, 'Evaluating NAFTA and the Commission for Environmental Cooperation' (2008) 28 *Saint Louis University Public Law Review* 201.

[43] Available at www.ecolex.org/server2.php/libcat/docs/TRE/Multilateral/En/TRE153663.pdf.

[44] For further information relating to MERCOSUR *cf* JP Schmidt, 'MERCOSUR' in R Wolfrum (ed), *Max Planck Encyclopedia of Public International Law* (Heidelberg/Oxford 2008), available at www.mpepil.com; on the MERCOSUR trade and environmental linkage debate *cf* F Morosini, 'The MERCOSUR Trade and Linkage Debate' (2010) 44 *Journal of World Trade* 1127–1144.

[45] *cf* U Beyerlin, 'Sustainable Use of Natural Resources—A Key to Combating Poverty' (2003) 63 *ZaöRV*, 430 *et seq*.

28.4 International Financial Institutions

International financial institutions are international bodies with a mandate related to the financial sector. The most prominent are the World Bank, the IMF and regional development banks. Although their objectives largely concern financial market governance and poverty alleviation, their activities often have significant environmental impacts. This is particularly true for the World Bank.[46] Projects performed or financed by the World Bank have come under scrutiny in light of costs arising from the destruction or degradation of the environment. In response to NGO and donor country pressure, policies and procedures were developed to offset some of the environmental risks. Meanwhile, the World Bank has its own environmental strategy. It mobilises financial resources for environmental concerns through the Global Environment Facility (GEF). The World Bank contributes to the administration and implementation of MEAs through, *inter alia*, the Multilateral Fund for the Implementation of the Montreal Protocol and through GEF compliance assistance. In order to manage conflicts between World Bank projects and environmental concerns, the Bank has established the World Bank Inspection Panel. The Panel is designed to increase the accountability of the World Bank and to improve compliance with its own environmental policies. It is available for locally affected people who believe that they have been or are likely to be adversely affected as a result of the Bank's policy violations.

28.5 Conclusions

Economic and environmental concerns are neither always compatible with each other nor in continuous conflict. There are, however, a number of conflicts that typically arise out of the distinct treatment of both areas by public international law. MEAs and WTO rules were not developed as a coherent body of international law. Rather, they constitute separate parts of what is still a fragmented and incomplete system of law. Increasingly, dispute-settlement bodies and negotiators have addressed these conflicts and have sought to manage them so as to harmonise competing obligations rather than giving preference to one of the objectives pursued. It is noteworthy that a large number of MEAs have intentionally chosen economic means to pursue environmental objectives. This brings the two areas of public international law even closer towards each other. Whether ideas of constitutionalisation will help to overcome existing conflicts is an open question. It seems more likely and more effective to deal with substantive and procedural conflicts by way of law-making, whether on the basis of treaties and treaty amendments, on the basis of interpretation of existing rules, or on the basis of non-legally binding instruments which may, however, in the long term have an impact on the interpretation and application of economic and environmental agreements alike.

[46] A Steer and J Mason, 'The Role of Multilateral Finance and the Environment' (1995) 31 *Indiana Journal of Global Legal Studies* 35.

Further Reading

FM Abbott, T Cottier and JH Jackson, 'The Limits of International Trade: Workers' Protection, the Environment and other Human Rights' (2000) 94 *Proceedings of the 94th Annual Meeting, American Society of International Law* 219–224.

MS Blodgett and RJ Hunter, 'The Environment and Trade Agreements: Should the WTO Become More Actively Involved?' (2010) 33 *Hastings International and Comparative Law Review* 1–19.

S Charnovitz, 'A New WTO Paradigm for Trade and the Environment' (2007) 11 *Singapore Yearbook of International Law* 15–40.

——, 'Trade and Climate Change' (2010) 9 *World Trade Review* 273–281.

DC Esty, 'Bridging the Trade–Environment Divide' (2001) 15 *Journal of Economic Perspectives* 113–130.

F Francioni, 'Recent WTO Cases on Trade and Environment' (2001) *The Global Community: Yearbook of International Law and Jurisprudence* 123–130.

D Gentile, 'International Trade and the Environment: What Is the Role of the WTO?' (2009) 20 *Fordham Environmental Law Review* 197–232.

A Goyal, *The WTO and International Environmental Law* (Oxford 2006).

H Horn and PC Mavroidis, 'Environment, Trade, and the WTO Constraint' (2009) 62 *Revue Hellénique de Droit International* 1–63.

PC Mavroidis, 'Trade and Environment after the Shrimps–Turtles Litigation' (2000) 34 *Journal of World Trade* 73–88.

A Rutgeerts, 'Trade and Environment—Reconciling the Montreal Protocol and the GATT' (1999) 33 *Journal of World Trade* 61–86.

EC Schlemmer, 'Compliance with WTO Obligations: Trade and the Environment Revisited' (2002) 27 *South African Yearbook of International Law* 272–285.

GC Shaffer, 'WTO Blue-Green Blues: The Impact of US Domestic Politics on Trade–Labor, Trade–Environment Linkages for the WTO's Future' (2000) 24 *Fordham International Law Journal* 608–651.

——, 'The World Trade Organization under Challenge: Democracy and the Law and Politics of the WTO's Treatment of Trade and Environment Matters' (2001) 25 *Harvard Environmental Law Review* 1–93.

R Skeen, 'Will the WTO Turn Green? The Implications of Injecting Environmental Issues into the Multilateral Trading System' (2004) 16 *Georgetown International Environmental Law Review* 161–199.

C Wold, 'Evaluating NAFTA and the Commission for Environmental Cooperation: Lessons for Integrating Trade and Environment in Free Trade Agreements' (2008) 28 *Saint Louis University Public Law Review* 201–252.

Part VII

Perspectives

In June 2012, 40 years after the Stockholm Conference and 20 years after the Rio Conference, the UN Conference on Sustainable Development (UNCSD), or 'Rio+20', will be held again in Rio de Janeiro. According to UN General Assembly Resolution 64/236,[1] the objective of this World Summit will be 'to secure renewed political commitment for sustainable development, assessing the progress to date and the remaining gaps in the implementation of the outcomes of the major summits on sustainable development and addressing new and emerging challenges'.[2] The states attending this conference will recount the success and failure of their endeavours to enhance international environmental and developmental co-operation. They will be likely to agree that the normative system of international environmental law is still far from perfect and shows severe gaps. They may also claim some success stories in individual fields, such as combating ozone depletion or transboundary air pollution. However, aware of the fact that humankind today faces an ever-growing number of global environmental problems with tremendous threat potential, progress achieved to date is too fragmentary and sporadic.

Current State of Global Environmental Co-operation

States and societies are faced with a multitude of global environmental problems. According to UNEP's fourth Global Environmental Outlook of 2007, increases in global average air and ocean temperature are causing rising sea levels, more frequent and intense heatwaves, storms, floods, and droughts, as well as loss of biodiversity; the 'ozone hole' is still alarming and only expected to recover from 2060 on; land degradation driven by unsustainable land use and climate change causes desertification and the disruption of biological cycles; global freshwater availability is declining; aquatic ecosystems are being overexploited; and valuable species of flora and fauna are increasingly threatened with extinction.[3] These and other problems threaten to degrade the earth's ecosystem to such an extent as to endanger the quality of life of current and future generations. Processes

[1] UNGA Res 64/236 (24 December 2009).

[2] *Ibid*, para 20(a).

[3] *Cf* U Beyerlin and J Grote Stoutenburg, 'Environment, International Protection' in R Wolfrum (ed), *Max Planck Encyclopedia of Public International Law* (Heidelberg/Oxford 2011), para 2, available at www.mpepil.com.

of man-made environmental degradation are often combined with natural disasters, such as droughts, floods, earthquakes and tsunamis, to pose a threat to the very existence of humankind. The disadvantaged and marginalised sectors of societies in the Third World often suffer from environmental degradation to such an extent that they feel forced to flee their homelands and take refuge in safer regions of their state or even abroad.

Therefore, protection of the global environment must become a common concern of humankind. Notwithstanding the increasing awareness of the urgent need for global environmental co-operation, states are still far from constituting a solidarity-driven community acting in concert as faithfully and intensively as needed to achieve this highly important objective.

Reasons for Deficient Environmental Co-operation

Notwithstanding promises made and concepts developed, states still stick with traditional perceptions of sovereignty. While occasionally promising to enhance co-operation for the common good and discussing the constitutionalisation of public international law, they too often tend to forget these enlightened approaches. In light of economic challenges, such as experienced at the end of the twenty-first century's first decade, national self-interest dominates their actions more often than common concerns. National interests still widely prevail over state community interests.

This is closely linked to their agenda setting. All too often, and largely irrespective of their form of government, the priorities set by states, nationally and internationally, do not reflect the idea of sustainability. Short-term economic gains are largely preferred to mid- and long-term objectives. Even in view of human suffering caused by man-made environmental disasters, states rather focus on the symptoms than carefully address the causes, not least because this might entail financial burdens or—even worse for most—political and behavioural changes in government and society.

One of the main problems is that very often the time span between environmentally harmful activities and the resulting environmental degradation is long. States and their organs perceive it to be inopportune to take mid- or long-term action in favour of the environment if there are conflicting policy objectives that can be reached within a short time. Even if states are formally committed to taking precautionary action, they will often do as little as possible if conflicting short-term objectives are at stake. This indicates that the effectiveness of such important concepts of international environmental law as sustainable development and precautionary action is rather limited.

North–South Dichotomy

Notwithstanding emerging economies such as Brazil, the People's Republic of China and India, humankind is still divided into prosperous industrialised societies, on the one hand, and marginalised societies in the South, on the other. Correspondingly, interstate co-operation in environmental and developmental matters continues to suffer from the so-called 'North–South divide'. Unfortunately, Mickelson's view that 'international environmental law . . . has failed to respond to Third World concerns in a meaningful fashion'[4] continues to be true. The South is still perceived 'as a grudging participant in environmental regimes rather than as an active partner in an ongoing discussion regarding what the fundamental nature of environmental problems is and what the appropriate responses should be'.[5]

'International justice' and 'international solidarity' could prove to be conceptual approaches for bridging the North–South dichotomy in international environmental law. Both ideas are important ethical sources for developing more concrete concepts, such as 'common but differentiated responsibilities' and 'intergenerational equity', which in turn lay the ground for consolidating and optimising the system of MEAs. The ultimate goal of all relevant endeavours must be to establish interstate relations, especially in the North–South context, that are more determined by co-equal partnership rather than by ideological confrontation.

As became obvious during the Copenhagen summit, one of the challenges today is that there are not only two distinct groups of states with their respective interests but at least three, namely developed states, fast industrialising countries and developing countries. While developed states will continue to be faced with legitimate requests for compliance assistance, as well as with legitimate calls to meet their environmental obligations, it will neither be adequate nor legitimate to treat emerging economies in the same way as developing countries. The concept of common but differentiated responsibilities necessitates differential treatment of groups of states to the extent possible, not only for reasons of legitimacy as an essential feature of international law, but also for reasons of its effectiveness:

> Whenever the preconditions of differential treatment cease to exist, the developing countries are no longer legitimised to take advantage of being dispensed from certain contractual obligations and getting compliance assistance from developed countries. Therefore, any differential treatment in treaty practice should be kept continuously under review.[6]

Current Challenges and Trends in Global Environmental Co-operation

Combating climate change has remained one of the most serious, and at the same time most pressing, challenges of global environmental co-operation. The 2009 Copenhagen

[4] M Mickelson, 'South, North, International Environmental Law, and International Environmental Lawyers' (2000) 11 *Yearbook of International Environmental Law* 52, 54.

[5] *Ibid*, 60.

[6] U Beyerlin, 'Bridging the North–South Divide in International Environmental Law' (2006) 66 *ZaöRV* 259, 295.

Accord failed to prescribe mandatory greenhouse gas emission cuts to achieve the goal of keeping the increase in global temperature below 2°C; it merely invited voluntary pledges for emission targets from developed countries and for nationally appropriate mitigation actions from developing countries. As already feared, COP/MOP 6 held at Cancun, Mexico, from 29 November to 10 December 2010, was not able to repair this failing. Adaptation obligations under the UNFCCC are gaining in importance. This should not, however, be at the expense of the need to continue with mitigation efforts. Otherwise, humankind will be heading for a climate catastrophe.

While efforts by states to stop the loss of biological diversity were for long rather in vain, the Strategic Plan of the Convention on Biological Diversity (the 'Aichi Target') adopted by COP 10 in October 2010 at Nagoya, Japan, may prove to become the starting point for new international and national initiatives to conserve biodiversity. Moreover, with the Nagoya Protocol on Access to Genetic Resources and the Fair and Equitable Sharing of Benefits Arising from Their Utilization, COP 10 succeeded in bringing the 2002 Bonn Guidelines into an international legal framework. Making use of economic incentives not only as a means to convince states of the need to protect and preserve biodiversity but also as a tool to implement pertinent MEAs has proven to be successful in this particular field of international environmental law. If it continues to be successfully applied, this far-sighted policy could serve as a model for addressing other global environmental challenges.

The need to protect the oceans and their resources has long been recognised but conservation efforts have largely been reactive rather than proactive. Today, especially at the regional level, there is a very dense network of international treaties dealing with specific sources of marine pollution or specific pollutants, including several instruments aimed at preventing, or at least regulating, oil pollution from tankers and offshore drilling platforms. Notwithstanding these efforts, in April 2010, the explosion of the BP *Deepwater Horizon* rig in the Gulf of Mexico caused 13 casualties, extensive damage to marine and wildlife habitats, as well as the Gulf's fishing industries, but also immense underwater plumes of dissolved oil not visible at the surface. This incident was the largest accidental oil spill in the history of the petroleum industry, and clearly shows how weak coastal states are in light of economic pressure from the natural resources industry, not only in preventing such oil disasters, but also in warding off their fatal consequences. States should feel prompted to engage in protecting the marine environment by taking actions which are more integrative than sectoral, and more precautionary than preventive. The stocks of marine fish, mammals or whales continue to be imperilled by overexploitation and degradation of their habitats. In order to achieve long-term sustainability of these stocks the many worldwide operating fisheries organisations should better co-ordinate their activities. Moreover, there is urgent need for providing a more effective enforcement of the existing rules on sustainable use and conservation of marine living resources. This should best be done by strengthening flag state jurisdiction and port state control, as advocated by the 2009 FAO Agreement on Combating IUU Fishing.

The continued availability of freshwater resources has become a global problem which is, however, normally addressed only at the transboundary or regional level. Even though the 1997 UN Watercourses Convention partly continues to serve as a model for regional agreements on non-navigational uses of transboundary water resources, its non-entry into force and the limited number of ratifications indicate that there is still a need to discuss the legal regime applicable to freshwater resources. Apart from the traditional hotspots known for their scarcity of water, conflicts have emerged in other areas, such as Central Asia's Syr Darya and Amu Darya river basins. In addition, there is a noticeable lack of genuine environmental provisions in pertinent agreements at the regional and at the transboundary level. With the inclusion of groundwater resources in the 2008 ILC Draft Articles on Transboundary Aquifers, there is continued activity at the international level. However, this needs to be translated into operational agreements.

The importance of forests for the local, regional and global environment as a whole and their contribution to combating desertification and climate change has been recognised since the 1992 Rio Conference. However, the lack of binding commitments continues to pose tremendous challenges. In particular, in light of the uncertainty about the further development of the climate change regime, it is a matter of urgency to develop a comprehensive strategy on forest protection at all levels.

In light of the fragmentation of international environmental law it has become a matter of concern to better co-ordinate or even harmonise pertinent international treaties. Synergies between major MEAs must be looked into and further developed in order to avoid conflicts between them and to improve their implementation.[7]

Ensuring More Effective Treaty Compliance

Deficient or non-compliance with MEAs more often arises from infrastructural shortages than from intentional policies. This is why an active treaty management combining elements of compliance control with compliance assistance is a better approach to bring a defaulting party back to treaty compliance than traditional means of law enforcement, such as state responsibility, reprisal and retorsion, or dispute settlement. The underlying ideas of compliance control, as first developed and implemented under the Montreal Protocol and then refined in subsequently adopted MEAs, are: (i) collective rather than unilateral enforcement; (ii) co-operation rather than confrontation; (iii) prevention rather than repression; and (iv) compliance assistance rather than sanctions.

However, ensuring compliance with MEAs begins with sound treaty-making, especially with framing clear-cut and rather precise obligations in order to facilitate compliance with them. The more abstract a particular treaty obligation is, the more difficult it is to ensure compliance with it. MEAs should always be conceptualised in such a way that the benefits that each party draws from compliance outweigh the costs of non-compliance. In light of the diversity of MEAs and the obligations contained therein, every single MEA has been equipped with tailor-made compliance-control mechanisms. Choosing the 'right' mechanism depends on the type of obligations. While compliance with specified

[7] *Cf* T Marauhn, 'The Potential of the Convention on Biological Diversity to Address the Effects of Climate Change in the Arctic' in T Koivoruva *et al* (eds), *Climate Governance in the Arctic* (Berlin *et al* 2009) 263.

environmental standards within a certain time frame ('result-oriented' obligation) can be easily controlled and thus ensured, compliance with a duty to take broadly designated action with an abstractly defined objective ('action-oriented' obligation) is difficult, if not impossible, to assess reliably.[8]

There is need for developing flexible mechanisms allowing meaningful reactions to cases of non-compliance, either by only responding in a spirit of co-operation and partnership, or by resorting to a mix of co-operative and confrontational means. In this respect, the non-compliance response mechanism available under the Kyoto Protocol may serve as a model: it combines confidence-building with 'deterrence'. In any case, co-operative methods of law enforcement should have precedence. Confrontational means should only be used after the co-operative procedures have been applied without success.

Compliance control must be necessarily combined with compliance assistance in the form of financial assistance, capacity-building and transfer of technology. The provision of some form of financial and technological assistance to developing countries aimed at ensuring compliance has become a common feature of modern MEAs. While *ex ante* assistance is aimed at inducing compliance with environmental agreements, *ex post* assistance will be resorted to in cases of non-compliance. The latter type of assistance aims at restoring compliance and thus ensuring continued co-operation between all parties, even in the case of non-compliance by some of them.[9]

Notwithstanding the need to promote co-operative compliance strategies, it is important to point out that transfers of finance, know-how and technology alone will not ensure compliance with MEAs by developing countries or countries in transition to a market economy. In the long run, there is a need to better co-ordinate traditional forms of development co-operation with compliance assistance as provided for under MEAs. Otherwise, the limited resources available will be unevenly split between these two policy objectives, and states may be less willing to co-operate.

Ways and Means to Enhance International Environmental Law

The steering capacity of MEAs requires a refined incentive structure since states are only intermediate addressees of environmental obligations; they must enact national legislation in order to achieve behavioural change at the level of private and business actors. It is important to balance carefully the costs and benefits flowing from every MEA, not only with a view to incentives which governments may perceive as positive or negative, but also with a view to include private and business considerations.

Proliferation and diversification of MEAs is not an objective which should be pursued

[8] *Cf* U Beyerlin, PT Stoll and R Wolfrum,'Conclusions drawn for the Conference on Ensuring Compliance with MEAs' in U Beyerlin *et al* (eds) *Ensuring Compliance with Multilateral Environmental Agreements. A Dialogue between Practitioners and Academia* (Leiden/Boston 2006) 359, 360 *et seq*.

[9] *Cf* L Boisson de Chazournes, 'Technical and Financial Assistance and Compliance: the Interplay' in *ibid*, 273, 277 *et seq* and 284 *et seq*.

as such. It is important in every case of a proposed new MEA to discuss its relationship with existing MEAs. In addition, it is suitable to integrate, as far as possible, legally binding and legally non-binding instruments.

Increasingly, in order to overcome fragmentation and in order to better integrate heterogeneous environmental considerations, a holistic rather than a sectoral approach towards the further development of international environmental law should be pursued. Some integrative and media-transcending instruments have already been adopted. Examples can be taken from the protection of biodiversity within the CBD and its ecosystem approach as well as from the protection of marine ecosystems and the preservation of marine biodiversity as a whole.

Current MEA practice still suffers from undue fragmentation. This flaw can best be remediated by providing for a better co-operation between treaty organs concerned. Such interinstitutional co-operation should be aimed at co-ordinating the respective treaty implementation measures as closely as possible. Thereby, overlaps and norm conflicts between the competing MEAs could be avoided or at least mitigated. Consolidation can best be achieved by adopting memoranda of understanding between various treaty organs, be they COPs or secretariats. There is ample practice to this end which may be easily further developed.

The highly complex multilevel system of international environmental norms consists of 'hard law' and 'soft law'. In order to better combine hard and soft law, MEAs should, much more than in the past, refer to standards adopted elsewhere. Thus, soft law may be integrated into hard law instruments, eventually obtaining binding force under certain circumstances. This is a promising approach since soft law agreements are easier to negotiate and to amend than international agreements.

Another structural weakness of international environmental law, apart from its substantive and procedural heterogeneity, is its lack of central authoritative institutions. The diversity of international environmental institutions, and the lack of transparency between them, calls for enhancing international environmental institution-building. It is doubtful whether any type of grand design will be achieved in the near future. UNEP and CSD are in place with their own structures and agendas, as well as their own share in protecting the global environment and promoting sustainable development. Attempts at establishing a new international organisation for the environment have failed in the past and it seems unlikely that they will be successfully taken up anew.

Since international environmental law must finally deploy its steering capacity upon individuals and business, it is important to strengthen public participation in international environmental decision-making. While the Aarhus Convention may be considered as an interesting model for further consideration, it is doubtful whether other regions will readily follow this model. Nevertheless, the role of NGOs may be easily strengthened, both at the level of international treaty-making and at the level of ensuring treaty compliance. In this context, the Johannesburg Summit has paved the way for increased public–private partnerships. Surprisingly or not, such partnerships have only been developed to a limited extent. Most relevant partnerships involve public institutions only. Fresh impetus is needed to increase not only the effectiveness but also the cost efficiency of MEAs.

Whether human rights protection is a useful means to make international environmental protection more efficient has been debated. There is a certain potential for international human rights law, in particular in the field of access rights to natural resources, including water and wildlife. Less promising is the ongoing debate about a general human right to (a healthy) environment, not least because it would be extremely difficult to enforce. Yet, it is beyond doubt that international human rights law has helped in enforcing those environmental standards which are directly linked to the human being. The jurisprudence of the European Court of Human Rights is a prominent example in this respect.

As regards international law applicable to indigenous peoples, human rights and international environmental law easily meet. While on the one hand indigenous peoples should fully benefit from general human rights law, there is a need to preserve their specific linkages to the environment. The challenge to US climate policies mounted by the Inuit is a telling example, combining human rights law with the particular protection provided for indigenous peoples in light of the close link which their traditional cultures demonstrate with nature.

The further development of international environmental law is multifaceted. It must take into account local, regional and global concerns alike, addressing the environment as such, as well as its human dimension.

Index